THE NEW AMERICAN NATION 1775–1820

A Twelve-Volume Collection of Articles on the Development of the Early American Republic

Edited by

★

PETER S. ONUF
UNIVERSITY OF VIRGINIA

A GARLAND SERIES

THE NEW AMERICAN NATION
1775–1820

Volume
6

RATIFYING, AMENDING, AND INTERPRETING THE CONSTITUTION

Edited with an
Introduction by

PETER S. ONUF

GARLAND PUBLISHING, INC.
NEW YORK & LONDON
1991

Library of Congress Cataloging-in-Publication Data

Ratifying, amending, and interpreting the Constitution / edited with an introduction by Peter S. Onuf.

p. cm. — (New American nation, 1776–1815 ; v. 6)

Includes bibliographical references.

ISBN 0-8153-0441-2 (alk. paper) : $49.99

1. United States—Constitutional history. 2. United States—Constitutional law—Interpretation and construction. 3. United States—Constitutional law—Amendments. 4. United States—Politics and government—Constitutional period, 1789–1809. I. Onuf, Peter S. II. Series.

E164.N45 1991 vol. 6
[KF4541]
973s—dc20
[342.73'029]
[973 s]
[347.30229] 91-3502
CIP

Printed on acid-free, 250-year-life paper.
Manufactured in the United States of America

THE NEW AMERICAN NATION, 1775–1820

★

EDITOR'S INTRODUCTION

This series includes a representative selection of the most interesting and influential journal articles on revolutionary and early national America. My goal is to introduce readers to the wide range of topics that now engage scholarly attention. The essays in these volumes show that the revolutionary era was an extraordinarily complex "moment" when the broad outlines of national history first emerged. Yet if the "common cause" brought Americans together, it also drove them apart: the Revolution, historians agree, was as much a civil war as a war of national liberation. And, given the distinctive colonial histories of the original members of the American Union, it is not surprising that the war had profoundly different effects in different parts of the country. This series has been designed to reveal the multiplicity of these experiences in a period of radical political and social change.

Most of the essays collected here were first published within the last twenty years. This series therefore does *not* recapitulate the development of the historiography of the Revolution. Many of the questions asked by earlier generations of scholars now seem misconceived and simplistic. Constitutional historians wanted to know if the Patriots had legitimate grounds to revolt: was the Revolution "legal"? Economic historians sought to assess the costs of the navigation system for American farmers and merchants and to identify the interest groups that promoted resistance. Comparative historians wondered how "revolutionary" the Revolution really was. By and large, the best recent work has ignored these classic questions. Contemporary scholarship instead draws its inspiration from other sources, most notable of which is the far-ranging reconception and reconstruction of prerevolutionary America by a brilliant generation of colonial historians.

Bernard Bailyn's *Ideological Origins of the American Revolution* (1967) was a landmark in the new historical writing on colonial politics. As his title suggests, Bailyn was less interested in constitutional and legal arguments as such than in the "ideology" or political language that shaped colonists' perception of and responses to British imperial policy. Bailyn's great contribution was to focus attention on colonial political culture; disciples and critics alike followed his lead as they explored the impact—and limits—of "republicanism" in specific colonial settings. Meanwhile, the social historians who had played a leading role in the transformation of colonial historiography were extending their work into the late colonial period and were increasingly interested in the questions of value, meaning, and behavior that were raised by the new political history. The resulting convergence points to some of the unifying themes in recent work on the revolutionary period presented in this series.

A thorough grounding in the new scholarship on colonial British America is the best introduction to the history and historiography of the Revolution. These volumes therefore can be seen as a complement and extension of Peter Charles Hoffer's eighteen-volume set, *Early American History*, published by Garland in 1987. Hoffer's collection includes numerous important essays essential for understanding developments in independent America. Indeed, only a generation ago—when the Revolution generally was defined in terms of its colonial origins—it would have been hard to justify a separate series on the "new American nation." But exciting recent work—for instance, on wartime mobilization and social change, or on the Americanization of republican ideology during the great era of state making and constitution writing—has opened up new vistas. Historians now generally agree that the revolutionary period saw far-reaching and profound changes, that is, a "great transformation," toward a more recognizably modern America. If the connections between this transformation and the actual unfolding of events often remain elusive, the historiographical quest for the larger meaning of the war and its aftermath has yielded impressive results.

To an important extent, the revitalization of scholarship on revolutionary and early national America is a tribute to the efforts and expertise of scholars working in other professional disciplines. Students of early American literature have made key contributions to the history of rhetoric, ideology, and culture; political scientists and legal scholars have brought new clarity and sophistication to the study of political and constitutional thought and practice in the founding period. Kermit L. Hall's superb Garland series, *United States Constitutional and Legal History* (20 volumes, 1985), is another fine resource for students and scholars interested in the founding. The sampling of recent work in various disciplines offered in these volumes gives a sense of the interpretative possibilities of a crucial period in American history that is now getting the kind of attention it has long deserved.

Peter S. Onuf

INTRODUCTION

Charles Beard argued in *An Economic Interpretation of the Constitution* (1913) that the framers of the Constitution were motivated by their economic interests, especially in what he called "personalty," or commercial, nonagricultural property. His conclusions were based on an analysis of delegates' property holdings and were compatible with the progressives' understanding of an ongoing struggle between "aristocratic" and "democratic" forces in American history. Although Beard's argument has been decisively refuted, most conclusively in Forrest McDonald's *We The People* (1958), an exhaustive economic profile of the state ratifying conventions, the main lines of his thesis remain influential.

The natural temptation for historians is to read too much into partisan polemics designed to persuade voters to support or reject the proposed national charter. Progressives sought to explain political rhetoric in terms of the underlying "interests" it was designed to promote, while neo-Whig historians and political theorists recast the framers as "founders" and philosophers. Meanwhile, cultural historians looked beyond articulations of high political principle for inadvertent and unintended signs of more profound changes. Clearly, this was a period of social dislocation and cultural transformation, and it is hardly surprising that Gordon S. Wood and other historians have found evidence for conflicting world views in debates over the Constitution.

The problem with all these approaches is that they fail to examine political rhetoric in its proper historical context. Our modern understanding of the ratification contest has benefited immeasurably from the debate among legal scholars over how to read the Constitution and contemporaneous writings revelatory of "original intent." The invocation of these intentions in modern jurisprudence may be naive and anachronistic, but it does direct our attention to what framers and ratifiers actually said and hoped to accomplish. In a similar, though more sophisticated, way, literary scholars, with their interest in how texts such as the Constitution are constructed and how they function, have also redirected attention toward rhetorical and political contexts.

Perhaps the most salutary result of the new interest in the ongoing process of constitutional interpretation has been the recognition of the key role of Antifederalists in shaping the original debate. Important early work by Cecelia Kenyon and Jackson Turner Main focused on whether or not opponents of the Constitution were "democratic." Publication of Herbert Storing's

What the Anti-Federalists Were For (1981) marked a new epoch in ratification scholarship. Critics of the Constitution raised a wide range of searching questions about the dangers of political centralization to the integrity of the state republics and the sanctity of individual liberties that no longer seem so fearful and reactionary. Most significantly, their concerns determined the kind of arguments the Federalists would deploy on behalf of their plan. The Antifederalists forced proponents of the Constitution to articulate a principled rationale for a federal regime that would secure states' rights. Efforts to preempt Antifederalist criticisms thus led Federalists to move beyond the original intentions of nationalists like Alexander Hamilton and to construct an "original interpretation" that shaped the reception and practical application of the constitutional text.

The most conspicuous instance of Antifederalist influence was in the drafting of the Bill of Rights, at Madison's urging, by the First Federal Congress. The Constitution was not only subject to conflicting interpretations, but it was also provisional and incomplete. The first ten amendments reassured skeptical Americans that the federal governments would not overbalance the states or jeopardize individual rights. The very fact that they played such a minor role in antebellum jurisprudence is indicative of the widespread acceptance of a strict constructionist, or essentially Antifederalist, understanding of the extent of federal powers.

Traditionally, ratification of the Constitution has been seen as the climax and conclusion of the colonial and Revolutionary period in American history and therefore as the beginning of our modern national history. It is now clear that the story is not so simple or straightforward. What began in 1787 was an ongoing debate over the meaning of the Constitution. But the outcome of the ratification controversy was a federal system that is hardly recognizable today. Despite the efforts of Hamiltonian centralizers, the United States was at first only a "more perfect union" of equal and self-governing republican states under a national government of limited powers.

Peter S. Onuf

Additional Reading

Charles Beard. *An Economic Interpretation of the Constitution.* New York: Macmillan, 1935; orig. pub., 1913.
Michael Gillespie and Michael Lienesch, eds. *Ratifying the Constitution.* Lawrence: University Press of Kansas, 1989.
Leonard Levy. *Original Intent and the Framers' Constitution.* New York: Macmillan, 1988.
Forrest McDonald. *We the People: The Economic Origins of the Constitution.* Chicago: University of Chicago Press, 1958.
Jackson Turner Main. *The Antifederalists: Critics of the Constitution, 1781–1788.* Chapel Hill: University of North Carolina Press, 1961.
Stephen L. Schecter and Richard B. Bernstein, eds. *Contexts of the Bill of Rights.* Albany: New York Commission on the Bicentennial, 1990.
Herbert Storing. *What the Anti-Federalists Were For.* Chicago: University of Chicago Press, 1981.
Gordon S. Wood. *The Creation of the American Republic, 1776–1787.* Chapel Hill: University of North Carolina Press, 1969.

CONTENTS

Volume 6—Ratifying, Amending, and Interpreting the Constitution

★

David T. Hardy, "The Second Amendment and the Historiography of the Bill of Rights," *Journal of Law and Politics*, 1987, 4(1): 1–62.

Steven R. Boyd, "The Contract Clause and the Evolution of American Federalism, 1789–1815," *William and Mary Quarterly*, 1987, 44(3)(Third Series):529–548.

Charles F. Hobson, "The Recovery of British Debts in the Federal Circuit Court of Virginia, 1790 to 1797," *Virginia Magazine of History and Biography*, 1984, 92(2):176–200.

Wythe Holt, "The First Federal Question Case," *Law and History Review*, 1985, 3(1):169–189.

James R. Perry, "Supreme Court Appointments, 1789–1801: Criteria, Presidential Style, and the Press of Events," *Journal of the Early Republic*, 1986, 6:371–410.

ACKNOWLEDGMENTS

Volume 6—Ratifying, Amending, and Interpreting the Constitution

William E. Nelson, "Reason and Compromise in the Establishment of the Federal Constitution, 1787–1801," *William and Mary Quarterly*, 1987, 44(3) (Third Series):458–484. Originally appeared in the *William and Mary Quarterly*. Courtesy of Yale University Sterling Memorial Library.

Frederick W. Marks, III, "Foreign Affairs: A Winning Issue in the Campaign for Ratification of the United States Constitution," *Political Science Quarterly*, 1971, 86(3):444–469. Reprinted with the permission of the Academy of Political Science. Courtesy of Yale University Sterling Memorial Library.

Steven R. Boyd, "Antifederalists and the Acceptance of the Constitution: Pennsylvania, 1787–1792," *Publius*, 1979, 9(2):123–137. Reprinted with the permission of the North Texas State University. Courtesy of *Publius*.

J. Thomas Wren, "The Ideology of Court and Country in the Virginia Ratifying Convention of 1788," *Virginia Magazine of History and Biography*, 1985, 93(4):389–408. Reprinted with the permission of the Historical Society of Pennsylvania. Courtesy of Yale University Sterling Memorial Library.

Jon Kukla, "A Spectrum of Sentiments: Virginia's Federalists, Antifederalists, and 'Federalists Who Are For Amendments,' 1787–1788," *Virginia Magazine of History and Biography*, 1988, 96(3):277–296. Reprinted with the permission of the Virginia Historical Society. Courtesy of Yale University Sterling Memorial Library.

Robert A. Ferguson, "'We Do Ordain and Establish': The Constitution as Literary Text," *William and Mary Law Review*, 1987, 29(1):3–25. Reprinted with the permission of the College of William and Mary. Courtesy of Yale University Law Library.

Michael Warner, "Textuality and Legitimacy in the Printed Constitution," *Proceedings of the American Antiquarian Society*, 1987, 97(1):59–84. Reprinted with the permission of the American Antiquarian Society. Courtesy of Yale University Sterling Memorial Library.

James H. Hutson, "The Creation of the Constitution: The Integrity of the Documentary Record," *Texas Law Review*, 1986, 65(1):1–39. Reprinted with the permission of the *Texas Law Review*. Courtesy of Yale University Sterling Memorial Library.

H. Jefferson Powell, "The Original Understanding of Original Intent," *Harvard Law Review*, 1985, 98(5):885–948. Reprinted with the permission of the *Harvard Law Review*. Courtesy of Yale University Law Library.

Thomas C. Grey, "Origins of the Unwritten Constitution: Fundamental Law in American Revolutionary Thought," *Stanford Law Review*, 1978, 30(5):843–893. Reprinted with the permission of the Board of Trustees of the Leland Stanford Junior University. Courtesy of Yale University Law Library.

Leslie Friedman Goldstein, "Popular Sovereignty, the Origins of Judicial Review, and the Revival of Unwritten Law," *Journal of Politics*, 1986, 48(1):51–71. Reprinted with the permission of the author and the University of Texas Press. Courtesy of Yale University Sterling Memorial Library.

Kenneth R. Bowling, "'A Tub to the Whale': The Founding Fathers and Adoption of the Federal Bill of Rights," *Journal of the Early Republic*, 1988, 8:223–251. Reprinted with the permission of Indiana University, Department of History. Courtesy of Yale University Sterling Memorial Library.

David T. Hardy, "The Second Amendment and the Historiography of the Bill of Rights," *Journal of Law and Politics*, 1987, 4(1):1–62. Reprinted with the permission of the University of Virginia, School of Law. Courtesy of Yale University Law Library.

Steven R. Boyd, "The Contract Clause and the Evolution of American Federalism, 1789–1815," *William and Mary Quarterly*, 1987, 44(3) (Third Series): 529–548. Originally appeared in the *William and Mary Quarterly*. Courtesy of Yale University Sterling Memorial Library.

Charles F. Hobson, "The Recovery of British Debts in the Federal Circuit Court of Virginia, 1790 to 1797," *Virginia Magazine of History and Biography*, 1984, 92(2):176–200. Reprinted with the permission of the Viriginia Historical Society. Courtesy of Yale University Sterling Memorial Library.

Wythe Holt, "The First Federal Question Case," *Law and History Review*, 1985, 3(1):169–189. Reprinted with the permission of the Cornell University Law School. Courtesy of Yale University Law School.

James R. Perry, "Supreme Court Appointments, 1789–1801: Criteria, Presidential Style, and the Press of Events," *Journal of the Early Republic*, 1986, 6:371–410. Reprinted with the permission of Indiana University, Department of History. Courtesy of Yale University Sterling Memorial Library.

Reason and Compromise in the Establishment of the Federal Constitution, 1787-1801

William E. Nelson

FEW historians today accept the view, outlined by Charles A. Beard and elaborated by Merrill Jensen, that the Federal Constitution was adopted for the purpose of enhancing the well-being of mercantile or aristocratic interest groups at the expense of agrarian or democratic groups. Indeed, what historians have labeled the Progressive interpretation has been widely disputed. One early challenge came from Forrest McDonald, who argued that intergroup conflict during the founding era was more complex than Beard and Jensen had imagined, with many diverse groups adopting a wide variety of sometimes antagonistic positions. Two important books, by Cecelia M. Kenyon and Herbert J. Storing, have argued that differences between the supporters and opponents of the Constitution were not socioeconomic but ideological. There have been yet other suggestions, such as that of James H. Hutson urging that conflict over the Constitution should be understood as between "court" and "country" parties.[1]

But, as Hutson himself reminds us, the Progressive interpretation has not died. It remains "evident in the identification of the Antifederalists as a discrete, socio-economic group in conflict with another discrete socio-

Mr. Nelson is Professor of Law and History, New York University. Research on this essay was supported by the John Simon Guggenheim Memorial Foundation and the Filomen D'Agostino Greenberg and Max E. Greenberg Faculty Research Fund of New York University School of Law. The helpful comments of David Thomas Konig and John Phillip Reid are gratefully acknowledged.

[1] See Beard, *An Economic Interpretation of the Constitution of the United States* (New York, 1913); Jensen, *The Articles of Confederation: An Interpretation of the Social-Constitutional History of the American Revolution, 1774-1781* (Madison, Wis., 1940), and *The New Nation: A History of the United States during the Confederation, 1781-1789* (New York, 1950); McDonald, *E Pluribus Unum: The Formation of the American Republic, 1776-1790* (Boston, 1965); Kenyon, ed., *The Antifederalists* (Indianapolis, Ind., 1966); Storing, *What the Anti-Federalists Were* For (Chicago, 1981); and Hutson, "Country, Court, and Constitution: Antifederalism and the Historians," *William and Mary Quarterly*, 3d Ser., XXXVIII (1981), 337-368. The extensive literature on the framing and ratification of the Constitution is discussed in Hutson's article and in many respects synthesized in Gordon S. Wood, *The Creation of the American Republic, 1776-1787* (Chapel Hill, N.C., 1969).

economic group."[2] While nearly all historians reject the simplistic view of the Constitution as a triumph of aristocrats over democrats, most still agree not only that the Constitution grew out of interest-group conflict, but also that it served as a vehicle through which some groups advanced their interests at the expense of others. Most historians understand that the political process by which the Constitution was adopted functioned largely as the political process now functions: through the construction of interest-group coalitions that obtain legal control of the machinery of government, enact their programs into law, and then rely on a bureaucracy, a police force, and ultimately an army to compel obedience to their law.

Although this understanding of the political process involved in the adoption of the Constitution has resulted in important contributions to historical knowledge, it is not without difficulties. One is that government in late eighteenth-century America did not possess bureaucracies, police forces, or professional soldiers armed with weapons markedly superior to the guns of ordinary citizens. As a result, government could enforce law only by persuading citizens of the law's rightness or by threatening a few dissidents with the power of the community at large.[3] This meant, in turn, that a person or group seeking to advance a political program could not do so simply by controlling existing governmental institutions and the enforcement mechanisms at their command.[4] Nor could the Founding Fathers practice politics as a science about the just distribution of wealth or influence or as a means through which particular interests could further their well-being at the expense of others. They had to work at framing a constitution that could command support from more than a narrow majority of the American people.

The received wisdom that the Constitution was designed to enable some groups to advance their interests at the expense of others also fails to account fully for the events of the founding era. It is true that, as the Constitution was being drafted, ratified, and put into operation, considerable conflict arose between interest groups. It is also true that many questions during drafting and ratification were resolved by narrow major-

[2] Hutson, "Country, Court, and Constitution," *WMQ*, 3d Ser., XXXVIII (1981), 356.

[3] On the difference between 18th- and 20th-century government compare William E. Nelson, "The Eighteenth-Century Background of John Marshall's Constitutional Jurisprudence," *Michigan Law Review*, LXXVI (1978), 893, 902-904, 917-924, with Nelson, *The Roots of American Bureaucracy, 1830-1900* (Cambridge, Mass., 1982), 2-3.

[4] The framers did not, in fact, proceed with the drafting of the Constitution or attempt to secure its ratification through manipulation of existing institutions; on the contrary, they worked outside existing procedures. The Articles of Confederation, it will be recalled, required that alterations in the frame of government be proposed by Congress and ratified by all 13 state legislatures; the framers, in contrast, used Congress only to transmit their proposals to the states and required ratification by nine state conventions instead of all 13 state legislatures.

ity votes. But, unlike the interest groups that suffer setbacks in the legislative process today, the losing minorities in the Constitution-making process quite readily accepted their defeat—a readiness demonstrated most strikingly by the disappearance of opposition to the Constitution within a few short years of its ratification.[5] Defeat was accepted, as we shall see, because majoritarian victories did not occur in matters where interest groups opposed each other; conflicts between groups were typically resolved by compromise. Majorities enjoyed their victories in other contexts where important interests were not at stake and little was lost by accepting defeat—a puzzle that historians have not explained.

New perspectives thus seem essential to a more precise understanding of the politics of the founding era. This essay will attempt to outline three such perspectives.

First, it will suggest that, although conflicts between interest groups did arise both at the Constitutional Convention and during the ratification debates, the framers dealt with them differently than modern leaders would. The Founding Fathers usually did not approach interest-group conflict by advancing one side's position, and when they did they were unsuccessful. Instead, as we know from familiar evidence about the compromises into which delegates entered during the drafting and the ratification processes, the framers strove for settlement and accommodation. What needs emphasis, however, is that their tendency to compromise was not accidental; it was embedded in the very structures of politics in which they carried on their activities.

Second, this essay will propose that interest-group conflict was neither the sole nor the most significant sort of disputation occurring at the Philadelphia and the ratifying conventions. What may be termed *instrumental-reasoning disputes* were even more important, as the Founding Fathers fought harder over questions of how to create the polity they all wanted than over how to advance the narrow interests of their constituents. Part II will examine how instrumental-reasoning disputes differed from other political conflicts and will give examples of important issues that fit within this category.

Third, the essay will urge that, once historians conceive of the Constitution not simply as a written document but also as a set of governmental customs and practices, they must understand the founding period not simply as the years 1787 and 1788 but as the decade and a half from the Philadelphia Convention to the inauguration of Thomas Jefferson and the meeting of his first Congress. Recognizing that the founding era extends into the early 1800s, in turn, further emphasizes the role of compromise and the importance of instrumental reason in the creation of the federal government.

In conjunction, these new perspectives will suggest that as the Founding Fathers drafted the Constitution, secured its ratification, and placed it into

[5] See Lance Banning, "Republican Ideology and the Triumph of the Constitution, 1789 to 1793," *WMQ*, 3d Ser., XXXI (1974), 167.

operation, they practiced a special sort of constitutional politics quite different from politics as we know it today. What made the framers' politics different was their recognition that constitutional law must resolve important issues of constitutional policy by means other than simply favoring the interests of dominant groups. By the use of reason and compromise the Founding Fathers were able to place in operation a Constitution that dominant groups in American society could not otherwise have imposed and that for two centuries has commanded wide popular support.

I: The Spirit of Compromise at the Constitutional Convention

It is unnecessary to recite in detail the conflicts between interest groups that arose at the Constitutional Convention: between the large and small states, between the agrarian South and mercantile North, and between antislavery and proslavery advocates. Nor is it necessary to write at length about the Great Compromise, giving each state two senators and apportioning representation in the House by population; about the three-fifths compromise, counting each slave as three-fifths of a white person; or about the interlocking compromises permitting the taxation of imports but not exports, barring the importation of slaves after but not before 1808, and authorizing Congress to enact commercial regulations by a simple rather than a two-thirds majority. Historians know this material too well for further discussion to serve any purpose.

But historians have tended to ignore the conciliatory habits of mind that most delegates to the convention possessed. They have also ignored the procedural rules promoting compromise that the delegates adopted at the convention's outset. These are small bits of evidence, but they are important because they suggest that the compromises were not the accidental acts of great statesmen. On the contrary, they show that the Founding Fathers cultivated a style of politics that strove for something other than the advancement of narrow group interests.

The framers were aware, of course, of the existence of interests. James Madison observed that "all civilized Societies would be divided into different Sects, Factions, & interests, as they happened to consist of rich & poor, debtors & creditors, the landed[,] the manufacturing, [and] the commercial interests," and so forth. Charles Pinckney divided Americans "into three classes—*Professional men*[,] . . . *Commercial men*, . . . [and] the *landed interest*," while others, such as Elbridge Gerry and James Wilson, thought the people had "two great interests, the landed interest, and the commercial including the stockholders."[6]

[6] Max Farrand, ed., *The Records of the Federal Convention of 1787* (New Haven, Conn., 1911), I, 135, 402, 152. On Wilson see *ibid.*, 154; see also 486-487, 491, 494-495, 604, II, 449.

Sometimes the proponents of particular interests became quite strident in their demands. For example, as soon as it was proposed that the states not have an equal vote in the new national legislature, a delegate from Delaware reminded his colleagues that his commission prohibited him "from assenting to any change of the rule of suffrage" and that the Delaware delegation might walk out rather than accept unequal voting in Congress. When the issue of representation came to a head six weeks later, the "little States" remained "fixt," as they "had repeatedly & solemnly declared themselves to be," in their demand for equality in at least one house; as William Paterson observed, no confederation "on the part of the smaller States" could occur "on any other ground than that of an equality of votes in the 2d. branch."[7]

Southerners made similarly fixed demands when the issue of slavery was discussed. Thus, when the convention was discussing a clause prohibiting the importation of slaves, John Rutledge announced that Georgia and the two Carolinas would never "agree to the plan, unless their right to import slaves be untouched"; they would "never be such fools as to give up so important an interest." Other southern delegates agreed. Likewise, when the delegates were deciding whether to count slaves in the basis for representation, William R. Davie stated that he "was sure that N. Carola. would never confederate on any terms that did not rate them at least as 3/5." On both questions, antislavery delegates responded in kind. Gouverneur Morris, for example, indicated that "the people of Pena. will never agree to a representation of Negroes," while Rufus King affirmed that "great & equal opposition" existed in the North to continued importation of slaves.[8]

The Founding Fathers' appreciation of the role of interest in politics and their sometimes strident insistence that their own interests be protected do not mean, however, that they resolved group conflict the same way political leaders resolve it today. Madison, whose advanced analysis of the politics of faction has become the starting point for subsequent American political theory, was atypical. Most delegates to the convention did not accept his view that popular rights could best be protected by dividing the community into a multiplicity of factions that could never coalesce into a stable majority and then threaten minorities.[9] They strove to preserve liberty not by promoting factional divisions but by arranging compromises that would accommodate all factions and ultimately transform them into a single homogeneous community.[10]

[7] *Ibid.*, I, 37, II, 18-19.

[8] For the debate on the importation of slaves see *ibid.*, II, 369-374. For the debate on including slaves within the basis of representation see *ibid.*, I, 591-596.

[9] Madison's theory of faction, elaborated in *Federalist* No. 10, was adumbrated at the Philadelphia Convention. See Farrand, ed., *Records*, I, 108, 134-136, 422-423, 446-447, II, 124.

[10] Unlike his fellow delegates in Philadelphia, Madison was unwilling to compromise on fundamental issues. See below, p. 465. Although he recognized that in theory factionalism could be avoided through compromise and accommodation—

Benjamin Franklin, whose role at the convention has sometimes been discounted,[11] was in fact quite important as the most persistent advocate of compromise. In the early weeks of the session, when discussion of the basis of representation was becoming heated, Franklin urged the delegates to carry on their debates "with great coolness & temper." "Positiveness and warmth," he cautioned, "tend to create and augment discord & division in a great concern, wherein harmony & Union are extremely necessary to give weight to our Councils, and render them effectual in promoting & securing the common good." Later he reminded his colleagues, "When a broad table is to be made, and the edges ⟨of planks do not fit⟩ the artist takes a little from both, and makes a good joint." Franklin's speech on the final day of the convention—the speech of an elder statesman sagely committed to traditional values of accommodation even while a young, brilliant theoretician such as Madison was foreseeing the new majoritarian form that politics would assume—typified his view in urging all the delegates to sign the Constitution and thereby "make manifest our unanimity," in spite of "all their prejudices, their passions, . . . their local interests, and their selfish views."[12]

Other delegates also put stock in methods of accommodation and compromise. When in early July the convention fell into bitter disagreement over whether to give each state equal representation in the Senate, Charles Cotesworth Pinckney seconded a motion of which, he said, he "did not entirely approve." He did so because "some compromise seemed to be necessary." Earlier, addressing the same broad issue, George Mason had expressed his "real concern" at the "difference of sentiment and opinion" that existed "in an assembly of the most respectable and confidential characters in America," while Jonathan Dayton noted his exasperation that "declamation" had been "substituted for argument." Hugh Williamson, agreeing that further debate on the convention floor was futile, favored appointment of a committee to work out a compromise because it would be "a smaller body" where "a compromise would be pursued with more coolness." Williamson was convinced that "if we do not concede on both sides, our business must soon be at an end."[13] Gerry agreed that "something must be done, or we shall disappoint not only America, but the whole world. . . . We must make concessions on both

"by giving to every citizen the same opinions, the same passions, and the same interests," Madison believed it "impracticable" to create such homogeneity (*Federalist* No. 10). He did not think the people of the United States could be regarded even in 1787 "as one homogeneous mass," and he foresaw the growth of even more factionalism in the future (Farrand, ed., *Records*, I, 422-423, II, 124). Madison's approach was thus not to try to create homogeneity but to promote a multiplicity of factions.

[11] See, for example, John P. Roche, "The Founding Fathers: A Reform Caucus in Action," *American Political Science Review*, LV (1961), 799, 808-809.

[12] Farrand, ed., *Records*, I, 197, 488, II, 641-643.

[13] *Ibid.*, I, 511, 161, 499, 515.

sides." Without concessions, he added, "the constitutions of the several States would never have been formed."[14]

What is most striking about these interest-centered debates is that claims of interest were always brought up by minorities that had no hope of triumph. The claims were a device by which defeated minorities insisted that they be accommodated through compromise. For example, the Delaware delegation reminded the convention of its instructions to insist on equality of representation in Congress at a time when a contrary plan, "being generally relished, would have been agreed to." Delaware's insistence on protection of its interest had precisely the effect that its delegates had expected when Gouverneur Morris "observed that the valuable assistance of those members could not be lost without real concern, and that so early a proof of discord in the convention as a secession of a State" was to be much regretted. Gunning Bedford's statement a month later in the same debate that the large states "no doubt" believed that they had "right on their side, but interest had blinded their eyes" likewise was designed to stop the majority from adopting a scheme of unequal representation, as was Paterson's insistence on equality of voting two weeks later; both statements had the desired effect, when Rutledge noted that all "the large States" could do in response to small-state demands for equal representation in the Senate was either "yield" or "abandon every thing to hazard." Similarly, southern intransigence on slavery led Gouverneur Morris and Roger Sherman to observe that it was "vain for the Eastern States to insist on what the Southn States will never agree to" and that it would be "better to let the S. States import slaves than to part with them."[15]

The willingness of majorities to accommodate minorities was a product, of course, of the realities of power. Nationalists of the 1780s did not have an army to coerce recalcitrant slaveholders or even a small state such as Delaware into accepting the Union. But ideology also played a role. The Founding Fathers were united in their fears that interest groups possessing untrammeled power would corrupt the polity. Thus Gouverneur Morris expressed a common sentiment when he observed that one group had "every thing" to "apprehend" from a hostile group's "getting the power into their hands." Bedford made the same point when he declared that, if they were deprived of voting equality, "the smaller States must be ruined." "The whole history of mankind," he declaimed, proved that if a majority were given power, "ambition will not fail to abuse it." Accordingly, it seemed obvious that when a minority believed some "restriction" to be "essential to liberty," while the majority felt "it of no importance," "the former" should "be indulged" by compromise.[16]

Considerations of this sort failed to persuade Madison, who urged the convention "to consider what was right & necessary in itself for the

[14] *Ibid.*, 515.
[15] *Ibid.*, 36-37, 491, II, 19, I, 593, II, 374.
[16] *Ibid.*, I, 605, 491, II, 297.

attainment of a proper Governmt." rather than to compromise. But Madison stood alone in his intransigence, for which he was upbraided by Elbridge Gerry and John Dickinson, who in mid-June, when divisions over the basis of representation were beginning "to produce serious anxiety for the result of the Convention," warned Madison that "you see the consequence of pushing things too far." Dickinson, like most of the delegates, expected that men would yield somewhat to attain agreement. The strength of this expectation is perhaps best attested by the statements of two men who refused at the convention's conclusion to sign the document: Edmund Randolph, who feared "that in refusing to sign the Constitution, he took a step which might be the most awful of his life," and Gerry, who as an earlier advocate of compromise now fully appreciated "the painful feelings of his situation."[17]

Thus, with occasional exceptions, the framers of the Constitution strove for accommodation and compromise. Indeed, they began the pursuit of agreement when, on the second day of the convention, they adopted rules for its proceedings that would facilitate accord.

These rules were designed not to enable a majority to triumph over a recalcitrant minority but to encourage discussion and to ensure that all delegates were as satisfied as possible with the convention's final decisions. One way the rules accomplished their objective was by requiring members to pay attention to each other: the delegates, for example, were prohibited from reading, milling about, or conversing while a member was speaking. Two more important rules prohibited hasty decision making when opposition existed. One provided that, although an issue had been "fully debated," its "determination" would "be postponed, if the Deputies of any State desire it, until the next day." Another directed that the delegates "not be precluded, by a vote upon any question, from revising the subject matter of it, when they see cause." Both rules encouraged pursuit of agreement by enabling defeated minorities to reopen issues until they were satisfied with their disposition. Another important decision encouraging compromise was the convention's rejection of a rule that would have authorized any member to call for the yeas and nays of individual delegates and have them recorded on the minutes. George Mason and Rufus King both opposed the rule. Mason held that "such a record of the opinions of members would be an obstacle to a change of them"—change that might be necessary to bring about compromises—and King objected because he anticipated that such "changes of opinion would be frequent in the course of the business" as differences were eliminated and agreement was established.[18]

The most prophetic decision concerned the rule by which the states were to vote in the convention. Delegates from Pennsylvania urged the large states to unite in denying the small states "an equal vote," but the Virginia delegation, "conceiving that such an attempt might beget fatal

[17] *Ibid.*, I, 215, 242, II, 646.
[18] *Ibid.*, I, 8-10; see also 65.

altercations between the large & small States, and that it would be easier to prevail on the latter, in the course of the deliberations, to give up their equality for the sake of an effective Government, than on taking the field of discussion, to disarm themselves of the right & thereby throw themselves on the mercy of the large States, discountenanced & stifled the project."[19] The Virginians, that is, recognized that to obtain the government they wanted it was necessary not to defeat the small states but to persuade them to agree, and that reason, not votes, could alone produce that result.

II: The Spirit of Reason at the Constitutional Convention

Modern political science, which contends that "at bottom, group interests are the animating forces in the political process,"[20] cannot account for all that occurred at the Philadelphia Convention. The conflicts between the large and small states and between northern and southern interests, and the compromises to which they led, consumed less than half the convention's time. In the remaining time the delegates dealt with disputes of another kind, in which no one's interests were at stake. These instrumental-reasoning disputes,[21] which produced lengthy and fiery debates, can be understood only by turning to eighteenth-century political theory.

The most helpful starting point is Jean-Jacques Rousseau's concept of the general will. The general will is not simply the unanimous will of all. The will of all is the sum of particular, private wills and hence of private interests; the general will, in contrast, "considers only the common interest" and "always . . . tends to the public advantage." Since the general will is not the same as the sum of private wills but exists independently, people may not even be aware of its existence. Accordingly, the general will is often hard to determine, and statesmen who use their powers of

[19] *Ibid.*, 11n.

[20] V. O. Key, Jr., *Politics, Parties, and Pressure Groups*, 5th ed. (New York, 1964), 17 (emphasis deleted). See also David B. Truman, *The Governmental Process: Political Interests and Public Opinion*, 2d ed. (New York, 1971), 45-65, and Robert A. Dahl, *Dilemmas of Pluralist Democracy: Autonomy vs. Control* (New Haven, Conn., 1982), 31-54, 207-209.

[21] To my knowledge, the only scholar who previously may have identified disputation of this type is John P. Roche. In his essay "The Founding Fathers: A Reform Caucus in Action," Roche distinguished between "ideological" and "structural" differences of opinion that arose at the Philadelphia Convention (*Am. Pol. Sci. Rev.*, LV [1961], 803). It may be that Roche would understand structural differences of opinion to be equivalent to what I label instrumental-reasoning disputes, but, if so, he and I reach somewhat different conclusions about the extent to which the debates at the convention and during ratification involved structural or instrumental-reasoning issues.

reasoning as an instrument for finding it "do not always see" how best to proceed and are "often deceived."[22]

Two factors make instrumental reasoning in search of the general will difficult. The first is identifying at a specific rather than a general level what constitutes the public good. For example, although Americans at the time of the Constitutional Convention understood that individual utilization of property rights promoted the public interest, this general principle gave little help to judges and lawyers striving to elaborate a myriad of specific doctrinal rules, such as which of two landowners along a stream ought to be held to own rights in the stream when each wanted to use its water in inconsistent fashions—the one for industrial and the other for agricultural purposes. The second is predicting whether the common interest will be the same in the long run as in the short. Thus judges might conclude, as they did in the late eighteenth century, that the best way to promote the public good in the case of the miller and the farmer was to recognize a property right in whichever party first used the stream, thereby giving security to investors and encouraging people to invest in economic development. A more long-range view, however, would suggest that a rule giving security to existing investors would by the 1830s retard economic growth by making it more difficult for people using new technologies to gain access to resources.[23]

[22] Rousseau, *The Social Contract and Discourses* (1762), trans. G.D.H. Cole (New York, 1950), 26. For a recent analysis of Rousseau's concept of general will as a device for distinguishing the public from private interest see Jim Miller, *Rousseau: Dreamer of Democracy* (New Haven, Conn., 1984), 61-65. The understanding of the public good as something distinct from private interest was widespread in the late 18th-century Anglo-American world. For one example see William Blackstone, *Commentaries on the Laws of England,* I (Oxford, 1765), 44, 124-128. See generally John Phillip Reid, *The Concept of Representation in the Age of the American Revolution* (forthcoming, 1987), chap. 4.

[23] These examples are drawn from law because legal reasoning is the best illustration available today of the broader category of instrumental reasoning. A recent effort to show in detail how sound legal analysis rejects the interest-group hypothesis of modern political science and attempts instead to refract precedent into coherent doctrine through the lenses of a vision of public good is Ronald Dworkin, *Law's Empire* (Cambridge, Mass., 1986). Of course, many legal scholars do not agree that the law pursues a neutral vision of the public good and instead believe that, when judges decide cases, they simply determine which of two or more contending interest groups to favor. For examples of this approach see William E. Nelson and John Phillip Reid, *The Literature of American Legal History* (Dobbs Ferry, N.Y., 1985), 261-266 (summarizing the scholarship of historians in the critical legal studies movement). For an analysis of changes in post-Revolutionary property law as a process of instrumental reasoning see William E. Nelson, *Americanization of the Common Law: The Impact of Legal Change on Massachusetts Society, 1760-1830* (Cambridge, Mass., 1975), 48-54, 121-133, 159-164. For an analysis of the same changes as a response to interest-group pressures see Morton J. Horwitz, *The Transformation of American Law, 1780-1860* (Cambridge, Mass., 1977), 31-139.

The Founding Fathers faced both these difficulties as they tried to reason instrumentally about a constitution that would serve the public not only in the 1780s and 1790s but for decades to come. How to structure and empower the national executive was perhaps the most difficult matter of instrumental reasoning that the convention faced. But it was not a matter that divided the delegates into opposing interests. Issues of presidential power, unlike those of representation, commercial regulation, or slavery, were not questions about which the delegates could know whether their constituents would benefit from particular outcomes. Predicting what groups in the nation would gain and what groups would lose from establishing either a strong or weak executive would require one piece of knowledge that the Founding Fathers could not possess—knowledge of which groups future chief executives would favor. Without this knowledge, the framers could not enter the debates on the executive branch from sharply competing points of view. On the contrary, they were united in two assumptions: first, that the new federal government would need a first magistrate sufficiently strong to provide effective leadership, and, second, that the magistrate's powers must be limited in ways that would prevent subversion of republican liberty.

The reasoned character of the debate over the executive emerged on its first day. Charles Pinckney "was for a vigorous Executive" but feared that if the chief magistrate had power to make war and peace, the new nation would become "a Monarchy, of the worst kind, towit an elective one." James Wilson "preferred a single magistrate, as giving most energy dispatch and responsibility to the office." Randolph, on the other hand, "strenuously opposed a unity in the Executive magistracy," which he regarded "as the foetus of monarchy," to which Wilson replied "that Unity in the Executive instead of being the fetus of Monarchy would be the best safeguard against tyranny."[24]

These remarks were generally offered with greater diffidence than remarks made during the discussions of representation. Indeed, after Pinckney and Wilson had opened the debate on the executive with their brief initial statements, there was a "considerable pause," which ended only when Franklin asked the delegates to "deliver their sentiments." Noting "the shyness of gentlemen," John Rutledge then commented that perhaps delegates were remaining silent because "they supposed themselves precluded by having frankly disclosed their opinions from afterwards changing them, which he did not take to be at all the case." Rutledge was plainly right: questions about the executive were matters on which, as Gouverneur Morris would later declare, his "opinion had been changed by the arguments used in the discussion," and on which Wilson could "never ma[k]e up an opinion . . . entirely to his own satisfaction."[25]

Opinions could so change because the subject of the executive was "in truth the most difficult of all on which [the convention] . . . had to decide."

[24] Farrand, ed., *Records*, I, 64-66.
[25] *Ibid.*, 65, II, 68, 501.

One's view on any particular question depended on one's other assumptions about how the executive would function—assumptions that could be elaborated only in part at the convention and would evolve in full only with the gradual development of the office of president. As Madison explained on the first day of the debate, whether the executive should be single or multiple depended on the powers granted it; accordingly, he urged the convention first to address its powers. The convention followed Madison's suggestion[26] but soon discovered that deciding what powers to grant the executive depended on whether it would be single or multiple.

Thinking about the presidency inevitably involved the delegates in such circular reasoning processes, and the question always was where to begin the circle. After the convention had been meeting for nearly three months, the problem remained unresolved. In apparent exasperation Nathaniel Gorham complained that "some could not agree to the form of Government before the powers were defined. Others could not agree to the powers till it was seen how the Government was to be formed." Rutledge agreed with Gorham about "the tediousness of the proceedings," while Oliver Ellsworth observed that "we grow more & more skeptical as we proceed. If we do not decide soon, we shall be unable to come to any decision."[27] Politics seen from such a perspective, where decisions must be made but leading figures cannot identify the best way to make them, is quite different from modern interest-group politics, where leaders know what they want and enact it into law as soon as they have the votes to do so.

The debate on July 24, dealing with the mode of selection of the president, illustrates the difference sharply. At issue was whether the president should be chosen by Congress. Gerry remarked that, if so, he should be ineligible for a second term "in order to render him independent of the Legislature." Indeed, ineligibility "appear[ed] a natural consequence of his being elected by the Legislature." But election by Congress also brought into question a second point—the length of the president's term. As Gerry later argued, "That the Executive shd. be independent of the Legislature is a clear point. The longer the duration of his appointment the more will his dependence be diminished—It will be better then for him to continue 10, 15, or even 20—years and be ineligible afterwards." Within the next few minutes several periods of tenure were proposed—eight years, eleven years, fifteen years, and even twenty years, which Rufus King called "the medium life of princes." King argued, however, that the president's term of office and reeligibility would have "small effect . . . on his dependence" on the legislature, "if impeachments are to lie." The effect of impeachment, he thought, would be to give the president "tenure during pleasure" and thereby transform the executive into a dependent of Congress.[28]

[26] *Ibid.*, II, 501, I, 67.
[27] *Ibid.*, II, 300-301.
[28] *Ibid.*, 100-102.

At this point Wilson commented on "the difficulties & perplexities into which the House is thrown," and Gerry observed that "we seem to be entirely at a loss on this head." Gouverneur Morris then summed up the convention's dilemmas. He noted that initially he "had been opposed to . . . impeachment" because giving Congress that power would make the president "the mere creature of it." He had become convinced, however, "that impeachments must be provided for," since "no man wd. say, that an Executive known to be in the pay of an Enemy, should not be removable in some way or other." Morris then discovered that a power of impeachment inevitably led to other difficulties—in particular, to "intrigues to get him [the president] out of office. Some leader of party will always covet his seat, will perplex his administration, will cabal with the Legislature, till he succeeds in supplanting him. . . . In order to get rid of the dependence of the Executive on the Legislature," Morris continued, "the expedient of making him ineligible a 2d. time had been devised," but he thought this expedient foolish since it would deprive the nation of the benefit of the president's experience. Nor did he favor ineligibility for a second term coupled with a long first term, since he feared that a long-term president "in possession of the sword" would be "unwilling to quit his exaltation," that "a civil war" would "ensue," and that "the Commander of the victorious army" would become "the despot of America." Morris's ultimate conclusion was that "it is ⟨the⟩ most difficult of all rightly to balance the Executive. Make him too weak: The Legislature will usurp his powers: Make him too strong. He will usurp on the Legislature."[29]

It is essential to observe how different this debate was from those between interest groups. What was in dispute was not what each delegate desired for his own group in the present but what the delegates expected or feared for the nation as a whole in the future. Their fears were not unreasonable, since the office they created was sufficiently amorphous to be subject, on the one hand, to subordination at the hands of Congress and to attain, on the other, almost dictatorial dominance over the other branches of government. Only the development of executive precedents and practices in the future could assure the framers of their unanimous desire—a strong and independent yet not tyrannical chief magistrate. Meanwhile all the Founding Fathers could do was to look dimly through the haze, to imagine problems the future might bring, and to reason about how to preclude or mitigate them. Their disagreements occurred not over competing ends but over the means best calculated to achieve their shared end.

Many issues, in addition to that of the executive, were discussed from this perspective of a politics of instrumental reason rather than a politics of conflicting interest. One was whether Congress should have a power to negative state laws. Madison, for one, "considered the negative . . . essential" to prevent the states from "pursu[ing] their particular interests in opposition to the general interest" and to keep them from encroaching

[29] *Ibid.*, 102-105.

on national authority as they had under the Articles of Confederation. Wilson agreed that the federal government needed more than the Supremacy Clause for its protection: "the firmness of Judges," he declared, "is not of itself sufficient." He thought it "better to prevent the passage of an improper law, than to declare it void when passed." Others were concerned that a power to negative state laws would be too broad. Williamson opposed "giving a power that might restrain the States from regulating their internal police," while Mason inquired, "Is no road nor bridge to be established without the Sanction of the General Legislature? Is this to sit constantly in order to receive & revise the State Laws?" Although a congressional negative was the most efficient means of ensuring Congress's supremacy over national matters, the danger was that the states would be deprived of control over merely local matters. Dickinson stated the dilemma most clearly when he observed that it was "impossible to draw a line between the cases proper & improper for the exercise of the negative" and added that the convention "must take our choice of two things"—"either subject the States to the danger of being injured by the power of the Natl. Govt. or the latter to the danger of being injured by that of the States." Dickinson "thought the danger greater from the States," but the convention disagreed when it ultimately rejected a congressional negative by a 6-5 vote.[30]

What demands emphasis is that the issue of a congressional negative, like every other issue concerning the relative power of state and federal institutions, could not become a subject of interest-group conflict until it was known which groups would control the federal and which groups would control the state governments. That could not be known in Philadelphia in 1787, and hence issues of federalism could not be debated there as interest-group conflicts. Such questions could be addressed only through reasoning about the proper balance between national and state powers under future circumstances that no one could perfectly predict.[31]

[30] *Ibid.*, 27-28, 391, I, 165, II, 390, I, 167, II, 391.

[31] But see Andrew Cunningham McLaughlin's argument in *The Confederation and the Constitution, 1783-1789* (New York, 1905), 208, that issues of federalism were related to the interest-group conflict over the basis of representation in Congress. According to McLaughlin, the delegates from the large states were strong nationalists, while many of those from the small states hoped to maintain state sovereignty as a check on national power. McLaughlin's argument finds some support in a speech by Ellsworth noting that "proportional representation . . . was conformable to the national principle" and "equality of voices was conformable to the federal principle" (Farrand, ed., *Records*, I, 468) and has been echoed in more recent scholarship. See, for example, Clinton Rossiter, *1787: The Grand Convention* (New York, 1966), 192-194.

The relationship suggested by McLaughlin fails to withstand analysis, however, when the votes on the Great Compromise are checked against the votes on the two key issues of federal power that most divided the convention: (1) whether Congress would have power to negative state laws, and (2) whether the Constitution *ex proprio vigore* would establish inferior federal courts. Of the four states that

This same sort of reasoned deliberation occurred in reference to a series of questions about the judiciary—what courts should exist, how judges should be chosen, and whether judges should be members of a Council of Revision with power to veto legislation. Since no one could predict which groups would gain and which would lose in future federal courts, questions about the judiciary could be apprehended only from a perspective of instrumental reasoning rather than interest-group politics. Thus the delegates inquired whether confining the federal judiciary to a single supreme court would be "sufficient to secure the national rights & uniformity of Judgmts." On the one hand, there were concerns that lower federal courts would encroach on state jurisdiction and be expensive, while, on the other, proponents of an inferior federal judiciary held that, if a supreme court were the only federal tribunal, "appeals would be multiplied to a most oppressive degree," and in many cases "an appeal would not . . . be a remedy." Moreover, they thought federal courts ought to have original jurisdiction over "cases not within the jurisdiction of particular states." In the upshot, the debate revealed the complexity of this issue of instrumental reasoning, and the framers wisely left to future Congresses the determination of what lower federal courts should exist.[32]

Another issue was whether judges should be appointed by the legislature or the executive. "Experience," said Wilson, "shewed the impropriety of such appointmts. by numerous bodies," where "intrigue, partiality, and concealment were the necessary consequences." On the other hand, delegates such as Rutledge were "by no means disposed to grant so great a power to any single person." Madison agreed with both views: he "disliked the election of the Judges by the Legislature or any numerous body," in which "many of the members were not judges of the requisite qualifications"; at the same time, he "was not satisfied with referring the appointment to the Executive." Early in the debate Madison proposed that

---

voted against equality of representation in the Senate, only one—Virginia—voted in favor of both the congressional negative and mandatory federal courts. Pennsylvania voted for lower federal courts but against the negative, while Georgia and South Carolina voted against both. A fifth large state—Massachusetts—voted in favor of the negative but was divided on the issues both of equality in the Senate and of mandatory lower courts. Of the five states voting in favor of equality in the Senate, only two—Connecticut and New Jersey—voted as McLaughlin's thesis would predict: against both the congressional negative and the lower federal courts. The other three—Delaware, Maryland, and North Carolina—supported one or the other of the proposals for enhancing national power but not both. Of the ten states that voted on all three issues, only three voted consistently for one or the other position identified by McLaughlin. See Farrand, ed., *Records*, I, 125, II, 15, 28. Given that the probability of obtaining a consistent run of either heads or tails on three consecutive flips of a coin is 25%, the pattern of voting identified above is better explained as random than as a reflection of some relationship between issues of federalism and the fight over the basis of representation in Congress.

[32] Farrand, ed., *Records*, I, 124-125.

"a blank [be] left to be hereafter filled on maturer reflection." The convention agreed and ultimately compromised on executive selection with senatorial confirmation.[33]

The third issue was whether judges should be joined to the president to form a Council of Revision with power to veto acts of Congress. "The aid of the Judges," it was thought, would "give more wisdom & firmness to the Executive." According to Madison, there was "a powerful tendency in the Legislature to absorb all power into its vortex," and this tendency "suggested the necessity of giving every defensive authority to the other departments." The objection to joining the judges to a Council of Revision was that this would weaken the judiciary. It was essential, according to Luther Martin, "that the Supreme Judiciary should have the confidence of the people," and that confidence, he thought, would "soon be lost, if they are employed in the task of remonstrating agst. popular measures of the Legislature." Nor, it was suggested, did judges "possess any peculiar knowledge of the mere policy of public measures," and, "as to the Constitutionality of laws, that point [would] come before the Judges in their proper official character." It was impossible, of course, to predict with certainty whether adding the judges to a Council of Revision would strengthen the executive or weaken the judiciary, and in that situation the convention acted in what was becoming a familiar pattern: by a narrow 4-3 margin, with two states divided, it reached a decision in which the three-state minority, which had no competing interest at stake, acquiesced, in this case declining to add the judges to a Council of Revision and leaving the president alone in the exercise of a qualified power of veto.[34]

Other issues also lent themselves to reasoned discussion and debate. Among them were whether legislators should be eligible for offices in the executive branch, whether federal force could ever be applied effectively against entire states as distinguished from individuals within those states, whether states should be barred from impairing the obligation of private contracts, and whether Congress should have authority to emit paper money.[35] The debates on all these issues were characterized by the framers' awareness that they could not resolve the issues simply by identifying an interest group, whether that group be debtors or creditors, on which to confer a short-term advantage. Rather, as Rutledge reminded them in another context, they were "laying the foundation for a great empire" and therefore had "to take a permanent view of the subject and not look at the present moment only." The delegates took a "permanent," instrumental-reasoning view even of the obligation of contract and paper money issues—matters of debtor-creditor law that had typically been the subject of intense interest-group conflict throughout eighteenth-century America. An illustration of the way instrumental-reasoning concerns could override interest-group affiliation comes from two speeches of

[33] *Ibid.*, 119-120.
[34] *Ibid.*, II, 73-80.
[35] See *ibid.*, 283-289, 489-492, I, 54, II, 439-440, 309-310.

George Mason, a creditor who favored enforcement of contracts and payment of debts in specie rather than in inflated paper money. Yet, in the midst of the debate on the contract clause, he argued that states should be left free to interfere with private contracts since "cases will happen that can not be foreseen, where some kind of interference will be proper, & essential." Similarly, he cautioned against preventing Congress from emitting paper money: although "he had a mortal hatred to paper money, yet as he could not foresee all emergences, he was unwilling to tie the hands of the Legislature."[36]

When the delegates took a long view, as they frequently did—so long, indeed, that they could not predict how their decisions would affect future configurations of interest-group conflict—they then had to decide issues not by determining the interest they favored but by reasoning how best to achieve the public good. When they came face-to-face with all the uncertainties that were inevitable in that process, they could and sometimes did debate with vehemence. But ultimately, they had to take one of three courses. They could, as with the Council of Revision and paper money proposals, decline to impose restrictions on the future. Or, as with the questions concerning a lower federal judiciary and state impairment of the obligation of contract, they could adopt general constitutional language and leave to future legislators or judges the tasks of working out the details. Finally, as with the presidency, they could, if an issue was sufficiently important to the success of the new government, think long and hard about its interrelated details, very often making judgments by narrow majority votes—votes that the losing minority could readily accept because all that had been at stake in the vote was its prediction about the future, not its fundamental group interests.

III: Ratifying the Constitution and Starting the New Government: The Continuing Role of Reason and Compromise

At least since Charles A. Beard's *An Economic Interpretation of the Constitution,* most historians have viewed the ratification process as one that pitted Federalists, who represented identifiable interest groups, against Antifederalists, who represented opposing groups. Likewise, historians have assumed that when Federalists and Republicans fought over issues of the Constitution's meaning during the early national period, they were standing as representatives of antagonistic interest groups.[37]

[36] *Ibid.,* II, 452, 440, 309.

[37] For the literature on ratification see Steven R. Boyd, *The Politics of Opposition: Antifederalists and the Acceptance of the Constitution* (Millwood, N.Y., 1979), and Hutson, "Country, Court, and Constitution," *WMQ,* 3d Ser., XXXVIII (1981), 337-368. The literature viewing political parties of the 1790s as surrogates for competing interest groups is usefully summarized in Daniel Sisson, *The American*

On the surface, key facts appear to support this view. Proponents of the Constitution secured its ratification in the four most important states—Massachusetts, New York, Pennsylvania, and Virginia—through manipulation of parliamentary procedure and by narrow majority votes of a sort familiar to modern interest-group politics. And key issues of constitutional interpretation, such as the propriety of a standing army and of federal prosecutions for seditious libel, did divide parties in the last years of the eighteenth century.[38] Nonetheless, during the 1787-1801 period, the politics of ratification and constitutional interpretation on the whole resembled the politics of instrumental reason and compromise that had been so prominent at the Philadelphia Convention.

Some familiar evidence should be noted at the outset. First there is the fact that the Constitution was ratified unanimously or by lopsided votes in seven states.[39] Close partisan battles were thus the exception rather than the rule. Then there is the pamphlet literature, especially *The Federalist,* one of the great examples in human history of the use of reasoned analysis to achieve a political end. While it was the most creative and insightful of the essays that were published, *The Federalist* was not unique: it was one of many similar efforts by both proponents and opponents of the Constitution to persuade the public by reason.[40] Finally there is the Bill of Rights, which is rightly understood as a Federalist effort at compromise designed to accommodate Antifederalist concerns that a strong national government might threaten individual liberties.

Even the opponents of ratification took note of the role that reasoned deliberation had played in their defeat. Several Massachusetts delegates observed that the debate there had been "govern[ed] . . . by principles of reason" and that the Constitution had been "carried by a majority of wise

---

Revolution of 1800 (New York, 1974), 3-24, despite his rejection of the received view.

[38] See Robert A. Rutland, *The Ordeal of the Constitution: The Antifederalists and the Ratification Struggle of 1787-1788* (Norman, Okla., 1966), 20, 110, 250, 255-256; Linda Grant De Pauw, *The Eleventh Pillar: New York State and the Federal Constitution* (Ithaca, N.Y., 1966), 183-254; Jonathan Elliot, ed., *The Debates in the Several State Conventions on the Adoption of the Federal Constitution* (Philadelphia, 1836), II, 181, III, 653-654; Richard H. Kohn, *Eagle and Sword: The Federalists and the Creation of the Military Establishment in America, 1783-1802* (New York, 1975), 191-255; and Leonard W. Levy, *Emergence of a Free Press* (New York, 1985), 280-281, 297-327.

[39] The vote was unanimous in Delaware, Georgia, and New Jersey. The vote in favor of the Constitution was 128-40 in Connecticut, 63-11 in Maryland, 149-73 in South Carolina, and 46-23 in Pennsylvania. See Boyd, *Politics of Opposition,* 46, and Rutland, *Ordeal of the Constitution,* 58, 157-158, 165, 168.

[40] The extent of the literature making reasoned arguments about the Constitution emerges in Merrill Jensen, John P. Kaminski, and Gaspare J. Saladino, eds., *The Documentary History of the Ratification of the Constitution* (Madison, Wis., 1976-), and Herbert J. Storing, *The Complete Anti-Federalist,* 7 vols. (Chicago, 1981).

and understanding men"; although they "had opposed adoption of the Constitution, upon the idea that it would endanger the liberties of . . . [the] country," they now hoped they would "be disappointed in their fears, and that the majority may reap the full fruition of the blessings they anticipate." Edmund Randolph, who refused to sign the Constitution at Philadelphia but ultimately voted to ratify it, explained that he "*still had objections to the Constitution*" but that he was supporting it because "the accession of eight states reduced our *deliberations* to the single question of *Union or no Union*." Many other opponents were similarly willing to "support the Constitution as cheerfully and as heartily as though [t]he[y] had voted on the other side of the question." Patrick Henry, who led the lost cause in Virginia and vowed to continue working to "remove the defects" of the Constitution, indicated that he would do so only "in a constitutional way" as "a peaceable citizen" who would "not . . . go to violence." As a result, according to one South Carolinian, "the Constitution went into operation with general consent," as "the minority not only acquiesced, but heartily joined in supporting the determination of the majority." A Massachusetts newspaper reported that "all appeared willing to bury the hatchet of animosity, and to smoke the calumet of union and love," while Connecticut, after "the federal party had obtained the superiority," was said to be "very quiet in its politics," with "both sides . . . quietly disposed to lay down their arms." Even in New York, observers commented upon "the spirit of amity and conciliation which prevail[ed] . . . among the people at large" by the close of the ratifying convention and reported that "all parties show a return of good humor, and a desire of once more becoming a united people."[41]

This acquiescence took place, in part, because Federalists and Antifederalists concurred on the main ends of government. Their disagreements, as Herbert Storing has observed, "were not based on different premises about the nature of man or the ends of political life." Rather, they "agreed that the purpose of government" was the protection of civil liberty and "that the best instrument for this purpose [was] some form of limited, republican government." Federalists and Antifederalists also agreed that the old structure of government was inadequate. As students of the ratification controversy have noted, there was "widespread support for some reform of the Articles," with "no substant[ial] group in Congress or in the state legislatures deny[ing] the need for reform."[42]

The meanderings of men like Elbridge Gerry and Edmund Randolph are important evidence that the Founding Fathers were working together to attain the public good but were uncertain how to do so. Gerry, for

[41] Elliot, ed., *Debates*, II, 181-183, III, 652, II, 183, III, 652, IV, 342; Russell's *Centinel*, quoted in Rutland, *Ordeal of the Constitution*, 111; Simeon Baldwin to James Kent, Mar. 8, 1788, quoted in Boyd, *Politics of Opposition*, 141; *New-York Journal*, July 21, 1788, quoted in De Pauw, *Eleventh Pillar*, 266.

[42] Storing, *What Anti-Federalists Were* For, 5; Boyd, *Politics of Opposition*, 4; De Pauw, *Eleventh Pillar*, 265.

example, revealed his ambivalence when, after he had acted contrary to the interests of his home state as a leading architect of the Great Compromise and thus kept the convention from failing, he refused to sign the document he had done so much to sustain. Randolph appears to have been even more confused: first, he presented the Virginia Plan for a strong national government; then he refused to sign the Constitution; finally, he voted in favor of its ratification. The wanderings of Gerry and Randolph were mirrored in the willingness of delegates elected to state conventions as Antifederalists to switch positions and vote for ratification when, upon reflection, they were persuaded by reasoned arguments that the Constitution did not threaten liberty.[43] These switches simply make no sense if divisions over the Constitution are perceived as deep cleavages of the sort that typically arise between aristocrats and democrats or between warring religious groups.

The best evidence of the circumscribed character of the debate concerns the issue that divided the key New York and Virginia conventions. It was a very narrow issue: whether to ratify the Constitution, put the federal government into operation, and then seek to correct its imperfections, or to push for a second general convention to improve the document before its final ratification. The issue grows even narrower when the amendments proposed by the Antifederalists in eight states are examined in detail.[44] Such examination discloses that the Antifederalists did not seriously question the need for a new central government exercising essentially the powers granted by the Constitution. And the Federalists' response to the proposed amendments indicates that they, on their part, did not, in the main, intend the new government to exercise the powers that the amendments were designed to limit or deny. Americans generally agreed upon the goal of a government strong enough to promote economic growth and protect them from foreign foes, yet not so strong as to endanger their liberty. They divided only on the means of attaining these objectives.

Many of the proposed amendments dealt with questions of personal liberty of the sort addressed in the first eight articles of the Bill of Rights. No one wanted a government that could quarter soldiers in private homes, compel citizens to incriminate themselves, subject them to cruel and unusual punishments, or establish a national religion. Nor did anyone want Congress to interfere with freedom of speech and press, whatever that might mean.[45] Accordingly, Federalists acceded to Antifederalist demands for the protection of personal rights as the price of ratification.

[43] See De Pauw, *Eleventh Pillar*, 250-254, and Rutland, *Ordeal of the Constitution*, 94, 109-110, 226-227, 233-234, 250.

[44] The proposals to amend the Constitution that are examined in the following pages are printed in Edward Dumbauld, *The Bill of Rights and What It Means Today* (Norman, Okla., 1957), 173-205.

[45] See Elwyn A. Smith, *Religious Liberty in the United States: The Development of Church-State Thought since the Revolutionary Era* (Philadelphia, 1972), 246-250, and Levy, *Emergence of a Free Press*, 234-269.

Other amendments dealt with questions of federal power as distinguished from individual rights. The most common concern was to control the military establishment and the war-making power. Six states proposed limitations on the power of Congress to maintain a standing army in time of peace, and five of these six sought to assure state control over the militia. Also proposed were limitations on the length of terms of military enlistment, a prohibition against the president's commanding the army in person, and a measure to prevent Congress from declaring war except with the concurrence of two-thirds of both houses.

Another common set of concerns focused on the power of the federal judiciary. Antifederalists in seven states desired amendments to guarantee the common law right to trial by jury and to limit the jurisdiction of inferior federal courts. Various limits on the scope of the federal judicial power were suggested: New York, for example, offered an amendment barring suits against a state, while Maryland proposed that "federal courts . . . not be entitled to jurisdiction by fictions or collusion."[46]

Such preoccupation with the judiciary and the military is not surprising given the structure of government to which eighteenth-century Americans were accustomed. Juries in the 1780s still possessed power to decide law as well as fact, thereby guaranteeing that the custom of the vicinage from which a jury was drawn would constitute the effective law of that vicinage.[47] Americans associated liberty with the preservation of local autonomy and had struggled for Independence from Great Britain partly in response to British efforts to restrict that autonomy. Federal judges and soldiers posed the same threat that imperial power had posed: the threat of a central government with the capacity to coerce local jurisdictions. The Antifederalist effort to check the rise of coercive government should not, however, be perceived as polarizing Americans. Most supporters of the Constitution did not want to destroy local autonomy any more than opponents wanted to see it destroyed; indeed, the Washington administration set precedents that preserved extensive local autonomy for four-score years. The issues of 1787-1801 concerning the military and the courts were not battles over whether a national government was needed but disputes about how to structure that government in order to provide the security Americans wanted without undermining liberty.

[46] Dumbauld, *Bill of Rights,* 178. An example of a fictitious or collusive suit would be one where both litigants agree that a federal court has jurisdiction of their case on grounds of diversity of citizenship even though both are, in fact, citizens of the same state. Federal courts actually heard such cases prior to *Bingham* v. *Cabot,* 3 U.S. (3 Dall.) 382 (1798), when the Supreme Court held that they were obliged to dismiss cases for want of diversity even when defendants failed to move for dismissal. See William E. Nelson, "The American Revolution and the Emergence of Modern Doctrines of Federalism and Conflict of Laws," Colonial Society of Massachusetts, *Publications,* LXII (Boston, 1984), 419, 454-456, 459-460.

[47] See Nelson, "Eighteenth-Century Background," *Mich. Law Rev.,* LXXVI (1978), 904-924.

Another common demand, in which seven states and the Antifederalist minority in Pennsylvania joined, was for a provision, the equivalent of the Ninth and Tenth Amendments, reserving to the people and to the states all rights not expressly granted to the federal government. The seven states and the Pennsylvania minority also requested limitations on the power of Congress to regulate elections and to levy direct taxes. Four states proposed to limit the treaty-making power, so that legal provisions contained in treaties would not automatically be superior to state law.

With the possible exception of the proposal to reserve rights to the people and the states, which has turned out to be meaningless, these were not trivial demands. Powers to tax, to regulate elections, and to make law through agreements with other nations could lead to national despotism over the states. No one, however, meant the federal government to exercise the powers in question. Neither Congress nor the president made any attempt to regulate elections during the 1790s, and the provision in the Jay Treaty making the federal government liable for debts that British creditors could not collect from their Revolutionary debtors set a precedent against using treaties as a mechanism for altering private rights held by individuals pursuant to state law—a precedent that continues to be honored today. Although the Washington administration used direct taxation, such as the tax on carriages, to obtain small amounts of revenue, it relied chiefly on import duties to finance the government; its practice, together with the repeal of all internal taxes at the outset of Jefferson's presidency, set a precedent allowing the use of direct taxation only in emergencies—a constitutional rule that was overturned only with the adoption of the Sixteenth Amendment. This rule was precisely what the Antifederalists wanted, as all their amendments proposing to limit the taxing power would have left Congress free to levy direct taxes in emergencies.[48]

In sum, the proposals to limit federal power to tax, regulate elections, and make law through treaties did not generate fundamental questions about the scope of national power. Nor did the proposals raise any sharp conflict among opposing interest groups. They merely raised a conflict over means, not over ends: was it better to prohibit the national government from ever exercising powers that Americans did not trust it to have or simply to say nothing about those powers and trust that the government would never use them?

Many less significant demands to limit the powers of Congress were also put forth. Three states demanded that congressional power over a future

[48] See Samuel Flagg Bemis, *Jay's Treaty: A Study in Commerce and Diplomacy*, rev. ed. (New Haven, Conn., 1962), 434-439; Article 6 of the Jay Treaty, *ibid.*, 460-463; Willard Bunce Cowles, *Treaties and Constitutional Law: Property Interferences and Due Process of Law* (Washington, D.C., 1941), 52-291; Noble E. Cunningham, Jr., *The Process of Government under Jefferson* (Princeton, N.J., 1978), 78, 155; and Sidney Ratner, *American Taxation: Its History as a Social Force in Democracy* (New York, 1942), 26-35, 64-98, 133-135, 140, 191-214, 298-307, 333-336.

federal district should extend only to regulations for police and good government. New York asked for an amendment barring Congress from constructing post offices and highways in a state without the consent of its legislature, and for a second amendment requiring a balanced budget unless two-thirds of each house agreed otherwise. The Pennsylvania minority sought protection of fishing rights in navigable waters and asked that the clause in Article I, Section 9, respecting vessels bound to or from any one of the states be explained. North Carolina joined Pennsylvania's Antifederalists in the latter request and further proposed that states be permitted to retain in circulation paper money that had already been emitted. North Carolina also proposed to bar Congress from declaring a state in rebellion or introducing foreign troops into the United States without the consent of two-thirds of each house. Two states proposed to limit the power of the president by prohibiting suspension of laws without the consent of Congress. None of these amendments touched an issue of any significance in 1788: all they did was raise again the question whether it was necessary explicitly to prohibit the national government from exercising powers that Americans did not trust it to have.

A large group of amendments dealt with housekeeping details. The most important of these proposed to limit the president's tenure to eight years. Another sought to deprive Congress of its power to allow foreign states to confer titles of nobility on American officeholders. Still others dealt with such matters as multiple officeholding, the keeping of national accounts, the creation of a presidential cabinet, the form of writs and processes, the size of congressional districts, federal regulation of the time and place of national elections, official salaries, and publication of the proceedings of Congress. As to these matters, the issue dividing the parties was whether to make provision in the Constitution or to deal with them by subsequent legislation.

Two subjects addressed by proposed amendments raised issues over which groups with divergent interests might have come into conflict. One was a proposal that Congress be barred from granting monopolies. This proposal did not, however, arise out of interest-group conflict, as is evidenced by the fact that it received support from Massachusetts, New Hampshire, New York, and North Carolina—four states that had few economic interests in common and were unlikely to be united, except fortuitously, on one side of any socioeconomic issue.

The second set of proposals addressed what could have been the most divisive of all issues in late eighteenth-century America—religion. Six states requested adoption of the equivalent of what became the First Amendment, barring an establishment of religion and prohibiting federal interference with its free exercise. Three states desired an amendment protecting conscientious objectors from compulsory military service. But although religious differences had great capacity to create conflict in the founding period, they did not in fact do so at the federal level. Some of the Constitution's strongest proponents, such as Madison, had fought for religious liberty and disestablishment. They had no plan to establish religion and quickly conceded the need for constitutional protection of the sort codified in the First Amendment.

Only two proposed amendments addressed matters of interest-group conflict and were designed to deprive Congress of important powers that the Founding Fathers intended it to have. One of the two was offered by Virginia, North Carolina, and a minority of the Maryland convention: "that no navigation law, or law regulating commerce, shall be passed without the consent of two thirds of the members present, in both houses."[49] At issue was whether a northern majority in Congress could adopt legislation to favor its own shipping interests at the expense of southern agriculture; requiring a two-thirds vote would ensure that no commercial legislation could be enacted without the help of southern votes. The two-thirds proposal had been advanced at the Philadelphia Convention but had been rejected as part of a compromise package in which southern interests in slavery were advanced in return for the advancement of northern shipping interests. Precisely because the proposal was a regional plank that upset a compromise that had brought benefit to the South, it attracted little support outside the region. Ultimately, it was an aberrant political effort that ran counter to the spirit of compromise and reasoned pursuit of the public good that characterized the constitution-making process.

The second of the two amendments seeking to protect special interests was offered by the Pennsylvania Antifederalists. It proposed to forbid the levy of excise taxes. New York provided support to the Pennsylvania minority with a proposal to ban all excise taxes except on ardent spirits. Two other states would have let Congress levy excises but would have permitted state governments to avoid the imposition of duties by paying to Congress the revenue expected from the excise. Antifederalists in three other states, however, took exactly the opposite position, specifically proposing that Congress be left with the same power to levy excise taxes as to impose import duties. Especially in view of these divisions among Antifederalists, it is not surprising that demands to restrict Congress's freedom to levy excise taxes were ignored. When opponents of the Constitution were even minimally united in opposition to the new government's exercise of some power, the Constitution's supporters could agree, either by formal constitutional amendment or by the informal establishment of constitutional precedent, that the power not be exercised. The Founding Fathers could not, however, guarantee protection for the interests of every small economic group; some interests required submersion if a nation was to be built. Thus the framers left future congressional majorities free both to impose excise taxes and to regulate commerce, even though the use of these powers immediately gave rise to substantial opposition.[50]

[49] Elliot, ed., *Debates*, III, 660.

[50] See Thomas P. Slaughter, "The Tax Man Cometh: Ideological Opposition to Internal Taxes, 1760-1790," *WMQ*, 3d Ser., XLI (1984), 566, 584-591, and

In most instances, however, the Federalists responded positively to Antifederalist demands for constitutional guarantees. Their response can be understood in two ways. First, the Federalists were willing to compromise and accede to Antifederalist demands for guarantees of liberty. During several state ratifying conventions, they agreed to press for constitutional amendments, and they did, in fact, bring to fruition amendments securing individual liberties such as freedom of religion and freedom of the press. Although they did not support formal amendments that would have limited the powers of Congress and the federal judiciary or otherwise restructured the new government, they made no efforts during Washington's administration to place in operation the kind of autocratic, coercive regime the Antifederalists feared. No standing army was created during the first years of the new republic, and only a bare-bones judiciary was put in place. Precedents in respect to such matters as the practices of Congress and the two-term limitation on the presidency, which had been sponsored by the Antifederalists in the form of explicit amendments, became established as custom. And when the Supreme Court in *Chisholm* v. *Georgia*[51] held that states were subject to suit in federal court, all political leaders quickly joined in reversing that ruling through the Eleventh Amendment.

The precedents set during the Washington administration would have the same enduring force as the constitutional text itself. They would be followed for nearly a century until the era of the Civil War. Of course, there was one exception. During the term of John Adams, proponents of strong national government adopted legislation suppressing freedom of speech and press, creating a standing army, and expanding the federal court system. But the exception merely proves the point that enduring constitutional customs were established during the Washington administration. The experiments of the Adams years aroused the indignation of many Americans, including former Federalists such as Madison who joined former Antifederalists to restore the original constitutional compromise by repealing the 1801 Judiciary Act and by allowing the Sedition Act and the legislation for a large military establishment to lapse.

The second way to understand the Federalists' positive response to Antifederalist demands is to perceive both groups not as antagonists who compromised matters about which they disagreed but as disinterested statesmen working together in pursuit of the public good. Their differences occurred only when, as they tried to reason toward that end, they recognized that their failure or success depended upon future contingencies that might or might not occur. So understanding their differences, both Federalists and Antifederalists were prepared to submerge them, to adopt constitutional amendments to protect rights against the contingencies most likely to occur, and otherwise to trust to future luck for the

---

Nelson, "Eighteenth-Century Background," *Mich. Law Rev.*, LXXVI (1978), 944-947.

[51] 2 U.S. (2 Dall.) 419 (1793).

preservation of a polity that both wanted and neither knew for certain how to attain.

Like the men who drafted the Constitution in the summer of 1787 at Philadelphia, the men who participated in its ratification and early interpretation during the closing years of the eighteenth century may at times have found themselves with conflicting interests that required compromise in order to promote a greater national interest. At other times, those who sat in the ratification conventions or served in the new national government engaged in vigorous and often brilliant debate about how best to effectuate fundamental principles on which they agreed. However, the outcome of these debates did not threaten vital interests of any substantial group, and thus the American people had no difficulty accepting that outcome, even though some may have doubted its wisdom.

IV: The Nature of Constitutional Law

If one accepts the conclusion that the proponents of the Constitution did not force a recalcitrant minority to accept a system favoring narrow interests but instead derived the system from first principles upon which most Americans agreed or from compromises that most could accept, an appreciation of the Founding Fathers' accomplishment falls readily into place. Their accomplishment was the differentiation of constitutional politics from normal politics. Although they could not eliminate all opposition to the Constitution or prevent debate about the wisdom of adopting it, they did succeed to a remarkable extent in separating the debate from ongoing interest-group conflicts. More important, they transformed the nature of the debate, causing participants to ask not what was good for them individually but what was best for the public as a whole.

Such an appreciation of the Founding Fathers' accomplishment can help to reaffirm the special place that constitutional law must enjoy in the American polity. Understanding that law represents nothing but the codified will of powerful interests may give satisfaction to those who have power and may also teach them how to maximize their well-being. But such a conception of law gives neither solace nor protection to the powerless. The nation cannot live up to its ideal of equal justice for the weak as well as the strong unless the Constitution and the law derived from it promote the good of all. Understanding that the founding generation could abandon an interest-oriented conception of politics and adopt a long-term disinterested view, and thereby draft and adopt a Constitution for the public good, serves to remind our generation that it too must make the same choice: it must interpret that Constitution not to achieve the narrow goals of interests but for the broad public good.

All this, in turn, warrants redirection of the course that the historiography of the Constitution has taken in this century. To the extent that historians understand that the debates over the Constitution were abstracted from the ongoing interest-group conflicts of normal politics, they ought not expend all their energies trying to relate the struggle over the Constitution either to those normal political conflicts or to deeper and more enduring divisions in American society. Rather, they should focus on the debates of 1787-1801 as an early step in the emergence of the classic American pattern of separation of constitutional law from politics. Finally, they should begin to analyze the Constitutional Convention and the state ratifying conventions as institutions that, like the Supreme Court under John Marshall,[52] derived constitutional law by reasoning instrumentally about the public good, not as institutions that made political decisions grounded in the self-interest of those in control.

[52] See Nelson, "Eighteenth-Century Background," *Mich. Law Rev.*, LXXVI (1978), 932-960.

Foreign Affairs: A Winning Issue in the Campaign for Ratification of the United States Constitution

FREDERICK W. MARKS III
Purdue University

If we are to be one nation in any respect, it clearly ought to be in respect to other nations.[1]

The work of the Philadelphia Convention in drafting the American Constitution during the hot summer of 1787 has been called a "miracle"—a miracle of statesmanship, of scholarly application, of political expertise.[2] Just as miraculous, however, was the skill with which the proponents of constitutional reform presented their case to the public. It has been suggested that they worked so quickly that the opposition never had time to organize, that they were favored by the newspapers, that they benefited from the superior prestige of their leaders, and that perhaps they succeeded through sheer good fortune. All of this may be true. But in light of the difficulties which lay before them, they waged a shrewd campaign. They had to sell the country a completely new frame of government. Many whose approval they sought, moreover, were unfamiliar with continental problems and therefore unappreciative of the remedies offered. Most were sensi-

[1] James Madison, *The Federalist Papers*, ed. Clinton Rossiter (New York, 1961), No. 42, p. 264; all subsequent references to the *Federalist Papers* are to this edition.

[2] Catherine Drinker Bowen, *Miracle at Philadelphia* (Boston, 1966).

tive to any threat, however remote, to their newly won freedom. In particular they would tend to be strongly biased against any plan which reminded them of the British imperial system, characterized by a strong central government with power to tax and maintain standing armies. Finally, state and local leaders were not anxious to see continental power augmented at their own expense.

Throughout the ratification campaign Antifederalists criticized the Constitution for concentrating too much power in the hands of the central government without sufficient checks and balances. State governments, they argued, would lose power. The country would fall into the hands of a privileged few. The rich would oppress the poor.[3] The Constitution would degenerate into a bill of tyranny. One geographical section would victimize another. Such arguments, stressing the cultural, economic, and political diversity of the country, were divisive and, as such, well suited to the obstructionist cause.[4]

Federalists, on the other hand, were obliged to emphasize unity and a harmony of interests. The question can therefore be put: how did they conduct their side of the great debate? Which arguments did they fasten upon as having the greatest common appeal for such a variety of people as lived between Maine and Georgia, and between the tidewater regions of Virginia and the Mississippi valley?

It appears that they found the key to consensus in several issues related to foreign affairs. In state ratifying conventions and in their propaganda, Federalists stressed the weak condition of American defense. The Constitution, with its provisions for a standing army and navy, would reduce the likelihood of invasion and increase America's ability to wage war. It would also bring relief from commercial distress by allowing Congress to retaliate against

[3] A classic example of this was the testimony of Amos Singletary in the Massachusetts ratifying convention; Jonathan Elliot, ed., *The Debates in the Several State Conventions on the Adoption of the Federal Constitution* (Philadelphia, 1861), II, 101-02, 147 (hereafter, *Debates*).

[4] For a good discussion of Antifederalist fears, see Cecilia M. Kenyon, "Men of Little Faith: The Anti-Federalists on the Nature of Representative Government," *William and Mary Quarterly*, XII, Third Series (1955), 3-43; see also Jackson Turner Main, *The Antifederalists: Critics of the Constitution, 1781-1788* (Chapel Hill, N.C., 1961), chaps. VI, VII.

British trade restrictions. Moreover, it promised to bolster national pride and to enable the United States to take a dignified place among the countries of the world. These were winning issues.

The 85 articles which make up *The Federalist Papers* reveal how the Constitution was presented.[5] Of the first 36 articles, 25 concerned the lack of national security. These 25 anticipated all the major arguments used during the campaign. The subject of military weakness was discussed in Numbers 3, 4, 14, 23-31, 34, and 36; the possibility of a dissolution of the Union and foreign intervention in Numbers 5-8 and 18-20; commercial distress and the need for congressional power to retaliate against foreign trade restrictions in Numbers 11-12, 22, and 23; national honor in Number 15; and treaty enforcement in Number 22. Nearly every argument sprang from the possibility of a foreign threat. Characteristic of these arguments was Madison's statement denying the Antifederalist claim that republican government could not be extended to the outlying areas of a country as large as the United States. Border communities, he pointed out, would be the first to benefit from a closer union because they would receive increased military support. He deplored the lack of protection for settlers on the frontier and condemned continued British occupation of the frontier posts, attributing these to two basic conditions, the lack of an adequate army and the depressed state of the treasury.[6] He cleverly replied to Antifederalist critics who feared that too

[5] *The Federalist* not only appeared in the most widely circulated newspapers, but was a chief source of reference in the Virginia and New York ratifying conventions and was more widely read than any other tract of the controversy. *Federalist Papers*, viii, xi; Frank Monaghan, *John Jay* (New York, 1935), 291. *The Federalist's* influence is also reflected in such letters as Richard Stuart to James Madison, Jan. 4, 1788; George Nicholas to James Madison, Apr. 5, 1788, Madison Papers, Library of Congress, Washington, D.C., Series I, Vol. VIII. Apparently, the series of articles was widely circulated in individual correspondence among Federalists. George Washington forwarded available issues of *The Federalist* to Richmond for publication, and the secretary of Congress, Charles Thomson, sent a copy of it to James McHenry, who exerted great influence on behalf of the Constitution throughout the Maryland ratifying convention; Washington to Madison, Dec. 7, 1787, John Clement Fitzpatrick, ed., *The Writings of George Washington from the Original Manuscript Sources, 1745-1799* (Washington, D.C., 1931-44), XXIX, 331 (hereafter, *Writings of Washington);* Thomson to McHenry, Apr. 19, 1788, Edmund Cody Burnett, ed., *Letters of Members of the Continental Congress*, (Washington, D.C., 1921-1936), VIII, 721-22 (hereafter, *Letters).*

[6] *Federalist Papers*, No. 14, p. 103.

strong a central government might undermine states' rights by pointing out that since the national government was intended primarily for the purpose of defense, its operations would be "most extensive and important in times of war and danger; those of the state government in times of peace and security." Therefore, if the Antifederalists proved correct in their prediction that war would not occur, the state governments would continue to hold sway. Indeed, the more power given to the national government to cope with a potential state of war, the less likely would be a state of war in which such power would be exercised.[7]

Hamilton, too, made much of this theme. He justified direct and unlimited taxation as a wartime necessity for obtaining foreign credit and a steady revenue; he affirmed that the government should not be disarmed "of a single weapon, which in any possible contingency might be usefully employed for the general defense and security."[8] In the same vein he asked, "Is public credit an indispensable resource in time of public danger?" America has very little. "Is respectability in the eyes of foreign powers a safeguard against foreign encroachments? . . . Our ambassadors abroad are the mere pageants of mimic sovereignty."[9]

The remainder of *The Federalist* was far more concerned with procedural clauses in the Constitution than with the underlying reasons for constitutional reform. Yet even here the subject of foreign relations was frequently injected.[10] Madison, defending the long House and Senate terms against those who desired a higher rate of turnover in public office, pointed out the problems of a high rate of change in government personnel:

> It forfeits the respect and confidence of other nations, and all the advantages connected with national character. An individual who is observed to be inconstant to his plans, or perhaps to carry on his affairs without any plan at all, is marked at once by all prudent people as a speedy victim to his own unsteadiness and folly. . . .[11]

John Jay referred especially to senators when he remarked that their diplomatic duties would demand that they take the time to

[7] *Ibid.*, No. 45, p. 293.
[8] *Ibid.*, No. 36, p. 223.
[9] *Ibid.*, No. 15, p. 107.
[10] *Ibid.*, Nos. 42, 53, 62-64, 75.
[11] *Ibid.*, No. 62, pp. 380-81.

acquire "exact information . . . to become perfectly acquainted with our national concerns, and to form and introduce a system for the management of them."[12] This point received additional clarification later in the New York ratifying convention when Robert R. Livingston defended lengthy terms for senators as essential for acquiring the experience necessary for the conduct of foreign affairs.[13]

The House term was also defended in a context of foreign relations. Federalists maintained that congressmen as well as senators would need a knowledge of foreign affairs because the regulation of commerce required an understanding of treaties and of the trade regulations of other nations. Newly elected congressmen would need sufficient time in office to acquire it.[14]

Any discussion of *The Federalist* in the context of foreign affairs would be incomplete without mentioning John Jay who, as Secretary for Foreign Affairs, was at the time the best known of its three authors. Jay had taken an important part in the peace negotiations, and his prestige was said to exceed the combined fame of his younger colleagues, Madison and Hamilton.[15] Because he was ill, Jay contributed only five articles to *The Federalist*. Yet, after an introductory article by Hamilton, it was Jay who actually launched the series, and his articles set the tone for the

[12] *Ibid.*, No. 64, p. 392.

[13] Alexander Hamilton supported Livingston on this issue, and James Iredell said the same thing in the North Carolina convention; *Debates*, II, 291, 302, 306; IV, 41.

[14] *Federalist Papers*, No. 53, p. 334. This argument came up again in the Massachusetts convention when Cabot of Beverly argued that the House would have to be specially qualified in its spending capacity to decide on the advisability of raising funds to support a war or implement a treaty; *Debates*, II, 25. John Dickinson wrote that the two houses of Congress would be "not only legislative bodies but also diplomatic bodies," requiring a "competent knowledge of foreign affairs relative to the states"; Dickinson, *The Letters of Fabius on the Federal Constitution*, No. 2, Paul Leicester Ford, ed., *Pamphlets on the Constitution of the United States, Published During its Discussion by the People, 1787-1788* (Brooklyn, 1888), 170 (hereafter, *Pamphlets*).

[15] Indicative of Jay's great popularity was the fact that out of a total of 2,833 votes cast in New York City for delegates to the state ratifying convention, he received 2,735 while Governor Clinton polled only 134; John Jay, *Second Letter on Dawson's Introduction to the Federalist* (New York, 1864), 26; Monaghan, 294. Jay assumed a prominent role at the state convention, being chosen by the Federalists to move the adoption of the Constitution and to draft New York's circular letter to the other states; Jay, *Second Letter*, 48.

rest of the series by emphasizing the foreign threat.[16]

In addition to his contribution to *The Federalist,* Jay published *An Address to the People of New York on the Subject of the Constitution,* which appeared in April 1788. An extremely popular and influential tract, it characteristically placed heavy emphasis on foreign affairs.[17] Congress could declare war, he pointed out, but could not raise men or money to wage it; it could make peace but could not enforce it; it could make commercial treaties but could not execute them. The result was:

> Our fur trade is gone to Canada and British garrisons keep the keys of it. Our shipyards have almost ceased to disturb the repose of the neighborhood by the noise of the axe and hammer; and while foreign flags fly triumphantly above our highest houses, the American stars seldom do more than shed a few feeble rays about the humble masts of river sloops and coasting schooners. The greater part of our hardy seamen are plowing the ocean in foreign pay; and not a few of our ingenious shipwrights are now building vessels on alien shores. Although our increasing agriculture and industry extend and multiply our productions, yet they constantly diminish in value; and although we permit all nations to fill our country with their merchandises, yet their best markets are shut against us.[18]

The convention which met to resolve these problems, continued Jay, drafted a plan which was the best possible under the circumstances. Should a future convention fail to agree on a plan—and the likelihood of this would increase as time passed and factions grew stronger—"then every state would be a little nation, jealous of its neighbors, and anxious to strengthen itself by foreign alliances against its former friends." New York State would be threatened by Connecticut and New Jersey, her great harbor im-

[16] *Federalist Papers,* Nos. 2-5, p. 64.

[17] Monaghan, 292. Washington recommended it for its "good sense, for able observations, temper and moderation." According to S. B. Webb, the pamphlet "had a most astonishing influence in converting anti-federalism to a knowledge and belief that the new constitution was their only political salvation"; and Noah Webster felt that it contained "a brief recapitulation of the most striking arguments in favor of adopting the Federal Constitution"; quoted in *Pamphlets,* 67. E. W. Spaulding agreed that the *Address* was one of the most influential of all Federalist works; Spaulding, *New York in the Critical Period, 1783-1789* (New York, 1932), 8.

[18] Jay, *Address,* in *Pamphlets.* 73.

periled, and the people of Long Island exposed.[19]

While Madison, Hamilton, and Jay were making their case for ratification in New York, other writers were presenting similar arguments elsewhere. Noah Webster's *Examination into the Leading Principles of the Federal Constitution* was not so much a defense of the Constitution as a rebuttal of specific criticisms. Nevertheless, mention was made of the foreign debt problem and the danger of foreign invasion. Alexander Hanson's *Remarks on the Proposed Plan of a Federal Government,* though mostly a defense of specific constitutional clauses, touched on the issue of war and national honor. In Pennsylvania, Tench Coxe applauded the new Constitution because of its safeguards against subversion and external attack. And John Dickinson's *Letters of Fabius on the Federal Constitution,* although mostly philosophical in tone, ended with a consideration of foreign hostility.[20]

From the South, also, came familiar arguments. Edmund Randolph's *Letter on the Federal Convention* concentrated almost entirely on the advantages of the new Constitution in the area of foreign relations. Randolph argued that war and defeat would be inevitable under the Articles. James Iredell, in answer to George Mason's objections, published a pamphlet on national honor and the threat of European and Indian attack. And David Ramsay, noted historian and politician, in his *Address to the Freemen of South Carolina on the Federal Constitution,* concerned himself mostly with the issue of defense against foreign aggression.[21]

I

Of the various issues related to foreign affairs, one in particular

[19] *Ibid.,* 81-84.

[20] Webster, *Examination;* Hanson, *Remarks;* Coxe, *An Examination of the Constitution for the United States of America;* Dickinson, *Letters,* Nos. 5, 9, *ibid.,* 29-61, 133-50, 188, 192-93, 215, 244-51.

[21] Randolph, *Letter;* Iredell, *Observations;* Ramsay, *Address,* in *ibid.,* 262-70, 365-70, 373-80. The heavy emphasis which the Federalists placed on the issues of national security, national honor, and foreign commerce is illustrated also in Oliver Ellsworth, *Landholder Letters;* Hugh Williamson, *Remarks on the New Plan of Government;* and Charles Pinckney, *Letter of a Steady and Open Republican,* in Paul Leicester Ford, ed., *Essays on the Constitution of the United States, Published During Its Discussion by the People, 1787-1788* (Brooklyn, 1892), (hereafter, *Essays).*

served the Federalists well: the military weakness and insecurity of the Confederation government. A letter from Henry Knox to George Washington reveals party strategy:

> As a war between France and England seems inevitable and a general war in Europe probable, the result may be highly beneficial to this country. . . . The war will impress on the fears of the people of the United States the necessity of a general government to defend them against the insults and invasions of the Europeans. . . . This subject being forcibly impressed on the public mind will have its full effect unless we are devoted to destruction.[22]

Other Federalists followed Knox's reasoning. The *New York Journal*, for example, argued:

> Wars have been, and, we must suppose, will continue to be frequent. A war has generally happened among the European nations as often as once in twelve or fifteen years, for a century past; and for more than one third of this period, the English, French and Spaniards have been in a state of war. The territories of two of these nations border upon our country. England is at heart inimical to us; Spain is jealous. . . . It would be no strange thing if within ten years the injustice of England or Spain should force us into a war; it would be strange, if it should not within fifteen or twenty years.[23]

Many theories were advanced to explain how the next war would come. The foreign debt was considered by some as a likely source of conflict. Foreign creditors would not be patient indefinitely while America continued to renege on its fiscal responsibilities; sooner or later they would seek revenge by attacking American commerce. British presence in the frontier posts was also cited as a powder keg to watch.[24]

Pelatiah Webster warned that the United States would become embroiled abroad unless some federal authority was established

[22] Henry Knox to Washington, Dec. 11, 1787, Washington Papers, Library of Congress, Series IV, Vol. CCXXXIX. This strategy would seem all the more likely in light of Forrest McDonald's observation that Federalists drew much of their support from the ranks of soldiers and officers who had fought in the Revolution; McDonald, "The Anti-Federalists, 1781-1789," *Wisconsin Magazine of History*, XLVI (1963), 207-09.

[23] *New York Journal*, Mar. 29, 1787.

[24] Jay, *Address*, in *Pamphlets*, 83; James Bowdoin in Massachusetts, *Debates*, II, 82; Alexander Hamilton, "Speech before the New York Assembly," Mar. 28, 1787, Harold Coffin Syrett, ed., *Papers of Alexander Hamilton* (New York, 1961), IV, 134-35.

"to punish any individual or state, who shall violate our treaties with foreign nations, insult their dignity or abuse their citizens, and compel due reparation in all such cases."[25] This was a common theme. William Davie echoed it in the North Carolina convention, recounting how Rhode Island, by refusing to hand over to Dutch authorities, a thief who had stolen a Dutch vessel, "might have involved the whole Union in a war."[26] But the great champion of this point of view was Edmund Randolph who insistently urged the need for some agency which would prevent war by enforcing the Law of Nations upon recalcitrant states. In a letter to the Virginia House of Delegates, he wrote:

> If we examine the Constitution and laws of the several states, it is immediately discovered that the law of nations is unprovided with sanctions in many cases which deeply affect public dignity and public justice. The letter, however, of the Confederation does not permit congress to remedy these defects. . . . Is it not a political phenomenon that the head of the Confederacy should be doomed to be plunged into war from its wretched impotency to check offenses against this law; and sentenced to witness in unavailing anguish the infraction of their engagements to foreign sovereigns?[27]

Once Federalists could demonstrate the likelihood of war, the next step was to show that the Confederation government would be unable to cope with it. James Madison in the Virginia ratifying convention pointed to the inadequacy of the Confederation during the late war and to Washington's postwar recommendations for a stronger central government. He argued that the state militias were no substitute for a federal army.[28] Under the old requisition system one section of the country, feeling less threatened than another, might be unwilling to pay its share of the cost of defense. There would be problems of partial payments, discipline, and federal finance should the usual state revenue from import duties dry up during hostilities.[29] Edmund Randolph warned that mili-

[25] P. Webster, *The Weakness of Brutus Exposed, or Some Remarks in Vindication of the Constitution Proposed by the Late Federal Convention against the Objections and Gloomy Fears of the Writer Humbly Offered to the Public.* Nov. 4, 1787, in *Pamphlets*, 121.

[26] *Debates*, IV, 19.

[27] Randolph, *Letter*, in *Pamphlets*, 262-63.

[28] *Debates*, III, 133, 90.

[29] *Ibid.*, III, 90-95, 248-49, 253. Similar remarks were made by John Marshall, Edmund Randolph, and Francis Corbin, *ibid.*, III, 109, 115, 227-29.

tias would be poorly trained and not as zealous as they had been in 1776. Recalling revolutionary days, he could not forget how the army, on a sudden challenge, marched into war "on the mere recommendation of Congress"; but he wondered if, in the future, the same enthusiasm would prevail. And, if not, "where shall we find protection?" Requisitions would be balked, and any attempt of Congress to coerce a particular state might induce that state to seek foreign support. Thus, "radical new powers must be entrusted to the national government and the Confederation must be altered in its very essence."[30]

When Antifederalists insisted that it would be time enough to organize a defense when war broke out, the reply was that a standing army would be necessary to strike an immediate blow against the enemy.[31] In a sneak attack, the enemy would allow no time for response: "Half a dozen regiments from Canada or New Spain, might lay whole provinces under contribution while we were disputing who has power to pay and raise any army."[32] Was America to wait until she was attacked? She was "circumscribed with enemies from Maine to Georgia." In an emergency, it would take precious time to obtain a representation of the required number of states in Congress, then to go through the process of pleading with the various state legislatures. The very power to lay direct taxes would itself act as a deterrent to invasion.[33]

Certain states were more impressed with the military benefits of the Constitution than others. The Southern states in particular evidenced a strong feeling of insecurity. They were faced with the prospect of full-scale Indian hostilities, and the experience of being conquered and occupied by British armies was still fresh in their memories. Georgia was actually involved in fighting Indians during the ratification campaign, and this no doubt contributed to her rapid and enthusiastic endorsement of the Constitution. Nor can it be doubted that Georgia's struggle influenced South Carolina's decision only a few months later. South Carolinians felt sufficiently threatened to authorize their own General Pickens

[30] Randolph, *Letter*, in *Pamphlets*, 263-67.

[31] *State Gazette of South Carolina*, Jan. 3, 1788.

[32] Ellsworth, *Letters*, No. 5, in *Essays*, 157.

[33] T. Sedgwick, Christopher Gore, and E. Pierce in Massachusetts, *Debates*, II, 61, 66-67, 76.

to raise a volunteer company for the defense of Georgia.[34] On May 5, 1788, just before South Carolina voted to accept the Constitution, a Charleston newspaper asked its readers: "How long can we be free from Indian cruelties and depredations sometime since begun in Georgia?"[35]

How the security issue was used in South Carolina is illustrated in the appeal made by David Ramsay:

> Our local weakness particularly proves it to be for the advantage of South Carolina to strengthen the federal government; for we are inadequate to secure ourselves from more powerful neighbors. . . . The Congress are authorized to provide and maintain a navy—our coast in its whole extent needs the protection thereof. . . . If this state is to be invaded by a maritime force, to whom can we apply for immediate aid? To Virginia and North Carolina? Before they can march by land to our assistance, the country may be overrun. The Eastern states, abounding in men and in ships, can sooner relieve us than our next door neighbors.[36]

If the foreign debt were not paid off, he warned, the Southern states would be the losers, for Southern exports, because they were the most valuable, would be the first to be captured in a war, and raids would be made on defenseless Southern coasts.

Charles Cotesworth Pinckney pleaded with the delegates to the South Carolina ratifying convention to allow Northern merchants a virtual monopoly of Southern commerce under the new Constitution in order to be assured of their naval support in case of attack. Hoping to soften the attitude of his fellow planters toward the New England manufacturing and commercial classes, he pointed out that because of the late war and the present state of commerce,

> they have lost everything but their country and freedom. It is notorious that some ports to the eastward which used to fit out one hundred and fifty sail of vessels do not now fit out thirty; that their trade of shipbuilding which used to be very considerable is now annihilated; that their fisheries are trifling, and their mariners in want of bread. Surely . . . we should let them in some measure,

[34] Savannah *Gazette of the State of Georgia*, Oct. 11, 1787.
[35] *State Gazette of South Carolina*, May 5, 1788.
[36] Ramsay, *Address*, in *Pamphlets*, 373-77.

partake of our prosperity.[37]

Pinckney was reminding his audience that Northern distress was in part the result of aiding the South during the war and that such aid might well be needed in the future.

In both North Carolina and Virginia, other Federalists echoed Pinckney. Iredell and Randolph, for example, emphasized the danger of foreign invasion and Indian attacks and the possibility of a slave uprising.[38]

The people of New England felt more secure than the Southerners. Though several coastal towns had been shelled and burned during the war, there had been no fighting on New England soil after the troops of George III had fled from Boston on St. Patrick's Day 1776. That New Englanders felt relatively strong and secure, however, did not deter Federalists from making use of the security issue. They called attention to the fact that New Hampshire, like Georgia, lay adjacent to enemy territory. A few regiments of Canadian troops could march through New Hampshire and put down all resistance along the way. Troops from other states would have to come to the rescue. But if New Hampshire refused to ratify, such out-of-state aid might be withheld.[39] Even though Massachusetts of all the states was the strongest militarily, Fisher Ames still argued along familiar lines in the state convention. Judge Francis Dana was certain that Nova Scotia and New Brunswick were full of Tories and refugees standing "ready to attack and devour these states, one by one."[40] Speaker after speaker urged that Congress be given the power to raise an army.[41]

In the Connecticut convention, national defense was cited as

[37] *Debates*, IV, 284-85. Charles Pinckney, not to be confused with his distant cousin, Charles Cotesworth Pinckney, argued the same way in the South Carolina convention (although he had spoken differently in Philadelphia); see *ibid.*, IV, 331, and Max Farrand, ed., *The Records of the Federal Convention of 1787* (New Haven, 1911), II, 449.

[38] Iredell in North Carolina, *Debates*, IV, 96. William Davie also concentrated heavily on the weakness of his state in case of attack; *ibid.*, IV, 17-19. Randolph in Virginia, *ibid.*, III, 72-73. For similar remarks by Randolph, Madison, Corbin, and Marshall, see *ibid.*, III, 76, 90-91, 95, 109, 112, 115-18, 226-27, 229, 231, 248-49.

[39] Ellsworth, *Letters*, No. 10, in *Essays*, 190-91.

[40] *Debates*, II, 43.

[41] See the remarks of William Phillips, *ibid.*, II, 158.

the most compelling reason for ratification. Oliver Ellsworth, referring to the geographical encirclement of America by foreign nations, pointed to the earlier encirclement of the Hebrew people and the infant Roman state, both of which had been conquered by inferior forces because of their lack of unity. He then appealed to Yankee thrift by reminding the delegates that the larger the nation, the less the cost of defense per person. England's burden of taxes, for example, was only about one-half that of the Netherlands.[42]

New York Federalists could capitalize on a past history of war, Indian raids, and occupation by British troops. New York was the one area that Washington had tried to hold at all costs but failed. Robert R. Livingston gave a detailed analysis of New York's exposure to attack in the state convention. He pointed out that Long Island and Staten Island were indefensible. New York was threatened on the west by hostile Indians, on the east by a potentially hostile Vermont, and it lay open to sudden attack from British-held posts, five of which were within the state's borders.[43] The Hudson River was an avenue of attack which would make New York the probable "theatre of operations" in wartime.[44] James Duane strongly resented the British troops which remained on New York soil and considered this "the highest insult to our sovereignty"; their presence created an immediate need for military power.[45]

Yet after all was said that could be said by the Federalists on the lack of preparation for another war, there were still those who remained unconvinced either because they did not believe another war likely or because they believed the existing system of defense adequate. For these, the Federalists modified their line of argument; they recommended a strong defense on the grounds that discouraging foreign powers from attacking the United States would prevent bloodshed. Weakness would invite attack.[46] Madison told the delegates to the Virginia ratifying convention that "the best way to avoid danger is to be in a capacity to withstand

[42] Ellsworth in Connecticut, *ibid.*, II, 185-86.

[43] *Ibid.*, II, 212. The vulnerability of New York and Long Island was also stressed in *The Federalist*, Nos. 25 and 41.

[44] Hamilton in Massachusetts, *Debates*, II, 232.

[45] *Ibid.*, II, 379.

[46] Hanson, *Remarks*, in *Pamphlets*, 244-45.

it." But, he asked, what would be the position of the United States as a neutral carrier believing in the principle of freedom of the seas if war broke out, as was most likely, between France and England?—"A neutral nation ought to be respectable or else it will be insulted and attacked."[47] Benjamin Rush of Philadelphia had the Quakers of his city in mind when he wrote that the new government would mean, among other things, "the prevention of war."[48] James Wilson, a neighbor of Rush in Philadelphia, made a similar appeal when he quoted the celebrated French statesman Necker to the effect that America was young, pure, and felicitous and should remain so by shunning involvement in European conflicts. "An efficient government," said Wilson, "will not hurry us into war; it is calculated to guard against it."[49]

For those New Englanders who saw no need for additional military resources, the Federalists had another argument. Yankee soldiers who had fought to liberate the Southern colonies during the Revolution and had borne a disproportionate burden of the war's cost would feel obligated in their own interest to do the same in any future invasion of the South. Therefore, even if they themselves were not in need of military assistance, would it not be in their interest to support a national army which would tap each state for a proportional number of troops? Had not Massachusetts and New Hampshire furnished half the Continental Army for the first two or three years of the war? Had not the Bay State in particular borne "an unequal burden" and "never been fairly compensated?"[50]

Federalists often ignored the subject of national defense alto-

[47] Gaillard Hunt, ed., *The Writings of James Madison* (New York, 1904), V, 150-51, 169. In the *Federalist*, No. 41, Madison had also stressed the idea that Virginia and Maryland could easily be attacked from the sea. For the same theme, see the *New York Journal*, Mar. 29, 1787; Pelatiah Webster, *Remarks on the Address of Sixteen Members of the Assembly of Pennsylvania to Their Constituents, Dated September 29, 1787*, in John Bach McMaster and Frederick Dawson Stone, eds., *Pennsylvania and the Federal Constitution* (Lancaster, Pa., 1888), 101; Richmond *Virginia Independent Chronicle*, June 13, 1787.

[48] *State Gazette of South Carolina*, Dec. 24, 1787.

[49] Wilson in Pennsylvania, *Debates*, II, 528.

[50] James Varnum and Reverend Mr. Thatcher in Massachusetts, *ibid*, II, 78, 142. Ellsworth also pointed this out in the Connecticut convention; *ibid*, II, 188.

gether and justified closer political ties because the Union was threatened with dissolution by outside forces. The residents of New Hampshire were warned that "your British neighbors . . . will not fail by their emmissaries to seminate such jealousies as favor their own designs."[51] Charles Pinckney maintained that George III had spies in every state and was hoping to separate the Southern states from the Confederacy and see them revert to his control.[52] And one newspaper, proclaiming that "every part of this federal empire was gained by the sword, by distress, and slaughter," asked, "What American can without horror, indignation and grief reflect that a fatal disunion may basely throw under foreign domination, the plains of Saratoga, Yorktown, or the Cowpens."[53] This argument appeared in pamphlets by Alexander Hanson and Edmund Randolph; it was used by John Jay. In the Virginia ratifying convention, it was used extensively by Madison and in the Massachusetts convention by the Reverend Mr. Thatcher.[54]

Federalists purported to know of various foreign plots which would succeed if the Constitution were not adopted. Britain and Morocco were said to have agreed to partition America and appoint such Tories and expatriates as Silas Deane, Joseph Galloway, and Benedict Arnold to the office of state governor.[55] The Antifederalists were furious at such tactics and tried to counteract them by printing Federalist-style propaganda so exaggerated as to be ludicrous. One pamphlet of this type described an Algerine spy who was prepared to offer Algerian support to both the Shaysites and Rhode Island if a dissolution of the Union could be effected. He would provide Rhode Island with a large sum of money accompanied by "one hundred thousand spahis and janizaries." And "in return for protection, Rhode Island would be permitted to pay their tribute to the Sultan in a certain number

[51] Ellsworth, *Letters*, No. 10, in *Essays*, 191.

[52] Charles Pinckney, *Letter*, in *ibid.*, 411-12. This charge also appeared in the *State Gazette of South Carolina*, May 5, 1788.

[53] *Trenton [N.J.] Mercury and Weekly Advertiser*, Sept. 25, 1787.

[54] Jay, *Address*, in *Pamphlets*, 82. Hanson, *Remarks;* Randolph, *Letter*, in *ibid.*, 248, 268-70. *Debates*, III, 79, 90-91, 129-30; II, 144, 146. The same theme was used in the New York convention; *ibid.*, II, 219.

[55] *Independent Gazetteer*, Sept. 20, 1787, quoted in McMaster and Stone, 122.

of virgins."[56] The Antifederalists accused the Federalists of deceiving the people into believing that opposition to the Constitution arose chiefly "from foreigners and foreign agents," of filling the papers "with ludicrous pieces under the signatures of 'Britons,' 'Gauls,' 'Spaniards,' and even 'Turks' "; whereas, in reality, foreign agents were in favor of the Constitution and "bellowing forth its praises."[57]

Both Federalist and Antifederalist charges were exaggerated. Foreign agents were not uniformly in favor of the Constitution, nor did they engage in the types of plot suggested by Federalist writers. But both friends and enemies of the Constitution tried to exploit the popular fear of subversion by identifying their adversaries with foreign influence. Antifederalists, labeled "the secret abettors of the interests of Great Britain," were said to be anxious for a return to prewar conditions. Twenty irreconcilables in the Massachusetts ratifying convention were accused of being British sympathizers because they had fought under Daniel Shays.[58] According to Oliver Ellsworth:

> The first to oppose a federal government will be the old friends of Great Britain who in their hearts cursed the prosperity of your arms and have ever since delighted in the perplexity of your councils. Many of these men are still with us and their hopes of a reunion with Britain have been high.[59]

On the other hand, the Federalists were said to be rich, haughty, and aristocratic, contemptuous of the common man and conspiring

[56] Peter Markoe, *The Algerine Spy in Pennsylvania: or Letters Written by a Native of Algiers on the Affairs of the United States of America, from the Close of the Year 1783 to the Meeting of the Convention* (Philadelphia, 1787), 105, 114-15.

[57] *Independent Gazetteer*, Oct. 15, 1787, quoted in McMaster and Stone, 163-64.

[58] *State Gazette of South Carolina*, Mar. 31, 1783; *Independent Gazetteer*, Sept. 20, 1787, quoted in McMaster and Stone, 121. It is interesting in this connection that many individuals, including Washington and Madison, regarded Shays' Rebellion as the work of British spies and sympathizers; see Boston *Massachusetts Centinel*, Apr. 2, May 21, 1785, for background; Trenton *New Jersey Gazette*, Oct. 9, 1786; *New York Journal*, Sept. 28, 1786; Philadelphia *Pennsylvania Gazette*, Sept. 27, Dec. 20, 1786; Washington to David Humphreys, Dec. 26, 1786, *Writings of Washington*, XXIX, 126; Madison to Edmund Pendleton, Jan. 9, 1787, *Writings of Madison*, II, 307.

[59] Ellsworth, *Letters*, No. 2, in *Essays*, 143; Isaac Lee to William Lee, July 18, 1785, Perkins Papers, William L. Clements Library, Ann Arbor, Mich.

with George III to destroy American liberty.[60]

II

In commercial centers such as Boston, New York, and Philadelphia, there was no doubt about the benefits of congressional regulation of commerce. Native fishermen, shipowners, shipbuilders, and a variety of craftsmen could be easily won over with the promise that a new constitution would help to revive the shipbuilding industry.[61] It was no coincidence that the principal theme of Federalist orators in the Massachusetts ratifying convention was American shipping.[62] It was pointed out, also, that manufacturers would benefit from national control of commerce by the passage of federal tariff legislation.[63]

In less commercial areas, where foreign trade was not as important, Federalists still went to great lengths to demonstrate that everyone had reason for concern. William Davie reminded the farmers and wealthy planters of North Carolina that commerce was "the nurse" of agriculture, and Madison reminded his fellow Virginians that the two were interdependent.[64] If the Constitution were adopted, wheat farmers would be able to ship their surplus produce to the British West Indies, and cheese and barley exports would increase. In general, farmers would escape from too heavy a tax burden since most revenue would come from import duties rather than land taxes.[65] Alexander Hamilton, appealing to a variety of groups including not only "the assiduous merchant," but also "the laborious husbandman, the active mechanic, and the industrious manufacturer," directed himself es-

[60] James Winthrop, *The Letters of Agrippa*, No. 11, in *Essays*, 89; *Independent Gazetteer*, Oct. 15, 1787, quoted in McMaster and Stone, 164.

[61] *Independent Gazetteer*, Sept. 20, 1787, quoted in McMaster and Stone, 121-22; *Charleston City Gazette*, Jan. 9, 1788.

[62] Thomas Dawes, J. Choate, James Bowdoin, and Thomas Russell in Massachusetts, *Debates*, II, 58-59, 79, 129-30, 139.

[63] Thomas Dawes in Massachusetts, *Debates*, II, 58-59; Jay, *Address*, in *Pamphlets*, 73. *Virginia Independent Chronicle*, June 13, Aug. 1, Dec. 5, 1787; June 2, 1788.

[64] *Ibid.*, III, 345; IV, 20.

[65] *Independent Gazetteer*, Sept. 20, 1787, quoted in McMaster and Stone, 121-23; *Pennsylvania Gazette*, Nov. 14, 1787; Bowdoin in Massachusetts, *Debates*, II, 130; *Federalist Papers*, No. 12, p. 92.

pecially to farmers when he argued that revenue from duties on commercial imports would render unnecessary all taxes on land. Land values would increase, agricultural produce would have a "free vent," and the supply of circulating specie would be more plentiful.[66]

In the South, where people were less interested in commerce and feared a Northern monopoly of the carrying trade, Federalists appealed to the popular hatred of Great Britain and the strong sense of national honor. St. George Tucker pointed to the folly of depending on the merchants, ships, and manufactures of "our natural enemy," the British.[67] Others argued that exclusion must be met by exclusion—foreign discrimination should be counteracted by appropriate retaliatory legislation in Congress.[68] In South Carolina David Ramsay insisted that "we certainly ought to have a navigation act, and we assuredly ought to give a preference though not a monopoly to our own shipping."[69] In the Virginia convention, Henry Lee and Edmund Randolph traced all evils to the stagnation of American foreign commerce and urged national measures to bring about a policy of reciprocity on the part of Great Britain.[70]

Such arguments were unanswerable because no one could deny that the commerce clause in the Constitution could be used to apply pressure on Great Britain. Even Patrick Henry, who minimized nearly every other Federalist argument, tacitly admitted that the new government would be a boon to commerce. James Monroe, who opposed the Constitution because it granted Congress direct taxing power, felt that the power to regulate commerce

[66] *Federalist Papers*, No. 12, p. 92. Typical of the broad Federalist appeal on the commercial issue was an article in the *Pennsylvania Packet* on Nov. 15, 1787, which predicted that the Constitution would encourage commerce, agriculture, manufactures, and immigration. Due to a labor shortage, immigrants were in great demand, and the new Constitution was viewed as a likely inducement to them because of its liberal voting and office-holding provisions.

[67] Tucker, *Reflections on the Policy and Necessity of Encouraging the Commerce of the Citizens of the United States . . .* (Richmond and New York, 1786), 4-6.

[68] Edmund Randolph's letter to the speaker of the Virginia House of Delegates, *Debates*, I, 484; William Davie in North Carolina, *ibid.*, IV, 18.

[69] Ramsay, *Address*, in *Pamphlets*, 376-77.

[70] *Debates*, I, 484; III, 43, 78.

should be a prerequisite for any "proper federal government." George Bryan of Pennsylvania, an Antifederalist, did not try to deny the commercial advantages of the Constitution. Nor did Samuel Adams have any doubts on this issue, although his support for the new government was less than total at first.[71]

The issues of commercial distress and national security were alike in many ways. Both appealed to the prevalent spirit of anglophobia: Britain must be compelled to drop its discrimination against American ships and British troops must evacuate American soil. Both depended in some measure upon granting Congress the power to fulfill its treaty commitments: Britain could not be deprived of its excuse for occupying the posts unless Congress enabled British merchants to collect the prewar debts owed them by Americans,[72] nor could the English be persuaded to negotiate a commercial treaty until Congress acquired the power to negotiate for all the states.[73] Finally, both issues appealed to a wide cross section of economic and geographic groups.

III

A comparison of Federalist and Antifederalist literature reveals that the Antifederalists rarely discussed foreign affairs. Richard Henry Lee's celebrated *Letters of a Federal Farmer* mentions the issue only once to assert that there was "no danger of invasions."[74] George Mason did not write a word on the subject in his *Objections to the Proposed Federal Constitution*. Patrick Henry in the Virginia ratifying convention, carefully separated domestic concerns from foreign pressures and addressed himself to the former. And Elbridge Gerry, in *Observations on the New Constitution*,

[71] *Ibid.*, II, 124. For evidence of Antifederalist recognition of Federalist arguments with regard to foreign commerce, see *ibid.*, III, 137-76, 214.

[72] For this argument, see Ellsworth in Connecticut, Livingston in New York, Wilson in Pennsylvania, Corbin and Nicholas in Virginia, *Debates*, II, 189, 213, 489-90; III, 104-05, 238-39; also the *Pennsylvania Packet*, which assured its readers on Nov. 23, 1787, that "in all probability the first good consequence arising from a firm and respectable government will be the relinquishment of the western posts."

[73] For examples of this argument, see Madison in Virginia, *Debates*, III, 135-36; Williamson, *Remarks*, in *Essays*, 402.

[74] Lee, *Letters*, No. 1, in *Pamphlets*, 281.

flatly denied the danger of foreign conquest, focusing nearly all his attention on the danger of aristocratic tyranny.[75]

When Antifederalists did turn to the subject of foreign affairs, they nearly always accepted Federalist arguments but questioned whether the good which would result from a stronger position in foreign affairs would outweigh the risks of central power, whether they should "swallow a large bone for the sake of a little meat."[76] The one related issue which Antifederalists did stress, particularly in the South, was the federal power to make treaties. They argued that the rule requiring approval of treaties by two-thirds of the Senate would not protect those who had an interest in the navigation of the Mississippi River. The North would gain the ascendancy over the South and would naturally favor its own commercial interests. Rather than aiding in the development of western lands, Northerners would consider further development a threat to their already scarce labor supply, and would try. to halt westward migration and keep the West dependent upon the East. They might also use their political power to conclude prejudicial treaties with the Indians. In the Virginia convention, Patrick Henry, William Grayson, and others laid great emphasis on these issues in an effort to woo the delegates from Kentucky. Throughout the first half of the convention, they returned repeatedly to "their favorite business" which, according to one delegate, was the "scuffle for Kentucky votes."[77] Yet their case was not, perhaps, as compelling as it might have been, since many Southern leaders such as Richard Henry Lee and George Washington had sided with John Jay in his negotiations with Gardoqui.[78] Others argued, moreover, that only a stronger federal government could

[75] Mason, *Objections*, in *Pamphlets*, 329-32; Gerry, *Observations*, in *ibid.*, 3-23.

[76] General Thompson in Massachusetts, *Debates*, II, 80-81.

[77] Nicholas in Virginia, *ibid.*, III, 502.

[78] Washington to Richard Henry Lee, July 26, 1786, *Writings of Washington*, XXVIII, 484-85; Richard Henry Lee to Washington, July 15, 1787, James Curtis Ballagh, ed., *The Letters of Richard Henry Lee* (New York, 1914), II, 426. They doubted that the United States could defend its right of navigation in view of Spain's superior military power. They also recognized the large economic benefit to be derived from increased trade with Spain. Finally, they hoped to keep the West dependent upon the East and to strengthen the bonds of union by extending river navigation inland and by building roads to link both sections of the country.

protect American rights.[79]

Only on rare occasions did the friends and enemies of the Constitution confront each other's arguments directly. Melancthon Smith, leader of the Antifederalists in the New York ratifying convention, attempted to refute every one of Jay's arguments point by point. He denied the benefit of commercial treaties with foreign nations and maintained strongly that no foreign nation threatened the United States.[80] One of the cleverest and most remarkable of all Antifederalist writers was James Winthrop, librarian at Harvard University and descendant of the first John Winthrop. He is one of the few Antifederalists who made good use of his enemy's weapon, turning the issue of foreign relations to his own advantage, by associating Federalists with foreigners. He accused them of favoring monarchy, and suggested that "some of their leaders . . . have formed pretty strong attachments to foreign nations, whether those attachments arose from their being educated under a royal government, from a former unfortunate mistake in politics, or from the agencies for foreigners." He pointed out that, for Federalists as well as monarchists, "power and high life are their idols."[81]

Winthrop echoed the Federalists' concern over the danger of subversion, but what they offered as a cure he argued would be a cause: foreign influence would result under the Constitution from the "multiplication of officers" as well as from the long terms proposed for representatives and senators.[82] The result, as he saw it, could only be American embroilment in European quarrels: "this is the only sense in which the Philadelphia system will render us more respectable in the eyes of foreigners."[83]

He conceded the Federalist argument that foreign commerce must be centrally regulated but claimed that a simple amendment to the Articles would suffice; thus the meat of reform could be eaten without swallowing the bone. He wanted, in addition, a

[79] John Marshall in Virginia, *Debates*, III, 223, 231; Madison to Nicholas, Apr. 8, 1788, Madison Papers, Series I, Vol. IX.

[80] Melancthon Smith, *Address to the People of the State of New York*, in *Pamphlets*, 91-115.

[81] *Agrippa*, No. 11, in *Essays*, 89. Federalist leaders did, in fact, tend to be relatively well-to-do and, as I shall indicate, a disproportionate number were indeed educated "under a royal government."

[82] *Ibid.*, 88.

[83] *Ibid.*, No. 14, p. 104; No. 11, pp. 88-89.

guarantee that Congress "shall not by treaty or otherwise give a preference to the ports of one state over those of another."[84]

Finally, he made light of the problem of treaty enforcement. The Dutch Confederacy never had any problems even though it had to consult all its states. The Federalists were mistaken, moreover, in believing that British reluctance to sign a commercial treaty was due to distrust. It was due, rather, to resentment. The British would place self-interest above pride once they recognized the desperate situation of Nova Scotia and their West Indian possessions.[85]

Winthrop alone among leading Antifederalists met his antagonists squarely on their own ground, arguing against their favorite issues and attacking their arguments on national security. Significantly, he avoided the military question. But, in a statement of fourteen reservations to the Philadelphia plan and in his advocacy of a simple commerce amendment to the Articles, he set forth a concrete and constructive plan of his own.

IV

One reason there were so few Winthrops among Antifederalists and so many Jays among Federalists was that the discussion of foreign affairs put the Constitution in the best light for most people. Federalists might have given more emphasis to the domestic anxiety aroused by Shays' Rebellion and spoken at greater length on the importance of law and order and the sanctity of private property. Issues such as fiscal responsibility, the rights of creditors, retiring the national debt would have attracted many, but these were divisive since they set poor against rich, debtors

[84] *Ibid.*, No. 10, p. 84. This was his strongest argument, although it could be argued that Congress had tried and failed to obtain such an amendment under the Articles. Federalists also argued that the commerce power was so radical in itself that it would necessitate many other innovations such as a national judiciary and some means of coercion, namely, taxation and an army.

[85] *Ibid.*, No. 11, pp. 89-90. In fact, what the Federalists claimed was the congressional inability to regulate trade provided Britain with an excuse for withholding trade concessions, but that her real motive was twofold: to strengthen her own merchant marine and naval power while injuring that of the United States. Hence congressional power, while eliminating possible distrust, was primarily intended to force British concessions by threat of retaliatory trade restrictions.

against creditors, West against East. For this reason Federalists wisely avoided them and sought to stress the ways in which the Constitution would benefit all people, concentrating on the issues of national security and commercial distress. Few in any part of the country would deny that external forces threatened the Confederation. Few would disapprove of a stronger national defense. There was little question of the disadvantages of America's commercial position or the need to strengthen the diplomatic bargaining power of Congress.

The Federalists' arguments on the issues related to foreign affairs carried conviction because they were often based on personal experience. Many Federalists were shipowners engaged in transatlantic trade, merchants anxious to penetrate European markets, or farmers who desired greater access to the British West Indies. They understood the advantages of a strong bargaining position in foreign affairs, not only for themselves but for the nation as a whole.[86]

Without exception, the men officially concerned with foreign affairs during this period also supported the Constitution. Robert R. Livingston, secretary for foreign affairs from 1781 to 1782, was a leading Federalist as was his successor, Elias Boudinot. Other supporters were James McClurg, whom Madison nominated as secretary for foreign affairs; Gouverneur Morris, who was deeply involved in diplomatic affairs and who later became American ambassador to France;[87] John Jay, a leading advocate on both the state and national level of constitutional reform, served throughout the postwar Confederation period as secretary for foreign affairs.[88] William Samuel Johnson, who led the Federal-

[86] This is clearly demonstrated in Forrest McDonald, *We the People: The Economic Origins of the Constitution* (Chicago, 1958). Main, 271, found the mercantile class to be the most outstanding and significant of all groups in support of the Constitution.

[87] Morris drafted the *Report on Lord North's Conciliation Offer* (1778), a public paper on the significance of the Franco-American alliance of that year; the instructions for Benjamin Franklin's mission to Paris; and the instructions for obtaining a treaty of peace and commerce with Great Britain (1779). See, David Saville Muzzy, "Gouverneur Morris," *Dictionary of American Biography* (New York, 1959), VII, 210.

[88] For Jay's influence, see Louis Guillaume Otto to Comte de Vergennes, Jan. 10, 1786, in George Bancroft, *History of the Formation of the Constitution of the United States of America* (New York, 1882), I, 479; Monaghan, chap. 13; Samuel Flagg Bemis, "John Jay, Secretary for Foreign Affairs for the Conti-

ist forces in Connecticut, had once defended his state's right to western lands as a colonial agent before the British House of Commons. Stephen Higginson, who mobilized support for the Constitution in Massachusetts, had testified before a Parliamentary committee on the subject of New England commerce and resources.[89] Other friends of the Constitution with outstanding diplomatic experience were John Adams, Benjamin Franklin, and Thomas Jefferson. All of these men had observed at close range the exigencies of foreign relations.

Men educated abroad might also be expected to have a deepened sense of the importance of foreign affairs. The Federalists who studied in Europe greatly outnumbered their counterparts among Antifederalists. They included Charles Pinckney, Charles Cotesworth Pinckney, Thomas Pinckney, Charles Rutledge, Arthur Lee, Joseph Jones, Hugh Williamson, Richard Dobbs Spaight, Daniel Carroll, Charles Carroll, John Dickinson, and Benjamin Rush (John Hancock received a year of training in London in the business of transatlantic shipping). The only prominent Antifederalists educated abroad were Theodorick Bland, William Grayson, Willie Jones, and Richard Henry Lee; and of these, Grayson opposed the Constitution in part because it was not strong enough in the area of treaty enforcement and Lee advocated a national government which would extend "exclusively to all foreign concerns."[90]

Men of foreign birth and upbringing were also more likely to be Federalists; Alexander Hamilton, James Wilson, Robert Morris, Thomas Fitzsimons, Pierce Butler, George Read, James McHenry, Samuel Johnston, William Davie, James Iredell, and St. George Tucker were Federalist leaders born outside the United States. Almost all Antifederalist notables were native born.[91]

Finally, many Federalist leaders had had experience on the na-

---

nental Congress, September 1, 1784 to September 15, 1789," in Bemis, ed., *The American Secretaries of State and their Diplomacy, 1776-1925* (New York, 1927), I, 202.

[89] Higginson played no major role in the ratification controversy, but he did recommend to General Knox a plan for the adoption of the Constitution; James Truslow Adams, "Samuel Higginson," *Dictionary of American Biography*, V, 16.

[90] William Grayson to William Short, Nov. 10, 1787, *Letters*, VIII, 678; Lee, *Letters*, No. 1, in *Pamphlets*, 287.

[91] Exceptions were George Bryan, Aedanus Burke, and Rawlins Lowndes.

tional level. Many had served during the Revolutionary War either as soldiers or as delegates to Congress.[62] In either capacity they would have been closer to the problems of foreign affairs than officials on the state and local levels.[63] Jefferson remarked to Madison that a term in Congress had an enlightening influence upon local politicians: "They see the affairs of the Confederacy from a high ground; they learn the importance of the Union and befriend federal measures when they return. Those who never come here [to Congress] see our affairs insulated."[64]

My argument assumes, of course, that the issues upon which the Federalists campaigned and won were real rather than merely semantic, an assumption that is, to a degree, supported by what has been said. It is an assumption which has been under fire for at least fifty years from the socio-economic school of interpretation pioneered by scholars such as J. Allen Smith and Charles A. Beard.[65] But it is an assumption which merits renewed emphasis.

To say that foreign affairs was a powerful weapon in the hands of Federalists is not to deny the importance of domestic issues.

[62] Cecilia M. Kenyon described the Antifederalist philosophy as one of localism rather than nationalism. Her ideas were then elaborated on in subsequent articles, including Stanley Elkins and Eric McKitrick, "The Founding Fathers, Young Men of the Revolution," *Political Science Quarterly*, LXXVI (1961), 202-10; John P. Roche, "The Founding Fathers: A Reform Caucus in Action," *American Political Science Review*, LV (1961), 799-816; McDonald, "The Anti-Federalists," 207-09.

[63] Roche, 801. According to Roche, "Congressmen were constantly forced to take the broad view of American prestige, were compelled to listen to frustrated envoys in Britain, France, and Spain. From considerations such as these, a 'continental' ideology developed which seems to have demanded a revision of our domestic institutions primarily on the ground that only by invigorating our general government could we assume our rightful place in the international arena."

[64] Jefferson to Madison, Feb. 20, 1784, in Bancroft, I, 345. Congressional experience in itself was, of course, not enough to assure unreserved support for the nationalist movement. Monroe encountered substantial congressional opposition in 1785 when he sponsored his amendment for congressional regulation of foreign commerce. Madison remarked at the time that even in Congress there were "minds unaccustomed to think nationally, let alone globally," and that these would be least sympathetic to the Monroe plan; Madison to Monroe, Aug. 7, 1785, *Writings of Madison*, II, 160. Nor did all congressmen support the Constitution. Exceptions were Richard Henry Lee, John Francis Mercer, Timothy Bloodworth, and William Grayson.

[65] See Richard B. Morris, "The Confederation Period and the American Historian," *William and Mary Quarterly*, XIII, Third Series (1956), 139-56. This is an excellent summary.

Without doubt, the desire for internal order and the protection of property motivated the constitutional movement from the beginning. However, because nearly everyone wanted the government strengthened in the area of foreign affairs, this issue provided the Federalists with the basis for a national consensus and with the primary theme of their campaign.

We might add that there was far more consensus on the existence of national ills than on the choice of remedies. For some, the Federalist prescription for a standing army and direct taxation was ominous.[96] There was a general repugnance to the idea that the central government could reach down to regulate life at the local level. Just as in the years prior to the Revolution, many colonists saw the use of British power at the local level as interference, so, now, many objected to the Constitution out of a similar fear that federal power would usurp the authority of local government. Thomas Jefferson wrote hopefully that the purpose of the central power should be "to make us one nation as to foreign concerns, and keep us distinct in domestic ones."[97] A principal task for Federalists, therefore, was to demonstrate that the exigencies of foreign affairs were sufficient to justify the significant and risky increase in national power represented by the Constitution. In this they succeeded.

[96] Main, 72, has written that direct taxation was the most divisive of all the issues.

[97] Jefferson to Madison, Dec. 16, 1787, Julian Parks Boyd, ed., *The Papers of Thomas Jefferson* (Princeton, N. J., 1954), X, 603.

Antifederalists and the Acceptance of the Constitution: Pennsylvania, 1787-1792*

Steven R. Boyd
University of Texas, San Antonio

When the Constitutional Convention adjourned on September 17, 1787, Federalists faced an uphill battle to secure a formal ratification of the Constitution by the required number of states. Potentially even more difficult was the problem of inducing the American people to accept the Constitution as a legitimate system of government for the nation. The difficulty of securing ratification had been early recognized and partially mitigated during the Convention itself by the decision to call special state conventions to consider the Constitution and by the requirement of the assent of only nine states as sufficient for the new government to be set into operation. The latter concession, even as it eased the problem of ratification, increased the difficulty of securing Constitutional acceptance, for it raised further questions about the legality of abolishing the old Confederation with less than unanimous consent. Federalists were, of course, able to secure ratification of the Constitution by eleven states by July 1788. Legitimacy did not come as quickly. Still by spring 1789, when the first Congress assembled in New York, the American people accepted the Constitution as the legitimate frame of government for the nation.

A key to this success was the manner by which Antifederalists chose to oppose the Constitution. During the ratification cam-

* Research for this article was completed while I was a member of the editorial staff of the Documentary History of the Ratification of the Constitution Project at the University of Wisconsin. I wish to thank Professor Merrill Jensen and the members of the project staff, particularly John P. Kaminski, for their assistance at all stages of my work. An earlier version of this article was presented at the annual meeting of the American Political Science Association, September 2-5, 1976.

Steven R. Boyd is assistant professor of history at the University of Texas at San Antonio. His book, *The Politics of Opposition: Antifederalists and the Acceptance of the Constitution* will be released August 1979 by Kraus Thomson Organization, New York.

paign, and again in the first federal elections, Antifederalists channeled their opposition to the Constitution into the political process. That in itself did not cause the demise of anticonstitutionalism (meaning the rejection of the Constitution as fundamental law) or insure the acceptance of the Constitution per se. But Antifederalists operated within the framework of the new Constitution, in 1787-1788 by accepting the proposal for special state conventions to consider the new Constitution and by working to elect Antifederalist majorities to them, and in 1788-1789 by channeling their efforts into the first federal elections. In addition, the Antifederalists' attack was early directed away from fundamentals. Thus, during the debate over ratification Antifederalists called for a second constitutional convention to revise the proposed Constitution. During the campaign for seats in the House of Representatives they stressed the need for amendments. Throughout, they operated within the framework of the new government. Furthermore, their effort drew thousands of voters into the framework of the Constitution as well in 1787, 1788, and 1789 when they again and again offered constitutional channels of opposition. This participation led, not only to an acceptance of the decisions of the state convention and the outcome of the first federal elections, but to an acquiescence to the Constitution as well. This in turn undercut any anticonstitutional or extra-legal challenge to the new government and transformed the opponents of the new Constitution into a "loyal opposition."

The circumstances by which Antifederalists moved into the camp of the Constitution varied. In some states, where Antifederalists were few in number, they were simply overwhelmed by Federalist majorities and accepted the constitution. In other states—e.g. New Hampshire, Massachusetts, New York, Pennsylvania, Virginia and South Carolina—Antifederalists were more numerous and better organized. In those states there were variations due to local circumstance—i.e. the timing of the elections for convention delegates, the presence or absence of intervening state elections, the date of the state's ratification, and the size of the Antifederalist block within the state. Despite these local variations the pattern evident in Pennsylvania provides an excellent example of how Antifederalists contributed materially to and in fact insured the acceptance of the Constitution.

By 1787 Pennsylvania politics were dominated by two well developed state parties. The Constitutionalists were predominately small farmers residing west of the Susquehanna River or urban artisans and shopkeepers. They were supporters of the state constitution of 1776, while the bulk of the Constitutionalists became opponents of the proposed federal Constitution. The leaders of the Constitutionalist party, who became the leaders of the Antifederalists in Pennsylvania, included an urban elite and western legislators. The former consisted of George Bryan, in 1787 the fourth judge of the Pennsylvania Supreme Court, his son Samuel, and Bryan's brother-in-law, Jonathan Bayard Smith. Blair M'Clenachan, a prominent Philadelphia merchant, and Jonathan Dickinson Sargeant were also part of this leadership group as were three members of the College of Philadelphia faculty—Dr. John Ewing, Dr. James Hutchinson and Dr. William Shippen. Western leaders included David Redick, James McLene and John Smiley, members of the Supreme Executive Council, and Robert Whitehill and William Findley, members of the Assembly.[1]

The Republicans were the opponents of the state constitution and supporters of the proposed federal one. Most Republicans resided east of the Susquehanna River with the party's strongest support in the city and county of Philadelphia and its immediate environs. The party included a large number of farmers, but a significantly larger portion were engaged either in trade or the professions. The leaders of the Republican party reflected these differences. Robert Morris, George Clymer, and James Wilson were prominent because of their extensive accumulated wealth and their speculations in land, commerce and government currency. All three men had been members of the Federal Convention, while Wilson was to serve in the state convention as well.[2]

The actual struggle over the Constitution in Pennsylvania began in August 1787, when George Bryan and other Constitutionalist leaders, alarmed by the persistent rumors of a new Constitution being prepared by the Convention (a Convention attended only by their political enemies), began to lay the groundwork for an organized, statewide attack on the work of the Convention. Thus, Bryan and Jonathan B. Smith allegedly prepared pamphlets "designed to excite prejudices against the new federal government, and thereby (to) prevent its adoption by this state."[3] Other Constitutionalists travelled westward to

[1] Jackson Turner Main, *Political Parties Before the Constitution* (Chapel Hill: Univ. of North Carolina in Press, 1973), chapter 8; Merrill Jensen, ed., *The Documentary History of the Ratification of the Constitution*, vol. 2; *Ratification of the Constitution by the States: Pennsylvania* (Madison: Univ. of Wisconsin Press, 1976); *Biographical Gazetteer*, pp. 727-34.

[2] Ibid.; Allen Johnson and Dumas Malone, eds., *Dictionary of American Biography*, 22 vols. (New York, 1928-44), 13: 219-23; 4: 234-45; 20:326-30.

[3] Philadelphia *Independent Gazetteer*, August 8, 1787.

prepare their constituents to view the work of the Convention, whatever it might be, "with a scrutinizing eye."[4] Once the Constitution was made public Constitutionalists urged delay. David Redick advised congressional delegate William Irvine to "deliberate and digest (the Constitution) thoroughly before recommending it to the states."[5] Similarly in the state legislature the Constitutionalist minority sought, first to delay action on the Constitution until the next legislative session, which followed upcoming state elections, and failing that, to delay the date of the elections and the meeting of the state convention as long as possible.[6] There were, of course, other alternatives theoretically available to Pennsylvania's Antifederalists. They could, as the Antifederalist majority in Rhode Island did later, oppose calling a convention, or, as some Massachusetts Antifederalists urged, press for a popular referendum on the Constitution in place of a state convention.[7] If Pennsylvania Antifederalists even considered these theoretical options, they rejected them. They acted as they did primarily because they were a minority in a state legislature which would not accept an alternative method of considering the Constitution. Furthermore, Antifederalists in the state legislature were handicapped by the overwhelming popularity of the Constitution in Philadelphia where the legislature was meeting. Thus, when the Antifederalist leadership tried to block action on the resolution establishing the date of the election of delegates to meet in a state convention by boycotting the legislative session and thereby preventing a quorum, an angry mob intervened, carried two Antifederalist legislators to the assembly, and held them there until a quorum was declared and the resolutions were adopted.[8]

With the passage of the convention election resolved, Pennsylvania's Antifederalists could have chosen to boycott the elections on the simple grounds that there was not sufficient time for the people to examine and evaluate the Constitution before

[4] A. Boyd Hamilton, ed., "An Autobiography: Extracts Taken from the Life of John Kean of Harrisburg," *Notes and Queries,* 3 vols., (Harrisburg, Pa., 1895-96), 3: 94.

[5] September 24, 1787, *Irvine Papers* (Pennsylvania Historical Society). This and much of the material cited below has, since I completed my research, been published in Merrill Jensen, ed., *The Documentary History,* vol. 2; and in Merrill Jensen and Robert A. Becker, eds., *The Documentary History of the First Federal Elections,* 1 vol. to date (Madison: Univ. of Wisconsin Press, 1976). These volumes constitute the starting point for any person seeking to understand the adoption of the United States Constitution.

[6] *Proceedings and Debates of the General Assembly* (Philadelphia, 1787), p. 115.

[7] William R. Staples, *Rhode Island in the Continental Congress, 1765-1790* (Providence, 1870), pp. 584-5; Report of debates in the Massachusetts legislature, Boston *Massachusetts Centinel,* October 27, 1787.

[8] The events are described in Tench Coxe to James Madison, September 29, *Madison Papers* (Library of Congress).

choosing delegates to the convention. They chose to participate, though, for Antifederalists believed that despite the short time between the passage of the convention resolutions and the elections, they could win a majority of the seats in the state convention. In the ensuing campaign Antifederalists proved to be formidable opponents. In the six weeks between the passage of the convention resolution and the election of delegates to the state convention, Antifederalists initiated a statewide propaganda and electoral effort. In a series of broadsides and newspaper articles the Antifederalists comdemned the Constitution as destructive of both the Articles of Confederation and the people's civil liberties. They also offered an alternative to unconditional ratification: a proposal for a second convention called by Congress where the Constitution as proposed "may be reconsidered, deliberately reviewed and corrected, (and) formed anew on the principles of a confederacy of free republics."[9]

This call for a second constitutional convention became the platform of the Pennsylvania Antifederalists and the issue on which they campaigned for convention delegates. Samuel Bryan, the most prolific of the Antifederalist writers, later claimed "many hundred pounds" were expended to defray the costs of publishing "Centinel" and other Antifederalist essays which were then distributed to supporters in the various counties.[10] George Bryan "constantly" sent packets of Antifederalist pamphlets to an ally in Chester county while further west in Franklin county, Federalist John King, in thanking Benjamin Rush for some Federalist material, commented that the influx of Antifederalist material into that county was so great that "we thought there were no 'Centinels' in Philadelphia but the one."[11] William Findley, a Constitutional representative from Westmoreland county, left Philadelphia "fraught with opposition papers" intended for distribution among his constituents in the west.[12]

The distribution of broadsides and pamphlets was designed to aid in the election of Antifederalist candidates who were nominated in at least fourteen of the state's nineteen electoral units (compared with Federalist nominations in eighteen electoral units). That effort met with some success for Federalist Benjamin Rush complained that in Berks county, where he expected

[9] "Old Whig," *To the People of Pennsylvania* (Philadelphia, 1787).

[10] To Albert Gallatin, December 18, 1790, *Gallatin Papers* (New York Historical Society).

[11] Robert Smith to George or Samuel Bryan, April 26, 1788, *Bryan Papers* (Pennsylvania Historical Society); November 5, 1787, *Rush Papers* (Library of Philadelphia).

[12] Richard Butler to William Irvine, October 11, 1787, *Irvine Papers,* (Pennsylvania Historical Society).

Federalists to do well, the voters chose Antifederalists, in large part because of the propoganda effort of George and Samuel Bryan.[13] Berks was, however, the exception, for the statewide returns reflected the popularity of the Constitution in Pennsylvania. Federalists won 46 of the 69 seats in the state convention.

Despite their poor showing in the elections, Antifederalists persisted. In November a group of Pennsylvania Antifederalists met with Richard Henry Lee, who had been in New York serving as a Virginia delegate to the Confederation Congress. In New York Lee had met with prominent Antifederalists, among them Governor George Clinton of that state and Elbridge Gerry of Massachusetts, to plot strategy and to plan the integration of efforts of state Antifederalists like those in Pennsylvania into a national plan. The outcome of those meetings was a proposal that the state legislatures delay action on the report of the Federal Convention until their spring sessions and that they schedule their conventions to meet simultaneously in April or May 1788 so that when the conventions did meet, they could communicate with one another, agree upon a specific list of amendments, and then petition Congress to call a second convention that "may weave them (the proposed amendments) into the proffered system."[14]

Lee informed William Findley, George Bryan and other Antifederalist leaders of this plan in November. Although the elections for convention delegates were already over, the latter initiated a petition campaign designed to bring Pennsylvania into line with that strategy. In Philadelphia county, where the Constitution was overwhelmingly popular, Antifederalists circulated a petition that asked only that the Pennsylvania convention adjourn until April or May 1788 "so that the deliberate sense of the people could be obtained."[15] In Cumberland county, where Antifederalists were stronger, the petition was more explicit, calling upon the convention "not to adopt" the Constitution until a bill of rights and other amendments were added to it.[16] The thrust of the two petitions was merged on December 12, 1787 when Robert Whitehill moved that the state convention adjourn so that the amendments outlined in the Cumberland

[13] To John Montgomery, November 9, 1787, *Rush Papers* (Library of Philadelphia).

[14] Richard Henry Lee to Samuel Adams, October 5, 1787; James C. Ballagh, ed., *The Letters of Richard Henry Lee,* 2 vols. (New York, 1911-1914), 2: 447. For Lee's role see Steven R. Boyd, "The Impact of the Constitution on State Politics: New York as a Test Case," in *The Human Dimensions of Nation Making: Essays on Colonial and Revolutionary America,* ed. James K. Martin (Madison: Univ. of Wisconsin Press, 1976), p. 273.

[15] Philadelphia *Pennsylvania Packet,* December 11, 1787.

[16] *Carlisle Gazette,* December 5, 1787.

County petition as well as those that "may be proposed by the other states may be offered to Congress and taken into consideration by the United States before the proposed Constitution shall be ratified." Clearly compatible with the plan as outlined by Lee, the motion failed 23 to 46.[17] A motion to ratify the Constitution passed by the same margin.

The fact of the Antifederalists defeat in the convention is, however, of less significance to this analysis than the impact of their electioneering in contributing to the acceptance of the Constitution. In the first place it should be noted that Pennsylvania Antifederalists did not explicitly (in most instances) call for the rejection of the Constitution, stressing instead the need for amendments that could be agreed upon at a meeting of a second constitutional convention. Delegates to a second constitutional convention could, emulating the Federal Convention, reject altogether the Constitution they were convened to revise and instead propose amendments to the Articles of Confederation. Some Antifederalists clearly hoped that it would do so. In that sense those Pennsylvania Antifederalists were anti-constitutionalists. But, during the fall of 1787, they operated within the framework of the very government which they opposed. That is, they accepted the ground rules of the new Constitution even before it was adopted and actively worked to elect Antifederalists to the state convention. One consequence of that campaign was to draw large numbers of people to the polls. And in December 1787, many of these voters, although they had voted against the Constitution, accepted the decision of the convention and declared their willingness to acquiesce to the will of the majority.

The extent of Antifederalist acquiesence at this time is unclear. The newspapers offer no adequate estimate for Philadelphia's newspapers were overwhelming partisan in their 'reporting'. Thus, the Federalist *Pennsylvania Journal* reported that the great majority of the people concurred in the decision of the convention and that only a handful of malcontents continued to oppose the Constitution. The Antifederalist *Independent Gazetteer* stated just the opposite, that the people did not accept the decision of the convention. Private comment was also contradictory, at least about public sentiment outside of Philadelphia, which all conceded was a Federalist stronghold. Thus, Thomas Scott, a Federalist, informed Benajmin Rush that "the voice of opposition is scarcely heard," while Benjamin Blythe, an Anti-

[17] Philadelphia *Pennsylvania Herald,* December 15, 1787.

federalist, claimed a majority of Pennsylvania's farmers were opposed.[18]

For those who did oppose—whatever the number—two options were available. They could resort to armed resistance or they could initiate political action—in state to annul Pennsylvania's ratification and elsewhere to block ratification by those states that had not yet adopted the proposed Constitution. In December 1787, Antifederalist John Nicholson, state comptroller general and an Antifederalist pamphleteer, initiated another petition campaign. In this petition Antifederalists called upon the legislature not to confirm the state convention's act of ratification because the Constitution and "the powers therein proposed to be granted to the government were too great as well as "dangerous and inimical to liberty and equality amongst the people."[19] Copies of the petition were circulated among the state's western counties during the winter months, and eventually over six thousand signatures were collected. For the petition to be approved, however, Antifederalists support alone was not sufficient. Federalists had to be convinced of the necessity of repeal as well. Toward that end Antifederalists embarked on another massive propoganda campaign, one with an added dimension.

Antifederalists believed that one of the most persuasive arguments for the Constitution was its promise to prevent further Shaysite actions like those that had appeared in Massachusetts in the winter of 1787. In the winter of 1788 Antifederalists tried to turn this fear to their advantage. They argued that the Constitution, rather than promising an end to armed resistance to governmental measures, was promoting it. Samuel Bryan, in "Centinel VII," for example, warned that the freemen of Pennsylvania would not submit to the new Constitution without a struggle. An unidentified correspondent in the Philadelphia *Freeman's Journal* made the same point when he declared that the Federalists must "immediately drop all proceeding in favor of the proposed Constitution . . . for should they persist in attempting to force it on the people, the peace of the country must inevitably be destroyed."[20] Such argument was, of course, a

[18] *Pennsylvania Journal,* December 26: *Independent Gazetteer,* December 22, 1787; Scott to Rush, March 15, *Rush Papers* (Library of Philadelphia); Blythe to John Nicholson, February 11, 1788, *Nicholson Papers* (Pennsylvania Historical and Museum Commission).

[19] "A draft of a petition in opposition to the actions of the Pennsylvania Convention," *Nicholson Papers* (Pennsylvania Historical and Museum Commission).

[20] Philadelphia *Independent Gazetteer,* December 29, 1787; Philadelphia *Freemans Journal,* January 16, 1788. See also "Versus Conciliator," *Independent Gazetteer,* January 19; and "Address of the Carlisle Town Meeting," *Freemans Journal,* February 13, 1788.

dangerous one and invited, not Federalist conversions, but attack. Thus, instead of being persuaded by Bryan's argument, Federalists condemned him for his refusal to accept the will of the majority as reflected in the state convention and warned that a strong central government was necessary to guard against civil strife being introduced by such anarchic and antidemocratic elements as Bryan.[21] The issue came to a head in March when the petitions calling for repeal were submitted to the state legislature. Despite the Antifederalists best effort no Federalist legislator was converted and the petitions were rejected.

The petition drive was, of course, only one aspect of the Antifederalists effort. During the winter Antifederalists shipped packets of "Centinel", "The Dissent of the Minority", and other pamphlets to Antifederalists in Maryland, Virginia and the Carolinas, where they were utilized by local candidates in their bid for seats in their respective state conventions. Bryan even shipped packets of "Centinel" and other essays to Georgia in March 1788, in the hope that state could be persuaded to repeal its earlier ratification.[22] Although that effort met with little support, Bryan's bid to assist in the election of Antifederalist delegates was more successful, particularly in the Carolinas where "pamphlets, speeches and protests of the disaffected in Pennsylvania . . . prejudiced the minds of (Carolina) citizens against the Constitution."

Pennsylvania Antifederalists were able to cooperate with their counterparts to the south because in the spring Antifederalists were working for the same immediate end—the election of Antifederalist convention delegates—and toward the same long term goal—interstate and interconvention cooperation in the call for a second constitutional convention. But effective interconvention cooperation did not materialize during June and July when the New Hampshire, New York, Virginia, and North Carolina conventions were in session. It did not in large part because of the failure of the Virginians to secure a substantial Antifederalist majority in their convention elections. Without a decisive majority, in Virginia, New York Antifederalists decided to act alone, thereby undercutting the plan for a united

[21] Philadelphia *Pennsylvania Mercury,* January 1; Philadelphia *Pennsylvania Herald,* January 16, 1788.

[22] Philadelphia *Pennsylvania Gazette,* March 12, 1788; Robert Smith to George or Samuel Bryan, April 26, 1788, *Bryan Papers* (Pennsylvania Historical Society).

[23] Charles C. Pinckney to Rufus King, May 24, 1788; Charles R. King, ed., *Life and Correspondence of Rufus King,* 6 vols. (New York, 1894-1900), 1: 328.

demand by all the non-ratifying states for amendments previous to ratification. However, Virginia's unconditional ratification altered the attitude of many New York Antifederalist delegates who in July carefully assessed the alternatives available to them: unconditional ratification with recommended amendments or rejection. Rejection would place the New Yorkers outside the union and therefore deprive them of any voice in the operation of the new government. Ratification, on the other hand, would give them another opportunity to try to secure amendments and a second constitutional covention. That consideration, based on an erroneous belief that Antifederalism was still strong in a majority of the states, and on the urgings of Pennsylvania Antifederalists who counseled ratification as the best alternative, induced a block of New York Antifederalists to agree to unconditional ratification which they combined with a circular letter to the states outlining the amendments supported by New York, and calling upon the states to petition Congress to convene a second constitutional convention to consider them.[24]

Ratification by New York and Virginia marked the practical completion of the new Union and prompted the Confederation Congress to begin work on an election ordinance calling for the states to choose senators, representatives, and electors. For the Antifederalists the elections provided, once again, a channel through which to direct their energies. Even before ratification by New York, Pennsylvania Antifederalists had called for a statewide conference to meet at Harrisburg in the fall, there "to consider and devise a plan the most likely to succeed in obtaining amendments to the new Constitution."[25] The Harrisburg Convention met on September 3, 1788. Its report recommended that the people of the state "acquiesce" in the organization of the new government, called for a speedy "revision of the said constitution" by a general convention, and proposed that a petition be presented to the state legislature calling upon that body to petition Congress to call a second constitutional convention in conformity with Article V of the new Constitution. Although not part of their formal report, the delegates to the convention also agreed upon a slate of Antifederalist candidates for the United States House of Representatives.[26]

[24] The New York Antifederalists decision to accept unconditional ratification is discussed in Boyd, "Impact of the Constitution," pp. 299-301.

[25] Proceedings of a Cumberland County Meeting, July 3, 1788, *Pennsylvania Papers, Harrisburg Convention* (New York Public Library).

[26] Philadelphia *Pennsylvania Packet,* September 15, 1788. The Antifederalist list of candidates was labeled the Harrisburg Ticket.

Between September and November 26, 1788 the Antifederalists, building on the organizing effort of the previous spring, duplicated their effort of the year before. In the first federal elections, however, Antifederalists were at a serious disadvantage. With ratification they experienced considerable loss of support. The petition campaign temporarily reversed that trend, yet the continuing success of Federalists in states other than Pennsylvania, and the fear, played upon by Federalists, that continued opposition in the state could indeed result in violence and conceivably even civil war, persuaded increasing numbers of Antifederalists, while still desiring amendments, to accept the new government and to look to Federalists to implement it.[27]

A second, smaller block of Antifederalists rejected that course. They argued that only a policy of non-cooperation could secure the desired goal. Thus, William Petriken retrospectively described a sentiment present in the fall of 1788. Petriken declared that decisive action rather than political participation was necessary. By that he meant the formation of county volunteer militia companies which could parade, exercise, and harass local Federalists, and, if these examples were emulated throughout the nation, compel Federalists to "rectify" the new government.[28]

Party leaders were well aware of these defections. As early as June 1788, Charles Pettit warned that the ratification of the Constitution, at that time by eight states, had legitimatized it in the eyes of the "large proportion of the people in every state." Pettit then urged that the only way to regain the support of those voters was for the party to accommodate itself to the changed mood of the people while making one final effort to secure amendments. Hence Pettit recommended that the states Antifederalists publicly declare their support of the new government, and work to be included among those that would implement it. Pettit recognized the risks inherent in such a strategy. If they failed election—and that was certainly a real possibility given the division of the party—there were no other options open to them. Even if they were elected it was far from certain that Congress could be persuaded to propose amendments. Pettit accepted those risks when he attended the Harris-

[27] See Benjamin Rush to Jeremy Belknap, May 29, 1788, *Belknap Papers* (Massachusetts Historical Society); Thomas Willing to William Bingham, June 29, Gratz Collection (Pennsylvania Historical Society); and the *Pennsylvania Gazette,* May 14, 1788.

[28] To John Nicholson, March 23, 1789, *Nicholson Papers* (Pennsylvania Historical and Museum Commission).

burg Convention and accepted nomination to the Harrisburg ticket.[29]

In the first federal elections, Pettit and other Antifederalist nominees for the House of Representatives worked to secure the support of all Antifederalists for their candidacy. In the report of the Harrisburg Convention (signed by the delegates, which included three nominees for the House) they declared that they possessed "sentiments completely Federal" even as they conceived "that amendments in some part of the plan are essential . . ."[30] This dual theme of support for the Constitution and amendments characterized the Antifederalists first federal election campaign. A "Friend to Liberty and Union," for example, assured the freemen of Pennsylvania that the Antifederalist nominees were committed to "effectuating the great object of the late Continetal Convention" even as they favored "carrying into execution the new government, and at the same time amending it." If, on the one hand, "A Friend" sought to placate those Antifederalists leaning toward Federalism, he also called upon the more radical wing of the party to support the ticket. Thus, repudiating the rhetoric of the previous spring, he admonished that "it has become the duty of all good citizens to make a beginning with the Constitution as it is, confiding in the hopes of obtaining all essential amendments in a constitutional manner (which) is certainly more eligible . . . than any violent or irregular opposition to attempt to overthrow it."[31]

As if these divisions were not enough, Antifederalists were also undermined by a block of German Americans who protested the absence of "German representation" on the Harrisburg and Lancaster (Federalist) tickets. To remedy this lack they proposed a revised Harrisburg ticket that removed Antifederalist Robert Whitehill and replaced him with a Federalist nominee for the House, Frederick Augustus Muhlenburg. Likewise the Lancaster ticket was altered by the deletion of two Federalist nominees and their replacement with two German Antifederalists, Peter Muhlenburg and Daniel Hiester.[32]

[29] To Robert Whitehill, June 5, 1788, *Whitehill Papers* (Cumberland County Historical Society).

[30] *Pennsylvania Packet,* September 15, 1788.

[31] Philadelphia *Federal Gazette,* November 7, 1788. This essay was originally printed as a broadside and "communicated to the inhabitants of the interior counties." See "A Friend to Truth and Freedom," ibid. No broadside copy of the essay is extant.

[32] *To the German Inhabitants of the State of Pennsylvania* (Philadelphia, 1787). Again no broadside copy of this essay is extant. It was reprinted in the *Gemeinnutziqe Philadelphische Correspondenz,* November 18; and the Philadelphia *Pennsylvania Packet,* November 19, 1788.

The outcome of the elections reflected both the decline of Antifederalist party support and the impact of the German nominations. Federalists won six of the eight seats for the House, the other two going to the Antifederalist German candidates. Equally devastating was the relatively low turnout for the elections in the western, and predominantly Antifederalist counties. James Madison, among others, commented on the "indifference" among Antifederalists, who in many instances "left it to the others (Federalists) and did not vote."[33] Only limited comparisons can be made because of the absence of complete electoral returns for the convention elections, but in Berks County, which elected Antifederalist convention delegates in November 1787, one-third fewer Antifederalists voted in the first federal election. In contrast Federalists in neighboring York increased their voter turnout by approximately one-third. The geographic distribution of the votes indicates continued Antifederalist strength in the western counties, but the absolute decline in the number of voters suggests a widespread continued antipathy toward the new Constitution.[34]

The first elections in Pennsylvania were not atypical. In each state where they had been a major force, Antifederalists faced the elections divided. Some, to the chagrin of their leadership declared "it (the Constitution) is adopted, let us try it."[35] Others, however, were either indifferent or explicity hostile, and refused to participate further in the new system by voting for Antifederalist candidates for federal office. Only in isolated districts in Massachusetts, New York, Virginia and South Carolina did Antifederalists have both the inclination and the ability to obtain federal office.[36] Overwhelmed by the nationwide Federalist victory, unsuccessful Antifederalist candidates moved quickly to declare their support for the new government and, with an eye to

[33] Madison to Henry Lee, November 30, 1788, *Madison Papers* (Library of Congress); Alexander McKeshan and George Logue to John Nicholson, January 8, 1789, *Nicholson Papers* (Pennsylvania Historical and Museum Commission). McKeshan and Logue were referring to the election of electors but their statement is equally applicable to the election of representatives.

[34] The returns were printed in various Philadelphia newspapers and like much of the data cited above, are now available in Jensen and Becker, eds., *The Documentary History of the First Federal Elections*.

[35] Joshua Atherton to John Lamb, February 23, 1789, *Lamb Papers* (New York Historical Society).

[36] The best account of the first federal elections pending the publication of additional volumes of *The Documentary History* is Kenneth R. Bowling, "Federalists and Antifederalists after Ratification, The First Congressional Election" (M.A. thesis, University of Wisconsin, 1964).

the future when Antifederalism might be equated with treason, to exculpate themselves from their Antifederalist part.[37]

When the new government met in April 1789, then it had the support of a majority of the American people and the acquiescence of the bulk of the minority. There was still considerable support for amendments and isolated pockets of overt hostility. The Bill of Rights, however, placated the demand for amendments while the response to the excise of 1791 brought the last group of opponents into the framework of the Constitution.

James Madison had initially opposed amending the Constitution. In February 1788 he deprecated the Massachusetts mode of ratification with recommended amendments, and he later opposed amendments in the Virginia ratifying convention. A seemingly Antifederalist upsurge in the fall 1788, however, coupled with a narrow victory over James Monroe in Virginia's fifth congressional district, convinced Madison that some amendments should be proposed by the first Congress. Consequently, he persuaded a hostile House and Senate of the expediency of some amendments, ultimately embodied in the Bill of Rights. The Bill of Rights did not, as has been recognized, meet the demands of those Antifederalists who wanted a substantive restructuring and debilitating of the powers of the central government. In the first federal election campaign, however, Antifederalists had stressed the civil liberties side of the amendments issue, and those guarantees were granted in the proposed amendments. Subsequently the Bill of Rights had the support of the general populace and their representatives promptly ratified it.[38]

Ultimately though it was Alexander Hamilton's excise bill of 1791 and the hostility that it engendered that drew the last of the Antifederalists of 1787-1788 into the framework of the Constitution. The excise bill, which levied a tax on all foreign and domestic "spirits", encountered immediate opposition in Pennsylvania and culminated in the Whiskey Rebellion of 1794. While the rebellion was a major test of strength for the new government, the initial impact of the excise was to draw the last

[37] As early as August 5, 1788 Charles Pettit explained to George Washington that he had consistently exerted his influence to insure the acquiescence of the Pennsylvania Antifederalists to the new government. He expressed similar sentiments in a second letter to Washington, March 19, 1791, *Washington Papers* (Library of Congress). In addition see his *An Impartial Review of the Rise and Progress of the Controversy Between the Parties* (Philadelphia, 1800).

[38] See "First Congress," chapter 5. Bowling, in my judgement, overemphasizes the impact of the Bill of Rights in sounding "the death watch of Antifederalism."

remnants of the opposition, concentrated in central and western Pennsylvania, into the framework of the new government.[39] Thus, in the 1792 federal elections these Pennsylvanians turned out to vote for candidates for the House of Representatives who opposed the excise and pledged to administer the government in a manner compatible with the wishes of the people.[40] At that point, with Antifederalists voting, not for amendments or a second convention that could, at least theoretically destroy the new government, but for a candidate that pledged a different policy of administration, the Constitution was secure.

In retrospect, Pennsylvania Antifederalists recognized the consequences of their participation in the framework of the new Constitution—that it directed their efforts away from "decisive action" while sanctioning the new government itself.[41] What they did not recognize was that "decisive action", like Shays Rebellion in 1786-1787, had proven singularly ineffective while political participation in Massachusetts in the spring 1787 elections led to some gains in the next legislative session.[42] In like manner, Antifederalists, by participating in the political process, won Federalist concessions in the form of the Bill of Rights and contributed materially to the acceptance of the Constitution as the legitimate basis of government. The latter proved to be their most enduring achievement.

[39] For the most recent dicussion of the Whiskey Rebellion see Richard H. Kohn, *Eagle and Sword* (New York: Free Press, 1975), chapter 8.

[40] The election is described in Harry Tinkcom, *The Republicans and Federalists in Pennsylvania, 1790-1801* (Harrisburg, 1950), chapter 4. The Constitutional character of the opposition to the excise is emphasized in Hugh H. Brackenridge, *History of the Western Insurrection* (Pittsburgh, 1859), passim.

[41] Reflecting his experience in the First Federal Elections, Albert Gallatin urged Constitutionalists to boycott the Republican's call for a convention to revise the state constitution rather than "sanction" an extra-legal measure. To Alexander Addison, October 7, 1789, *Gallatin Papers* (New York Historical Society).

[42] Van Beck Hall, *Politics Without Parties: Massachusetts, 1789-1790* (Pittsburgh: Univ. of Pittsburgh Press, 1971), pp. 235-49.

THE IDEOLOGY OF COURT AND COUNTRY IN THE VIRGINIA RATIFYING CONVENTION OF 1788

by J. THOMAS WREN*

IN an article recently published in the *William and Mary Quarterly*, James H. Hutson suggested that the debate between Federalists and Antifederalists over the ratification of the Constitution can best be viewed in terms of contemporary British political language; that is, within the framework of a "Court" versus "Country" approach.[1] In suggesting this form of analysis, Hutson built upon a similar perception articulated by John M. Murrin in an earlier essay.[2] In proposing the Court versus Country dichotomy, both Hutson and Murrin were attempting to bridge the gap between the neo-progressive historians, who view the ratification debate as one between distinct socioeconomic groups, and those historians who emphasize ideological similarities between Federalists and Antifederalists.[3] Moreover, Hutson acknowledged that he sought "to offer a more serviceable definition of Antifederalism than now exists, and show how Antifederalism can be more intelligibly differentiated from Federalism."[4] Both Hutson and Murrin agreed on the terms that best meet these requirements. The appellation that most accurately portrays the Antifederalists is "Country." Its antonym, "Court," best denotes the Federalists.[5]

This essay seeks to apply the interpretive framework of these scholars to the Virginia ratifying convention of 1788. In the process, the perceptions of Hutson and Murrin will be substantially borne out: it is indeed possible to trace the debate in terms of traditional Court versus Country language and concepts. The Virginia debate, however, also demonstrates the degree to which both sides adhered to the same basic assumptions, varying only in

---

*J. Thomas Wren is a member of the Ohio bar and a doctoral candidate in American history at the College of William and Mary. The author would like to thank Michael McGiffert, John E. Selby, and Robert C. Palmer for their comments on an early draft of this essay. He also expresses his appreciation for the constructive criticisms of John M. Murrin and Lance Banning.

[1] James H. Hutson, "Country, Court and Constitution: Antifederalism and the Historians," *William and Mary Quarterly* (hereafter cited as *WMQ*), 3d ser., XXXVIII (1981), 337.

[2] John M. Murrin, "The Great Inversion, or Court versus Country: A Comparison of the Revolution Settlements in England (1688-1721) and America (1776-1816)," in *Three British Revolutions: 1641, 1688, 1776*, ed. J. G. A. Pocock (Princeton, 1980), p. 376.

[3] Hutson, "Country, Court and Constitution," p. 356; Murrin, "The Great Inversion," p. 375.

[4] Hutson, "Country, Court and Constitution," p. 338.

[5] Ibid., p. 356; Murrin, "The Great Inversion," p. 376.

THE VIRGINIA MAGAZINE OF HISTORY AND BIOGRAPHY
Vol. 93 No. 4 (October 1985)

the application of those shared notions. As J. G. A. Pocock stated in regard to British politics, "Both [Country] and [Court] accept the same historical scheme . . . but what the [Country] rejects as corruption, the [Court] accepts as the foundation of a new order."[6] Although Hutson acknowledged the frequency of agreement between Court and Country partisans, the discussions of the Virginia ratifying convention highlight this underlying congruence in ideology with remarkable clarity.[7]

To understand the debates of the Virginia convention in their proper context, it is necessary to trace the meaning of Court and Country as those concepts came down to the delegates of 1788. The Court was the "collective designation of the monarch, his residence, council, officials and courtiers."[8] After the accession of William III in 1688, the Whigs gradually emerged as the party in power and therefore the Court party. As the ruling party, the Whigs sought the means to restrain opposition at home while conducting a vigorous foreign policy against France. This course involved Court support of numerous expedients. The French policy entailed the support of a standing army and a huge navy. The financial exigencies of government demanded acceptance of a national debt, the establishment of the Bank of England, and an increased reliance on the business and professional classes. To administer the government a reasonably effective bureaucracy was required, together with increased patronage to guarantee the docility of Parliament.[9]

The adversary of the Court was the Country. By the end of the seventeenth century, Country was a widely used term in England with a generally accepted meaning: "opposition to the exercise of power by government."[10] Pocock best summarizes the world view of the Country faction in England. The Country vision of English politics saw society as consisting of the Court, or administration, and the Country, or the men of independent property. The business of Parliament (representing the Country) was to preserve the independence of property, in which was founded all human liberty and excellence. The business of administration (the Court) was to govern. Of course this was a legitimate activity, but to govern is to wield power, and power has a natural tendency to aggrandize itself. It was more

[6] J. G. A. Pocock, "Machiavelli, Harrington, and English Political Ideologies in the Eighteenth Century," *WMQ*, 3d ser., XXII (1965), 577.

[7] Hutson, "Country, Court and Constitution," pp. 360, 363, 367-68.

[8] Ibid., p. 357.

[9] Murrin, "The Great Inversion," pp. 379-81; Hutson, "Country, Court and Constitution," p. 357; J. H. Plumb, *The Origins of Political Stability: England, 1675-1725* (Boston, 1967), pp. 134-35.

[10] Hutson, "Country, Court and Constitution," p. 356.

Colonial Williamsburg Foundation

The constitutional balance of king, lords, and commons represented in a 1755 English engraving

important to supervise government than to support it, because the preservation of independence was the ultimate political good. To the "Country-man," there existed an ancient constitution in England, which consisted of a balance or equilibrium between the various organs of government. Within this balance, the function of Parliament was to supervise the executive. But the executive possessed means of distracting Parliament from its proper function by seducing members with offers of places and pensions and by persuading them to support measures—standing armies, national debt, excise schemes—whereby the activities of administration would grow beyond Parliament's control. These means of subversion were known collectively as "corruption," and if ever Parliament should become wholly corrupt, it would mean the end of independence and liberty. To combat the aggressions of the Court, the Country must redouble its suspicion—the eighteenth-century term was "jealousy"—of government. Moreover, an active program must be undertaken (such as holding frequent elections and the abolition of placemen) that would stop the government's strides toward tyranny.[11]

The English political system of the late seventeenth and early eighteenth centuries was resisted, then, by a Country opposition that remained faithful to the ideals of the 1680s. This opposition occasionally extracted concessions from the government, but it never acquired enough strength to regain control of Parliament, despite highly articulate support for its position from the press.[12] But it was quite a different story in England's North American colonies. Historians have generally accepted Bernard Bailyn's thesis that in America the Country ideology played a major role in shaping colonial thought. In the colonies, "altered conditions of life made what in England were considered to be extreme, dislocating ideas seem like simple statements of fact." British opposition thought, in the form it acquired at the turn of the seventeenth and early eighteenth centuries, was devoured by the colonists. As the eighteenth century progressed, this ideology "nourished their political thought and sensibilities." By the 1770s, as the colonists struggled to work out their beliefs in the years before independence, the republicans employed Country ideology profusely (for example, frequently citing their fear of influence and corruption).[13]

By the time the fighting ended, the revolutionary issues had given way

---

[11] Pocock, "English Political Ideologies," pp. 565-66; Hutson, "Country, Court and Constitution," p. 358.

[12] Murrin, "The Great Inversion," pp. 382-83.

[13] Bernard Bailyn, *The Ideological Origins of the American Revolution* (Cambridge, Mass., 1967), pp. 43, 51; Hutson, "Country, Court and Constitution," pp. 361, 367; Murrin, "The Great Inversion," pp. 397-98.

to new ones created by inflation, high taxation, and military confiscations. Murrin and Hutson agree that the disputes of the 1780s "fit neatly within the old Court-Country paradigm." Whichever end of the spectrum was accepted, the issues seemed obvious. On the Court side, the War for Independence had produced groups of men who had become frustrated at congressional ineptitude in conducting hostilities and who admired eighteenth-century Whig statecraft. Alarmed at the swirl of disorder around them, these men advocated the shift to Court policies and espoused energetic government served by professional bureaucrats and armies and buttressed by modern financial methods that could mobilize the full resources of the state. On the Country side, "virtuous farmers struggled desperately to protect their land and hence their independence against a corrupt, grasping and... mysterious money power."[14] By 1787, the political situation was desperate. It appeared that the Country principles that had stoked the fires of revolution were self-destructing, and there was an urgent need to remedy the situation. In Murrin's words, there was a "splendid opportunity to attempt traditional Court politics on a continental scale."[15] The result was the Constitutional Convention in Philadelphia.

The stage has now been set for our review of the deliberations of the Virginia ratifying convention. The hypothesis is that the debates will reveal expressions of Court conceptualizations by the supporters of the Constitution and that Country ideology will dominate the arguments of the Anti-federalists. The Virginia proceedings, particularly in the early going, were so unfocused as to defy useful chronological analysis. Nevertheless, the major focal points of debate through the course of the session can be identified and analyzed. By this subject-matter approach, it is possible to come to some conclusions about the effect of Court-Country ideology upon the delegates to the Virginia ratifying convention.

One of the fundamental differences between Court and Country partisans was their view of human nature. Cecilia Kenyon has demonstrated that a key aspect of the Country ideology was the belief that "the dominant motive of human behavior was self-interest, [which] found... political expression in an insatiable lust for power." If this drive were not placed under the strongest restraints, it would be fatal to liberty.[16] Likewise, Bailyn suggests

---

[14] Murrin, "The Great Inversion," pp. 400-403; Hutson, "Country, Court and Constitution," p. 367.

[15] Murrin, "The Great Inversion," p. 404.

[16] Cecilia M. Kenyon, "Men of Little Faith: The Anti-Federalists on the Nature of Representative Government," *WMQ*, 3d ser., XII (1955), 13-15; Hutson, "Country, Court and Constitution," p. 363.

Virginia Historical Society

Former Virginia Governor Patrick Henry (1736-1799), shown here in a portrait by Thomas Sully, took the cynical, Country view of human nature. "If you are safe, it is not from the Constitution, but from the virtues of men in government. If gentlemen are willing to trust themselves and posterity to so slender and improbable a chance, they have greater strength of nerves than I."

Virginia Historical Society

Henry Lee (1756-1818), who had served as governor of Virginia from 1791 to 1794, believed with Edmund Pendleton that "there is no quarrel between government and liberty. The former is the shield and protector of the latter. The war is between government and licentiousness. . . . I dread more from the licentiousness of the people than from the bad government of the rulers."

that those in America who followed opposition tradition had "a general sense that they lived in a conspiratorial world in which what the highest officials professed was not what they in fact intended, and that their words masked a malevolent design."[17] This cynical view of human nature is reflected in the words of the Antifederalists at the Virginia convention. "This [government] . . . will be composed of some bad and some good men," opined George Mason, "and considering the natural lust of power so inherent in man, I

[17] Bailyn, *Ideological Origins*, p. 98.

fear the thrust of power will prevail to oppress the people." George Grayson added, "Power ought to have such checks and limitations, as to prevent bad men from abusing it. It ought to be granted on a supposition that men will be bad; for it may be eventually so." Patrick Henry concurred. "If you are safe, it is not from the Constitution, but from the virtues of men in government. If gentlemen are willing to trust themselves and posterity to so slender and improbable a chance, they have greater strength of nerves than I."[18]

The Federalists responded to such outcries with a much more optimistic portrayal of human nature. James Madison answered Henry:

> I have observed, that gentlemen suppose that the [federal government] will do everything mischievous they possibly can, and that they will omit to do everything good which they are authorized to do. If this were a reasonable supposition, their objections would be good.... But I go on this great republican principle, that the people will have virtue and intelligence to select men of virtue and wisdom. Is there no virtue among us? If there be not, we are in a wretched situation.

John Marshall indicated the conclusion of most Federalists when he said, "I think the virtue and talents of the members of the general government will tend to the security, instead of the destruction, of our liberties."[19]

Bailyn has demonstrated that fear of power was central to Country ideology. The Country-men's discussion of power focused on its "essential characteristic of aggressiveness; its endlessly propulsive tendency to expand... beyond legitimate boundaries."[20] The tradition was carried on by Antifederalist John Tyler: "When I consider the constitution in all its parts, I cannot but dread its operation. It contains a variety of powers too dangerous to be vested in any set of men whatsoever."[21] From the basic Country premises on the nature of power and man's weaknesses in facing its temptations there followed a series of important corollaries.

Country ideologues in Britain preached the necessity of vigilance and suspicion, comprehended by the term "jealousy," as the first line of defense against the abuse of power. They called for vigilance against the government, insisting that government—by its very nature—was hostile to liberty and happiness. The Antifederalists in Virginia echoed this exhortation, defiantly defending jealousy and proclaiming their intention of employing it ag-

---

18 George Mason, in Jonathan Elliot, ed., *The Debates in the Several State Conventions on the Adoption of the Federal Constitution*..., III (2d ed.; Philadelphia, 1863), p. 32; George Grayson, in ibid., p. 563; Patrick Henry, in ibid., p. 387.

19 James Madison, in ibid., pp. 536-37; John Marshall, in ibid., p. 236.

20 Bailyn, *Ideological Origins*, p. 56; Hutson, "Country, Court and Constitution," p. 363.

21 John Tyler, in Elliot, ed., *Debates*, III, 641.

*National Portrait Gallery,
Smithsonian Institution, Washington, D.C.*

Antifederalist James Monroe (1758-1831), shown here in a portrait by John Vanderlyn, maintained that the new federal government would usurp the power of the states. "If you give the resources of the several states to the general government, in what situation will the states be left? I . . . think the general government will preponderate."

gressively.[22] Patrick Henry asserted that "suspicion is a virtue as long as its object is the preservation of the public good." He exhorted his fellow delegates to "guard with jealous attention the public liberty. Suspect everyone who approaches that jewel." Virginians were told to be "extremely cautious, watchful [and] jealous of your liberty; for instead of securing your rights, you may lose them forever."[23] The Federalists accepted the need for vigilance but questioned the zealotry of the opposition. "I will agree," said Governor Edmund Randolph, "in the necessity of political jealousy to a certain extent; but we ought to examine how far this political jealousy ought to be carried." Indeed, the Federalists turned the Antifederalist logic on its head, arguing that the people's jealousy would keep the proposed government in line. "Another security is that. . . I know this government will be cautiously watched. The smallest assumption of power will be sounded in alarm to the people, and followed by bold and active opposition."[24]

The fear of power also comprehended concern with the locus of that power, that is, the question of sovereignty, which is the question of the nature and location of the ultimate power in the state.[25] Country spokesmen preferred to rely upon local resources and institutions for the preservation of domestic order. In the pre-Revolutionary period, most powers were enjoyed by the local, colonial organs of government, and this autonomy figured largely in the debates with Parliament.[26] This opposition ideology appeared again in Richmond at the Virginia ratification convention. Rarely were the Antifederalists in the Virginia convention more vocal than in their outrage at the specter of a new general government usurping the power of the states. Mason charged that "these two concurrent powers cannot exist long together; the one will destroy the other." "If you give the resources of the several states to the general government," James Monroe added, "in what situation will the states be left? I therefore think the general government will preponderate." As usual, the last word went to Patrick Henry: "The whole history of human nature cannot produce a government like that before you. . . . [It] seems to me calculated to lay prostrate the states, and the liberties of the people."[27]

[22] Hutson, "Country, Court and Constitution," pp. 363-64; Bailyn, *Ideological Origins*, p. 47; James H. Hutson, "The Origins of 'The Paranoid Style in American Politics': Public Jealousy from the Age of Walpole to the Age of Jackson," in *Saints and Revolutionaries: Essays on Early American History*, ed. David D. Hall et al. (New York, 1984), pp. 336-38, 346-47.

[23] Patrick Henry, in Elliot, ed., *Debates*, III, 45, 22.

[24] Edmund Randolph, in ibid., pp. 70, 206-7.

[25] Bailyn, *Ideological Origins*, pp. 55, 198.

[26] Murrin, "The Great Inversion," p. 379; Bailyn, *Ideological Origins*, pp. 203-4.

[27] George Mason, in Elliot, ed., *Debates*, III, 29-30; James Monroe, in ibid., p. 216; Patrick Henry, in ibid., p. 579.

The friends of the Constitution disputed the Antifederalist conclusion, however, claiming that the new government would not override the states. Madison agreed that "were all the powers vested in the general government, it would be a consolidated government; but the powers of the federal government are enumerated; it can only operate in certain cases . . . beyond which it cannot extend its jurisdiction." Francis Corbin agreed. "Liberty is secured . . . by the limitation of [the federal government's] powers, which are clearly and unequivocally defined."[28] In any event, the loyalty of the people would assure the continued dominance of state government. "The people will be attached to their state legislatures from a thousand causes; and into whatever scale the people at large throw themselves, that scale will preponderate." Edmund Pendleton added that "our dearest rights—life, liberty, and property—as Virginians, are still in the hands of our state legislature."[29]

The Federalists borrowed from the ideology of the Revolutionary generation to support their cause. In the prewar years, Americans had brought into question the entire concept of absolute governmental sovereignty; in its place had come the assumption that ultimate sovereignty rested with the people.[30] Madison best articulated how this concept related to the locus of power. "The people at large are the common superior of the state governments and the general government. . . . The people would not support [the general government], were it to impose oppressive burdens." Henry Lee elaborated. "This new system shows, in stronger terms than words can declare, that the liberties of the people are secure. It goes on the principle that all power is in the people, and that rulers have no powers but what are enumerated in [the Constitution]."[31] Here, as in the case of the need for jealousy of government, there is agreement between Federalist and Antifederalist on fundamental principles. Each side of the dispute over the locus of power acknowledged the importance of maintaining state and local power; the dispute was over the degree to which the proposed general government would infringe on that local sovereignty. This continuing disagreement underlay many of the subsequent disputes over the specifics of the Constitution.

Federalists and Antifederalists alike expressed concern over the degree of virtue to be found in man, while fundamentally agreeing—in principle, if not in practice—on the dangers of unrestrained power in government.

---

[28] James Madison, in ibid., p. 95; Francis Corbin, in ibid., p. 110.

[29] James Madison, in ibid., p. 258; Edmund Pendleton, in ibid., p. 301.

[30] Bailyn, *Ideological Origins*, p. 228; see also Gordon S. Wood, *The Creation of the American Republic, 1776-1787* (Chapel Hill, 1969), pp. 530-32, 545-47.

[31] James Madison, in Elliot, ed., *Debates*, III, 256; Henry Lee, in ibid., p. 186.

Their differences in perspective became—inevitably—more pronounced when they turned from more theoretical matters to the issue at hand: What sort of government was needed to govern the new nation? Their debate clearly illuminated the Court versus Country dichotomy.

The nature of government had ever been the fundamental issue of disagreement between Court and Country. England's revolutionary settlement of 1688 had created a centralized system of Court politics closely tied to the new world of high finance. After William III's accession, the Whigs aligned themselves with those elements in society that participated in and profited from the recent changes in the English scene. They embraced commerce. As Hutson notes, "The Court Whigs were patrons not only of commerce but also of strong government. They were interested in administrative efficiency in the operation and manipulation of the powers of government. [The Court party was] prepared to exploit the fruits of the new commercial-bureaucratic society, strengthening the executive with increased revenues and asserting control over competing power centers like the House of Commons."[32] In Murrin's words, "Court apologists were intensely statist . . . and tried to endow the government with the resources and vigor necessary to command great respect abroad and maintain order at home."[33] We have seen how this philosophy of government was resurrected in America in the 1780s in the aftermath of the War for Independence.

On the Country side, the Tories (and some "real Whigs") tended overwhelmingly after 1688 to assume the attitudes of a Country opposition. They defended the Glorious Revolution, according to Murrin, "not as a new departure, but as the restoration of the ancient and virtuous constitutional balance of King, Lords and Commons, once threatened by James II and now menaced from a new and more sinister direction by the fiscal revolution and the patronage politics of [the Whigs]." Hutson added that the Country's major tenet, the danger of government and governmental power, now appeared to have an empirical basis because the landed interest was under heavy financial pressure from the government.[34] Pocock summarized it well when he said that the Country "really is talking about the rise of the modern state and the effect of money upon society. . . . What moves [them] is an increasing—and hostile—awareness of the importance of money in government: of public finance, of the professionalization of army and bureaucracy, of the inducements which a well-financed court

[32] Murrin, "The Great Inversion," p. 382; Hutson, "Country, Court and Constitution," p. 357.
[33] Murrin, "The Great Inversion," p. 379.
[34] Ibid., p. 382; Hutson, "Country, Court and Constitution," p. 358.

bureaucracy can offer the subject to co-operate."[35] This concern had been transmitted directly to America by a group of early eighteenth-century radical publicists and opposition politicians in England.[36]

The arguments of the Federalists in Richmond were clearly congruent with Court attitudes toward strong and effective government. Castigating the Confederation government as unequal to the task of governing, the Federalists insistently championed the thesis that only a strong government would serve the interests of the United States.[37] In response, the Antifederalists could only assert that their opponents had gone too far toward consolidated government, thereby threatening the liberties of all.[38] In the course of the debates, however, some Federalists and Antifederalists rose above the immediate issue and clearly stated the philosophical underpinnings for their view of the Constitution. Pendleton and Lee espoused the creed of the Federalist: "There is no quarrel between government and liberty; the former is the shield and the protector of the latter. The war is between government and licentiousness. . . . I dread more from the licentiousness of the people than from the bad government of rulers."[39] Given the fear of anarchy, there could be but one remedy. "Government must . . . have its complete powers, or be ineffectual," stated Marshall. "It would not be effectual if the means were not adequate to the power. . . . Arguments [to the contrary] go in direct opposition to the government, and in recommendation of anarchy."[40] It is significant that the Federalists cited as their source for this theory of strong government such theorists as Montesquieu, Sidney, and Harrington—the lodestones of Country ideology. "These writers," asserted Pendleton, "point out licentiousness as the natural off spring of liberty, and that, therefore, all free governments should endeavor to suppress it, or else it will ultimately overthrow that liberty of which it is the result."[41]

The Antifederalist opposition replied in kind, citing the Country version of events. "In 1688, the British nation expelled their monarch for attempting to trample on their liberties. . . . He wanted to possess, without control, the sword and the purse. The attempt cost him his crown. This government demands the same powers. I see reason to be more and more alarmed. I fear

[35] Pocock, "English Political Ideologies," p. 577.

[36] Bailyn, *Ideological Origins*, p. viii.

[37] Edmund Randolph, in Elliot, ed., *Debates*, III, 26-27, 67, 71, 78, 80-81, 197; George Wythe, in ibid., pp. 586-87; Henry Lee, in ibid., p. 43; John Marshall, in ibid., p. 227; Edmund Pendleton, in ibid., p. 36.

[38] Patrick Henry, in ibid., p. 22; George Mason, in ibid., p. 33.

[39] Edmund Pendleton, in ibid., p. 37; Henry Lee, in ibid., p. 185.

[40] Edmund Pendleton, in ibid., p. 39; John Marshall, in ibid., p. 226.

[41] Edmund Pendleton, in ibid., p. 294.

Federalist Edmund Pendleton (1721-1803) believed licentiousness was "the natural offspring of liberty, and that, therefore, all free governments should endeavor to suppress it, or else it will ultimately overthrow that liberty of which it is the result."
Colonial Williamsburg Foundation

it will terminate in despotism."[42] John Dawson also reverted to Country principles when he predicted that "when a confederation of independent states shall be converted into a consolidated government . . . we shall afford one more proof to the favorite maxim of tyrants, that 'mankind cannot govern themselves.' "[43]

This reference to America's Country heritage on the part of both Federalists and Antifederalists highlights an important perception about the ideology underlying the debate. Something more sophisticated than a mere Court-Country split is revealed. Both sides were still firmly entrenched in the opposition mindset that Bailyn has traced to the Revolution. That the Federalists had grafted onto it an undeniably Court overlay by 1788 alters the way in which one may evaluate the debate. The differences between the parties may seem no less real, particularly to them; but the depth of their disagreement suddenly becomes less threatening to the ultimate functioning of a continental society (perhaps this explains the virtually universal acceptance of the Constitution scant years after its stormy ratifica-

[42] Patrick Henry, in ibid., p. 396.
[43] John Dawson, in ibid., p. 606.

tion).[44] The debate itself yields ample evidence that differences between Federalist and Antifederalist were more tactical than strategic. "We acknowledge the defects of the confederation and the necessity for reform," admitted Mason. "We ardently wish for a union with our sister states on terms of security. This I am bold to declare is the desire of most of the people. On these terms we will most cheerfully join with the warmest friends of this Constitution." Even Patrick Henry condescended to admit some common ground. "I acknowledge that licentiousness is dangerous, and that it ought to be provided against. I acknowledge also, the new form of government may effectually prevent it: yet there is another thing it will effectually do—it will oppress . . . the people."[45]

Of course all was not harmonious, and as the convention got down to specifics the specters of Court and Country continued to haunt the deliberations. The delegates took up the legislative, executive, and judicial powers of the proposed government in turn. Regarding the powers of Congress, the general issue involved the familiar differences of opinion. Federalists spoke of the necessity of vesting sufficient power in the general government to secure tranquillity and good order, while the opposition thundered warnings about consolidated government and the dire consequences of entrusting "such unbounded powers" to the "frailties of human nature."[46] The voices of Court and Country were particularly clear in the specific instance of direct taxation.[47] Madison best stated the position of the friends of the Constitution when he commented that the provision "which gives the general government the power of laying and collecting taxes [is] indispensable, and essential to the existence of any efficient or well-organized system of government."[48] But Bailyn has traced the opposition conception of taxes as a tool of corrupt governments to enslave the people with burdensome debts.[49] Grayson reflected this view admirably. "As to direct taxation—give up this, and you give up everything, as it is the highest act of sovereignty: surrender up this inestimable jewel, and you throw away a pearl richer than all your tribe."[50]

[44] See Lance Banning, "Republican Ideology and the Triumph of the Constitution, 1789 to 1793," *WMQ*, 3d ser., XXXI (1974), 167-88.

[45] George Mason, in Elliot, ed., *Debates*, III, 272; Patrick Henry, in ibid., p. 46.

[46] Edmund Randolph, in ibid., p. 82; George Mason, in ibid., p. 29; Patrick Henry, in ibid., p. 437.

[47] See Thomas P. Slaughter, "The Tax Man Cometh: Ideological Opposition to Internal Taxes, 1760-1790," *WMQ*, 3d ser., XLI (1984), 590-91.

[48] James Madison, in Elliot, ed., *Debates*, III, 128.

[49] Bailyn, *Ideological Origins*, p. 9.

[50] George Grayson, in Elliot, ed., *Debates*, III, 280.

Another aspect of the legislative power that reverberated with Court-Country connotations was the debate over the threat of a standing army and the role of the militia under the Constitution. The dangers of a standing army had long been axiomatic in Country thought. Bailyn noted that perhaps the most important conclusion to be derived from the opposition's central premise about the nature of power and man's weakness in the face of its temptations was the danger of a standing army. Because the supreme power is "ever possessed by those who have arms," the danger to liberty lay in the absolute supremacy of standing armies. Beyond the fear of dictatorship, the Country mentality saw such an army as a source of corruption—an entity filled with placemen beyond parliamentary control. Instead, reliance should be upon an independent militia. On the other hand, traditional Court writers defended standing armies, contending that there must be a permanent military establishment with sufficient financial resources behind it to meet the realities of modern warfare. According to Lawrence Cress, there was also a moderate Court position, which held that a standing army was compatible with free government if proper constitutional safeguards (such as the power of the purse residing in the legislature) existed.[51]

The position taken by the Federalists on this issue demonstrates again the danger in unthinkingly tagging the Virginia antagonists with Old World Court and Country labels. The Antifederalists lived up to their billing. "I abominate and detest the idea of a government, where there is a standing army," thundered Mason. "When once a standing army is established in any country, the people lose their liberty." And John Dawson brought up the connection with corruption. "A standing army will introduce idleness and extravagance, which will be followed by their sure concomitant vices . . . and dissipation."[52] But the Federalists, although supporting a role for the general government in the discipline of the militia, came down four-square on the Country side of the question of a standing army. Randolph noted, "With respect to a standing army, I believe there was not a member in the federal convention, who did not feel indignation at such an institution." Madison chimed in. "I most cordially agree that a standing army is one of the greatest mischiefs that can possibly happen."[53] Again, we see the Federalists maintaining a Country philosophy with a Court overlay.

The final aspect of the legislative power that evoked a Country response

[51] Bailyn, *Ideological Origins*, pp. 50, 61; Pocock, "English Political Ideologies," pp. 566, 577; Lawrence D. Cress, *Citizens in Arms: The Army and the Militia in American Society to the War of 1812* (Chapel Hill, 1982), pp. 25-26.

[52] George Mason, in Elliot, ed., *Debates*, III, 380; John Dawson, in ibid., p. 611.

[53] Edmund Randolph, in ibid., p. 401; James Madison, in ibid., p. 381.

Bowdoin College Museum of Art, Brunswick, Maine

Father of the Constitution James Madison (1751-1836) was optimistic in his view of human nature. "I have observed, that gentlemen suppose that the [federal government] will do everything mischievous they possibly can, and that they will omit to do everything good which they are authorized to do. If this were a reasonable supposition, their objections would be good. . . . But I go on this great republican principle, that the people will have virtue and intelligence to select men of virtue and wisdom. Is there no virtue among us? If there be not, we are in a wretched situation."

related to the concept of representation. The question of representation was key to the Country ideology. In Country thought, local communities bound their representatives to local interests in every way possible: by requiring local residency, by instructing representatives minutely, and by making them strictly accountable for all actions taken in the name of their constituents.[54] In the Virginia convocation, Mason parroted the party line faithfully. "To make representation real and actual, . . . representatives . . . ought to mix with the people, think as they think, feel as they feel—ought to be perfectly amenable to them, and thoroughly acquainted with their interest and condition. Now, these great ingredients are either not at all, or in a smaller degree, to be found in our federal representatives."[55] Again, the Federalists for their part acknowledged the principle espoused by the Antifederalists, while disputing its application. "It is an established maxim that such a body [as Congress] ought . . . to be well acquainted with the interests of the people, to prevent corruption and to give a chance to men of merit to be elected. If the number be not sufficient for these purposes, I confess it to be a defect." But most Federalists concluded with John Marshall that liberty was secure under the Constitution, "where the people hold all powers in their own hands, and delegate them cautiously, for short periods, to their servants, who are accountable for the smallest mal-administration."[56]

The debate over the executive and judicial branches can be passed over more quickly, in part because the Virginia delegates spent proportionately less time on these topics. The chief fear of the executive was that he would, in Henry's words, "easily become King. . . . If [he] be a man of ambition and abilities, how easy is it for him to render himself absolute!"[57] The Federalists responded with arguments about the necessity of an executive and the limits on his power.[58]

The debate over the judiciary article did evoke some opposition principles. Henry was at his Country best. "The purse is gone; the sword is gone; and here is the only thing of importance that is to remain with us. . . . The judiciary are the sole protection against a tyrannical execution of the laws. But if by this system we lose our judiciary, and they cannot help us, we must sit down quietly, and be oppressed." Mason reiterated the effect upon the locus of power: "What is left to the state courts? . . . When we consider the nature of the [federal courts] we must conclude that their effect

---

54 Bailyn, *Ideological Origins*, pp. 161-63.
55 George Mason, in Elliot, ed., *Debates*, III, 32.
56 Edmund Randolph, in ibid., p. 125; John Marshall, in ibid., p. 232.
57 Patrick Henry, in ibid., p. 59.
58 Edmund Randolph, in ibid., pp. 200-201.

George Mason (1725-1792), author of the Virginia Declaration of Rights, declared, "When we consider the nature of the [federal courts] we must conclude that their effect and operation will be utterly to destroy the state governments."

Virginia Historical Society

and operation will be utterly to destroy the state governments." And Grayson raised again the ghost of corruption. "Our federal judges are placed in a situation as liable to corruption as they could possibly be [because of the possible augmentation of their salary]. Throughout the whole page of history, you will find the corruption of judges to have always arisen from that principle—the hope of reward." [59] The Federalists fired their usual returning salvos of necessity and sufficient safeguards to protect abuse.[60]

One matter that came up repeatedly during the debates over the various branches of government strikes to the heart of Country ideology: the corrupt use of patronage to destroy the balance of government. In Country thought, the secret of the success of the British constitution lay in its peculiar capacity to balance and check the basic forces within society (royalty, nobility, and commons). So long as each component checked all efforts of the others to transcend their proper sphere, there would be a stable equilibrium that con-

[59] Patrick Henry, in ibid., p. 539; George Mason, in ibid., p. 521; George Grayson, in ibid., p. 564.

[60] James Madison, in ibid., pp. 530, 537-38; John Marshall, in ibid., p. 551; Edmund Pendleton, in ibid., p. 303.

tributed to the preservation of the rights of all. In this scheme it was for the crown to govern and for Parliament to exercise a jealous surveillance of government. But corruption would follow if the crown discovered any means of attaching members of Parliament to the crown's interests. In the eighteenth century, opposition leaders were convinced of the systematic corruption of Parliament by the executive.[61] The Antifederalist opposition perceived the constitutional balance of powers in just such a suspicious light. Henry saw not real, but only ideal, balances in the Constitution. Dawson noted that under the proposed plan, the legislative and executive branches were not distinct, but closely united. And worst of all, Mason detected in the ability of the president and Congress to create offices "as wide a door for corruption as in any government in Europe. There is the same inducement for corruption, there is the same room for it, in this government, which they have in the British government." [62]

The chief remaining opportunity for the mobilization of Country ideology in the Virginia convention concerned the related issues of implied powers and individual rights. The idea of individual rights was a late-blooming phenomenon in the opposition tradition. Yet during the eighteenth century there had been a steadily increasing emphasis on the universal, inherent, indefeasible qualities of rights. As this conception of rights developed, there was a parallel perception emerging that these rights should somehow be specified and codified if they were to serve effectively as limits on the actions of courts and legislatures. By 1776 it was accepted that all great rights should be guaranteed by the terms of a written constitution.[63] These developments were greatly in evidence in Virginia in 1788. The Antifederalists attacked the "general welfare" and the "necessary and proper" clauses of the Constitution as "very dangerous. Our great unalienable rights ought to be secured from being destroyed by such unlimited powers, either by a bill of rights, or by an express provision in the body of the constitution." [64] The Federalists heartily agreed with the principle of individual rights but maintained that the Constitution did not infringe upon them. The Federalists held that all the powers not expressly delegated to the federal government were reserved to the states, thus preserving both state governments and individual rights.[65] In this discussion, as in so many others, the Federalists

---

[61] Bailyn, *Ideological Origins*, pp. 70, 48; Pocock, "English Political Ideologies," p. 571.

[62] Patrick Henry, in Elliot, ed., *Debates*, III, 165; John Dawson, in ibid., p. 608; George Mason, in ibid., p. 263.

[63] Bailyn, *Ideological Origins*, pp. 186-89.

[64] James Monroe, in Elliot, ed., *Debates*, III, 218.

[65] George Nicholas, in ibid., p. 246.

are found agreeing with Country assumptions of the Antifederalists but are at odds over the interpretation of the Constitution with respect to those principles.

This essay began by positing Hutson's belief that the terms Court and Country serve to "show how Antifederalism can be more intelligibly differentiated from Federalism" and that these competing ideologies provide a framework for understanding the debate over the ratification of the Constitution. And indeed the evidence is overwhelming that elements of Court and Country thought were central to the contest. This article has demonstrated, however, that there was a more sophisticated relationship between the two ideologies. Instead of Court versus Country, the ideological division was rather Country versus Court-Country. Even the strongest advocates of the Constitution placed only an overlay of Court principles upon an essentially Country ideology. This is not to gainsay that the Court language of the Federalists was sincerely expressed; it undoubtedly was. Despite the heritage of Country principles, the events of the 1780s and the promise of a strong federal government under the Constitution evoked a genuine Court response and precipitated a Court-Country split in the ratifying debate. But the important point is that the underlying ideology was Country; the Federalists repeatedly had to come to grips with a legacy shared by all. The debate struck chords of that common Country heritage that simply could not be denied. The rhetoric of the debate underscores the uniformity of that underlying value structure.

This suggests possibilities for further study. Although the Court-Country dichotomy has assisted in focusing attention on the differentiation between supporters and opponents of the Constitution, its real contribution may be to open yet another window onto Virginia society in the late eighteenth century. The question of the depth of divisions in Virginia society in this period is still an open one. The ratification debate suggests that there remained a significant degree of common ground between Virginians in the 1780s. Alternatively, it is possible that the Virginia convention was not representative of the social and intellectual forces emerging in its society. The opportunity for further work by historians is abundant.

No matter in which direction the truth lies, its discovery will provide a significant step forward in our understanding of eighteenth-century Virginia.

A SPECTRUM OF SENTIMENTS
Virginia's Federalists, Antifederalists, and "Federalists Who Are For Amendments," 1787–1788

by Jon Kukla

On 2 June 1988 the Virginia Historical Society inaugurated "Reluctant Ratifiers: Virginia Considers the Federal Constitution," an exhibition commemorating the bicentennial of the ratification of the federal Constitution in the Old Dominion. In conjunction with the opening of the exhibition, the Society was pleased to sponsor a lecture by Jon Kukla, assistant director for publications at the Virginia State Library and Archives. The text of Mr. Kukla's lecture, with accompanying notes, is printed below.

With characteristic acumen, James Madison sized up Virginia's contest over ratification of the United States Constitution six months before the convention of 1788 met in Richmond. "My information leads me to suppose there must be three parties in Virginia," he reported to Thomas Jefferson: "The first for adopting without attempting Amendments[,] . . . the 2d. party which urges amendments[,] . . . [and] a third Class, at the head of which is Mr. Henry." Then, six weeks before the convention, Edward Carrington reported to Jefferson that "very active opposition is made and the event is uncertain" even with the elections of delegates completed: "We have a party that is truly antifederal headed by Mr. Henry, but it will be limitted to a few, unless the federalists who are for amendments, should, from a mistaken view of the probability of the measures being carried into effect by Nine States, be drawn into steps favouring the antifederal scheme.—Mr. H[enry] does not openly declare for a dismemberment of the union, but his Arguments in support of his opposition to the constitution go directly to that issue."[1]

The private assessments by these statesmen warn against hasty summaries of Virginia's ratification of the United States Constitution, and especially they warn against the deeply rooted American habit of

[1] James Madison to Thomas Jefferson, 9 Dec. 1787, in Robert A. Rutland et al., eds., *The Papers of James Madison* (15 vols. to date; Chicago and Charlottesville, 1962–), X, 312; Edward Carrington to Thomas Jefferson, 24 Apr. 1788, in Julian P. Boyd et al., eds., *The Papers of Thomas Jefferson* (23 vols. to date; Princeton, 1950–), XIII, 101. These letters are also printed in Merrill Jensen, John P. Kaminski, et al., eds., *The Documentary History of the Ratification of the Constitution* (7 vols. to date; Madison, Wisc., 1976–), XIV, 408; XIII, 396.

The Virginia Magazine of History and Biography
Vol. 96 No. 3 (July 1988)

defining public issues as clear, two-sided, yes-no choices. Historians certainly have tried to look at both sides of this story, but their effort to impose a dichotomy of federalists and antifederalists has obscured as much as it explained about Virginia's role in shaping the Constitution and the political heritage of the new nation. The debates from Virginia's ratification can be quoted to display contrasts as stark as George Bancroft's good versus evil,[2] as Charles Beard's personalty versus realty,[3] as Jackson Turner Main's localists versus nationalists,[4] as Stanley Elkins and Eric McKitrick's youth versus age,[5] as James H. Hutson's and J. Thomas Wren's court versus country,[6] or as Forrest McDonald's adher-

---

[2] George Bancroft, *The History of the United States of America, from the Discovery of the Continent: The Author's Last Revision*, IV (New York, 1885), pp. 6–7, 207, 367.

[3] Charles A. Beard, *An Economic Interpretation of the Constitution of the United States* (New York, 1913). Madison's view "that whilst in Virga. and some of the other States in the middle & Southern Districts of the Union, the men of intelligence, patriotism, property, and independent circumstances, are . . . divided; all of this description, with few exceptions, in the Eastern States, & most of the Middle States, are zealously attached to the proposed Constitution" (James Madison to Thomas Jefferson, 9 Dec. 1787, in Rutland et al., eds., *Madison Papers*, X, 312) is confirmed by Robert E. Thomas, "The Virginia Convention of 1788: A Criticism of Beard's *An Economic Interpretation of the Constitution*," *Journal of Southern History*, XIX (1953), 63–72, and Norman K. Risjord, "Virginians and the Constitution: A Multivariant Analysis," *William and Mary Quarterly* (hereafter cited as *WMQ*), 3d ser., XXXI (1974), 613–32.

[4] Jackson Turner Main, *The Antifederalists: Critics of the Constitution, 1781–1788* (Chapel Hill, 1961) and *Political Parties before the Constitution* (Chapel Hill, 1973). In the latter book, Main used only recorded voting lists on money-related questions and assumed that 70% voting agreement defined the membership of a political group. To test this assumption for Virginia I conducted a Rice-Beyle cluster-bloc analysis of the 74 extant division lists on all questions recorded in the journals of the state Senate from October 1783 through November 1789 and found that Main's 70% concurrence describes two large groups of senators but that 85% agreement identifies four tight clusters. The latter pattern suggests the complex political networks in revolutionary Virginia recognized by many historians, while Main's dichotomy reflects the Progressive interpretation of his mentor, Merrill Jensen, who wrote that "there were men who veered from side to side, but their number is relatively small and their veering is of little significance as compared with the fact that from the outset of the Revolution there were two consistently opposed bodies of opinion as to the nature of the central government" (Jensen, *The New Nation: A History of the United States during the Confederation, 1781–1789* [New York, 1950], p. 425).

[5] Stanley Elkins and Eric McKitrick, "The Founding Fathers: Young Men of the Revolution," *Political Science Quarterly*, LXXVI (1961), 181–216, and *The Founding Fathers: Young Men of the Revolution* (Washington, D.C., 1962) promoted the idea that the federalists were youthful reformers, but they were not the first to suggest it. Charles Warren remarked about age differences in his *Making of the Constitution* (Boston, 1928), as did Forrest McDonald in *We the People: The Economic Origins of the Constitution* (Chicago, 1958), p. 260n, and earlier someone named Putnam, whose work I have not found, inspired a speaker at the 1927 annual meeting of the Virginia Bar Association to find "interesting . . . the average youthfulness of the delegates [to the Philadelphia convention]. Thirty-five of them, according to Putnam, were over forty; but twenty of them were under" (George Latham Fletcher, "Sidelights on the Federal Constitutional Convention," *Proceedings of the 38th Annual Meeting of the Virginia Bar Association* [Richmond, 1927], p. 413). Of the 97 members of the Virginia convention of 1788 whose ages are known, the 53 men who voted for the Constitution on 25 June 1788 had an average age of 43.20 years compared to 45.32 years for the 44 men who voted against them—a difference of 2.12 years (see also note 24, below). Pauline Maier explored the converse idea and provided a fine interpretation of Richard Henry Lee in *The Old Revolutionaries: Political Lives in the Age of Samuel Adams* (New York, 1980).

[6] James H. Hutson, "Court, Country, and the Constitution: Antifederalism and the Historians," *WMQ*, 3d ser., XXXVIII (1981), 337–68, and J. Thomas Wren, "The Ideology of Court and Country in the Virginia Ratifying Convention of 1788," *Virginia Magazine of History and Biography* (hereafter cited as *VMHB*), XCIII (1985), 389–408, adopted the court-country dichotomy used effectively to illuminate long-term tendencies and

ents and nonadherents to the doctrine of Original Sin.[7] Such dichotomies may fit the circumstances of the ratifications by Massachusetts or Pennsylvania, but the effort to impose a two-party outline on Virginia seems futile. Virginians displayed a full spectrum of sentiments about the Constitution, from ardent support through wary acquiescence to defiant resistance, and to see the subtle gradations along this continuous spectrum we need something better than the blunt instrument of American dichotomies. By helping us avoid dichotomy, Madison's framework of "three parties in Virginia" encourages a clearer view of the Virginia statesmen who wrote and ratified the Constitution and Bill of Rights and of Virginia's central role in the American Revolution and the new nation. Grouped toward opposite ends of our spectrum are the federalists and their "truly antifederal" opponents, but in the middle we dare not overlook those Virginians whom Carrington called "federalists who are for amendments."[8]

1

> "There must be three parties in Virginia. The first for adopting without attempting Amendments. This includes Genl. W[ashington] and the other deputies, who signed the Constitution."[9]

Virginia's nationalists were eager to ratify the Constitution without amendments, but these federalists never composed a majority in the state or its convention. At the nationalist extreme of Virginia's political spectrum in 1787 and 1788—indeed "in the forefront of the advocates of national consolidation"—stood the martial figure of Henry ("Light-Horse Harry") Lee. Distinguishing between "the people" and "our great men," and putting his faith in the latter, Lee seems an archetype of the military hero impatient with civilian institutions and sovereignty. "It was my fortune to be a soldier of my country," he reminded Patrick Henry in the

themes of comparative history by Perez Zagorin in *The Court and the Country: The Beginnings of the English Revolution* (London, 1966); J. G. A. Pocock in *The Machiavellian Moment: Florentine Political Thought and the Atlantic Republican Tradition* (Princeton, 1975); and John M. Murrin in "The Great Inversion, or, Court versus Country: A Comparison of the Revolution Settlements in England (1688–1721) and America (1776–1816)," in J. G. A. Pocock, ed., *Three British Revolutions: 1641, 1688, 1776* (Princeton, 1976). Wren's bid "to apply the interpretive framework of these scholars to the Virginia ratifying convention of 1788" proved unsuccessful and ended with a warning against "the danger in unthinkingly tagging the Virginia antagonists with Old World Court and Country labels" (p. 403) and the conclusion that country rhetoric was so common in Virginia that "instead of Court versus Country, the ideological division was rather Country versus Court-Country" (p. 408).

[7] Forrest McDonald, *E Pluribus Unum: The Formation of the American Republic* (Boston, 1965), p. 1. McDonald's specific reference was to 1776.

[8] Edward Carrington to Thomas Jefferson, 24 Apr. 1788, in Boyd et al., eds., *Jefferson Papers*, XIII, 101.

[9] James Madison to Thomas Jefferson, 9 Dec. 1787, in Rutland et al., eds., *Madison Papers*, X, 312.

Virginia convention: "I saw what the honorable gentleman did not see—our men fighting. . . . I have seen proofs of the wisdom of that paper on your table. I have seen incontrovertible evidence."[10] To listeners of like mind, Lee's arguments were irrefutable, while others envisioned horrors against which the Second and Third Amendments were designed to protect the republic and its citizens.[11]

George Washington, whose military experience excited fewer misgivings,[12] influenced many with his firm belief "that, in the aggregate, it is the best Constitution that can be obtained at this Epocha, and that this, or a dissolution of the Union awaits our choice, and are the only alternatives before us." Although showing in public a reticence befitting the presidential role to which the nation expected to summon him, in his private correspondence Washington wrote of the Constitution as enthusiastically as he did of improved plows and seeds. "The establishment of an energetic general Government will disappoint the hopes and expectations of those who are unfriendly to this Country," he wrote in 1787, "give us a national respectability, and enable us to improve those commercial and political advantages which Nature and situation have placed within our reach."[13]

Madison, too, sought unconditional ratification of the Constitution, despite private misgivings "that the plan should it be adopted will neither effectually answer its national object nor prevent the local mischiefs which every where excite disgusts ag[ain]st the state governments." Madison contended that "no regard ought to be had to local prejudices or temporary considerations," for with the intuition of a statesman he sensed that a decisive moment in history was at hand to be grasped or lost: "the public mind will now or in a very little time receive any thing that

---

[10] Charles Royster, *Light-Horse Harry Lee and the Legacy of the American Revolution* (New York, 1981), pp. 89, 96, 100; Jonathan Elliot, ed., *The Debates in the Several State Conventions, on the Adoption of the Federal Constitution*. . . (2d ed., 5 vols.; Washington, D.C., 1836–59), III, 178. Kenneth M. Stampp found that Lee made the only public "formulation of a case against state sovereignty . . . in the Federalist period" (Stampp, "The Concept of Perpetual Union," *Journal of American History*, LXV [1978–79], 22–23).

[11] Lawrence Delbert Cress, *Citizens in Arms: The Army and Militia in American Society to the War of 1812* (Chapel Hill, 1982).

[12] The former commander-in-chief did raise a controversy with an unguarded private comment about constitutional revision by *ultima ratio* (final argument, or force) that found its way into newspapers throughout the country (John C. Fitzpatrick, ed., *The Writings of George Washington* . . . , XXIX (Washington, D.C., 1939), pp. 340, 380, 396, 403–4; Jensen, Kaminski, et al., eds., *Ratification*, XV, 135–37; XVI, 27–28, 128, 463–66.

[13] George Washington to Sir Edward Newenham, 25 Dec. 1787, George Washington to Edmund Randolph, 8 Jan. 1788, in Fitzpatrick, ed., *Writings of Washington*, XXIX, 346, 358. Washington described his views at length to Lafayette on 7 Feb. 1788 (ibid., pp. 409–12).

promises stability to the public Councils & security to private rights."[14] Writing as Publius in *The Federalist* he cloaked in newly minted theory his disappointment that the proposed central government lacked power to veto state laws and pressed the argument that a bill of rights was dangerous. Comfortable with the "tough-minded interest-centered political philosophy" that is his contribution to American political theory, Madison stood in 1787 and 1788 at the nationalist end of the spectrum. From Paris Jefferson stood nearer to Virginia's middle ground, eager for a bill of rights and ambivalent about "a system rigged to substitute the countervailing forces of self-interest for the defect of public virtue and supposed dangers of majority rule." The American ambassador to France wrote that "as to the new Constitution I find myself nearly a Neutral."[15]

In Richmond John Marshall saw a "deep shade over that bright prospect which the revolution in America and the establishment of our free governments had opened to the votaries of liberty throughout the globe" and began 1787 in gloom. "I fear, and there is no opinion more degrading to the dignity of man, that these have truth on their side who say that man is incapable of governing himself," he wrote. "I fear we may live to see another revolution." Marshall greeted the Constitution as nothing less than the country's salvation, "a great improvement on that system from which we are now departing." Dr. James McClurg worked on the Constitution in Philadelphia and said he was "so fearful of it's Loss, that I should be willing to trust the remedy of it's defects to the reason moderation & experience of the future Congress."[16]

From Richmond in October 1787 federalist Zachariah Johnston wrote home to Rockbridge County that there was "nothing of A publick Nature to relate worth while but our New Confederated Co[n]stitution I find has its friends and its Enemies." Throughout the Valley, Piedmont, and Southside counties, men and women of steadfast dissenting religious convictions—Baptists, Presbyterians, Lutherans, Quakers, and Mennonites—feared that the Constitution and a stronger central government might lead to a re-established church. Because he had served as chairman of the Committee on Religion when the House of Delegates passed the

[14] James Madison to Thomas Jefferson, 6 Sept. 1787, in Rutland et al., eds., *Madison Papers*, X, 163–64. Madison detailed his private reservations about the Constitution in a long letter to Jefferson on 24 Oct. 1787 (ibid., pp. 205–20).

[15] Merrill D. Peterson, *Jefferson and Madison and the Making of Constitutions* (Charlottesville, 1987), pp. 9–10; Thomas Jefferson to Edward Carrington, 21 Dec. 1787, in Boyd et al., eds., *Jefferson Papers*, XII, 446.

[16] John Marshall to James Wilkinson, 5 Jan. 1787, in Herbert Johnson et al., eds., *The Papers of John Marshall* (5 vols. to date; Chapel Hill, 1974–), I, 201; Elliot, ed., *Debates*, III, 551; James McClurg to James Madison, 31 Oct. 1787, in Rutland et al., eds., *Madison Papers*, X, 233–34.

Virginia Statute for Religious Freedom, the staunch Presbyterian Johnston had great influence among fourteen Upper Valley delegates without whose votes Virginia would not have ratified the Constitution.[17] In able speeches at the Virginia convention of 1788, Albemarle County delegate George Nicholas attempted a similar, though unsuccessful, effort to persuade the fourteen Kentucky delegates to vote for ratification.[18]

Madison owed his presence in the Virginia convention to dissenters whose trust he had earned in the struggle for religious liberty. The Baptists of Orange County had become "Very formi[da]ble in p[o]int of Elections" and were decidedly antifederalist. "What is dearest of all—religious liberty, is not sufficiently secured," wrote their leader John Leland in his widely circulated objections to the Constitution. On 7 March 1788 the General Baptist Committee met in Goochland County and unanimously resolved against the Constitution. Two weeks later, however, on his way home for the election, Madison met with Leland and convinced him that religious liberty was not endangered. Leland's new-found assurance reached only the voters of Orange, perhaps at the courthouse itself; in other counties Baptist votes sent opponents to the convention of 1788.[19]

---

[17] Zachariah Johnston to Mrs. Ann Johnston, 26 Oct. 1787, Zachariah Johnston Papers, 1742–1856, Virginia State Library and Archives, Richmond (hereafter cited as Vi); Freeman H. Hart, *The Valley of Virginia in the American Revolution, 1763–1789* (Chapel Hill, 1942), pp. 178–89. In a serious political miscalculation, William Graham, of Rockbridge County, invited Johnston to join with him, Arthur Campbell, and William McKee in "a vigorous opposition" to the Constitution by distributing where "newspapers dont circulate in the back parts" two thousand copies of a pamphlet he had "been solicited to write . . . to open the Eyes of the People" (William Graham to Zachariah Johnston, 3 Nov. 1787, William Fleming Papers, Vi). Graham had backed Patrick Henry's Bill for the Support of Teachers of the Christian Religion and wrote provisions restricting office-holding to men of virtue and good character in his 1784 draft constitution for the state of Franklin; see the sketch by Wesley Frank Craven in Richard A. Harrison, ed., *Princetonians, 1769–1775: A Biographical Dictionary* (Princeton, 1980), pp. 289–94. Graham's ally William McKee voted with the "middle group" (see note 24, below), and Arthur Campbell was involved in separatist intrigue and the state of Franklin (see James William Hagy, "Arthur Campbell and the Origins of Kentucky: A Reassessment," *Filson Club Historical Quarterly*, LV [1981], 367–74, and "Arthur Campbell and the West, 1743–1811," *VMHB*, XC [1982], 464–69).

[18] Elliot, ed., *Debates*, III, 236–47, 449–51, 482–83, 499, 502, 506–7; Richard H. Caldemeyer, "The Career of George Nicholas" (Ph.D. diss., Indiana University, 1951), pp. 13–28; Charles Gano Talbert, "Kentuckians in the Virginia Convention of 1788," *Register of the Kentucky Historical Society*, LVIII (1960), 187–93.

[19] Joseph Spencer to James Madison, 28 Feb. 1788, in Rutland et al., eds., *Madison Papers*, X, 540–42; Lyman C. Butterfield, "The Elder John Leland," *Proceedings of the American Antiquarian Society*, n.s., LXII (1952), 187–88. Wesley Marsh Gewehr (*The Great Awakening in Virginia, 1740–1790* [Durham, 1930], p. 189 n. 8) incorrectly identified Leland as a candidate for the convention of 1788, and Alan Heimert (*Religion and the American Mind: From the Great Awakening to the Revolution* [Cambridge, Mass., 1966], p. 559) incorrectly identified him as a delegate to the convention.

Philosophically, everyone on Virginia's political spectrum agreed with Francis Corbin when he told the Virginia convention that "coercion is necessary in every government." The question was, How best to entrust that power to government? Corbin and the nationalist end of the political spectrum differed from their contemporaries in their insistence that "a superintending coercive power [was] absolutely indispensable" to the central government and in their zeal to ratify the Constitution without conditions or alterations.[20]

2

> "At the head of the 2d. party which urges amendments are the Govr. & Mr. Mason. These do not object to the substance of the Governt. but contend for a few additional Guards in favor of the Rights of the States and of the people."[21]

The pivotal figures in Virginia's ratification of the Constitution occupied the middle of the spectrum of political sentiments in Virginia in 1787 and 1788. As statesmen who fought for modifications to the Constitution but were willing to accept most of the plan, Virginia's "federalists who are for amendments" found it difficult to reduce the complex issues of national destiny and regional interests, liberty and power, statecraft and the public good, to a single aye or nay vote in Richmond on 25 June 1788.

On the spectrum of sentiments, Edmund Pendleton holds the spot at which the federalist and middle groups converge. As Virginia's preeminent jurist, Pendleton was widely respected. He had chaired several revolutionary conventions and the Committee of Safety, and it was no surprise when he was chosen president of the convention of 1788. One suspects that his hesitations about the Constitution fostered the atmosphere of open-minded debate that Virginians enjoyed between September 1787 and June 1788. Although convinced that Congress needed "additional Powers," he found himself unable to "suppress my fears of giving that of regulating Commerce." He was "led into these suspicions by the Eastern Publications, where the avowed purpose of excluding the British trade is to prevent their underselling their Manufacturers, a thing which may not suit them, . . . but which I am sure would not displease a Virginian." "The project for Bartering away the Navigation of the

[20] Elliot, ed., *Debates*, III, 106.
[21] James Madison to Thomas Jefferson, 9 Dec. 1787, in Rutland et al., eds., *Madison Papers*, X, 312.

Mississippi . . . ," he continued, "is not calculated to remove the above fears."[22]

By December 1787 Pendleton's initial admiration for the Constitution had cooled, and "Light-Horse Harry" Lee lamented to Madison that "Judge Pendleton . . . continues amidst the strange change of opinion on the worth of the foederal Government," while Governor Edmund Randolph, astride the same fence, wrote that Pendleton had "expressed himself to this effect: that the constitution is very full of radical faults, & that he would adopt it with a protest as to its imperfections, in order that they may be corrected at a future day." Midway through the Virginia convention Pendleton described his views to Richard Henry Lee: "You have been truly informed of my Sentiments being in favor of Amendments, but against the insisting on their Incorporation previous to and as a sine qua non of Adoption, or of a Convention being previously called to consider them."[23]

In the end, Pendleton and the governor both voted for ratification, but historians generally have overlooked Pendleton's reservations. How much correction did he think the Constitution needed? The answer turns on how one interprets the 27 June 1788 vote by which Pendleton and twelve others who had voted for the Constitution recommended an amendment about powers of taxation that such nationalists as Madison vigorously opposed.[24] On this point I must reluctantly part company with Pendleton's superb biographer, David John Mays, who regarded the vote as a gesture to "mollify Henry and Mason";[25] the issue seems too serious for that. Faced with the tactical dilemma of whether to demand amendments before or after ratification, Pendleton agreed with Randolph that Virginia "ought to ratify it, in order to secure the Union," but in

[22] Edmund Pendleton to James Madison, 19 Dec. 1786, in David John Mays, ed., *The Letters and Papers of Edmund Pendleton, 1734–1803*, Virginia Historical Society Documents, VII, VIII (2 vols.; Charlottesville, 1967), pp. 492–93.

[23] Henry Lee to James Madison, ca.20 Dec. 1787, Edmund Randolph to James Madison, [29] Oct. 1787, in Rutland et al., eds., *Madison Papers*, X, 339, 230; Edmund Pendleton to Richard Henry Lee, 14 June 1788, in Mays, ed., *Letters and Papers of Pendleton*, p. 530.

[24] Elliot, ed., *Debates*, III, 653–55, 662. The delegates who voted for the Constitution on 25 June and for Amendment Three on 27 June were Burwell Bassett and William Clayton, of New Kent County; Paul Carrington, of Charlotte County; William Fleet, of King and Queen County; William Fleming, of Botetourt County; James Gordon, of Lancaster County; John Hartwell Cocke, of Surry County; Miles King, of Elizabeth City County; William McKee, of Rockbridge County; Edmund Pendleton, of Caroline County; Solomon Shepherd, of Nansemond County; Walker Tomlin, of Richmond County; and David Patteson (who also voted for previous amendments on 25 June), of Chesterfield County. Birthdates for eight of these cross-over voters are known; their average age was 44.87 years, compared to 42.90 years for 45 federalists and 45.32 years for 44 antifederalists (see note 5).

[25] David John Mays, *Edmund Pendleton, 1721–1803: A Biography* (1952; 2 vols., Richmond, 1984), II, 270.

supporting all the recommended amendments, Pendleton voted like an experienced Virginia statesman who wanted structural change. Pendleton exemplified the finest tradition of Virginia statecraft. "In all . . . Political cases," he wrote, "if we can't get the very best, we must take the best we can get, provided it be preferable to the thing to be changed."[26]

Near Pendleton at mid-spectrum were the young Fredericksburg law partners James Monroe, whom Madison called "a friend [to the Constitution] though a cool one," and John Dawson. In Congress Monroe had witnessed the dealings with Spain over navigation of the Mississippi River, and he gave the Virginia convention an even-handed summary of those proceedings. Monroe sought a stronger union without putting the "rights and interests" of either "states or individuals" in jeopardy. "May not some middle course be struck," he asked in a pamphlet issued on the eve of the Virginia convention, "some plan be adopted to give the general government those rights of internal legislation necessary for its safety, and well being . . . and yet leave to the states other powers they might exercise to advantage?" Declaring himself "a warm friend to a firm, federal, energetic government," Dawson called for a bill of rights and wanted the treaty-making provisions of Article II, section 2, changed to require concurrence by "three fourths of all the senators" (rather than "two-thirds of the Senators present") for any treaty that involved territorial or navigational rights. Only one thing separated Pendleton from Dawson and Monroe on the political spectrum: the latter "could not conceive that a conditional ratification would, in the most remotest degree, endanger the Union." Prior amendments were "harmless," Monroe argued. "They secure our rights without altering a single feature." Without them, Dawson and the future president voted against ratification.[27]

George Mason was author of the Virginia constitution of 1776 and its Declaration of Rights, delegate to the Philadelphia convention, independent man of principle, and a prudent farmer who managed his business affairs profitably—in all Mason was Virginia's epitome of a country whig.

[26] Edmund Pendleton to James Madison, 19 Dec. 1786, in Mays, ed., *Letters and Papers of Pendleton*, p. 491; Jon Kukla, "Order and Chaos in Early America: Political and Social Stability in Pre-Restoration Virginia," *American Historical Review*, XC (1985), 297–98.

[27] James Madison to Thomas Jefferson, 22 Apr. 1788, in Rutland et al., eds., *Madison Papers*, XI, 28; Elliot, ed., *Debates*, III, 207–22, 334–39, 606, 610, 630; Harry Ammon, *James Monroe: The Quest for National Identity* (New York, 1971); Charles Ellis Dickson, "Politics in a New Nation: The Early Career of James Monroe" (Ph.D. diss., Ohio State University, 1971), p. 34; Edward Carrington to Thomas Jefferson, 24 Apr. 1788, Jensen, Kaminski, et al., eds., *Ratification*, XIV, 408.

At Philadelphia he and Randolph had moved for a second convention and refused to sign the Constitution. "There is no Declaration of Rights," Mason's widely circulated objections began, "and the laws of the general government being paramount to the laws and constitution of the several States, the Declarations of Rights in the separate States are no security." He declared publicly in October 1787 "that altho' he is for amendments, he will not quit the union, even if they should not be made," and throughout most of the contest he was the most visible of those who "would adopt it sooner than jeopardize the union."[28]

Today, Mason's efforts toward the creation of our Bill of Rights are rightly celebrated. Two hundred years ago, however, with Pendleton and Randolph resigned to subsequent amendments and Richard Henry Lee absent, Mason found himself uncomfortably allied with Patrick Henry at the New Academy on Shockoe Hill. Mason sought "to give the [national] government sufficient energy, on real republican principles; but . . . to withhold such powers as are not absolutely necessary in themselves, but are extremely dangerous." After antifederalist Benjamin Harrison "moved that all the papers relative to the Constitution should be read" and antifederalist John Tyler suggested that "rules and regulations should be established," Randolph proposed the rules of the House of Delegates. Mason then promptly moved that the convention proceed "clause-by-clause, before any general previous question be put." Hugh Blair Grigsby thought Mason "went beyond his legitimate purpose, and played into the hands of his opponents," because debating individual clauses undermined the "anti-Federalists [who] believed that the Constitution in its general scope was false to liberty." Trapped by the familiar dichotomy, Grigsby failed to see this was precisely Mason's plan—to protect his middle ground both against federalists who sought to accept the Constitution without amendments and against Henry's intention of challenging the Philadelphia convention's decision to draft "an entirely new government."[29]

Mason coordinated the compilation of the forty amendments, a bill of rights and twenty structural changes, adopted by the convention on the

---

[28] Robert A. Rutland, ed., *The Papers of George Mason, 1725–1792* (3 vols.; Chapel Hill, 1970), p. 991; Edmund Randolph to James Madison, [29] Oct. 1787, in Rutland et al., eds., *Madison Papers*, X, 230.

[29] Elliot, ed., *Debates*, III, 2–3, 271; Hugh Blair Grigsby, *The History of the Virginia Federal Convention of 1788 . . .*, ed. R. A. Brock, Virginia Historical Society Collections, IX, X (2 vols.; Richmond, 1890–91), I, 71–73; Helen Hill Miller, *George Mason: Reluctant Revolutionary* (Chapel Hill, 1975), pp. 287–89. Mason and Richard Henry Lee had agreed upon this strategy (Richard Henry Lee to George Mason, 7 May 1788, in James Curtis Ballagh, ed., *The Letters of Richard Henry Lee* [2 vols.; New York, 1911–14], II, 466–69, and George Washington to James Madison, 10 Oct. 1787, in Jensen, Kaminski, et al., eds., *Ratification*, XIII, 358.

day it adjourned.[30] If a fatigued and gout-ridden sixty-three-year-old George Mason got a bit testy during his long and lonely campaign, the reason is surely because, despite the coolness of longtime friends with whom he differed, Mason believed with all his heart in the urgency of a declaration of rights and "had no expectation of gaining amendments if the Constitution were ratified unconditionally."[31] On the latter point, the example of Mason's profound commitment helped prove him wrong.

Governor Edmund Randolph, "an open, easy character, affable and popular," had nominally led Virginia's delegation to the Philadelphia convention. Upon learning that he and Mason refused to sign the Constitution, Virginians reacted with a rapid change in their favorable opinion that frightened Washington, Madison, and other nationalists.[32] In Randolph's estimation, the Constitution needed amendments to clarify its delegations of power and remove "all ambiguities of expression," to limit presidential, congressional, and judicial powers, and to distinguish clearly between state and federal powers in order to avert "dangerous disputes." This mid-spectrum longing for precise definitions of state and central powers was at once a clear-eyed diagnosis of potential conflict and an intellectual and political impossibility that would have shattered the understandings achieved at Philadelphia.[33]

Before the Philadelphia convention Randolph had hoped that new powers might be "grafted on the old confederation" (Madison cagily agreed that it would "be well to retain as much as possible of the old Confederation") and that a method of ratification could be devised with "the points of power . . . so detached from each other, as to permit a state to reject one part, without mutilating the whole." When the convention failed to protect southern agricultural states by requiring two-thirds

[30] Miller, *George Mason*, pp. 291, 298. Successive drafts of these amendments are printed in Rutland, ed., *Mason Papers*, pp. 1054–57, 1068–72, 1115–20.

[31] Rutland, ed., *Mason Papers*, p. 1044; Miller, *George Mason*, pp. 270–74, 281, 287, 298. "The liberty or misery of millions yet unborn are deeply concerned in our decision," Mason felt (Elliot, ed., *Debates*, III, 271).

[32] J. Rives Childs, "French Consul Martin Oster Reports on Virginia, 1784–1796," *VMHB*, LXXVI (1968), 37; John J. Reardon, *Edmund Randolph: A Biography* (New York, 1974), pp. 121–36; Richmond *Virginia Independent Chronicle*, 31 Oct. 1787; Paul Leicester Ford, ed., *Pamphlets on the Constitution of the United States* (Brooklyn, 1888), pp. 259–76; Elliot, ed., *Debates*, III, 603; Edmund Randolph to James Madison, 30 Sept. 1787, in Rutland et al., eds., *Madison Papers*, X, 182; Rutland, ed., *Mason Papers*, p. 1012; Moncure Daniel Conway, *Omitted Chapters of History Disclosed in the Life and Papers of Edmund Randolph* . . . (New York and London, 1889), p. 71.

[33] Ford, ed., *Pamphlets on the Constitution*, p. 275. Mason, too, sought "such amendments as will point out what powers are reserved to the state governments . . . and those given to the general government, so as to prevent future disputes and clashing of interests" (Elliot, ed., *Debates*, III, 271). Randolph accepted the federalist argument that a bill of rights was unnecessary and dangerous in a government of carefully delegated powers, and he focused on defining those powers precisely (John P. Kaminski and Gaspare H. Saladino, "Edmund Randolph and the Constitution," in Jensen, Kaminski, et al., eds., *Ratification*, XV, 117–21).

majorities for commercial regulations, Randolph's doubts overtook him, and on 17 September he withheld his signature. On the way home he outlined plans to finesse those whose opposition would be "formidable, if they must take altogether or reject" by asking the General Assembly both to call a state convention and circulate a list of amendments to the other states. "Before the meeting of the convention an answer may be obtained," he suggested, and if there were agreement upon a slate of amendments, Virginia's ratification could be made conditional upon their adoption. By mid-winter, however, Randolph placed his hopes on a second national convention rather than conditional ratification because he saw the call for previous amendments giving "cover" to those willing to see "the spirit of the Union extinguished."[34]

When the General Assembly called for a state convention to come to order on the first Monday in June 1788, it also authorized "communications with any of the sister states" and "delegates to another general Federal Convention, should such a body be convened."[35] Randolph knew of Jefferson's idea that nine states could ratify and the others hold out for satisfactory changes, but what if the new government began without Virginia's leaders? What if Robert Morris (whose machinations with les Fermiers Generaux and the tobacco market terrified Virginians), not Washington, became the first president? And what were satisfactory changes? The Massachusetts amendments that allies of Meriwether Smith thought "proper to make . . . the Basis of such as may finally be agreed on" disgusted Randolph. On the other hand, Article V of the proposed Constitution provided for amendment by convention without the dangers of conditional ratification. When Maryland ratified unconditionally in April 1788, Randolph's mind finally was settled. "With me," he maintained at the Virginia convention, "the only question has ever been, between previous, and subsequent amendments." Virginia could no longer demand previous amendments without endangering the Union; "the accession of eight states reduced our deliberations to the single question of union or no union." Randolph voted for union on 25 June

[34] Edmund Randolph to James Madison, 24 Mar., 29 Oct. 1787, James Madison to Edmund Randolph, 8 Apr. 1787, in Rutland et al., eds., *Madison Papers*, IX, 335, 369; X, 230; Reardon, *Edmund Randolph*, pp. 121–36; Ford, ed., *Pamphlets on the Constitution*, pp. 259–76. A sound assessment of Randolph's actions and indecision is Charles F. Hobson, "The Early Career of Edmund Randolph" (Ph.D. diss., Emory University, 1971), esp. pp. 253, 297–99, 306–11.

[35] William Waller Hening, ed., *The Statutes at Large; Being a Collection of all the Laws of Virginia . . .* (13 vols.; Richmond, Philadelphia, and New York, 1809–23), XII, 462–65; Reardon, *Edmund Randolph*, p. 128; *Journal of the House of Delegates of the Commonwealth of Virginia; Begun . . . the Twentieth Day of October . . . in the Year of Our Lord, One Thousand Seven Hundred and Eighty-seven* (Richmond, 1828), p. 77.

1788 and then, as Linda De Pauw showed us fifteen years ago, worked hard but unsuccessfully for a second national convention.[36]

Health forced Richard Henry Lee, who was a veteran of Congress, to decline to attend both the Philadelphia and Virginia conventions, but Lee found himself in the thick of the ratification contest anyway, even if we no longer think he wrote the *Letters from the Federal Farmer*. James Gordon, of Orange County, asked Lee "whether the United States had not better receive than reject the Constitution." Lee replied that although Gordon's "question implies a necessity of either adopting or rejecting," because "the happiness or misery of mankind depends so essentially upon government . . . the right of the people cannot be questioned, of so acting with plans proposed, as to adopt them, reject them, or propose amendments to them." The Confederation was "well calculated," Lee told John Adams (whose *Defence of the Constitutions* he had just read), if only the states would do their duty. He wondered, however, whether Americans could make a mild government effective. "A popular government cannot flourish without virtue in the people," he declared. Lee hoped that virtue could be inculcated by religion and education.

He distrusted the spirit of commerce and the "8 interested States" whose advocacy of congressional power to regulate trade threatened to create "a most pernicious and destructive Monopoly." Monopolies always worry farmers, but what Lee saw was a moral problem, too. "The Spirit of Commerce through out the world is a spirit of Avarice" that weakened the virtue, self-restraint, and wisdom required of a free people. If the country's plight stemmed from flaws in the structure of government, Lee reasoned, altering the Constitution might work. "But, alas! sir," he wrote Mason, "I fear it is more in vicious manners, than in mistakes in form, that we must seek for the causes of the present discontent." Lee felt it would have been "sufficient so to alter the Confederation as to allow Congress full liberty to make Treaties," regulate trade, and establish an impost, but because the proposed Constitution had "many good regulations," he was willing to see it properly amended and ratified. Beyond strengthening Articles VI and IX of the Confederation (commerce and

[36] Edmund Randolph to James Madison, 17 Apr. 1788, in Rutland et al., eds., *Madison Papers*, XI, 26–27; Reardon, *Edmund Randolph*, p. 135; Alan Schaffer, "Virginia's 'Critical Period,' " in Darrett B. Rutman, ed., *The Old Dominion: Essays for Thomas Perkins Abernethy* (Charlottesville, 1964), pp. 152–70; Meriwether Smith to John Lamb, 9 June 1788, Virginia Historical Society, Richmond (hereafter cited as ViHi); Elliot, ed., *Debates*, III, 652; Linda Grant De Pauw, "The Anticlimax of Antifederalism: The Abortive Second Convention Movement, 1788–89," *Prologue: The Journal of the National Archives*, II (1970), 98–114.

treaties) and improving the system by which revenues were collected from the states, Lee thought "no form of government whatever, short of force, will answer." His comment speaks volumes. Richard Henry Lee refused to abandon the hope that government could depend upon the states' willing compliance with their obligations, and he declined to join the federalists in giving the federal government coercive power to enforce such obligations, because Richard Henry Lee refused to surrender the revolutionary dream that a free people might be induced to govern themselves without coercion. From Edmund Pendleton to Richard Henry Lee, the Virginians in the middle of the spectrum balanced the federalists' commitment to union against the antifederalists' watchful devotion to the liberties, virtues, and interests of the states and people.[37]

On 27 June 1788, two days after Virginia's vote to ratify, George Wythe, another moderate, reported twenty "essential and unalienable rights of the people" (based on the Virginia Declaration of Rights) and twenty "Amendments to the Constitution."[38] Of these forty items, federalists objected only to one, the proposed Amendment Three, which outlined a requisition system for national revenue. Congress would apportion quotas among the states according to population and give the states opportunity to raise the money; only if a state failed to comply could Congress resort to direct federal taxation.[39] This idea—an impost with

[37] Richard Henry Lee to Samuel Adams, 18 Nov. 1784, to James Madison, 26 Nov. 1784, 11 Aug. 1785, to George Mason, 15 May 1787, to Francis Lightfoot Lee, 14 July 1787, to Thomas Lee Shippen, 22 July 1787, to John Adams, 5 Sept. 1787, to Samuel Adams, 5 Oct. 1787, to James Gordon, 26 Feb. 1788, to John Lamb, 27 June 1788, in Ballagh, ed., *Letters of Richard Henry Lee*, II, 294, 307, 383, 419, 424, 427, 434, 447, 460, 475; Gordon S. Wood, *The Creation of the American Republic, 1776–1787* (Chapel Hill, 1969), pp. 418–25; Maier, *Old Revolutionaries*, pp. 165–200, 282–94. Lee had heartily supported local efforts to establish schools as well as Henry's bill for a general assessment for religious teachers (Richard Henry Lee to Martin Pickett, 5 Mar. 1786, in Ballagh, ed., *Letters of Richard Henry Lee*, II, 411–12), and his work for amendments is apparent in his correspondence from October 1787 through the meeting of the First Congress. The traditional attribution of the *Federal Farmer* essays was challenged in Gordon S. Wood, "The Authorship of the *Letters from the Federal Farmer*," *WMQ*, 3d ser., XXXI (1974), 299–307.

[38] Elliot, ed., *Debates*, III, 657–63; George Wythe, "Report of the Committee of the Whole," 27 June 1788, ViHi. Wythe had not been a candidate for the convention but was elected unanimously in absentia by the citizens of York County as their respected elder statesman, "impartial" and "aloof from the warm conflict" (Alonzo Thomas Dill, *George Wythe: Teacher of Liberty* [Williamsburg, 1979], pp. 66–70).

[39] "When the Congress shall lay direct taxes or excises, they shall immediately inform the executive power of each state, of the quota of such state, according to the census herein directed, which is proposed to be thereby raised; and if the legislature of any state shall pass a law which shall be effectual for raising such quota at the time required by Congress, the taxes and excises laid by Congress shall not be collected in such state" (Elliot, ed., *Debates*, III, 659). Recent historians agree on the basic working of the Confederation impost but differ about linking the reformers of the early 1780s with the movement for the Constitution: Main, *Antifederalists*, pp. 72–74; E. James Ferguson, *The Power of the Purse: A History of American Public Finance, 1776–1790* (Chapel Hill, 1961), pp. 140–41; Jack N. Rakove, *The Beginnings of National Politics: An Interpretive History of the Continental Congress* (New York, 1979), pp. 337–42. Similar amendments were recommended by Pennsylvania, New York, and North Carolina (Thomas P. Slaughter, "The Tax Man Cometh: Ideological Opposition to Internal Taxes, 1760–1790," *WMQ*, 3d ser., XLI [1984], 585).

teeth—allowed the states to avoid federal collectors and choose the kinds of taxes that suited them but gave Congress power of internal taxation as a last resort. This amendment offered local control of administration and central revenues sufficient for national purposes. Amendment Three expressed mid-spectrum goals in careful legal language. It distinguished sovereignty from solvency, and the Virginia delegates' decision on 27 June to recommend this change in the Constitution reveals attitudes toward government more accurately than the vote on ratification itself, which was affected by questions of amendment tactics and nationhood. On 27 June federalists eager to grant substantial powers to a central government could not cloak that ambition with memories of an impoverished Continental Congress and freezing soldiers at Valley Forge, while the Virginians who supported Amendment Three—including Pendleton and twelve others who had voted for ratification[40]—saw this and the other amendments as means both to uphold local administration without emasculating the nation and threatening the Union and to empower the central government without undermining virtue and threatening the republic.

Concern about giving away the powers incident to direct taxation was common among Virginians at the middle of the spectrum.[41] Typically, when Monroe sought "some middle course," he specifically challenged the dangers of a Constitution "intended to comprehend the right of direct taxation and excise," for "upon this point, between the two governments, will their balance depend." For Monroe, the prospect of conflict between state and federal governments seemed "a more perilous and stormy sea, than even a complete annihilation of the state governments."[42]

---

[40] See note 24, above.

[41] "Not that Confederation," Pendleton reminded the convention in rebuttal to Henry's assertion that the Articles of Confederation had sustained the nation through the Revolutionary War, "but common danger, and the spirit of America, were bonds of union: . . . 'United we stand—divided we fall!' echoed and reechoed through America—from Congress to the drunken carpenter." Warming to the subject, Pendleton pilloried Rhode Island for failing to honor congressional requisitions and concluded that "if a sufficient revenue be not otherwise raised, recurrence must be had to direct taxation" (Elliot, ed., *Debates*, III, 38–40). Edmund Randolph did not favor the requisition system and voted against Amendment Three (Jensen, Kaminski, et al., eds., *Ratification*, XV, 127).

[42] Stanislaus Murray Hamilton, ed., *The Writings of James Monroe* (7 vols.; New York, 1898–1903), I, 320–21. Monroe had *Some Observations on the Constitution* printed in Petersburg to distribute to his constituents several days before the Virginia convention, but the edition was late and Monroe suppressed it (Charles Evans, *American Bibliography*, VII [Chicago, 1912], item 21263). Hamilton attributed to Monroe a pamphlet entitled *Observations upon the Proposed Plan of the Federal Government. With an Attempt to Answer Some of the Principal Objections That Have Been Made to It* (Petersburg, 1788), but style and internal evidence support Charles Evans's doubts about Monroe's authorship (Hamilton, ed., *Writings of Monroe*, I, 347–99; Evans, *American Bibliography*, item 21264, and VII, 238; Herbert J. Storing, ed., *The Complete Anti-Federalist*, V [Chicago, 1981], p. 280 n. 5).

3

"A third Class, at the head of which is Mr. Henry . . . concurs at present with the patrons of Amendments, but will probably contend for such as strike at the essence of the System, and must lead to an adherence to the principle of the existing Confederation . . . or to a partition of the Union into several Confederacies."[43]

The preeminent voice of Virginia's resolute opponents to the Constitution was Patrick Henry, who spoke for many when he enumerated the order of his priorities at the convention of 1788. "The first thing I have at heart is American liberty: the second thing is American union." The forest-born Demosthenes was a power to be reckoned with—"you know the force of this wonderful mans oratory upon a Virginia house of Delegates," a federalist warned. In eloquent speeches familiar to readers of the published *Debates*, Henry denounced the Constitution as a consolidated government rather than a confederation, demanded a bill of rights, and championed the twenty substantial amendments, including "the single amendment . . . respecting direct taxes" that he thought "worth all the rest."[44]

William Grayson—Confederation congressman and future senator—held resolute antifederalist positions before, during, and after the convention of 1788. He drafted substantive amendments about the presidency and the militia, and his democratic faith was the antifederalist counterpoint to John Marshall's fears. "There are two opinions prevailing in the world," Grayson told the convention of 1788, "the one, that mankind can only be governed by force; the other, that they are capable of freedom and a good government. Under a supposition that mankind can govern themselves," he concluded, "I would recommend that the present Confederation should be amended," even though eight states already had ratified.[45]

---

[43] James Madison to Thomas Jefferson, 9 Dec. 1787, in Rutland et al., eds., *Madison Papers*, X, 312. "Mr. Henry . . . ," John Marshall had advised Arthur Lee on 5 March 1787, "has been heard to say that he would rather part with the confederation than relinquish the navigation of the Mississipi—but as we have been fortiter in modo, I dare say we shall be suaviter in re" (that is, strongly in manner, gently in deed) (in Johnson et al., eds., *Marshall Papers*, I, 206).

[44] Elliot, ed., *Debates*, III, 22, 30–31, 57, 148–49, 320–21, 593, 659–62; David Stuart to George Washington, 12 Sept. 1789, quoted in Alpheus Thomas Mason, *The States Rights Debate: Antifederalism and the Constitution* (Englewood Cliffs, N.J., 1964), p. 96. On 10 November 1788 Edmund Randolph reported to Madison that the latter's candidacy for a Senate seat in the First Congress had failed after his supporters "acknowledged, that it was doubtful, whether you would obey instructions, which should direct you to vote against direct taxation" (in Rutland et al., eds., *Madison Papers*, XI, 339).

[45] Elliot, ed., *Debates*, III, 278; Jon Kukla, ed., "William Grayson's Notes on the United States Constitution," *Virginia Phoenix*, VII, no. 1 (1974), 2–14; Jon Kukla, " 'Freedom and Good Government':

Benjamin Harrison of Berkeley, signer of the Declaration of Independence, Speaker of the House of Delegates, and former governor, had supported Henry's bill for religious teachers and thought the Constitution "unwarrantable, precipitate, and dangerously impolitic." Its commerce provision would render the southern states "little more than appendages," and Harrison objected that in giving powers for taxation, commerce, and the judiciary, "the sword and such powers . . . must sooner or later establish a tyranny." At the Virginia convention Harrison was chairman of the Committee on Elections, whose long deliberations over contested seats testifies to the uncertainties of all parties about the outcome.[46]

Harrison's neighbor and sometime rival John Tyler, former Speaker of the House of Delegates and proponent of the Annapolis convention, also opposed the Constitution. "Do let me know," a convention-watcher wrote from New Kent County in June 1788, "as soon as Messrs. Henry and Tyler have fixed the question in the negative." Tyler thought the Constitution's "tendency must be, either a revolt, or a destruction of the state governments, and a consolidation of them all into one general system" and warned that the document's ambiguities would "be used to serve particular purposes." Tyler declared that unless the elastic ("necessary and proper") clause of Article I, section 8, "were expunged, he would vote against the Constitution." Most vehemently, however, the statesman from Charles City County condemned the clause offering twenty years of protection to the slave trade. "Nothing could justify it," Tyler proclaimed. "I want it to be handed down to posterity that I opposed that wicked clause."[47] Theodorick Bland, Confederation congressman and Henry's candidate for governor in 1786, advocated "interior amendments" and did "not think it prudent to mount a high-blooded, fiery steed, without a bridle."[48]

Critics who think the antifederalists were unlettered provincials are hard put to account for the learned and deliberate localism of such Virginians as Spencer Roane, who had read law with George Wythe and

Antifederalist William Grayson's Intended Amendments to the United States Constitution," *Virginia Cavalcade*, XXXVI (1986–87), 184–91.

[46] Elliot, ed., *Debates*, III, 628–29; Benjamin Harrison to George Washington, 4 Oct. 1787, in U.S. Department of State, *Documentary History of the Constitution of the United States of America* . . . (5 vols.; New York, 1894–1905), IV, 313; James Madison to Thomas Jefferson, 9 Dec. 1787, in Rutland et al., eds., *Madison Papers*, X, 312; Howard W. Smith, *Benjamin Harrison and the American Revolution*, Virginia Independence Bicentennial Commission, No. 13 (Williamsburg, 1978), pp. 76–82.

[47] "Letters of John Dandridge to John Hopkins," *WMQ*, 1st ser., XX (1911–12), 153; Elliot, ed., *Debates*, III, 454–55; 638–42; [Lyon G. Tyler], *Judge John Tyler, Sr., and His Times* (Richmond, 1927), p. 18.

[48] Theodorick Bland to Arthur Lee, 13 June 1788, in Richard Henry Lee, *Life of Arthur Lee, LL.D.* . . . (2 vols.; Boston, 1829), II, 337–38.

won the admiration of his father-in-law, Patrick Henry, as "a man of honor, talents, and of an open generous disposition." The twenty-six-year-old had already served in the House of Delegates and resigned from the Executive Council to protest an assertion of state executive authority in the local judiciary. Federalists recognized the "Plain Dealer" as "bitter in principle vs. the Constitution."[49] Foreshadowing his later national role as jurist and Jeffersonian, Roane favored more effective government (he believed that the Union was "too loosely banded together") but thought the Constitution gave away powers that should have been withheld and far too vaguely stipulated the powers retained by the states and people. It made no "sense to accept a Constitution, knowing it to be imperfect," Roane thought. "A Constitution ought to be like Caesar's wife, not only good; but unsuspected, since it is the highest compact which men are capable of forming, and involves the dearest rights of life, liberty and property." Nor did Roane suffer gladly Edmund Randolph's willingness to accept the Philadelphia plan. "Good God!" he exclaimed. "How can the first Magistrate . . . after a feeble parade of opposition, and before his desired plan of amendments has been determined upon, declare that he will accept a Constitution which is to beget either a monarchy or an aristocracy?" "His Excellency has let the cat out of the bag," Roane sneered.[50]

Many formidable politicians were silent on the convention floor but active in a powerful antifederalist caucus working with the Federal Republican Committee of New York, headed by Governor George Clinton's lieutenant, John Lamb. George Mason was titular chairman, but the organizer of this Virginia caucus was Meriwether Smith, the Essex County veteran of the Confederation Congress and Annapolis convention whom George Washington dismissed as "bad company."[51]

[49] "Letters of Spencer Roane, 1788–1822," *Bulletin of the New York Public Library*, X (1906), 167; Edmund Randolph to James Madison, 9 Feb. 1788, in Rutland et al., eds., *Madison Papers*, X, 543; Clyde Christian Gelbach, "Spencer Roane of Virginia, 1762–1822: A Judicial Advocate of State Rights" (Ph.D. diss., University of Pittsburgh, 1955), pp. 18–23; Margaret Eileen Horsnell, "Spencer Roane: Judicial Advocate of Jeffersonian Principles" (Ph.D. diss., University of Minnesota, 1967), pp. 16–20. Roane's dissent from the dismissal of a county justice is recorded in Wilmer L. Hall, ed., *Journals of the Council of the State of Virginia*, III (Richmond, 1952), pp. 542, 577.

[50] [Spencer Roane], "A Plain Dealer," Richmond *Virginia Independent Chronicle*, 13 Feb. 1788; also reprinted in Paul Leicester Ford, ed., *Essays on the Constitution of the United States* (New York, 1892), pp. 385–92. Randolph was also the target of Roane's epigram adapted from Horace, "Mons parturiens et ecce nascitur mus"—roughly, a mountain labored and brought forth a mouse.

[51] Emory L. Carlton, "Col. Meriwether Smith and His Time, 1730–1794," *Essex County Historical Society Bulletin*, XXI (1982), 1–5; George Washington to James Madison, 10 Jan. 1788, Fitzpatrick, ed., *Writings of Washington*, XXIX, 372. The 9 June 1788 letter warned Lamb to correspond through Richmond merchant

Smith's caucus of "several respectable Gentlemen of the Convention now met in this City, who are opposed to the Adoption without previous Amendments," surely included William and Samuel Jordan Cabell, of Amherst County. Father and son had "declared themselves opposed to the Federal Constitution in the present form" before the election of delegates in Amherst. When the poll was "stopped at the request of Col. Hugh Rose," they had 327 and 313 votes, respectively, to 23 and 5 for Rose and the other federalist, "and those who were prevented from voting, loudly and openly declared themselves in favor of the Gentlemen elected."[52]

When the Virginia convention acquiesced to the scheme of recommended amendments, Spencer Roane reported that "the Decision has been distressing & awful to great Numbers; & it is generally believed will be so received by the people. . . . There is no rejoicing on Acc[oun]t of the vote of ratification—it would not be prudent to do so; & the federalists behave with moderation and do not exult in their Success." Meriwether Smith yielded "to the Determination of the Majority, as the only rule by which free Societies can be supported," but warned the freeholders of Essex that

> to rest satisfied with the Adoption of the new Constitution may be fatal to you. . . . It should be critically examined and not suffered by precedents founded on the Construction of loose and inaccurate Expressions, to speak a Language and assume a principle, neither understood nor foreseen by the People, when they adopted it. . . . I own I don't like the Constitution in the present Dress. I fear it is a wolf in Sheep's clothing, that will seek & find opportunity to devour us.

To preserve state governments, individual rights, or both, the most reluctant ratifiers at the antifederalist end of Virginia's political spectrum hastily became strict constructionists.[53]

George Fleming "in Order to prevent any Interruption that Curiosity might give." Smith's draft is at the Virginia Historical Society; the recipient's copy over Mason's signature is printed in Rutland, ed., *Mason Papers*, pp. 1057–58, from a manuscript at the New-York Historical Society. Letters to Lamb on the same date from Patrick Henry and William Grayson are published in Isaac Q. Leake, *Memoir of the Life and Times of General John Lamb* (Albany, N.Y., 1850), pp. 307–8, 311–12.

[52] Richmond *Virginia Independent Chronicle*, 19 Mar. 1788.

[53] "Letters of Spencer Roane," p. 167; Meriwether Smith, "To the Freeholders of the County of [Essex, Virginia]," 1788, ViHi; I am grateful to E. Lee Shepard for calling this manuscript to my attention. Two centuries of shifting tensions between individual liberties and states' rights and between the relative powers of state and federal governments suggest that these tensions will remain as long as the republic endures, for as John Randolph of Roanoke said, "You can cover whole skins of parchment with limitations, but power alone can limit power" (quoted in Mason, *States Rights Debate*, p. 194).

Last year Americans celebrated the convention of 1787, and soon we will mark the passage of our Bill of Rights, maneuvered through Congress by James Madison and adopted when Francis Corbin secured Virginia's ratification on 15 December 1791 over the objections of William Grayson and Richard Henry Lee. This summer we venerate all the Virginians who were parties to the heated public debate over the Constitution. The intensity of that discussion in 1787 and 1788 melded thirteen separate arguments into a substantial debate about the lessons of America's shared past and the course of its common future—a debate whose specific terms may vary but that is now entering its eleventh generation. Even Virginians dubious about the stronger central government became, in their opposition to ratification, participants in a national political arena that had not existed a few years earlier. The vigilant antifederalists who dominated the General Assembly as it gathered in the new capitol in October 1788 made no attempt to isolate Virginia from the other states. Quite to the contrary, they insisted on strict adherence to the document they had opposed, fought hard for alterations in it, and even prepared for a second national convention to remedy the handiwork of Philadelphia.[54] Foreshadowing many of the great themes of the new nation's antebellum years, the ratification contest in Virginia reminds us again of America's profound dependence on the Old Dominion's complex and fascinating political heritage, a birthright already one hundred eighty years old when Patrick Henry reminded the convention of 1788 that "the example of Virginia is a powerful thing."[55]

[54] Brent Tarter, "Virginians and the Bill of Rights," in Jon Kukla, ed., *The Bill of Rights: A Lively Heritage* (Richmond, 1987), pp. 14–15; Richard Beeman, Stephen Botein, and Edward C. Carter II, eds., *Beyond Confederation: Origins of the Constitution and the American National Identity* (Chapel Hill, 1987), pp. 17–19, 293–94, 344–48; *Journal of the House of Delegates of the Commonwealth of Virginia . . . in the Year of Our Lord, One Thousand Seven Hundred and Eighty-eight* (Richmond, 1789), p. 13.

[55] Elliot, ed., *Debates*, III, 315.

Textuality and Legitimacy in the Printed Constitution

MICHAEL WARNER

IN OUR SOCIETY, outfitted as it is with unprecedented technologies of discipline, the forms of coercion are innumerable; but the supreme means of deriving force over the will of others is to win the appeal to a written text. Let us consider this state of affairs. Why is the ground of legality—and thus of coercion—an official hermeneutics of a written text? What establishes *its* legality, and what is the significance of its textuality? The question is complicated because the Constitution's textuality was an issue even before conflict over the text's meaning was institutionalized in the role of the court system. The act of writing constitutions had been an American innovation, and one that had taken place only on the assumption that the constitutional text would be a printed one. The subject that I wish to take up, therefore, is that of the meaning of the writtenness and printedness of constitutions in the culture of republican America, and of the relation between textuality, so considered, and the changing criteria of legitimacy that produced our official hermeneutics.

For Americans of the Revolutionary period, the written constitution was a way of literalizing the doctrine of popular sovereignty. That literalization was a complex strategy, giving sub-

This paper, in somewhat different form, was given on April 21, 1987, as a public lecture under the auspices of the Society's Program in the History of the Book in American Culture and as one of several activities related to the Society's commemoration of the bicentennial of the Federal Constitution.

MICHAEL WARNER is an assistant professor in the Department of English and the Program in Comparative Literature and Theory at Northwestern.

stance to the people's authority but doing so only by the agency of writing. It was also, therefore, a deeply problematic strategy, since the sovereignty of the people is obviously not identical to the official hermeneutics entailed by the constitutive text. On the other hand, if popular sovereignty seems to be a doctrine beyond question in our society, I shall argue that its literalization articulated its already problematic nature. The writtenness of the constitution mediated a central and paradoxical problem in revolutionary politics: that of sovereignty in a legal order—or more generally, the legality of law.

Of course, the British had believed their polity to be founded, in theory, on the sovereignty of the people as well. Sovereignty lay in Parliament, or the king-in-Parliament, but it did so because all Englishmen were represented there and could therefore be said to have consented to Parliament's laws. The imperial crisis leading to the Revolution came about when Americans, refusing their consent to the laws of Parliament, denied that they were represented there. In doing so, they disclosed a tautology deployed in England to legitimate the order of law: although what gave authority and legality to parliamentary law was its claim to represent the people, the only warrant for its claim to represent the people was parliamentary law. No one questioned the appeal to sovereignty; it was axiomatic that law required some authority for its legality. But since Americans were denying that they themselves, in representation, were the authority for law's legality, it became obvious that parliamentary law was its own authority. The American rhetoric of contestation, which identified parliamentary law as arbitrary power, thus derived its categories and its power from the British rhetoric of legitimation.[1]

Working out that rhetoric of contestation could be dangerous. Since it was (and could only have been) worked out within the

1. The best source on American constitutionalism remains Gordon Wood's *The Creation of the American Republic* (Chapel Hill, 1969; repr. New York, 1972). For a comparative history of the state constitutions, see Willi Paul Adams, *The First American Constitutions* (Chapel Hill, 1980).

paradigm of representational legitimation, having identified the tautology of representational politics left the Americans with a heavily invested challenge to the legitimacy of their own governments. Recognizing that their challenge to the British was not just a challenge to particular rulers, but rather to the fundamental validity of a legal order, the Continental Congress issued on May 15, 1776, a decree calling for the suppression of the authority of the Crown and for the establishment of new state governments 'on the authority of the people.' A peculiar crisis ensued. The present governments, like Parliament, already claimed the authority of the people in their representational character, though of course their claim to that authority became problematic because revolutionary politics depended on suspicion toward the circularity of such claims. But it also seemed that any *legal* procedures for claiming the authority of the people would have to be void along with the rest of the Crown-derived legal order. Far from being a lawyer's debate internal to law, this was a political crisis involving the legality of law. In a time of increasing military violence and crowd actions, the legal order as a whole was losing legitimacy.

In Philadelphia, as soon as word had spread of the May 15 decree, a pamphlet called *The Alarm* appeared, asking the hard question of who the 'proper persons' could be to establish a government 'on the authority of the people,' and what could be the proper 'mode of authorizing such persons?' The Assembly was claiming that right, but as the *Alarm* pointed out, the Assembly derived its legal warrant from the proprietary charter, the authority of which was now void. Were the Assembly to suppress the authority of the Crown and institute the authority of the people, it would be suppressing its own authority and instituting its own authority, and thus the Assemblymen might be 'continually making and unmaking themselves at pleasure' (p. 1). The Assembly, in other words, wasn't legal enough precisely because it was *already legal.*

For all the splendor of the argument, one has to wonder what ideal standard is being invoked against the Assembly. The very posing of the problem in the *Alarm*, in fact, offers us the spectacle of a legal order trying to legalize itself. 'It is now high time,' says the pamphlet, 'to come to some settled point, that we may call ourselves a people; for in the present unsettled state of things we are only a decent multitude. . . . We are now arrived at a period from which we are to look forward as *a legal people*' (p. 3). From decent multitude to legal people—how could this transformation come about? Better yet, how could it come about without law being there already?

The crisis symptomatized an irresolvable problem in the sovereignty of the people. The sovereignty of the people had to be appealed to as the ground for a legal order, but it could only be represented from within that legal order. As James Otis had put it in 1764, 'An original supreme Sovereign, absolute and uncontroulable, *earthly* power *must* exist in and preside over every society; from whose final decisions there can be no appeal but directly to Heaven. It is therefore *originally* and *ultimately* in the people.'[2] Originally, ultimately—but in the meantime? One reason why the Revolution has struck many observers as not being very revolutionary is that the Americans insisted at every point on the continuity of law; new governments could not be established by fiat. The common-law tradition, of course, continued; as a sphere of customary law rather than of positive, bureaucratic law, it required no original authority.[3] What needed original authority was a state

2. James Otis, *Rights of the British Colonies Asserted and Proved* (Boston, 1764).

3. The tension between revolutionary rhetoric and forms of continuity such as the doctrine of state succession is explored in Peter Onuf's *The Origins of the Federal Republic* (Philadelphia, 1983). By concentrating on the derivation of law in constitutionalism, I have not afforded space to the American understanding of state sovereignty, a subject well treated by Onuf. Although the doctrine of state succession allowed Americans to continue the legal arrangements of their pre-Revolutionary governments, they clearly regarded themselves as needing a more transcendent ground for the legitimacy of the new governments and their systems of law, and it is with the latter that I am concerned.

The distinction between customary and bureaucratic law follows Roberto Mangabeira Unger's comparative theory of law, *Law and Modern Society* (New York, 1976). One of the main differences between customary and bureaucratic law, in Unger's view, is the separation of state and society in a system of bureaucratic law. The common-law tradition did not observe that separation, as has been amply shown by William Nelson in *Americanization of the Common Law* (Cambridge, Mass., 1975). The emergence of a paradigm of sovereignty

apparatus and the legal order in which it would operate. It was in this sphere of positive, bureaucratic law that revolutionary rhetoric insisted that law had been abrogated. Some in New Hampshire, for example, believed that once royal prerogative was annulled, 'they never were a body politic in any legal sense whatever.'[4]

There is a delirious theatricality about such claims; the American crisis of law was acting out, through time, the eighteenth century's narrative of legitimation: the social contract. Once law had been relegalized by the Massachusetts constitution, for example, an orator named Thomas Dawes proclaimed that the people had successfully 'convened in a state of Nature.' 'We often read,' he said, 'of the original Contract, and of mankind, in the early ages, passing from a state of Nature to immediate Civilization. But *what eye* could penetrate through the gothic night and barbarous fable to that remote period? . . . And yet the people of Massachusetts have reduced to practice the wonderful theory.' By enacting the founding of the legal-political orders that would represent them, the people would render the origin within history and the transcendent source of law as its present practice.[5]

The crisis is therefore revealing because the difficulties encountered in generating law from nature are symptomatic of difficulties in the legal order's claim to transcendent justification; that is, to law's character of duty as opposed to force. Many of the period's most vexing problems, such as the problematic character of popular sovereignty, continue to haunt law's account of itself. As H. L. A. Hart argues in *The Concept of Law*, the people cannot be said to lay down the rules, and thus to be sovereign, because 'the rules are *constitutive* of the sovereign. . . . So we cannot say that . . . the rules specifying the procedure of the electorate represent the conditions under which the society, as so many individuals, obeys itself as an electorate; for 'itself as an electorate' is not a reference to a

in constitutionalism, along with the consequent replacement of the customary legitimacy of common law, can therefore be seen as part of the emergence of the modern state.

4. Quoted in Wood, *Creation of the American Republic*, p. 289.

5. Thomas Dawes, *Oration Delivered March 5th 1781* (Boston, 1781), pp. 20–21.

person identifiable apart from the rules.'[6] Hart concludes that a legal system cannot have a sovereign, an origin of law not itself legally constrained. Rather, it can have only rules.

Hart argues against sovereignty because he identifies it with coercion, with an account of law as orders backed by threats. Sovereignty, to him, is that point at which legality must derive from orders backed by threats, or, what comes to the same thing, from politics. His solution, however, will be subject to the same problem. Hart argues that primary rules, such as statutory law, are made law by means of secondary rules—rules of recognition that enable certain people under special conditions to establish law. In these terms, Americans of the Revolutionary period were trying, in their debates about constitution forming, to establish the secondary rules. But what rule of recognition allows one to establish or adjudicate or even reproduce a rule of recognition? Rules, as Hart himself remarks in another context (p.123), cannot provide for their own interpretation. Unless, therefore, the modern Cato is destined to plunge philosophically onto the dagger of infinite regress, it will be necessary to concede that the legality of law is not itself guaranteed by law or rules. The effectiveness of any claim to be operating according to rules will depend in the last analysis not on autonomous or self-modifying rules but on the politics of rhetoric in which rules are reproduced and altered. Hart struggles to imagine a self-contained and self-authorizing system of legality because, for him, when law's authority is seen to derive from the contingencies and irregularities of political culture it can no longer be exempt from the character of coercion.

Eighteenth-century Americans had the same dream of a self-contained system of positive law; where Hart dreams of law regulated by its own regularity, Americans pictured law justified by its derivation from the will of the people. The legal-political order would be transcendent in its authority but immanent in its source. The trick was to see how law could be given to the people transcendently and received from it immanently at the same time. Like

6. H. L. A. Hart, *The Concept of Law* (Oxford, 1961), p. 75.

Hart's, the *Alarm*'s solution for the legal origination of law was predictably disappointing. The committees of inspection, 'agreeable to the power they are already invested with,' were to call a convention for the drafting of a constitution. The pamphlet regards the authority of the committees as unproblematic, a tendency that should not be astonishing, since at some point the authority of law must always be seen as 'already invested.' Similar crises were resolved in similar ways in other colonies. The 1778 Massachusetts constitution, for example, was voted down primarily because it originated from the old House of Representatives and not a special convention; two years later, a convention-drafted constitution succeeded. Only a national pest like Noah Webster would follow the critique to its conclusion, pointing out that a convention must inevitably be 'chosen by the people in the manner they choose a legislature."[7]

If the argument for constitutional conventions thus lacked a legal and theoretical consistency—and no argument for the legal establishment of law *could* have had such a consistency—the question of how they were legitimated could only be answered politically. Why, having mounted a brilliant challenge against the Assembly's claim to originate law, did the *Alarm* simply turn around and accord that right to conventions established by virtually the same legal procedures? The explanation lies in one of the most brilliant insights in Gordon Wood's history of the period: given the colonial tradition of extralegal conventions, says Wood, the new constitutional conventions could fill their legitimating role precisely because of their inferior legality. Formed in imitation of assemblies, the conventions had long been denounced as subversions of law. They could therefore be described, as Tom Paine describes them in *Common Sense*, as 'some intermediary body between the governed and the governors, that is, between the Congress and the people.'[8] In the political culture of Revolutionary

7. Quoted in Wood, *Creation of the American Republic*, p. 379.
8. *The Complete Writings of Thomas Paine*, ed. Philip Foner, 2 vols. (New York, 1945), 1:28.

America, then, the convention was sufficiently dubious to appear unconstrained by law, and thus it could stand in the place of the sovereign.

But this is also where writing comes in. Paine's notion that the constitutional conventions would stand between 'the governed and the governors' is an invocation of the contract theory of written law, in which bills of rights or charters or the Magna Carta were supposed to embody agreements mutually constraining rulers and ruled. Yet, as Wood points out, 'bills of rights in English history had traditionally been designed to delineate the people's rights against the Crown or the ruler, not against Parliament which presumably represented the people' (p. 272). The bizarre new American project of writing charters as fundamental law for all government aimed at removing the circular legitimation of representative assemblies. But the constitutions, themselves generated 'on the authority of the people,' prescribed the procedures for claiming the authority of the people. By constituting the government, the people's text literally constitutes the people. In the concrete form of these texts, the people decides the conditions of its own embodiment. The text itself therefore becomes not only the supreme law but the only original embodiment of the people. In this act of literalization, the meaning of the charters' writtenness has been transformed; no longer merely a better way of keeping records, writing gives original existence to its author. Ecriture would save the republic.

Because the writtenness of the constitution has its source in the legitimating—and, by the same token, delegitimating—tenet of popular sovereignty, it shares a history with crowd actions, extra-legal conventions, and the intense localism of community assemblies in the 1770s and 1780s. Yet these latter movements, though motivated by the desire to maintain political sovereignty in the people rather than in the kind of supreme institution that Parliament had become, were distinctly outside the legal order. They were perceived not as manifestations of the sovereign body but rather as the breakdown of government altogether. In these contexts, 'the people' functioned as a legitimating signifier that did not entail the regularity of law. It interpellated subjects into a political world without interpellating them into the juridical order.[9] In some regions, such as Vermont and the western counties of Massachusetts, people began regularly to disobey the courts, and defended doing so by means of rigorous republican constitutional theory. Undesirable as this delegitimizing result was for American revolutionaries, it was the practical fulfillment of the necessary conditions under which the signifier of 'the people' could *legitimate* a juridical order.

Like any signifier, of course, the people could never be realizable *as such*. Yet in the Revolutionary years a wide range of collectivities, especially local assemblies, were able to recognize themselves, in action, as the people. Moreover, they were often able to sustain that self-identification legitimately in their dealings with other, similarly identified collectivities. This should not surprise us, since a people recognizing itself as the people is like a king recognizing himself as the king; we do not have to indulge in a sentimental populism to see these groups as realizations of the people. The difficulty of doing so lies in that our society's representational polity rests precisely on a recognition of the abstract and definitionally nonempirical character of the people. It is the invention of the written constitution, itself now the original and literal embodiment of the people, that ensures that the people will henceforward be nonempirical by definition. The opacity of signification has become a political fact.

By means of their customarily extralegal status, the constitutional conventions repeated the revolutionary realizations of the people, so that writing could be summoned, from a position not yet law, to become already law. It could do so partly on the very grounds of a traditional logocentric anxiety: whereas in speech

9. The term 'interpellation' comes from Louis Althusser's 'Ideology and Ideological State Apparatuses,' in his *Lenin and Philosophy* (New York, 1971), pp. 127–86. It designates the hailing of the individual that always renders the individual as a subject within an ideology. (See note 22 below.)

persons, hearing themselves speak, are present to themselves and therefore responsible for their language, writing migrates from persons arbitrarily. Rousseau, for example, cites this determination of language to argue for the necessity of speech for any realization of the people in a republic. 'I maintain,' he writes in the *Essay on the Origin of Languages*, 'that any language in which it is not possible to make oneself understood by the people assembled is a servile language; it is impossible for a people to remain free and speak that language.' The classical republics survived because 'among the ancients it was easy to be heard by the people in a public square'; by contrast, writing is the mark of modern corruption: 'Popular languages have become as thoroughly useless as has eloquence. Societies have assumed their final forms: nothing can be changed in them anymore except by arms and cash, and since there is nothing left to say to the people but *give money*, it is said with posters on street corners or with soldiers in private homes; for this there is no need to assemble anyone; on the contrary, subjects must be kept scattered; that is the first maxim of modern politics.'[10] As Derrida observes of Rousseau, 'Praise of the "assembled people" at the festival or at the political forum is always a critique of representation. The legitimizing instance, in the city as in language—speech or writing—and in the arts, is the representer present in person: source of legitimacy and sacred origin.'[11]

In contrast, the Americans who prevailed in the constitutional movement were those who regarded their task not as getting rid of representation, but of deriving representation in the first place. The presence of the people to themselves in oral assembly was for them not legitimate enough precisely because it was recognized as the *source* of legitimacy. As source, or sovereign, it was by definition not legally constrained. The speech heard by the assembled people, in the words of the Boston *Independent Chronicle*, could only come from men 'with the *vox populi vox Dei* in their mouths.'[12]

10. Jean-Jacques Rousseau, *The First and Second Discourses and Essay on the Origin of Languages*, trans. Victor Gourevitch (New York, 1986), pp. 294–95.

11. Jacques Derrida, *Of Grammatology*, trans. Gayatri Spivak (Baltimore, 1976), p. 296.

12. Quoted in Wood, *Creation of the American Republic*, p. 369.

In this view, the vox populi, in order to be the vox Dei, cannot be in anybody's mouth because the owner of the mouth, as embodiment of the sovereign, would not be a constrained subject. What was needed was the derivative afterwards of writing. By articulating a nonempirical agency to replace empirical realizations of the people, writing came to be the hinge between a delegitimizing revolutionary politics and a nonrevolutionary, already legal signification of the people.

Written constitutions, including the federal Constitution of 1787, completed a deployment of writing that had already begun with the Declaration of Independence. The best account of that earlier deployment comes to us from the unlikely source of Jacques Derrida, in a set of prefatory and not entirely serious remarks given at the University of Virginia during the Declaration's bicentennial. Derrida notes the paradox that documents such as the Declaration, or the Constitution, should be signed. 'In principle,' he observes, 'an institution is obliged, in its history and in its tradition, in its permanence and thus in its very institutionality, to render itself independent from the empirical individuals who have taken part in its production'; nevertheless, 'the founding act of an institution—the act as archive equally with the act as performance—must retain the signature within it.' Derrida will attribute the felt need for the founding signature to 'the structure of the institutive language.' But for such a purpose, he asks, 'whose signature could be legitimate?'[13]

Derrida observes that although Jefferson wrote the Declaration, he did so not in his own right but by delegation from the other delegates, who then revised his draft and put their names to it. But they in turn put their names to it not in their own right but 'in the name and by authority of the good people of these . . . free and independent states':

> By rights, then, the signatory is the people, the 'good' people. . . . It is the 'good people' that declares itself free and independent by the relays of its representatives of representatives. One cannot decide—

13. Jacques Derrida, *Otobiographies* (Paris, 1984), p. 17 (my translation).

> and it is all the interest, the strength, and the impact of such a declarative act—whether the independence is stated or produced by this statement. . . . Is it the case that the good people is already freed in fact and does nothing but acts out its emancipation by the Declaration? Or rather does it liberate itself at the instant and by the signature of the Declaration? . . . Such then is the 'good people' which is not engaged and only engaged in signing, in causing to sign its own declaration. The 'we' of the Declaration speaks 'in the name of the people.' But this people does not exist. It does not exist *before* this declaration, not *as such*. If it is given birth, as a free and independent subject, as a possible signatory, that can only depend on the act of this signature. The signature invents the signatory. The latter can only authorize to sign once it has arrived at the goal, so to speak, of its signature, in a sort of fabulous retroactivity. Its first signature authorizes to sign. . . . In signing, the people speaks—and does what it says to do, but in deferring it by the intermediation of its representations, whose representativeness is only fully legitimated by the signature, and thus after the fact. . . . By this fabulous event, by this fable which is implicated in the trace and is in truth possible only by the inadequacy of a present to itself, a signature is given a name. (pp. 20–23)

In this mention of the trace and the inadequacy of the present, Derrida's philosophical concerns become visible, and he will pursue his teasing remarks only in that direction, through a discussion of Nietzsche. Yet the paradox he identifies in the Declaration is perhaps not just a tease or a philosopher's puzzle, and Derrida indicates in passing a couple of ways in which it raises a serious issue. The puzzle of the relation between the authorizing people and the authorized signature that creates the people's authority, Derrida remarks, 'is not a matter here of an obscurity or a difficulty of interpretation, a problematic on the way toward a solution. It is not a matter of a difficult analysis that founders before the structure of implied acts and the overdetermined temporality of events. This obscurity, this indecidability between, let us say, a performative structure and a constative structure, is *required* in order to produce the effect sought for. It is essential to the very position of law [droit] as such, that one speaks here of hypocrisy, of equivocation, of indecidability or of fiction' (p. 21).

Derrida suggests, in other words, that the paradox of the authorized and authorizing signature replicates the contradiction that we have already observed in the notion of sovereignty. By saying that it is 'essential to the very position of law as such,' however, he means that the effect is not simply that of the founding moment produced by the Americans' theatrical claim that they had reverted to the state of nature. The word 'droit,' essential for his assertion here, denotes at once law and right, commandment and authorization to command. In the systems of positive law that characterize modern society—systems of law, let us say, not underwritten by God—law is defined by its derivation of authority from itself.

The contrast with divine authority may clarify the position of the written constitution as fundamental American law. Paine refers to the written constitution, in *The Rights of Man*, as a 'political bible.' It is no accidental turn of phrase. When the Declaration asserts that the states 'are and ought to be' free and independent, Derrida notes (p.27) that the 'and,' which 'articulates and conjoins here the two discursive modalities of is and ought, statement and prescription, fact and law,' occupies the position of God. 'Are and ought to be' is like the divinely imperative and creative 'Be,' which human authority can approximate in an indicative 'is' or a subjunctive 'ought.'[14] For a legal system to derive its legality immanently rather than transcendently, therefore, requires the effect of textuality that collapses the two modes. The Constitution deploys that effect most notably in the preamble: 'We the People . . . do constitute. . . .' Legality rides on the inability to decide whether the people constitute the government already—that is, in fact—or in the future, as it were by prescription.

In order to be the law to the law, however, the people must

14. William Nelson's study of the law in Massachusetts affords an illustration of this point. According to Nelson, pre-Revolutionary legislation was almost always justified by preambles that explained the continuity of the statute with common law. Beginning with the ratification of a written constitution, however, the legislature began to shift its self-understanding so that by the 1790s 'legislation was coming to rest solely on a "be it enacted" clause—a naked assertion of sovereign legislative power.' Nelson, *Americanization of the Common Law*, p. 91.

occupy this textual position themselves, and not by the relays of representatives who sign for them in the Declaration. It is for this reason that it was of utmost importance that the legal political order be constituted not just by a written text, but by a printed one. In the important 1776 pamphlet called *Four Letters on Interesting Subjects*, which along with *Common Sense* was among the first to argue for a written constitution, we read that 'all constitutions should be contained in some written Charter, but *that* Charter should be the act of *all* and not of *one man*.' The specific negative reference here is to Pennsylvania's proprietary charter, granted by the Crown; such charters are inappropriate models, the pamphlet suggests, because they emanate from the authority of persons, and are thus 'a species of tyranny, because they substitute the will of ONE as the law for ALL.'[15] Since it is not clear how any concrete act could be the act of all, the obscurity of agency in print was helpful as the enabling pretext for a constitution.

In *Common Sense*, Paine similarly suggests that the people might charter their own government. It is this suggestion that occasions the famous passage in which he imagines a solemn day for 'proclaiming the charter,' on which the charter will be brought forth and crowned so that the world will know that 'in America the law is king.' 'But lest any ill use should afterwards arise,' he adds in a revealing afterthought, 'let the crown at the conclusion of the ceremony be demolished, and scattered among the people whose right it is.' The political motives for this vivid image of the smashed and scattered crown would become the meaning of the printed artifact on the constitution. By the time of *Rights of Man*, Paine would be laying great emphasis on the constitution's printed condition, detailing carefully the procedures of printing proposed constitutions for the people's approval. Similarly, he notes with satisfaction that, once approved in Pennsylvania, the state constitution had been properly scattered. 'Scarcely a family was without

15. Anonymous, *Four Letters on Interesting Subjects* (Philadelphia, 1776), reprinted in Charles S. Hyneman and Donald S. Lutz, eds., *American Political Writing during the Founding Era*, 2 vols. (Indianapolis, 1983), 1:381–82.

it. Every member of the Government had a copy; and nothing was more common when any debate arose on the principle of a bill, or on the extent of any species of authority, than for the members to take the printed Constitution out of their pocket, and read the chapter with which such matter in debate was connected.'[16] When every representative is able to pull the people out of his pocket to receive his charter, then is law law.

The procedure of printing the Constitution for reference was undergone twice during the proceedings of the federal convention (after the reports of the committees of detail and style), in order that each delegate might be sure of identical wording. The procedure guaranteed that the Constitution would be a general creation. Franklin's motion for unanimity similarly indicates the importance of nonparticular authorship; when his famous speech failed to obtain the assent of every delegate, Franklin proposed that the document be signed by 'unanimous consent' of the states. By this stratagem, signing the Constitution did not amount to endorsing it personally. And thus, whereas the climactic moment for the Declaration of Independence was the signing, for the Constitution the climactic moment was the maneuver that deprived signing of personal meaning. For the same reason, where the signed copy of the Declaration continues to be a national fetish, from which printed copies can only be derived imitations, the Constitution found its ideal form in every printed copy, beginning—though not specially—with its initial publication, in the place of the weekly news copy of the *Pennsylvania Packet*.

The printedness of the Constitution allows it to emanate from no one in particular and thus from the people. It is worth stressing, however, that this meaning for print is a determinate feature of political culture, not a transcendently secured logic.[17] The Con-

16. Paine, *Rights of Man*, in Foner, ed., *Complete Writings*, 1:378.

17. I emphasize that even the nature of print is a contingent element of culture in order to distinguish my argument from the technological determinism that one finds in studies of print by Elizabeth Eisenstein, Marshall McLuhan, Walter Ong, Jack Goody, and Alvin Kernan. These studies, different though they are, have in common the assumption that print exerts a causative force independent of the political/cultural determinations of print discourse.

stitution derives from particular persons as much as speech or script do. We know their names—compilers, printers, and printing-shop journeymen included. Only contingent structures of meaning ensure that such filiations will lack the status of the filiatons of other kinds of language. Among these structures we may count the emergent paradigm of representational legitimacy, with its newly literal and literalizable notion of the sovereignty of the people. We may also include a republican paradigm of public discourse that for several decades had informed perceptions of print in America.

Developed in practices of literacy that included the production and consumption of newspapers, broadsides, pamphlets, legal documents, and books, the republican ideology of print arranged the values of generality over those of the personal. In this cognitive vocabulary, the social diffusion of printed artifacts took on the investment of the disinterested virtue of the public orientation, as opposed to the corrupting interests and passions of particular and local persons.[18] *The Alarm*, quoted earlier, is a good example. It argues that one reason why the Assembly should be disqualified from writing a constitution is that its members have a 'private interest' in the positions to be established under such a constitution. Offering itself as a contrast, the anonymous *Alarm* proclaims: 'The persons who recommend this, are Fellow-Citizens with yourselves. They have no private views; no interest to establish for themselves. Their aim, end and wish is the happiness of the Community. He who dares say otherwise, let him step forth, and prove it; for, conscious of the purity of our intentions, we challenge the world' (p. 3). 'We,' however, do so anonymously, in print, while the doubtless corrupt challenger is imagined to speak and stand forth in person. Anonymity, in the republican culture of print, does not designate cowardice, but public virtue. The arguments of the

18. I have argued this point in more detail in 'Franklin and the Letters of the Republic,' *Representations* 16 (1986): 110–30. For an excellent discussion of the interest/disinterest opposition in the constitutional period, see Gordon Wood, 'Interests and Disinterestedness in the Making of the Constitution,' in Richard Beeman et al., eds., *Beyond Confederation: Origins of the Constitution and American National Identity* (Chapel Hill, 1987), pp. 69–109.

The Pennsylvania Packet, *and Daily Advertiser.*

[Price Four-Pence.] WEDNESDAY, SEPTEMBER 19, 1787. [No. 2690.]

WE, the People of the United States, in order to form a more perfect Union, establish Justice, insure domestic Tranquility, provide for the common Defence, promote the General Welfare, and secure the Blessings of Liberty to Ourselves and our Posterity, do ordain and establish this Constitution for the United States of America.

ARTICLE I.

Sect. 1. ALL legislative powers herein granted shall be vested in a Congress of the United States, which shall consist of a Senate and House of Representatives.

Sect. 2. The House of Representatives shall be composed of members chosen every second year by the people of the several states, and the electors in each state shall have the qualifications requisite for electors of the most numerous branch of the state legislature.

No person shall be a representative who shall not have attained to the age of twenty-five years, and been seven years a citizen of the United States, and who shall not, when elected, be an inhabitant of that state in which he shall be chosen.

Representatives and direct taxes shall be apportioned among the several states which may be included within this Union, according to their respective numbers, which shall be determined by adding to the whole number of free persons, including those bound to service for a term of years, and excluding Indians not taxed, three-fifths of all other persons. The actual enumeration shall be made within three years after the first meeting of the Congress of the United States, and within every subsequent term of ten years, in such manner as they shall by law direct. The number of representatives shall not exceed one for every thirty thousand, but each state shall have at least one representative; and until such enumeration shall be made, the state of New-Hampshire shall be entitled to chuse three, Massachusetts eight, Rhode-Island and Providence Plantations one, Connecticut five, New-York six, New-Jersey four, Pennsylvania eight, Delaware one, Maryland six, Virginia ten, North-Carolina five, South-Carolina five, and Georgia three.

When vacancies happen in the representation from any state, the Executive authority thereof shall issue writs of election to fill such vacancies.

The House of Representatives shall chuse their Speaker and other officers; and shall have the sole power of impeachment.

Sect. 3. The Senate of the United States shall be composed of two senators from each state, chosen by the legislature thereof, for six years; and each senator shall have one vote.

Immediately after they shall be assembled in consequence of the first election, they shall be divided as equally as may be into three classes. The seats of the senators of the first class shall be vacated at the expiration of the second year, of the second class at the expiration of the fourth year, and of the third class at the expiration of the sixth year, so that one-third may be chosen every second year; and if vacancies happen by resignation, or otherwise, during the recess of the Legislature of any state, the Executive thereof may make temporary appointments until the next meeting of the Legislature, which shall then fill such vacancies.

No person shall be a senator who shall not have attained to the age of thirty years, and been nine years a citizen of the United States, and who shall not, when elected, be an inhabitant of that state for which he shall be chosen.

The Vice-President of the United States shall be President of the senate, but shall have no vote, unless they be equally divided.

The Senate shall chuse their other officers, and also a President pro tempore, in the absence of the Vice-President, or when he shall exercise the office of President of the United States.

The Senate shall have the sole power to try all impeachments. When sitting for that purpose, they shall be on oath or affirmation. When the President of the United States is tried, the Chief Justice shall preside: And no person shall be convicted without the concurrence of two-thirds of the members present.

Judgment in cases of impeachment shall not extend further than to removal from office, and disqualification to hold and enjoy any office of honor, trust or profit under the United States; but the party convicted shall nevertheless be liable and subject to indictment, trial, judgment and punishment, according to law.

Sect. 4. The times, places and manner of holding elections for senators and representatives, shall be prescribed in each state by the legislature thereof; but the Congress may at any time by law make or alter such regulations, except as to the places of chusing Senators.

The Congress shall assemble at least once in every year, and such meeting shall be on the first Monday in December, unless they shall by law appoint a different day.

Sect. 5. Each house shall be the judge of the elections, returns and qualifications of its own members, and a majority of each shall constitute a quorum to do business; but a smaller number may adjourn from day to day, and may be authorised to compel the attendance of absent members, in such manner, and under such penalties as each house may provide.

Each house may determine the rules of its proceedings, punish its members for disorderly behaviour, and, with the concurrence of two-thirds, expel a member.

Each house shall keep a journal of its proceedings, and from time to time publish the same, excepting such parts as may in their judgment require secrecy; and the yeas and nays of the members of either house on any question shall, at the desire of one-fifth of those present, be entered on the journal.

Neither house, during the session of Congress, shall, without the consent of the other, adjourn for more than three days, nor to any other place than that in which the two houses shall be sitting.

Sect. 6. The senators and representatives shall receive a compensation for their services, to be ascertained by law, and paid out of the treasury of the United States. They shall in all cases, except treason, felony and breach of the peace, be privileged from arrest during their attendance at the session of their respective houses, and in going to and returning from the same; and for any speech or debate in either house, they shall not be questioned in any other place.

No senator or representative shall, during the time for which he was elected, be appointed to any civil office under the authority of the United States, which shall have been created, or the emoluments whereof shall have been encreased during such time; and no person holding any office under the United States, shall be a member of either house during his continuance in office.

Sect. 7. All bills for raising revenue shall originate in the house of representatives; but the senate may propose or concur with amendments as on other bills.

Every bill which shall have passed the house of representatives and the senate, shall, before it become a law, be presented to the president of the United States; if he approve he shall sign it, but if not he shall return it, with his objections to that house in which it shall have originated, who shall enter the objections at large on their journal, and proceed to reconsider it. If after such reconsideration two-thirds of that house shall agree to pass the bill, it shall be sent, together with the objections, to the other house, by which it shall likewise be reconsidered, and if approved by two-thirds of that house, it shall become a law. But in all such cases the votes of both houses shall

Fig. 1. *The first publication of the Constitution, in the* Pennsylvania Packet, *September 19, 1787. Note the relative type size of the preamble. American Antiquarian Society.*

Alarm are vouched for by the claim to disinterested concern for the general good, and that claim is in turn vouched for by the perceived conditions of the very medium in which it is made. And if such assumptions on the part of the unnamed 'we' of the *Alarm* seem to be determinate features of a political culture, it will be remembered that the same assumptions enable the unnamed 'we' of the Constitution. They will also be seen animating the ratification debates, especially in the aggressive print campaign of the 'Publius' who stands forth in the Federalist papers.

For all the power of the republican paradigm of print discourse, it hardly replaced the more familiar logocentric determinations of language. Readers of the *Alarm*, even while according validity to its rhetorical self-presentation, might have speculated about the authors' identities and their private views. The same is true, as we know, of the Constitution. Its composers, unlike those of the *Alarm*, did not refuse to subscribe their names, though after Franklin's motion they deliberately ambiguated the significance of their subscriptions. It was not unusual for copies of the Constitution to omit the names, printing only the approved resolutions of unanimity. That the generality of the printed language be seen as more important than the signatures was crucial to the legitimation of the document.

Some of the document's detractors, from that time to the present, have not refrained from reading its significance as determined by the private interests of those men. By the same token, many of the document's professed admirers also adduce, for *their* interpretations, views about the private interests of the subscribing individuals, though interests in this case are redescribed as intentions. The present attorney general of the United States, for one, believes the proclaimed derivation of the Constitution's authority in the preamble to be uncreditable. In his view, all official hermeneutics of the text should be governed by the intentions of the particular men who signed it on September 17, 1787, in Philadelphia—long before its ratification. Given the eighteenth-century republican understanding of the Constitution as fundamental law expressing the authority of the people, Attorney General Meese's understanding of constitutional validity would have to be seen as transforming the document into the kind of charter that *Four Letters on Interesting Subjects* calls tyranny, for the simple reason that it derives authority in the last instance from the will of the so-called founders—specifically, from the supposed mental contents of those founders—rather than from the people, who were at the time the only legitimate founders. In other words, the Constitution would never have been ratified had it been perceived as the kind of document that Meese thinks it is. The Meese brand of intentionalism could only take hold once a nationalist filiopietism had supplanted the radical republicanism that initially legitimated the constitutional order. The amnesia of that shift in legitimacy paradigms demonstrates the historical specificity of the cultural assumptions that allowed the printed constitution to embody the will of all. As one South Carolinian put it in 1783, 'What people in their senses would make the judges, who are fallible men, depositaries of the law; when the easy, reasonable method of printing, at once secures its perpetuity, and divulges it to those who ought in justice to be made acquainted with it.'[19]

But, as this last passage makes clear, in allowing the expression of the will of all, the printedness of the constitution not only underwrites, so to speak, the popular *authorship* of the constitution, but also summons the *readership* of the print audience to recertify it continually and universally. As with the authorship, the readership of the constitution is more than a convenience or mere exigency, and in an important sense is structurally required by representational legitimacy. The same textuality that was essential to the constitution of law's authority inhabits equally the position of the subject under the law, in that it provides a necessary ambiguation of consent. For the constitution, readership is to authorship as consent is to sovereignty. Popular sovereignty, which avoids domination by allowing that all subjects of the legal order will take their place as the sources of law, necessarily requires a notion of

19. Quoted in Wood, *Creation of the American Republic*, pp. 302–3.

consent, in which the people who give law vow that they will take their place as its subjects. The two parts of sovereignty and consent correspond, then, to the compulsory and voluntary aspects of duty. It is to give law the character of duty that republican political rhetoric insists on the foundation of politics in popular sovereignty and popular consent. Thus the predicament of sovereignty in the Revolutionary period was everywhere implicated with a problem of consent.

Revolutionary rhetoric required Americans to be very good at using the word 'consent' to mean both authorization and compliance at once, as when the *Boston Evening Post* proclaimed in 1765 that 'the only moral foundation of government is, the consent of the people'; in that phrase, 'consent' must be redundant for 'moral foundation' or redundant for 'government'—or rather, both simultaneously.[20] On one hand, to say that people consent to the law is tautologous, since consent from this point of view designates what Weber calls 'validity': the belief in a norm by the members of a society. Consent of this variety does not confer any lasting authority on law, but just *is* the authority of law; it is either continually reproduced or law loses legitimacy. On the other hand, in a system of positive law and popular sovereignty, consent is adduced to justify the enforcement of norms even where they are not believed—that is to say, where they are not taken as duty—or those norms obviously would not be law. But this second variety of consent is narrativized; it is the moment at the origin of law in which the coercive character of law is forsworn in advance. Unlike the voluntary aspect of duty, which by nature cannot be instituted as positive law, authorizing consent is thus consent to one's own coercion, contradiction in terms though that might be.

For the American republicans, it was self-evident that a law could not be law by reason of someone else's consent; in a letter to Madison in 1789, Jefferson took this to mean that 'no society can make a perpetual constitution, or even a perpetual law.' Madison's response astutely realizes that a doctrine of actual consent

20. Ibid., p. 182.

would not only prevent one generation from legislating for another—this, it will be recalled, is Paine's justification for revolution—but will prevent the majority from legislating for the minority. 'Strict Theory,' he observes, 'at all times presupposes the assent of every member to the establishment of the rule itself.' But, asked John Adams, when he sensed the same implications, 'Shall we say that every individual of the community, old and young, male and female, as well as rich and poor, must consent, expressly, to every act of legislation?' 'I find no relief from these consequences,' Madison wrote, 'but in the received doctrine that a tacit assent may be given to established Constitutions and laws, and that this assent may be inferred, where no positive dissent appears.' Indeed, he went on, 'May it not be questioned whether it be possible to exclude wholly the idea of tacit assent, without subverting the foundation of civil Society?' Madison, Adams, and Jefferson were understandably worried about this conclusion, because it retroactively denied the legitimacy of the Revolution and, more to the point, left the present order without transcendent legality. *Every* extant legal order is justified by tacit assent, which is to say that no legal order is *justified* at all.[21]

The written constitution mediates this crisis in perpetuity—the only way it could be mediated. In the preamble, the reading citizen interpellates himself—even herself—into the juridical order precisely at its foundation. Whereas Meese's sacralizing intentionalism makes the foundational moment the finite intentions of the patriarchs, the ongoing consumption of the preamble in print makes the moment of foundation perpetual and socially undifferentiated. Not only does it enact the consent of every citizen—male and female, old and young, black and white, rich and poor—it also reads that consent as the transcendent grounds of subjection. We might say that the printedness of the constitution here restores

21. Jefferson to Madison, September 6, 1789, *The Papers of Thomas Jefferson*, ed. Julian Boyd et al., (Princeton, 1950–), 15:392–97; Madison to Jefferson, February 4, 1790, *The Papers of James Madison*, ed. William Hutchinson et al., (Chicago, 1962–77 [vols. 1–10]; Charlottesville, 1977–), 13:18–21; John Adams, quoted in Wood, *Creation of the American Republic*, p. 182.

to the dutifulness of law the permanence that consent had narrativized. By the same token, the 'we' of the constitution—and this is essential for its legitimating effect—is speaking *to itself.* The evidently untraced origins and universal audience of the printed text allow the people always to be both authoring and reading, and thus giving and receiving its commands at once. Unlike Rousseau's general will, which similarly derives its obligatory character from the simultaneity of its common origin and common object, the printed constitution is a mechanism whereby the transcendent conditions of legality are translated into a system of positive law. In this sovereign interpellation the people are always coming across themselves in the act of consenting to their own coercion.

I say 'their' own coercion, but of course this is what the Constitution will not allow me to say. There is no legitimate representational space outside of the constitutive we. When someone calls out to the people, you will answer.[22] You inhabit the people, but this is not true of any group to which you belong, the people being the site where all lesser collectivities are evacuated. For this reason, the preamble contributes to a nationalist imagination in the same way that Benedict Anderson has argued for novels and print in general.[23] It is by means of print discourse that we have come to imagine a community simultaneous with but not proximate to ourselves: separate persons having the same relation to a corporate body realized only metonymically. The national community of the constitutional 'we' is thus an aspect of the people's abstractness, and may be contrasted with the intense localism of the popular assemblies that were its main rival for the role of the people.[24]

22. My wording here is meant to echo Althusser's explanation of interpellation (see note 9 above). Ideology, he writes, 'transforms the individuals into subjects (it transforms them all) by that very precise operation which I have called interpellation or hailing, and which can be imagined along the lines of the most commonplace everyday police (or other) hailing: "Hey, you there!" Assuming that the theoretical scene I have imagined takes place in the street, the hailed individual will turn round. By this mere one-hundred-and-eighty-degree physical conversion, he becomes a ***subject***. Why? Because he has recognized that the hail was "really" addressed to him, and that "it was ***really him*** who was hailed" (and not someone else)' (p .174).

23. Benedict Anderson, ***Imagined Communities*** (London, 1983).

24. The ratification parades that were held in some cities, notably in Boston, provide

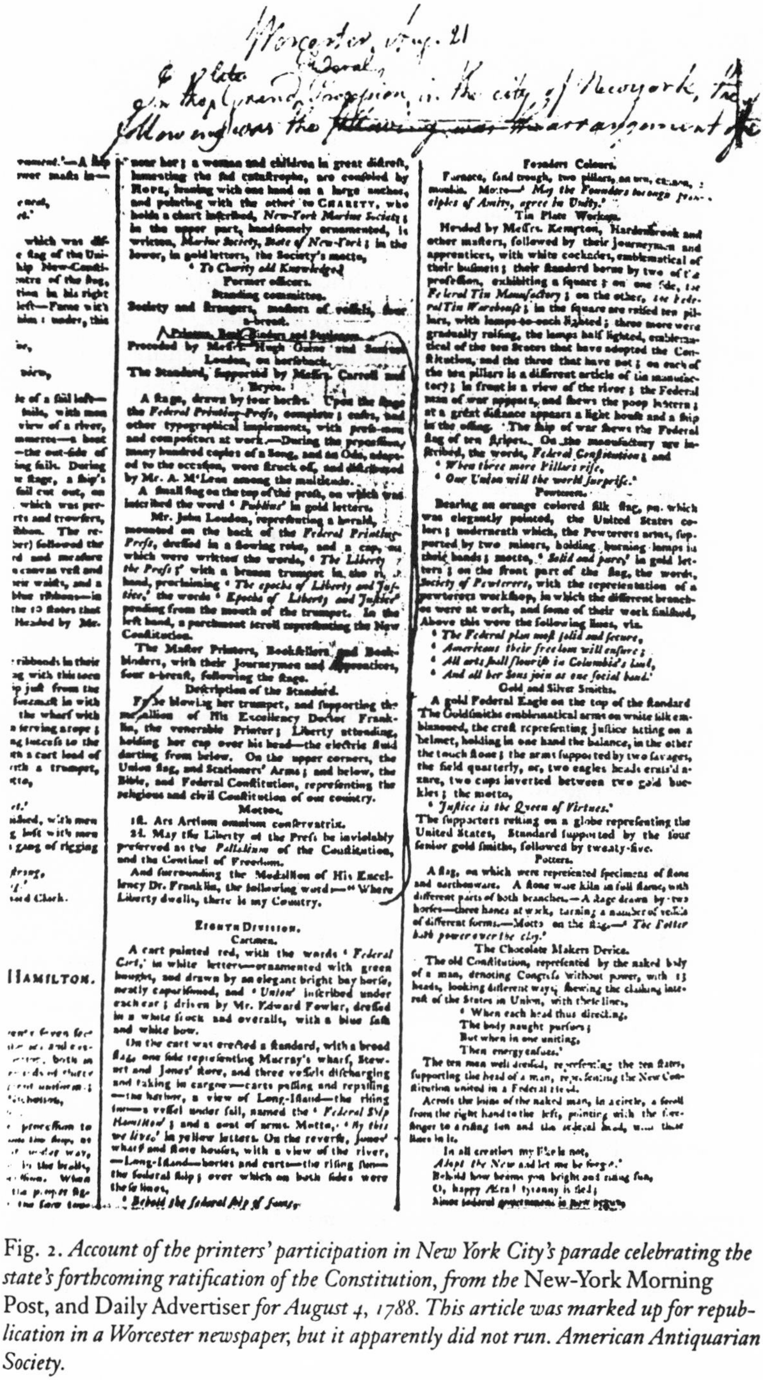

Worcester, Aug. 21

in the Grand Procession in the city of Newyork, the following was the arrangement

near her; a woman and children in great distress, lamenting the sad catastrophe, are consoled by HOPE, leaning with one hand on a large anchor, and pointing with the other to CHARITY, who holds a chart inscribed, *New-York Marine Society*; in the upper part, handsomely ornamented, is written, *Marine Society, State of New-York*; in the lower, in gold letters, the Society's motto,

'*To Charity add Knowledge*'

Former officers.

Standing committee.

Society and strangers, masters of vessels, four a-breast.

Printers, Book-binders and Stationers.

Preceded by Messrs. Hugh Gaine and Samuel Loudon, on horseback.

The Standard, supported by Messrs. Carroll and Bryce.

A stage, drawn by four horses. Upon the stage the *Federal Printing-Press*, complete; cases, and other typographical implements, with press-men and compositors at work.—During the procession, many hundred copies of a Song, and an Ode, adapted to the occasion, were struck off, and distributed by Mr. A. M'Lean among the multitude.

A small flag on the top of the press, on which was inscribed the word '*Publius*' in gold letters.

Mr. John Loudon, representing a herald, mounted on the back of the *Federal Printing-Press*, dressed in a flowing robe, and a cap, on which were written the words, '*The Liberty of the Press*;' with a brazen trumpet in the right hand, proclaiming '*The epocha of Liberty and Justice*,' the words '*Epocha of Liberty and Justice*' pending from the mouth of the trumpet. In the left hand, a parchment scroll representing the New Constitution.

The Master Printers, Booksellers, and Book-binders, with their Journeymen and Apprentices, four a-breast, following the stage.

Description of the Standard.

Fame blowing her trumpet, and supporting the medallion of His Excellency Doctor Franklin, the venerable Printer; Liberty attending, holding her cap over his head—the electric fluid darting from below. On the upper corners, the Union flag, and Stationers' Arms; and below, the Bible, and Federal Constitution, representing the religious and civil Constitution of our country.

Mottoe.

1st. Ars Artium omnium conservatrix.

2d. May the Liberty of the Press be inviolably preserved as the *Palladium* of the Constitution, and the Centinel of Freedom.

And surrounding the Medallion of His Excellency Dr. Franklin, the following words—"Where Liberty dwells, there is my Country.

EIGHTH DIVISION.

Cartmen.

A cart painted red, with the words '*Federal Cart*,' in white letters—ornamented with green boughs, and drawn by an elegant bright bay horse, neatly caparisoned, and '*Union*' inscribed under each ear; driven by Mr. Edward Fowler, dressed in a white frock and overalls, with a blue sash and white bow.

On the cart was erected a standard, with a broad flag, one side representing Murray's wharf, Stewart and Jones' store, and three vessels discharging and taking in cargoes—carts passing and repassing—the harbor, a view of Long-Island—the rising sun—a vessel under sail, named the '*Federal Ship Hamilton*'; and a coat of arms. Motto, '*By this we live*,' in yellow letters. On the reverse, Jones' wharf and store houses, with a view of the river,—Long-Island—horses and carts—the rising sun—the federal ship; over which on both sides were these lines,

'*Behold the federal ship of fame*,

Founders Colours.

Furnace, sand trough, two pillars, an urn, cannon, mould. Motto—'*May the Founders through principles of Amity, agree in Unity*.'

Tin Plate Workers.

Headed by Messrs. Kempton, Hardenbrook and other masters, followed by their journeymen and apprentices, with white cockades, emblematical of their business; their standard borne by two of the profession, exhibiting a square; on one side, *the Federal Tin Manufactory*; on the other, *the Federal Tin Warehouse*; in the square are raised ten pillars, with lamps to each lighted; three more were gradually raising, the lamps half lighted, emblematical of the ten States that have adopted the Constitution, and the three that have not; on each of the ten pillars is a different article of tin manufactory; in front is a view of the river; the Federal man of war appears, and shews the poop lantern; at a great distance appears a light house and a ship in the offing. The ship of war shews the Federal flag of ten stripes. On the manufactory are inscribed, the words, *Federal Constitution*; and

'*When three more Pillars rise,*

'*Our Union will the world surprise*.'

Pewterers.

Bearing an orange colored silk flag, on which was elegantly painted, the United States colors; underneath which, the Pewterers arms, supported by two miners, holding burning lamps in their hands; motto, '*Solid and pure*,' in gold letters; on the front part of the flag, the words, *Society of Pewterers*, with the representation of a pewterers workshop, in which the different branches were at work, and some of their work finished, Above this were the following lines, viz.

'*The Federal plan most solid and secure,*

'*Americans their freedom will ensure;*

'*All arts shall flourish in Columbia's land,*

'*And all her Sons join as one social band*.'

Gold and Silver Smiths.

A gold Federal Eagle on the top of the standard The Goldsmiths emblematical arms on white silk emblazoned, the crest representing Justice sitting on a helmet, holding in one hand the balance, in the other the touch stone; the arms supported by two savages, the field quarterly, or, two eagles heads erais'd azure, two cups inverted between two gold buckles; the motto,

'*Justice is the Queen of Virtues*.'

The supporters resting on a globe representing the United States, Standard supported by the four senior gold smiths, followed by twenty-five.

Potters.

A flag, on which were represented specimens of stone and earthenware. A stone ware kiln in full flame, with different parts of both branches.—A stage drawn by two horses—three hands at work, turning a number of vessels of different forms.—Motto on the flag—'*The Potter hath power over the clay*.'

The Chocolate Makers Device.

The old Constitution, represented by the naked body of a man, denoting Congress without power, with 13 heads, looking different ways, shewing the clashing interest of the States in Union, with these lines,

'When each head thus directing,
The body naught pursues;
But when in one uniting,
Then energy ensues.'

The ten men well dressed, representing the ten states, supporting the head of a man, representing the New Constitution united in a Federal Head.

Across the loins of the naked man, in a circle, a scroll from the right hand to the left, pointing with the fore-finger to a rising sun and the federal head, were these lines in it.

In all creation my like is not,
Adopt the New and let me be forgot.'
Behold how beams you bright and rising sun,
O, happy Æra! tyranny is fled;
Since federal government is now begun.

Fig. 2. *Account of the printers' participation in New York City's parade celebrating the state's forthcoming ratification of the Constitution, from the* New-York Morning Post, and Daily Advertiser *for August 4, 1788. This article was marked up for republication in a Worcester newspaper, but it apparently did not run. American Antiquarian Society.*

For several decades before the Constitution, print had in its political uses been acquiring the ability to serve as a means of imagining the public sphere. The simultaneity of the artifacts of political print discourse expressed the identity of this sphere that was no longer local. Eventually, although this abstract public sphere was articulated with republican categories of generality, disinterested virtue, and civic liberty, it would enable a modern national state that was more appropriate to liberal individualism. By way of conclusion, then, I would like to suggest that the deployment of textuality in the Constitution, though itself profoundly republican, marks the emergence also of a new mode of textuality.

The commission of sovereignty to its literalization in print required from American political culture a high degree of confidence in the transparency of language and the undifferentiated universality of print. 'No man is a true republican,' says *Four Letters on Interesting Subjects*, 'or worthy of that name, that will not give up his single voice to that of the public.'[25] The voicing strategies of the written constitution are registered here as the liberty of the social contract. Here also we can see most clearly the relation between the legitimating drama of sovereignty that gave rise to the Constitution and the official hermeneutics that resulted from it. Hermeneutics, as John Marshall makes clear in his analysis of the Constitution's writtenness, gives the law exactly in the act of receiving the law: 'The powers of the legislature are defined and limited; and that those limits may not be forgotten, the constitution is written. . . . Certainly, all those who have framed written constitutions contemplate them as forming the fundamental and paramount law of the nation, and consequently, the theory of every such government must be, that an act of the legislature, repugnant to the constitution, is void. This theory is essentially

---

an interesting case in which these two modes for the realization of the public are sutured together. In the parades, printing presses were dragged through the streets on wagons, being worked en route by pressmen who distributed the products to the crowd. The civic populace and the abstract public of print are here called to bear witness to each other in a way that may be without parallel. (See fig. 2.)

25. In Hyneman and Lutz, *American Political Writing*, 1:386.

attached to a written constitution, and is, consequently, to be considered, by this court, as one of the fundamental principles of our society.'[26] Marshall's decision establishes the principle of judicial review precisely by denying that the court can make law: 'the courts, as well as other departments, are bound by' the written Constitution. Giving the law in receiving it, official hermeneutics repeats, albeit in a very different mode, the sovereign consent of the Constitution.

Official hermeneutics thus constructs a relation between the subject and the text that must be registered as mediation. There language, far from being transparent, has become in its ambiguity the site of conflict even while the resolution of that conflict must be received from an authority immanent in the language. In a letter of 1814, Gouverneur Morris expresses disbelief at the new state of constitutional textuality. For him, the existence of 'a written constitution containing unequivocal provisions and limitations' should have eliminated all difficulty of meaning. Interpreting the Constitution, he writes, 'must be done by comparing the plain import of the words with the general tenor and object of the instrument.' He then adds, evidently in support of his position, 'That instrument was written by the fingers which write this letter.' The curious thing about it is that he does *not* appeal to his intentions as founder, but to the act of writing as testament to the clarity of the written text. But because authority was now to be received from its already mediated condition, Morris's somewhat comical confidence in, as it were, the indexical value of his fingers had become deeply anachronistic. Legality is to be registered under the bureaucratic nationalist state as an alienation within experience. This characteristically modern relation to an authoritatively mediated hermeneutics, I would suggest, helps to determine a newly representative relation between literary textuality and the nature of subjectivity in the bureaucratic nation. More appropriate than Morris's appeal to his fingers, then, is Poe's *Narrative of*

26. *Marbury v. Madison*, in John Marshall, *Major Opinions and Other Writings*, ed. John P. Roche (New York, 1967), pp. 87–88.

Arthur Gordon Pym, published fifty years after the Constitution. There, the unfingered text that has mysteriously but authoritatively materialized on the island of Tsalal—without author but with the full prophetic weight of law—is encountered both as fate and as the pure resonance of signification. It is the romantic scandal of hermeneutics, now to inhabit the law.

Texas Law Review

Volume 65, Number 1, November 1986

The Creation of the Constitution: The Integrity of the Documentary Record*

James H. Hutson**

I. Introduction

In 1911, the Yale University Press published the *Records of the Federal Convention of 1787*, edited by Max Farrand. Farrand's edition of the *Records* was published in three volumes and, because of its comprehensive and meticulous scholarship, quickly supplanted all competing editions of Convention records. Yale reprinted the volumes in 1923, 1927, and 1934, and reissued them a final time in 1937 with the addition of a fourth, supplementary volume that contained documents discovered since the first three volumes were published in 1911. Because of the surprising number of new Convention documents that have come to light since 1937, another Farrand supplement is necessary. This Article resulted from research conducted for the preparation of such a supplement.

Some of the newly discovered documents raise questions concerning the reliability of the principal printed sources of information about the drafting and ratification of the Constitution: the Convention journal, kept by Secretary William Jackson;[1] Robert Yates' notes of debates at the Convention;[2] James Madison's notes;[3] and Jonathan Elliot's collection of

** Chief, Manuscript Division, Library of Congress; Executive Secretary, Council of Scholars, Library of Congress. Ph.D 1964, Yale University. The author's most recent book, JOHN ADAMS AND THE DIPLOMACY OF THE AMERICAN REVOLUTION (1980), won the Gilbert Chinard Prize in 1981.

1. JOURNAL, ACTS AND PROCEEDINGS OF THE CONVENTION, ASSEMBLED AT PHILADELPHIA, MONDAY, MAY 14, AND DISSOLVED, SEPTEMBER 17, 1787, WHICH FORMED THE CONSTITUTION OF THE UNITED STATES (Boston 1819) [hereinafter CONVENTION JOURNAL].

2. SECRET PROCEEDINGS AND DEBATES OF THE CONVENTION ASSEMBLED AT PHILADELPHIA, IN THE YEAR 1787, FOR THE PURPOSE OF FORMING THE CONSTITUTION OF THE UNITED STATES OF AMERICA. FROM NOTES TAKEN BY THE LATE ROBERT YATES, ESQUIRE, CHIEF JUSTICE OF NEW YORK, AND COPIED BY JOHN LANSING, JUN., ESQUIRE, LATE CHANCELLOR OF THAT STATE, MEMBERS OF THAT CONVENTION (Albany 1821) [hereinafter SECRET PROCEEDINGS].

3. THE PAPERS OF JAMES MADISON (H. Gilpin ed. 1842).

debates at the state ratifying conventions.[4] The question of the integrity of the documentary record[5] is related to the current controversy about the advisability of interpreting the Constitution according to the original intention of the Framers. If Convention records are not faithful accounts of what was said by the delegates in 1787, how can we know what they intended? The purpose of this Article is to issue a caveat about Convention records, to warn that there are problems with most of them and that some have been compromised—perhaps fatally—by the editorial interventions of hirelings and partisans. To recover original intent from these records may be an impossible hermeneutic assignment.

The Constitutional Convention proceedings were conducted in secrecy.[6] No publication of the speeches, resolutions, or votes of the delegates occured until 1819, when, as the result of a joint congressional resolution of the previous year,[7] the official *Journal* of the Convention, kept by Secretary William Jackson, issued from the press. Two years later, the Convention notes of New York delegate Robert Yates appeared, covering the debates from May 25 to July 5. Jonathan Elliot began publishing his *Debates* in the state ratifying conventions in 1827. Not until 1840, more than fifty years after Washington took the presidential oath, were James Madison's notes of the debates, a full record of the Convention's proceedings, published.

How did the Supreme Court function during its first thirty years, when it was compelled to construe the Constitution without the benefit of a published record that described the motives and intentions of the delegates? The answer, as Professor Powell has explained recently, is that in the early years of the Republic, written records about the gestation of the Constitution were considered irrelevant.[8] To establish its meaning, the "Philadelphia framers . . . assumed that future interpreters

4. THE DEBATES IN THE SEVERAL STATE CONVENTIONS, ON THE ADOPTION OF THE FEDERAL CONSTITUTION, AS RECOMMENDED BY THE GENERAL CONVENTION AT PHILADELPHIA, IN 1787 (J. Elliot ed. 1827, 1828 & 1830) [hereinafter ELLIOT'S DEBATES].

5. Documentary sources also exist in the form of letters written by delegates during and after the Convention and in fragmentary notes of debates, motions, and other proceedings. The delegate letters, a few of which Farrand published, discuss personal and family matters, private business, Philadelphia society—everything but activities on the Convention floor. The delegates' silence about the Constitution was the result of a secrecy rule, adopted by the Convention on May 29, 1787, and observed with fidelity throughout the proceedings. The fragmentary notes of debate, which also are published in Farrand, supplement Madison's and Yates' notes, but suffer the same defects as these fuller accounts, which will be described in the course of this Article. There were reports about the Convention in contemporary newspapers, but because of the delegates' self-imposed gag rule, and because the Convention was closed to the public, they were merely guesses and rumors.

6. *See supra* note 5.

7. 3 Stat. 475 (1818), *reprinted in* 3 THE RECORDS OF THE FEDERAL CONVENTION OF 1787, at 425 (M. Farrand rev. ed. 1937) [hereinafter M. FARRAND].

8. Powell, *The Original Understanding of Original Intent*, 98 HARV. L. REV. 885, 904 (1985).

would adhere to the then-prevalent methods of statutory construction."[9] These methods obliged those construing statutes to effectuate the intention of the drafters, to discover their "intent" by consulting the words of the instrument and, if these were ambiguous, the common law.[10] Professor Powell finds no indication that the framers "expected or intended future interpreters to refer to any extratextual intentions revealed in the convention's secretly conducted debates."[11] The "legislative history" of the Constitution could, in short, be ignored.

At first, the Supreme Court honored this "interpretative intention" of the Framers. The Court generally eschewed the use of extrinsic aids in construing the Constitution. Summarizing their early practices, Chief Justice Marshall claimed in *Ogden v. Saunders*[12] that the Court had taken "frequent occasion to declare its opinion . . . that the intention of the instrument must prevail; that this intention must be collected from its words; [and] that its words are to be understood in that sense in which they are generally used by those for whom the instrument was intended."[13] But, as Professor tenBroek has demonstrated, the Court early permitted exceptions to its rule against using extrinsic aids to construe the Constitution.[14] Because this rule was formulated in "conditions that made it only a dictum," not a "vital doctrine,"[15] the Court permitted itself to use records of the debates of the Philadelphia Convention almost as soon as they were in print. In 1854, for example, in *Carpenter v. Pennsylvania*,[16] the Court cited the recently published edition of Madison's notes to prove that "the debates in the federal convention upon the Constitution" demonstrated that the constitutional prohibition against ex post facto laws was restricted to criminal cases,[17] thus reversing a posi-

9. *Id.* at 904.

10. *See, e.g.*, Letter from Gouverneur Morris to Timothy Pickering (Dec. 22, 1814), *reprinted in* 3 M. FARRAND, *supra* note 7, at 419, 420 ("What can a history of the Constitution avail towards interpreting its provisions? This must be done by comparing the plain import of the words with the general tenor and object of the instrument.").

11. Powell, *supra* note 8, at 903.

12. 25 U.S. (12 Wheat.) 213 (1827) (Marshall, C.J., dissenting).

13. *Id.* at 332.

14. tenBroek, *Admissibility and Use by the United States Supreme Court of Extrinsic Aids in Constitutional Construction* (pt. 1), 26 CALIF. L. REV. 287, 290 (1938).

15. *Id.* at 307. Professor tenBroek noted:

> [T]he doctrine of the United States Supreme Court that the meaning of the Constitution is to be derived from the text itself unless internal factors create a doubt survives in a great state of infirmity. Never a vital doctrine, its present weakness represents the course of its history and results from its origin, its intrinsic character, the nature of its use and the development of antithetical doctrines. Formulated in *dictum*, it never overcame the stigma of its unfortunate birth.

Id. (italics in original).

16. 58 U.S. (17 How.) 456 (1854).

17. *Id.* at 463.

tion Justice Johnson had taken in 1829 in *Satterlee v. Matthewson*,[18] when Madison's notes were unavailable.

Professor Powell has argued that, by 1840, the "earlier scruples against the use of 'extrinsic evidence' in constitutional interpretation" had become sufficiently relaxed to allow a "modern" approach to the discovery of intent, involving "historical reconstruction" of the motives of document drafters.[19] Professor tenBroek did not assign any specific date for this transition to modernity, but, writing in 1938, he cited dozens of cases that spanned a century in which the Supreme Court employed the printed records of the debates and proceedings of the Convention to establish the Framers' intentions.[20] The "propriety of considering the proposals and debates of the Constitutional Convention," Chief Justice Vinson wrote in 1949, had long been a respected practice.[21] That such historical citation continues unabated is attested by recent cases like *Bowsher v. Synar*,[22] in which Chief Justice Burger cited "the debates in the Constitutional Convention" to demonstrate the "dangers of congressional usurpation of Executive Branch functions . . . ."[23]

Professor tenBroek concluded that the most frequent use by the Court of the proceedings at Philadelphia was "to affirm a conclusion which apparently, and sometimes assertedly, rests chiefly upon other grounds."[24] The perception that Convention records are used principally to "rationalize" decisions[25] and "create an illusion" that the Framers are guiding the judges,[26] has bred cynicism about them. Witness a recent

18. 27 U.S. (2 Pet.) 380, 416 (1829) ("The whole of this difficulty arises out of that unhappy idea, that the phrase 'ex post facto,' in the constitution of the United States, was confined to criminal cases exclusively; a decision which leaves a large class of arbitrary legislative acts without the prohibitions of the constitution.").

19. Powell, *supra* note 8, at 946-47.

20. tenBroek, *Use by the United States Supreme Court of Extrinsic Aids in Constitutional Construction* (pt. 2), 26 CALIF. L. REV. 437, 437-54 (1938). In this second of two articles, *see* tenBroek, *supra* note 14, Professor tenBroek analyzes such cases by dividing them into five categories—cases in which the court:

(a) places primary reliance on convention debates and proceedings;
(b) relies on the proceedings to support a doctrine previously established without them;
(c) utilizes the debates by way of affirmation;
(d) examines them to show they do not contradict a result reached; and
(e) renders a decision in conflict with revealed debates and proceedings.

Id. at 437.

21. National Mut. Ins. Co. v. Tidewater Transfer Co., 337 U.S. 582, 631 n.8 (1948) (Vinson, C.J., dissenting).

22. 106 S. Ct. 3181 (1986).

23. *Id.* at 3189 (citing Buckley v. Valeo, 424 U.S. 1 (1976)).

24. tenBroek, *supra* note 20, at 443.

25. *Id.* at 448.

26. Perry, *Interpretivism, Freedom of Expression, and Equal Protection*, 42 OHIO ST. L.J. 261, 265 (1981).

article about an attorney who defends his client by citing "selected snippets from Farrand's Records of the Federal Convention of 1787,"[27] not because he subscribes to their contents, but because he knows they will impress the judge and better justify his fee;[28] the judge, described in the same article, cites Farrand, not because he grounds his decision on the intentions of the Framers, but because references to them will make his opinion sound more learned and convincing.[29] If Convention records are no more than eye-catching, judicial wrapping paper, it is not surprising that their reliability has escaped rigorous scrutiny.

But what if the records are more than ornamental? A growing movement has called for the intentions of the Framers—presumed to be discoverable in Convention documents—to be binding on the Court. The campaign mounted in recent years by some scholars and judges, and now embraced by public officials, to convert the courts to what has been called a "Jurisprudence of Original Intention"[30] has received so much publicity that it is familiar even to readers of mass circulation newspapers.[31] Few of these readers may be aware, however, that the success of such a campaign would dictate, as Professor Perry explains, that "virtually all of the constitutional doctrine regarding human rights fashioned by the Supreme Court in this century must be adjudged illegitimate."[32] Constitutional scholars to whom such a result would be repugnant have challenged the doctrine of original intent, variously called "interpretivism," "originalism," or "intentionalism,"[33] on epistemological or other grounds.[34]

27. Leedes, *A Critique of Illegitimate Noninterpretivism*, 8 DAYTON L. REV. 533, 542-43 (1983).

28. *Id.* at 543.

29. *See id.*

30. Address by Attorney General Edwin Meese III, American Bar Association Meeting (July 9, 1985, Washington, D.C.); *see Meese Assails High Court for Church-State Rulings*, Wash. Times, July 10, 1985, at A1, col. 4. For recent expressions of the Attorney General's views, see Meese, *Toward a Jurisprudence of Original Intention*, 2 BENCHMARK 1 (1986); Meese, The Attorney General's Views of the Supreme Court: Toward a Jurisprudence of Original Intention, 45 PUB. ADMIN. REV. 701 (1985).

31. *See* USA Today, Oct. 17, 1985, at 14A, col. 3.

32. M. PERRY, THE CONSTITUTION, THE COURTS, AND HUMAN RIGHTS 91 (1982).

33. *See, e.g.*, J. ELY, DEMOCRACY AND DISTRUST: A THEORY OF JUDICIAL REVIEW 1-11 (1980) ("interpretivism"); Brest, *The Misconceived Quest for the Original Understanding*, 60 B.U.L. REV. 204, 204 (1980) ("originalism"); Grey, *Do We Have an Unwritten Constitution?*, 27 STAN. L. REV. 703, 705 (1975) (analyzing the "interpretive model"); Powell, *supra* note 8, at 886 ("intentionalism").

34. *See* Brest, *supra* note 33, at 218-22; Tushnet, *Following the Rules Laid Down: A Critique of Interpretivism and Neutral Principles*, 96 HARV. L. REV. 781, 786-804 (1983). Both Professors Brest and Tushnet disavow the belief that the past is unknowable, but occasionally their views approach such a conclusion.

> Even when the interpreter performs the more conventional historian's role, one may wonder whether the task is possible. There is a hermeneutic tradition . . . which holds that we

An equally promising way to explore the viability of interpretivism is to scrutinize the condition of constitutional texts. Lawyers, judges, and legal scholars have been inclined to accept whatever is in print as a faithful rendition of what occurred at the Philadelphia and state ratifying conventions. Professor Crosskey, it is true, in his first two volumes of *Politics and the Constitution in the History of the United States*,[35] impugned the documentary record of the Convention by charging that Madison's notes were little better than fiction.[36] But Crosskey's controversial reputation evidently has inhibited legal scholars from marshalling his arguments during the current debate, profound though their implications are for a theory of original intent. Professor Wofford also raised serious questions about the reliability of Convention records in an article published in 1964.[37] Since then, however, little has been written about constitutional documentation. The current debate over original intent calls for a fresh examination of the historical evidence. To ascertain what weight lawyers, judges, and scholars should give to which records relating to the creation of the Constitution, this Article examines the Convention records in the chronological order in which they were published.

II. The Accuracy and Reliability of Convention Records

A. The Journal of the Convention

The Convention journal was published in 1819. Secretary William Jackson, after "burning all the loose scraps of paper which belong[ed] to

> can never understand the past in its own terms, free from our prejudices or preconceptions. We are hopelessly imprisoned in our own world-views; we can shed some preconceptions only to adopt others, with no reason to believe that they are the conceptions of the different society that we are trying to understand. One need not embrace this essentially solipsistic view of historical knowledge to appreciate the indeterminate and contingent nature of the historical understanding that an originalist historian seeks to achieve.
>
> None of this is to disparage doing history and other interpretive social science. It suggests, however, that the originalist constitutional historian may be questing after a chimera.

Brest, *supra* note 33, at 221-22 (footnotes omitted).

> The intellectual world of the framers is one that bears some resemblance, which is more than merely genetic, to ours. A hermeneutic interpretivism would force us to think about the social contexts of the resemblances and dissimilarities. It would lead us not to despair over the gulf that separates the framers' world from ours, but rather to the crafting of creative links between their ideals and our own. But in recognizing the magnitude of the creative component, we inevitably lose faith in the ability of interpretivism to provide the constraints on judges that liberal constitutional theory demands.

Tushnet, *supra*, at 803-04.

35. W. CROSSKEY, POLITICS AND THE CONSTITUTION IN THE HISTORY OF THE UNITED STATES (2 vols. 1953).

36. 1 *id.* at 12-13; 2 *id.* at 1009, 1012, 1020.

37. Wofford, *The Blinding Light: The Uses of History in Constitutional Interpretation*, 31 U. CHI. L. REV. 502, 503-06 (1964).

the convention,"[38] handed "the Journal and other papers" generated by the Convention to George Washington on the evening of adjournment, September 17, 1787.[39] On March 19, 1796, Washington turned these documents over to the State Department. According to a receipt executed that day by Secretary of State Timothy Pickering, Washington delivered a

> journal of the general or fœderal convention, in one hundred & fifty three pages; together with a journal of the proceedings of the Committee of the Whole House; a book exhibiting on eight pages a detail of yeas & nays on questions taken in the Convention & two loose sheets & a half sheet, containing nine pages of the like yeas and nays.[40]

In 1818, Congress passed a joint resolution ordering the Convention journal printed.[41] The task of preparing it for publication fell to Secretary of State John Quincy Adams, who found the demands of editing exasperating. "The journals and papers were very loosely and imperfectly kept,"[42] he complained on June 2, 1818. "They were no better than the daily minutes from which the regular journal ought to have been, but never was, made out."[43]

Farrand was equally vexed by the condition of the journals and papers. He scored Jackson for "carelessly" keeping his notes[44] and excused "mistakes" in Adams' edition of the journal as "inevitable" because of the disordered materials he was using.[45] In 1964, Professor Wofford charged that the "accuracy" of the Convention journal "leaves a great deal to be desired."[46]

38. 3 M. FARRAND, *supra* note 7, at 82.

39. *Id.*

40. *Id.* at 370. The manuscript journal and related documents are now at the National Archives and Records Administration, Washington, D.C., where they may be consulted by scholars.

41. 3 Stat. 475 (1818), *reprinted in* 3 M. FARRAND *supra* note 7, at 425.

42. John Quincy Adams: Memoirs (May 13 - June 2, 1819), *reprinted in* 3 M. FARRAND, *supra* note 7, at 430, 433.

43. *Id.* Farrand printed excerpts from John Quincy Adams' memoirs that traced the custodial history of the *Journal*. As shown there, and still commonly believed, George Washington had confidential care of the *Journal* papers from the Convention adjournment until March 19, 1796. *Id.* at 431. It has recently come to light, however, that during this time, Washington lent the *Journal* to Madison who copied it, and thus had the convention information long before anyone else. Such possession is a significant blow to those who argue that Madison corrupted his account of the proceedings with much later reminiscences. *See supra* notes 144-49 and accompanying text.

44. 1 M. FARRAND, *supra* note 7, at xiii.

45. *Id.* at xii ("As Adams had nothing whatever to guide him in his work of compilation and editing, mistakes were inevitable, and not a few of these were important.").

46. Wofford, *supra* note 37, at 504. Confidence in Wofford's judgment would be stronger had he not, some lines later, identified Washington as "president of the Congress of the Confederation," *id.*, a body in which he never served. Washington served in the First and Second Continental Congresses, 1774-1775, but held no offices; the "Congress of the Confederation" began with the adoption of the Articles of Confederation in 1781.

The inaccuracies with which Farrand and Wofford taxed the Convention journal need to be put in perspective. The journal proper—the 153 page journal of the Convention and the 28 page journal of the Committee of the Whole—was not the problem. The trouble was the seventeen-odd pages, detached from the journal, which recorded the "ayes and noes on the various questions"[47] taken in the Convention. Jackson kept these detached votes in tabular form, by delegation not individuals. In at least ninety percent of the cases, the questions on which the votes were taken were given but the dates on which the voting occurred were not. This system of recording, though nettlesome to both Adams and Farrand, posed no insuperable editorial problems because the questions for which the votes were recorded could be found by searching through the chronologically organized journal. Once the questions were found, the votes could be added at the appropriate dates. For example, Jackson's table indicated that three states voted yea, eight nay, on the question whether Congress should have power to make sumptuary laws. The journal, when examined, revealed that a motion "to make sumptuary laws" had been considered on August 20. In preparing the journal for publication, the three-to-eight vote could be matched with the August 20 motion.[48]

The real problems arose with a handful of "ayes and noes" in the detached sheets that were accompanied by no contextual information, and which Jackson had keyed to neither questions nor dates. Through considerable editorial ingenuity, Adams and Farrand succeeded in matching these votes with the appropriate motions, but the possibility that errors had been made, in a few instances, caused Farrand, ever the perfectionist, to warn that the printed edition of the journal "cannot be relied upon absolutely."[49] Another trifling problem was that, in a few instances, Jackson may have counted the votes inaccurately. Hugh Wil-

47. 1 M. FARRAND, *supra* note 7, at xiii.

48. As Farrand explained:

> The secretary's minutes consist of the formal journal of the Convention, the journal of the Committee of the Whole House and, partly on loose sheets and partly in a bound blank book, a table giving the detail of ayes and noes on the various questions. The detail of ayes and noes offers the greatest difficulty, for no dates are given and to about one tenth of the votes no questions are attached. The photograph of the first loose sheet of this table reveals the difficulties at a glance; the later pages are not as bad as the first, for the secretary evidently profited by experience, but uncertainty and confusion are by no means eliminated. For convenience of reference, in the present edition a number in square brackets is prefixed to each vote, and the editor has taken the liberty of dividing the detail of ayes and noes into what are, according to his best judgment, the sections for each day's records. The sections are retained intact, and a summary of each vote in square brackets is appended to that question in the Journal to which, in the light of all the evidence, it seems to belong.

1 M. FARRAND, *supra* note 7, at xiii (footnote omitted).

49. *Id.*

liamson, for example, noted on his copy of the Committee of Detail report that the vote on August 31 to require nine states to ratify the Constitution before it could become operative was seven-to-four; using Jackson's tables, Farrand made the vote eight-to-three.[50] It was the possibility of such inconsequential computational differences or a misattributed vote that caused Farrand to issue his warning about the accuracy of the printed journal.[51] However, the slight probability of error—and the understanding that none of it relates to what the delegates said—permits confidence in the journal, as published by John Quincy Adams or Max Farrand, as a reliable text. No such confidence is possible, however, in Yates' notes, considered next.

B. Yates' Notes

Farrand called Robert Yates' notes the source "next in importance" to Madison's notes for information about the Philadelphia Convention.[52] The frequency with which they have been cited, from the *Legal Tender Cases* in which they were curiously identified by the appellant Potter as "Yates's Minute"[53] to more recent cases,[54] confirms the accuracy of his assessment.

The notes were published in Albany in 1821 under the title *Secret Proceedings and Debates of the Convention Assembled at Philadelphia in the year 1787, ... From Notes taken by the late Robert Yates, Esquire, Chief Justice of New York and copied by John Lansing, Jun., Esquire, Late Chancellor of that State, Members of that Convention*. The title page listed no editor. Washington newspapers plausibly but erroneously speculated that Lansing had seen the volume through the press.[55] The identity of the editor would have startled the country's newspaper readers, for he was none other than Citizen Genet[56]—Edmond C. Genet—the

50. 2 *id.* at 477. Williamson's copy of the Committee of Detail report is in the Manuscript Division, Library of Congress.

51. Farrand said:

> In the judgment of the editor, however, a word of warning seems necessary. With notes so carelessly kept, as were evidently those of the secretary [William Jackson], the Journal cannot be relied upon absolutely. The statement of questions is probably accurate in most cases, but the determination of those questions and in particular the votes upon them should be accepted somewhat tentatively.

1 *id.* at xiii-xiv.

52. 1 *id.* at xv.

53. Legal Tender Cases, 79 U.S. (12 Wall.) 457, 497 n.* (1870).

54. *See, e.g.*, Goldberg v. Kelly, 397 U.S. 254, 273 (1970) (Black, J., dissenting) (citing "Yates' Minutes" for support); National Mut. Ins. Co. v. Tidewater Transfer Co., 337 U.S. 582, 634 n.13 (1948) (Vinson, C.J., dissenting) ("The sense of the Convention at this point was expressed in Yates' Notes . . . .").

55. Albany Argus, Sept. 11, 1821 (referring to commentary in Washington newspapers).

56. 3 M. FARRAND, *supra* note 7, at 410 n.1.

tempestuous minister of revolutionary France who convulsed American politics in 1793.[57] Fearing the guillotine, Genet refused to return to France when recalled. He married a daughter of Governor George Clinton of New York and settled on a farm in Long Island, later removing to Greenbush, near Albany. Among Clinton's political lieutenants were Yates and Lansing. They went to the Philadelphia Convention to protect the interests of New York State as the Clintonians parochially defined them. Both men withdrew on July 10 when it became apparent that they could not prevent the adoption of a strong national government. Introduced to the circle of Clinton's friends by marriage, Genet, nevertheless, was distrusted because of the tumultuous scenes he had precipitated in 1793 and because in his occasional forays into political journalism on behalf of his father-in-law, he displayed a penchant for character assassination that produced notorious libels such as one charging Rufus King, a model of probity and a pillar of the New York establishment, with robbing a widow in the settlement of an estate.[58]

Upon Yates' death in 1801, his Convention notes passed to his wife who retained them until 1808. Genet then tried to get them from Mrs. Yates to conduct a political smear campaign. Fearing for their safety in the Frenchman's hands, Lansing intervened and rescued the original manuscript from the widow, promising that she would receive a copy. Lansing completed the copy within a month, making the "transcript verbatim, without the least mutilation or other alteration."[59] Genet then extracted Lansing's copy of Yates' notes from the widow to use in promoting Clinton's political ambitions.[60]

In 1808, Clinton challenged Madison for the presidential nomination on the Jeffersonian Republican ticket.[61] Over the signature of a "Citizen of New York," Genet wrote a polemic against Madison, entitled *A Letter to the Electors of the President and Vice President of the United States*.[62] The raw material for Genet's screed was Lansing's copy of Yates' notes, which Genet edited so drastically and tendentiously that

57. In 1793, Genet fitted out privateers in American ports to sail against British shipping in violation of American neutrality. When the government protested, Genet threatened to go over Washington's head by appealing to the American people. Such actions caused even Genet's friends to distance themselves from him. For an accurate, short sketch of Genet, see 7 DICTIONARY OF AMERICAN BIOGRAPHY 207-09 (1931).

58. D. FOX, THE DECLINE OF ARISTOCRACY IN THE POLITICS OF NEW YORK 81 (1919).

59. Letter from John Lansing to Edmond C. Genet (July 6, 1821), *reprinted in* Albany Argus, Aug. 24, 1821.

60. Albany Argus, Sept. 11, 1821.

61. Morison, *The First National Nominating Convention, 1808*, 17 AM. HIST. REV. 744, 746 (1912).

62. E. Genet, A Letter to the Electors of the President and Vice President of the United States (1808) (available in the Rare Book and Special Collections Divisions, Library of Congress).

Lansing, who had evidently anticipated just such a reckless manipulation of the sources, later congratulated himself on "getting possession of the original . . . in opposition to some ardent politicians, adverse to the election of Mr. Madison as president."[63]

In his broadside against Madison, Genet promised that the full text of Yates' notes would "soon be offered to the people,"[64] but he withheld the document for thirteen years until another set of political ends could be served by its publication. Such an opportunity presented itself on August 28, 1821, when a convention met in Albany to revise the constitution of the state of New York. Genet published what purported to be a complete version of Yates' notes—his *Secret Proceedings*, the version we now have in Farrand—shortly before the convention convened. His purpose was to influence the convention's deliberations, as he admitted in a letter, presenting his *Secret Proceedings* to President James Monroe.[65] The states "being now engaged in the revisal or foundation of their organic laws, I have," he informed the President, "thought the moment propitious to supply their Legislatures with the various opinions, views, and principles of the sages who framed the federal constitution."[66] Because of the murky nature of New York politics in the 1820s, it is not clear on whose behalf Genet produced Yates' notes. He may have been working for his father-in-law's nephew, DeWitt Clinton, who according to an older view of New York history, opposed the calling of the convention and the reforms proposed by its proponents, the Bucktail Republicans, who were suspected of scheming "to revolutionize everything."[67] Certainly, Genet's statement in his letter to Monroe that he intended Yates' notes to divulge "admonitory facts and observations that will render them less liable to be led astray by erroneous doctrines and guard them against the danger of exchanging for adventurous innovation real and substantial good,"[68] suggests that he was no friend of reform. On the other hand, recent revisionist historians who have studied the Convention have portrayed the Clintonians as matching their opponents' ardor for progressive change and exceeding it in certain areas such as concern for the welfare of the black population.[69] It is conceivable,

63. Lansing letter, *supra* note 59.

64. E. Genet, *supra* note 62, at 3-4.

65. Genet's letter, of which there are two drafts—one dated simply August, the other August 27, 1821—may be found in his papers at the Library of Congress.

66. *Id.*

67. *See* A. KASS, POLITICS IN NEW YORK STATE, 1800-1830, at 89 (1965).

68. Genet letter, *supra* note 65.

69. *See, e.g.*, A. KASS, *supra* note 67, at 88 ("[A]t the outset the primary *raison d'être* of the [Clintonians] had been to achieve universal manhood suffrage and to abolish laws for the imprisonment of debtors.").

therefore, that in opposing "adventurous innovation," perhaps in race relations, Genet was cooperating with the Clintonian opposition, the Bucktail Republicans, whose power base was in Tammany Hall. We simply do not know the precise nature of his political agenda in 1821.

What is known is that, in publishing the *Secret Proceedings*, Genet took liberties with Lansing's copy of Yates' notes, liberties that appear to have exceeded those he permitted himself in the anti-Madison polemic in 1808. Lansing's copy of Yates' notes were thought to have been lost until two sheets from July 5, 1787 were discovered recently in Genet's papers at the Library of Congress.[70] By comparing the contents of those sheets—the only ones known to exist—with what Genet actually published as occurring on July 5, 1787, it can be seen that he omitted half of the material on the sheets and altered every sentence that he published (see pages 14-19). If Genet inflicted similar depredations on the remainder of Yates' notes, those notes as now printed in the *Secret Proceedings* cannot be considered a reliable record of what occurred at the Philadelphia Convention and cannot be consulted as a source of the intentions of the Framers. When Madison read extracts from Genet's publication in August 1821, he protested its "extreme incorrectness."[71] The plaything of an unscrupulous partisan, Yates' notes as published by Genet fully deserved Madison's condemnation.

C. *The Debates in the State Ratifying Conventions*

Because many of the members of the Federal Convention sought seats in the ratifying conventions of their respective states to explain and defend the work done at Philadelphia, and because men like John Mar-

70. The manuscript of Yates' notes that Lansing obtained from Mrs. Yates and from which he made the copy Genet used also has disappeared.

71. Letter from James Madison to Joseph Gales (Aug. 26, 1821), *reprinted in* 3 M. FARRAND, *supra* note 7, at 446.

> I thank you for your friendly letter of the 20th. inclosing an extract from notes by Judge Yates, of debates in the Convention of 1787, as published in a N.Y. Paper [Commercial Advertizer, Aug. 18, 1821]. . . .
>
> If the extract be a fair sample, the work about to be published will not have the value claimed for it. . . . [The] intrinsic evidence alone ought to satisfy every candid reader of the extreme incorrectness of the passage in question. . . .
>
> Whatever may have been the personal worth of the 2 delegates from whom the materials in this case were derived, it cannot be unknown that they represented the strong prejudices in N.Y. agst. the object of the Convention which was among other things to take from that State the important power over its commerce and that they manifested, untill they withdrew from the Convention, the strongest feelings of dissatisfaction agst. the contemplated change in the federal system and as may be supposed, agst. those most active in promoting it. Besides misapprehensions of the ear therefore, the attention of the note taker wd naturally be warped, as far at least as, an upright mind could be warped, to an unfavorable understanding of what was said in opposition to the prejudices felt.

Id. at 446-47.

shall served in these conventions, the state proceedings have always been regarded as a storehouse of information about the intentions of the Framers. Debates in the state conventions, Professor tenBroek has explained, have "frequently [been] utilized . . . in arguments before the United States Supreme Court,"[72] a fact demonstrated by Justice White's use of the debates in the Pennsylvania and North Carolina ratifying conventions in his opinion in *Nixon v. Fitzgerald.*[73] Indeed, some recent scholars such as Professor Brest have suggested that the members of the state conventions were the true framers,[74] because it was their action in ratifying the Constitution that brought it to life and transformed it from a mere proposal to the supreme law of the land. This line of argument appears to be designed to discredit the theory of original intent by multiplying the number of framers exponentially—to a majority in each of nine ratifying conventions or, in the case of a constitutional amendment, to a majority in each of three-fourths of the state legislatures. Nevertheless, it does emphasize the importance of the state ratifying conventions as a source for ascertaining the intentions of the drafters of the Constitution.

Our information about the proceedings in the state ratifying conventions comes from a single source: Jonathan Elliot's *The Debates in the several State Conventions, on the adoption of the Federal Constitution, as recommended by the General Convention at Philadelphia, in 1787.*[75] First published in four volumes between 1827 and 1830, Elliot's work is a bibliographical brainteaser, for it was republished in at least seven more editions, in differing numbers of volumes, with the contents of individual volumes differing in many cases from edition to edition. Elliot was not a scholar. Rather, he was a Washington political journalist turned editor, whose press was for sale to the highest bidder. John Quincy Adams, who cancelled a government printing contract held by Elliot because he suspected price gouging, described him as "an Englishman, having no character of his own—penurious and venal—metal to receive any stamp."[76] It appears that in the 1830s, Elliot was promoting the political fortunes of John C. Calhoun, although he had opposed the South Carolinian earlier.[77] Some scholars believe that one of Elliot's purposes in preparing his *Debates* was to advance Calhoun's cause, for Elliot supplemented proceedings in the conventions with such states' rights classics as the Virginia and Kentucky Resolves and deleted from the 1836 second

72. tenBroek, *supra* note 20, at 454.
73. 457 U.S. 731, 774-75 (1981) (White, J., dissenting).
74. Brest, *supra* note 33, at 214-15.
75. *See* ELLIOT'S DEBATES, *supra* note 4.
76. 6 DICTIONARY OF AMERICAN BIOGRAPHY 93 (1931).
77. *Id.*

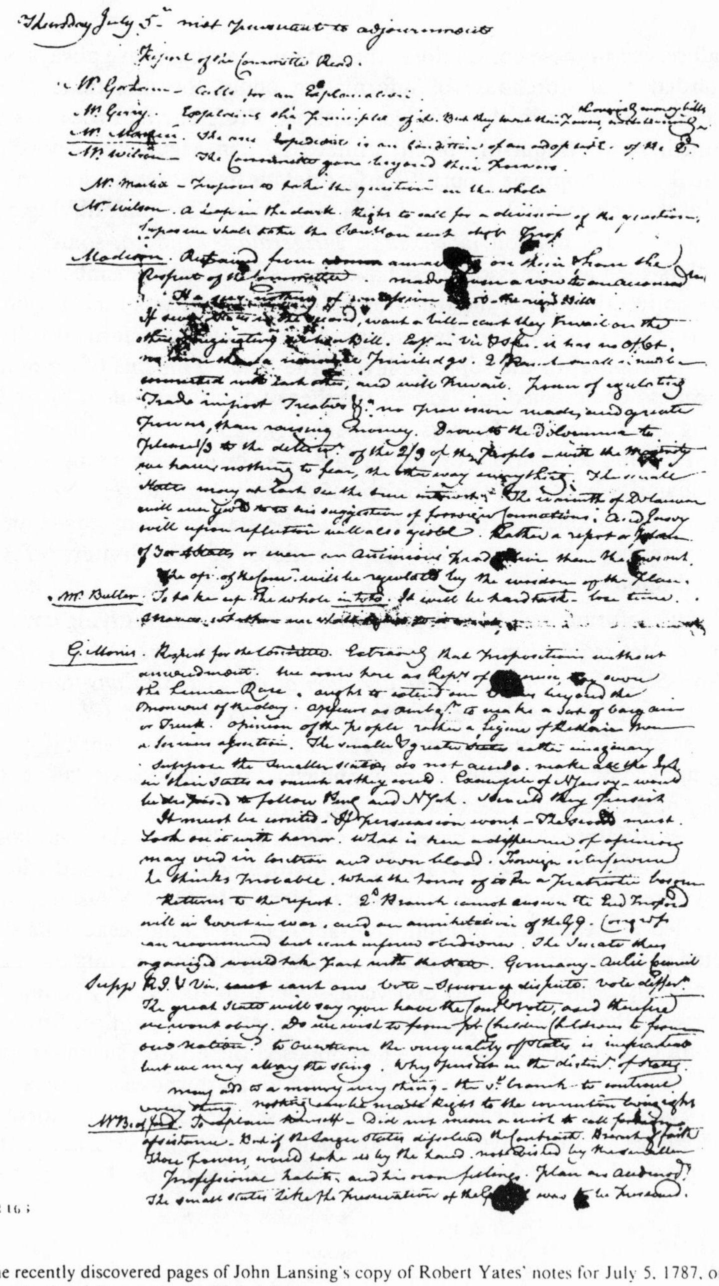

Thursday July 5th met pursuant to adjournment
Report of the Committee Read.
Mr. Gorham — Calls for an Explanation.
Mr. Gerry. Explaining the Principle of it. [illegible]
Mr. Martin. [illegible]
Mr. Wilson — The Committee gone beyond their Powers.
Mr. Martin — Proposes to take the question on the whole
Mr. Wilson. A leap in the dark. Right to call for a division of the question. [illegible]
[illegible]

The recently discovered pages of John Lansing's copy of Robert Yates' notes for July 5, 1787, on the Constitutional Convention in Philadelphia.

Judge [illegible]worth.

Rutledge.

Mr. Paterson — Was with Rounds not to recom. convention — nor will the sword or Bayonet do it. The manner of the Govt. of Pennsylvania and Virginia have given occasion of the Alarm.

Mr. Mason — The report recommends no more, in order to see whether it could not be the basis of an accommodation. Knows how the question of Representation was agitated in Convention.
Some Gent. will appeal to the world at large rather agree
If an agreemt. could be made, he would stay till he was [illegible]...

Mr. Butler — agd. by propositions as they stand — Property not represented. Taxation and Representation ought to go together — if otherwise suppose they tax away my property — and would be like a Tartar, with liberty indeed, but a beggar. Rather would not have a second Branch.

G. Morris — Thinks property ought to have weight — Liberty most enjoyed by the savages — numbers will answer the dogmatist & metaphysician but not reducable to practice.

Mr. Butler — Holland grumbling, because she has only one vote — and pays one half of the Expense.

G. Morris. — Is for det. the number of votes for each state in Representation. [illegible] better for small States. R.I. now one of 13. would she not agree to this rather than to have 1/57 votes agt. etc.

Mr. Gorham — Has no objn. to the motion of S.C. provided the property could be ascertained. It cannot be done by any way. In short. Practical?

Thursday July 5.	Met pursuant to adjournment. Report of the Committee Read.
Mr. Gorham.	Calls for an Explanation.
Mr. Gerry.	Explains the principle of it. But they want their powers, in determining the original money bills.
Mr. Martin.	The one Expedient is on Condition of an adoption of the 2d.
Mr. Wilson.	The Committee gone beyond their powers.
Mr. Martin.	proposes to take the question on the whole.
Mr. Wilson.	A Leap in the dark. Right to call for a division of the question, hopes we shall take the Senti[ment]s on each dist[inct] prop[osal].
Madison.	Restrained from animadverting on them from the Respect of the Committee. Made from a view to an accommodation. He sees nothing of concession in it, the orig[inating] Bills. If seven States in the second, want a bill—cant they prevail on the other of originating such a Bill. Exp[erience] in Vi[rginia] and S[outh] C[arolina]. it has no effect. no more than a nominal priviledge. 2 Branch small in number connected with each other, and will prevail. power of regulating Trade impost Treaties etc. no provisions made, and greater powers, than raising money. Drove to the dilemma to please $1/3$ to the detriment of the $2/3$ of the people—with the Majority we have nothing to fear, the other way everything. The small states may at last see the true interest. The warmth of Delaware will ever yield to his suggestion of foreign Connections. And Jersey will upon reflection will also yield. Rather a report or plan of 3 or 4 States or even an [anonymous?] production than the [present?]. The op[inion] of the Com[mittee] will be regulated by the wisdom of the plan.
Mr. Butler.	To take up the whole *in toto*. It will be hard task—lose time. Moves whether we shall agree to it as wrote.
G. Morris.	Respect for the Committee. Extraordinary that propositions without amendment. We come here as Rep[resentatives] of America, nay even human Race. ought to extend our Views beyond the Moment of the day. Appears as Ambas[sador] to make a sort of bargain or truck. Opinion of the people rather a figure of Rethoric than a serious assertion. The small and greater states rather imaginary. suppose the smaller states do not accede. make all the Int[erest] in their states as much as they could. Example of N Jersey would be disposed to follow Penn and N York. [one word indecipherable] they persist. It must be united. IF persuasion wont—the sword must. Look on it with horror. What is here a difference of opinion may end in Contrav[ersy] and even blood. Foreign interference he thinks probable. What the horros of it [in?] a patriotic bosom.

Transcription of Lansing's copy of Yates' notes, July 5, 1787

16

Returns to the report. 2d. Branch cannot answer the End proposed. Will in [Event?] in war and an annihilation of the G[eneral] G[overnment]. Congress can recommend but cant enforce obedience. The Senate thus organized would take part with the state. Germany. Aulic Council. Suppose RI and Vir cast one vote—Source of dispute. vote different. The great State will say you have the Con [rest of word indecipherable] vote, and therefore we wont obey. Do we wish to [one word indecipherable] for Children Childrens to form our nation? to overturn the inequality of the states is impractical but we may allay the sting. Why persist in the distinct[ion] of states.

May add to a [one word indecipherable] everything the 1st branch to controul everything. Nothing can be m ade right to the conviction being right.

Mr. Bedford. To explain himself—Did not mean a wish to call foreign assistance. But if the larger states dissolved the Contract. Breach of faith. Those powers would take us by the hand. not wished by the smaller. professional habits and his own feelings. Plan are Accomod[ation?]. The small states like the preservation of the G[eneral] G[overnment] was to be preserved.

Judge Elsworth.

Rutlegde.

Mr. Paterson. Warmth tends not to recom[mend] conviction—nor will the sword or Bayonet do it. The manner of the G[entlemen?] of Pennsylvania and Virginia have given cause of the Alarm.

Mr. Marson. The report [recommending?] no more, in order to see whether it could not be the basis of our accomodation. shews how the question of Representation was agitated in Convention. Some Gent[lemen] will appeal to the world at large rather agree. If an agreement could be made, he would stay till he was burryed here.

Mr. Butler. Against both propositions as they stand—property not represented Taxation and representation ought to go together—if otherwise suppose they tax away my property and wander like a Tartar, with Liberty indeed, but a baggor. Rather would not have a second Branch.

G. Morris. Thinks property ought to have weight—Liberty most enjoyed by the savages—Numbers will amuse the Logycian and Matephysician but not reducable to practice.

Mr. Butler. Holland grumbling, because she has only one vote and pays one half of the Expence.

G. Morris. Is for defining the number of votes for each state in pepetuity. It is better for small States. R.I. now one of 75. would she not agree to this rather than have 757 votes against it.

Mr. Gorham Has no obj[ection] to the Motion of SC provided the property could be ascertained. It cannot be done by any way. In past. partial.

17

That the subsequent propositions be recommended to the convention, on condition that both shall be generally adopted.

That in the first branch of the legislature, each of the states now in the union, be allowed one member for every 40,000 inhabitants, of the description reported in the seventh resolution of the committee of the whole house—That each state, not containing that number, shall be allowed one member.

That all bills for raising or apportioning money, and for fixing salaries of the officers of government of the United States, shall originate in the first branch of the legislature, and shall not be altered or amended by the second branch; and that no money shall be drawn from the public treasury, but in pursuance of appropriations to be originated in the first branch.

That in the second branch of the legislature, *each state shall have an equal vote.*

THURSDAY, JULY 5th, 1787.

Met pursuant to adjournment.

The report of the committee was read.

Mr. Gorham. I call for an explanation of the principles on which it is grounded.

Mr. Gerry, the chairman, explained the principles.

Mr. Martin. The one representation is proposed as an expedient for the adoption of the other.

Mr. Wilson. The committee has exceeded their powers.

Mr. Martin proposed to take the question on the whole of the report.

Mr. Wilson. I do not chuse to take a leap in the dark. I have a right to call for a division of the question on each distinct proposition.

Mr. Madison. I restrain myself from animadverting

Edmond C. Genet's version of John Lansing's copy of Robert Yates' notes for July 5, 1787 as published in *Secret Proceedings*.

on the report, from the respect I bear to the members of the committee. But I must confess I see nothing of concession in it.

The originating money bills is no concession on the part of the smaller states, for if seven states in the second branch should want such a bill, their interest in the first branch will prevail to bring it forward—it is nothing more than a nominal privilege.

The second branch, small in number, and well connected, will ever prevail. The power of regulating trade, imposts, treaties, &c. are more essential to the community than raising money, and no provision is made for those in the report—We are driven to an unhappy dilemma. Two thirds of the inhabitants of the union are to please the remaining one third by sacrificing their essential rights.

When we satisfy the majority of the people in securing their rights, we have *nothing* to fear; in any other way, *every thing*. The smaller states, I hope will at last see their true and real interest.—And I hope that the warmth of the gentleman from Delaware will never induce him to yield to his own suggestion of seeking for foreign aid.

[At this period Messrs. YATES and LANSING left the convention, and the remainder of the session was employed to complete the constitution on the principles already adopted. See the revised draft of the constitution and the constitution of the United States, with all the ratified amendments as at present existing, in the appendix.]

☞ The preceding Notes of the late Chief Justice YATES, contained in two hundred and forty-five pages,* of two volumes, were copied by me, literally, from the original manuscript in his hand writing.—The several papers referred to did not accompany his notes.

JOHN LANSING, Jun.

* The number of pages in the manuscript.

edition a letter from Madison, which appeared in the first edition, attacking nullification.[78] Whether Elliot went as far as Genet and doctored the *Debates* to promote the politics of a patron is not clear, but so obvious were their shortcomings that Elliot himself apologized for them in the preface to the first edition, confessing that "the sentiments they contain may, in some instances, have been inaccurately taken down, and, in others, probably, too faintly sketched, fully to gratify the inquisitive politician."[79]

To know why the debates were "inaccurately taken down," it is necessary to know how and by whom they were recorded. Unlike the Philadelphia Convention, the state ratifying conventions were open to the public. Enterprising men recorded the debates in shorthand and then published them as commercial ventures in the newspapers and in book form. Elliot's *Debates* are a collection of these publications, generated in the first instance by shorthand reporters. And precisely here was the problem, for the technique of shorthand was in its infancy in the United States and did not provide the means of recording public discourse accurately.

Most of those stenographers who recorded the state conventions are known to us: Benjamin Russell in Massachusetts, Enoch Perkins in Connecticut, Francis Childs in New York, Thomas Lloyd in Pennsylvania and Maryland, and David Robertson in Virginia and North Carolina. Lloyd's career is better documented than those of his colleagues.[80] He claimed to have learned shorthand from the Jesuits at St. Omers, Flanders, but his system has been shown to be identical to one published by Graves and Ashton in York, England, in 1775,[81] which was in turn based on Thomas Gurney's popular method.[82] Whatever the source of Lloyd's system, like all "[e]ighteenth-century shorthand [it] was inadequate to the task of recording speeches verbatim."[83] "Like most systems of his day," Lloyd's technique left "much to the imagination of the transcriber. There is much similarity between symbols for different letters, and there are no vowels. Lloyd omitted most articles and connectives, and used many abbreviations peculiar to him alone."[84] In short, he was technically unable to capture accurately most of what speakers said.

78. Leonard Rapport, senior archivist at the National Archives and Records Administration, intends to illuminate the Elliot-Calhoun connection in a forthcoming article.

79. 1 ELLIOT'S DEBATES, *supra* note 4, at v.

80. Tinling, *Thomas Lloyd's Reports of the First Federal Congress*, 18 WM. & MARY Q. 519 (1961).

81. *Id.* at 541.

82. E. BUTLER, THE STORY OF BRITISH SHORTHAND 79 (1951).

83. Tinling, *supra* note 80, at 530.

84. *Id.*

The other stenographers of the state conventions were in all probability even less capable of accurately conveying the proceedings than was Lloyd. By 1787, Lloyd had been dabbling in shorthand for some years. Given his inadequacies, it is hard to believe that the records of his colleagues could be considered reliable when they were mere neophytes in a technique that took at least five years to master.[85] No wonder, then, that Elliot was compelled to admit that the proceedings of the ratifying conventions were "inaccurately taken down."[86]

A survey of the records in states for which information is available shows that in some cases insufficient stenographic skills may have been the least of problems. From New Hampshire, Elliot published only a fragment of the Convention debates, the centerpiece of which was a speech by Joshua Atherton.[87] According to the historian of the New Hampshire Convention, Atherton's speech apparently was "written out from tradition, by a hand other than his own, long after the Convention."[88] In fact, it appears to have been composed by parties unknown in 1827, when it was first published as antislavery propaganda in a New Hampshire newspaper.[89]

Elliot reprinted the debates in the Massachusetts Convention from a volume published in Boston in 1788 by Benjamin Russell.[90] In a publisher's note, Russell apologized for " 'some inaccuracies, and many omissions,' due to the 'inexperience' of the reporters."[91] Contemporaries testified that Russell and his colleagues inserted speeches in the published debates that they themselves had written for some of the delegates—General William Thompson of Billerica, for example, was said to have been one of the beneficiaries of their ghostwriting. "The Printers here have really mended the diction and some of the Sentiments" of the Convention delegates, a Bostonian wrote a friend on March 4, 1788.[92]

Political partisanship in Connecticut and New York, more than the shortage of stenographic expertise, compromised the quality of the record of convention debates in those states. In Connecticut, the *Connecti-*

85. E. BUTLER, *supra* note 82, at 60.
86. 1 ELLIOT'S DEBATES, *supra* note 4, at v.
87. 2 *id.* at 203-04.
88. J. WALKER, A HISTORY OF THE NEW HAMPSHIRE CONVENTION 4-5 (1888).
89. *Id.*
90. B. RUSSELL, DEBATES, RESOLUTIONS AND OTHER PROCEEDINGS OF THE CONVENTION . . . TOGETHER WITH THE YEAS AND NAYS ON THE DECISION OF THE GRAND QUESTION (Boston 1788), *reprinted in* 1 ELLIOT'S DEBATES, *supra* note 4, at 25-184.
91. S. HARDING, THE CONTEST OVER THE RATIFICATION OF THE FEDERAL CONSTITUTION IN THE STATE OF MASSACHUSETTS 177 (1896 & photo. reprint 1970) (quoting B. RUSSELL, *supra* note 90).
92. Letter from David Sewell to George Thatcher (Mar. 4, 1788), *reprinted in* 6 HIST. MAG. 343 (1869).

cut Courant and the *American Mercury*, both Federalist newspapers, hired Enoch Perkins, a young Federalist lawyer, to report the debates at Hartford. The results were egregiously partisan—only one short summary of one Anti-Federalist speech was published, and at least one Federalist speech was said to have been "particularly erroneous."[93] For New York, Elliot published Francis Childs' *Debates and Proceedings of the Convention of the State of New York . . . .* that appeared in December 1788.[94] A fledgling stenographer, Childs apologized to the delegates he recorded

> for the imperfect dress in which their arguments are given to the Public. Not long accustomed to the business, he cannot pretend to as much accuracy as might be expected from a more experienced hand,—and it will easily be comprehended how difficult it must be to follow a copious and rapid Speaker, in the train of his reasoning, much more in the turn of his expression.[95]

Childs further impaired his credibility by recording and publishing the debates for only two of the Convention's six weeks, and by allowing speakers to revise their remarks after the event.[96] The most damaging charge against his reliability as a reporter, however, was the accusation that he was a "partyman,"[97] a Federalist who manipulated his notes to promote factional interests.

This charge was made with more vehemence against Thomas Lloyd, the reporter of the Pennsylvania and Maryland debates. An ardent Federalist, Lloyd probably had no qualms about taking money from Pennsylvania Federalist leaders to delete all the Anti-Federalist speeches in the Convention,[98] as he in fact did in his *Debates of the Convention of the*

93. 3 Documentary History of the Ratification of the Constitution 336, 573 (M. Jenson ed. 1978) [hereinafter Documentary History].

94. 1 Elliot's Debates, *supra* note 4, at 185-358. Commenting on the work of Childs and other reporters of the debates in the ratifying conventions, Elliot wrote Madison that he was "fully sensible of the imperfections of many of the materials." Letter from Jonathan Elliot to James Madison (Aug. 19, 1830) (available in Madison Papers, Library of Congress).

95. 5 Papers of Alexander Hamilton 12 (H. Syrett ed. 1962).

96. Letter from John Lansing to Abraham Yates and Melancton Smith (Oct. 3, 1788) (available in Lamb Papers, New York Historical Society).

97. G. Saladino, *A Guide to Sources for Studying the Ratification of the Constitution by New York State*, in The Reluctant Pillar, New York and the Adoption of the Federal Constitution 133, 188 (S. Schecter ed. 1985).

98. On Lloyd's being "bought up by the Federalists," see Pennsylvania and the Federal Constitution 14-15 (J. McMaster & F. Stone eds. 1888).

> Of the proceedings of the [Pennsylvania] convention no full and satisfactory record is known to exist. . . . The minutes are exceedingly meagre; but from them it appears that Thomas Lloyd applied to the convention for the place of assistant clerk. Lloyd was a shorthand writer of considerable note, and, when the convention refused his request, determined to report the debates and print them on his own account. His advertisement promised that the debates should be accurateiy [sic] taken in shorthand, and published in one volume octavo at the rate of one dollar the hundred pages. These fine promises, however, were never fulfilled. Only one thin volume ever came out, and that contains merely the

State of Pennsylvania, published on February 7, 1788, and reprinted by Elliot.[99] In addition to suppressing the Anti-Federalists, Lloyd eliminated all Federalist speeches except those by Thomas McKean and James Wilson, the latter of which had obviously been corrected and "improved" after the Convention because they were printed with footnotes.[100] The Anti-Federalists correctly charged that Lloyd's *Debates* had been "afterwards altered, dressed and undressed by, and at the pleasure of his benefactors,"[101] and were nothing more than Federalist campaign literature. In December and January of 1787-1788, Federalist stalwarts Timothy Pickering and Tench Coxe sent prepublication excerpts from Lloyd's *Debates* to partisans in other states to furnish Federalist orators arguments for ratification.[102] Even Elliot deprecated Lloyd's notes by advising his readers that although he was publishing them, he had sought in vain to obtain better accounts of the Pennsylvania Convention.[103]

The reporter of the Virginia debates, one David Robertson, inspired little confidence in some citizens of the Old Dominion. "The Debates are not Yet published; nor is there any Cause to expect that they will be authentic; the Short Hand Man," wrote George Mason, "being a *federal* Partizan, [the notes] will probably be garbled, in some such Partial Manner as the Debates of the Pennsylvania Convention have been by Lloyd."[104] Robertson's *Debates and Other Proceedings of the Convention of Virginia*, published in 1788 and reprinted by Elliot,[105] shared the weaknesses of the works of his stenographic colleagues. "I find passages," wrote Madison, "some appearing to be defective, others obscure, if not unintelligible, others again which must be more or less erroneous."[106] John Marshall, whose speeches at the Virginia Convention

> speeches of Wilson and a few of those of Thomas M'Kean. The reason is not far to seek. He was bought up by the Federalists, and, in order to satisfy the public, was suffered to publish one volume containing nothing but the speeches made by the two federal leaders.

Id.

99. T. Lloyd, Debates of the Convention of the State of Pennsylvania on the United States Constitution, Proposed for the Government of the United States (Philadelphia 1788), *reprinted in* 3 Elliot's Debates, *supra* note 4, at 221-322.

100. Pennsylvania and the Federal Constitution, *supra* note 98, at 765-85.

101. Peep Junior, Independent Gazetteer (Philadelphia), Feb. 5, 1788.

102. 2 Documentary History, *supra* note 93, at 41-42.

103. This notice was contained in the preface to volume 3 of the first edition (1830) of *Elliot's Debates*; it was deleted in subsequent editions.

104. 3 Papers of George Mason: 1725-1792, at 1126 (R. Rutland ed. 1970).

105. D. Robertson, Debates and Other Proceedings of the Convention of Virginia (1788), *reprinted in* 2 Elliot's Debates, *supra* note 4, at 33-487.

106. Letter from James Madison to Jonathan Elliot (November 1827) (available in Madison Papers, Library of Congress).

are frequently cited in the legal literature,[107] was so distressed by Robertson's inaccuracies that he complained that "as to what is given to me . . ., if my name had not been prefixed to the speaches [sic] I never should have recognized them as productions of mine."[108]

The Virginia Convention adjourned on June 27, 1788; Robertson was then hired by James Iredell and William Davie, the Federalist chieftains in North Carolina, to come to Hillsboro and record the action in the ratifying convention in the Tarheel state.[109] Apparently Robertson did not please his employers, for he refused to make a "fair copy" of his shorthand notes. This task then fell to "a little boy the son of Mr. Turnbull," who to no one's surprise, performed the work "most defectively."[110] Various Federalist speakers tinkered with the lad's work before the debates were published by Iredell and Davie. They hoped that the dissemination of the debates "would produce a salutary change in the opinions of the people,"[111] whose representatives had failed to ratify the Constitution but were scheduled to try again in 1789. Thus, the North Carolina debates as reported were designed, like those in Pennsylvania, to serve as Federalist campaign literature.

Reviewing the ratification proceedings on the floor of Congress in 1791, Elbridge Gerry asserted that "[t]he debates of the State Conventions, as published by the short-hand writers, were generally partial and mutilated . . . ."[112] Gerry's assessment applies with equal force to Genet's edition of Yates' notes. Documents as corrupt as these cannot be relied upon to reveal the intentions of the Framers.

D. Madison's Notes

1. Their History of Controversy.—Although often entreated to publish his notes on the Philadelphia Convention, James Madison never relented in his conviction that they should appear posthumously. At his death in 1836, the notes passed to his widow who sold them to the federal government, which commissioned their publication in 1840;[113] "at once," wrote Farrand, "all other records paled into insignificance."[114]

107. *See, e.g.*, R. BERGER, GOVERNMENT BY JUDICIARY: THE TRANSFORMATION OF THE FOURTEENTH AMENDMENT 304 (1977).

108. 1 PAPERS OF JOHN MARSHALL 256 n.7 (H. Johnson ed. 1974).

109. Letter from William Davie to James Iredell (Dec. 19, 1788) (available in Iredell Papers, Duke University).

110. *Id.*

111. 2 G. MCREE, LIFE AND CORRESPONDENCE OF JAMES IREDELL 235 (1858).

112. 2 ANNALS OF CONG. 2005 (1791).

113. The document's history is chronicled in correspondence in 1 THE PAPERS OF JAMES MADISON, *supra* note 3, at xii-xxiv.

114. 1 M. FARRAND, *supra* note 7, at xv.

So comprehensive and convincing did the notes appear that most readers accepted them as authoritative. Partisans of Alexander Hamilton, however, challenged their veracity and an undercurrent of skepticism about their accuracy has continued ever since. Gaillard Hunt, for example, in a preface to an edition of Madison's notes published in 1920, commented on "the suspicious investigator, who thinks that Madison may have made alterations in his original record so as to suppress or distort the truth or give a coloring to the facts."[115]

The suspicious investigators found their champion three decades later in Professor William Winslow Crosskey of the University of Chicago Law School. Crosskey revealed his true feelings about Madison and his notes to his constitutional law classes. According to the reminiscence of a student, Crosskey would begin his class by slamming Farrand's *Records* on his desk and promising "to demonstrate to you that Madison was a forger—he tampered with the notes he kept of the debates at the federal constitutional convention in order to suit his own political advantage and that of his party."[116] Crosskey was more circumspect in the first two volumes of his opus, *Politics and the Constitution in the History of the United States*,[117] published in 1953, merely suggesting "the possibility that his [Madison's] testimony may have been, not inadvertently, but deliberately false and misleading."[118] Elsewhere in the volume, however, Crosskey became more explicit, declaring that Madison "presented falsely the sentiments of other men"[119] and inserted "spurious" dialogue in his notes.[120] Crosskey argued that Madison's motive in doctoring his manuscript was to play politics—to make his Convention notes support the doctrines of the Jeffersonian-Republican party that coalesced in the 1790s and that Madison helped to lead for the remainder of his career. If we accept Crosskey's account, Madison's notes, no less than Genet's and Lloyd's, were the product of political partisanship and were, on that account, corrupt.

Crosskey's volumes aroused conflicting passions. Admirers praised them enthusiastically;[121] detractors accused the author of McCarthyism on the grounds that Crosskey made unproven charges and innuendos

115. THE DEBATES IN THE FEDERAL CONVENTION OF 1787 WHICH FRAMED THE CONSTITUTION OF THE UNITED STATES OF AMERICA at xxi (G. Hunt & J. Scott eds. 1920) [hereinafter THE DEBATES].

116. Krash, *William Winslow Crosskey*, 35 U. CHI. L. REV. 232, 232 (1968).

117. W. CROSSKEY, *supra* note 35.

118. 2 *id.* at 1009.

119. 2 *id.* at 1012.

120. 1 *id.* at 313.

121. *See, e.g.*, Heinmann & Kelso, Politics and the Constitution—*A Dual Review* (Book Review), 39 IOWA L. REV. 139 (1953).

against Madison.[122] Mixed reviews did not discourage Professor Crosskey.[123] He completed most of a third volume, published posthumously by his disciple William Jeffery in 1980,[124] bringing his account up to the eve of the Convention. Crosskey also finished some sections on the Convention itself, including one on the ex post facto and contract clauses that was published posthumously as a law review article in 1968.[125] Crosskey characteristically charged Madison with fabricating passages in his notes and further distorting them by deliberately omitting relevant information.[126]

Although potentially a formidable weapon in the debates over the validity of attempting to discern the Framer's "original intent," Crosskey's thesis has not been wielded by legal scholars. Some historians and biographers, however, have embraced it with enthusiasm. In 1970, for example, Paul Clarkson and Samuel Jett, biographers of *Luther Martin of Maryland*,[127] charged that "scores of . . . serious (and often demonstrably inaccurate) 'corrections,' alterations, and additions, made over a period of fifty years . . . raise a serious question as to accuracy of [Madison's] record."[128] The treatment Madison's notes receive in Christopher and James Collier's 1986 monograph, *Decision in Philadelphia: The Constitutional Convention of 1787*,[129] demonstrates the persistence of Crosskey's influence.[130] The Colliers draw on the scholarship of S. Sidney Ulmer, himself an adherent of Crosskey, who in 1958 charged that Madison's "objectivity" as a reporter of the Convention debates was "corrupted beyond repair,"[131] to assert that "Charles Pinckney of South Carolina was cheated of credit for his role in modeling the Constitution" by Madison's having "suppressed" evidence of Pinckney's activities in

122. For the charge of McCarthyism, see Hart, *Professor Crosskey and Judicial Review*, 67 HARV. L. REV. 1456, 1475 (1954).

123. Crosskey promised to present fully documented proof in later volumes. 2 W. CROSSKEY, *supra* note 35, at 1175.

124. 3 W. CROSSKEY & W. JEFFREY, POLITICS AND THE CONSTITUTION IN THE HISTORY OF THE UNITED STATES (1980).

125. Crosskey, *The Ex-Post-Facto and the Contracts Clauses in the Federal Convention: A Note on the Editorial Ingenuity of James Madison*, 35 U. CHI. L. REV. 248 (1968).

126. *Id.* at 252-53.

127. P. CLARKSON & S. JETT, LUTHER MARTIN OF MARYLAND (1970).

128. *Id.* at 95.

129. C. COLLIER & J. COLLIER, DECISION IN PHILADELPHIA: THE CONSTITUTIONAL CONVENTION OF 1787 (1986).

130. *See id.* at 69, 81. Other scholars have relied on Crosskey's work. In 1984, John Murrin praised portions of Crosskey's work. About Crosskey's attacks against Madison, however, Murrin concluded, "To this reviewer, Crosskey's accusation seems tortured and unconvincing. Madison's memorandum is hardly a 'clear' instance of falsification. . . . Crosskey's attempt to indict Madison is premised on pure speculation." Murrin, Book Review, 58 N.Y.U. L. REV. 1254, 1263-64 (1983) (reviewing 3 W. CROSSKEY & W. JEFFREY, *supra* note 124).

131. Ulmer, *Charles Pinckney: Father of the Constitution*, 10 S.C.L.Q. 225, 245 (1958).

Philadelphia.[132] And, in a passage of pure Crosskey, the Colliers charge that after 1800, Madison became interested in "controlling as much as he could the history" of the creation of the Constitution and "altered his own speeches" to accomplish his objective.[133] Madison, they conclude, "improved his own arguments and abbreviated those of his opponents."[134]

Crosskey himself was more severe with Madison, charging that Madison invented dialogue at the Convention exactly as would a writer of fiction. Thus, he argued that John Dickinson's speech on August 29, explaining Blackstone's definition of the scope of ex post facto laws, was "a later Madisonian fabrication";[135] that debates on August 21 on the imports and exports clause contained "certain spurious passages";[136] and that a colloquy between Dickinson and Gouverneur Morris on August 15 had "very much the appearance of a later interpolation."[137]

No visual evidence supports these charges—an examination of the relevant manuscript pages of Madison's notes reveals no significant alteration of the text on any of these dates. Therefore, Crosskey's allegations must be based on a theory that Madison completely rewrote his notes (or parts of them) at a later date using a fresh supply of paper and substituted the newly composed sheets for the ones he had prepared earlier. Does an examination of the paper used in Madison's manuscript support such a theory?

2. *Their Accuracy Confirmed.*—Watermarks on the pages of Madison's manuscript notes reveal that he used British papers, predominantly those of the celebrated Kentish manufacturer James Whatman, whose family has been called the "most eminent British paper makers of the eighteenth century."[138] On all but seven days of the Convention Madison used Whatman paper, recognized by three watermarks: (1) J Whatman, (2) a crown and post horn with a pendant cursive W, or (3) a crown and post horn with a pendant GR. The only days Madison did not use Whatman paper were June 26, June 29, July 17, and July 18 when he employed paper with the watermark T French; and September 7, 15, and 17, when he used paper marked Budgen. All of this paper must have been manufactured before 1794 because none of it is dated,

132. C. Collier & J. Collier, *supra* note 129, at 64, 69.
133. *Id.* at 66-67.
134. *Id.* at 81.
135. Crosskey, *supra* note 125, at 252.
136. 1 W. Crosskey, *supra* note 35, at 313.
137. 2 *id.* at 1021.
138. T. Balston, James Whatman: Father and Son 1 (1957).

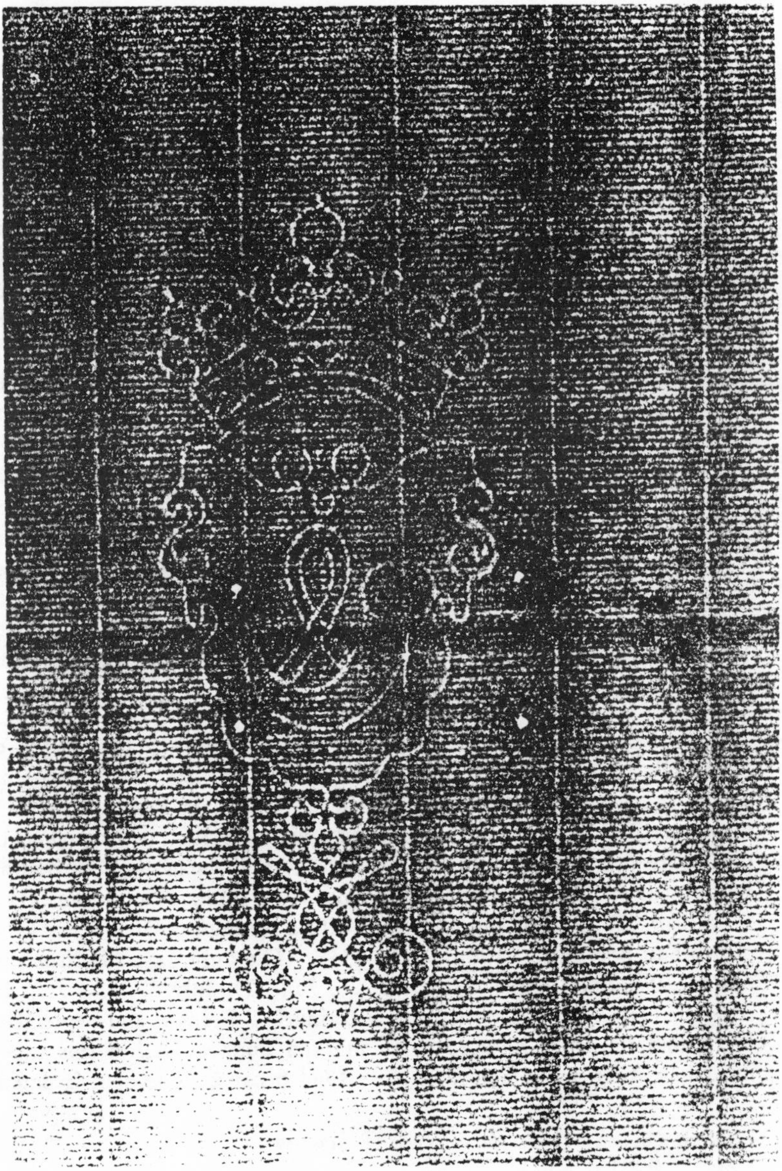

Watermark on paper used by James Madison in taking notes on Wednesday, July 18, 1787. This watermark, across the horizontal center of the open sheet, is a "W" (James Whatman) cypher appended to crowned shield with post horn.

28

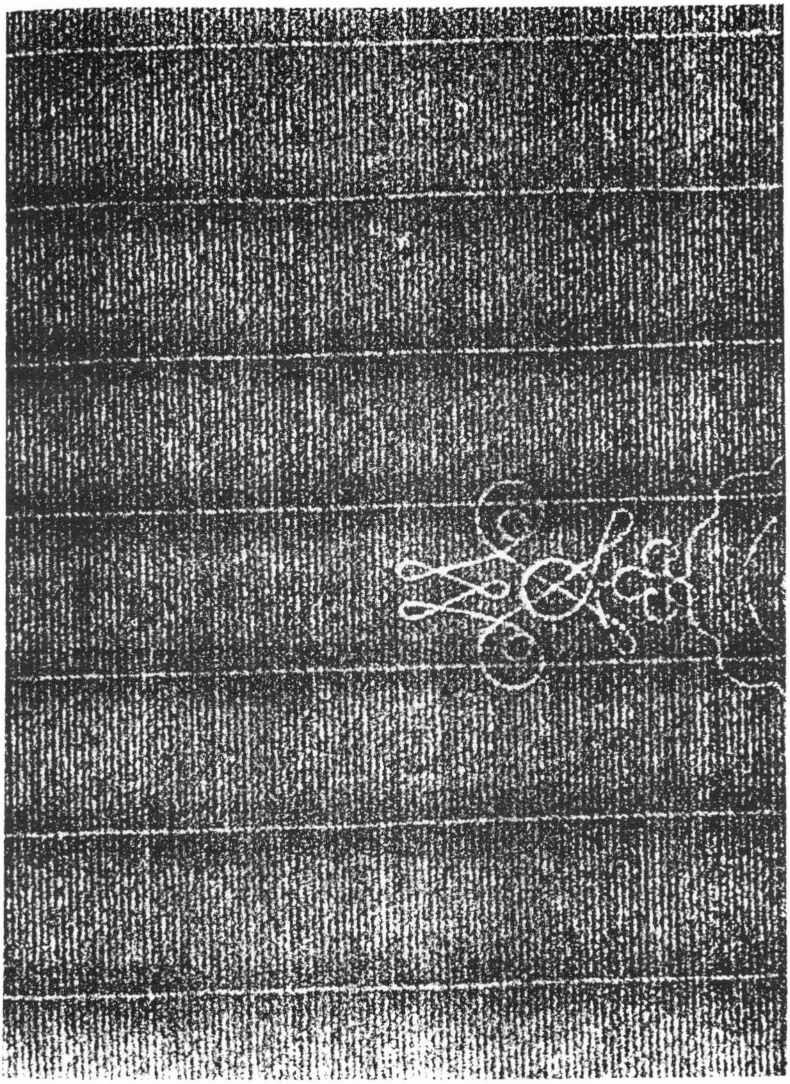

Watermark on paper used by James Madison in writing to Thomas Jefferson on July 18, 1787. The watermark is identical to the one on the facing page. Chain and laid line comparison proves the letter and note sheets to be identical.

and a British law of 1794 required all paper to be dated to obtain a rebate on the export excise tax.[139]

A comparison of Madison's notes with letters he wrote during the Convention demonstrates that on every date such a comparison is possible, the paper used for the notes and letters is identical. For example, on July 18, Madison wrote Jefferson a letter on paper with Whatman's crown, post horn, and cursive W watermark; the July 18 pages in the notes bear the same watermark. When chain lines and laid lines are compared, using betaradiography, the letter and note sheets prove to be identical (see pages 28-29). Similar results are obtained by comparing other letters written during the summer, for example, Madison to Pendleton on May 27, to Jefferson on June 6, to Monroe on June 10, to Madison, Sr., on July 28 and September 4, to Convention notes composed on each of these days. Paper studies indicate that Madison's notes were written out, as he later claimed they were, as soon as possible after he took them on the floor of the Convention.[140]

Also militating against the theory of a later, massive adulteration of Madison's notes is the recent discovery of the "Eppes copy" of those notes. Probably in the summer of 1791, though possibly as late as 1793, John Wayles Eppes, Thomas Jefferson's nephew, who was living at the time with his uncle in Philadelphia, transcribed Madison's notes.[141] Eppes' transcription, less the pages from June 21 to July 18, has been

139. *Id.* at 157.

140. 1 M. FARRAND, *supra* note 7, at xvi.

> In a preface to the Debates, written before his death, Madison had explained with what care the material was gathered and written up:
>
> "I chose a seat in front of the presiding member, with the other members, on my right and left hand. In this favorable position for hearing all that passed I noted in terms legible and in abbreviations and marks intelligible to myself what was read from the Chair or spoken by the members; and losing not a moment unnecessarily between the adjournment and reassembling of the Convention I was enabled to write out my daily notes during the session or within a few finishing days after its close."
>
> Indeed Madison was evidently regarded by his fellow-delegates to the Convention as a semi-official reporter of their proceedings, for several of them took pains to see that he was supplied with copies of their speeches and motions.

Id. (footnotes omitted).

141. For a discussion of Eppes' transcription, see 19 PAPERS OF THOMAS JEFFERSON 549-51 (J. Boyd ed. 1974) and 10 PAPERS OF JAMES MADISON 8-9 (R. Rutland, C. Hobson, W. Rachal & F. Teute eds. 1977) [hereinafter R. RUTLAND]. Both Boyd and Rutland give the history behind the "Eppes copy." In what was probably the summer of 1791, Thomas Jefferson was tutoring his nephew, John Wayles Eppes, and as an exercise Jefferson had Eppes copy Madison's convention notes. R. RUTLAND, *supra*, at 7. The seriousness of the task impressed Eppes such that he later revealed that

> [t]he particular and confidential manner in which he entrusted them to me prevented my making the smallest extract from any part of them—and so careful was I of preserving sacred a document the importance of which to posterity I could not but feel, that I never suffered the papers to mix either with my own or any others entrusted to my care.

19 PAPERS OF THOMAS JEFFERSON, *supra*, at 549.

found in the Edward Everett papers at the Massachusetts Historical Society. A comparison of the Eppes transcription with Madison's notes for August 15, 21, and 29, dates on which Professor Crosskey claimed Madison "fabricated" and "interpolated" the proceedings, demonstrates that the two documents are identical, proving no changes were made in Madison's notes (on these dates, at least) after Eppes executed his copy in 1791 or 1793. It appears, then, that Madison did not rewrite the story of the Constitutional Convention later in life.

As Farrand pointed out, however, Madison did make some changes in his notes in the years after the Convention.[142] Failing to understand Madison's purposes, Professor Wofford misjudged his alterations. There is no explanation, however, for Wofford's fabrication of the statement he attributed to Farrand, that Madison's emendations "seriously impaired the value of his notes."[143] Wofford asserted that "after the publication of the official—and inaccurate—*Journal*, Madison went over his notes and made numerous changes in them."[144] It has been shown above, however, that the mistakes in the *Journal* were so inconsequential—involving only a few computational and assignment of vote errors—that even if Madison included all of the *Journal* errors, he would not have significantly compromised the value of his notes. Madison, however, did not use the printed *Journal* as the sole source of his emendations. Unbeknownst to Wofford, Madison had a *copy* of Secretary William Jackson's manuscript journal years before its publication in 1819; by using it he avoided incorporating any editorial errors that John Quincy Adams may have introduced.

In taking notes at the Convention, Madison had the good sense not to try to do too much.[145] If a set speech was being delivered, in many cases he did not try to record it. Instead, he sought copies from the speakers, who usually obliged, either immediately or later in the proceedings.[146] Madison followed the same practice with motions and resolu-

142. 1 M. FARRAND *supra* note 7, at xvi-xix; *see infra* note 149.

143. Wofford, *supra* note 37, at 505 (citing 1 M. FARRAND, *supra* note 7, at xvii). This statement does not occur in any of the editions of Farrand's *Records*.

144. *Id.*

145. In a letter to John Adams, Jefferson wrote:

> Do you know that there exists in manuscript the ablest work of this kind ever yet executed, of the debates of the constitutional convention of Philadelphia in 1788? The whole of everything said and done there was taken down by Mr. Madison, with a labor and exactness beyond comprehension.

Letter from Thomas Jefferson to John Adams (Aug. 10, 1815), *reprinted in* 3 M. FARRAND, *supra* note 7, at 421.

146. The manuscript of Madison's notes at the Library of Congress contains motions and speeches, such as Randolph's of May 29 introducing the Virginia Plan, in the handwriting of the authors who gave them to Madison to incorporate into his notes.

tions. Short ones he recorded on the spot; longer ones he obtained from their movers after the session. It is obvious he anticipated having access to Jackson's journal, for during the introduction of long motions such as that of August 18, which he did not at the time record, he reminded himself to "see Journal of Convention."[147] Madison thus expected that Jackson, as secretary of the Convention, would preserve in his journal all the motions and resolutions made and that after the Convention he could borrow Jackson's journal and remedy the omissions in his notes. This is precisely what happened. In 1789, Washington lent Jackson's manuscript journal to Madison and Madison made a copy.[148] Then, Madison compared his notes to his copy and inserted in the notes, on slips of paper of varying sizes, the texts of the motions and resolutions that he had not recorded in 1787. When the journal was printed in 1819, Madison compared it with his notes, as expanded by the 1789 collation, and made some additional corrections in the interest of further improving the record.[149] Thus, insofar as existing evidence permits a judgment, Madison's notes are a faithful account of what he recorded at the Convention in 1787—augmented by motions, resolutions, and votes that he believed to be, and in the vast majority of cases were, accurately recorded by Jackson and accurately printed by John Quincy Adams in 1819.

We see, then, that unlike Yates' notes and the state ratifying debates, Madison's notes and the Convention journal do not suffer from editorial interventions by their authors or others, disqualifying them as sources of information about the Convention. But the question of how accurately these works reveal the intentions of the Framers remains, for

147. This reminder in Madison's manuscript of the notes of debates at the Library of Congress was not reprinted by Farrand.

148. On Madison's copy of the official journal and the use to which he put it, see Pierson & Keller, *A New Madison Manuscript Relating to the Federal Convention of 1787*, 36 AM. HIST. REV. 17-30 (1930).

149. Farrand discovered that, when Genet published his edition of Yates' notes in 1821, Madison collated it with his notes and incorporated some of Yates' material. 1 M. FARRAND, *supra* note 7, at xviii. The amount of borrowing from Yates turns out, on examination, to be minimal.

> Another extensive set of corrections is to be found in the speeches made in debate. These are generally in the form of additions to Madison's original record. Because of misquotations of his own remarks, Madison condemned Yates's notes severely, as being a "very erroneous edition of the matter". It is more than surprising, then, to discover that these additions were taken from Yates.

Id. at xviii (footnote omitted). Hunt and Scott explain such a curious borrowing by minimizing the information that Madison was willing to take from Yates.

> The chief source of Madison's corrections of his notes was the official *Journal* of the convention which was printed in 1819 and Yate's *Secret Proceedings and Debates of the Federal Convention* which appeared in 1821. Whenever Madison thought either of these records were more correct than his he changed or added to his; but he noted more frequently errors in the official *Journal* itself. Yate's record he regarded as having little value. Nevertheless, he derived from it a few lesser motions which had escaped him.

THE DEBATES, *supra* note 115, at xxi-xxii.

although they are faithful accounts of what Madison and Jackson recorded in 1787, it is necessary to know if what Madison and Jackson recorded was a faithful account of what occurred on the floor of the Convention. In short, how good were they as reporters?

3. Lingering Questions.—The Convention journal consists of little more than a chronological list of motions. It is, in one of Genet's few accurate statements about a constitutional document, a mere "diplomatic skeleton" that needs the discourse of delegates to "fill up . . . its vital parts."[150] Why did the journal lack debates that would explain the objectives of the delegates in making their motions, as well as the meaning they attached to such motions? Secretary Jackson did keep shorthand notes of the debates using his own idiosyncratic system. He was preparing to publish these notes in 1827 to flesh out his skeleton,[151] but no publication appeared and the notes have disappeared. The journal, therefore, reveals little about the delegates' intent.

Madison's notes, then, stand alone as the key to the Framers' intentions. If his notes on any given day are compared to the fragmentary records of debates left by other delegates that Farrand printed or that have been discovered more recently, a rough approximation between the different accounts is evident—demonstrating that Madison was not inventing dialogue, but was trying to capture what was said. Still, there is an enigma about Madison's note-taking methods. The Convention was in session from 10:00 A.M.[152] to mid-afternoon every day except Sunday—"not less than five, for a large part of the time Six and sometimes 7 hours sitting every day," Washington wrote on September 17, 1787.[153] These were full sessions of the Convention; committees, as Madison and others attested, met before or after the day's business, and there is no

150. Proposals for Publishing the *Secret Debates of the Convention* (Albany, New York Mar. 30, 1821) (available in Genet Papers, Library of Congress).

151. Memorandum of Timothy Pickering (Aug. 11, 1827) (available in Pickering Papers, Massachusetts Historical Society).

152. Max Farrand noted:

> It seems to have been the practise of the Convention at the close of the day's session to adjourn until the next morning at ten o'clock. Apparently the hours were somewhat irregular, and on August 18, it was agreed to meet precisely at 10 A.M., and no motion to adjourn was to be in order until 4 P.M. On August 24, the hour of adjournment was fixed at 3 P.M.

1 M. FARRAND, *supra* note 7, at 2 n.1.

153. 5 DIARIES OF GEORGE WASHINGTON 185 (D. Jackson & D. Twohig eds. 1979). In a letter of September 20, 1787, to Mrs. Jane Mecom, Benjamin Franklin confirmed that the Convention met for at least five hours per day. 3 M. FARRAND, *supra* note 7, at 98 ("The Convention finish'd the 17th Instant. I attended the Business of it 5 Hours in every Day from the Beginning; which is something more than four Months.").

evidence that the Convention took breaks, although individual members must have excused themselves now and again.

If read aloud, Madison's notes for any particular day consume only a few minutes, suggesting that he may have recorded only a small part of each day's proceedings. An experiment was tried to verify this hypothesis. On April 17-19, 1986, the Council of Scholars of the Library of Congress sponsored a symposium on scholarship. A portion of the final day was devoted to a discussion of the symposium papers previously delivered. Thirty-odd people participated in the symposium, roughly the number present on any one day during the Convention. A chairman moderated exchanges about issues raised earlier in the symposium. The debates were recorded on electromagnetic tape and transcribed verbatim. One hour's discussion yielded 8,400 words. Comparing this figure to the 6,000-7,000 words used in a typical, fifty minute undergraduate lecture[154] demonstrates its plausibility. For comparison purposes a word count was made of Madison's debates for each day the Convention was in session in June. June was chosen because it was Madison's most productive month as a recorder. The weather was cool, he was fresh, and the Convention was talking rather than incessantly voting on motions as it did in August and September. Madison averaged 2,740 words per session in June. Because sessions lasted five hours—the Convention did not go to a longer schedule until August[155]—he averaged 548 words per hour, a figure which can be rounded up to 600 words per hour to simplify calculations. At this rate Madison recorded only 600 of a possible 8,400 words per hour, or seven percent of each hour's proceedings. Even if the possible words per hour are reduced to 6,000, Madison recorded only ten percent of each hour's proceedings.

This experiment, it will be objected, is impressionistic, unscientific, and flawed. And so it is. Yet conceding every shortcoming, it demonstrates that there is a significant quantitative difference between what Madison recorded and what was said at the Convention, even if the shortfall cannot be expressed in a mathematical percentage precise enough to please the more pedantic. Because Madison's raw Convention notes—his "abbreviations and marks intelligible to myself"[156]—have not survived, it is not known if he recorded all or nearly all of each session and then severely compressed the results or if he followed stenographer

154. Twenty typed pages, more or less, of 350-odd words.

155. On August 18, the Convention voted to begin meeting from 10:00 A.M. to 4:00 P.M. to relieve the "extreme anxiety of many members of the Convention to bring the business to an end." 2 M. FARRAND, *supra* note 7, at 328.

156. 1 *id.* at xvi.

Robertson's practice in the Virginia Convention of ignoring everything that seemed "desultory" or "irregular."[157] Whatever the case, much appears to be missing.

Another feature of Madison's notes is troublesome. His own remarks at the Convention occupy a considerable portion of the notes, yet they cannot have been delivered as they are now recorded in print. Madison could not speak and record at the same time. Because he did not prepare his speeches in advance—"having never written one before hand," as he reported late in life[158]—dialogue attributed to him must have been composed after the day's proceedings. After a few hours reflection, Madison may have written a good deal more and a good deal that differed from what he said earlier. Consider his speech of June 6 that some political scientists regard as among the most important delivered at the Convention. In it, Madison presented his theory of the benefits of an expanded republic, which he elaborated in *Federalist 10.*[159] As it appears in Farrand's printed version of Madison's notes, the speech occupies approximately two pages.[160] Lansing did not report it at all; Genet-Yates and Hamilton gave it six lines;[161] Pierce five;[162] and King four.[163] The speech as delivered must have been far briefer than the one Madison inserted in his notes. Speeches written and "improved" after the event and large-scale deletions are reminiscent of Genet, Lloyd, and the shorthand reporters, however different Madison's motives may have been.

Madison's notes are not a forgery, but they are far from a verbatim record of what was said in the Convention. They omit much of what happened in Philadelphia. The extent of their omission is the measure of the difficulty in using them to discover the delegates' intentions.

III. A Note on the Documentation of the Bill of Rights

The First Congress under the new federal government, meeting

157. 11 PAPERS OF JAMES MADISON 75 (R. Rutland & C. Hobson eds. 1977). "David Robertson's effort to preserve the Richmond debates in stenographic form was noble but flawed. He was absent on at least one occasion, and on others he admittedly could not hear the speaker, or he skimmed over parts of speeches which struck him as 'desultory,' or 'some irregular conversation.' " *Id.* Yet, Rutland and Hobson write, "With all these shortcomings, Robertson's work (despite Anti-Federalists' objections that he was a Federalist partisan) still provides the most comprehensive record of what occurred in any of the state ratifying conventions." *Id.* at 76.

158. Letter from James Madison to Gales and Seaton (Aug. 5, 1833) (available in Madison Papers, Library of Congress).

159. THE FEDERALIST No. 10 (J. Madison).

160. 1 M. FARRAND, *supra* note 7, at 134-36.

161. 1 *id.* at 141, 146.

162. 1 *id.* at 147.

163. 1 *id.* at 143-44.

from early April through the end of September 1789, sent twelve amendments to the states for ratification on September 25, 1789. The ten amendments eventually ratified are known, of course, as the Bill of Rights.

In 1789, the Senate did not permit its proceedings to be reported.[164] The documentary record of debates on the Bill of Rights consists, therefore, of deliberations in the House of Representatives. These were published in 1834 by the Washington firm of Gales & Seaton under the title, *The Debates and Proceedings in the Congress of the United States*, known to and cited by scholars as *Annals of Congress*.[165] For the first session of the First Congress, the period covering the gestation of the Bill of Rights, the *Annals of Congress* is a reprinting of a publication called the *Congressional Register*,[166] prepared by none other than Thomas Lloyd, the shorthand reporter of the debates in the Pennsylvania and Maryland ratifying conventions.

Far from improving by 1789, Lloyd's technical skills had become dulled by excessive drinking.[167] In 1940, the Library of Congress acquired the manuscript of Lloyd's shorthand notes of the debates from April 8 to May 15, 1789, and from January 19 to June 3, 1790. These notes were transcribed, insofar as they could be, by a shorthand expert, and the transcription was compared to the debates printed by Lloyd in the *Congressional Register*. It was discovered that what Lloyd published "bears only slight resemblance to the literal transcript of his own notes. Sometimes a speech is printed for which no notes or only very brief notes exist; sometimes a long speech reported in the manuscript is printed very briefly or not at all."[168] Another investigator has reported that Lloyd's reports were frequently "garbled" and that he neglected to report speeches whose texts are known to exist elsewhere.[169] Lloyd's manuscript also demonstrates a wandering mind, for it is periodically interrupted by doodling, sketches of members, horses, and landscapes, and by poetry (see facing page). It is thus little wonder that on May 9, 1789, Madison condemned the *Congressional Register* as exhibiting "the strongest evidences of mutilation & perversion"[170] and that Elbridge

164. A NATIONAL PROGRAM FOR THE PUBLICATION OF HISTORICAL DOCUMENTS: A REPORT TO THE PRESIDENT BY THE NATIONAL HISTORICAL PUBLICATIONS COMMISSION 93 (1954) [hereinafter NATIONAL PROGRAM].

165. *Id.*

166. 12 PAPERS OF JAMES MADISON 63 (C. Hobson, W. Rachal, J. Sisson & R. Rutland eds. 1977).

167. Tinling, *supra* note 80, at 537-38.

168. *Id.* at 530.

169. NATIONAL PROGRAM, *supra* note 164, at 93-94.

170. Tinling, *supra* note 80, at 533 (quoting from Madison Papers, Library of Congress).

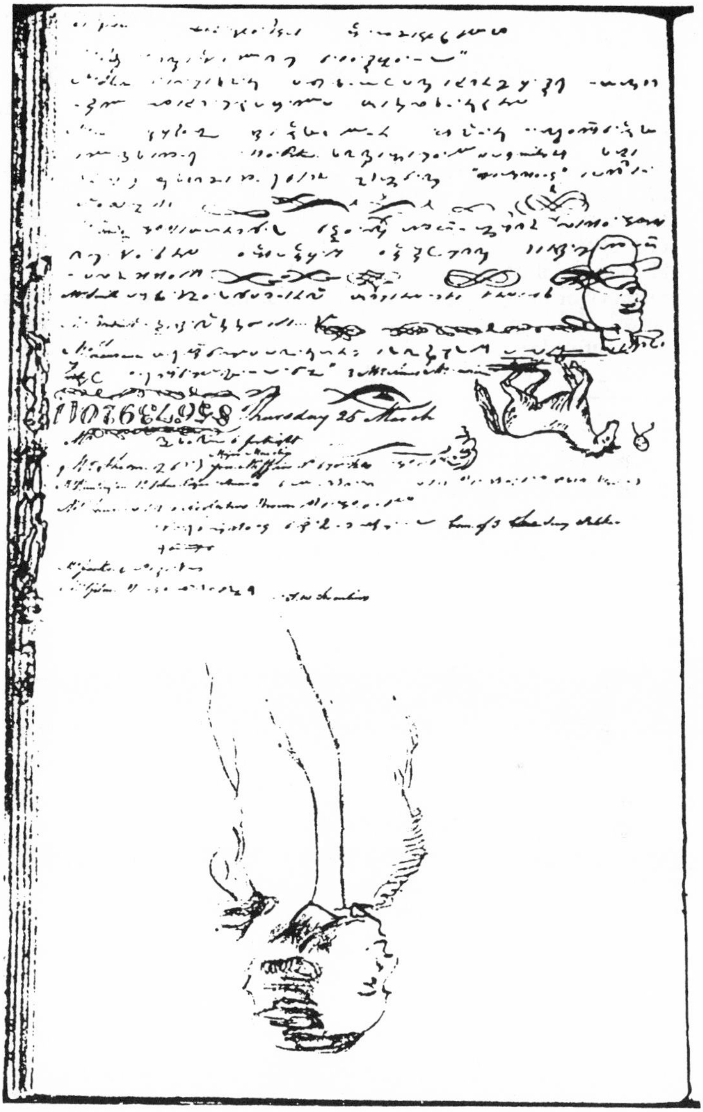

Page from Thomas Lloyd's notes of deliberations in the First Congress in the House of Representatives.

Gerry, after accusing Lloyd of persisting in his Federalist partisanship, complained that "[s]ometimes members were introduced as uttering arguments directly the reverse of what they had advanced."[171] The accuracy of Lloyd's reports "is not to be relied on," Madison advised a correspondent.

> The face of the debates shews that they are defective, and desultory, where not revised, or written out by the Speakers. In some instances, he makes them inconsistent with themselves, by erroneous reports of their speeches at different times on the same subject. He was indolent and sometimes filled up blanks in his notes from memory or *imagination*. I recollect that he put into my mouth, a speech, drawn much from the latter and in its style suited rather to a youthful declaimer than to me in my situation. He finally, became a votary of the bottle and perhaps made too free use of it sometimes at the period of his printed debates.[172]

Some Congressmen did not censure Lloyd quite so severely, but even his apologists admitted that his reports abounded with error.[173]

Therefore, in seeking to ascertain the intentions of the drafters of the Bill of Rights, scholars should know that the *Annals of Congress*—the source traditionally relied upon for that purpose—is the voice of Thomas Lloyd, a voice even less reliable in 1789 than it was at the Pennsylvania ratifying convention.

IV. Conclusion

This Article has examined the most important documentary records surrounding the creation of the Constitution and has found them to be defective in varying degrees. In some cases recorders were incompetent. In others, documents were separated from their compilers and published by editors with partisan agendas who revised and deleted the original material. And in yet others, compilers retained control over their records but still produced alterations and omissions. There were differences in the extent of editorial alteration and in the motives of the editors. But in all cases the resulting documents are not full, reliable records of the debates at the Constitutional and ratifying conventions.

If we conclude that this array of defects has corrupted the historical documentation of the Constitution, it would appear to be impossible to rely upon the documentary record to discover the intentions of the Framers. A jurisprudence of original intention is not precluded by these find-

171. Tinling, *supra* note 80, at 532, 536.

172. Letter from James Madison to Edward Everett (Jan. 7, 1832) (available in Edward Everett Papers), *quoted in* Tinling, *supra* note 80, at 537-38.

173. Tinling, *supra* note 80, at 533-36.

ings, but it would be obliged to seek the intention of the Framers in the words of the Constitution, as the Framers themselves intended. Whether so restrictive a requirement would promote or retard the goals of the proponents of original intent is beyond the scope of this inquiry. The author will be satisfied if lawyers, judges, historians, and legal scholars are reminded, as they periodically need to be, that the mere fact that a record is in print does not make it reliable.

VOLUME 98 MARCH 1985 NUMBER 5

HARVARD LAW REVIEW

THE ORIGINAL UNDERSTANDING OF ORIGINAL INTENT

*H. Jefferson Powell**

When interpreting the Constitution, judges and commentators often invoke the "original intent of the framers" in support of their positions. Many claim that such an interpretive strategy is not only currently desirable, but indeed was the expectation of the Constitution's drafters and early interpreters. In this Article, Professor Powell examines the historical validity of the claim that the framers of the Constitution expected future interpreters to seek the meaning of the document in the framers' intent. He first examines the various cultural traditions that influenced legal interpretation at the time of the Constitution's birth. Turning to the history of the Constitution's framing, ratification, and early interpretation, Professor Powell argues that although early constitutional discourse did contain references to "original intention" and the "intent of the framers," the meaning of such terms was markedly different from their current usage. He concludes that modern resort to the "intent of the framers" can gain no support from the assertion that such was the framers' expectation, for the framers themselves did not believe such an interpretive strategy to be appropriate.

I. INTRODUCTION

"The world must construe according to its wits. This Court must construe according to the law."[1]

CONTEMPORARY discussion of the theory and methodology of constitutional interpretation exhibits no general agreement on the proper role either of history in general, or of the history of the Constitution's framing and ratification in particular. A few scholars argue that the latter is essentially irrelevant to the task of establishing constitutional norms;[2] a more common position is to recognize an obli-

---

* Associate Professor of Law, University of Iowa. University of Wales, B.A., 1975; Duke University, A.M., 1977; Yale Divinity School, M. Div., 1979; Yale Law School, J.D., 1982. This Article was written while I was a research associate at Yale Law School; I appreciate the school's support. For their comments, criticisms, and encouragement, I am greatly indebted to Mary Dudziak, Owen Fiss, Burke Marshall, Jan Powell, and George Priest.

[1] R. BOLT, A MAN FOR ALL SEASONS 152 (1962) (speech of Sir Thomas More at his trial).

[2] *See, e.g.*, Sandalow, *Constitutional Interpretation*, 79 MICH. L. REV. 1033 (1981) (arguing that historical evidence of the framers' intent cannot constrain modern interpretation). Michael Perry admits the theoretical legitimacy of judicial enforcement of the framers' intentions, but argues that in practice modern constitutional decisionmaking does not, and need not, depend

gation to avoid direct contradiction of the intentions and expectations of the Constitution's framers.[3] Finally, a minority of legal scholars,[4] and a substantial and influential group of judges,[5] maintain that the historically demonstrable intentions of the framers should be binding on contemporary interpreters of the Constitution. This last group not only invokes history ("the original understanding at Philadelphia"[6]) as a normative guide to the Constitution's meaning, but also claims historical warrant for this interpretive strategy.[7] Raoul Berger, for example, has assured us that "current indifference to the 'original intention' . . . is a relatively recent phenomenon."[8] The Constitution, according to Berger and others, "was written against a background of interpretive presuppositions" — chiefly, that the goal of future interpreters would be to carry out the framers' intent.[9] As a consequence, Berger argues, the intention of the framers should control interpretation, because it is only by examining their "original intent" that the interpreter can discover the normative meaning of the Constitution. In modern discussions, this view of constitutional decision-making has acquired a number of different labels; I shall call it "intentionalism."

The purpose of this Article is to examine the historical validity of the claim that the "interpretive intention"[10] informing the Constitution was an expectation that future interpreters would seek the instrument's meaning in the intentions of the delegates to the 1787 Constitutional Convention in Philadelphia. I am not concerned, then, with the historical question of what we would say early interpreters actually did in construing the Constitution, but with what they said they and others should do. I am also unconcerned in this Article with what contemporary interpreters should do, although my conclusions obviously have normative implications for strict intentionalists, who presumably regard the framers' interpretive intentions as binding for

---

on historical argument. *See* M. PERRY, THE CONSTITUTION, THE COURTS, AND HUMAN RIGHTS 19, 75 (1982).

3 *See, e.g.*, J. CHOPER, JUDICIAL REVIEW AND THE NATIONAL POLITICAL PROCESS at xvii–xviii (1980).

4 *See, e.g.*, 3 W. CROSSKEY & W. JEFFREY, POLITICS AND THE CONSTITUTION IN THE HISTORY OF THE UNITED STATES (1980); B. SIEGAN, ECONOMIC LIBERTIES AND THE CONSTITUTION 11–14 (1980).

5 *See* Bork, *Neutral Principles and Some First Amendment Problems*, 47 IND. L.J. 1 (1971); Rehnquist, *The Notion of a Living Constitution*, 54 TEX. L. REV. 693 (1976).

6 Trimble v. Gordon, 430 U.S. 762, 778 (1977) (Rehnquist, J., dissenting).

7 *See* Monaghan, *Our Perfect Constitution*, 56 N.Y.U. L. REV. 353, 375–76 (1981).

8 R. BERGER, GOVERNMENT BY JUDICIARY 363 (1977).

9 *Id.* at 365–66. Modern intentionalists, of course, do not claim that the legislators' personal motives, as distinguished from their intentions as lawmakers, are relevant. *See* Palmer v. Thompson, 403 U.S. 217, 224–25 (1971); *cf.* Fletcher v. Peck, 10 U.S. (6 Cranch) 87 (1810) (first Supreme Court case rejecting inquiry into legislators' motives).

10 On the concept of "interpretive intention," see Brest, *The Misconceived Quest for the Original Understanding*, 60 B.U.L. REV. 204, 215–16 (1980).

the same reasons they believe the framers' substantive opinions should control.

The Article first explores the various cultural resources available to late eighteenth century Americans seeking to conceptualize the unprecedented task of interpreting a written constitution.[11] The cultural influences of Enlightenment rationalism and British Protestantism combined in an unlikely alliance to engender a suspicion of any sort of interpretation at all. The rich interpretive tradition of the English common law, in contrast, offered a plethora of hermeneutical suggestions, sometimes conflicting with one another and usually peculiar to the specific type of instrument being construed. Turning to the views on constitutional interpretation expressed during and immediately after the ratification process, I conclude that there was a tension during this period between a global rejection of any and all methods of constitutional construction and a willingness to interpret the constitutional text in accordance with the common law principles that had been used to construe statutes.[12]

A consensus on the proper approach to construing the Constitution later emerged out of the political struggle between Federalists and Republicans during the administration of John Adams. To the embattled Republicans, conceiving the Constitution as a compact of sovereign states not only had an intellectual appeal, but also seemed a politically expedient means to challenge the activities of the Federalist-controlled national government. This substantive conception of the Constitution's nature was justified by, and in turn entailed, resort to an extratextual source: the "original intent" underlying the Constitution. The Republican constitutional theory swiftly became the common property of almost all American constitutionalists after the Republicans' electoral triumph in 1800.

Contemporary intentionalists are correct, therefore, in claiming that resort to "original intent" is an interpretive strategy of great antiquity in American constitutional discourse. Despite verbal similarities, however, modern intentionalism cannot be equated with the early Republican theory. As understood by its late eighteenth and

[11] Pre-Revolutionary constitutional discourse frequently referred to colonial charters and parliamentary documents, such as Magna Carta and the 1688 Bill of Rights, as evidence of the meaning of the English constitution. *See* G. WOOD, THE CREATION OF THE AMERICAN REPUBLIC: 1776–1787, at 259–73 (1969). The use of constitutions as written fundamental laws subject to judicial interpretation and enforcement, however, was an essentially new creation of the American Revolutionary period. *See id.* at 291. The practice, as applied to the state constitutions, was still in the embryonic stage in 1787.

[12] Eighteenth century criticism of traditional hermeneutical methods usually described what was being criticized as "construction" rather than "interpretation" of the text, perhaps because even the most literal and text-bound approach is still an interpretation. This distinction in usage, however, is not absolute. *See, e.g., infra* note 34; *see also* S. JOHNSON, A DICTIONARY OF THE ENGLISH LANGUAGE (London 1755) (entries for "construction" and "interpretation") (indicating that the two words can be used synonymously).

early nineteenth century proponents, the original intent relevant to constitutional discourse was not that of the Philadelphia framers, but rather that of the parties to the constitutional compact — the states as political entities. This original "original intent" was determined not by historical inquiry into the expectations of the individuals involved in framing and ratifying the Constitution, but by consideration of what rights and powers sovereign polities could delegate to a common agent without destroying their own essential autonomy. Thus, the original intentionalism was in fact a form of structural interpretation.[13] To the extent that constitutional interpreters considered historical evidence to have any interpretive value, what they deemed relevant was evidence of the proceedings of the state ratifying conventions, not of the intent of the framers. Only later, during the breakdown of the Republican consensus, did the attention of constitutional interpreters gradually shift from the "intention" of the sovereign states to the personal intentions of individual historical actors.

II. Hermeneutical Traditions in 1787

"There is more ado to interpret interpretations than to interpret things."[14]

We cannot appreciate how the task of interpreting the Constitution was originally understood unless we first know something about the intellectual tools that were available.[15] The Americans who wrote, debated, denounced, and ratified the Constitution of 1787 were thoroughly familiar with argument over the meaning and implications of "constitutions"; the "patriots" of the previous decade had understood the Revolution itself, in part, as the final, violent phase of a sustained effort to vindicate the true meaning of the ancient English constitution.[16] But pre-Revolutionary constitutional discourse differed in one obvious and vitally important manner from the constitutional task that independent America set for itself: the new federal Constitution,

---

[13] For a discussion of the concept of structural interpretation, see C. Black, Structure and Relationship in Constitutional Law (1969) (arguing that constitutional rules may be inferred from the structural relationships the Constitution ordains among governmental institutions).

[14] M. Montaigne, Of Experience (1588), *reprinted in* The Essays of Michel Eyquem de Montaigne III.13, at 518 (W. Hazlitt ed., C. Cotton trans. 1952).

[15] *But see* P. Bobbitt, Constitutional Fate 10 (1982) (contemporaneous British canons of construction are "largely beside the point"). To whatever extent Professor Bobbitt is making the historical assertion that late 18th century Americans regarded contemporaneous canons of construction as "beside the point," the abundant evidence to the contrary, *see infra* pp. 902–24, suggests that he is mistaken.

[16] *See generally* B. Bailyn, The Ideological Origins of the American Revolution (1967) (arguing that American resistance to Britain was often justified by the claim that Americans were defending English liberties and the ancient constitution); P. Maier, From Resistance to Revolution (1972) (same).

like those of the individual states, consisted not of a Burkean tradition of historical custom and political principle, but of a written document. As a result, constitutional argument in the new republics naturally and necessarily assumed the form of dispute over the proper interpretation of the constitutional texts. But Americans did not approach this novel task of constitutional interpretation free of all presuppositions about the appropriate method for construing a written instrument. They instead drew overtly on the various approaches to interpretation embedded in their cultural heritage.[17] The two most obvious sources of hermeneutical wisdom were the anti-interpretive tradition of Anglo-American Protestantism and the accumulated interpretive techniques of the common law.

A. The Cultural Rejection of Interpretation

One of the central themes of the Protestant Reformation of the sixteenth century was summed up in the Reformers' slogan, "*sola Scriptura*" (Scripture only).[18] In Britain, *sola Scriptura* became even more important than on the continent as a unifying principle for Protestants: the role of the English translation of the Bible in the spread of Protestantism in Britain, and Anglicanism's de-emphasis of substantive doctrine, made a professed adherence to biblical authority the main point of agreement for British Protestants.[19] In the name of obedience to the Bible, Protestants rejected the rich medieval tradition of interpretation, according to which literal exposition of the text was only one (and by no means necessarily the most important) methodology; likewise, they spurned the medieval acceptance of Pope and council as authoritative interpreters.[20] In the eyes of the British Protestants, the only authoritative, and indeed the only safe, interpreter of Scripture was Scripture itself.[21] Any exposition of the text that went beyond the text was, of necessity, a "human invention,"[22]

---

[17] *See, e.g.*, F. DWARRIS, A GENERAL TREATISE ON STATUTES *646 (in United States, interpretation of a constitution "requires the exercise of the same legal discretion as the interpretation or construction of a law"); THE FEDERALIST No. 78 (A. Hamilton) (courts, in construing the Constitution, will follow the familiar rules of interpretation).

[18] *See* R. BROWN, THE SPIRIT OF PROTESTANTISM 67 (1965).

[19] *See* A. DICKENS, THE ENGLISH REFORMATION 189–93 (rev. ed. 1971). Instead of a detailed examination of the ordinand's Protestant orthodoxy, the Anglican Book of Common Prayer asked of men about to be made priests whether they were resolved to teach as doctrine nothing "but that you shalbe perswaded may be concluded, and proued by the scripture?" FIRST BOOK OF COMMON PRAYER OF EDWARD VI, Ordinal 309 (Everyman's Library ed. 1968) (1st ed. London 1549).

[20] *See* R. GRANT, A SHORT HISTORY OF THE INTERPRETATION OF THE BIBLE 92–109 (rev. ed. 1984).

[21] *See, e.g.*, Westminster Confession of Faith I.9 (1647), *reprinted in* UNITED PRESBYTERIAN CHURCH IN THE UNITED STATES OF AMERICA, BOOK OF CONFESSIONS 6.009 (2d ed. 1970) [hereinafter cited as BOOK OF CONFESSIONS].

[22] J. SELDEN, TABLE-TALK: BEING THE DISCOURSES OF JOHN SELDEN ESQ. 25 (London

"which a discreet Man may do well; but 'tis his Scripture, not the Holy Ghost['s]."[23]

From this position it was but a short step, already taken with respect to medieval and contemporary Catholic interpretation, to the conclusion that such "human invention" is, necessarily and always, a corruption of the text's meaning.[24] For example, the Scots Confession of 1560, discussing the authority of general councils, granted that conciliar decrees might be accepted when confirmed "by the plain Word of God." But this did not mean that a council could develop doctrines beyond the letter of Scripture, "or even [offer] the true interpretation of it, which was not expressed previously by his holy will in his Word."[25] The distinction between a decree confirmable by a text and "the true interpretation" of that text is subtle, and from a modern viewpoint perhaps vacuous. The fact remains, however, that British Protestants fervently believed that such a distinction could and should be drawn, and that their own version of Christianity could be described truthfully as a presentation of the plain Word rather than as an interpretation — even a "true interpretation" — of Scripture. British Protestant writers in the post-Reformation era delighted in contrasting their own chaste literalism to the delusive and unscriptural interpretations of their theological opponents.[26]

1699). A 17th century jurist and member of Parliament, Selden participated in the parliamentary resistance to Charles I; this role gave him a place in the pantheon of Whig defenders of liberty whom the American revolutionaries regarded as constitutional authorities. *See* B. BAILYN, *supra* note 16, at 315; P. MAIER, *supra* note 16, at 48.

[23] J. SELDEN, *supra* note 22, at 45.

[24] "If I give any Exposition but what is express'd in the Text, that is my invention: if you give another Exposition, that is your invention, and both are Human." *Id.* at 25. Protestant insistence that interpretation is corruption was linked with the rejection of the "multiple sense" approach of medieval exegesis. *See* Westminster Confession of Faith I.9 (1647), *reprinted in* BOOK OF CONFESSIONS, *supra* note 21, at 6.009.

[25] Scots Confession ch. XX (1560), *reprinted in* BOOK OF CONFESSIONS, *supra* note 21, at 3.20.

[26] *See, e.g.*, Owen, Book Review (c. 1650), *reprinted in* INTRODUCTION TO PURITAN THEOLOGY: A READER 141 (E. Hindson ed. 1976) (criticizing Thomas More's 1643 work, *The Universality of God's Free Grace*). John Owen concludes his own elaborate interpretation of the Bible's teaching on the scope of divine grace with an attack on More for presenting "allegations and interpretations of Scripture" instead of the plainly revealed "mind and will of God." *Id.* at 170.

Critiques such as this by Protestant theologians planted the seeds of the deconstruction of Protestant orthodoxy undertaken by religious "liberals" in the late 17th and 18th centuries. Orthodox and liberal alike agreed with John Locke's claim that the sober and unprejudiced reader would find little need to interpret Scripture because such a reader would have no difficulty in understanding the plain meaning of the text. *See* J. Locke, Essay for the Understanding of St. Paul's Epistles, *reprinted in* 8 WORKS OF JOHN LOCKE at iii (11th ed. London 1812). Contemporary deistic and rationalistic critics of Protestant dogma thus could draw on the deeply ingrained literalism of British Protestantism in order to "demonstrate" the absurdities of traditional Christianity. *See generally* H. FREI, THE ECLIPSE OF BIBLICAL NARRATIVE 51–54, 66–85 (1974) (discussing the use of literalism by deists and others to attack Protestant orthodoxy).

Attacks on the legitimacy of scriptural interpretation spilled over easily into the political sphere.[27] Reform of the law emerged as a major theme of seventeenth century Puritan politics both in the American colonies and in interregnum England, and reformers saw the elimination of confusion and complexity in the law as a primary goal.[28] To the Puritans, the Bible could govern theological discourse because its meaning was lucid to the ordinary reader. Legal texts, in contrast, were usually obscure, and thus no explanation of their meaning could simply be "confirmed" by reference to their plain words. As a result, the Puritans argued, these supposedly authoritative texts could not in fact constrain judicial interpretation, and the elaborate interpretive techniques of the common law served only to justify judges' imposition of their personal views. Puritan lawyer William Sheppard was both prominent among and typical of the reformers. In 1656 Sheppard published a program for law reform entitled *Englands Balme*.[29] The centerpiece of his criticism of the existing statutory and common law was the claim that the law was so obscure that "it is not to be understood, when it is read," and was therefore "incertain," because not even judges could agree on its proper interpretation. Sheppard advocated a kind of codification that would make the law "cleer and certain" and would require judges to disavow traditional modes of interpretation and to pledge to follow the code's wording henceforth as "the setled law."[30]

The Puritan attack on traditional legal hermeneutics was largely unsuccessful in the mother country, but in the following century its main themes were absorbed into an ideology of opposition (the "Country" ideology) that served as an important intellectual foundation for both the American revolutionaries of the 1760s and 1770s and the Jeffersonian Republicans of the 1790s.[31] For the "Country" writers,

---

This type of British religious radicalism was influential in the thinking of many 18th century Americans. *See* D. BOORSTIN, THE LOST WORLD OF THOMAS JEFFERSON 151–66 (1948).

[27] *See generally* C. HILL, THE WORLD TURNED UPSIDE DOWN (2d ed. 1974) (discussing relationship between religious radicalism and political and social criticism in 17th century England).

[28] *See* E. DUMBAULD, THOMAS JEFFERSON AND THE LAW 146–55 (1978).

[29] *See id.* at 146.

[30] *See id.* at 148.

[31] This school of thought, which modern historians usually label the "Country" ideology, emerged in England in the early 18th century in reaction to the policies of the dominant "Court" Whigs. The Court leadership favored executive dominance in an increasingly powerful and centralized government. It supported a permanent military establishment and the encouragement of commerce through the Bank of England, and maintained a docile parliamentary majority through the use of patronage. Opposition leaders, both Tories and "Real Whigs" (who regarded the Court Whigs as apostates from the Whig heritage of 1688), developed an ideology of opposition based on suspicion of government in general and of a strong national executive in particular. The Country spokesmen identified the Court's manipulation of patronage and of the national debt as a process of "corrupting" English society that would culminate in the replacement of traditional free government by despotism on a continental model. Following 1760,

clarity and simplicity were necessary if law was to serve rather than smother liberty,[32] but these advantages of a known and written law would be lost if the law's meaning could be twisted by means of judicial construction. Furthermore, just as the Pope had usurped the authority of God by claiming the power to interpret His Word, so the judiciary could undermine the legislative prerogatives of the people's representatives by engaging in the corruptive process of interpreting legislative texts.

For cosmopolitan Americans, the influence of the *philosophes*[33] — the rationalist intellectuals and social critics of the Enlightenment era — reinforced the anti-interpretive tradition of British Protestantism. The *philosophes*, sometimes borrowing from earlier intellectual movements such as sixteenth century humanism,[34] perceived traditional interpretation of Scripture as one of the chief props supporting the theological absurdities and religious oppression perpetrated by the established churches, and saw the niggling interpretation of complicated or obscure laws as a relic of feudal misrule and political tyranny.[35] In addition, they condemned judicial interpretation of statutes as a violation of the separation of governmental powers many believed

---

Country thought became increasingly influential among the American colonists, both as an explanation for London's apparent drift toward tyranny and as a justification for resistance. Having victoriously expelled the "Court" from America by the Revolution, American Country thinkers like Thomas Jefferson were horrified to see it reemerge in the Federalist policies of the Washington and Adams administrations. Once again, the Country themes of localism and opposition to "energetic" government seemed relevant. *See* Murrin, *The Great Inversion, or Court versus Country: A Comparison of the Revolution Settlements in England (1688–1721) and America (1776–1816)*, in THREE BRITISH REVOLUTIONS: 1641, 1688, 1776, at 368, 379–83, 397–401, 404–11 (J. Pocock ed. 1980); *see also* L. BANNING, THE JEFFERSONIAN PERSUASION (1978) (tracing the development of Jeffersonian Republicanism from Country ideology).

[32] *See* L. FRIEDMAN, A HISTORY OF AMERICAN LAW 79 (1973); P. MILLER, THE LIFE OF THE MIND IN AMERICA 99–109, 239–49 (1965).

[33] The use of a single term such as *philosophes* for the predominantly French propagandists of the 18th century Enlightenment is misleading to the extent that it obscures the real disagreements — political, philosophical, and theological — among such figures as Voltaire, Diderot, Condorcet, and Rousseau. It suggests accurately enough the American tendency to treat the views of those sages as a collective body of "enlightened" (we would say "progressive") opinion and to select specific intellectual positions from them in an eclectic manner.

[34] One example of this humanist thought is Sir Thomas More's *Utopia*. More's Utopians considered the "simple and apparent sense of the law" the correct interpretation since it is "open to everyone." T. MORE, UTOPIA 69 (R. Adams trans. 1975) (1st ed. Louvain 1516). The *philosophes* were also influenced by the opposition to legal interpretation exhibited by English political thought. *See, e.g.*, J. GRAY, THE NATURE AND SOURCES OF THE LAW 172 (2d ed. 1921) (quoting Whig controversialist Benjamin Hoadly, who warned George I of the dangers inherent in interpretation in a sermon delivered before the King in 1717: "Whoever hath an *absolute authority* to *interpret* any written or spoken laws, it is *he* who is truly the *Law giver* to all intents and purposes, and not the person who first wrote or spoke them.").

[35] *See, e.g.*, VOLTAIRE, PHILOSOPHICAL DICTIONARY 289 (T. Besterman trans. 1971) (1st ed. Geneva 1764) (entry for "Civil and ecclesiastical laws") ("to interpret" the law "is nearly always to corrupt it").

necessary to a rational and free polity.[36] In his enormously influential essay on criminal law, the Italian jurist Cesare Beccaria wrote that judges in criminal cases must not be allowed the authority to interpret the laws because that would make them de facto legislators.[37] Beccaria contrasted "the constant fixed voice of the law" with "the erring instability of interpretation," and his firm conclusion — "the interpretation of laws is an evil" — expressed a view widely shared by educated and "progressive" individuals in the late eighteenth century.[38]

Either British biblicism or Enlightenment rationalism or both formed part of the mental furniture of virtually all literate Americans in the half-century from the Declaration of Independence through the presidency of John Quincy Adams.[39] It is therefore unsurprising that one can often discern the anti-interpretive biases of those traditions in American discussions of grand political issues,[40] as well as of private legal affairs.[41] For example, the Essex County convention, in rejecting the proposed Massachusetts constitution of 1778, explained that the document provided inadequate safeguards against "artful constructions" of the laws, with potentially tragic results.[42] The county's solution was a rigid separation of powers scheme that would enable each branch of government to check the others.[43] Such cultural reluctance to admit the legitimacy of significant interpretation of writ-

---

[36] *See, e.g.*, MONTESQUIEU, THE SPIRIT OF LAWS VI.3, at 34–35 (T. Nugent & J. Prichard trans. 1952) (1st ed. Geneva 1748) (in a republican polity the very nature of the constitution requires judges to follow the letter of the law).

[37] C. BECCARIA, ON CRIMES AND PUNISHMENTS 14–18 (H. Paolucci trans. 1963) (1st ed. Livorno 1764).

[38] *See id.*; *see also* G. WOOD, *supra* note 11, at 301–02 (discussing American objections to judicial interpretation).

[39] *Cf.* G. WOOD, *supra* note 11, at 17 (noting influence of Puritan theology and Enlightenment rationalism on Revolutionary thought).

[40] "Our peculiar security is in the possession of a written Constitution. Let us not make it a blank paper by construction." Letter from Thomas Jefferson to Wilson C. Nicholas (Sept. 7, 1803), *reprinted in* THE POLITICAL WRITINGS OF THOMAS JEFFERSON 144, 144 (E. Dumbauld ed. 1955) [hereinafter cited as POLITICAL WRITINGS]. Many Americans during this period believed that the great political desideratum was a means of protecting the Constitution from what Edmund Pendleton called "the wiles of construction," Pendleton, *The Danger Not Over*, Richmond Examiner, Oct. 20, 1801, *quoted in* L. BANNING, *supra* note 31, at 282.

[41] George Washington's final will exemplified the fear of construction. The will included an elaborate arbitration provision designed, in the event of a dispute over the will's terms, to allow a determination of Washington's (subjective) intentions "unfettered by law or legal constructions." 4 ANNALS OF AMERICA 115, 119 (1968). Criticizing the Virginia Court of Appeals for a decision involving the interpretation of a will, Washington's fellow Virginian George Wythe analogized the evils of testamentary construction to the confusion scriptural interpretation had wrought on the understanding of the Bible. Aylett v. Minnis, Wythe 219, 234 n.*l* (Va. Ch. 1793), *rev'd*, 1 Va. (1 Wash.) 300 (1795); *see infra* pp. 896–97 & note 59.

[42] Essex Result (1778), *reprinted in* MASSACHUSETTS, COLONY TO COMMONWEALTH 73, 79–80 (R. Taylor ed. 1961).

[43] *See id.* at 80–89.

ten documents strongly influenced Americans in their conceptualization of the task of interpreting their new Constitution. Yet despite this reluctance, the necessity of judicial construction had already engendered a second — and conflicting — source of influence: the rich common law traditions of legal interpretation.

B. *Interpretation and the Common Law*

Although they lacked a significant tradition of interpreting written constitutions, the newly independent Americans possessed almost an embarrassment of hermeneutical riches in the common law's centuries of dealing with wills, deeds, contracts, and statutes. By 1787, the English legal system had produced a wealth of reflection on the process of construing normative documents.[44] Moreover, the common law considered these canons of interpretation to be themselves a part of the law, and to be equally binding on the maker and the interpreter of a document.[45]

The concept central to the common law's hermeneutic, and to later American discussion of constitutional interpretation, was the notion of the "intention" or "intent" underlying a text.[46] "[A]s touching construction of words," Chief Justice Fleming of the Court of King's Bench explained in 1611, "they shall be taken according to the . . . intent of parties."[47] This simple principle, however, concealed a significant ambiguity, because its salient term — intent — was by no means unequivocal in meaning.[48] The English nouns "intention" and

---

44 Besides being familiar with common law traditions, some Americans were also conversant with the work done on questions of legal interpretation in the Continental international law tradition, especially that of Hugo Grotius, *see* H. GROTIUS, DE IURE BELLI AC PACIS (Paris 1625), Emerich de Vattel, *see* E. DE VATTEL, LE DROIT DES GENS (London 1758), and Jean Jacques Burlamaqui, *see* J. BURLAMAQUI, PRINCIPES DU DROIT NATUREL ET POLITIQUE (Geneva 1748). *Cf.* B. BAILYN, *supra* note 16, at 26–29 (noting American reliance on these authors for the laws of nations and of nature).

45 *See* 2 T. JARMAN, A TREATISE ON WILLS *738 (citing 18th century cases); Porter, Book Review, 27 N. AM. REV. 167, 179 (1828), *reprinted in* THE LEGAL MIND IN AMERICA 161, 167 (P. Miller ed. 1962) (the common law supplies "the principles of interpretation" used in "every branch and department of jurisprudence").

46 In an 1819 newspaper essay, John Marshall remarked that he could cite from the common law "the most complete evidence that the *intention* is the most sacred rule of interpretation." Marshall, *A Friend of the Constitution*, Alexandria Gazette, July 2, 1819, *reprinted in* JOHN MARSHALL'S DEFENSE OF MCCULLOCH V. MARYLAND 155, 167 (G. Gunther ed. 1969) [hereinafter cited as JOHN MARSHALL'S DEFENSE]. In applying "intention" language to constitutional interpretation, Marshall explicitly drew on the traditional hermeneutic of the common law. Charles Miller's observation that "intention" properly applies only to people whereas "intent" may refer to both people and documents, *see* C. MILLER, THE SUPREME COURT AND THE USES OF HISTORY 154 n.12 (1969), correctly states current usage, but is inaccurate as applied to 18th and early 19th century authors, who used the terms interchangeably, *see, e.g.*, S. JOHNSON, *supra* note 12 (entries for "intent" and "intention" (second definition)).

47 Hewet v. Painter, 1 Bulstrode 174, 175, 80 Eng. Rep. 864, 865 (1611).

48 Indeed, Chief Justice Fleming went on to explain that "this intention and construction of words shall be taken, according to the vulgar and usual sense, phrase and manner of speech of

"intent" were derived from the Latin *intentio*, which in medieval usage could refer either to individual, subjective purpose or to what an external observer would regard as the purpose of the individual's actions.[49] The English derivatives of *intentio* inherited a similar ambiguity: the "intent" or "intention" of a document could denote either the meaning that the drafters wished to communicate or the meaning the reader was warranted in deriving from the text. The two might or might not be identical. Thus, to understand the import of the common law's focus on "intent," we must determine in what sense the word itself was used.

The use of "intent" in common law interpretive discourse is well illustrated in the *Table-Talk* of seventeenth century jurist and parliamentary hero John Selden.[50] Although Selden insisted that the "one true sense" of a document is that which "the Author meant when he [wrote] it" (the modern intentionalist's definition of "intent"), he also asserted that the court determines "the intention of the King" solely on the basis of the words of the law, and not by investigating any other source of information about the lawgiver's purposes.[51] A century and a half later, John Joseph Powell's treatise on contract law displayed the same usage of "intent." According to Powell, "the law always regards the intention of the parties" to an agreement. But it does so, he immediately continued, by applying the parties' words "to that which, in common presumption, may be taken to be their intent."[52] The law of contracts is not concerned with anyone's "internal sentiments," Powell wrote, but only with their "external expression."[53] At common law, then, the "intent" of the maker of a legal document and the "intent" of the document itself were one and the same; "intent" did not depend upon the subjective purposes of the author.[54] The

---

these words," not according to any particular meaning the parties may have intended. *Id.* at 175–76, 80 Eng. Rep. at 865.

[49] *See, e.g.*, Langton, Fragments on the Morality of Human Acts (c. 1200), *reprinted in* A SCHOLASTIC MISCELLANY: ANSELM TO OCKHAM 355–56 (E. Fairweather ed. 1956). The ambiguity of *intentio* is likely to have continued to affect the use of its English derivatives in legal discourse because virtually all lawyers were familiar with Latin.

[50] J. SELDEN, *supra* note 22.

[51] *Id.* at 4, 44.

[52] 1 J. POWELL, ESSAY UPON THE LAW OF CONTRACTS AND AGREEMENTS 244 (London 1790).

[53] *Id.* at 372–73.

[54] "[A]lthough it is the duty of the Court to ascertain and carry into effect the intention of the party, yet there are, in many cases, fixed and settled rules by which that intention is determined; and to such rules the wisest judges have thought proper to adhere, in opposition to their own private opinions as to the probable intention of the party . . . ." H. BROOM, A SELECTION OF LEGAL MAXIMS *427 (rev. ed. London 1848) (1st ed. London 1845).

Some modern students of hermeneutics attack non-author-based interpretation as an abstract and ultimately hopeless search for a text's meaning apart from any human context or usage. *See, e.g.*, J. BRUNER, IN SEARCH OF MIND 165–66 (1983) (any message must be interpreted in terms of the intent of its originators; it is a "nice question as to whether any save linguists, logicians, lawyers and pedants ever processed a locution for its 'timeless meaning'"); E. HIRSCH,

late eighteenth century common lawyer conceived an instrument's "intent" — and therefore its meaning — not as what the drafters meant by their words but rather as what judges, employing the "artificial reason and judgment of law,"[55] understood "the reasonable and legal meaning" of those words to be.[56]

Although the common law tradition identified the purpose of interpreting any document as the determination of that document's "intent," it also insisted that the proper means of carrying out this task varied according to the type of instrument to be construed. By the late eighteenth century, statutes, wills, deeds, and contracts had become the objects of what seemed at least superficially to be increasingly different interpretive methodologies. Courts treated statutes and wills similarly by purporting to pay particular attention to the subjective intentions of their drafters.[57] This concern for the drafters' purposes was, however, largely illusory. Blackstone's description of the proper approach to the construction of a will is typical: "the construction [should] be favorable, and as near the minds and apparent intents of the parties, as the rules of law will admit."[58] But Blackstone did not mean that in interpreting what lay in the testator's mind a court was free to disregard the rule of law governing the "apparent intent" of the testator's words: "the construction must also be reasonable, and

---

VALIDITY IN INTERPRETATION 12–14 (1967) (attacking non-author-based interpretive methodologies as incoherent). Eighteenth century common lawyers did not hold precisely the view of interpretation that Bruner and Hirsch assail. They did not deny the existence of authors' personal intentions, nor did they argue that a text can be said to have a "meaning" in itself apart from any human act of expression or understanding. Rather, they believed that the meaning *relevant* to *legal* analysis of an instrument is that understood by its interpreters, not that entertained by its drafters.

[55] *See* Prohibitions del Roy, 12 Co. Rep. 63, 65, 77 Eng. Rep. 1342, 1343 (1608).

[56] Talbot *qui tam* v. Commanders and Owners of three Brigs, 1 Dall. 95, 100 (Pa. 1784). The court went on to explain that on the basis of the words' "legal meaning" the judges could reach a "construction, by which positive words may be properly and justly modified." *Id.* Eighteenth century lawyers were aware, of course, that the words of a text mean something (subjectively) to the text's framers. Yet the 18th century usage of "intent(ion)" melded semantic nuances that modern usage segregates much more cleanly; it thereby blurred for 18th century English speakers differences of meaning that we regard as clear. Failure to recognize the difference between modern and circa-1800 usage undermines Raoul Berger's attempt to ground his form of intentionalism in the generally accepted "interpretive intention" of the constitutional era. *See supra* p. 886. Berger cites James Madison and Joseph Story in support of his contention, *see* R. BERGER, *supra* note 8, at 364–66, but this citation reflects a striking misinterpretation of the two men's views. Although Madison did refer at times to "the intention of the framers," he made it clear on numerous occasions that he was not an "intentionalist" in Berger's sense. *See infra* pp. 935–41. Story's attack on the practical possibility and theoretical propriety of intentionalism was equally thorough. *See* 1 J. STORY, COMMENTARIES ON THE CONSTITUTION OF THE UNITED STATES 388–92 (Boston 1833); *infra* pp. 942–43 & note 325; *see also* Powell, *Joseph Story's Commentaries on the Constitution: A Belated Review*, 94 YALE L.J. 1285 (1985) (discussing Story's theory of constitutional interpretation).

[57] *See* F. DWARRIS, *supra* note 17, at *688–90.

[58] 2 W. BLACKSTONE, COMMENTARIES *379 (emphasis omitted).

agreeable to common understanding."[59] Blackstone was cautioning against hypercritical readings of the words of unlearned laypersons, not endorsing an extratextual search for the purposes underlying those words.

The courts likewise looked to "rules of law" and to "common understanding" when interpreting statutes. The modern practice of interpreting a law by reference to its legislative history was almost wholly nonexistent, and English judges professed themselves bound to honor the true import of the "express words" of Parliament.[60] The

---

[59] *Id.* (emphasis omitted). Wills were to receive special treatment because the law assumed them to be the creations of ignorant testators at death's door. *See* Throckmerton v. Tracy, 1 Plowden 145, 162, 75 Eng. Rep. 222, 251 (C.P. 1555). The case of Aylett v. Minnis, Wythe 219 (Va. Ch. 1793), *rev'd*, 1 Va. (1 Wash.) 300 (1795), illustrates the limits on the common law's willingness to seek the testator's subjective purposes. In his will, the testator left his son Philip, the plaintiff, "all [his] lands in Kingwilliam [County]," *id.* at 220 (emphasis omitted), and directed the equal division of the residuary estate among the testator's widow and children. The testator, at death, owned certain lands in the named county in fee simple and was engaged in legal action to secure possession of other property to which he held a 999-year lease. After his father's executors obtained possession, Philip laid claim to the land under lease. The defendants relied on an old English case with similar facts, Rose v. Bartlett, Croke Car. 292, 79 Eng. Rep. 856 (K.B. 1631), in which the court had interpreted the will's language to cover only lands held in fee simple. Chancellor George Wythe refused to follow the English precedent on the grounds that the reasoning of the justices was unpersuasive and that, in light of the Aylett will as a whole, the testator clearly had meant to leave Philip all of his real property, of whatever legal character, in King William County. Wythe cautioned, however, that his interpretation was not based on extratextual considerations, but rather "exactly corresponded with the meaning of William Aylett's *words* . . . [because the Court was] convinced that *they* only ought to be consulted for discovering it." *Aylett*, Wythe at 233–34. Finding Wythe's opinion too daring a departure from traditional legal hermeneutics, the Virginia Court of Appeals subsequently reversed and held that, on this issue, the legal meaning of Aylett's 1780 will was fixed by the 1631 English decision. *See* 1 Va. (1 Wash.) 300 (1975). A few years later Wythe, admitting that he was flouting legal tradition, launched a direct and thoroughgoing attack on the use of judicial precedents in discerning the intention of wills. *See* Wilkins v. Taylor, Wythe 338, 347–54 (Va. Ch. 1799), *rev'd*, 9 Va. (5 Call) 150 (1804).

[60] "And the Judges said they ought not to make any construction against the express letter of the statute; for nothing can so express the meaning of the makers of the Act, as their own direct words, for *index animi sermo* ["the word is the sign or indicator of the soul"]." Edrich's Case, 5 Co. Rep. 118a, 118b, 77 Eng. Rep. 238, 239 (C.P. 1603). During the great debate in the fourth Congress over the House of Representatives' right of access to the executive branch's diplomatic files, Nathaniel Smith observed that proper statutory interpretation did not involve reference to anything other than the text of the act:

> This was the universal practice of the Courts of Law, who, when called on to expound an act of the Legislature, never resorted to the debates which preceded it — to the opinions of members about its signification — but inspected the act itself, and decided by its own evidence.

5 ANNALS OF CONG. 462 (1796); *accord id.* at 441 (remarks of Rep. William Smith) (in construing a federal act, the Supreme Court does not "call for the Journals of the two Houses, or the report of the Committee of Ways and Means, in which the law originated, or the debates of the House on passing the law"). Discussing statutory construction in the 1820s, Massachusetts legal scholar Nathan Dane wrote that "such a construction ought to be put on a statute, as may best answer the intention which the makers of it had in view"; he added, somewhat ironically, that "the only difficulty is in finding this intention," and listed the means available for discovering

"intent of the act" and the "intent of the legislature" were interchangeable terms; neither term implied that the interpreter looked at any evidence concerning that "intent" other than the words of the text and the common law background of the statute.[61] Political and legal scholars in both Britain and the American colonies viewed strict judicial adherence to the legislature's language as a constitutional necessity, because the "known, fixed laws" could be properly established or altered only by "the whole legislature," which spoke only through its enactments.[62]

The common law tradition did admit the propriety of looking beyond the statute's wording where the text was defective on its face. In such situations judges were free to substitute coherence for gibberish.[63] A more serious interpretive problem occurred when the statute's wording was ambiguous, rather than clear but in conflict with its apparent intent. It was generally agreed that such *ambiguitas patens* could not be resolved by extrinsic evidence as to Parliament's purpose; in Francis Bacon's classic formulation, ambiguity "shall bee holpen by construction . . . but never by averrement" of the purposes of the members of Parliament.[64] This did not mean, however, that "construction" was viewed as an unstructured exercise of judicial choice. Instead, courts were bound to read acts of Parliament against the background of the common law. The Barons of the Exchequer resolved in *Heydon's Case*[65] that all statutes concerned a "mischief and defect for which the common law did not provide," and for which

---

the legislators' intent. "Legislative history" was not on his, or anyone else's, list at the time. 6 N. DANE, GENERAL ABRIDGMENT AND DIGEST OF AMERICAN LAW 600 (Boston 1824).

61 "So the Judge speaks of the King's Proclamation, this is the intention of the King, not that the King had declared his intention any other way to the Judge, but the Judge examining the Contents of the Proclamation, gathers by the Purport of the words, the King's Intention, and then for shortness of expression says, this is the King's intention." J. SELDEN, *supra* note 22, at 44.

62 L. LEDER, LIBERTY AND AUTHORITY 86–87 (1968) (quoting charge to Philadelphia grand jury in 1723 case).

63 *See* H. BROOM, *supra* note 54, at *534–36 (citing authorities); *cf.* 6 N. DANE, *supra* note 60, at 596 (noting that only "where the *meaning of a statute is doubtful* . . . can courts of law look to consequences in construing it"). In cases of defective wording, English judges followed the policy of upholding the validity of written instruments, *see* H. BROOM, *supra* note 54, at *413 (citing Lord Coke), by searching for the general purpose of the document as a guide to construction. *See, e.g.*, The Earl of Clanrickard's Case, Hobart 273, 277, 80 Eng. Rep. 418, 423 (C.P. 1613) (expressing approval of judges "that are curious and almost subtil . . . to invent reasons and means to make Acts, according to the just intent of the parties"); *see also* F. DWARRIS, *supra* note 17, at *689–90 (arguing that in the construction of deeds, "such exposition should, if possible, be made, as is most agreeable to the intention of the grantor," and citing the *Earl of Clanrickard's Case* approvingly). But the curiosity and subtlety of the judges were tempered by their abhorrence of making "exposition against express words." *Id.* at *706 (quoting Lord Coke).

64 F. BACON, *Containing a Collection of Some Principall Rules and Maximes of the Common Law*, in THE ELEMENTS OF THE COMMON LAWES OF ENGLAND 1, 92 (London 1630).

65 3 Co. Rep. 7a, 76 Eng. Rep. 637 (1584).

Parliament had ordained a remedy.[66] Therefore, "the office of all the Judges is always to make such construction as shall suppress the mischief, and advance the remedy."[67] In the performance of this office, the courts might consult the statute's preamble, which, although not an operative provision of the act, was the "key" to the purposes of its makers.[68] In seeking a statute's proper construction, courts would also admit the practical exposition of the statute supplied by usage under it.[69] But judicial precedent served as the most important source of information about an act's meaning beyond its actual text.[70] This followed almost by definition from the basic notion of "intent" as a product of the interpretive process rather than something locked into the text by its author. A prior construction of a statute provided certainty as to the meaning because, in Lord Coke's words, it was not the "private interpretation[ ]" of an individual, but rather the authoritative "resolution[ ] of judges in Courts of Justice."[71]

Whereas the common law tradition at least purported to implement the desires of the drafters in interpreting wills and statutes, the common law approach to the interpretation of contracts was blatantly unconcerned with the subjective purposes of the parties. With minor exceptions,[72] contracting parties were conclusively presumed to have meant what their words said,[73] and to have been aware of the law's

---

66 *Id.* at 7b, 76 Eng. Rep. at 638.

67 *Id.* According to Professor Lon Fuller, "mischief" in this case meant something like "repugnancy" or "inconvenience." *See* L. FULLER, THE MORALITY OF LAW 83 n.38. (rev. ed. 1969). The formula in *Heydon's Case*, as reported by Coke, has been extremely influential. *See* 1 W. BLACKSTONE, *supra* note 58, at *87; 6 N. DANE, *supra* note 60, at 600; F. DWARRIS, *supra* note 17, at *694–95; L. FULLER, *supra*, at 82–83; J. HURST, DEALING WITH STATUTES 41 (1982); T. SEDGWICK, A TREATISE ON THE RULES WHICH GOVERN THE INTERPRETATION AND APPLICATION OF STATUTORY AND CONSTITUTIONAL LAW 235–37 (New York 1857).

68 Sir James Dyer, a 16th century chief justice of the Court of Common Pleas, asserted, in an oft-repeated passage, that the preamble of a statute is "a key to open the minds of the makers of the act, and the mischiefs which they intended to redress." H. BROOM, *supra* note 54, at *439. A supplementary guide to the construction of a statute was provided by its classification as public and remedial rather than private or penal, a matter often noticed in the preamble. Statutes "concerning the public good," as opposed to private and penal acts, were to be construed "liberally; that is . . . in an enlarged manner." 6 N. DANE, *supra* note 60, at 599 (citing cases).

69 *See* H. BROOM, *supra* note 54, at *719 (citing Lord Coke); 6 N. DANE, *supra* note 60, at 596.

70 *See* Letter from Thomas Jefferson to Skelton Jones (July 28, 1809), *quoted in* D. MALONE, JEFFERSON THE VIRGINIAN 261–62 (1948) (meaning of statutes is "in the air" until "settled by decisions").

71 E. COKE, *Proeme* to SECOND PART OF THE INSTITUTES OF THE LAWS OF ENGLAND (London 1642); *accord* Kamper v. Hawkins, 3 Va. (1 Va. Cas.) 20, 93 (Gen. Ct. 1793) (Tucker, J.) (decisions of Virginia supreme court of appeals by definition expound Virginia's constitution and laws "in their truest sense"); *see also* 6 N. DANE, *supra* note 60, at 597 (commonly used expressions "by being often used in statutes, and so construed, have acquired their meaning").

72 *See* 1 J. POWELL, *supra* note 52, at 387 ("ordinary import of words may be restrained" where there is "an original defect in the will of the speaker, so that it is not co-extensive with his words," or where there is "some collateral accident inconsistent with the speaker's design").

73 *See id.* at 372–73. Chief Justice Popham's observations in The Countess of Rutland's

canons of interpretation.[74] The view of contract prevalent before the American Revolution, a view that emphasized considerations of equity and substantive justice over contractual freedom and the will of the parties,[75] went hand in hand with the courts' lack of concern with subjective intention. Judges generally construed agreements in light of the ordinary meaning of the terms and with an eye toward the nature of the contract and the identity of the parties to it.[76]

During the same period in which Americans were drawing on these common law traditions to respond to the novel challenges posed by constitutional interpretation, certain changes were occurring within the traditional branches of the common law. A new self-consciousness about the process of interpretation developed toward the end of the eighteenth century, and the sixty years following 1800 saw a remarkable outpouring of scholarly discussion of hermeneutical issues in both Great Britain and America.[77] Judicial opinions also reflected ostensible shifts in emphasis. Statutory interpretation became even more frankly literalistic.[78] A judicial opinion of New York Senator John Young in 1835 captures the spirit of the age: "To understand the statute, it is only necessary to know the meaning of the words which

---

Case, 5 Co. Rep. 25b, 77 Eng. Rep. 89 (K.B. 1604), became proverbial, and others generalized them to include written documents of a noncontractual nature. Coke reported Chief Justice Popham to have stated that parol evidence was not admissible to vary or add to a writing, because

> every contract or agreement ought to be dissolved by matter of as high a nature as the first deed. . . . Also it would be inconvenient, that matters in writing made by advice and on consideration, and which finally import the certain truth of the agreement of the parties should be controlled by averment of the parties, to be proved by the uncertain testimony of slippery memory.

Id. at 26a, 77 Eng. Rep. at 90. It is clear that the exclusion of extrinsic evidence of intent, both in the contractual and in the statutory areas, rested on a substantive view of what (legally significant) "intent" is. *See* 1 W. BLACKSTONE, *supra* note 58, at *62; 1 J. POWELL, *supra* note 52, at 372–73.

[74] *See* Throckmerton v. Tracy, 1 Plowden 145, 162, 75 Eng. Rep. 222, 251 (C.P. 1555).

[75] *See* P. ATIYAH, THE RISE AND FALL OF FREEDOM OF CONTRACT 169–77 (1979); M. HORWITZ, THE TRANSFORMATION OF AMERICAN LAW: 1780–1860, at 161–73 (1977); W. NELSON, AMERICANIZATION OF THE COMMON LAW 54–63 (1975).

[76] *See* 2 J. POWELL, *supra* note 52, at 40–41; 3 N. DANE, *supra* note 60, at 574–75.

[77] Good examples are H. BROOM, *supra* note 54; F. DWARRIS, *supra* note 17; 1–4 J. KENT, COMMENTARIES ON AMERICAN LAW (New York 1826–1830); F. LIEBER, LEGAL AND POLITICAL HERMENEUTICS (Boston 1839); T. SEDGWICK, *supra* note 67; 1 J. STORY, *supra* note 56, at 383–443; Hawkins, *On the Principles of Legal Interpretation*, 2 JURID. SOC'Y PAPERS 298 (1860).

[78] Broom summarized the trend toward literalism thus: in construing a statute "to ascertain and carry out the intention of the legislature . . . the judges will bend and conform their legal reason to the words of the act, and will rather construe them literally, than strain their meaning beyond the obvious intention of Parliament." H. BROOM, *supra* note 54, at *117; *see also* F. DWARRIS, *supra* note 17, at *708 (noting that "[r]ecently" English judges had manifested an intention "to adhere more closely . . . to the words of the act of Parliament"); T. SEDGWICK, *supra* note 67, at 382–83 (arguing that the "only safe rule" is to trace the legislative intent "as expressed *by the words which the legislature has used*").

are used."[79] Rather than take advantage of the increasing availability of legislative history in the form of committee reports and legislative journals, courts emphatically rejected any consideration of such "extrinsic evidence."[80]

On the surface, the interpretation of contracts took the opposite course. The will theory of contracts gained ascendancy in the early nineteenth century, and the courts accepted as their task the simple enforcement of whatever bargain the parties had made.[81] Ironically, though, the rise of the will theory was accompanied by an increasingly "objective" approach to the discovery of the parties' intent.[82] Thus, the ideology of freedom of contract did not entail any essential modification of the law's traditional hermeneutic.

Despite the anti-interpretive influences of British Protestantism and Enlightenment rationalism, the sheer necessity of judicial construction gave rise to a substantial common law tradition of legal interpretation by the end of the eighteenth century.[83] Most of the Americans influential in the framing, ratification, and early interpretation of the federal Constitution were intimately familiar with the common law,[84] and they gleaned from it not only a general approach to constitutional

---

79 Coster v. Lorillard, 14 Wend. 265, 375 (N.Y. 1835); *cf.* O.W. HOLMES, *The Theory of Legal Interpretation*, in COLLECTED LEGAL PAPERS 203, 207 (1920) ("We do not inquire what the legislature meant; we ask only what the statute means."). The legitimacy of resort to legislative history was only imperfectly established in Holmes's period, *see, e.g.*, Davis v. Pringle, 268 U.S. 315, 318 (1925) (Holmes, J.), and he often resisted its use as contrary to the proper, "external principle of construction." *See* O.W. HOLMES, *supra*, at 208; *see also* Frankfurter, *Some Reflections on the Reading of Statutes*, 47 COLUM. L. REV. 527, 538 (1947) (quoting letter from Holmes in which the latter recalls having said, while hearing oral argument, "I don't care what [the legislature's] intention was. I only want to know what the words mean.").

80 "[T]he journals [of the legislature's proceedings] are not evidence of the meaning of a statute, because this must be ascertained from the language of the act itself, and the facts connected with the subject on which it is to operate." Southwark Bank v. Commonwealth, 26 Pa. 446, 450 (1856); *see also* T. SEDGWICK, *supra* note 67, at 243 (noting that "the intention of the legislature is to be found in the statute itself") (emphasis omitted).

81 *See, e.g.*, M. HORWITZ, *supra* note 75, at 180–85.

82 *See* P. ATIYAH, *supra* note 75, at 459. The triumph of the will theory and the spread of an "objective" approach to contracts did not proceed at precisely the same pace, of course. *See* G. GILMORE, THE DEATH OF CONTRACT 39–40 (1974) (noting persistence of "subjective" approach into latter part of 19th century).

83 An early Delaware case, Laws v. Davis, 1 Del. Cas. 256 (1800), illustrates the strength of the cultural distrust of interpretation even within the legal profession. One of the lawyers warned against carrying the potentially "unlimited power of contruction" beyond narrow limits. The interpretations of judges, he feared, threaten "the law" on which "our rights hang and society depends." *Id.* at 258. In another Delaware case, Brown v. Brown, 1 Del. Cas. 188 (1798), Chief Justice Richard Bassett warned that judicial restraint in the exercise of a power to construe statutes was necessary in order to protect the constitutional separation of powers. *See id.* at 191.

84 *See, e.g.*, A. Hamilton, Opinion on the Constitutionality of an Act to Establish a Bank (1791), *reprinted in* 8 PAPERS OF ALEXANDER HAMILTON 97, 111 (H. Syrett ed. 1965) (referring to "the usual and established rules of construction").

interpretation — one centering on a search for the Constitution's "intention" — but also a variety of specific interpretive techniques. The common law, however, did not yield ready responses to a number of preliminary questions that required answers before constitutional interpretation could be assimilated to the familiar patterns of legal construction. What kind of document was the Constitution — a statute, a contract, an instrument *sui generis*? Who were its makers — the Philadelphia framers, the state conventions, the states, "We the People"? What, if any, extrinsic evidence of its meaning would be admissible in case of uncertainty — records of the federal and state conventions, statements made by its supporters, general principles of political philosophy? Without answers to these and other inquiries, the common law's hermeneutical tradition could contribute only chaos to American constitutional discourse.

III. Early Views on Interpreting the Constitution

Friend: "You have given us a good Constitution."
Gouverneur Morris: "That depends on how it is construed."[85]

A. The Framers and the Battle for Ratification

Constitutional debate was not the invention of Revolutionary America, and the invocation of written documents was a wholly traditional move in English high political controversy.[86] America's innovation was to identify "the Constitution" with a single normative document instead of a historical tradition, and thus to create the possibility of treating constitutional interpretation as an exercise in the traditional legal activity of construing a written instrument.[87] The proceedings of the Philadelphia convention reflect the delegates' awareness of this innovation and their desire to craft a document that would be understood, at least in part, through the traditional processes of legal interpretation.

---

[85] This exchange is quoted in A. Mason, The States Rights Debate 107 (2d ed. 1972).

[86] *See* C. Bowen, The Lion and the Throne 452–53, 482–84, 495–99 (1957); L. Leder, *supra* note 62, at 95–117.

[87] *See* H. Commager, The Empire of Reason 227–35 (1977); G. Wood, *supra* note 11, at 454–63. The Articles of Confederation were also regarded by the courts as amenable to traditional hermeneutical techniques. *See* Talbot *qui tam* v. Commanders and Owners of three Brigs, 1 Dall. 95, 100 (Pa. 1784). In an 1824 book review, Henry Sedgwick contrasted American constitutional discourse with its British counterpart:

> [O]ur written constitutions have furnished a comparatively easy and definitive test, for the resolution of doubts and decision of controversies. In England also there have been constitutional disputes, and the disputants have appealed to theoretic reasoning, vague maxims, obsolete charters, ancient usages, half forgotten statutes, concerning which it has been [a] matter of doubtful discussion, whether they were or were not in force . . . .

Sedgwick, Book Review, 19 N. Am. Rev. 411, 438 (1824), *reprinted in* The Legal Mind in America, *supra* note 45, at 135, 145.

The Philadelphia framers' primary expectation regarding constitutional interpretation was that the Constitution, like any other legal document, would be interpreted in accord with its express language. This expectation is evident in the framers' numerous attempts to refine the wording of the text, either to eliminate vagueness[88] or to allay fears that overprecise language would be taken literally and that the aim of a given provision would thus be defeated.[89] Debates over the language of the document were abundant,[90] yet in none of them did any delegate suggest that future interpreters could avoid misconstruing the text by consulting evidence of the intentions articulated at the convention. Although the Philadelphia framers certainly wished to embody in the text the most "distinctive form of collecting the mind" of the convention,[91] there is no indication that they expected or intended future interpreters to refer to any extratextual intentions revealed in the convention's secretly conducted debates.[92] The framers shared the traditional common law view — so foreign to much hermeneutical thought in more recent years — that the import of the document they were framing would be determined by reference to the

---

[88] *See, e.g.*, J. MADISON, JOURNAL OF THE FEDERAL CONVENTION 83 (E. Scott ed. 1893) (proceedings of May 31, 1787) (provision giving Congress powers in cases in which state legislatures are individually "incompetent" is criticized as vague); *id.* at 133 (June 8) (provision giving Congress power to negate "improper" state laws is criticized as indefinite); *id.* at 562 (Aug. 20) (necessary and proper clause is criticized as too vague in respect to Congress's power to establish federal offices); *id.* at 614 (Aug. 27) (provision concerning impeachment and removal of President in case of "disability" is criticized as too vague).

[89] Some delegates suggested that the Committee of Detail's draft provision giving each house of Congress "in all cases . . . a negative on the other" would give the House of Representatives a veto on treaties despite the later provision giving the Senate alone power to ratify treaties. *Id.* at 463 (Aug. 7). Others criticized the committee's draft of the presidential veto provision because it referred to "bills" and could thus be evaded simply by styling congressional acts as "resolutions." *See id.* at 536–37 (Aug. 15). Some delegates feared that the draft provision empowering Congress "to make war" would render the President incompetent to order defensive operations in the event of a surprise attack, while others thought the proposed substitution ("to declare war") left Congress's power too narrow. *See id.* at 548 (Aug. 17).

[90] The debate over the provision giving Congress legislative authority over maritime crimes exemplifies the convention's concern for precision. As proposed by the Committee of Detail, the provision empowered Congress "[t]o declare the law and punishment of piracies and felonies committed on the high seas." *Id.* at 454 (Aug. 6). When the provision came up for consideration by the full convention, James Madison moved to strike the words "and punishment" as superfluous. George Mason opposed the motion because he feared that the omission would leave Congress capable only of defining maritime crimes, and not of setting penalties for them. Edmund Randolph did not regard the removal of "punishment" as significant, but expressed concern over "the efficacy" of the verb "declare." Gouverneur Morris preferred "designate" to "declare," while Madison and James Wilson debated the precision of "felonies." Only after considerable discussion was the final wording settled upon. *See id.* at 544–46 (Aug. 17).

[91] *Id.* at 173 (June 16).

[92] At the convention's close, the delegates decided not to publish the journal and other papers, but rather to entrust them to convention president George Washington, subject to future action by Congress under the proposed Constitution. *See id.* at 748 (Sept. 17).

intrinsic meaning of its words or through the usual judicial process of case-by-case interpretation.[93]

In accepting the common law's objective approach to discerning the meaning of a document, the framers did not endorse strict literalism as the proper stance of future interpreters. The framers were aware that unforeseen situations would arise, and they accepted the inevitability and propriety of construction.[94] When a motion was made to extend the jurisdiction of the Supreme Court to cases arising under "this Constitution" as well as under "the laws of the United States," James Madison expressed concern that this would extend the Court's power to matters not properly within judicial cognizance:

> Mr. MADISON doubted whether it was not going too far, to extend the jurisdiction of the Court generally to cases arising under the Constitution, and whether it ought not to be limited to cases of a judiciary nature. The right of expounding the Constitution, in cases not of this nature, ought not to be given to that department.
>
> The motion of Docr. JOHNSON [to extend the Court's jurisdiction] was agreed to, *nem. con.* [without dissent], it being generally supposed, that the jurisdiction given was constructively limited to cases of a judiciary nature.[95]

Although the Philadelphia framers did not discuss in detail how they intended their end product to be interpreted, they clearly assumed that future interpreters would adhere to then-prevalent methods of statutory construction.

The political struggle over the ratification of the Constitution elicited, both in print and on state convention floors, a considerable body of commentary on the Constitution's "intent," and on the means that future interpreters would use to determine that "intent." Americans generally agreed that the Articles of Confederation were a compact among the several states.[96] The Federalist proponents of the Constitution identified the contractual basis of the Articles as one of their chief weaknesses.[97] One of the Constitution's virtues, in the Federalists' view, lay in its rejection of a contractual model for the polity of the United States.[98] The Federalists analogized the ratification

[93] *See, e.g.*, *id.* at 625–26, (Aug. 29) (meaning of "ex post facto law" not controlled by intentions of delegates to convention); *id.* at 727–28 (Sept. 14) (same).

[94] *See, e.g.*, *id.* at 220 n.* (June 22) (Massachusetts concurs in deletion of phrase because its purpose would be achieved without express wording); *id.* at 726 (Sept. 14) (James Wilson argues that power to create monopolies is implicit in commerce power).

[95] *Id.* at 617 (Aug. 27).

[96] *See, e.g.*, L. Martin, The Genuine Information Delivered to the Legislature of the State of Maryland (1788), *reprinted in* 2 THE COMPLETE ANTI-FEDERALIST 19, 75–76 (H. Storing ed. 1981) [hereinafter cited as STORING]; THE FEDERALIST No. 15, at 70–71 (A. Hamilton) (G. Wills ed. 1982); THE FEDERALIST No. 22, at 111 (A. Hamilton) (G. Wills ed. 1982).

[97] *See, e.g.*, THE FEDERALIST No. 18 (J. Madison) (comparing the Articles to confederations of the past).

[98] *See, e.g.*, THE FEDERALIST No. 15 (A. Hamilton); *infra* pp. 929–30.

process to the passage by a legislature (the people) of a statute (the Constitution) drafted by a committee (the Philadelphia convention). Without the people's approval, the convention's work would remain a mere proposal lacking any intrinsic authority.[99] This analogy led many Federalists to assume or assert that the Constitution would be construed in accord with the same basic principles that the common law had developed for statutory interpretation.[100] Perhaps for their own polemical purposes, the Anti-Federalists usually agreed with the statutory analogy for the proposed Constitution, and with the corollary analogy between constitutional and statutory interpretation.[101] Their complaint was that this methodology, applied to the sweeping language of the Constitution, would lead inexorably to the effective consolidation of the states into a single body politic with a single, omnipotent government.[102]

Once the Constitution was proposed to the states, a central element of the campaign to prevent ratification was the charge that the Constitution would be the object of interpretation and that judges and legislators would read into it doctrines present only "constructively" and not textually.[103] All of the anti-hermeneutic resources of Protestant biblicism and Enlightenment rationalism were enlisted in an effort to show that the Constitution was an open invitation to political corruption and oligarchic usurpation. The Constitution was ambiguous by design, the Anti-Federalists claimed, and thereby invited con-

---

[99] *See, e.g.*, THE FEDERALIST No. 40, at 199–200 (J. Madison) (G. Wills ed. 1982) (although Anti-Federalists attack convention as if it had sought the "establishment" of the Constitution, its powers were in fact "merely advisory and recommendatory").

[100] *See, e.g.*, THE FEDERALIST No. 78, at 395–96 (A. Hamilton) (G. Wills ed. 1982).

[101] *See, e.g.*, Letters from the Federal Farmer No. 4 (Oct. 12, 1787), *reprinted in* 2 STORING, *supra* note 96, at 248 (assuming analogy between statutory and constitutional interpretation); Essays by Cincinnatus No. 2 (Nov. 8, 1787), *reprinted in* 6 STORING, *supra* note 96, at 12 (applying principles of "legal construction" to Constitution).

[102] The Federalists maintained that the states' autonomy was secure because the text of the Constitution did not purport to abolish it and indeed contained only a few explicit restrictions on state power. The Anti-Federalists countered that the supremacy clause and the expansive definitions of congressional authority would reduce the states to insignificance. *See* 3 THE DEBATES, RESOLUTIONS, AND OTHER PROCEEDINGS, IN CONVENTION, ON THE ADOPTION OF THE FEDERAL CONSTITUTION 159 (J. Elliot ed. 1827, 1828 & 1830) [hereinafter cited as ELLIOT'S DEBATES] (reporting the first North Carolina convention, in which Timothy Bloodworth claimed that these provisions would "produce an abolition of the state governments"). Massachusetts Anti-Federalist Amos Singletary summarized the view of those opposed to ratification when he complained that he "wished [the Federalists] would not play round the subject with their fine stories, like a fox round a trap, but come to it," and admit that after ratification "the states will be like towns in this state. Towns . . . have a right to lay taxes to raise money, and the states possibly may have the same." 1 ELLIOT'S DEBATES, *supra*, at 111.

[103] *See, e.g.*, *The Address and Reasons of Dissent of the Minority of the Convention of Pennsylvania To Their Constituents*, Pennsylvania Packet and Daily Advertiser, Dec. 18, 1787, *reprinted in* 3 STORING, *supra* note 96, at 145, 154–57 (criticizing Constitution for permitting Congress to assume effectively unlimited powers by construction, and intimating that the instrument would allow similar self-aggrandizement by the federal judiciary).

struction.[104] Through such construction the new federal rulers would gradually extend their power and so finally subvert American liberties.[105] The Supreme Court's power to interpret the Constitution would make the Court, not the people or their representatives, the true lawgiver.[106] Disputes over the scope of the Constitution's grants of power, the Anti-Federalists argued, showed that no one could predict how the instrument would be interpreted once adopted.[107] The good intentions of the Philadelphia delegates, or of the proponents of the Constitution in the state conventions, were irrelevant, because the *Constitution's* intention was expressed "[s]o loosely . . . [and] inaccurately" that misconstructions were certain to occur.[108] The Protestant tradition taught that God's Word is its own interpreter, and the *philosophes* had warned against the dangers of any law not plainly comprehensible on its face; the proposed Constitution, however, contained no acceptable internal criteria to guide its interpreters.[109] Some Anti-Federalists viewed the document in an even darker light: to them it revealed a conscious desire on the part of the Philadelphia delegates, who had clothed their proceedings in a veil of secrecy, to overthrow the free and republican constitutions of the states and substitute for them a centralized despotism.[110]

The Federalist supporters of ratification offered a variety of responses to the barrage of criticism leveled against the Constitution and its alleged susceptibility to corrupting interpretation. First, to those who questioned the good faith of the Philadelphia delegates, the Federalists responded by invoking not only the great names of Washington and Franklin, but also the common law's understanding of "intent." The Anti-Federalists' fears were misguided, they asserted, because whatever the private sentiments of the Philadelphia delegates

---

[104] *See* G. WOOD, *supra* note 11, at 538; 1 STORING, *supra* note 96, at 54.

[105] *See, e.g.*, Letters of Centinel No. 5 (Nov. 30, 1787), *reprinted in* 2 STORING, *supra* note 96, at 166, 167–69.

[106] *See* 1 STORING, *supra* note 96, at 50.

[107] This assertion was made repeatedly by Anti-Federalists in the state conventions. *See, e.g.*, 3 ELLIOT'S DEBATES, *supra* note 102, at 57 (remarks of Timothy Bloodworth at the first North Carolina convention) ("no one can say what construction congress will put upon" article I); *id.* at 156 (noting remarks of Andrew Bass at the first North Carolina convention) ("[Bass] observed that gentlemen of the law and men of learning did not concur in the explanation or meaning of this constitution. . . . From the contrariety of opinions, he thought the thing was either uncommonly difficult, or absolutely unintelligible.").

[108] A. MASON, *supra* note 85, at 134 (quoting remarks of John Smilie at the Pennsylvania ratifying convention).

[109] *See id.*; Letters of Centinel No. 2 (1787), *reprinted in* 2 STORING, *supra* note 96, at 147 (Federalist claim that unenumerated powers are not granted to the federal government is "a speculative unascertained rule of construction" that would prove "a *poor* security for the liberties of the people"); 3 ELLIOT'S DEBATES, *supra* note 102, at 164 (remarks of Timothy Bloodworth at the first North Carolina convention) (Constitution is flawed because it grants "indefinite power" about which "members of Congress will differ").

[110] *See generally* L. BANNING, *supra* note 31, at 105–13 (discussing Anti-Federalist arguments); 1 STORING, *supra* note 96, at 3–76 (same).

had been, those sentiments would not be the legally significant "intent" of the Constitution.[111] The members of the federal convention had been mere scriveners or attorneys appointed to draw up an instrument; the instrument's true makers were the people of the United States assembled in state conventions.[112] It was thus the people's unquestionably republican intention, evinced in the plain, obvious meaning of the text, that would control future interpretations. The Federalists additionally denied allegations that they were already corrupting the meaning of the Constitution. It was not they but their opponents, the Federalists claimed, who were engaged in lawyers' quibbles over the language of an instrument that the common sense of the people found perfectly clear.[113] As John Jay explained, Federalist statements of the document's meaning were not products of a suspect hermeneutical process; they involved "no sophistry; no construction; no false glosses, but simple inferences from the obvious operation of things."[114] Finally, Federalists argued that the Anti-Federalist attack on the Constitution's indeterminacy ignored the limits of human communicative powers: "no compositions which men can pen, could be formed, but wh[ich] would be liable to the same charge [of ambiguity]."[115] When interpretation was necessary, it would take place in accord with the rules of "universal jurisprudence," subject to correction by the amendment process provided for in article V.[116]

A series of essays published in the *New York Journal* from October 1787 through April 1788 under the byline "Brutus" constituted by far the most powerful and sustained attack on the Constitution from an anti-hermeneutical perspective.[117] "Brutus" read the first sentence of the second section of article III ("The judicial power shall extend to

---

[111] *See* G. WOOD, *supra* note 11, at 524–43.

[112] *See, e.g.*, 3 ELLIOT'S DEBATES, *supra* note 102, at 37 (remarks of Archibald Maclaine at the first North Carolina convention) ("The constitution is only a mere proposal. . . . If the people approve of it, it becomes their act."); THE FEDERALIST No. 40 (J. Madison). In asserting the Philadelphia convention's authority to propose a new constitution instead of mere amendments to the Articles of Confederation, in justifying the lack of a bill of rights, and in defending against the charge that the Constitution had bypassed the states (by beginning with "We the People" instead of "We the States"), the Federalists relied on the basic proposition that the Constitution would be, if adopted, the act of the people, not of the state governments or of the federal convention.

[113] *See* 3 ELLIOT'S DEBATES, *supra* note 102, at 71 (remarks of Archibald Maclaine at the first North Carolina convention).

[114] 1 *id.* at 255 (remarks of John Jay at the New York convention).

[115] *Id.* at 115 (remarks of Theophilus Parsons at the Massachusetts convention); *see* THE FEDERALIST No. 37 (J. Madison).

[116] *See* 3 ELLIOT'S DEBATES, *supra* note 102, at 74 (remarks of John Steele at the first North Carolina convention) ("universal jurisprudence" and a "plain obvious" construction will be applied to the Constitution); A. MASON, *supra* note 85, at 160 (remarks of Edmund Randolph at the Virginia convention) (improper construction of ambiguous parts of Constitution can be remedied through amendment); *cf.* THE FEDERALIST No. 44, at 230 (J. Madison) (G. Wills ed. 1982) (remedy for misconstructions by Congress is electoral).

[117] *See* 2 STORING, *supra* note 96, at 358.

all cases, in law and equity, arising under this Constitution . . . .") to authorize the federal courts to give the Constitution both "a legal construction" and an interpretation "according to the reasoning spirit of it, without being confined to the words or letter."[118] Courts frequently would employ the latter "mode of construction" out of necessity, because the Constitution's grants of authority were "conceived in general and indefinite terms, which are either equivocal, ambiguous, or which require long definitions to unfold the extent of their meaning."[119] The courts' exercises in construction "according to the reasoning spirit," therefore, would necessarily amount to the creation of constitutional norms by judges themselves.[120]

"Brutus" felt that the courts' interpretations "according to the rules laid down for construing a law"[121] would be just as unfortunate. The common law tradition of statutory interpretation, he pointed out, permitted and even required the court to take the end or purpose of the statute into account.[122] Like many statutes, the Constitution declared its purpose in a Preamble, the wording of which made it "obvious," to "Brutus," that the Constitution "has in view every object which is embraced by any government," leaving no separate sphere of responsibility for the state authorities and reducing the present confederation to a single, consolidated nation.[123] Most horrifying of all to "Brutus" was the realization, gathered from the Preamble, from the grants of power to Congress,[124] and from the interpretive authority entrusted to the federal judiciary, that the Constitution identified the separate existence and autonomy of the states as the mischief and defect it was to cure.[125] "Brutus" insisted that the most disinterested judge, interpreting the Constitution with strict regard for the proprieties of common law statutory construction, would agree that the document "was calculated to abolish entirely the state governments, and to melt down the states into one entire government."[126] And of course, he argued, judges would not in fact be disinterested. Elec-

---

[118] Essays of Brutus No. 11, *reprinted in* 2 STORING, *supra* note 96, at 417, 419 (footnote omitted).

[119] *Id.* at 420–21.

[120] *See id.* at 422 ("This power in the judicial, will enable them to mould the government, into almost any shape they please.").

[121] *Id.* at 419.

[122] *See id.*

[123] Essays of Brutus No. 12, *reprinted in* 2 STORING, *supra* note 96, at 422, 424.

[124] "Brutus" thought the "most natural and grammatical" interpretation of article I, section 8, was that it authorized Congress to do "any thing which in their judgment will tend to provide for the general welfare, and [that] this amounts to the same thing as general and unlimited powers of legislation in all cases." *Id.* at 425.

[125] *See id.* at 424–25.

[126] Essays of Brutus No. 15, *reprinted in* 2 STORING, *supra* note 96, at 437, 441; *see* Essays of Brutus No. 12, *reprinted in* 2 STORING, *supra* note 96, at 422, 424–25 (courts will be authorized to interpret the Constitution "according to its spirit," which is "to subvert and abolish" all state powers).

torally irresponsible, endowed with that absolute authority to interpret against which English religious and political tradition warned, the federal judges would be from the beginning the final lawgivers of the system, and in the end its absolute rulers.[127]

"Brutus" therefore saw the Constitution as flawed at a deeper level than that reached by criticisms of its ambiguities or of its broad grants of power to the federal legislature. Its basic evil was its framers' misconception, deliberate or not, of the nature of fundamental law in a free society. The Philadelphia convention had devised a constitution patterned after a statute, a command issued by a legal superior and subject to technical interpretation in accord with the traditional rules of construction. But for "Brutus," a constitution should be a contract, "a compact of a people with their rulers," framed in simple and nontechnical language and enforced by the people's right to remove those rulers "at the period when the rulers are to be elected."[128] A constitution, for "Brutus," should articulate in plain terms the agreement of the community on the rightful powers of government, not establish a superior authority to determine what those powers are. Under such a political compact there could be no danger of effective usurpation by the rulers, save by force, for the compact's meaning would be clear to all and would be interpreted by the equal parties to the compact, not by a legal superior. The Philadelphia framers, unfortunately, had followed a different model. Their proposed constitution did not express consensus; it issued commands — mandates at once so complicated and so obscure that it would be impossible to give them meaning without resort by the federal political bodies to the artificial techniques of traditional legal hermeneutics. By drafting an instrument requiring such interpretation, the Philadelphia framers had ensured that future authority over the parameters of American political society would ultimately be transferred from the ordinary people to a small coterie of legal quibblers.

Commentators have suggested that Alexander Hamilton's discussion of article III in *The Federalist* Nos. 78 through 83, which appeared in late May 1788, was written as a direct response to the *Essays* of "Brutus."[129] Whether or not intended as such, those papers

---

127 *See* Essays of Brutus No. 15, *reprinted in* 2 STORING, *supra* note 96, at 437, 437–41.

128 *Id.* at 442. The views of "Brutus" were not unique; throughout this period American writers invoked the image of "compact" in explaining and defending the basis of the American political order. *See, e.g.*, Amicus Republicae, Address to the Public (Exeter 1786), *reprinted in* 2 STORING, *supra* note 96, at 638, 639–40 (each state was constituted by "civil compacts"; the Articles are a further "solemn covenant" between the states); Hart, Liberty Described and Recommended: in a Sermon Preached to the Corporation of Freemen in Farmington (Hartford 1775), *reprinted in* 1 AMERICAN POLITICAL WRITING DURING THE FOUNDING ERA: 1760–1805, at 305, 308–10 (C. Hyneman & D. Lutz eds. 1983) (human society is founded on "compact[] or mutual agreement").

129 *See, e.g.*, L. LEVY, JUDICIAL REVIEW AND THE SUPREME COURT 6 (1967) (discussing *The Federalist* No. 78). *But see* G. WILLS, EXPLAINING AMERICA: THE FEDERALIST 130–50 (1981) (suggesting alternative interpretation of Hamilton's purposes).

in fact offered the most coherent Federalist rebuttal of the arguments of "Brutus." Hamilton had already observed in *The Federalist* No. 22 that one of the defects of the Articles of Confederation was their failure to establish an effective federal judiciary.[130] In addition, in *The Federalist* No. 37 James Madison had launched a devastating counterattack on the standard Anti-Federalist charge of ambiguity.[131] Madison stressed the inescapable fallibility and tentativeness of all human acts of discrimination — sensory, mental, or experiential — and responded to the religious overtones in the Anti-Federalist critique with the observation that the meaning even of God's Word "is rendered dim and doubtful, by the cloudy medium through which it is communicated" when He "condescends to address mankind in their own language."[132] Mortals' efforts at the framing of law obviously could not be hoped to better those of Omnipotence; Madison thus concluded that "[a]ll new laws, though penned with the greatest technical skill, and passed on the fullest and most mature deliberation, are considered as more or less obscure and equivocal, until their meaning be liquidated and ascertained by a series of particular discussions and adjudications."[133] Madison's argument, which Hamilton had anticipated in *The Federalist* No. 22,[134] was of course a restatement in somewhat abstract terms of the old common law assumption, shared by the Philadelphia framers, that the "intent" of any legal document is the product of the interpretive process and not some fixed meaning that the author locks into the document's text at the outset. In his *Essays* "Brutus" underscored this confession that the Constitution would be subject to judicial construction whose results were not completely foreseeable at present, and he labored with considerable success to demonstrate that the necessary consequence was judicial tyranny.

In *The Federalist* Nos. 78 through 83, Hamilton returned his attention to the legal character of the Constitution and its provisions for a federal judiciary. He steadfastly reiterated *The Federalist*'s earlier claims that it was appropriate and necessary for the courts to "liquidate and fix [the] meaning and operation" of laws, including the Constitution.[135] Hamilton rejected the inference that the future fed-

---

[130] "Laws are a dead letter without courts to expound and define their true meaning and operation." THE FEDERALIST No. 22, at 109 (A. Hamilton) (G. Wills ed. 1982).

[131] *The Federalist* No. 37 (J. Madison) appeared on January 11, 1788, well before the main body of the *Essays*' attack on article III and its implications.

[132] THE FEDERALIST No. 37, at 180 (J. Madison) (G. Wills ed. 1982).

[133] *Id.* at 179.

[134] "The treaties of the United States to have any force at all, must be considered as part of the law of the land. Their true import as far as respects individuals, must, like all other laws, be ascertained by judicial determinations." THE FEDERALIST No. 22, at 109 (A. Hamilton) (G. Wills ed. 1982).

[135] THE FEDERALIST No. 78, at 396 (A. Hamilton) (G. Wills ed. 1982).

eral courts would find in the Constitution anything shocking or surprising to the ordinary reader: "The rules of legal interpretation are rules of *common sense*, adopted by the courts in the construction of the laws. . . . In relation to such a subject [a constitution of government], the natural and obvious sense of its provisions, apart from any technical rules, is the true criterion of construction."[136]

Faced with the argument of "Brutus" that the courts' powers of constitutional interpretation and judicial review of legislative acts would inexorably result in uncontrollable and ultimately despotic oligarchy, Hamilton countered by suggesting that "Brutus" had not taken the statutory analogy seriously enough. Both agreed, Hamilton approvingly and "Brutus" disapprovingly, that the Constitution was to be viewed as a quasi-statute, a command from a legal superior to those under its authority. According to this view, Hamilton argued, the legal superior issuing the command must be considered the ultimate repository of sovereignty in a republic: the people. But "the nature and reason of the thing," Hamilton wrote,

> teach us that the prior act of a superior ought to be preferred to the subsequent act of an inferior and subordinate authority; and that, accordingly, whenever a particular statute contravenes the constitution, it will be the duty of the judicial tribunals to adhere to the latter, and disregard the former.[137]

Far from exalting the judiciary over all, the doctrine of judicial review based on the courts' construction of the Constitution simply safeguarded the authority of the people who had "ordained and established" the Constitution in the first place.[138]

Hamilton and "Brutus" therefore disagreed primarily over the nature of legal interpretation. "Brutus" feared that interpretation would inevitably convert the Constitution's open-textured language into a license for omnipotent federal government. Hamilton countered that legal interpretation was simply the application of common sense to text. Because the people can exercise common sense, they could tell for themselves what the Constitution meant — and no sensible reader would take it to be a charter for tyranny. Hamilton scornfully dismissed the notion that judges could exploit their interpretive authority to make themselves despots: lacking influence "over either the sword or the purse,"[139] he remarked, courts would possess "neither Force nor Will, but merely judgment."[140] The insulation of judges from

---

[136] THE FEDERALIST No. 83, at 422 (A. Hamilton) (G. Wills ed. 1982).

[137] THE FEDERALIST No. 78, at 396 (A. Hamilton) (G. Wills ed. 1982).

[138] *See id.* at 395–96 ("[W]here the will of the legislature declared in its statutes, stands in opposition to that of the people declared in the constitution, the judges ought to be governed by the latter, rather than the former.").

[139] *Id.* at 393.

[140] *Id.* at 394.

electoral accountability was not a threat to liberty, but rather an essential condition to the judiciary's role as independent guardian of the Constitution's limitations on power.[141] In reality, as Hamilton had argued earlier,[142] the seeds of tyranny lurked not within the statutory analogy proposed by the Federalists, but within the contract analogy favored by "Brutus." A government with no justification other than a contractual meeting of the minds could not long endure without resorting to force to resolve the disagreements that would inevitably splinter society. The debate between Hamilton and "Brutus" was ultimately irresolvable, for they started from different premises that paralleled the conflicting hermeneutical perspectives discussed above in Part II. "Brutus" assumed the validity of the anti-interpretive tradition's equation of construction and corruption. In sharp contrast, Hamilton accepted the validity of the common law's hermeneutical techniques as means to discovering a document's "intent."

The public debate over the adoption of the Constitution thus revealed that Americans of all political opinions accepted the applicability to constitutional interpretation of hermeneutical views developed in relation to quite different documents — the Bible, parliamentary statutes, and private contracts. But there were sharp disagreements over which interpretive approach was acceptable.[143] An important element in the Anti-Federalists' critique was their implicit appeal to the distrust of interpretation cultivated by the British

---

[141] *See id.*; THE FEDERALIST No. 79 (A. Hamilton).

[142] *See* THE FEDERALIST No. 16 (A. Hamilton). At the New York convention, Hamilton argued that to "take the old confederation" and entrust it with the minimal powers virtually all Anti-Federalists conceded should be placed in federal hands "would be establishing a power which would destroy the liberties of the people," because the Confederation government, lacking the legal power to act directly on individuals, could carry out its new responsibilities only by using military force. 1 ELLIOT'S DEBATES, *supra* note 102, at 210 (remarks of Alexander Hamilton at the New York convention).

[143] The complex response evoked in many Americans by the proposed Constitution is exemplified in the behavior of Edmund Randolph of Virginia. A delegate and active participant at the Philadelphia convention, Randolph found himself unable at the end to sign the convention's finished product. After his return to Virginia, however, Randolph's fears that rejection would spell the end of the union between the states, and that disunion would lead to anarchy, overcame his misgivings about the Constitution, and he played an important role in securing Virginia's ratification. *See* R. RUTLAND, THE BIRTH OF THE BILL OF RIGHTS: 1777–1791, at 167–68, 174 (rev. ed. 1983). At the state ratifying convention, Randolph assailed the Anti-Federalists' dire prophecies as the product of "extravagant" misconstructions of the Constitution's text. But he agreed that at certain important points the Constitution was unhappily vague, and noted his special concern with the vagueness of the necessary and proper clause in defining the scope of congressional powers:

> My objection is, that the clause is ambiguous, and that that ambiguity may injure the states. My fear is, that it will by gradual accessions gather [power to Congress] to a dangerous length. . . . I trust that the members of congress themselves will explain the ambiguous parts: and if not, the states can combine in order to insist on amending the ambiguities. I would depend on the present actual feeling of the people of America, to introduce any amendment which may be necessary.

A. MASON, *supra* note 85, at 160 (remarks of Edmund Randolph at the Virginia convention).

Protestant tradition and Enlightenment thought. The Federalists, on the other hand, treated the availability of common law hermeneutics as a positive good: precisely because there was a developed tradition of legal interpretation, they argued, the people could predict with confidence the results of future constitutional construction.

B. The Beginnings of Constitutional Interpretation

Upon convening in the spring of 1789 to inaugurate the new government created by the ratification of the Constitution, the first Congress found itself engaged almost at once in the task of explaining the Constitution's ambiguities. The Congress's most famous exercise in constitutional interpretation was the formulation and proposal to the states of a federal bill of rights, embodied in twelve proposed amendments to the 1787 text.[144] But almost every significant issue considered by the Congress (and some arguably not so significant[145]) required some excursion into the fields of constitutional construction. The establishment of the executive departments, the debates over a protective tariff and a national bank, the consideration of a memorial against the slave trade and of the proper means of handling the public debt — all involved the resolution of issues of constitutional authority not plainly answered on the face of the document.[146] Despite their almost constant involvement with the reality of constitutional interpretation, however, many members of Congress attacked the theoretical propriety of such construction and insisted that they were merely applying the Constitution's terms. Rep. Elias Boudinot of New Jersey declared: "For my part, I shall certainly attend to the terms of the Constitution in making a decision [on whether the President's removal power could be exercised constitutionally only with the concurrence of the Senate]; indeed, I never wish to see them departed from or construed, if the Government can possibly be carried into effect in any other manner."[147] Rep. Elbridge Gerry of Massachusetts was dogmatic: "[A]ll construction of the meaning of the Constitution, is

---

[144] Leading members of Congress regarded the amendments not as modifying the 1787 text, but merely as making explicit the original instrument's solicitude for individual liberties. *See, e.g.*, 1 ANNALS OF CONG. 432 (J. Gales ed. 1789) (remarks of Rep. James Madison on June 8, 1789) (Congress ought to adopt amendments that will "expressly declare the great rights of mankind secured under this Constitution"); *id.* at 715 (remarks of Rep. Roger Sherman on Aug. 13, 1789) ("The amendments reported are a declaration of rights; the people are secure in them, whether we declare them or not . . . .").

[145] The premier example of the latter is the famous dispute over the appropriate address for the President. *See* L. BANNING, *supra* note 31, at 117–21.

[146] *See* 4 ELLIOT'S DEBATES, *supra* note 102, pt. II, at 139–232 (collecting opinions on constitutional questions expressed by members of the first Congress).

[147] 1 ANNALS OF CONG. 526 (J. Gales ed. 1789) (remarks of Rep. Elias Boudinot on June 18, 1789).

dangerous or unnatural, and therefore ought to be avoided."[148] Other prominent members joined in the repetition of the old anti-hermeneutical arguments.[149] More realistic about what Congress actually was doing, and concerned only that Congress should interpret well, were men like James Madison. Rising to address the scope of the President's removal power, Madison stressed the far-reaching consequences of Congress's decision on the question. "The decision that is at this time made," he declared, "will become the permanent exposition of the Constitution . . . ."[150]

The passage by the first Congress of a bill to establish a national bank,[151] drafted by Secretary of the Treasury Hamilton, provoked an elaborate debate over constitutional interpretation within the executive branch. President Washington, troubled by doubts over the constitutionality of the measure, requested formal opinions on its validity from Hamilton, Attorney General Edmund Randolph, and Secretary of State Thomas Jefferson. The opinions of Hamilton and Jefferson became classic statements of the expansive and restrictive views, respectively, of the constitutional scope of congressional power.

Both Hamilton and Jefferson purported to rely on "the usual & established rules of construction."[152] Their opposing conclusions and

---

[148] *Id.* at 574 (remarks of Rep. Elbridge Gerry on June 19, 1789). Early in his remarks, Gerry asserted that he was "decidedly against putting any construction whatever on the Constitution." *Id.* at 573. Like Edmund Randolph of Virginia, Gerry had refused to sign the Constitution at the close of the Philadelphia convention. Unlike Randolph, he opposed its ratification. *See* 2 STORING, *supra* note 96, at 4–8.

[149] Roger Sherman expressed a preference "to leave the Constitution to speak for itself wherever occasion demands," rather than for Congress to "attempt to construe the Constitution." 1 ANNALS OF CONG. 538 (J. Gales ed. 1789) (remarks of Rep. Roger Sherman on June 18, 1789). Abraham Baldwin, a proponent of the view that Congress could make executive officers removable by unilateral actions of the President, responded to opponents' claims that his position violated article II, section 2 (which provides that the appointment power is exercisable "by and with the advice and consent of the Senate") with the hope that "gentlemen will change their expression, and say, we shall violate their construction of the Constitution, and not the Constitution itself." For himself, Baldwin remarked, "[W]hen gentlemen tell me that I am going to construe the Constitution, . . . I am very cautious how I proceed. I do not like to construe over much." *Id.* at 556 (remarks of Rep. Abraham Baldwin on June 19, 1789).

[150] *Id.* at 495 (remarks of Rep. James Madison on June 17, 1789). In defending the constitutionality of Hamilton's bank bill, Fisher Ames contrasted "the letter of the constitution" with the instrument's "meaning and intention"; the latter, he argued, was properly and necessarily to be determined by "the doctrine of implication" and the use of "a reasonable latitude of construction." 4 ELLIOT'S DEBATES, *supra* note 102, at 220–23 (remarks of Fisher Ames on Feb. 3, 1791); *see also* 2 ANNALS OF CONG. 1903–09 (1791) (alternative version of Ames's remarks).

[151] Act of Feb. 25, 1791, ch. 10, 1 Stat. 191.

[152] A. Hamilton, *supra* note 84, at 111. Jefferson's opinion includes a similar reference. *See* T. Jefferson, Opinion on the Constitutionality of a National Bank (1791), *reprinted in* 5 THE WRITINGS OF THOMAS JEFFERSON 284, 286 (P. Ford ed. 1892–1899) [hereinafter cited as WRITINGS]. Both papers make clear use of traditional interpretive strategies. *See infra* pp. 915–17.

radically different approaches to the problem, however, demonstrated that the two men held incompatible views about the nature of the Constitution and consequently about the proper application to it of the "usual" rules of construction. Hamilton clearly remained committed to the statutory analogy he had adopted in *The Federalist*. He insisted, in good common law fashion, that the Constitution's text was to be given its "grammatical" and "popular" meaning:

> [W]hatever may have been the nature of the proposition or the reasons for rejecting it concludes nothing in respect to the real merits of the question. The Secretary of State will not deny, that whatever may have been the intention of the framers of a constitution, or of a law, that intention is to be sought for in the instrument itself, according to the usual & established rules of construction. Nothing is more common than for laws to *express* and *effect*, more or less than was intended. If then a power to erect a corporation, in any case, be deducible by fair inference from the whole or any part of the numerous provisions of the constitution of the United States, arguments drawn from extrinsic circumstances, regarding the intention of the convention, must be rejected.[153]

This absolute rejection of what modern intentionalists would regard as evidence of "intent" was perfectly consistent with language prescient of modern intentionalism. A few pages earlier, Hamilton had referred to "the intent of the [Philadelphia] convention."[154] Such locutions were common.[155] They did not in any way indicate that the writer was rejecting the traditional common law understanding of "intent" as the apparent "meaning of the text" in favor of more modern, subjective notions. Indeed, in the passage last quoted from Hamilton, the context makes it plain that he derived his knowledge of "the intent of the convention" from the "obvious & popular sense" of the constitutional expression under consideration ("necessary and proper") and from the "whole turn of the clause containing it."[156]

Just as a statute is to be construed so as to advance the remedy proposed by the legislature and revealed in the statute's preamble and provisions, so the Constitution, Hamilton wrote, must be interpreted in accord with the expansive purposes outlined in its Preamble.[157] The Constitution plainly intended to create a government capable of

---

[153] A. Hamilton, *supra* note 84, at 111. This point was made in response to Jefferson's unusual resort to "legislative history" from the Philadelphia convention's nominally secret proceedings. Jefferson referred to the well-known fact that the convention had rejected a proposal to give Congress explicit power to charter corporations. *See* T. Jefferson, *supra* note 152, at 287.

[154] A. Hamilton, *supra* note 84, at 103.

[155] *See, e.g.*, *infra* note 267 (illustrating similar usage by Madison).

[156] A. Hamilton, *supra* note 84, at 102–03.

[157] *See id.* at 105.

the "advancement of the public good."[158] The "sound maxim of construction" required, therefore, that the Constitution's grants of power be "construed liberally."[159] This conclusion from the general principles of legal interpretation was confirmed, Hamilton added, by the text itself, in the necessary and proper clause:[160] "The whole turn of the clause containing [the phrase 'necessary and proper'], indicates, it was the intent of the convention, by that clause to give a liberal latitude to the exercise of the specified powers."[161]

Jefferson, too, treated the task of constitutional construction as analogous to common law interpretation of statutes and as requiring a determination of the document's "intent." He began, however, from a different point within the tradition — from the maxim that a statute is to be construed as changing the substance of the common law only to the extent that that conclusion is plainly required.[162] Jefferson's opinion began with a list of the preexisting rules of state law that he believed the establishment of a national bank would abrogate.[163] He returned to this theme toward the end of his paper:

> Can it be thought that the Constitution intended that for a shade or two of *convenience*, more or less, Congress should be authorised to break down the most ancient and fundamental laws of the several States; such as those against Mortmain, the laws of Alienage, the rules of descent, the acts of distribution, the laws of escheat and forfeiture, the laws of monopoly?[164]

Jefferson's opening point was wholly traditional, but, as the quoted sentence indicates, his argument subtly shifted ground during the course of his opinion. The aberrant positions of Lord Coke and a few others to one side,[165] the common law presumption against change was only that — a commonsense assumption that legislatures do not transform whole areas of legal custom by implication.[166] But Jefferson

---

[158] *Id.*

[159] *Id.*

[160] *See* U.S. CONST. art. I, § 8 ("The Congress shall have Power . . . [t]o make all Laws which shall be necessary and proper for carrying into Execution the foregoing Powers and all other Powers vested by this Constitution in the Government of the United States, or in any Department or Officer thereof.").

[161] A. Hamilton, *supra* note 84, at 102–03.

[162] *See* H. BROOM, *supra* note 54, at *28.

[163] *See* T. Jefferson, *supra* note 152, at 284–85.

[164] *Id.* at 289.

[165] Coke suggested in Dr. Bonham's Case, 8 Co. Rep. 107, 118, 77 Eng. Rep. 638, 652 (C.P. 1610), that "when an Act of Parliament is against common right and reason, or repugnant, or impossible to be performed, the common law will controul it, and adjudge such Act to be void." Whatever Coke may have meant by this remark, British legal opinion at the time of the American Revolution was overwhelmingly against any possibility of judicial review of Parliament's acts, in the name of the common law or otherwise. *See, e.g.*, 1 W. BLACKSTONE, *supra* note 58, at *156–57 (what Parliament does, "no authority upon earth can undo").

[166] *See* F. DWARRIS, *supra* note 17, at *695.

wanted to establish a more radical interpretive principle: that the presumption in constitutional construction was against *any* change, not only in particular substantive laws but also in spheres of legislative competence.[167] Here Jefferson's argument left behind traditional common law notions of statutory interpretation.[168]

Jefferson implicitly accepted Hamilton's statutory analogy for constitutional interpretation yet provided no real justification for departing from the familiar patterns of statutory interpretation that Hamilton manipulated so well. Jefferson asserted that the Constitution was based on the principle embodied in the tenth amendment: that powers "not delegated" to the federal government are "reserved to the States respectively, or to the people."[169] He did not explain, however, how that amendment's denial to Congress of any undelegated powers necessarily carried with it an attitude of strict construction toward the powers that were delegated. Hamilton, by contrast, presented a clear picture of what the Constitution was and how it should be construed, a picture that fit easily into the traditional interpretive wisdom of the common law.

The most sustained early congressional discussion of constitutional hermeneutics arose out of the controversial treaty with Great Britain negotiated by Chief Justice John Jay. To enable the House of Representatives fully to consider the treaty's expediency and constitutionality, the powerful Republican opposition in the fourth Congress proposed a resolution calling on President Washington to transmit to the House the executive branch's files concerning Jay's negotiations. Federalist opponents of the resolution initially attacked it as unnecessary.

> I will admit, that if the PRESIDENT has assumed powers not delegated to him by the people in making and proclaiming this Treaty, it is void

---

[167] Jefferson wrote that he "consider[ed] the foundation of the Constitution as laid on this ground: That 'all powers not delegated to the United States, by the Constitution, nor prohibited by it to the States, are reserved to the States or to the people.'" T. Jefferson, *supra* note 152, at 285. Hamilton did not deny the principle on which Jefferson relied, but he viewed its significance quite differently. For Hamilton, the tenth amendment merely restated the first principle of republican government, that all governmental power is a delegation from the sovereign people. But mere acceptance of this principle did not indicate what powers the people had in fact delegated to the national government. This was the real question at issue, and Hamilton answered it with his arguments, textual and hermeneutical, for a "liberal" construction of the delegation. *See* A. Hamilton, *supra* note 84, at 99–100. For Jefferson, on the other hand, the tenth amendment was not a mere truism, but expressed a genuine presumption against the legitimacy of federal power, at least in the domestic sphere. *See* Letter from Thomas Jefferson to Justice William Johnson (June 12, 1823), *reprinted in* POLITICAL WRITINGS, *supra* note 40, at 148 ("The States supposed that by their tenth amendment they had secured themselves against constructive powers.").

[168] Jefferson's argument was paralleled, however, by the strict-construction approach taken by 18th century international public law in regard to cessions of power by sovereigns. *See* Tucker, *Appendix* to 1 BLACKSTONE'S COMMENTARIES, note D, at 143 (St.G. Tucker ed. & comm. 1803).

[169] U.S. CONST. amend. X.

in itself; but of what use can those papers be to us in determining that question? Are we to explain the Treaty by private and confidential papers, or by anything extraneous to the instrument itself? I conclude not. . . .

. . . .

. . . [I]f the articles of the instrument be constitutional, can the preparatory steps make them not so?[170]

The debate soon moved, however, to a heated discussion of the House's role in considering or implementing treaties, with the Federalists arguing that the resolution would be an unconstitutional intrusion upon the exclusive treaty powers of the President and Senate. During the debate, a number of Representatives (most but not all of them opponents of the resolution) referred to or quoted from the discussions of the Constitution's meaning that had taken place during the framing and ratification period, and thus provoked a subsidiary debate on the question of constitutional hermeneutics. Asserting that the Constitution itself "must be our sole guide," William Smith of South Carolina argued that "the general sense of the whole nation at the time the Constitution was formed" could be consulted when "the words" of the text were being construed.[171]

This use of history was related but not identical to that of modern intentionalism. The "contemporaneous expositions" on which Smith and others relied were not confined to the debates at Philadelphia, or at the state conventions, but included the defenses of the Constitution published by its proponents and even the critical interpretations of its opponents.[172] In addition, those who cited evidence from the ratification period almost invariably linked it with other expressions of constitutional opinion.[173] Typical of the caution with which these Representatives advanced historical materials as evidence of the Constitution's meaning was the tack taken by Uriah Tracy of Connecticut. Tracy began his attack on the resolution by observing that the House's present decision would probably fix the course of constitutional interpretation in future cases; he consequently urged caution on his colleagues.[174] After setting forth an elaborate analysis of the constitu-

[170] 5 ANNALS OF CONG. 432 (1796) (remarks of Rep. Daniel Buck); *id.* at 441 (remarks of Rep. William Smith).

[171] *Id.* at 495 (remarks of Rep. William Smith); *see also id.* at 519–21, 523–27 (remarks of Rep. Theodore Sedgwick); *id.* at 574–75 (remarks of Rep. Benjamin Bourne).

[172] *See id.* at 495–96 (remarks of Rep. William Smith) (the relevant "general opinion of the public" is that manifested uniformly by both friend and foe of ratification); *id.* at 523 (remarks of Rep. Theodore Sedgwick) (same); *id.* at 580-81 (remarks of Rep. Richard Brent) (same).

[173] *See id.* at 496 (remarks of Rep. William Smith) (subsequent "practice of Congress"); *id.* at 528 (remarks of Rep. Theodore Sedgwick) ("well understood" opinion of Supreme Court); *id.* at 574 (remarks of Rep. Benjamin Bourne) (resolutions of state legislatures on earlier treaties); *id.* at 615–16 (remarks of Rep. Uriah Tracy) (views expressed of federal powers under Articles of Confederation).

[174] *See id.* at 612 (remarks of Rep. Uriah Tracy).

tional text and of American practice under the Articles of Confederation, Tracy quoted from the Virginia ratification convention debates as an illustration of the "almost unanimous understanding of the members of the different [state] Conventions."[175] Tracy "acknowledged, that, from such debates, the real state of men's minds or opinions may not always be collected with accuracy," and explained that he relied on the state proceedings not to prove an affirmative assertion, but only to show that "no one took such extensive ground as is now contended for by some of the supporters of the resolution under consideration."[176]

Although Tracy and others placed only modest weight on materials from the framing and ratification process, they were vigorously attacked by the resolution's supporters for "conjur[ing] up" such "extraneous sources."[177] Their opponents contended that the proper method of interpretation was "to attend to and compare"[178] the text's various provisions in accordance with the "ancient" rules for "the interpretation and construction of laws or Constitutions."[179] In the view of Republican spokesmen, the suggestion that the correct interpretation of the Constitution must conform to "the opinion which prevailed when the Constitution was adopted"[180] misconstrued both the nature of interpretation and the value of the available evidence. Edward Livingston of New York, who introduced the resolution, said that a construction based on history cannot be "conclusive . . . because . . . we [are] now as capable at least of determining the true meaning of that instrument as the Conventions were: they were called in haste, they were heated by party, and many adopted [the Constitution] from expediency."[181] The House, it was argued, must seek "the intrinsic meaning of the Constitution. . . . from the words of it,"[182] while recognizing that the text was unavoidably ambiguous on many issues and that its framers had anticipated that those questions would "be settled by practice or by amendments."[183]

Resort to materials from the ratification era as one species of evidence as to the Constitution's context was in fact only mildly innovative, although proponents of the House resolution strove to make it appear a flagrant violation of the established canons of con-

---

175 *Id.* at 616.

176 *Id.* at 617.

177 *Id.* at 727 (remarks of Rep. Albert Gallatin).

178 *Id.*

179 *Id.* at 603 (remarks of Rep. William Lyman).

180 *Id.* at 574 (remarks of Rep. Benjamin Bourne).

181 *Id.* at 635 (remarks of Rep. Edward Livingston).

182 *Id.* at 505 (remarks of Rep. William Branch Giles).

183 *Id.* at 537 (remarks of Rep. Abraham Baldwin); *see also id.* at 538–39 (it is no objection to a fair construction of the text that it was not anticipated in the ratification era).

struction. One congressman, however, seems to have come much closer to modern intentionalism. Maryland's William Vans Murray, speaking late in the three-week-long debate, expressed surprise that those privy to information about the Philadelphia convention (especially James Madison) had not shared with the House the understanding prevalent at that convention. Vans Murray regarded the Constitution as, on the whole, so "explicit[]" that the text itself left no room for arguments of "expediency or sophistry."[184] But the existence, so soon after the Constitution's adoption, of "doubts upon some of its plainest passages" made it the duty of a man "known to have been in the illustrious body that framed the instrument [to] clear up difficulties by [communicating] his contemporaneous knowledge."[185] Vans Murray himself made no attempt to locate or use such information and expressed doubt about the propriety of consulting the official journal of the Philadelphia convention.[186]

On the following, final day of the debate, one of the leading Republicans in the House, Albert Gallatin of Pennsylvania, recapitulated the argument for the resolution. Its opponents had turned to extraneous evidence of various types, Gallatin said, only when they had recognized that "the letter and spirit of our Constitution" were against them.[187] Even so, Gallatin stated that he "little expected to have heard such an appeal as was made yesterday" by Vans Murray, an appeal he described as the doctrine that "the opinions and constructions of those persons who had framed and proposed the Constitution, opinions given in private, constructions unknown to the people when they adopted the instrument, should, after a lapse of eight years, be appealed to."[188] Even if it were proper to use the views expressed in the debates of a legislative body in interpreting that body's acts — a proposition Gallatin doubted — the opinions of the Philadelphia framers were as irrelevant as those of the legislative clerk who penned a statute. Gallatin conceded that the proceedings of the state conventions might serve as a source of corroborative evidence, but insisted that the House could and should resolve the question of its role with respect to treaties "by the letter of the instrument alone."[189]

The *Annals of Congress* record only one voice raised in (at least partial) support of Vans Murray, that of George Washington.[190] The

---

[184] *Id.* at 701 (remarks of Rep. William Vans Murray). Vans Murray noted that "contemporaneous opinions [that were] still fresh" and the contents of the Philadelphia convention's official journal could serve as additional checks on misconstruction. *Id.*

[185] *Id.* at 701–02.

[186] *See id.* at 701.

[187] *Id.* at 733 (remarks of Rep. Albert Gallatin).

[188] *Id.* at 734.

[189] *Id.* at 738.

[190] President Washington's written response to the House resolution was made part of the congressional record. *See id.* at 760–61.

resolution passed by a lopsided majority (62 to 37) and was presented to President Washington; after a few days' deliberation, Washington declined to carry out the Representatives' request. He explained in a written message to the House that delivery of the administration's files on the treaty would intrude on the confidentiality necessary to the President's successful exercise of his diplomatic responsibilities. Washington went on to reject the argument that the execution of at least some treaties demanded the concurrence of the House. He based this position on his own knowledge of the Philadelphia convention's views, on the practice of the government from 1789 to 1796, on the "plain letter" of the Constitution, and on the convention's rejection of a motion to require all treaties to be confirmed by statute — a rejection recorded in the convention's official journal.[191] The backers of the House resolution criticized Washington's conclusion and his interpretive methodology, and secured the passage of another resolution reaffirming their position.[192] During the debate over this resolution, James Madison took issue with the invocation of the Philadelphia convention by Vans Murray and Washington. Vans Murray's speech had caused Madison "some surprise, which was much increased by the peculiar stress laid on the information expected," and Madison's amazement had reawakened when Washington too appealed to the Philadelphia proceedings "as a clue to the meaning of the Constitution."[193] Personal impressions of "the intention of the whole body," whether his own or Washington's, were of little value according to Madison, and were likely in any case to conflict.[194] Madison dismissed Washington's citation of the convention's journal as an attempt to draw an affirmative conclusion from an unexplained, negative, and "abstract vote."[195] Madison stated that he "did not believe a single instance could be cited in which the sense of the Convention had been required or admitted as material [to] any Constitutional question" discussed either in Congress or in the Supreme Court.[196]

C. The Constitution and the New Supreme Court

While the members of the executive and legislative branches were busily engaged in the process of constitutional interpretation during the Constitution's first decade, the Supreme Court found relatively few opportunities to address constitutional issues. But in its first great case, *Chisholm v. Georgia*,[197] the Court signaled its approval of a

[191] *See id.*

[192] *See id.* at 771–72 (reprinting the text of the resolution); *id.* at 782–83 (noting affirmative vote on the resolution).

[193] *Id.* at 775 (remarks of Rep. James Madison).

[194] *Id.*

[195] *Id.* at 776.

[196] *Id.*

[197] 2 U.S. (2 Dall.) 419 (1793).

traditional statutory approach to construing the nation's fundamental law. *Chisholm* was an action in assumpsit against the state of Georgia, brought under the Court's original diversity jurisdiction. Georgia denied the Court's authority to hear the case and refused to enter an appearance.[198] Plaintiff's counsel Edmund Randolph argued that both "the letter" and the "genuine and necessary interpretation" of the Constitution sustained the Court's jurisdiction.[199] His argument as to the Constitution's proper "interpretation" disavowed reliance on the "history" of the instrument or on its Preamble, resting instead on two distinct pillars: the existence in the Constitution of various prohibitions on state action, and the American experience of a "government of supplication" under the "deceased" Articles of Confederation.[200] Randolph's argument was thus wholly traditional: he sought the intent of the document by examining the text in the light of the evil it was meant to correct.

The question of state amenability to suit in federal court had been raised repeatedly during the ratification campaign, and the virtually unanimous Federalist response had been to deny that the Constitution would affect the states' sovereign immunity.[201] If the Court had regarded itself as bound by the expectations of the Constitution's framers and supporters, a decision in Georgia's favor obviously would have been warranted. A majority of the Justices, however, agreed with Randolph that a "genuine interpretation" was not to be based on such external evidence,[202] but rather was to be reached by use of

---

[198] *See id.* at 419.

[199] *Id.* at 421. Randolph was Attorney General of the United States at the time, but was representing the plaintiff in his private capacity.

[200] *See id.* at 421–25.

[201] *See, e.g.*, THE FEDERALIST No. 81 (A. Hamilton).

[202] Justice Iredell dissented on statutory grounds and indicated that he disagreed with Randolph's view of the constitutional question as well. *See Chisholm*, 2 U.S. (2 Dall.) at 429, 449–50 (Iredell, J., dissenting). Justice Iredell's constitutional disagreement with the majority was not based, however, on his acceptance of evidence about the Constitution's "history," but on the 18th century public-law presumption against the delegation of sovereign power. *See id.* at 435–36.

Justice Iredell's acceptance of the common law approach to legal interpretation is exemplified by a grand jury charge he delivered in 1799. In addressing the constitutionality of the Alien and Sedition Acts, Justice Iredell noted the Republicans' view that the Alien Act violated the "migration and importation" clause of article I, section 9. Although some Federalists rebutted the accusation by referring to the clause's well-known connection with the importation of slaves, Justice Iredell rejected this line of defense as contrary to proper legal interpretation:

> I am not satisfied, as to [the Republican] objection, that it is sufficient to overrule it, to say the words do not express the real meaning, either of those who formed the constitution, or those who established it, although I do verily believe in my own mind that the article was intended only for slaves . . . . But, though this probably is the real truth, yet, if in attempting to compromise, they have unguardedly used expressions that go beyond their meaning, and there is nothing but private history to elucidate it, I shall deem it absolutely necessary to confine myself to the written instrument.

G. MCREE, LIFE AND CORRESPONDENCE OF JAMES IREDELL 551, 558 (New York 1857) (quoting charge delivered by Justice Iredell to grand jury in 1799).

the "ordinary rules for construction."[203] These rules required that the intent of the Constitution's maker, "the people of the United States,"[204] be sought in the people's own, authoritative words: the constitutional text.[205] The majority believed that these rules of construction, when applied to the Constitution, indicated that the document was intended to allow the action against the state. The proposal and ratification of the eleventh amendment[206] swiftly overturned the holding of *Chisholm*, but the majority's highly traditional and strikingly nationalistic approach to constitutional interpretation foreshadowed the jurisprudence of John Marshall.

* * *

Although most Americans in public life in the 1790s accepted the propriety of a statutory analogy for constitutional construction, disagreements over substantive constitutional doctrine became more glaring as opposing political parties coalesced during the later years of Washington's administration. Constitutional issues, and in particular the split between Hamilton and Jefferson over liberal versus strict construction, played an important role in the parties' efforts to define themselves.[207] Federalists like Hamilton, applying the traditional tools of statutory construction to the Constitution's sweeping generalities, found in the text the basis for an expansive view of federal power. The Republicans, in contrast, took up the cudgels of the religious and philosophical opposition to interpretation and warned that the "wiles of construction"[208] could be controlled only by a narrow reading of the Constitution's expansive language.[209] It was in the course of their political guerrilla warfare against the dominant Federalists during the administration of Washington's successor, John Adams, that the two greatest Republican leaders, Jefferson and Madison,[210] formulated the theory of the Constitution, and of its proper

---

203 *Chisholm*, 2 U.S. (2 Dall.) at 476 (Jay, C.J.).

204 *Id.* at 464 (Wilson, J.); *see id.* at 466–68 (Cushing, J.); *id.* at 470–72 (Jay, C.J.).

205 *See id.* at 450 (Blair, J.); *id.* at 466 (Wilson, J.); *id.* at 467 (Cushing, J.); *id.* at 476–77 (Jay, C.J.). Indeed, Chief Justice Jay and Justice Wilson went a step beyond Randolph by relying in part on the Preamble to illuminate the Constitution's meaning. *See id.* at 463 (Wilson, J.); *id.* at 474–75 (Jay, C.J.).

206 *See* U.S. CONST. amend. XI ("The Judicial power of the United States shall not be construed to extend to any suit . . . commenced or prosecuted against one of the United States by Citizens of another State, or by Citizens or Subjects of any Foreign State.").

207 *See* L. BANNING, *supra* note 31, at 201–02.

208 Pendleton, *The Danger Not Over*, Richmond Examiner, Oct. 20, 1801, *quoted in* L. BANNING, *supra* note 31, at 282; *see also* Letter from Thomas Jefferson to Wilson C. Nicholas (Sept. 7, 1803), *reprinted in* POLITICAL WRITINGS, *supra* note 40, at 144 (warning of the dangers of construction).

209 *See generally* L. BANNING, *supra* note 31, at 126–245 (discussing the rise of Republican opposition to the Federalist administration).

210 Madison's emergence as a key figure in the development of the state-sovereignty theory

interpretation, that became the basis of consensus for a quarter-century of constitutional discourse. In addition, the constitutional hermeneutic they proposed became, remotely and rhetorically, the precursor of modern intentionalism.

IV. SOVEREIGN STATES AND LATER THEORIES OF CONSTITUTIONAL INTENT

"A system like ours, of divided powers, must necessarily give great importance to a proper system of construction."[211]

In 1798, the Federalist-controlled Congress, alarmed by the radical and increasingly hostile behavior of revolutionary France and fearful of subversion by a fifth column composed of foreign immigrants and Francophile Republicans,[212] enacted the series of measures known collectively as the Alien and Sedition Acts.[213] Congress passed the

---

of the Constitution in the 1790s is, on the surface, somewhat surprising in light of his nationalist sympathies in the 1780s. *See* G. WOOD, *supra* note 11, at 473 (noting that by 1787, Madison was "a thorough nationalist, intent on subordinating the states as far as possible to the sovereignty of the central government"). Madison's view of federal power during his Presidency can be seen as a partial return to this pre-ratification nationalism. *See* Madison, Message to Congress (Dec. 5, 1815), *reprinted in* THE MIND OF THE FOUNDER: SOURCES OF THE POLITICAL THOUGHT OF JAMES MADISON 297 (M. Meyers rev. ed. 1981) [hereinafter cited as MIND OF THE FOUNDER] (suggesting an expansive view of congressional power). *But see* Madison, Veto Message (Mar. 3, 1817), 30 ANNALS OF CONG. 1061 (vetoing internal improvements bill on ground that it exceeded powers delegated to Congress). In the final constitutional struggle of his life, the nullification crisis of 1828 to 1832, Madison forcefully repudiated the extreme state sovereignty views of the nullifiers. *See, e.g.*, J. Madison, Notes on Nullification (1835–1836), *reprinted in* MIND OF THE FOUNDER, *supra*, at 417. Madison, of course, may simply have been inconsistent; a more sympathethic interpretation is that Madison's consistency lay in his constant desire to preserve the federal republic as a just and free society. *See* A. KOCH, MADISON'S 'ADVICE TO MY COUNTRY' (1966) (developing such an interpretation).

211 J. Calhoun, South Carolina Exposition (original draft, Dec. 1828), *reprinted in* 6 THE WORKS OF JOHN C. CALHOUN 1, 40 (R. Crallé ed. 1855).

212 *See generally* J. MILLER, CRISIS IN FREEDOM 3–73 (1951) (discussing historical setting of Alien and Sedition Acts).

213 Congress raised the residency requirement for naturalization from five to 14 years. Act of June 8, 1798, ch. 54, 1 Stat. 566; (repealed by Act of April 14, 1802, ch. 28, § 5, 2 Stat. 153, 155). The Alien Enemies Act, ch. 66, 1 Stat. 577 (1798) (current version at 50 U.S.C. §§ 21–22 (1982)), provided for the arrest and "removal" of resident aliens in the event of hostilities between their native country and the United States. The Alien Act, ch. 58, 1 Stat. 570 (1798) (expired 1800), gave the President "virtually unlimited power over all aliens in the United States," J. MILLER, *supra* note 212, at 52, permitting him to order their surveillance, arrest, deportation, and (if they returned) imprisonment, with little judicial supervision. The Sedition Act, ch. 74, 1 Stat. 596 (1798) (expired 1801), settled doubts over the existence of a federal common law offense of seditious libel by making it a statutory crime to defame the government or incite resistance to the laws of the United States. The Act's defenders pointed to its requirement that malice be proved, its allowance of truth as a defense, and its provisions for jury trial as evidence that the statute in fact allayed the common law's rigor. The Republicans, who did not think there was rightfully any federal common law to change for better or worse, saw the Act as "an experiment on the American mind to see how far it will bear an

Sedition Act on July 14, 1798, and federal prosecutors swiftly pressed it into action against critics of the government; at least twenty-five arrests, in most cases of editors of Republican journals, were made under either the Act or the federal common law crime of seditious libel. The government eventually succeeded in procuring several convictions and permanently shutting down a number of opposition presses.[214]

The Alien and Sedition Acts alarmed the Republican leadership on both theoretical and practical grounds. They regarded passage of the Acts as a patent transgression of both the principle of limited federal government and the liberties guaranteed by the Bill of Rights, as well as proof that the process of corruption their ideology led them to expect in any government was proceeding at an alarming rate in the United States.[215] On a practical, political level, the federal suppression of criticism was an obvious and potentially effective attempt to perpetuate Federalist control of the Presidency and Congress. The Republicans saw that a vigorous response was necessary, but the appropriate means were not obvious. Attacking the Acts through the Republican press was likely to prove self-defeating by bringing down upon the newspaper the rigor of the Sedition Act itself. Petitioning Congress for redress of grievances clearly would be futile. Public statements by prominent Republicans would put the speakers at risk — even before the Acts were passed, a Federalist-dominated grand jury had indicted a Republican congressman for communicating to his own constituents his negative evaluation of administration policies.[216] The vigor of the Federalist attempt to choke off dissent, and the Republican commitment to decentralization of power in the Union,[217] drove the Republicans to the only sphere of political power still somewhat insulated from federal retribution: the Republican-controlled legislatures of the Southern states.

---

avowed violation of the Constitution," to be followed if successful by an open repudiation of republicanism. Letter from Thomas Jefferson to Stephens Mason (Oct. 11, 1798), *reprinted in* POLITICAL WRITINGS, *supra* note 40, at 156.

[214] *See* T. EMERSON, THE SYSTEM OF FREEDOM OF EXPRESSION 100 (1970) (recounting arrests under the Acts); C. HAINES, THE ROLE OF THE SUPREME COURT IN AMERICAN GOVERNMENT AND POLITICS: 1789–1835, at 159–60 (1944) (discussing federal common law crime of seditious libel).

[215] *See* L. BANNING, *supra* note 31, at 246–70; A. KOCH, JEFFERSON AND MADISON: THE GREAT COLLABORATION 174–211 (1950). Jefferson referred to the Acts as "violations of the Constitution" because they attempted "to silence by force and not by reason the complaints or criticisms, just or unjust, of our citizens against the conduct of their agents." Letter from Thomas Jefferson to Elbridge Gerry (Jan. 26, 1799), *reprinted in* POLITICAL WRITINGS, *supra* note 40, at 47, 47.

[216] *See* A. KOCH, *supra* note 215, at 182–83.

[217] *See, e.g.*, Madison, *Consolidation*, Nat'l Gazette, Dec. 5, 1791, *reprinted in* MIND OF THE FOUNDER, *supra* note 210, at 181; Letter from Thomas Jefferson to Gideon Granger (Aug. 13, 1800), *reprinted in* POLITICAL WRITINGS, *supra* note 40, at 96, 97 (arguing against "assumption of all the State powers into the hands of the General Government").

In utter secrecy, Jefferson and Madison prepared two sets of resolutions denouncing the Alien and Sedition Acts as tyrannical and unconstitutional. Jefferson's draft, originally intended for submission to the North Carolina legislature, was instead proposed to the Kentucky legislature by John Breckinridge and, with certain changes, was passed by that body in November 1798.[218] Republican legislator John Taylor[219] introduced Madison's draft in the Virginia General Assembly, which approved it in late December 1798.

The initial response to the "Virginia and Kentucky Resolutions" disappointed the Republican leadership. No other state endorsed them, and several Federalist legislatures replied with strongly nationalist resolutions denying the right of state assemblies to pass on the validity of federal statutes.[220] The Kentucky legislature replied to the criticisms in 1799 by adopting a second, briefer set of resolutions reiterating the constitutional views expressed in its original resolutions.[221] The Virginia General Assembly followed suit in January 1800 by adopting a resolution approving a report, written by Madison, that reaffirmed the views expressed in its own 1798 resolutions.[222]

The Virginia and Kentucky Resolutions and Madison's "Report of 1800"[223] did not achieve their immediate goal of mobilizing opposition

---

[218] *See* A. KOCH, *supra* note 215, at 186–94.

[219] Taylor became in later years one of the leaders of the "Old Republicans," the extreme wing of the Jeffersonian movement whose adherents regarded Jefferson's second term as somewhat compromised and the administrations of Madison and Monroe as continual apostasy from the true principles of 1798. Of the commentaries written before Calhoun began his series of state papers in 1828, Taylor's works — especially his NEW VIEWS OF THE CONSTITUTION OF THE UNITED STATES (Washington City 1823) — represent the most powerful and sustained vindication of an uncompromising states' rights interpretation of both the Virginia and Kentucky Resolutions and the Constitution.

[220] *See* STATE DOCUMENTS ON FEDERAL RELATIONS 16–26 (H. Ames ed. 1906) [hereinafter cited as STATE DOCUMENTS] (collecting the most important of the replies). Ironically, having denied the right of states to judge the constitutionality of federal laws, several Federalist legislatures went on to review the Alien and Sedition Acts and to uphold their validity. *See id.* at 18–20 (Massachusetts); *id.* at 20–22 (Pennsylvania); *id.* at 24–25 (New Hampshire).

[221] The draftsman of the 1799 Resolutions is unknown, although the Resolutions strongly reflect the ideas of both Jefferson and Madison. *See* A. KOCH, *supra* note 215, at 201.

[222] Previously, while circulating the 1798 Resolutions to its fellow legislatures, the General Assembly had published an "Address to the People" that justified its action as an attempt to "exhibit to the people the momentous question, whether the Constitution of the United States shall yield to a construction which defies every restraint and overwhelms the best hopes of republicanism." Address of the General Assembly to the People of the Commonwealth of Virginia (1799), *reprinted in* 4 LETTERS AND OTHER WRITINGS OF JAMES MADISON 509, 509 (Philadelphia 1865) [hereinafter cited as MADISON LETTERS]. In the Report of 1800, Madison, who had left Congress in March 1798 and entered the Virginia legislature in December 1799, *see* A. KOCH, *supra* note 215, at 172, provided a point-by-point commentary on the 1798 Resolutions and concluded with a proposed resolution that the legislature renew its protest against the Alien and Sedition Acts. The General Assembly approved both the Report and the resolution. *See* Report on the Virginia Resolutions, *reprinted in* 4 MADISON LETTERS, *supra*, at 515, 555.

[223] References in the text to "the Virginia and Kentucky Resolutions" are meant to include all three sets of resolutions as well as the Report of 1800. Debates over the proper interpretation

to the "reign of witches."[224] In the longer term, however, the Resolutions proved to be among the most influential extraconstitutional, nonjudicial texts in American constitutional history. They presented a vision of the United States as a league of sovereign states, a vision that in many respects was closer to the position of the Anti-Federalists than to the view espoused by the Constitution's supporters.[225] They created a vocabulary with which to express that vision.[226] And they proposed, in justification of their substantive constitutional doctrines, an interpretive strategy centered on a search for the Constitution's underlying and original "intent." The detailed implications of this strategy were spelled out over the next several decades by Madison, and were criticized by the United States Supreme Court under the leadership of Federalist Chief Justice John Marshall. Even the final passage into history of the Federalist-Republican controversies did not end the Resolutions' influence. The rhetoric of "original intent" has endured, and indeed flourished, long after the universal rejection of most of its accompanying complex of ideas.

A. The "Doctrines of '98"[227]

The Resolutions defined the Constitution in contractual terms, as a "compact" to which "each State acceded as a State, and is an integral

---

of the Resolutions, including whether the Kentucky documents present a more extreme states' rights position than do Madison's products, have raged since the Old Republicans began their critique of the official — and in their view crypto-Federalist — Republicanism of Madison and Monroe. The argument put forward in this Article does not require resolution of these issues. My primary assumption has been that the interpretation placed on the Resolutions by Jefferson and Madison should be respected. Both men maintained throughout their lives that their actions in office had been consistent with the constitutional position staked out in the Resolutions and with one another's views. *See* J. Madison, Notes on Nullification (1835–1836), *reprinted in* MIND OF THE FOUNDER, *supra* note 210, at 418–42 (defending continuity of his views on nullification and the doctrines of the Resolutions, and denying difference between his and Jefferson's views on federalism); Letter from Thomas Jefferson to Edward Everett (Apr. 8, 1826), *reprinted in* POLITICAL WRITINGS, *supra* note 40, at 151 (federal Constitution is "a compact of independent nations subject to the rules acknowledged in similar cases"); Letter from Thomas Jefferson to James Madison (Feb. 17, 1826), *reprinted in* 10 WRITINGS, *supra* note 152, at 375, 377 (referring to the half-century of "harmony of our political principles"); Letter from James Madison to William Eustis (May 22, 1823), *reprinted in* 9 THE WRITINGS OF JAMES MADISON 135, 135 (G. Hunt ed. 1910) (denying charge that the Republican leaders had "abandoned their Cause, and gone over to the policy of their opponents").

[224] Letter from Thomas Jefferson to John Taylor (June 1, 1798), *reprinted in* 7 WRITINGS, *supra* note 152, at 263, 265.

[225] For discussions of the Anti-Federalist views of the Union, see A. MASON, *supra* note 85, at 69–100, and 1 STORING, *supra* note 96, at 24–37.

[226] References to the constitutional "compact" and to the continued "sovereignty" and "independence" of the states, as well as the notions of "interposition" and "nullification," were among the Resolutions' important contributions to antebellum constitutional rhetoric.

[227] In later years Republicans often referred to the constitutional theory put forward in the Resolutions as the "doctrines of '98." *See, e.g.*, THE VIRGINIA AND KENTUCKY RESOLUTIONS OF 1798 AND '99, at 1 (J. Elliot ed. 1832) [hereinafter cited as RESOLUTIONS].

party; its co-States forming, as to itself, the other party."[228] This constitutional contract did not affect the "sovereign and independent" character of the parties to it.[229] Before the Revolution the colonies and Great Britain had been de jure equal and "coördinate members . . . of an empire united by a common executive sovereign, but not united by any common legislative sovereign."[230] Therefore, upon rejecting the royal executive the states became discrete bodies politic, united only to the extent that they had delegated certain powers to a common agent, the federal government. The political society created by the Constitution was a purely artificial product of the states' compact, and the federal government was a creature of the states with absolutely no powers except those "resulting from the compact."[231] As in other cases of international compacts among independent nations, each state was necessarily an equal and final judge over constitutional disputes because there was no legal authority superior to the states to which such disputes could be referred. The federal instrumentalities of the compact obviously could not serve as umpire, at least with respect to disputes concerning the line between federal and state power, because to allow them to do so would be to permit the agent, rather than the principal, to determine the agent's duties.[232]

The constitutional vision expressed in the Resolutions was by no means original, but the first application of that vision was not to the Constitution but to the Articles of Confederation. With the exception of a few ultranationalist Federalists,[233] all the participants in the

---

228 Kentucky Resolutions of 1798 (T. Jefferson draft 1798), *reprinted in* RESOLUTIONS, *supra* note 227, at 61, 61.

229 Kentucky Resolutions of 1799, *reprinted in* RESOLUTIONS, *supra* note 227, at 19, 20.

230 Madison's Report of 1800, *reprinted in* MIND OF THE FOUNDER, *supra* note 210, at 231, 245–46.

231 Virginia Resolutions of 1798, *reprinted in* RESOLUTIONS, *supra* note 227, at 5, 5.

232 *See* Kentucky Resolutions of 1798, *reprinted in* RESOLUTIONS, *supra* note 227, at 15, 15–16; Madison's Report of 1800, *reprinted in* MIND OF THE FOUNDER, *supra* note 210, at 231, 237.

233 Ironically, in light of later history, ultranationalist sentiment at the time of the Constitution's ratification was especially strong in the South Carolina convention. Responding to Anti-Federalist arguments that the link between the states existed solely on the basis of the Articles of Confederation and the ad hoc military alliance that had preceded their ratification, South Carolina Chancellor John Mathews asserted that the authority of the Continental Congress from the beginning was derived from the American people and that consequently Congress's resolutions had possessed "the force of law" quite apart from and before the approval of the Articles by the state legislatures. 4 DEBATES IN THE SEVERAL STATE CONVENTIONS ON THE ADOPTION OF THE FEDERAL CONSTITUTION 298, 298 (J. Elliot 2d ed. 1836) (remarks of John Mathews at the South Carolina convention). Charles Cotesworth Pinckney, a South Carolina delegate to the Philadelphia convention, claimed that "[t]he separate independence and individual sovereignty of the several states were never thought of by the enlightened band of patriots who framed this Declaration [of Independence]." *Id.* at 300, 301 (remarks of Charles Cotesworth Pinckney at the South Carolina convention). Pinckney regarded the belief that "each state is

dispute over the Constitution's ratification in the previous decade had regarded the Articles as a compact among the states as independent sovereigns, and the Confederation Congress as the agent, not the superior, of the states. The Anti-Federalist charge that the Constitution plainly was intended to replace that existing league (based on a compact) with a "consolidated" government had been a central point of dispute in the ratification campaign.[234] Although the Federalist response had taken several different tacks,[235] in the end the supporters of the Constitution could not, and did not wish to, deny the noncontractual character of the instrument.[236] As James Wilson observed at the Pennsylvania convention, the Constitution was not a contract, poorly drafted or otherwise:

> I cannot discover the least trace of a compact in that system. . . .
> . . . This, Mr. President, is not a government founded upon compact; it is founded upon the power of the people. They express in their name and their authority, *"We the people do ordain and*

separately and individually independent, as a species of political heresy." *Id.* Most Federalists, however, conceded that the Articles made the United States no more than a league of sovereignties; the virtue of the Constitution, in their eyes, was that it would remedy this political anomaly. *See supra* pp. 904–05.

234

> "We the people of the United States," is a sentence that evidently shows the old foundation of the union is destroyed, the principle of confederation excluded, and a new and unwieldy system of consolidated empire is set up, upon the ruins of the present compact between the states. Can this be denied? No, sir: It is artfully indeed, but it is incontrovertibly designed to abolish the independence and sovereignty of the states individually . . . .

Remarks of Robert Whitehill at the Pennsylvania Ratifying Convention (1787), *quoted in* A. MASON, *supra* note 85, at 135, 135.

235 The most conciliatory Federalist position, and the one most familiar to modern lawyers through its incorporation in *The Federalist Papers*, held that the Constitution preserved a residuum of state sovereignty. *See* THE FEDERALIST No. 32 (A. Hamilton); THE FEDERALIST No. 39 (J. Madison). These verbally moderate Federalists pointed to equal representation in the Senate, the limitation and enumeration of federal powers, and the states' closer links with the people as significant safeguards of state autonomy. *See* 1 ELLIOT'S DEBATES, *supra* note 102, at 225, 230–31 (remarks of Alexander Hamilton at the New York convention); *id.* at 281, 282–84 (same); 2 *id.* at 95 (remarks of James Madison at the Virginia convention); 2 *id.* at 197, 203–05 (same); 3 *id.* at 122, 123 (remarks of James Iredell at the first North Carolina convention). Other Federalists were not willing to make even these concessions. *See supra* note 233. But even the most conciliatory Federalist would not and could not deny that the Constitution gave final and uncontrollable authority to the people's national organs of expression. *See* 1 ELLIOT'S DEBATES, *supra* note 102, at 319, 321 (remarks of Alexander Hamilton at the New York convention); THE FEDERALIST No. 39, at 194 (J. Madison) (G. Wills ed. 1982).

236 The common Federalist position of turning aside attacks on the federal convention's authority or on the language of the Preamble by describing the Constitution as a grant of authority from the sovereign people implicitly repudiated all contractual images of the Union's fundamental law. *See* G. WOOD, *supra* note 11, at 532–47. Not all Federalists were completely aware of this, however, and the Resolutions were to show that the document could be read from a contractual perspective.

establish," &c. from their ratification alone, it is to take its constitutional authenticity; without that, it is no more than *tabula rasa*.

. . . .

I have already shewn, that this system is not a compact or contract; the system itself tells you what it is; it is an ordinance and establishment of the people. [237]

The Resolutions simply ignored the recent and well-known debates over the Constitution's character, as well as the absence within its text of references to a compact or to the states as sovereign contracting parties.[238] Jefferson and Madison offered instead a coherent reading of the Constitution based on the contractual imagery still familiar from the Confederation era. The force of the authors' styles, together with the infancy of the Constitution and the lingering memories of the Confederation, enabled the Resolutions to overcome these historical and textual obstacles and gain political acceptance.

The Resolutions explained that their substantive constitutional doctrines were legitimated by an inquiry into "the plain intent and meaning in which [the compact] was understood and acceded to by the several parties,"[239] and "the plain sense and intention of the instrument constituting that compact."[240] Because the Constitution is a

---

[237] 3 ELLIOT'S DEBATES, *supra* note 102, at 286–88 (remarks of James Wilson at the Pennsylvania convention).

[238] The only textual hook on which to hang the ideas of state sovereignty and constitutional compact was the tenth amendment: "The powers not delegated to the United States by the Constitution, nor prohibited by it to the States, are reserved to the States respectively, or to the people." U.S. CONST. amend. X. How little support even that provision provided a theory of state sovereignty can be seen by comparing its text to that of the second of the Articles of Confederation, which declared: "Each State retains its sovereignty, freedom and independence, and every power, jurisdiction, and right, which is not by this confederation expressly delegated to the United States, in Congress assembled." The tenth amendment lacks the earlier provision's positive declaration of state autonomy and its restriction of federal powers to those "expressly" delegated. Instead, the amendment notes that the Constitution denies certain powers to the states, and makes an ambiguous reference to powers "reserved . . . to the people." Nineteenth century advocates of state sovereignty bridled at the possibility that this last phrase could be construed as a reference in the constitutional text to the nationalist idea of a unitary American people, rather than a citizenry comprising the separate peoples of the several states. *See* 1 J. DAVIS, THE RISE AND FALL OF THE CONFEDERATE GOVERNMENT 158 (1881). The ambiguity was resolved by the framers of the Confederate States Constitution, who rewrote the tenth amendment to read: "The powers not delegated to the Confederate States by the Constitution, nor prohibited by it to the States, are reserved to the States, respectively, or to the people *thereof*." CONFEDERATE STATES CONST. art. VI, § 6 (emphasis added); *see also id.* preamble ("We, the people of the Confederate States, each State acting in its sovereign and independent character . . ."); *id.* art. VI, § 5 (rewritten version of ninth amendment) ("The enumeration, in the Constitution, of certain rights, shall not be construed to deny or disparage others retained by the people *of the several States*." (emphasis added)).

[239] Kentucky Resolutions of 1798, *reprinted in* RESOLUTIONS, *supra* note 227, at 15, 18; *see also* Kentucky Resolutions of 1799, *reprinted in* RESOLUTIONS, *supra* note 227, at 19, 20 (referring to the Constitution's "obvious and real intention").

[240] Virginia Resolutions of 1798, *reprinted in* RESOLUTIONS, *supra* note 227, at 5, 5.

contract, they argued, it is to be interpreted according to the "intent" of the contracting parties. But, as discussed above, in late eighteenth century Anglo-American legal discourse, references to the "intent of a legal instrument" and to the "intent of its makers" were interchangeable, and in neither case did the term refer to the subjective purposes of the human authors. One construed a contract's "intent" not by embarking on a historical inquiry into what the parties actually wished to accomplish, but by applying legal norms to the contract's terms — that is, by construing the contract in accordance with the common understanding[241] of its terms, and in light of its nature and the character of the contracting parties.[242]

When the Resolutions announced that the Constitution, like an ordinary contract, should be construed according to its original and "plain intent," they were not proposing that interpreters investigate the proceedings of the Philadelphia framers. They were instead arguing for an interpretive strategy whereby the Constitution would be read against the background of eighteenth century notions about sovereignty and the behavior of sovereign entities. As explained by St.George Tucker a few years later, the justification for giving the Constitution's grants of power to federal instrumentalities "the most strict construction that the instrument will bear"[243] was not that such an approach would conform to the general expectation of the individual delegates to Philadelphia or even those in the state conventions. Rather, strict construction was justified by reference to the "maxim of political law" that a sovereign can be deprived of any of its powers only by its express consent narrowly construed.[244] The intentionalism of the Resolutions was therefore a form of structural interpretation carried out largely by inference from the nature both of compacts and of sovereignty.[245] It was the "intent" of the states as political entities that the Resolutions deemed normative for purposes of constitutional interpretation.[246]

---

[241] *See supra* note 52.

[242] *See supra* pp. 894–96, 899–900.

[243] Tucker, *supra* note 168, note D, at 154.

[244] *Id.*

[245] *See* Madison's Report of 1800, *reprinted in* MIND OF THE FOUNDER, *supra* note 210, at 231, 232–35; Letter from Thomas Jefferson to Edward Everett (Apr. 8, 1826), *reprinted in* POLITICAL WRITINGS, *supra* note 40, at 151, 151; Tucker, *supra* note 168, note A, at 3–6; *id.* note D, at 141–46, 151–56, 170–72.

[246] Many years later, Jefferson prepared a protest for possible use by the Virginia legislature as a response to the nationalist policies of the administration of John Quincy Adams. In this protest Jefferson recapitulated the history of the Revolution and of the establishment of the Constitution, describing all these events as actions, decisions, and intentions of the states. *See* Jefferson, The solemn Declaration and Protest of the Commonwealth of Virginia on the principles of the Constitution of the United States of America and on the violation of them (1825), *reprinted in* POLITICAL WRITINGS, *supra* note 40, at 167, 167–69. Madison, too, remained faithful to the idea that the Constitution was the creation of the states acting as sovereign communities.

The Resolutions' reliance on the common law method of interpreting contracts was for the most part traditional, but in one respect Jefferson and Madison broke new ground. By emphasizing that the Constitution's proper meaning was that understood and acceded to by the states during a particular period of time in the past, the Resolutions suggested the possibility that some extratextual historical evidence might be relevant to constitutional interpretation. Indeed, the Resolutions explicitly recognized a form of direct "evidence" of the intent of the states: the proposed amendments and declarations of reserved rights that accompanied several of the states' ratification resolutions.[247] For instance, the Virginia convention's recommendation of an amendment safeguarding freedom of religion and of the press was cited in the Virginia Resolutions as an express declaration, made at the time Virginia assented to the contract, that the state did not intend to delegate authority over those subjects to the federal government.[248] Consistent with the contractual model of the Constitution, the Resolutions treated these accompanying documents as conditions attached to the state's subscription to the federal compact. By accepting Virginia's expressly conditioned ratification, the other states necessarily agreed to those conditions.[249] This use of historical evidence in constitutional interpretation is therefore not identical to mod-

---

See Letter from James Madison to Daniel Webster (Mar. 15, 1833), *reprinted in* 4 MADISON LETTERS, *supra* note 222, at 293, 293–94.

[247] The Virginia convention, for example, included in its ratification resolution a declaration that the Constitution's powers could be resumed by "the people of the United States," 4 B. SCHWARTZ, THE ROOTS OF THE BILL OF RIGHTS 839 (1980), and that the Constitution did not grant the federal government power to infringe certain essential rights (specifically naming "the liberty of conscience and of the press"), *id.* In addition, the convention formally approved, and transmitted to Congress along with the ratification resolution, a lengthy declaration of "unalienable rights of the people" and a set of proposed amendments to the Constitution. *See id.* at 840–46.

[248] *See* Virginia Resolutions of 1798, *reprinted in* RESOLUTIONS, *supra* note 227, at 5, 6.

[249] The Virginia convention's ratification of the Constitution was embodied in a document that included not only the text of the Constitution, but also Virginia's declaration of reserved rights. Resort to the latter, therefore, was not consultation of a source of evidence extrinsic to the contract. Virginia, as it were, had exercised its powers as master of its offer to make that offer conditional on acceptance of Virginia's terms. *Cf.* Pinnel's Case, 5 Co. Rep. 117a, 117b, 77 Eng. Rep. 237, 238 (C.P. 1602) (discussing conditions on acceptances of contract offers). Madison does not discuss the consequences of other states' insisting on contradictory conditions, perhaps because the possibility of "final" but discordant interpretations by different states did not concern him, or perhaps because neither he nor Jefferson completely explored the implications of their contractual vision of the Constitution.

During the ratification campaign, a key issue had been the Anti-Federalist demand that the Constitution either be amended before adoption or ratified conditionally. The Federalists held out for unconditioned ratification, and successfully insisted that amendment propositions be recommendatory and explanatory only. *See, e.g.*, B. SCHWARTZ, THE GREAT RIGHTS OF MANKIND 135–38, 144–47 (1977). Madison's implicit analysis of the proposed amendments in 1798 was therefore in partial conflict with the view he took of them in 1788. But, as noted on pp. 933–34, Jefferson and Madison were not purporting to engage in historical research, but rather in legal analysis of the "intent" of the parties to the constitutional compact.

ern intentionalism: it directs attention not to evidence concerning discussions preceding the framing or adoption of the text, but rather to recommendations that were themselves part of the official document constituting Virginia's ratification of the constitutional compact. Nevertheless, by focusing attention on a past historical event Jefferson and Madison raised the possibility that other historical documents might be relevant to determining the state's *original* intent.

In Republican hands, the intentionalist hermeneutic of the Resolutions became a powerful tool in the fight against the expansive, "liberal" construction of the Constitution favored by the Federalists. As a form of the traditional approach to contract interpretation, that intentionalism was even more familiar than Hamilton's use of common law techniques of statutory interpretation: for Hamilton, the Constitution could at most be regarded as analogous to a statute; but for Jefferson and Madison, it actually was a contract.[250] Furthermore, the interpretive strategy suggested by the Resolutions enabled the Republicans to wield the anti-hermeneutic tradition against Federalist "construction" of the Constitution even as they insisted that their own equally extratextual interpretation involved mere adherence to the "obvious and real intention" of the compact.[251] As Madison wrote in the Report of 1800, it did "not seem possible that any just objection [could] lie against" the Virginia Resolutions' invocation of intent, because that invocation "amounts merely to a declaration that the compact ought to have the interpretation plainly intended by the parties to it."[252]

The Republicans insisted that the Resolutions' version of intentionalism called simply for the application of the "acknowledged rule[s] of construction"[253] to the Constitution in order to expound that contract "according to the true sense in which it was adopted by the States, that in which it was advocated by its friends, and not that which its enemies apprehended."[254] The "friends" of the Constitution during the ratification era, however, had denied that the instrument was contractual and that the new federal government would be subordinate to the states.[255] The striking dissimilarity between this view and the one advanced by Jefferson and Madison in 1798 — that the

---

250 The states created the federal government, according to the Kentucky Resolutions of 1798, "by compact under the style and title of a Constitution for the United States . . . each State acced[ing] as a State." Kentucky Resolutions of 1798, *reprinted in* RESOLUTIONS, *supra* note 227, at 15, 15.

251 *See* Kentucky Resolutions of 1799, *reprinted in* RESOLUTIONS, *supra* note 227, at 19, 20.

252 Madison's Report of 1800, *reprinted in* MIND OF THE FOUNDER, *supra* note 210, at 231, 234.

253 *Id.* at 253.

254 Letter from Thomas Jefferson to Elbridge Gerry (Jan. 26, 1799), *reprinted in* POLITICAL WRITINGS, *supra* note 40, at 47, 47.

255 *See supra* pp. 929–30 (Constitution not contractual); *supra* note 235 (final authority under Constitution lies in federal, not state, hands).

Constitution was a compact among the states and that the states possessed final authority under it — demonstrates that the Resolutions' brand of intentionalism did not in fact lead to a historically valid reconstruction of the views of the original proponents of ratification. Moreover, the interpretive strategy employed in the Resolutions was an integral part of the substantive constitutional doctrine it was designed to justify. To agree that proper constitutional interpretation involves an examination of the intent of sovereign states forming a compact, we must first agree that this is what the Constitution truly is — a contract among sovereigns. The Resolutions rested on a circularity, justifying substance by a mode of interpretation justified only by that same substance.

Circular or not, the Resolutions were triumphantly vindicated, at least in Republican eyes, by the results of the election of 1800, in which the Republicans seized control of both Congress and the Presidency from the Federalists. The victors viewed the "revolution of 1800"[256] as the people's endorsement of the approach to constitutional interpretation embodied in the "doctrines of '98." The champions of "the Republican Ascendency" were quick to paint themselves as the heirs to a line of apostolic succession extending back to the heroes of the colonial struggles against British tyranny.[257]

With remarkable speed, the constitutional theory of the Virginia and Kentucky Resolutions established itself as American political orthodoxy. Even the state legislatures that had denounced the Resolutions in the strongest terms and decried the Virginia and Kentucky assemblies as improper arbiters of federal constitutional questions were, within a decade, preaching the pure Republican doctrines. The General Assembly of Rhode Island, for example, had replied to the Virginia Resolutions in 1799 by describing them as an "infraction of the Constitution of the United States, expressed in plain terms."[258] By 1809, however, the Rhode Island legislature was of a different mind, resolving

> [t]hat the people of this State, as one of the parties to the Federal compact, have a right to express their sense of any violation of its provisions and that it is the duty of this General Assembly as the organ of their sentiments and the depository of their authority, to

---

[256] Letter from Thomas Jefferson to Judge Spencer Roane (Sept. 6, 1819), *reprinted in* POLITICAL WRITINGS, *supra* note 40, at 151, 152.

[257] Letter from James Madison to William Eustis (May 22, 1823), *reprinted in* 9 THE WRITINGS OF JAMES MADISON, *supra* note 223, at 135, 136; *see* Elliot, *Preface* to RESOLUTIONS, *supra* note 227, at 2, 2 (the Resolutions "embody the principles of the old Republicans of the Jeffersonian school, the genuine disciples of the Whigs of '76"). This invocation of "Whiggism" by Elliot evoked even more distant but equally hallowed memories of the struggle of free Englishmen against Stuart despotism.

[258] State of Rhode Island and Providence Plantations to Virginia (1799), *reprinted in* STATE DOCUMENTS, *supra* note 220, at 17, 17.

> interpose for the purpose of protecting them from the ruinous inflictions of usurped and unconstitutional power.[259]

Acceptance of the compact theory (and of its accompanying intentionalism) spread throughout the country and, beyond the confines of John Marshall's Supreme Court, stood virtually unquestioned until the nullification crisis of 1828 through 1832.[260] Even if it were not actually coeval with the Constitution, the rhetoric of that document's original "intent" acquired an aura of age and self-evident truth all its own.

B. James Madison's Theory of Constitutional Interpretation

Although the Virginia and Kentucky Resolutions expressed an approach to constitutional construction that soon achieved canonical status in American politics, they did not themselves set forth a detailed interpretive methodology. That task remained for James Madison. As one of the prime movers in the Philadelphia convention of 1787 and in the Virginia ratifying convention the following year, as one of the authors of *The Federalist*, and as the draftsman of both the Virginia Resolutions of 1798 and the Report of 1800, Madison played a critical role both in the process of framing and ratifying the Constitution and in the formulation of a consensus about its meaning. Although he would have been quick to distinguish his personal opinions from the public meaning of the Constitution, the coherent interpretive theory Madison expressed in speeches and letters over many years has special value for anyone seeking to discern the "interpretive intent" underlying the Constitution.

Madison's interpretive theory rested primarily on the distinction he drew between the public meaning or intent of a state paper, a law, or a constitution, and the personal opinions of the individuals who had written or adopted it. The distinction was implicit in the common law's treatment of the concept of "intent," but Madison made it explicit and thereby illuminated its implications and underlying rationale. Madison's reliance on this basic hermeneutical premise is evident in his correspondence with Secretary of State Martin Van Buren in 1830. Responding to President Andrew Jackson's citation of a veto message Madison had sent Congress in 1817, Madison wrote

---

259 Report and Resolutions of Rhode Island on the Embargo (1809), *reprinted in* STATE DOCUMENTS, *supra* note 220, at 42, 43–44.

260 States' rights constitutionalists of a later era looked back on the first three decades of the 19th century as a halcyon period of consensus on basic constitutional issues, although they recognized, of course, that there had been disagreements on particulars. *See, e.g.*, 1 J. DAVIS, *supra* note 238, at 128–29 (the heresies of the Federalists were first revived around 1830 by Webster and Story); 1 A. STEPHENS, A CONSTITUTIONAL VIEW OF THE LATE WAR BETWEEN THE STATES 503–05 (1868) (Tucker's state-sovereignty reading of the Constitution "was not gainsayed or controverted by any writer of distinction, that I am aware of, until Chancellor Kent's Commentaries appeared in 1826, and Story's, in 1833").

that Jackson's use of his message had misconceived his personal views. But Madison conceded that Jackson might have correctly interpreted the public meaning of the message:

> On the subject of the discrepancy between the construction put by the Message of the President [Jackson] on the veto of 1817 and the intention of its author, the President will of course consult his own view of the case. For myself, I am aware that the document must speak for itself, and that that intention cannot be substituted for [the intention derived through] the established rules of interpretation.[261]

Madison applied the same distinction between public meaning and private intent to statutes,[262] to the Report of 1800,[263] and to the Constitution. With respect to the Constitution, Madison described his knowledge of the views actually held by the delegates to the Philadelphia and Virginia conventions as a possible source of "bias" in his constitutional interpretations,[264] and cautioned a correspondent against an uncritical use of *The Federalist*, because "it is fair to keep in mind that the authors might be sometimes influenced by the zeal of advocates."[265] He explained that he had decided to delay publication of his notes of the Philadelphia convention until after his death

> or, at least, . . . till the Constitution should be well settled by practice, and till a knowledge of the controversial part of the proceedings of its framers could be turned to no improper account. . . . As a guide in expounding and applying the provisions of the Constitution, the debates and incidental decisions of the Convention can have no authoritative character.[266]

---

[261] Letter from James Madison to Martin Van Buren (July 5, 1830), *reprinted in* 4 MADISON LETTERS, *supra* note 222, at 89, 89. In an earlier letter to Van Buren, on June 3, 1830, Madison had written that he believed his own present understanding of the 1817 veto message "was the general understanding" in 1817, but conceded that "[w]hether the language employed duly conveyed the meaning of which J.M. retains the consciousness, is a question on which he does not presume to judge for others." Letter from James Madison to Martin Van Buren (June 3, 1830), *reprinted in* 4 MADISON LETTERS, *supra* note 222, at 88, 88; *see also* Letter from James Madison to N.P. Trist (June 3, 1830), *reprinted in* 4 MADISON LETTERS, *supra* note 222, at 87, 87 (Madison again speaks of the meaning of the 1817 veto "[t]o my consciousness," while admitting that "the entire text" of the message may have conveyed that meaning faultily).

[262] *See* Letter from James Madison to Edward Livingston (July 10, 1822), *reprinted in* MIND OF THE FOUNDER, *supra* note 210, at 338, 338–39.

[263] *See* Letter from James Madison to N.P. Trist (Feb. 15, 1830), *reprinted in* 4 MADISON LETTERS, *supra* note 222, at 61, 61 (acknowledging distinction between "the object of the member who prepared the documents in question" and their "fair import," while asserting in that particular case the identity of the two).

[264] Letter from James Madison to Henry St.George Tucker (Dec. 23, 1817), *reprinted in* 3 MADISON LETTERS, *supra* note 222, at 53, 54.

[265] Letter from James Madison to Edward Livingston (Apr. 17, 1824), *reprinted in* 3 MADISON LETTERS, *supra* note 222, at 435, 436.

[266] Letter from James Madison to Thomas Ritchie (Sept. 15, 1821), *reprinted in* 3 MADISON LETTERS, *supra* note 222, at 228, 228.

Madison employed the distinction between public meaning and private intent to differentiate the relative value of the various sources of information to which constitutional interpreters might turn for evidence on "the intention of the States."[267] The text itself, of course, was the primary source from which that intention was to be gathered, but Madison's awareness of the imperfect nature of human communication[268] led him to concede that the text's import would frequently be unclear.[269] Madison thought it proper to engage in structural inference in the classic contractual mode of the Virginia and Kentucky Resolutions, and to consult the direct expressions of state intention available in the resolutions of the ratifying conventions.[270] He regarded the debates in those conventions to be of real yet limited value for the interpreter: evidentiary problems with the surviving records[271] and Madison's insistence on distinguishing the binding public intention of the state from the private opinions of any individual or group of individuals, including those gathered at a state convention,

---

[267] Letter (not posted) from James Madison to John Davis (c. 1832), *reprinted in* 4 MADISON LETTERS, *supra* note 222, at 232, 243–44. This letter illustrates well the variety of uses Madison could make of the rhetoric of "intention" without indicating any change or uncertainty in his basic interpretive stance: within a few paragraphs, Madison refers to "the intention of those who framed, or, rather, who adopted the Constitution"; he immediately states that the interpreter "must decide that intention by the meaning attached to the terms by the '*usus*' [governmental and judicial precedent]"; he remarks that it "need scarcely to be observed that" the intention so determined "could not be overruled by any latter meaning put on the phrase, however warranted by the grammatical rules of construction"; and he finally mentions the "intention of the parties to the Constitution" and the "intention of the States." *Id.* at 242–43 (emphasis omitted). The apparent inconsistency of Madison's use of the term to the modern reader is due to the fact that for Madison the word still retained its traditional common law meaning. *See supra* pp. 895–96.

[268] *See* THE FEDERALIST No. 37 (J. Madison); Letter from James Madison to N.P. Trist (Mar. 2, 1827), *reprinted in* 3 MADISON LETTERS, *supra* note 222, at 565, 565; *supra* p. 910.

[269] *See* Letter from James Madison to N.P. Trist (Mar. 2, 1827), *reprinted in* 3 MADISON LETTERS, *supra* note 222, at 565, 565; Letter from James Madison to Judge Spencer Roane (Sept. 2, 1819), *reprinted in* 3 MADISON LETTERS, *supra* note 222, at 143, 145; *cf.* Letter from James Madison to Thomas Grimké (Jan. 15, 1828), *reprinted in* 3 MADISON LETTERS, *supra* note 222, at 611, 611 (laws are "always liable, more or less, till made technical by practice, to discordant interpretations").

[270] *See* Letter from James Madison to Judge Spencer Roane (May 6, 1821), *reprinted in* 3 MADISON LETTERS, *supra* note 222, at 217, 220 (advocating structural inference about the intentions of the states); Letter from James Madison to Joseph Cabell (Mar. 22, 1827), *reprinted in* 3 MADISON LETTERS, *supra* note 222, at 571, 571–72 (same); Letter from James Madison to Andrew Stevenson (Nov. 27, 1830), *reprinted in* 4 MADISON LETTERS, *supra* note 222, at 121, 129–30 (amendments proposed by state ratifying conventions are evidence of states' intentions); *supra* p. 932. Madison also made reference at times to the weaknesses in the previous federal system that the Constitution was intended by the states to correct — a combination of the intentionalism of the Resolutions and the traditional common law approach to statutory interpretation. *See* Letter from James Madison to Joseph Cabell (Oct. 30, 1828), *reprinted in* 3 MADISON LETTERS, *supra* note 222, at 648, 655.

[271] *See* Letter from James Madison to Jonathan Elliot (Feb. 14, 1827), *reprinted in* 3 MADISON LETTERS, *supra* note 222, at 552, 552.

led him to conclude that the state debates could bear no more than indirect and corroborative witness to the meaning of the Constitution.[272] Madison allowed that contemporaneous expositions of the document by its supporters were of some value, but he cautioned that such statements were to be regarded strictly as private opinions, useful chiefly in shedding light upon the meaning of words and phrases that the fluidity of language might gradually change over time.[273] Last and least in value were the records of the Philadelphia convention. Once again, there were significant evidentiary problems,[274] but Madison's objection to treating the framers' views as authoritative was based chiefly on theoretical grounds.

> Mr. [Madison] said, he did not believe a single instance could be cited in which the sense of the Convention had been required or admitted as material in any Constitutional question. . . .
>
> But, after all, whatever veneration might be entertained for the body of men who formed our Constitution, the sense of that body could never be regarded as the oracular guide in expounding the Constitution. As the instrument came from them, it was nothing more than the draft of a plan, nothing but a dead letter, until life and validity were breathed into it by the voice of the people, speaking through the several State Conventions.[275]

Madison was quite insistent that a distinction must be drawn between the "true meaning" of the Constitution and "whatever might have been the opinions entertained in forming the Constitution."[276] The distinction did not imply a refusal to recognize the purposive character

---

[272] *See id.*; Letter from James Madison to Andrew Stevenson (Nov. 27, 1830), *reprinted in* 4 MADISON LETTERS, *supra* note 222, at 121, 128 (interpreter must look for the meaning given the text "by the Conventions, or, rather, by the people, who, through their Conventions, accepted and ratified" the text).

[273] *See* Letter from James Madison to H. Lee (June 25, 1824), *reprinted in* 3 MADISON LETTERS, *supra* note 222, at 441, 442–43 (arguing that literal meaning of text varies as language changes); Letter from James Madison to Andrew Stevenson (Mar. 25, 1826), *reprinted in* 3 MADISON LETTERS, *supra* note 222, at 520, 521–22 (noting value of "contemporary expositions"); Letter from James Madison to N.P. Trist (Mar. 2, 1827), *reprinted in* 3 MADISON LETTERS, *supra* note 222, at 565, 565 (Constitution affected by the imprecision and mutability of language).

[274] *See* Letter from James Madison to Robert Garnett (Feb. 11, 1824), *reprinted in* 3 MADISON LETTERS, *supra* note 222, at 367, 367; Letter (not posted) from James Madison to John Davis (c. 1832), *reprinted in* 4 MADISON LETTERS, *supra* note 222, at 232, 253–54 (noting difficulties in interpreting convention's proceedings); Letter (not posted) from James Madison to John Tyler (1833), *reprinted in* 4 MADISON LETTERS, *supra* note 222, at 280, 288–89 (criticizing as biased and inaccurate Robert Yates's and Luther Martin's accounts of the convention). The problem of accuracy could of course have been cured, at least to Madison's satisfaction, by publication of his journal, which he regarded as "a pretty ample view of what passed in that Assembly." Letter from James Madison to Thomas Ritchie (Sept. 15, 1821), *reprinted in* 3 MADISON LETTERS, *supra* note 222, at 228, 228.

[275] 5 ANNALS OF CONG. 776 (1796) (remarks of Rep. James Madison).

[276] Letter from James Madison to John Jackson (Dec. 27, 1821), *reprinted in* 3 MADISON LETTERS, *supra* note 222, at 243, 245.

of the instrument;[277] it simply denied that the framers' subjective intent was the purpose that mattered.[278]

The dichotomy between public meaning and private intent also informed Madison's view of constitutional precedent. He consistently thought that "*usus*,"[279] the exposition of the Constitution provided by actual governmental practice and judicial precedents,[280] could "settle its meaning and the intention of its authors."[281] Here, too, he was building on a traditional foundation: the common law had regarded usage as valid evidence of the meaning of ancient instruments, and had regarded judicial determinations of that meaning even more highly.[282] Applying this view of interpretation to the Constitution, Madison felt himself compelled to change his position on the controversial issue of Congress's constitutional power to incorporate a national bank.[283] In the first Congress, Representative Madison opposed

---

[277] *See* THE FEDERALIST No. 37, at 179 (J. Madison) (G. Wills ed. 1982) ("The use of words is to express ideas.").

[278]

> But whatever respect may be thought due to the intention of the Convention which prepared and proposed the Constitution, as presumptive evidence of the general understanding at the time of the language used, it must be kept in mind that the only authoritative intentions were those of the people of the States, as expressed through the Conventions which ratified the Constitution.

Letter from James Madison to M.L. Hurlbert (May, 1830), *reprinted in* 4 MADISON LETTERS, *supra* note 222, at 73, 74.

In 1791, in the heat of the congressional debate over Hamilton's bank bill, Madison, like other opponents of the bill, occasionally referred to the Philadelphia convention's failure to adopt a proposal giving Congress the power to charter corporations. *See* 2 ANNALS OF CONG. 1937–60 (1791) (remarks of Rep. James Madison). Thereafter, Madison's understanding of the task of constitutional interpretation remained remarkably consistent over a period stretching from 1796 (when he was a leader of the embattled Republican opposition that was resting its hopes on the states as a counterweight to the federal government) until the early 1830s (when, as an elder statesman, he was contributing his prestige to the support of federal authority against a states' rights challenge by self-proclaimed followers of the "doctrines of '98").

[279] Letter (not posted) from James Madison to John Davis (c. 1832), *reprinted in* 4 MADISON LETTERS, *supra* note 222, at 232, 242.

[280] *See* Letter from James Madison to Judge Spencer Roane (Sept. 2, 1819), *reprinted in* 3 MADISON LETTERS, *supra* note 222, at 143, 143 (a constitution's meaning, "so far as it depends on judicial interpretation," is established by "a course of particular decisions"); Letter from James Madison to Joseph Cabell (Sept. 7, 1829), *reprinted in* 4 MADISON LETTERS, *supra* note 222, at 45, 47 ("definitive power" to settle constitutional questions on the allocation of power between federal and state governments is lodged in federal Supreme Court).

[281] Letter (not posted) from James Madison to John Davis (c. 1832), *reprinted in* 4 MADISON LETTERS, *supra* note 222, at 232, 249.

[282] *See supra* p. 899. Madison also referred to this legal background in *The Federalist Papers*. *See* THE FEDERALIST No. 37, at 179 (J. Madison) (G. Wills ed. 1982); *supra* p. 910.

[283] In later life Madison was accused by state's rights advocates of inconsistency in his constitutional opinions — a charge that he denied. *See* Letter from James Madison to W.C. Rives (Oct. 21, 1833), *reprinted in* 4 MADISON LETTERS, *supra* note 222, at 309, 309–10. He would admit to even the *appearance* of inconsistency only in the national bank case. *See* Letter from James Madison to N.P. Trist (Dec. 1831), *reprinted in* 4 MADISON LETTERS, *supra* note 222, at 204, 211.

on constitutional grounds the bill establishing the First Bank of the United States;[284] as President, Madison twenty years later signed into law the act creating the Second Bank.[285] "But even here the inconsistency," Madison assured a correspondent, "is apparent only, not real." His own "abstract opinion of the text" remained unchanged: the words of the Constitution did not authorize Congress to establish the bank.[286] Nevertheless, he recognized that Congress, the President, the Supreme Court, and (most important, by failing to use their amending power) the American people had for two decades accepted the existence and made use of the services of the First Bank, and he viewed this widespread acceptance as "a construction put on the Constitution by the nation, which, having made it, had the supreme right to declare its meaning."[287] He had signed the Second Bank bill, Madison declared, in accordance with his "early and unchanged opinion" that such a construction by usage and precedent should override the intellectual scruples of the individual,[288] and he explained to his friend the Marquis de LaFayette that "I did not feel myself, as a public man, at liberty to sacrifice all these public considerations to my private opinion."[289] In Madison's eyes, precedents — at least those derived from "authoritative, deliberate, and continued decisions" — served to "fix the interpretation of a law."[290] Furthermore, Mad-

---

[284] *See* A. KOCH, *supra* note 215, at 108–10.

[285] *See id.* at 254.

[286] Letter from James Madison to C.E. Haynes (Feb. 25, 1831), *reprinted in* 4 MADISON LETTERS, *supra* note 222, at 164, 165.

[287] Letter from James Madison to Marquis de LaFayette (Nov. 1826), *reprinted in* 3 MADISON LETTERS, *supra* note 222, at 538, 542; *see also* Letter from James Madison to Thomas Jefferson (Feb. 17, 1825), *reprinted in* 3 MADISON LETTERS, *supra* note 222, at 483, 483 (stating that Congress, in legislating in accordance with the Constitution, will inevitably reflect the will of the people).

For Madison, the most unequivocal exercise by the people of their power "to declare [the Constitution's] meaning" was the formal procedure of amendment or constitutional convention. *See, e.g.*, Madison, Veto Message (Mar. 3, 1817), 30 ANNALS OF CONG. 1061 (1817) (in vetoing on constitutional grounds an internal improvements bill, Madison expressed his approval of the bill's object, "cherishing the hope" that an amendment rendering the bill constitutional would be secured). But Madison feared the unsettling effects of resorting too frequently to formal constitutional revision. *See* Letter from James Madison to Thomas Jefferson (Feb. 4, 1790), *reprinted in* 1 MADISON LETTERS, *supra* note 222, at 503, 504. In Madison's view, the ordinary and indeed preferable mode for popular declaration of the Constitution's meaning was the deliberate contruction put on it by the people's organs of government and confirmed by the acquiescence of officials and voters. *See* Letter from James Madison to C. J. Ingersoll (June 25, 1831), *reprinted in* 4 MADISON LETTERS, *supra* note 222, at 183, 183–87.

[288] Letter from James Madison to C.E. Haynes (Feb. 25, 1831), *reprinted in* 4 MADISON LETTERS, *supra* note 222, at 164, 165; Letter from James Madison to N.P. Trist (Dec. 1831), *reprinted in* 4 MADISON LETTERS, *supra* note 222, at 204, 211.

[289] Letter from James Madison to Marquis de LaFayette (Nov. 1826), *reprinted in* 3 MADISON LETTERS, *supra* note 222, at 538, 542.

[290] Letter from James Madison to N.P. Trist (Dec. 1831), *reprinted in* 4 MADISON LETTERS, *supra* note 222, at 204, 211. The obligation of legislator or judge henceforth was to follow the meaning as construed, and not his "solitary opinions." Letter from James Madison to C.J. Ingersoll (June 25, 1831), *reprinted in* 4 MADISON LETTERS, *supra* note 222, at 183, 184–86.

ison claimed, this view represented not just his opinion, but the general expectation — the "interpretive intention"[291] — that prevailed at the time of the Constitution's framing and ratification:

> It could not but happen, and was foreseen at the birth of the Constitution, that difficulties and differences of opinion might occasionally arise in expounding terms and phrases necessarily used in such a charter . . . and that it might require a regular course of practice to liquidate and settle the meaning of some of them.[292]

The public character of long-settled precedent was for Madison the key to reconciling his acceptance of views inconsistent with his "abstract opinion" of the bare text and his commitment to the Republican version of the old anti-interpretive tradition. To the end of his life, Madison warned his fellow citizens against expansive innovations in constitutional interpretation, "new principles and new constructions, that may remove the landmarks of power."[293] But however strongly he might have fought constitutional error when it first appeared, for Madison there could be no return to the unadorned text from interpretations that had received the approbation of the people.[294] The Constitution is a public document, and its interpretation, for Madison, was in the end a public process.

---

[291] *See supra* note 10.

[292] Letter from James Madison to Judge Spencer Roane (Sept. 2, 1819), *reprinted in* 3 MADISON LETTERS, *supra* note 222, at 143, 145.

[293] Letters of Helvidius No. 4 (1793), *reprinted in* MIND OF THE FOUNDER, *supra* note 210, at 209, 210; *see also* Letter from James Madison to James Monroe (Dec. 27, 1817), *reprinted in* 3 MADISON LETTERS, *supra* note 222, at 54, 56 ("Serious danger seems to be threatened to the genuine sense of the Constitution . . . by an unwarrantable latitude of construction."); Letter from James Madison to Joseph Cabell (Sept. 18, 1828) (published with Madison's approval in the *Washington National Intelligencer* in December 1828), *reprinted in* MIND OF THE FOUNDER, *supra* note 210, at 370, 375 (contrasting congressional power to enact a protective tariff, sanctioned by 40 years' exercise, with a "novel construction however ingeniously devised"). Madison's reluctance to categorize a constitutional development as sufficiently erroneous to warrant resistance was based in part on his belief that interpretation is only partially "objective." *See, e.g.*, 5 ANNALS OF CONG. 494 (1796) (remarks of Rep. James Madison) (acknowledging that "[n]o construction" can be "perfectly free from difficulties," but recommending his own as "subject to the least").

[294] Madison's view of interpretation is exemplified in his warning to one correspondent that "some care in discussing the question of a distinction between literal and constructive meanings may be necessary in order to avoid the danger of a verbal character to the discussion." Letter from James Madison to N.P. Trist (Mar. 1, 1829), *reprinted in* 4 MADISON LETTERS, *supra* note 222, at 16, 17. For Madison, the (legitimate) "constructive" meaning of the Constitution is no less that instrument's "intention" than is the "literal"; and indeed the former may be the legally appropriate "intention" in the event of a conflict. Madison did not deny that some constructions of the Constitution would so transform the nature of the federal compact that nothing less than a formal exercise of the amending power could justify them, but in his view such a case would be "of a character [so] exorbitant and ruinous" as to justify revolution. *See* Letter from James Madison to Joseph Cabell (Oct. 30, 1828), *reprinted in* MIND OF THE FOUNDER, *supra* note 210, at 380, 387; J. Madison, Notes on Nullification (1835–1836), *reprinted in* MIND OF THE FOUNDER, *supra* note 210, at 417, 418. Madison himself was confident that "the barrier" against any such usurpation was now "happily too strong in the text of the

C. The Marshall Court and Constitutional Construction

The "revolution of 1800" that swept away Federalist nationalism and vindicated the "doctrines of '98" left one pocket of resistance to Jeffersonian Republicanism intact: the Supreme Court and its newly appointed Federalist Chief Justice, John Marshall. Over the three and a half decades of Marshall's tenure, his rhetorically moderate[295] yet staunchly nationalistic views prevailed on a Court increasingly populated by Republican Justices.[296] Marshall and his learned Republican friend, Justice Joseph Story, regarded the state-sovereignty and constitutional-compact themes of Republican constitutional thought as strands of wild-eyed political theory, "the cobwebs of sophistry and metaphysics."[297] Instead of searching for the intent of sovereign contracting parties, the Marshall Court followed the path, staked out in the Constitution's first years, of applying traditional methods of statutory construction to that instrument.

Marshall's conventional view of statutory construction is illustrated by his opinion in *United States v. Fisher*,[298] a case involving the interpretation of a federal act giving the United States priority over general creditors in bankruptcy proceedings.[299] Marshall noted the difficulties attendant upon construing an ambiguous statutory provision, and he stressed the need to cast a wide net in seeking evidence as to "the intention of the legislature": "Where the mind labors to discover the design of the legislature, it seizes every thing from which aid can be derived."[300] Although in this case Marshall perceived clarity where the defendants had seen confusion, he agreed that in interpreting ambiguous terms the Court might properly use "all the means recommended by the counsel for the defendants."[301] Cranch's report of the arguments shows that the suggested means included consultation of the act's title, preamble, and "general scope and design,"[302] and consideration of the methodology prescribed in *Heydon's*

Instrument, in the uniformity of official construction, and in the maturity of public opinion, to be successfully assailed." Letter from James Madison to C.J. Ingersoll (Nov. 27, 1827), *reprinted in* 3 MADISON LETTERS, *supra* note 222, at 601, 601.

[295] *See, e.g.*, Marshall, *A Friend to the Union*, Philadelphia Union, Apr. 24, 1819, *reprinted in* JOHN MARSHALL'S DEFENSE, *supra* note 46, at 78, 87–91 (denying difference between his views in *McCulloch v. Maryland* and Madison's in the Report of 1800).

[296] After 1811 only two Justices (Marshall and Bushrod Washington) were Federalists.

[297] Letter from Joseph Story to Stephen White (Mar. 3, 1819), *reprinted in* 1 W. STORY, LIFE AND LETTERS OF JOSEPH STORY 325 (1851); *cf.* Letter from John Marshall to Joseph Story (July 31, 1833), *reprinted in* 2 W. STORY, *supra*, at 135 (describing states' rights views as "political metaphysics").

[298] 6 U.S. (2 Cranch) 358 (1805).

[299] Act of April 4, 1800, ch. 19, § 62, 2 Stat. 19, 36.

[300] *Fisher*, 6 U.S. (2 Cranch) at 386.

[301] *Id.* at 389.

[302] *Id.* at 368, 372.

Case,[303] of other federal statutes,[304] and of the consequences of taking the act literally.[305] Although Marshall considered all of these means legitimate, he placed the most weight on a close analysis of the wording and structure of the statute's text.[306] Neither the attorneys nor the Chief Justice suggested an investigation of the congressional debates. In light of Marshall's traditional view of statutory construction and his acceptance of a statutory analogy for the Constitution, there appears to have been no inconsistency between his insistence that "the great duty of a judge who construes an instrument, is to find the intention of its makers,"[307] and his belief that a construction "within the words" of a constitutional provision is legitimate regardless of whether the framers foresaw or intended it.[308]

The Marshall Court's response to constitutional arguments based on invocations of the extratextual "intent" of the states was a renewed emphasis on the supremacy of the text, read in light of the Constitution's purposes as set forth in its Preamble:

> [T]he enlightened patriots who framed our Constitution, and the people who adopted it, must be understood to have employed words in their natural sense, and to have intended what they have said. . . . [We] know of no rule for construing [the Constitution] other than is given by the language of the instrument . . . taken in connection with the purposes for which [federal powers] were conferred.[309]

The Marshall Court's approach to constitutional interpretation was strikingly similar to Madison's, despite their different starting points. Both Marshall and Madison accepted the common law understanding that the intent of a document is, at least in part, the product of the

---

303 *See id.* at 368, 372–73.

304 *See id.* at 374–75.

305 *See id.* at 368–69.

306 *See id.* at 387–89.

307 Marshall, *A Friend of the Constitution*, Alexandria Gazette, July 2, 1819, *reprinted in* JOHN MARSHALL'S DEFENSE, *supra* note 46, at 155, 168–69. Like earlier common lawyers, and like Madison, *see supra* note 267, Marshall could refer to the intention of "the framers" or of "those who gave these powers," McCulloch v. Maryland, 17 U.S. (4 Wheat.) 316, 415 (1819), without thereby implying that he was relying on any extratextual evidence of that intention. Marshall shared Madison's view that the Philadelphia framers were merely drafters whose views were not binding. *See id.* at 403; *see also* 1 J. STORY, *supra* note 56, at 383 (assessing "intention," in the words of Blackstone, from "the words, the context, the subject-matter, the effects and consequence, or the reason and spirit of the law").

308 Trustees of Dartmouth College v. Woodward, 17 U.S. (4 Wheat.) 518, 644–45 (1819); *cf.* Marshall, *A Friend to the Union*, Philadelphia Union, Apr. 28, 1819, *reprinted in* JOHN MARSHALL'S DEFENSE, *supra* note 46, at 78, 102–03 (necessary and proper means may be unforeseeable by framers).

309 Gibbons v. Ogden, 22 U.S. (9 Wheat.) 1, 188–89 (1824) (Marshall, C.J.); *cf.* Martin v. Hunter's Lessee, 14 U.S. (1 Wheat.) 304, 326 (1816) (Story, J.) (Constitution should receive a "reasonable construction, according to the import of its terms"); Satterlee v. Matthewson, 27 U.S. (2 Pet.) 380, 414–16 (1829) (Johnson, J., concurring) (insisting that a literal reading of the ex post facto clause correctly construes what "the Constitution most clearly intended").

interpretive process; both accepted the authority of practice and precedent;[310] and neither regarded historical evidence of the framers' personal intentions as a definitive or even particularly valuable guide to constitutional construction.

D. *Aftermath*

The constitutional consensus created by the "doctrines of '98" and the "revolution of 1800" endured at least until the nullification crisis of Andrew Jackson's first term,[311] but cracks in its facade began to appear in the 1820s. New England Federalists' resistance to the foreign policies of Presidents Jefferson and Madison culminated in the Hartford convention of 1815, which was widely seen as a first step toward secession.[312] However politically divisive, the convention signaled that the heirs of Hamilton had accepted a key constitutional dogma of his enemies: it served notice that if the grievances voiced were not redressed, New England Federalists were prepared to invoke state sovereignty against the assertion of federal power.[313] Despite this general acceptance of the Republican account of the Constitution's nature and origin, constitutional argument continued: the political debates in the 1810s and '20s over federal tariff policy and over congressional power to further internal improvements prompted proponents of federal power to search for means of altering the antinationalist legacy of the Virginia and Kentucky Resolutions. From the other end of the political spectrum, the devotees of an extreme states' rights constitutionalism criticized the more moderate policies of

---

[310] *See* 1 J. KENT, COMMENTARIES ON AMERICAN LAW 242 n.a (3d ed. New York 1836) (1st ed. New York 1826) (commending Marshall and Story for their allegiance to text and precedent); 1 J. STORY, *supra* note 56, at 392.

[311] *See supra* note 260.

[312] Federalist delegates from the New England states convened in Hartford in December 1814 and January 1815 to discuss means of opposing the unpopular war measures of the Republican administration. Among the convention's resolutions, which were approved only by the legislatures of Massachusetts and Connecticut and were rejected by nine other states, were a series of amendments to the Constitution designed to enhance New England influence on national affairs and check the power of the federal government. An additional resolution — that the New England states should meet again in June if their reforms were not achieved — was widely interpreted as a threat of secession, but was mooted by the news of peace. *See* Resolutions Adopted by the Hartford Convention (1815), *reprinted in* STATE DOCUMENTS, *supra* note 220, at 83, 85; Reply of the Legislature of New Jersey (1815), *reprinted in* STATE DOCUMENTS, *supra* note 220, at 86 (condemning the resolutions); Extract from the Reply of the Legislature of New York (1815), *reprinted in* STATE DOCUMENTS, *supra* note 220, at 87 (same).

[313] During the nullification crisis, New England nationalist Nathan Dane wrote: "[*S*]*tates rights* and *state sovereignty*, are expressions coined for party purposes, often by minorities, who happen to be dissatisfied with the measures of the General Government, and as they are afterwards used, they produce only state delusion. In this business each large minority has had its turn." 9 N. DANE, GENERAL ABRIDGMENT AND DIGEST OF AMERICAN LAW app. 32–33 (Boston 1829).

Madison and his successor, James Monroe, as apostasy from the Republican faith.[314]

Faced with a political need to develop new modes of constitutional interpretation to supplement or supplant the eroding Republican consensus, interpreters of the Constitution redefined the central hermeneutical concept of that consensus, the Constitution's "intent." As employed in the Virginia and Kentucky Resolutions, that term was an invitation to structural, not historical,[315] interpretation: witness how thoroughly Madison, one of the greatest of the Republican thinkers, excluded from his understanding of normative constitutional intent any trace of the historically ascertainable purposes and expectations of the Philadelphia framers. But this traditional, Republican understanding of "intent" was gradually replaced by the modern, subjective use of the word. In other areas of law, "intent" increasingly meant the historical intentions of *someone*, however much evidentiary rules might be used to frustrate a genuine search for those intentions.[316] A similar change became evident in constitutional discourse. With the growing availability of original materials revealing the actions and opinions of the individual actors who played roles in the Constitution's framing and adoption, popular and legal interest in that episode of history markedly increased.[317]

The watershed in the history of constitutional interpretation was the crisis provoked by South Carolina's strident response to the passage of a protective tariff by Congress in May 1828. Although the so-called "tariff of abominations" was extremely unpopular throughout most of the South, the reaction to it was exceptionally vigorous in South Carolina. A state convention assembled in November 1832 and passed an ordinance "nullifying" the federal act.[318] President Jackson responded with a vigorous assertion of federal supremacy and his resolve to uphold the tariff — and a potentially violent collision between federal authority and states' rights was averted only narrowly.[319] Two conflicting approaches to constitutional interpretation

---

[314] *See* A. SCHLESINGER, THE AGE OF JACKSON 18–29 (1946).

[315] The Resolutions, to be sure, did presuppose a simple and stylized model of American history in which separate, semi-sovereign colonies threw off the British yoke to become fully sovereign republics that subsequently linked themselves in a confederation through a compact. The final stage in American constitutional development was the renegotiation of the contract in 1787 through 1790. This static picture of "history," however, did not depend on any particular historical research and was not subject to revision. It was taken as a first principle.

[316] *See, e.g.*, P. ATIYAH, *supra* note 75, at 459.

[317] *See* J. HIGHAM, HISTORY 69 (1965).

[318] *See* Ordinance of Nullification of South Carolina (1832), *reprinted in* STATE DOCUMENTS, *supra* note 220, at 169.

[319] In early 1833 Congress passed both an act empowering the President to use federal power to collect the tariff, Act of Mar. 2, 1833, ch. 57, 4 Stat. 632, and a compromise tariff act, Act of Mar. 2, 1833, ch. 55, 4 Stat. 629, which alleviated the South Carolinians' economic objections to the "tariff of abominations." South Carolina, in convention, then repealed its repudiation of

emerged as the intellectual product of the crisis. The nationalist school of constitutional thought, with Daniel Webster leading the way in the Senate and Justice Joseph Story serving as scholar and consultant,[320] explicitly rejected the definition of the Constitution as a compact among sovereign states. The nationalists identified the text, as construed by precedent, as the authoritative source of constitutional meaning and regarded the Supreme Court as the final and authoritative interpreter of the Constitution.[321] The states' rights school, with John C. Calhoun playing the roles of both Webster and Story, subscribed to an extreme version of the compact theory and insisted that final interpretive authority rested with the states.[322] Adherents of both camps increasingly expressed their views as explications of the "original intent" of the framers,[323] and earlier scruples against the use of "extrinsic evidence" in constitutional interpretation gradually lost their force.

The new use of the rhetoric of constitutional intention is illustrated by Judge Abel Parker Upshur's *A Brief Enquiry into the True Nature and Character of our Federal Government*,[324] published in 1840. Upshur, a distinguished Virginia jurist and states' rights politician, wrote the *Brief Enquiry* as a "review" of Story's treatise on constitutional law; the result was a closely argued critique of Story's nationalism and a reformulation of states' rights constitutionalism in light of Story's argument.[325] Although Upshur accepted and employed the interpre-

---

federal tariff laws and nullified the Force Act. *See* South Carolina's Final Action (1833), *reprinted in* STATE DOCUMENTS, *supra* note 220, at 188. Both sides having saved face, the crisis subsided. *See* A. SCHLESINGER, *supra* note 314, at 94–97.

320 Webster and Story were friends as well as political allies, and some believe that the latter's hand can be seen in Webster's famous speeches against the compact theory on the Senate floor. *See* 2 V. PARRINGTON, MAIN CURRENTS IN AMERICAN THOUGHT: THE ROMANTIC REVOLUTION IN AMERICA 300 (1927).

321 *See* 1 J. STORY, *supra* note 56, at 344–75.

322 Calhoun, although originally a nationalist, secretly authored some of the early justifications of nullification adopted by South Carolina during the crisis. An open advocate of South Carolina's position by 1830, Calhoun was quickly recognized as the most powerful thinker on the states' rights side of the dispute, and Jonathan Elliot included extracts from two of his addresses in his 1832 collection of the canon of "documents in support of the Jeffersonian Doctrines of '98." *See* RESOLUTIONS, *supra* note 227, at 41.

323 Interestingly, both Story and Calhoun avoided the "original intention" terminology for the most part — the former because of his textualism and regard for precedent, *see infra* note 325, the latter because of his almost pure "intentionalism" in the original sense, *see* Calhoun, Fort Hill Address (1831), *reprinted in* 6 THE WORKS OF JOHN C. CALHOUN, *supra* note 211, at 59, 60–61.

324 A. UPSHUR, A BRIEF ENQUIRY INTO THE TRUE NATURE AND CHARACTER OF OUR FEDERAL GOVERNMENT (Petersburg 1840).

325 In his treatise, Justice Story criticized states' rights constitutionalists on substantive and hermeneutical grounds. Responding to the emergence of modern intentionalism, Story roundly attacked the notion that historical evidence from the framing and ratification process could determine the Constitution's meaning. Such evidence, he thought, can reveal only "the private interpretation of any particular man, or body of men" — an interpretation that others have no

tive tools made familiar by the Resolutions, he did not characterize his inferences from structure and from the political theory of sovereignty as evidence of the "intent" of the Constitution.[326] Upshur, instead, was an intentionalist in the modern sense: "The strict construction for which I contend applies to the *intention* of the framers of the Constitution; and this may or may not require a strict construction of their words."[327] Upshur thought that the determination of that intention was an essay in historical reconstruction, to be carried out by investigating the proceedings and opinions of the Philadelphia framers.[328]

By the outbreak of the Civil War, intentionalism in the modern sense reigned supreme in the rhetoric of constitutional interpretation. In his inaugural address, Jefferson Davis described the Confederate constitution as "the Constitution formed by our fathers," a document that differed from the older instrument's text only "insofar as it is explanatory of their well-known intent."[329] Sen. Charles Sumner of Massachusetts, one of the most radically nationalist members of the Union Congress, stated: "Every Constitution embodies the principles of its framers. It is a transcript of their minds. If its meaning in any place is open to doubt . . . we cannot err if we turn to the framers . . . ."[330] The implicit repudiation of the original understanding of "original intent" was complete.

---

reason to accept. 1 J. STORY, *supra* note 56, at 388. The people sanctioned not the debates of the various conventions, but the text only. *See id.* at 389 ("Nothing but the text itself was adopted by the people."); *see also id.* at 388–90 (attacking use of "legislative history" in constitutional interpretation). Story contended that constitutional interpretation, like statutory construction, is a matter of construing the text "according to its fair intent and objects, as disclosed in its language," and not of arguing over the "probable meaning" of the personal intentions of historical actors. *Id.* at 390 n.1.

Story's brilliant polemic against the modern form of intentionalism (which he ascribes to Jefferson) attacks it not only on evidentiary, but also on theoretical grounds (it elevates private views over the expressed will of the public). The one striking deviation from this strongly textualist approach during the Marshall years was Chief Justice Marshall's opinion in Barron v. Mayor of Baltimore, 32 U.S. (7 Pet.) 243 (1833). Barron sued the city of Baltimore for violating his fifth amendment right to receive just compensation for a public taking of his property. Despite the open-ended character of the amendment's text, which had led some commentators to suggest that it applied to state as well as federal action, *see, e.g.*, W. RAWLE, A VIEW OF THE CONSTITUTION 120–21, 129–30 (1825), a unanimous Court limited the amendment's scope to federal takings, at least partly because the "universally understood . . . history of the day" showed that the amendments were not intended to apply to the states. 32 U.S. (7 Pet.) at 250.

[326] *See, e.g.*, A. UPSHUR, *supra* note 324, at 58, 71 (describing his constitutionalism as based on political theory, without referring to "intent").

[327] *Id.* at 94. Upshur never discusses the possibility that the framers' intentions might conflict with his political theory.

[328] *See, e.g.*, *id.* at 51–53 (using history of the proceedings of the Philadelphia convention to establish the meaning of the Preamble).

[329] Address of Jefferson Davis at Montgomery, Alabama (Feb. 18, 1861), *reprinted in* 9 ANNALS OF AMERICA 238, 240–41 (1968).

[330] CONG. GLOBE, 39th Cong., 1st Sess. 677 (1866).

V. Conclusion

It is commonly assumed that the "interpretive intention" of the Constitution's framers was that the Constitution would be construed in accordance with what future interpreters could gather of the framers' own purposes, expectations, and intentions. Inquiry shows that assumption to be incorrect. Of the numerous hermeneutical options that were available in the framers' day — among them, the renunciation of construction altogether — none corresponds to the modern notion of intentionalism. Early interpreters usually applied standard techniques of statutory construction to the Constitution. When a consensus eventually emerged on a proper theory of constitutional interpretation, it indeed centered on "original intent." But at the time, that term referred to the "intentions" of the sovereign parties to the constitutional compact, as evidenced in the Constitution's language and discerned through structural methods of interpretation; it did not refer to the personal intentions of the framers or of anyone else. The relationship of modern intentionalism to this early interpretive theory is purely rhetorical.[331]

In defending their claim that the "original understanding at Philadelphia" should control constitutional interpretation, modern intentionalists usually argue that other interpretive strategies undermine or even deny the possibility of objectivity and consistency in constitutional law. Critics of this position typically respond with a battery of practical and theoretical objections to the attempt to construe the nation's fundamental law in accord with historical reconstructions of the purposes of the framers. There may well be grounds to support either of these positions. This debate cannot be resolved, however, and should not be affected, by the claim or assumption that modern intentionalism was the original presupposition of American constitutional discourse. Such a claim is historically mistaken.

---

[331] To be faithful to the interpretive intentions of the generation of the framers, the modern intentionalist would have to abandon his or her intentionalism and adopt the common law view of the "intention" of a statute, or disavow the legitimacy of any extratextual interpretation in the manner of the anti-hermeneutical traditions of British Protestantism and European rationalism, or accept the substantive constitutional doctrines of compact and state sovereignty that grew out of the original intentionalism of the Virginia and Kentucky Resolutions.

Origins of the Unwritten Constitution: Fundamental Law in American Revolutionary Thought

Thomas C. Grey*

In the first comprehensive treatise on advocacy,[1] Aristotle distinguishes between the written law, the rules governing a particular community, and the unwritten law, those equitable principles "supposed to be acknowledged everywhere."[2] Aristotle advises advocates that when the written law supports their cases, they should stress the virtue of respect for authority and the vice of "trying to be cleverer than the laws."[3] Conversely, when the written law tells against their cases, lawyers "must appeal to the universal law, and insist on its greater equity and justice"[4]—a legitimate as well as an effective appeal, Aristotle suggests, since "there really is, as everyone to some extent divines, a natural justice and injustice that is binding on all men."[5]

This Aristotelian dialogue permeates American constitutional law. On the one hand, Americans have always tended to assume that laws perceived as violating basic national values are unconstitutional, whether or not they conflict with actual provisions of the written constitution. On the other hand, democratic values and fear of unbridled judicial discretion counsel against granting courts the power to disregard the enactments of an elected legislature in favor of judges' views of justice or national ideals. The historical origins of

---

* A.B. 1963, Stanford University; LL.B. 1968, Yale University. Associate Professor of Law, Stanford University. My special thanks to the editors of the *Stanford Law Review* and to my colleagues Lawrence Friedman and Gerald Gunther for their detailed and helpful criticism of a draft of this article; thanks also to those other colleagues and friends, too many to list here, who made useful comments and suggestions. Thanks are also due to Robert Weisberg and Robin B. Johansen for valuable research assistance and to the National Endowment for the Humanities and the Mellon Foundation for financial support.

1. ARISTOTLE, RHETORIC, in THE BASIC WORKS OF ARISTOTLE (R. McKeon ed. 1941).
2. *Id.* at 1359.
3. *Id.* at 1375.
4. *Id.* at 1374.
5. *Id.* at 1370.

the American constitutional version of this Aristotelian dialogue, and its development before 1776, are the subject of this article.

I. INTRODUCTION: THE PROBLEM OF THE UNWRITTEN CONSTITUTION

It is almost universally accepted that our system recognizes no higher legal authority than the written constitution; explicit constitutional text cannot be overriden by unwritten natural or fundamental law.[6] The Aristotelian dialogue in our constitutional law is played out around the issue of whether the formal enacted Constitution, conceded to be legally supreme, is the *exclusive* legitimate source of judicially enforceable constitutional law. Our judges have, as a matter of unarguable historical fact, developed a body of unwritten constitutional law—doctrine whose normative content cannot be derived from examining the language of the Constitution or investigating the intent of its framers. The question is whether this mode of review—which I have called "noninterpretive"[7]—is, in its various manifestations,[8] a legitimate part of our scheme of government.

---

6. On a few occasions, it has been argued that provisions of the Constitution itself were invalid on general ethical or political grounds. *See* The National Prohibition Cases, 235 U.S. 350 (1920) (counsel suggesting that the 18th amendment was invalid because it was "subversive of fundamental principles" and would "do violence to" a "fundamental maxim of republican government"). *See also* L. SPOONER, THE UNCONSTITUTIONALITY OF SLAVERY 14 (Boston 1860) ("*[C]onstitutional law, under any form of government, consists only of those principles of the written constitution that are consistent with natural law, and man's natural rights.*" (emphasis in original)).

7. Grey, *Do We Have An Unwritten Constitution?*, 27 STAN. L. REV. 703 (1975).

8. The purest form of noninterpretive review, a form virtually moribund today, invokes general principles of republican government, natural justice or human rights as confining legislative authority regardless of the terms or even the existence of a written constitution. *See generally* Corwin, *The Basic Doctrine of American Constitutional Law*, 12 MICH. L. REV. 247 (1914). Modern constitutional law includes three other forms of noninterpretive review; these surviving forms all claim some connection to the constitutional text, but their actual normative content is not derived from the language of the Constitution as illuminated by the intent of its framers.

The first such modern form licenses judges to read normative content into such general phrases in the Constitution as "due process" and "equal protection" in order to prevent legislative infringement on individual rights the judges deem fundamental. *See, e.g.*, Bullock v. Carter, 405 U.S. 134 (1972) (access to ballot); Kramer v. Union Free School Dist., 395 U.S. 621 (1969) (equality in voting); Griswold v. Connecticut, 381 U.S. 479 (1965) (right of privacy); Lochner v. New York, 198 U.S. 45 (1905) (liberty of contract). A second surviving mode of noninterpretive review allows courts to invoke more specific constitutional provisions as judicial instruments for applying contemporary social and moral norms as restraints on legislative power, even though the framers would have read these provisions as embodying different and narrower restraints. A prime example is the contemporary doctrine that the

The resort to noninterpretive judicial review echoes the "unwritten law" side of the Aristotelian dialogue. When a statute conflicts with some felt principle of justice or ideal of good government, noninterpretive review provides lawyers and judges with an argument for holding that the statute is not binding law. At the same time, this invocation of an unwritten constitution stimulates the fears—and the sensible cautions—expressed in the "written law" side of the dialogue. Judges who believe themselves authorized to enforce unwritten constitutional law may more readily usurp the primary political functions of governing and lawmaking. This possibility is a special concern of those who disbelieve the existence of principles of natural justice or shared national ideals, or doubt the special capacity of judges to discern or apply them. Under either of these skeptical views, judges purporting to apply unwritten constitutional principles are only carrying on a personal constitutional amendment process rooted in personal will and judgment.[9]

Respect for the authority of enacted law and distrust of judicial discretion thus underlie what I have called the "pure interpretive

---

eighth amendment prohibition against "cruel and unusual punishment" imposes *evolving* standards of decency on penal legislation. *See* Trop v. Dulles, 356 U.S. 86, 101 (1958).

A final contemporary mode of noninterpretive judicial review reads into a general provision of the Constitution a body of constitutional law developed under other constitutional provisions which would not otherwise apply to the case at hand. One example is the application of 14th amendment equal protection doctrine to the federal government through the medium of the fifth amendment due process clause. *See* Buckley v. Valeo, 424 U.S. 1, 93 (1976); Bolling v. Sharpe, 347 U.S. 497 (1954). Another is the concept of the "selective incorporation" into the 14th amendment of the due process clause of most of the provisions of the Bill of Rights. *See, e.g.*, Duncan v. Louisiana, 391 U.S. 145, 149 (1968). Some may object that, except for the substantive due process and equal protection cases, the constitutional developments I have ascribed to the noninterpretive mode are in fact intelligent *interpretations* of the constitutional text, aimed at the modern versions of old legislative evils that the framers themselves addressed. In my view, significant new constitutional developments are rarely just extensions of framer-intended norms to novel fact situations. The framers of the first amendment were quite aware of the suppression of erotic literature, just as the framers of the equal protection clause were aware of school segregation and miscegenation laws. For a further discussion of this point, see Grey, *supra* note 7, at 713 n.46.

9. Thus Learned Hand has said that judges engaging in noninterpretive judicial review "wrap up their veto in a protective veil of adjectives such as 'arbitrary,' 'artificial,' 'normal,' 'reasonable,' 'inherent,' 'fundamental,' or 'essential,' whose office usually, though quite innocently, is to disguise what they are doing and impute to it a derivation far more impressive than their personal preferences, which are all that in fact lie behind the decision. If we do need a third chamber, it should appear for what it is, and not as the interpreter of inscrutable principles." L. HAND, THE BILL OF RIGHTS 70 (1962). *See* Rehnquist, *The Notion of a Living Constitution*, 54 TEX. L. REV. 693, 698 (1976) (Judges purporting to enforce a "living constitution" are simply "a small group of fortunately situated people with a roving commission to second-guess Congress, state legislatures, and state and federal administrative officers concerning what is best for the country.").

model" of judicial review.[10] According to that model, legitimate constitutional adjudication is limited to the application of concrete norms derivable from the written constitution itself. The written constitution is conceived of as supreme positive law, the most direct legal expression of the popular will. Applying its commands in litigated disputes simply requires ordinary judicial expertise in construing statutes or other documents. Judicial review, if so confined, involves no serious tension with the theory of popular sovereignty, no departure from the jurisprudence of positivism, and no controversial philosophical claims about the existence of principles of justice or unwritten law or the capacity of reason to discern them.[11]

Not surprisingly, the Supreme Court's persistently active resort to noninterpretive review over the last quarter century has recently called forth an unusual number of explicit affirmations of the pure interpretive theory.[12] These affirmations have, in turn, stimulated rejoinders by the defenders of noninterpretive review,[13] generally in defense of the recent recognition of a constitutional right to privacy.[14] The issue of the legitimacy of noninterpretive judicial review thus has come to be identified with the debate over the new privacy cases. However, the more general theoretical question of whether the courts may ever properly give constitutional force to

10. *See* Grey, *supra* note 7, at 703-06. Note the caveat: "The pure interpretive model should not be confused with *literalism* in constitutional interpretation, particularly with 'narrow' or 'crabbed' literalism. The interpretive model, at least in the hands of its sophisticated exponents, certainly contemplates that the courts may look through the sometimes opaque text to the purposes behind it in determining constitutional norms. Normative inferences may be drawn from silences and omissions, from structures and relationships, as well as from explicit commands." *Id.* at 706 n.9. Further, the pure interpretive model does not exclude the judicial implementation of one concept of a living constitution—the application by the courts of norms intended by the framers to factual circumstances that the framers did not foresee. *See* Rehnquist, *supra* note 9, at 694-95; note 8 *supra*.

11. The classic expositions of this interpretive mode of judicial review are those of Alexander Hamilton in *Federalist No. 78* and Chief Justice Marshall in Marbury v. Madison, 5 U.S. (1 Cranch) 137 (1803).

12. *See* R. BERGER, GOVERNMENT BY JUDICIARY (1977); Bork, *Neutral Principles and Some First Amendment Problems*, 47 IND. L.J. 1 (1971); Ely, *The Wages of Crying Wolf: A Comment on* Roe v. Wade, 82 YALE L.J. 920 (1973); Linde, *Judges, Critics, and the Realist Tradition*, 82 YALE L.J. 227 (1972); Monaghan, *Of "Liberty" and "Property,"* 62 CORNELL L.J. 405 (1977); Rehnquist, *supra* note 9; Strong, *Bicentennial Benchmark: Two Centuries of Evolution of Constitutional Processes*, 55 N.C.L. REV. 1 (1976).

13. A. COX, THE ROLE OF THE SUPREME COURT IN AMERICAN GOVERNMENT (1976); Black, *The Unfinished Business of the Warren Court*, 46 WASH. L. REV. 1, 31–45 (1970); Perry, *Abortion, The Public Morals and The Police Power: The Ethical Function of Substantive Due Process*, 23 U.C.L.A. L. REV. 689 (1976).

14. Griswold v. Connecticut, 381 U.S. 479 (1965).

extra-constitutional norms is one which should be addressed on its own terms.

In my earlier essay, I noted several levels on which the issue of an unwritten constitution might be investigated.[15] First, there is the question of the extent to which the pure interpretive model conforms to judicial practice. In that essay, I argued that the logic of the pure interpretive model condemns not only decisions of the "substantive due process" variety—against which its exponents generally direct their specific criticism—but also a much larger body of existing constitutional doctrine which cannot be attributed to the value choices of the framers. If logically implemented, the interpretive model would entail a virtual revolution in constitutional doctrine—and this prospect provides a sound conservative argument against the model.[16]

But such an argument from consequences is not itself an entirely satisfying resolution of so basic a question of constitutional theory as the propriety of noninterpretive review. Old or established practices can and should be changed—particularly if they lack utility, theoretical justification and original legitimacy. One may ask whether noninterpretive review on the whole does more practical good than harm. One may ask whether it is congruent with some acceptable theory of adjudication.[17] And finally, one must ask the question addressed in this article—the question of lawful authority.

Even if judicial development of an unwritten constitution is good for a country and fits an appropriate theory of the judicial function, each legal system retains the choice whether to grant so impressive a power to its judges. The pure interpretive model rests in large part on the claim that the framers made no such grant to American courts—that under our constitutional scheme as originally intended, judges were meant to invalidate statutes only on the basis of values chosen by the framers and enacted in the written constitution.[18]

15. Grey, *supra* note 7, at 714–15.

16. *Id.* at 710–14.

17. *Id.* at 714–15. At the time I noted the kinship between the nonpositivist jurisprudential theories of Ronald Dworkin and noninterpretive judicial review. *Id.* at 715 n.48. *See generally* R. DWORKIN, TAKING RIGHTS SERIOUSLY (1977).

18. I suspect that some will wish to say that they are interpretivists, not because of any intent of the framers, but rather because the "discovery theory of adjudication" on which the framers depended has since been exploded by legal realism and other advances in jurisprudential wisdom. Those holding such a position hence consider themselves confined to the interpretation of the written constitution on every question except the very question of whether they are confined to the interpretation of the written constitution. This is perhaps not a self-contradiction, but it is certainly an odd position.

Judicial review that goes beyond this and rests on values chosen by judges themselves, or purportedly drawn by them from the unwritten moral code of their contemporary society, would then invite the criticism voiced against the judicial implementation of a flexible fairness test of due process by Mr. Justice Black—that it "alters the form of government our Constitution provides."[19]

This article addresses the question raised by Mr. Justice Black—the question of the historical legitimacy of noninterpretive judicial review—by examining the view of law, constitutionalism and judicial function dominant among the generation of Americans who framed the Constitution. That view was partly inherited from the more remote past, and then was shaped by two great controversies—the American colonists' struggle with England that led to the decision for independence in 1776, and the internal controversies within the newly independent nation that led to the framing and ratification of the Federal Constitution and the Bill of Rights by 1791. In this article, I focus on the legacy of the pre-1776 independence struggle for the American concept of a judicially enforceable unwritten constitution.

The evidence I will be reviewing is not new; it has been thoroughly examined by two groups of historians, though in neither case with a view toward answering the same questions as have stimulated this study. First, the constitutional theories of the 1760's and 1770's have been a favorite subject of the intellectual and political historians of the American Revolution.[20] The primary focus of those historians has been the longstanding dispute over whether the Revolution grew primarily out of ideas and ideals on the one hand, or out of material interests masked in the rhetoric of natural and constitutional rights on the other.[21]

In my discussion of the ideas of the period, I am not interested in pursuing this dispute. My purpose is rather to investigate the

19. International Shoe v. Washington, 326 U.S. 310, 326 (1945) (Black, J., concurring).

20. Surveys by historians of the political ideas of the revolutionary period include B. Bailyn, The Ideological Origins of the American Revolution (1968); C. Mullett, Fundamental Law and the American Revolution (1933); C. Rossiter, Seedtime of the Republic (1953).

21. This one-sentence summary of the controversy necessarily oversimplifies a complex debate. For the position that ideas counted, see B. Bailyn, *supra* note 20; C. McIlwain, The American Revolution: A Constitutional Interpretation (1923). For the contrary position, see P. Davidson, Propaganda and the American Revolution (1941); A. Schlesinger, The Colonial Merchants and the American Revolution (1917). A good historiographical review of that debate is J. Greene, The Reinterpretation of the American Revolution 1–59 (1968).

American view of unwritten constitutional law during the revolutionary period for the light it casts on the ideas held by the framers of the first American constitutions. The best evidence of these views is to be found in what leading American spokesmen said—particularly to their fellow Americans—during the struggle with England. The rhetoric used by successful politicians and advocates tends to indicate the dominant belief-structure of their audience, whether or not that conscious belief-structure was the primary causal force on the audience's behavior. Otis, Dickinson, John and Samuel Adams, Jefferson, and other leaders of the struggle for independence were successful politicians and advocates. There must be a very strong presumption that the arguments they used rested on widely shared beliefs and invoked widely shared values.

In addition to the historians of the Revolution, constitutional historians have examined much of the evidence that I reexamine in this article, searching for anticipations of *Marbury v. Madison*.[22] Their primary concern has been the extent to which "judicial review" (conceived as a single unitary practice) was already familiar at the adoption of the Constitution. They have been engaged, that is, in the traditional inquiry into whether judicial review *of any kind* is consistent with the intent of the framers.

Again, my own focus is different. My aim is to examine the *relative* acceptability of interpretive and noninterpretive modes of constitutional adjudication for the generation of Americans who framed the Constitution. These familiar antecedents of judicial review are cast in a different light when one accepts *Marbury* as a given, and asks whether an unwritten as well as a written constitution was intended to be enforced by judges.

II. The English and Continental Background of American Fundamental Law Conceptions

The constitutional ideas of the American Whigs[23] of the revolutionary era arose primarily out of the traditional English conception of fundamental law. The original colonists were 17th-century Eng-

---

22. *See, e.g.*, E. Corwin, The "Higher Law" Origins of American Constitutional Law (1955); C. Haines, The American Doctrine of Judicial Supremacy 29–121 (2d ed. 1959); A. McLaughlin, The Courts, The Constitution and Parties 3–107 (1912); Plucknett, *Bonham's Case and Judicial Review*, 40 Harv. L. Rev. 30 (1926).

23. In line with common convention, I have called Americans who eventually supported independence "Whigs" and have generally treated them as holding a monolithic set of views. This is an oversimplification, but not a serious one in the context of this article, where my effort is to uncover the broad outlines of American constitutional thought.

lishmen, and their political thought was formed by the institutions and beliefs characteristic of 17th-century England. Ideas of fundamental law superior to all organs of government—ideas that had dominated the century of civil war and revolution in their homeland—were to provide the moral and intellectual background for the colonists in the struggle that ultimately led to independence. While the traditional English conception of fundamental law lost institutional support in 18th-century English politics, this conception was renewed and fortified, particularly for Americans, by the political and legal theories of the Enlightenment. These theories, as developed by writers such as Pufendorf, Burlamaqui and Vattel, stressed limitations upon legislative power imposed both by general natural law and by the particular provisions of each nation's constitution.

A. *The English Fundamental Law Tradition*

The traditional concept of fundamental law had three separable components. First, fundamental law was *legally* supreme. It placed binding legal limitations on all the organs of government so that no single institution could claim total sovereignty. Second, fundamental law was unwritten; it drew its content from sources other than enactment, whether usage and custom, or reason and natural justice. Finally, fundamental law was at least in some circumstances *judicially* enforceable, even against the highest legislative and executive organs of government.[24]

1. *The supremacy of the law.*

The English 17th-century conception of fundamental law was

24. That fundamental law is legally binding does not entail that it must be judicially enforceable. *See* notes 129–35 *infra* and accompanying text. Numerous critics of Chief Justice Marshall's opinion in *Marbury v. Madison* have pointed this out. *See, e.g.*, Eakin v. Raub, 12 Serg. & Rawl. 330, 345 (Pa. 1825) (Gibson, J., dissenting); A. BICKEL, THE LEAST DANGEROUS BRANCH 1–14 (1962). The fundamental law may be left to other agencies of government for final interpretation—as are the limitations of our own Federal Constitution with respect to "political questions," *see* Wechsler, *Toward Neutral Principles of Constitutional Law*, 73 HARV. L. REV. 1, 8 (1959). Throughout this study I have applied the term "legal" to elements of fundamental law that possess the first component—binding force on all organs of government—whether or not they possess the second—specifically judicial enforceability. The claim of legally binding force is typically expressed by condemnation of statutes or measures in such terms as "illegal," "unlawful," "ultra vires," "unauthorized," "void," or the like. I apply the term "extra-legal" to fundamental law restrictions intended to bind governments only by *ethical* force. Such extra-legal restrictions typically appear in the legal and political literature in condemnations of enacted laws as "unjust," "improper" or "wrongful." Terms such as "unconstitutional" and "rights" stand ambiguously between the legal and extra-legal concepts of fundamental law, and their intended force must be found in their context.

itself the offspring of medieval ideas. The medieval view of law recognized no unlimited political sovereignty; even the King, the highest earthly power, was, as Bracton wrote in the 13th century, "not under man, but under God and the law."[25] In England, this medieval view of the supremacy of law survived the Renaissance, retaining much of its power even through the enhancement and centralization of state power that characterized the Tudor era.[26]

But where the Tudor monarchs had consolidated their actual power without making novel theoretical claims to sovereignty, James I, in the early years of the 17th century, asserted for himself the very absolute legal authority which traditional law had denied to royalty.[27] Against his claims were arrayed the forces of the House of Commons, asserting sovereignty not in Parliament itself, but rather in the ancient and fundamental laws which established the respective rights of monarch, Lords, Commons, and people. As John Pym said of the proposal to insert into the 1628 Petition of Right a recognition of the "sovereign power" of the King: "All our petition is for the Laws of England. . . . I know how to add sovereign to his Person but not to his Power . . . we cannot leave to him a sovereign power . . . we were never possessed of it."[28]

After the failure of those early theoretical claims of the Stuart kings to be above the law in all things, the great constitutional controversies of the period were debated in the traditional terms of fundamental law. Parliamentarians like Coke and Pym argued that the King's as well as Parliament's authority was limited by fundamental law.[29] Royalists argued that the broad scope they claimed for the royal prerogative was itself guaranteed against parliamentary interference by fundamental law.[30] After the overthrow of royal

25. H. BRACTON, ON THE LAWS AND CUSTOMS OF ENGLAND 33 (S. Thorne trans. 1968). *See generally* F. KERN, KINGSHIP AND LAW IN THE MIDDLE AGES (1956); C. MCILWAIN, CONSTITUTIONALISM: ANCIENT AND MODERN 67–87 (rev. ed. 1947).

26. *See* J. GOUGH, FUNDAMENTAL LAW IN ENGLISH CONSTITUTIONAL HISTORY 12–29 (1955); M. JUDSON, THE CRISIS OF THE CONSTITUTION 80–85 (1964); C. MCILWAIN, *supra* note 25, at 93–122.

27. James I, *The Trew Law of Free Monarchies*, in THE POLITICAL WORKS OF JAMES I at 53–70 (C. McIlwain ed. 1918). *See* J. ALLEN, ENGLISH POLITICAL THOUGHT, 1603–1660, at 3–12 (1938); J. GOUGH, *supra* note 26, at 51–54; M. JUDSON, *supra* note 26, at 107–70.

28. 1 J. RUSHWORTH, HISTORICAL COLLECTIONS 562 (London 1682).

29. *Id.*

30. When Charles I's advisor Strafford was attainted by the Long Parliament in 1640, he defended on the ground that his policies involved proper exercise of the prerogative, itself protected by fundamental law. The charge against Charles in his own trial in 1649 was his breach of fundamental law; he defended on the ground that the special court established to try him was unconstitutional. J. GOUGH, *supra* note 26, at 74–77.

government, the "left opposition" to the Cromwellian regime itself invoked fundamental law to protest against parliamentary absolutism.[31] Though 17th-century England produced two important theoretical proponents of the concept of unlimited sovereignty, Filmer and Hobbes, their ideas won little acceptance in the arena of legal and political controversy.[32]

2. *The unwritten law: reason and custom.*

For the 17th-century parliamentarians, Magna Carta was a particularly revered embodiment of fundamental law. Sir Edward Coke, for example, considered Magna Carta sacred and unalterable; he insisted that "Magna Carta is such a Fellow, that he will have no Sovereign,"[33] and that an act of Parliament in violation of the charter would be "holden for none."[34] Coke considered Magna Carta supreme, however, not as a written constitution in the modern sense, binding by virtue of some peculiarly authoritative process of enactment, but rather as a statement "declaratory of the principal grounds of the fundamental laws of England."[35]

According to 17th-century myth, a myth later fully embraced by the American Whigs, the origins of these fundamental unwritten laws themselves were buried beyond recovery in the Saxon past.[36] The authority of the fundamental laws rested partly on this imagined immemorial antiquity, but also partly on their asserted reasonableness. As had their medieval predecessors, 17th-century lawyers blended custom and reason into a single system of fundamental

31. Throughout the period of the Civil War and Interregnum (1640–1660), not only royalist but Leveller and other "left" critics attacked Parliament for illegal and unconstitutional arrogations of authority. *See id.* at 98–116. John Lilburne was particularly explicit on this point; he quoted Coke's judgment in Dr. Bonham's Case, 77 Eng. Rep. 647 (C.P. 1610), for the proposition that Parliament was limited by "reason and nature" as incorporated into English fundamental law. J. Gough, *supra* note 26, at 110–11.

32. M. Judson, *supra* note 26, at 14–15; J. Pocock, The Ancient Constitution and the Feudal Law 54–55 (1957).

33. 1 J. Rushworth, *supra* note 28, at 562.

34. 3 E. Coke, Institutes of the Laws of England *111.

35. 2 E. Coke, Institutes of the Laws of England *Proeme (unpaged). Coke here is referring to the confirmation of the Charter in 1368, in which it was enacted, "That the Great Charter and the Charter of the Forest be holden and kept in all points; and if any Statute be made to the contrary, that shall be holden for none." 42 Edw. 3, c.1 (1368), *translated in* C. McIlwain, The High Court of Parliament and Its Supremacy 59 (1910).

36. On the 17th century belief in a fixed unwritten constitution of immemorial antiquity, see J. Pocock, *supra* note 32, at 30–55 (1957); on the influence of these ideas on the American revolutionaries, see T. Colbourn, The Lamp of Experience 25–39 (1965).

law. The two sources were not seen as in conflict—the old was the reasonable and the reasonable was the old.[37]

As Christopher St. Germain had noted in the 16th Century, the common lawyers' resort to what was considered "reasonable" as a source of law was the English equivalent of the natural law arguments of the scholastics and the Roman and canon lawyers.[38] By the early 17th Century, not only the substance but also the vocabulary of natural law argument had entered into the fabric of English law. Thus Coke stated in *Calvin's Case* that the law of nature was part of the law of England and took precedence over earthly law, since it was of Divine origin, eternal and unchanging.[39] And the leading introductory treatise on English law to appear in the 17th Century, Sir Henry Finch's *Law*, firmly declared that positive laws contrary to natural law "lose their force, and are no laws at all."[40]

Though 17th-century fundamental law theory was associated with revolutionary developments, including the deposing and beheading of a king, it was in a sense profoundly conservative. The same Coke who asserted the supremacy of the fundamental law made clear that the "law of reason" did not refer to the untutored reason of everyman, but to a special "artificial reason" of the law, infused with the dictates of custom, experience and the professional training of lawyers.[41] Sir John Davies, writing in 1612, said that

37. F. KERN, *supra* note 25, at 70–72. Kern's description of medieval law and constitutionalism, *id.* at 149–205, is particularly valuable. *See also* J. POCOCK, THE MACHIAVELLIAN MOMENT (1975).

38. C. ST. GERMAIN, DOCTOR AND STUDENT 4, 9 (n.p. 1580).

39. 77 Eng. Rep. 377, 391–92 (K.B. 1609). For this proposition, Coke cites Bracton and St. Germain.

40. H. FINCH, LAW, A DISCOURSE THEREOF 75 (4th ed. D. Pickering 1759). On the importance of Finch's work, see 5 W. HOLDSWORTH, HISTORY OF ENGLISH LAW 400–01 (3d ed. 1966). Finch's treatise was reissued in a newly annotated edition in London in 1759, and was known to American lawyers of the colonial and revolutionary period. *See* 1 THE WORKS OF JOHN ADAMS 46 (C. Adams ed. 1856); THE LAW PRACTICE OF ALEXANDER HAMILTON 857 (J. Goebel ed. 1969). It had earlier been cited in the important 1657 Massachusetts case of Giddings v. Browne, *reported in* 2 HUTCHINSON PAPERS 1–25 (reprinted Albany, N.Y., 1865) (1st ed. Boston 1769).

41. For the phrase "artificial reason," see Prohibitions del Roy, 77 Eng. Rep. 1342, 1343 (1608). In the introduction to the fourth volume of his reports, Coke says that the common law "hath been refined and perfected by all the wisest men in former succession of ages, and proved and approved by continual experience to be good and profitable for the commonwealth." 4 Coke's Reports *vi. *Compare* 5 W. HOLDSWORTH, *supra* note 40, at 500, 502–06 (reproducing Sir Matthew Hale's panegyrics to the common law as the perfect blend of reason and experience in his criticism of Hobbes), *and* 1 W. BLACKSTONE, COMMENTARIES *69–70, *with* K. LLEWELLYN, THE COMMON LAW TRADITION (1960). For a discussion of the links between this legal ideology and the political philosophy of Burke, see J. POCOCK, *supra* note 32, at 242–243, and particularly, J. POCOCK, POLITICS, LANGUAGE AND TIME 202–32 (1971).

while "the Law of Nature . . . is better than all written Laws in the world," it was "the Customary Law of England," not the raw good sense of the common man's mind, that came "nearest to the law of Nature . . . ."[42] Custom—the special professionally tested custom of the common law—was thus the most reliable *evidence* of the content of natural law. Finally, Finch, who had asserted the supremacy of natural over positive law, cautioned that "the law of reason is known only to such as are able to judge aright, and that but imperfectly," so that it was no easy matter to determine "what laws may be said agreeable and what repugnant thereunto. . . ."[43]

3. *Judicial review.*

Modern discussion of the existence of judicial review in 17th-century England tends to focus around Coke's opinion in *Dr. Bonham's Case*[44] and its few progeny,[45] which asserted judicial power to disregard an act of Parliament violating common right and reason. These relatively isolated cases were indeed important precedents, particularly for the American colonists, but they did not represent the only, or even the principal, instances of what we should consider judicial enforcement of fundamental law against otherwise sovereign agencies of state in 17th-century England. Judicial rulings on constitutional questions of what we could call separation of powers were common. From *Bate's Case* in 1606,[46] to the *Five Knights' Case* in 1628[47] to *Godden v. Hales* in 1686,[48] the courts

42. J. Davies' Reports 4 (1762).

43. H. FINCH, *supra* note 40, at 75–76.

44. 77 Eng. Rep. 647, 652 (C.P. 1610).

45. Day v. Savadge, 80 Eng. Rep. 235 (K.B. 1614); City of London v. Wood, 88 Eng. Rep. 1592 (K.B. 1701).

46. 145 Eng. Rep. 267 (Ex. 1606). James I had imposed a duty upon the import of currants, which Bates refused to pay as a tax not consented to by Parliament. The Court of Exchequer decided in favor of the legality of the impost under the royal prerogative on the ground that the legal incidence of the tax was not upon the subject Bates but upon the foreign exporters. *Id.* at 274.

47. 3 Howell's State Trials 1 (1628). The King imposed forced loans on named subjects without parliamentary approval. Sir Thomas Darnel and four other knights who refused to pay and were imprisoned by order of the King brought a writ of habeas corpus challenging the legality of their detention on the ground of the fundamental law requirement expressed in the "law of the land" provision of Magna Carta that imprisonment could only follow indictment or presentment for crime. *Id.* at 18. Attorney-General Heath argued that "the law of the land" included a royal prerogative to imprison by special mandate. *Id.* at 36. Lord Chief Justice Hyde denied the writ, on the ground "that if no cause of the commitment be expressed, it is to be presumed to be for the matter of state, which we cannot take notice of . . . ." *Id.* at 57.

48. 89 Eng. Rep. 1050 (K.B. 1686). Sir Edward Hales took office as colonel of a foot-regiment without taking the oaths of supremacy and allegiance, which were required by

frequently determined the boundary between Parliament's authority and the royal prerogative.[49] In the greatest of these cases, the *Ship-Money Case* of 1637,[50] a divided Exchequer chamber upheld the royal power to raise money for national defense without the consent of Parliament in emergency circumstances. In his opinion supporting the King, Lord Chief Justice Finch wrote "[A]cts of Parliament to take away his royal power in defense of his kingdom, are void . . . ."[51]

It is in this general context of judicially enforceable supreme law—a fundamental though unwritten law, compounded of reason and experience—that *Dr. Bonham's Case* should be considered. In that case, decided in 1610, Coke made his celebrated declaration that "when an act of Parliament is against common right and reason, or repugnant, or impossible to be performed, the common law will control it, and adjudge such act to be void."[52]

There has been much debate over whether Coke meant this passage as an assertion of a full power of judicial review in the modern sense.[53] On the one hand, the full modern concept of the separation of legislative, executive and judicial power had not developed in the early 17th Century. The King, the courts (which were the King's courts) and Parliament (still considered the "High Court") all were thought of as institutions controlled by an overarching fundamental law to which they were all jointly responsible. The hierarchical relationship among these institutions was not clear; while all agreed that the law was supreme, there was no consensus on who should have the last word in interpreting it. Coke, for example, while never repudiating the doctrine of *Dr. Bonham's Case*,

statute, and designed to bar Catholics from public offices. King James II issued Sir Edward letters-patent purporting to discharge him from his statutory duty, and Sir Edward invoked the letters as a defense to his indictment for violation of the statute. Counsel for the plaintiff argued that the King lacked constitutional authority to dispense with the statute. *Id.* Counsel for the King argued that the royal prerogative included power to dispense with statutes punishing *malum prohibitum* (which this was), though not *malum in se*. *Id.* at 105. The Lord Chief Justice ruled for Sir Edward (and the King). *Id.*

49. The decision in Calvin's Case, 77 Eng. Rep. 377 (K.B. 1609), is another example.

50. 3 Howell's State Trials 825 (1637).

51. *Id.* at 1235.

52. 77 Eng. Rep. 646, 652 (K.B. 1610).

53. *See, e.g.*, R. BERGER, CONGRESS V. THE SUPREME COURT 349–68 (1969); E. CORWIN, *supra* note 22, at 43–51; J. GOUGH, *supra* note 26, at 30–40; M. JUDSON, *supra* note 26, at 92–102; C. MCILWAIN, *supra* note 25, at 286–300; Plucknett, *Bonham's Case and Judicial Review*, 40 HARV. L. REV. 30 (1926); Thorne, *The Constitution and the Courts: A Reexamination of the Famous Case of Dr. Bonham*, in THE CONSTITUTION RECONSIDERED 15–24 (C. Read ed. 1937).

elsewhere described the power and jurisdiction of Parliament as "transcendent and absolute."[54] Such an assertion cannot be taken as a claim of Hobbesian sovereignty for Parliament, overriding either the legitimate claims of prerogative or those rights based on natural justice involved in *Dr. Bonham's Case*. Rather Coke seems to have been speaking of Parliament in what we would consider its judicial role, as the highest court in the land.[55] In *that* role, Coke probably did not regard Parliament as bound by the ruling of the King's lesser courts that an act of Parliament was void. In this limited sense, the doctrine of *Marbury v. Madison*, which asserts the final authority of ordinary courts on constitutional questions, was probably not suggested by *Dr. Bonham's Case*.

On the other hand, Coke's language in *Dr. Bonham's Case* undeniably claims for the ordinary courts the power to disregard the plain import of statutes where these conflicted with "common right and reason." Statutes violating common right and reason were "utterly void."[56] This is not the usual language of statutory construction; here is no mere assertion of a power to interpret statutes in light of equitable principles. Given the widespread acceptance of fundamental law as both superior to all government and applicable by the courts, we should grant Coke's words their natural implication: judicial review in the full sense over Parliament in what we would call the latter's *legislative* capacity.[57]

4. *Eighteenth-century developments.*

The ideas of fundamental law, so dominant in 17th-century England, were subtly undermined in that country by the course of

54. *See* E. COKE, INSTITUTES OF THE LAWS OF ENGLAND *36.

55. That this was Coke's meaning is argued convincingly in C. MCILWAIN, *supra* note 25, at 139–43. *See also* J. GOUGH, *supra* note 26, at 41–44.

56. 77 Eng. Rep. 647, 652 (C.P. 1610).

57. The view that in *Dr. Bonham's Case* Coke was merely asserting a power in the courts to construe statutes so as to avoid inequitable results has been advanced by Thorne, *supra* note 53, at 15–24. For criticism of that view, see R. BERGER, *supra* note 53, at 349–68. It is clear that Coke accepted the view, perfectly standard in his time, that natural law or the law of reason was a higher law, controlling King, Parliament and all earthly authority. He had asserted that view a year earlier in Calvin's Case, 77 Eng. Rep. at 392, citing St. Germain's *Doctor and Student*. That *Dr. Bonham's Case* was regarded as asserting the same doctrine is made equally clear by the decision of Lord Hobart, Coke's successor as Chief Justice of Common Pleas 4 years later in the case of Day v. Savadge, 80 Eng. Rep. 235 (K.B. 1614). Hobart asserted the precise doctrine of *Dr. Bonham's Case*—that an act of Parliament making a man judge in his own case would be "void in itself"—because "*jura natura sunt immutabilia*." These were the same words, taken from Bracton, which Coke had himself used to assert the doctrine of binding higher law in *Calvin's Case*. See the discussion in Plucknett, *supra* note 53, at 49–50.

political history. The events of the Cromwellian period, the Restoration and the Revolution of 1688, and finally the evolution of the system of ministerial government under the Hanoverian Kings, all tended to create a practical legal supremacy in Parliament. Whig theory and practice made royal authority subordinate to Parliament, and *Godden v. Hales*[58] in 1686 represented the court's last imposition of a constitutional limit on parliamentary authority in the name of the royal prerogative. The constitution came to be seen less as a body of principles limiting governmental power, and more as a set of institutions headed by a Parliament that possessed ultimate authority to change customary arrangements by legislation.[59]

But the rhetoric of fundamental law persisted. Even after the Glorious Revolution, in 1701, we find Lord Chief Justice Holt asserting in dictum:

> [W]hat my Lord Coke says in Dr. Bonham's Case . . . is far from any extravagancy, for it is very reasonable and true saying, that if an act of parliament should ordain that the same person should be party and judge . . . it would be a void act of parliament.[60]

Outside the courts, the notion of a fundamental law binding even on Parliament retained its place in the framework of political argument. Thus, in the debates over the Septennial Act in 1716, the opposition continued to assert that a bill might go through the proper forms of enactment and yet "not obtain the force of a law" because as "warranted by one of our greatest lawyers . . . an act of parliament may be void of itself."[61]

Well into the period of the American revolution itself, leading English lawyers and statesmen continued to assert that a fixed constitution and fundamental law limited even Parliament. Opposing the Declaratory Act in the House of Lords in 1766, Lord Camden denounced taxation without representation in exactly the terms the Americans were using themselves, as "illegal, absolutely illegal, contrary to the fundamental laws of nature, contrary to the fundamental laws of this constitution . . . [a] constitution grounded on the external and immutable laws of nature."[62] Camden was no

58. 89 Eng. Rep. 1050 (K.B. 1686).

59. *See* J. Gough, *supra* note 26, at 160-91.

60. Day v. Savadge, 80 Eng. Rep. 235 (K.B. 1614). For another example, see J. Fortescue, The Difference Between an Absolute and Limited Monarchy at xxix (1714).

61. Speech by Archibald Hutcheson (April 24, 1716), *reprinted in* 7 Parl. Hist. Eng. 349 (1811).

62. Speech by Lord Camden (Feb. 10, 1766), *reprinted in* 16 Parl. Hist. Eng. 178 (1813). He had earlier in the same debate said: "The sovereign authority, the omnipotence of the legislature, my lords, is a favourite doctrine, but there are some things they cannot do. They

political rebel or deviant, but a former Chancellor and Lord Chief Justice. His views were echoed by the greatest English statesman of the age, William Pitt the Elder, Lord Chatham.[63] Another member of Parliament, Alderman Beckford, directly invoked the authority of Coke: "[A]n Act of Parliament against common right is a nullity; so says Lord Coke."[64]

Thus, the old idea of a fundamental law, a fixed constitution standing above and limiting the working institutions of government, remained a respectable idea in England in the 1760's. Nevertheless, the notion that courts or other governmental institutions could disregard unconstitutional acts of Parliament was in decline. Blackstone stated what was doubtless the prevailing English view in the *Commentaries*, first published in 1765. Describing the relationship between Parliament and the courts, he repudiated the broader implications of Coke's doctrine that judges could treat unreasonable acts of Parliament as void.[65]

Blackstone recognized Cokean judicial review in its broadest sense as a prevalent doctrine, albeit a fallacious one; it was still what was "generally laid down." Blackstone himself, moreover, had earlier in the *Commentaries* stated the standard doctrine that "the law of nature is of course superior in obligation to all others . . . . No human laws are of any validity, if contrary to this."[66] But his en-

---

cannot enact any thing against the divine law. . . . They cannot take away any man's private property without making him a compensation." *Id.* at 168.

63. Speech by Lord Chatham (Jan. 20, 1775), *reprinted in* 18 PARL. HIST. ENG. 165 (1813). The occasion was Chatham's motion in 1775 to withdraw British troops from Boston. On the place of the Camden-Chatham position in the English politics of the period, see G. GUTTRIDGE, ENGLISH WHIGGISM AND THE AMERICAN REVOLUTION, 14–16, 63–66, 142–43 (1942).

64. 1 H. CAVENDISH, DEBATES OF THE HOUSE OF COMMONS 1768–1770, at 83–84 (1841), *quoted in* J. GOUGH, *supra* note 26, at 194.

65. "[A]cts of parliament that are impossible to be performed are of no validity: and if there arise out of them collaterally any absurd consequences, manifestly contradictory to common reason, they are, with regard to those collateral consequences, void. I lay down the rule with these restrictions; though I know it is generally laid down more largely, that acts of parliament contrary to reason are void. But if the parliament will positively enact a thing to be done which is unreasonable, I know of no power in the ordinary forms of the constitution, that is vested with authority to control it; and the examples usually alleged in support of this sense of the rule do none of them prove, that, where the main object of a statute is unreasonable, the judges are at liberty to reject it: for that were to set the judicial power above that of the legislature, which would be subversive of all government." 1 W. BLACKSTONE, COMMENTARIES *91. There was articulate contemporaneous dissent from Blackstone's view. Furneaux, *Letters to Blackstone*, *82 n., in PALLADIUM OF CONSCIENCE (Philadelphia 1773); *see* J. GOUGH, *supra* note 26, at 196-200 (Granville Sharp's tracts on the Irish question (1774) and the proposed suspension of habeas corpus (1778)).

66. 1 W. BLACKSTONE, COMMENTARIES *41.

dorsement of the superiority of natural law was perfunctory and not repeated.

By contrast, Blackstone called upon his unrivaled gift for sonorous and redundant vehemence in his assertions of parliamentary supremacy.[67] He did not merely refuse to recognize judicial review in defense of the constitution or the natural rights of the subject; he believed that the constitution was subject to the legislative authority of Parliament, and that the violation of even natural rights was subject to no remedy within the legal system.[68] Finally, there is nothing at all to be found in the *Commentaries*, nothing even comparable to the lip-service Blackstone pays natural law, suggesting that traditional and customary common law or constitutional principles were binding upon Parliament.[69] All that survives in Blackstone of the 17th-century conception of the sovereignty of the law is his passing obeisance to natural justice.

Despite all this, it would be a mistake to suppose that this obeisance, however out of harmony with the main thrust of the *Commentaries* it seems to us, was not meant or taken seriously. It was an essential component of the conventional wisdom of Blackstone's day, and Bentham himself took it seriously enough to make it the target of his first work, the *Fragment on Government*.[70] The statement of the legal supremacy of natural justice was certainly the passage in the *Commentaries* that the American colonists quoted most often.[71]

B. *Enlightenment Legal and Political Philosophy*

Blackstone's popularity can be attributed to his smooth transformation of the crabbed particularities of the English law into the

---

67. In every form of government, "there is and must be . . . a supreme, irresistible, absolute, uncontrolled authority, in which the *jura summi imperii*, or the rights of sovereignty, reside." *Id.* at *49. Under the English constitution, Parliament has the "supreme and absolute authority of the state," *id.* at *147, which is the "sovereign and uncontrolable authority in the making, confirming, enlarging, restraining, abrogating, repealing, reviving and expounding of laws. . . ." *Id.* at *160. Parliamentary power is not only "absolute," but "despotic." *Id.* Finally, (for the reader who might thus far have missed the point) Parliament "can change and create afresh even the constitution of the kingdom and of parliaments themselves. . . . It can . . . do everything that is not naturally impossible. . . . True it is, that what the parliament doth, no authority upon earth can undo." *Id.* at *161 (footnote omitted).

68. *Id.* at *161–62.

69. Trial by jury and habeas corpus are apparently within the power of Parliament to alter or abolish. *Id.* at *134–36.

70. Bentham himself, the arch-positivist, recognized the concept of fundamental law as probably ineradicable from legal and political discourse, however incoherent in theory and deplorable in practical result it might be. *See* Bentham, *A Fragment on Government, reprinted in* 1 THE WORKS OF JEREMY BENTHAM 260, 291 (1838).

71. *See* C. ROSSITER, SEEDTIME OF THE REPUBLIC 356, 367–68 (1953).

abstract and universal language demanded by the intellectual fashions of the Enlightenment. His theoretical bow to the ultimate supremacy of natural law was dictated by the same fashions—fashions which, in England, reflected the continuing prestige of the great figure of Locke. Locke's influence in America may have been even greater than in his own country. His theory of natural rights and revolution supplied the conceptual framework for the two great American documents of 1776—Thomas Paine's *Common Sense* and the Declaration of Independence.

Yet it is possible to overemphasize Locke's pre-eminence as ideological father of the American Revolution. Careful students of revolutionary literature have noted that Locke was cited by colonial spokesmen no more often than a number of other writers, including Coke and Blackstone.[72] These other writers fulfill needs that Lockean theory could not meet. The very elements that made Locke's theory so appropriate as the justification of the extra-legal break with England in 1776 at the same time lessened its usefulness in the disputes that led up to the break. These disputes were conducted in the language of law and constitutionalism. While Locke's theory elevated the traditional common law rights to life, liberty and estate into universal human rights, he did not mean these rights to operate as legal checks upon the supremacy of the legislature, but rather only as moral and political justifications for revolution.[73]

While Americans drew on the natural rights rhetoric of Locke and Blackstone, they found the best contemporary support for their own more traditional constitutional views in those curious products of the Age of Reason, the systematic treatises on the law of nature and nations. Except for Grotius, the authors of these public law treatises are little known and almost never read today, but in the 18th and early 19th centuries, the works of Pufendorf, Burlamaqui, Vattel and Rutherforth had prestige and influence, and helped shape the constitutional ideas of the American colonists.

The contribution of these public law theorists was twofold. First, like Locke and Blackstone, they stressed the importance of natural law and natural rights. Unlike Locke, however—and more seriously

72. C. Mullett, Fundamental Law and the American Revolution 78 (1933); C. Rossiter, *supra* note 71, at 357–58.

73. Locke speaks of intrinsic limitations on legislative authority, J. Locke, Second Treatise of Government 67–73 (J. Gough ed. 1956) (1st ed. London 1689), but Locke's language suggests that he regarded the limitations as moral and political only. *See generally* W. Kendall, John Locke and the Doctrine of Majority Rule (1965).

than Blackstone—they claimed *legally binding* force for the law of nature. They insisted that legislative power could not lawfully infringe the first principles of morality and politics. In this respect, they revitalized the natural law component of traditional English fundamental law theory.

Secondly, these Enlightenment treatise-writers reinforced and partly reformulated the idea of a fixed and binding constitution placing legal limitations upon legislative power in addition to those imposed by natural law. According to their theory of the origins of the state, individuals first united into a nation or a society, then established a government, and limited that government's lawful authority in a constitution. Just as the lawful powers of the nation itself were confined by natural law, so the powers of the government—the nation's agent—were legally limited by the constitution.

Pufendorf's *On the Law of Nature and Nations*, first published in 1672, spelled out this theory of governmental legitimacy in complex detail. First, according to Pufendorf, individuals in a state of nature agreed with each other to form a society, in which each would be bound by the decision of the majority concerning the kind of government to be established.[74] Only then did the group establish and decree the form of government. Finally, all the members of the society contracted with those whom they chose as their rulers, the rulers promising to "take care of the common security and safety" and the people promising to obey.[75] The people could grant the ruling king or assembly full sovereignty, or they could condition their own obligation of obedience on the government's compliance with the constitution. Pufendorf clearly distinguished between these constitutional restraints, established by the people of a particular society, and the requirements of natural law, which were equally binding on all governments. He made clear that acts by a ruler violating either natural law or the constitution were not merely wrongful or unjust but were void—without legal effect.[76]

Pufendorf's writings inspired John Wise's celebrated *A Vindication of the Government of New England Churches* in 1717, the first great American whig political tract,[77] which was republished shortly before the Revolution.[78] Wise's adoption of Pufendorf so early in the

74. S. PUFENDORF, ON THE LAW OF NATURE AND NATIONS 974-75 (Oldfather & Oldfather trans. 1964).

75. *Id.* at 975.

76. *Id.* at 1070.

77. C. ROSSITER, *supra* note 71, at 212.

78. A. MCLAUGHLIN, FOUNDATIONS OF AMERICAN CONSTITUTIONALISM 72-73 (1932).

18th Century demonstrates that the ultimately revolutionary fusion of traditional English ideas of fundamental law and more theoretical Enlightenment concepts of constitutionalism had formed in the American mind long before 1763.

But of even more immediate influence than Pufendorf on Americans of the revolutionary generation were the later Swiss theorists, Burlamaqui and Vattel. Burlamaqui's *Principles of Natural and Politic Law* first appeared in French in 1747, and was translated into English in 1752.[79] Its success in America was immediate and long-lasting.[80] One student of the literature of the revolutionary period tells us that this now little-known theorist shares with Locke and Coke the distinction of being among the authors most cited by the colonial polemicists.[81]

Burlamaqui followed Pufendorf in concluding that the people, once organized by mutual compact, were free to delegate their sovereign power to either an absolute or a limited government.[82] He recommended the latter course, since "absolute power easily degenerates into despotism."[83] The limits on a "limited" sovereignty were "the fundamental laws of the state . . . which regulate the manner of governing, and by which the supreme authority is limited."[84] These fundamental laws were limitations additional to natural law; they were "more particular precautions, taken by the people, to oblige sovereigns more strongly to employ their authority, agreeably to the general rule of the public good."[85] They had "the force of law," so whatever rulers did in violation of them should be "void and of no effect."[86]

Vattel's *Law of Nations*, published in 1758 and translated into English in 1759, was largely concerned with international law,[87] but

---

79. R. HARVEY, JEAN JACQUES BURLAMAQUI 188–89 (1937).

80. For a detailed discussion of the dissemination and influence of Burlamaqui's work in America, see *id.* at 79-176. Blackstone's passages on political theory were virtually copied from Burlamaqui. *See* E. Barker, *Blackstone on the British Constitution*, in *Essays on Government* 136 (1945).

81. C. MULLETT, *supra* note 72, at 78. Rossiter, who like Mullett has exhaustively canvassed the American political literature of the Revolutionary Era, ranks Burlamaqui, Pufendorf, Vattel, and Montesquieu as the Continental philosophers most often cited by the Americans. C. ROSSITER, *supra* note 71, at 359.

82. 2 J. BURLAMAQUI, THE PRINCIPLES OF NATURAL AND POLITIC LAW 45 (5th ed. T. Nugent trans. 1807).

83. *Id.*

84. *Id.* at 46.

85. *Id.* at 47.

86. *Id.*

87. E. VATTEL, THE LAW OF NATIONS at lvi, lvii (Fenwick trans. 1916).

its short introduction on the internal constitution of the state provided American spokesmen with a much quoted passage on the limited nature of legislative power. Vattel wrote that the nation could grant its legislative power to a prince, an assembly, or both conjointly,

> and they are thereby empowered to make new laws and to repeal old ones. The question arises whether their power extends to the fundamental laws, whether they can change the constitution of the State. The principles we have laid down lead us to decide definitely that the authority of these legislators does not go that far . . . . In a word, it is from the constitution that the legislators derive their power; how, then, could they change it without destroying the source of their authority?[88]

The English counterpart of Burlamaqui and Vattel was Rutherforth, whose *Institutes of Natural Law* appeared in 1750.[89] Like the continental writers, Rutherforth viewed the original sovereign power as held by the "whole collective body" of the nation. This body established a "civil constitution," which delegated power to a legislative and executive authority.[90] The "fundamental laws" of the constitution established the power of the legislative and were understood "not to be alterable by its authority."[91] Legislative authority was limited by "the laws of nature and God" as well as by the constitution, and when the government transgressed either of these limitations, "the people [were] under no obligation to obey or submit."[92]

In a strikingly English twist, Rutherforth combined standard Enlightenment theory with traditional notions of *customary* fundamental law. He noted that the content of a nation's constitution was a question of fact, to be determined by considering the history and present customs of the people.[93] Law, including fundamental law, did not arise solely from legislation. Rather, usage that "has obtained in any civil society for time immemorial . . . may be presumed to have obtained with its consent . . . . But whatever is

88. *Id.* at 19. This passage was a favorite of the Americans. *See* B. BAILYN, *supra* note 20, at 29; C. MULLETT, *supra* note 72, at 30-32.

89. T. RUTHERFORTH, INSTITUTES OF NATURAL LAW (2d American ed. 1832). Rutherforth's work was based on a course of lectures delivered at Cambridge University in 1750. C. MULLETT, *supra* note 72, at 64. Rutherforth was not nearly so often cited in Revolutionary America as Pufendorf, Burlamaqui or Vattel, but he was known. *See id.*; THE LAW PRACTICE OF ALEXANDER HAMILTON, *supra* note 40, at 864.

90. T. RUTHERFORTH, *supra* note 89, at 285.

91. *Id.* at 399.

92. *Id.* at 453–54.

93. *Id.* at 296.

consented to by a civil society, becomes a law of such society . . . ."[94] This legally binding unwritten constitution, based upon consent as revealed by usage, was precisely the English constitution that the American colonists were to invoke in the controversies of the 1760's and 1770's.

The public law theorists of the Enlightenment thus reaffirmed the traditional English idea of binding fundamental law that included but was not limited to the requirements of natural law, while blending these old ideas with 18th-century political theory. Enlightenment fashion required that social and governmental institutions be justified by imaginative reconstruction from a state of nature through one or more actual or hypothetical contracts or agreements. Recasting fundamental law in the language of social contract lent new support to the idea of fundamental law at a time when it was in decline in England, and when its original medieval theological foundations were eroding. Traditional fundamental law theory was thus refurbished and reformulated in an up-to-date vocabulary, and so became an effective ideological weapon in the coffee-houses, salons and public meeting places of the Age of Reason.

Further, the public law theorists helped lay a theoretical foundation for constitutional developments yet to come. They saw a constitution as a body of law authorized by the agreement or promulgation of a people acting together. In this they anticipated, and helped shape, the idea that a nation or society, in a kind of prepolitical act of legislation, could frame and adopt its own fundamental law through an extraordinary assembly of the whole people. This idea was to erupt into practice in the new American states immediately after independence was declared in 1776, and was to achieve practical embodiment in that American innovation, the constitutional convention.

But what is important (and difficult) for us to remember is that this idea of an enacted constitution was relatively novel in 1760, while the idea of an ancient unwritten constitution compounded of custom and reason was comfortable and familiar in the English-speaking world. It was still this traditional idea that sprang to the minds of Americans when they read in Burlamaqui or Vattel of "constitutions" and "fundamental laws," and it was this traditional idea which Rutherforth explicitly invoked.

Finally, while the public law treatise-writers nowhere explicitly

94. *Id.* at 396.

argued for judicial review, their doctrines did indirectly suggest that the enactments of a supreme legislative body might be subject to judicial scrutiny for their consistency with fundamental law. Unlike Locke, the treatise-writers spoke of fundamental law in the language of lawyers. The constitution "had the force of law"; legislators "lacked power" to pass statutes contrary to the constitution; such enactments were "void," without legal effect. Language of this sort, combined with the general notion that it was the business of courts to enforce the law and the 17th-century English tradition of judicial enforcement of fundamental law, naturally suggested to Americans the full-fledged conception of judicial avoidance of unconstitutional legislation.

III. American Revolutionary Constitutionalism

The phase of the colonists' struggle with England that culminated in independence in 1776 was organized around a theoretical position that combined the English tradition of fundamental law and the doctrines of Enlightenment public law theory. That position was concisely stated by James Otis at the outset of the struggle, in 1764, in a passage for which he cited two authorities, Coke in *Dr. Bonham's Case* and Vattel:

> 'Tis hoped it will not be considered as a new doctrine that even the authority of the Parliament of Great Britain is circumscribed by certain bounds which if exceeded their acts become those of mere power without right, and consequently void. The judges of England have declared in favor of these sentiments when they expressly declare that acts of Parliament against natural equity are void. That acts against the fundamental principles of the British constitution are void.[95]

A. *The Colonial Heritage*

The Cokean aspect of Otis' argument was well-rooted in the prerevolutionary colonial past. Although during the colonial period Americans had not been much given to debate over issues of constitutional theory, their few pronouncements reflected their intellectual debt to 17th-century England, and its ideas of fundamental law. Thus, for example, when the dissident freemen of Massachusetts Bay Colony attacked the sovereignty of the governing magistrates, they did so in the name of the traditional legal rights of

---

95. Otis, *The Rights of the British Colonies Asserted and Proved*, in 1 PAMPHLETS OF THE AMERICAN REVOLUTION 409, 476 (B. Bailyn ed. 1965) (emphasis omitted) [hereinafter cited as PAMPHLETS].

Englishmen.[96] And when in the case of *Giddings v. Browne*[97] a Massachusetts court invalidated a town meeting's appropriation of public money for a minister's house as an impermissible confiscation of taxpayers' property it held that the appropriation was "against the fundamental law and therefore void."[98] Colonial charters spoke the language of fundamental law, guaranteeing to the colonists the rights of Englishmen,[99] and colonial spokesmen argued that these legal rights were equally guaranteed by unwritten law "without any declaration of grant."[100] Particularly during the home government's assertion of increased control over the colonies in the late 1600's, the colonists invoked the fundamental legal rights of Englishmen to challenge the policies of proprietors and royal governors.[101]

As Parliament achieved practical supremacy in 18th-century England, new constitutional theory gave it unlimited legal sovereignty. According to the new theory, England's constitution was no more than the set of laws, institutions and traditional principles for governing the nation and was legally subject to alteration by Parliament at any time.[102] This theory was geared to practical polit-

---

96. G. HASKINS, LAW AND AUTHORITY IN EARLY MASSACHUSETTS 36, 56–57 (1960).

97. The judge's opinion is reproduced in 2 HUTCHINSON PAPERS 1–25 (reprinted Albany, N.Y., 1865) (1st ed. Boston 1769).

98. 2 HUTCHINSON PAPERS at 5. The judge deciding the case cited Finch's *Law, supra* note 40, at 74, for the proposition that positive laws in violation of natural law "doe lose their force and are noe lawes at all." 2 HUTCHINSON PAPERS at 5.

99. For example, the charter of Massachusetts Bay Colony guaranteed the colonists "all liberties and immunities of free and natural subjects . . . as yf they and everie of them were borne within the realme of England." 3 F. THORPE, THE FEDERAL AND STATE CONSTITUTIONS, COLONIAL CHARTERS AND OTHER ORGANIC LAWS 1857 (1909). For similar provisions in early colonial charters, see 1 *id.* at 533 (Connecticut); 7 *id.* at 3788 (Virginia); 6 *id.* at 3220 (Rhode Island); 3 *id.* at 1681 (Maryland); 5 *id.* at 2747 (Carolina); 2 *id.* at 773 (Georgia).

100. *See* D. LOVEJOY, THE GLORIOUS REVOLUTION IN AMERICA 39 (1974).

101. C. ANDREWS, THE COLONIAL BACKGROUND OF THE AMERICAN REVOLUTION 53–54 (1931). Andrews tends to downplay these early protests, in line with his general view that the constitutional protests of the 1760's and 1770's were innovations, *see, e.g., id.* at 55–56, 62–63. *But see* D. LOVEJOY, *supra* note 100, at 376–78. In his comprehensive study of American protest at the time of the Revolution of 1688, Lovejoy finds the appeal by Americans to rights based on a conception of legal equality with Englishmen within the realm pervasive during the period.

102. This is the standard English conception of the "flexible" constitution, consisting not of laws but "conventions." *See* 1 J. BRYCE, STUDIES IN HISTORY AND JURISPRUDENCE 124–215 (1901); A. DICEY, THE LAW OF THE CONSTITUTION 417–74 (10th ed. 1959). According to this conception, "things might be legal and yet unconstitutional." The Wensleydale Peerage, 5 House of Lords Cases 958, 969 (1856). For the 18th century American expressions of this conception, see L. LEDER, LIBERTY AND AUTHORITY 88–89, 91 (1976). Also relevant is John Adams' statement in 1773: "If the king should suffer no parliament to sit for twelve years, by reason of continual prorogations, this would be an unconstitutional exercise of prerogative. If the commons should grant no supplies for twelve years, this would be an unconstitutional

ical reality, but was slow to gain full intellectual force and supplant the traditional theory of fundamental law as a limitation on legislative authority. Even in England such leading statesmen as Camden and Chatham continued to rely on the older theory as late as the 1760's.[103]

The theory of parliamentary sovereignty was transmitted to the American colonies,[104] but it less accurately mirrored the realities of colonial government than of English government. It thus made less headway against traditional notions of fundamental law in America than in England. In the colonies, actual governing power was divided; governors and colonial legislatures contested for local power with the theoretically supreme English Parliament exercising only an incomplete and sporadic control that, in Bernard Bailyn's words, "touched only the outer fringes of colonial life."[105] The Americans were therefore generally unpersuaded by the new theory of the flexible constitution, whose only fixed doctrine was that Parliament was legally free to do as it liked. Before the revolutionary struggle began in the 1760's, American discussions of the issues of sovereignty and fundamental law were less frequent and intense than they were to become during the revolutionary period. But in those discussions, the traditional view that legislative authority was legally confined by fundamental law continued to predominate over the new notion of parliamentary supremacy.[106]

---

exertion of their privilege. Yet the king has power *legally* to do one, and the commons to do the other." Letter from John Adams to Printer of Boston Gazette (Feb. 8, 1773), *reprinted in* 3 THE WORKS OF JOHN ADAMS 556 (C. Adams ed. 1851) (emphasis added).

103. *See* notes 62–63 *supra* and accompanying text.

104. *But see* G. SABINE, A HISTORY OF POLITICAL THEORY 490 (3d ed. 1963): "After the Restoration in 1660 the exchange of political ideas between England and America was much restricted, in comparison with what it had been earlier. In consequence the newer idea of parliamentary sovereignty never spread among the English in America . . . ." Sabine's curious notion that some fortuitous Atlantic quarantine prevented the transmission of new constitutional ideas cannot be sustained. *See* L. LEDER, *supra* note 102.

105. B. BAILYN, *supra* note 20, at 203. Elsewhere Bailyn points out additional factors making it less likely that colonial Americans would see their own governments as centering around a single "sovereign" organ—the absence of a strong executive and of a recognized leadership class, with consequent party strife and persistent legalistic dispute about the conflicting authority of different organs of government. B. BAILYN, THE ORIGINS OF AMERICAN POLITICS 59–105 (1967).

106. See L. LEDER, *supra* note 102, at 80–94, for a collection of prerevolutionary American contributions to the ongoing debate between the opposed conceptions of parliamentary sovereignty on the one hand, and the fixed constitution or binding fundamental law on the other. Leder's findings seriously undermine Bernard Bailyn's view that at the outset of the revolutionary period, American constitutional thinking was so dominated by the idea of parliamentary supremacy that the colonists' first arguments against Parliament's new assertions of power were "necessarily, fumbling and unsure efforts, for there were no arguments—

Otis' statement of the American position in 1764 suggests not only that legislative authority should be subject to theoretical legal restraints, but also that those restraints should be enforceable in court. For the colonists, judicial supervision of legislative activity was a familiar concept. For one thing, the laws of the colonial legislatures were subject to a kind of judicial review before the Privy Council in England, which could invalidate measures in conflict with English law.[107] Further, prerevolutionary Americans still thought of courts as responsible for deciding questions of the constitutional allocation of power between executive and legislature, as the English courts had done in the *Ship-money Case* and other great cases of the Stuart era.[108] Joseph Galloway illustrated the persistence of this latter view in his 1759 attack on the English disallowance of a Pennsylvania statute that granted judges tenure during good behavior. Galloway argued that judicial independence was essential to the judicial task of maintaining the ultimate distribution of power between "the sovereign's prerogative and the people's liberties" in accordance with the "fundamental laws and rules of the constitution."[109]

The tradition of a judicially enforceable higher law of "common right and reason"—the tradition of *Dr. Bonham's Case*—had been implemented during the early colonial period in *Giddings v. Browne*.[110] *Dr. Bonham's Case* itself was familiar to American lawyers of the late colonial period through the most up-to-date English law books, which reasserted Coke's doctrine as sound authority.[111]

The vitality of Coke's version of judicial review tradition in America on the eve of the revolutionary struggle is illustrated by

---

there was no vocabulary—to resort to: the ideas, the terminology had to be invented." B. BAILYN, *supra* note 20, at 204–05. Quite the contrary, the theory of fundamental law confining parliamentary authority was still alive, though in decline, even in England, *see* notes 62–65 *supra* and accompanying text, and, for reasons which Bailyn himself has well stated, was much more vigorous in the colonies than in the mother country. *See* note 105 *supra*.

107. J. SMITH, APPEALS TO THE PRIVY COUNCIL FROM THE AMERICAN PLANTATIONS (1950) (chronicling workings of this appellate jurisdiction). The influence of Privy Council jurisdiction on judicial review in America is assessed in J. GOEBEL, HISTORY OF THE SUPREME COURT OF THE UNITED STATES: ANTECEDENTS AND BEGINNINGS TO 1801, at 95 (1971).

108. *See* notes 46-51 *supra* and accompanying text.

109. *A Letter to the People of Pennsylvania*, in 1 PAMPHLETS, *supra* note 95, at 257.

110. The 1657 opinion is reproduced in 2 HUTCHINSON PAPERS 1–25 (reprinted Albany, N.Y., 1865) (1st ed. Boston 1769).

111. *See* 19 C. VINER, ABRIDGMENTS 513 (2d ed. Aldershot 1793). Viner's *Abridgments*, which first appeared in 1742–1753 was the leading law encyclopedia of the time. It was from Viner that James Otis was to take his citation of Coke in the Writs of Assistance Case. John Adams' notes of Otis' argument are reprinted in 2 THE WORKS OF JOHN ADAMS 521 (C. Adams ed. 1850).

James Otis' own legendary attack in 1761 on the writs of assistance. Opposing issuance of the writs, which gave royal customs officials sweeping powers to search for smuggled contraband, Otis argued to a Massachusetts court that such powers violated "the fundamental principles of Law," under which a man "is as secure in his House, as a Prince in his Castle."[112] Even if the writs had been authorized by act of Parliament, the court should not have issued them, because:

> As to Acts of Parliament, an Act against the Constitution is void: an Act against natural Equity is void: and if an Act of Parliament should be made, in the very Words of this Petition, it would be void. The Executive Courts must pass such Acts into disuse.[113]

Of Otis' argument, the aged and nostalgic John Adams was to say nearly 60 years later: "Every man of a crowded audience appeared to me to go away, as I did, ready to take arms against writs of assistance . . . . Then and there the child Independence was born."[114] In sober fact, the writs were eventually issued and enforced as before, and there is no contemporary evidence that Otis' words had any immediate effect outside the courtroom.[115] But the idea he articulated—the idea that according to English law itself, Parliament's authority was legally limited by an unwritten constitution incorporating natural law—was to animate the struggle for independence. The corollary notion that fundamental law could be argued *to a court* as ground for disregarding an act of the supreme legislature was itself to play an appreciable, if lesser, role in the Revolution. John Adams' romanticized recollection has more than anecdotal significance; it shows that one of the central figures in the founding of the nation could look back and find in such an argument the first articulation of the essential spirit of the Revolution.

B. *Constitutional Protest Against the Sugar Act*

The revolutionary struggle broke out in 1764, when the British government began to implement its new policy of taxing the American colonies to reduce the debts from the Seven Years' War. The first step was the Sugar Act, which raised the duty payable by Americans on imported molasses. At the same time, the administration announced its intention to introduce a stamp tax on the colonies the following year.

---

112. 2 THE WORKS OF JOHN ADAMS 521.

113. *Id.* at 522. Otis cited *Dr. Bonham's Case* for this proposition.

114. Letter from John Adams to William Tudor (Mar. 29, 1817), *reprinted in* 10 THE WORKS OF JOHN ADAMS 247–48 (C. Adams ed. 1856).

115. B. KNOLLENBERG, ORIGINS OF THE AMERICAN REVOLUTION 1759–1766, at 69 (1960).

Otis' statement of 1764 was a response to these actions by the British government.[116] That statement was only part of an unprecedented outbreak of articulate American protest against the new taxes. Some of the protest was expressed in terms of policy; the taxation policy was said to be harsh, uneconomic, unfair, and destructive of imperial harmony.[117] But as will be shown below, the greater part of the opposition sounded the note struck by Otis. The new taxes were said to violate fundamental law, and to be unconstitutional and void, as taxation without representation. According to prevailing English doctrine, taxation of the subject required consent—at least in the fictional sense that it required approval by a body in which the subject was represented.[118] Since Americans were not represented in Parliament, they insisted that parliamentary taxation violated their natural and constitutional property rights.[119]

An issue subsidiary to taxation, but also of constitutional status, was the colonists' insistence on a right to jury trial. Violations of the Sugar Act and the Stamp Act were subject to prosecution in the Vice-Admiralty courts, where trial was before a judge alone; further, a Vice-Admiralty court in Halifax, Nova Scotia, was given jurisdiction over offenses in all the American colonies, so that trials could be held entirely free from the check of local opinion. According to the entirely mythical version of history which Coke and other founders of English Whiggery constructed, and to which colonial spokesmen firmly adhered, Englishmen had from immemorial antiquity enjoyed the right to be punished only upon the verdict of a jury of their peers.[120] Smuggling offenses in England had long been subject to trial by jury in the common law courts. Accordingly, colonial spokesmen considered the admiralty jurisdiction an unconstitutional violation of the Englishman's right to jury trial.[121]

---

116. *See* Otis, *supra* note 95.

117. *See, e.g.*, Dickinson, *The Late Regulations Respecting the British Colonies*, in 1 PAMPHLETS, *supra* note 95, at 669–91.

118. This ancient doctrine, which had been invoked in Bate's Case, 145 Eng. Rep. 267 (Ex. 1606), and the Ship-money Case, 3 Howell's State Trials 825 (1637), was reflected in the English Petition of Right, 3 Carl. 1, c. 1 (1627), and the Bill of Rights, 1 W. & M., 2d Sess., c.2 (1688). Crown spokesmen conceded the force of the principle, but argued that the new taxes complied with it on the ground that the colonists were "virtually represented" in Parliament.

119. *See* notes 125–28 *infra* and accompanying text.

120. On the supposed roots of trial by jury in Magna Carta, see F. THOMPSON, MAGNA CARTA 72–97, 185, 242 (1948).

121. *See* Lovejoy, *"Rights Imply Equality": The Case Against Admiralty Jurisdiction in America, 1764–1766*, in THE REINTERPRETATION OF THE AMERICAN REVOLUTION 181–206 (J. Greene ed. 1968).

The claim of constitutional protection for jury trial has particular theoretical interest, since it shows that the colonists viewed the unwritten fundamental law limiting Parliament's power as including matters of custom independent of natural law. As McIlwain has said, "It would be difficult indeed . . . to insist that so entirely English a thing as trial by jury was founded on the 'immutable law of nature.'"[122] Indeed, while in the literature of protest the basis for the principle of "no taxation without representation" was founded in the natural right of property, arguments for the right of jury trial were generally based upon its antiquity alone.[123] As John Dickinson was later to put it: "It was not Reason that discovered or ever could have discovered the odd and in the eye of those who are governed by reason, the absurd mode of trial by Jury. Accidents probably produced these discoveries and experience has given a sanction to them."[124]

Among the protests made against the new British policies in 1764 before the Stamp Act was actually passed, the best known at the time and the most celebrated and controversial since was Otis' pamphlet, *The Rights of the British Colonies Asserted and Proved*.[125] Otis flatly condemned taxation without representation as a violation of "the law of God and nature," "the common law"[126] and property rights that "no man or body of men, not excepting the Parliament . . . consistently with . . . the constitution can take away."[127] And echoing his argument in the *Writs of Assistance Case*, he asserted that courts could declare "void" acts that violated natural equity.[128]

Yet in the same pamphlet, Otis urged that Americans had a duty to obey the unconstitutional act if Parliament insisted on it:

> [T]he power of Parliament is uncontrollable but by themselves, and we must obey. . . . There would be an end of all government

---

122. C. McIlwain, The American Revolution: A Constitutional Interpretation 163 (1923).

123. C. Rossiter, *supra* note 71, at 388–91.

124. 2 M. Farrand, Records of the Federal Convention 278 (1911). *See also* 1 Annals of Cong. 437 (Madison ed. 1789). Dickinson's argument was echoed as recently as a decade ago by the United States Supreme Court when it ruled that the due process clause of the 14th amendment required jury trial in criminal cases. Duncan v. Louisiana, 391 U.S. 145 (1968). The Court held that even though jury trial is not essential to a scheme of civilized criminal justice, it is fundamental to "the common law system that has been developing contemporaneously in England and in this country" and is "necessary to an Anglo-American regime of ordered liberty." *Id.* at 149 n.19.

125. Otis, *supra* note 95, at 409.

126. *Id.* at 444.

127. *Id.*

128. *Id.* at 449, 455.

> if one or a number of subjects . . . should take upon them so far to judge of the justice of an act of Parliament as to refuse obedience to it. . . . Therefore, let the Parliament lay what burdens they please on us, we must, *it is our duty* to submit and patiently bear them till they will be pleased to relieve us.[129]

The juxtaposition of Otis' claim that the taxes were void with his assertion of a duty of compliance has created confusion about the American constitutional position at the outset of the taxation controversy. Charles Mullett finds Otis self-contradictory,[130] while Bernard Bailyn finds him consistent but anachronistic. In Bailyn's view, Otis' mind was still rooted in the Middle Ages—he saw Parliament as still essentially a judicial body, the highest court in the land, adjudicating under a static body of unwritten law rather than exercising legislative functions. According to Bailyn's version of Otis' theory, an unconstitutional act of Parliament was thus like an erroneous decision of a highest court which had to be accepted as final until the court (or Parliament) could be persuaded to see the error of its ways.[131]

In my view, Otis' position was neither inconsistent nor anachronistic. To take the charge of inconsistency first, there is no logical contradiction between the proposition that Parliament is legally subject to fundamental law, and the proposition that it nevertheless has the last word in determining the meaning of that law. Binding constitutions need not be judicially enforceable; a legislature as well as a court can have the final authority to construe a constitution, written or unwritten.[132] As for Bailyn's charge of anachronism there was no suggestion in Otis' pamphlet that Parliament lacked genuinely legislative powers. Quite the contrary, it was "the supreme legislative,"[133] with authority to determine the meaning of the fundamental law that defined its own powers. The notion of a legislature bound by a constitution but not subject to judicial review is scarcely medieval. It is a notion that reflects distrust of judicial oligarchy and a most modern respect for politically responsible legislative institutions.

---

129. *Id.* at 448 (emphasis added).

130. C. MULLETT, *supra* note 82, at 83.

131. B. BAILYN, *supra* note 20, at 176–81, 205–09; 1 PAMPHLETS, *supra* note 95, at 412–17. Bailyn argues that Otis' theory illustrates the "fumbling" and "unsure" quality of colonial constitutional argument early in the revolutionary struggle, which in his view is linked to the colonists' supposed inability to escape the imprisoning vocabulary of parliamentary sovereignty. *See* note 106 *supra*.

132. *See* note 24 *supra*.

133. Otis, *supra* note 95, at 455.

If Otis thought of Parliament as ultimately supreme in its construction of the constitution, in what sense did he think courts could declare acts of Parliament void? One possible answer is suggested by his description of the relation between courts and Parliament: "The supreme legislative and the supreme executive are a perpetual check and balance to each other. If the supreme executive errs it is informed by the supreme legislative in Parliament. If the supreme legislative errs it is informed by the supreme executive in the King's courts of law."[134] Otis may have seen the courts as possessing an initial power to invalidate unconstitutional statutes, while believing that if Parliament persisted in supporting a statute declared unconstitutional, it should have the last word.

In any event, Otis' remarks on parliamentary supremacy were made, not in the context of discussion of judicial review, but as a counsel against popular disobedience to the unconstitutional taxes. That tactical position, though it was to appear conservative in later years, was quite general among American spokesmen in 1764. The Stamp Act had not yet been enacted, and the colonists still hoped to persuade Parliament against its enactment. Conspicuous colonial leaders were not yet ready to advocate publicly more drastic measures.[135] But Otis' cautious advice on the remedy to be applied against Parliament's unlawful assertion of power was in no way inconsistent with his unequivocal conclusion that the new taxes *were* unlawful.

Other American spokesmen prominent in the brief period preceding enactment of the Stamp Act were more equivocal than Otis on the question of Parliament's *legal* power to tax the colonists. Connecticut Governor Thomas Fitch, for example, asserted that a fundamental "right" of self-taxation was "the chief excellency of the British Constitution," but nowhere denied Parliament the legal authority to violate that "right".[136] According to Fitch, it was "to be presumed" that the "wise and vigilant" Parliament would not permit "such an essential right" to be infringed.[137] With similar ambiguity, Otis' Massachusetts colleague, Oxenbridge Thacher, spoke of the

134. *Id.*

135. None of the other well-known American protests against the Sugar Act advocated resistance or disobedience. *See* notes 146–52 *infra* and accompanying text. And even after enactment of the Stamp Act, cautious American spokesmen continued to refrain from calls for resistance. *See* note 149 *infra*.

136. Fitch, *Reasons Why the British Colonies in America Should Not Be Charged with Internal Taxes*, in 2 PAMPHLETS, *supra* note 95, at 379, 386.

137. *Id.* at 387.

"essential British right" of self-taxation, and of the "darling privilege" of trial by jury, guaranteed by the "common law," that "birthright of every subject".[138] Those words, too, fall short of an unequivocal claim that the taxes or the Vice-Admiralty courts were illegal. Stephen Hopkins, Governor of Rhode Island, came closer to outright assertion that the proposed stamp tax was legally invalid: "If the British House of Commons are rightfully possessed of a power to tax the colonies in America, this power must be vested in them by the British constitution . . . ."[139] Hopkins was unable to see that this power had been granted, and he spoke of self-taxation as an "inherent, indefeasible right," but even he did not unequivocally assert it as a *legal* limitation on parliamentary power.[140]

As a means of official protest against the proposed Stamp Act, a number of colonial assemblies framed petitions to the Crown and the houses of Parliament in 1764. Beyond attacking the Act as inexpedient and unjust, these petitions charged that the tax would violate the "rights" of the colonists and the "principles of the constitution." The New York petition, for example, spoke of the right of self-taxation as "the natural Right of Mankind," and a right of Englishmen.[141] The Virginia House of Burgesses stated that the proposed tax would be "inconsistent with the fundamental Principles of the Constitution,"[142] and expressed its confidence that the House of Lords "will not think any Reason sufficient to support such a Power in the British Parliament."[143]

The language of these petitions, like that of some of the protesting pamphlets, might be read as mere appeals to the colonists' moral or traditional rights and privileges, rather than as claims of legal restriction on Parliament's authority to tax. But the House of Commons itself clearly read these petitions as challenging its actual legal power to tax the colonies. During their debate on the Stamp Act, members of the House of Commons opened but did not read the American petitions, because, as a spokesman said, they were

138. Thacher, *The Sentiments of a British American*, in 1 PAMPHLETS, *supra* note 95, at 483, 491–92.

139. Hopkins, *The Rights of Colonies Examined*, in 1 PAMPHLETS, *supra* note 95, at 518.

140. *Id.* at 511.

141. New York Petition to the House of Commons (Oct. 18, 1764), *reprinted in* PROLOGUE TO REVOLUTION: SOURCES AND DOCUMENTS ON THE STAMP ACT CRISIS, 1764–1766, at 9–10 (E. Morgan ed. 1959) [hereinafter cited as PROLOGUE].

142. Virginia Petitions to the King and Parliament (Dec. 18, 1764), *reprinted in id.* at 17.

143. *Id.* at 15.

"positively and directly questioning the authority and jurisdiction of parliament over the properties of the people in the colonies."[144]

C. *The Attack on the Legality of the Stamp Act*

The actual passage of the Stamp Act in 1765 demonstrated to many colonists the ineffectiveness of petitions and constitutional arguments directed to Parliament. Much American protest took on a new and more vehement tone—but its underlying theory, that taxation without representation violated the unwritten fundamental law, remained unchanged.

Of the innumerable American polemics against the Stamp Act published after its enactment, none was more influential than the pamphlet by Daniel Dulany.[145] Dulany's arguments were chiefly directed against the constitutional justification for the Stamp Act offered by English spokesmen. Conceding the principle of no taxation without representation, the government spokesmen had argued that American colonists—like disenfranchised Englishmen—were "virtually" represented by the members of the House of Commons, each of whom was conceived of as representing *all* British subjects.[146] In the course of his widely echoed attack on this theory of virtual representation, Dulany described the principle of self-taxation as "an essential principle of the English constitution,"[147] a right derived from "the common law" and "enforced by the declaration of the Great Charter and the Bill of Rights, neither the one nor the other introducing any new principle."[148] If the theory of virtual representation was fallacious, as he believed he had shown, "the principle of the Stamp Act must be given up as indefensible on the point of representation, and the validity of it rested upon the *power* which they who framed it have to carry it into execution."[149] He viewed it, in short, as an act of raw power without legal right.

144. Knox, *The Claim of the Colonies, reprinted in id.* at 97.

145. Dulany, *Considerations on the Propriety of Imposing Taxes in the British Colonies*, in 1 PAMPHLETS, *supra* note 95, at 610. On the influence of Dulany's pamphlet, see E. & H. MORGAN, THE STAMP ACT CRISIS 71–87 (1953).

146. *See, e.g.*, Whately, *The Regulations lately Made concerning the Colonies and the Taxes Imposed upon Them, reprinted in* PROLOGUE, *supra* note 141, at 20–21.

147. Dulany, *Considerations on the Propriety of Imposing Taxes in the British Colonies*, in 1 PAMPHLETS, *supra* note 95, at 612.

148. *Id.* at 635.

149. *Id.* at 616. Dulany also noted "the opinion of a great lawyer" that "an act of Parliament may be void" and that "no legislative authority" could deprive freemen of their legal rights. *Id.* at 609. But later he echoed Otis' reluctance to urge resistance to the illegal

The view that the Stamp Act was unconstitutional (in the full sense of "illegal") provided the organizing principle for a new and vigorous movement of popular protest against the tax. Mobs forced stamp collectors from office and destroyed stamped paper, yet their actions were conceived as justified resistance to an illegal exercise of power, not as revolutionary attack on English rule. Thus, sober and law-abiding anti-stamp leaders like John Adams endorsed the mob violence in Boston on August 14, 1765, violence that forced the resignation of stamp collector Andrew Eliot. Yet, two weeks later, those same leaders firmly condemned the mob for wrecking the house of Lieutenant-Governor Thomas Hutchinson: they could not justify this action as legal resistance to the Stamp Act itself, but viewed it as simply an expression of popular hatred against a visible symbol of crown authority.[150]

The theme of the illegality of the Stamp Act emerged as well in the resolutions the colonial assemblies adopted as their official response to the new taxes. The first and most influential of these, the June 1765 resolves of the Virginia House of Burgesses, was in its finally adopted form a relatively mild protest that avoided explicit assertion of the legal invalidity of the tax, and merely described self-taxation as a traditional English right.[151] But a false version of the resolves, published in colonial newspapers and represented as authentic, included three provisions that had actually been voted down by a majority of the Burgesses as too radical.[152] The first of these additional resolves articulated the full theory of the legally binding fundamental law, already familiar from Otis' pamphlet, concluding that the stamp taxes were "illegal, unconstitutional and unjust."[153] The two other "false" resolves went far beyond Otis in drawing practical consequences from the assertion of illegality. They stated that the colonists were "not bound to yield Obedience" to the uncon-

taxes: "[W]ho would rely upon the authority of opinions . . . for his protection against the penalties of *any* positive law? . . . But though it might be dangerous to declare against the authority of Parliament, we are not bound to acknowledge its inerrability . . . ." *Id.*

150. Reid, *In a Defensive Rage: The Uses of the Mob, the Justification of the Law, and the Coming of the American Revolution*, 49 N.Y.U. L. REV. 1043, 1047 (1974). Professor Reid argues that American Whigs saw the anti-stamp riots as actual legal remedies for the illegal stamp taxes. For an account that places riotous resistance to unlawful official action within the general context of 18th-century opposition theory, see P. MAIER, FROM RESISTANCE TO REVOLUTION 27–50 (1972).

151. Virginia Resolutions, *reprinted in* PROLOGUE, *supra* note 141, at 47–48.

152. E. & H. MORGAN, *supra* note 145, at 120–32.

153. Virginia Resolutions (as printed in The Newport Mercury, June 24, 1765), *reprinted in* PROLOGUE, *supra* note 141, at 49.

stitutional tax, and went on to denounce any person who supported the legal authority of Parliament to tax the colonies as "an Enemy to this his Majesty's Colony."[154] This striking call to resistance, justified by a claim of illegality and bearing the imprimatur of the prestigious Virginia House of Burgesses, infused what the Massachusetts Tory Thomas Hutchinson called "[a] new spirit" of radicalism into the anti-stamp tax movement.[155]

Subsequent official protests of the other colonial assemblies fell into a fairly consistent doctrinal pattern. They were stronger than the actual Virginia resolves, in that they repeated the claim that the Stamp Act was "unconstitutional."[156] On the other hand, except for the Rhode Island resolves, they were weaker than the false Virginia resolves in that they did not make explicit that unconstitutionality meant legal invalidity. And none of them proclaimed the right of the people to disobey, much less condemned supporters of British taxing power as enemies of the people.

Similar moderation and caution marked the resolves of the first great united assembly of the colonies, the Stamp Act Congress, which met in October of 1765. Although the assembled delegates declared that "no Taxes ever have been, or can be Constitutionally imposed on [the colonies], but by their respective Legislature,"[157] they voiced no explicit claim that the Stamp Act was invalid or illegal, nor did they call for resistance. The structure of the Congress' petition to the House of Commons does implicitly show, however, that the delegates conceived their constitutional claims as legal in nature. After forcefully urging those claims, the petition went on to state as an alternative position that even if "in Law" the British claims were correct, nevertheless there were other good reasons based upon "[i]nconvenience, . . . true Policy, and . . . the Spirit of the *British* Constitution" for repealing the Stamp Act.[158]

The restrained language used by the Stamp Act Congress and the colonial assemblies—apart from the false Virginia Resolves—

154. *Id.*

155. Hutchinson recalled that before the circulation of the Virginia Resolves, the idea that parliamentary taxation was wholly illegal was common among the Whig vanguard, but not yet dominant among the people. Letter from Thomas Hutchinson to Thomas Pownall (Mar. 8, 1766), *reprinted in id.* at 124.

156. Rhode Island Resolves (Sept. 1765), *reprinted in id.* at 51; Pennsylvania Resolves (Sept. 21, 1765), *reprinted in id.* at 51–52; Maryland Resolves (Sept. 28, 1765), *reprinted in id.* at 53; Connecticut Resolves (Oct. 25, 1765), *reprinted in id.* at 55; New Jersey Resolves (Nov. 30, 1765), *reprinted in id.* at 60; New York Resolves (Dec. 18, 1765), *reprinted in id.* at 61.

157. Declarations of the Stamp Act Congress, *reprinted in id.* at 63.

158. Petition to the House of Commons, *reprinted in id.* at 67 (emphasis added).

does not fully capture the spirit of the extraordinarily effective popular movement that eventually resulted in the effective nullification of the Stamp Act. For the expression of that spirit, one must look to the words of the Sons of Liberty, the unofficial bodies which organized and directed the Anti-Stamp riots and the boycott against British goods.

The resolutions adopted at meetings of the Sons of Liberty clearly asserted the illegality of the Stamp Act, and were replete with calls to resistance and threats against colonists who complied with the Act. Thus the Sons of Liberty of Wallingford, Connecticut resolved to oppose the "unconstitutional" act "to the last extremity, even to take the field."[159] The New York Sons of Liberty resolved that those complying with the Act would "incur the highest Resentment of this Society, and be branded with everlasting Infamy."[160] The New Brunswick Sons would "resist . . . all *illegal* attempts to deprive us of our indubitable rights".[161] The resolves of New London, Connecticut, expressed in concise form the fundamental law theory of Burlamaqui and Vattel: "[T]he Boundaries set by the People in all Constitutions, are the only Limits within which any Officer can lawfully exercise authority."[162] When that authority was exceeded, as with the Stamp Act, "the People have a Right to reassume" governmental authority.[163] Another Sons of Liberty statement describes the Stamp Act as "a certain pamphlet" which "has appeared in America in the form of an act of parliament," but which can "never [be] legally . . . introduced" because of its violation of "the British constitution."[164]

As Otis' pamphlet had shown, denunciation of the English taxes as illegal and void did not necessarily entail a call for resistance or disobedience.[165] But American spokesmen who urged the most forceful measures against the taxes were also likely to be most explicit in asserting the claim of illegality. The doctrinal link between the legal right to be free of taxes, which Otis had vigorously

159. Resolves of the Sons of Liberty, Wallingford, Connecticut (Jan. 13, 1766), *reprinted in id.* at 114.

160. Resolutions of the Sons of Liberty, New York (Jan. 11, 1766), *reprinted in id.* at 115.

161. Resolves of the Sons of Liberty, New Brunswick, New Jersey (Feb. 25, 1766), *reprinted in id.* at 115.

162. Resolves of the Sons of Liberty, New London, Conn. (Dec. 10, 1765), *reprinted in id.* at 114.

163. *Id.*

164. Sons of Liberty Agreement, New London, Conn. (Dec. 25, 1765), *reprinted in id.* at 117, 118.

165. *See* note 135 *supra* and accompanying text.

pressed, and the remedy of disobedience, which he had disavowed, was stated by the cautious Whig Lawyer John Dickinson in November 1765. In his view, to comply with the Stamp Act would establish a "detestable precedent" that the English would later cite as evidence of American acceptance of the legality of taxation.[166] Even to suspend business requiring the use of stamped paper would be "nearly the same acknowledgement of the Validity of the Stamp Act, and of its legal Obligation upon you, as if you use the Papers."[167] Thus resistance and disobedience were not merely justified by the illegality of the Act, but were virtually required if the claim of illegality was not to be waived. Here is the paradoxical revolutionary legalism of the American Whigs—which Edmund Burke was later to memorialize[168]—in its clearest form. The Tory Hutchinson captured the close linkage of constitutional theory to political action in his concise summary of the emerging vanguard Whig position: "An act of Parliament against our natural rights was ipso facto void and the people were bound to unite against the execution of it. . . ."[169]

D. *The Stamp Act and Judicial Review*

The sharpest practical test for the Whig claim that the Stamp Act was of no legal effect was the question of whether colonial courts should remain open for business without the stamped papers required by the Act. Following Dickinson's line of argument, Whigs urged that the courts should use unstamped paper rather than close, since, if they closed, they would acknowledge the binding force of the unconstitutional Stamp Act.[170]

Nowhere was the Whig constitutional case made more forcefully than in Boston.[171] In December of 1765, John Adams and James Otis appeared for the lawyers of Boston before Governor Bernard to urge that the courts be opened despite the absence of stamped

166. I THE WRITINGS OF JOHN DICKINSON 202 (P. Ford ed. 1895).

167. *Id.* at 204.

168. *See* SELECTED WRITING AND SPEECHES OF EDMUND BURKE 161 (P. Stanlis ed. 1963).

169. Letter from Thomas Hutchinson to Thomas Pownall (Mar. 8, 1766), *reprinted in* PROLOGUE, *supra* note 141, at 124.

170. Thus Maryland's Charles Carroll of Carrollton argued that allowing courts to remain closed because of the absence of stamped paper implied that Parliament had the power to impose such laws. E. & H. MORGAN, *supra* note 145, at 178.

171. The Boston lawyers had from the first invoked *Dr. Bonham's Case*, with its implications of judicial review, in their attacks on the Stamp Act. As Thomas Hutchinson summarized the Bostonian Whig position: "The prevailing reason at this time is, that the Act of Parliament is against Magna Charta, and the natural rights of Englishmen, and therefore, according to Lord *Coke*, null and void." Quincy's Reports 527 n.28.

paper. With his usual cloudy eloquence, Otis appealed to first principles, liberties and fundamental maxims, noting "that there are Limits, beyond which if Parliaments go, their Acts bind not."[172] But it was Adams who most clearly invoked the power of the governor and the courts to disregard an Act of Parliament which violated fundamental law:

> The Stamp-Act, I take it, is utterly void, and of no binding Force upon us; for it is against our Rights as Men, and our Privileges as Englishmen . . . . Parliaments may err; they are not infallible; they have been refused to be submitted to. An act making the King's Proclamation to be Law, the Executive Power adjudged absolutely void . . . . This Act has never been received from Authority, therefore in a legal sense we know Nothing of it.[173]

Significantly, the governor did not reject these arguments out of hand; he advised counsel to present them before the ordinary courts, where they "would be very pertinent to induce the judges of the Superior Court to think the Act of no Validity, and that therefore they should pay no Regard to it."[174] This response was in part a disingenuous attempt to pass a very unpopular issue to the courts. But it also showed that a royal governor could openly acknowledge as worthy of consideration the idea that judges might refuse to enforce the Stamp Act on the grounds that it violated the fundamental unwritten law of the British constitution.

The appeal to the courts to proceed in disregard of the unconstitutional Stamp Act was not confined to Massachusetts. In most of the colonies, Whig lawyers argued that courts could and should open for business without stamped documents, and in many colonies the courts did.[175] Thus the New Haven town meeting agreed that the Stamp Act was unconstitutional "and therefore not binding on the conscience," and thus that the courts should proceed

172. *Id.* at 205.

173. *Id.* at 200–01.

174. *Id.* at 206.

175. In some cases, Whig lawyers did not force opening of the courts, but for reasons of prudence rather than because of doubts over the claim of the legal invalidity of the Stamp Act. Thus at the meeting of Philadelphia lawyers called to consider the question, it was thought justified to open the courts, but it was concluded that if Parliament should determine to enforce the Act, it would immediately prosecute officers who had proceeded without stamps. E. & H. MORGAN, *supra* note 145, at 173–74 (citing letter from Edward Shippen, Jr., to Edward Shippen (Oct. 17, 1765)). Further, there was the risk that judicial actions taken in stampless proceedings would later be nullified, to the prejudice of clients' interests. Finally, there were those, debtors particularly, who for their own reasons preferred to see the courts remain closed. *See id.* at 163–79.

with business as usual without stamps.[176] In South Carolina, the lawyers petitioned the chief justice to open the courts, declaring that they could not be bound by a law that "annihilates our natural as well as constitutional rights."[177] In Caroline County, Virginia, the solidly conservative judge Edmund Pendleton wrote that he considered it his duty as a magistrate to sit and decide cases "according to law" and that he would never consider the Stamp Act as having the character of law "for want of power (I mean constitutional authority) in the Parliament to pass it . . . ."[178] His words matched those of the court in Patrick Henry's own Louisa County[179] and an official judgment of the court in Northampton County.[180]

These rulings by courts and the arguments supporting them provide the clearest illustrations that the colonists regarded the fundamental law as binding in the fullest possible sense on the legislature. By the time the Stamp Act became effective, the standard American Whig position was that parliamentary taxes were not only bad or unjust, but legally invalid. During the remainder of the revolutionary struggle, Whig lawyers had few practical opportunities to invoke that position in courts of law as a justification for judicial review, but that they did so when possible confirms what Otis' argument in the *Writs of Assistance Case* had already strongly suggested: that the idea of judicial review on the basis of an unwritten constitution was part of the common intellectual heritage of revolutionary Americans.

One must not, however, overstate the importance of judicial review to the colonial Whigs. It played a minor role in the conflict with Britain during the 1760's and 1770's, as it did in American life generally. After the repeal of the Stamp Act, there were to be few further occasions when courts of law served as an important forum for the Americans' constitutional arguments.[181] But the basic idea

176. P. MAIER, *supra* note 150, at 99.

177. M. JENSEN, THE FOUNDING OF A NATION 142 (1968).

178. 1 D. MAYS, EDMUND PENDLETON 170 (1952).

179. *Id.* at 172.

180. The Northhampton Court's order read: "On the motion of the Clerk, and other Officers of this Court, praying their opinion whether the act entitled 'an act for granting and applying certain Stamp Duties, and other Duties, in America & c.' was binding on the inhabitants of this colony, and whether they the said officers should incur any penalties by not using stamped paper, agreeable to the directions of the said act, the Court unanimously declared it to be their opinion that the said act did not bind, affect, or concern the inhabitants of this colony, inasmuch as they conceive the same to be unconstitutional, and that the said several officers may proceed to the execution of their respective offices without incurring any penalties by means thereof; which opinion doth court doth order to be recorded." Richmond Gazette, Mar. 21, 1766.

181. One further occasion was John Adams' argument to the courts in Massachusetts in

that underlies judicial review—the idea of a fundamental law or constitution limiting legislative authority—was to remain central to the colonists' cause up to the moment of independence.

E. *The Case Against the Townshend Act*

After the repeal of the Stamp Act in 1766, two actions by the home government stimulated another round of constitutional polemic by the colonists. The first was Parliament's suspension of the New York legislature for the New Yorkers' failure to comply with the Quartering Act.[182] The second was the enactment of the Townshend Duties of 1767, which taxed the importation of glass, lead and tea.[183] These events provoked the most popular single expression of the colonial position that was to appear in America before 1776, John Dickinson's *Letters of a Pennsylvania Farmer*, which "ran through the Colonies like wildfire" in 1768.[184] The first of the letters attacked the suspension of the New York legislature, while the others focused on the duties themselves. Dickinson's main point was to deny the British charge that the colonists had acquiesced in duties or "external taxes" in the past by objecting only to the "internal tax" imposed by the Stamp Act and were therefore inconsistent in now claiming exemption from external taxes as well. His rather fine-spun argument was that all duties previously imposed were adopted not for the purpose of raising revenue but rather as part of the comprehensive scheme of imperial trade regulation, which the colonists accepted as within Parliament's proper authority. The Townshend Duties, by contrast, were admittedly revenue measures, and hence violated the prohibition against taxation without representation.

1768 in the case of John Hancock's ship *Liberty*. *See* 2 THE LEGAL PAPERS OF JOHN ADAMS 198 (L. Wroth & H. Zobel eds. 1965). Another was the argument of counsel in the 1770 Rhode Island case of Freebody v. Brenton, which is reproduced in J. SMITH, *supra* note 107, at 336–41. For a domestic case involving an appeal for judicial review on the basis of an unwritten constitution, see Robin v. Hardaway, Jeff. (Va.) 109 (1772).

182. The Quartering Act required the colonies to provide supplies to British troops stationed in America; the requirement was regarded as simply another illegal tax, and none of the colonial legislatures complied. In retaliation, the Townshend ministry suspended the New York assembly, which had defied the requirement more explicitly than most, until it should comply with the Act. M. JENSEN, *supra* note 177, at 68–69, 225–26.

183. The Townshend Act imposed duties expressly for the purpose of revenue; provided that the revenue was used to pay the salaries of local officials formerly paid by the colonial assemblies themselves; and granted the courts the power to issue writs of assistance in enforcement of the taxes. *Id.* at 226–27.

184. 1 THE WRITINGS OF JOHN DICKINSON, *supra* note 166, at 279.

The *Farmer Letters* were filled with the language of revolutionary legalism. The Quartering Act was a tax; if Parliament had "legal authority" to require supply for troops, then it could impose *any* tax.[185] The people of New York could not "be legally taxed but by their own representatives," and thus could not "legally" be punished for insisting on their right of self-taxation.[186] The Townshend Duties themselves were "unconstitutional"[187] violations of the principle of self-taxation, which had always been a crucial "legal curb" on the power of English rulers.[188] British officials were entitled to obedience as long as they conducted themselves "according to the laws,"[189] but when they acted beyond the "due limits" of their "authority" they should be resisted.[190] Indeed, the colonists would establish a disastrous precedent if they were to "admit the legality" of the tax.[191]

Dickinson, the lawyerly revolutionary, continually warned of the potential shaping effect of precedent upon fundamental law. He feared that acquiescing in official illegality would eventually convert it to legality by the force of prescription. Many people had "no other idea of the legality of power, than that it is founded on the exercise of power."[192] The British ministry was proceeding on this principle; its interest in the Townshend Duties was not the relatively minor revenue which could be raised, but the establishment of the principle of taxation: "Nothing is wanted at home but a precedent . . . ."[193] The fact that the tax was light should not tempt the colonists into compliance; even if the duties could be paid with ease, and the purposes to which the revenue would be applied were "reasonable and equitable," still "these colonies ought to regard the act with abhorence."[194] Dickinson's explanation of this view captured the essence of the colonial position: "For who are free people? Not *those*, over whom government is reasonably and equitably exercised, but *those*, who live under a government so constitutionally

185. *Id.* at 309.
186. *Id.* at 309–10.
187. *Id.* at 312, 359.
188. *Id.* at 365.
189. *Id.* at 404.
190. *Id.*
191. *Id.* at 319.
192. *Id.* at 390.
193. *Id.* at 382. For a general analysis of the place of precedent in the debate over the Stamp Act, see Reid, *In an Inherited Way: English Constitutional Rights, The Stamp Act Debates, and the Coming of the American Revolution*, 49 S. CAL. L. REV. 1109 (1976).
194. I THE WRITINGS OF JOHN DICKINSON, *supra* note 166, at 356.

checked and controlled, that proper provision is made against its being otherwise exercised."[195]

Some historians have found Dickinson's legalism an atypically conservative strand of colonial Whig thought.[196] Yet Samuel Adams, generally characterized as one of the radical leaders of the revolutionary movement, employed a similar legalism in that other most celebrated document of colonial protest against the Townshend Duties, the Massachusetts *Circular Letter* of 1768.[197] The *Circular Letter* stated clearly, in terms derived from Burlamaqui and Vattel, the theory of the legislatively unalterable constitution: "In all free States the Constitution is fixed; and as the supreme Legislative derives its Power and Authority from the Constitution, it cannot overlap the Bounds of it without destroying its own foundation . . . ."[198] Part of the fixed British constitution was the right of self-taxation, based on the natural right of property:

> It is an essential unalterable right in nature, ingrafted into the British Constitution, as a fundamental Law and ever held sacred and irrevocable by the Subjects within the Realm, that what a man has honestly acquired is absolutely his own, which he may freely give, but cannot be taken from him without his consent . . . American Subjects may therefore . . . assert this natural and constitutional right.[199]

Like the *Farmer Letters*, the *Circular Letter* concluded that because the new duties were "for the sole and express purpose of raising a Revenue," they infringed these rights.[200] Thus the legalistic distinction supplied by the careful Dickinson was echoed by the inflammatory propagandist Adams.

F. *Evolution of the Constitutional Argument: From "No Taxes" to "No Laws"*

A colonial boycott of goods subject to the Townshend Duties forced the British government to rescind all except the tea duty in 1770.[201] Militant Whigs eventually responded to the tea duty by feeding East India Company tea to the fish of Boston Harbor in the

---

195. *Id.*

196. *See, e.g.*, 1 V. PARRINGTON, MAIN CURRENTS IN AMERICAN THOUGHT 219–33 (1927).

197. The *Circular Letter*, which called for intercolonial cooperation in resistance to the home government's policies, was found so inflammatory that the ministry ordered the colonial assembly to rescind it on pain of being dissolved; the House refused. M. JENSEN, *supra* note 177, at 250–264.

198. 1 THE WRITINGS OF SAMUEL ADAMS 185 (H. Cushing ed. 1904).

199. *Id.*

200. *Id.*

201. J. MILLER, ORIGINS OF THE AMERICAN REVOLUTION 278 (1943).

great Tea Party of 1773. In response, the British government enacted the "Coercive" or "Intolerable" Acts of 1774, which closed Boston to all trade and unilaterally altered the traditional governmental structure of Massachusetts. These measures led to the calling of the First Continental Congress in 1774, to the arming of the back-country men of Massachusetts, and thence to Lexington and Concord, Bunker Hill, and war.[202]

In the course of these events, the Whig constitutional position evolved from "no taxation without representation" to a rejection of all British legislative authority over the internal affairs of the colonies. The basis for this natural evolution in theory appeared in the home government's own semi-official constitutional justification for the stamp tax itself, Thomas Whately's *The Regulations Lately Made*, published in London in 1765.[203] Whately had noted that the colonists' constitutional objection to the stamp tax rested upon the right of British subjects to be taxed only through their representatives. He pointed out that the principle behind that objection applied not only to taxation but to all parliamentary legislation: "No new Law whatever can bind us that is made without the Concurrence of our Representatives."[204] His argument was intended as a *reductio ad absurdum*; if the stamp tax was unconstitutional, so was the whole body of parliamentary legislation regulating the trade of the colonies—and this was (in 1765) an untenable position. Whately's solution was that *both* taxation *and* legislation were authorized on the theory that the colonists were "virtually" represented in the House of Commons.

Rejection of the theory of virtual representation, of course, was an essential part of the Whig argument that the Stamp Act and the Townshend Duties were illegal. How could Whigs then consistently maintain their position of 1768, articulated in the *Farmer Letters* and the Massachusetts *Circular Letter*, which distinguished between valid regulation and invalid taxation? This inconsistency was pointed up by Tories like Thomas Hutchinson, who kept reiterating that logically Parliament must either have *total* authority over the colonies or *no* authority.[205] The natural but radical implications began to be drawn in the late 1760's by venturesome Whigs like William Hicks, who in a 1768 pamphlet rejected all parliamentary authority over

---

202. For the events of the period, see D. AMMERMAN, IN THE COMMON CAUSE (1974); M. JENSEN, *supra* note 177, at 461-601; J. MILLER, *supra* note 201, at 355-442.

203. *See* 1 PAMPHLETS, *supra* note 95, at 601-02; Whately, *supra* note 146, at 17-23.

204. *Id.* at 19.

205. *See* B. BAILYN, *supra* note 20, at 219-22.

the colonies. Denying the distinctions drawn by Dickinson and the *Circular Letter* in America and by Chatham and Camden in England, Hicks pointed out that Americans had not consented to Parliament's laws any more than to its taxes, and that the colonists could be "as effectually ruined by the powers of legislation as by those of taxation."[206]

That measures other than taxes might infringe the deeply felt liberties of Americans was illustrated that year. In 1768, responding to the repeated calls of the hapless Governor Bernard for force sufficient to allow him to deal with the rebellious Bostonians, the home government dispatched two regiments of regular British troops to Massachusetts. The presence of a standing army in time of peace violated one of the central constitutional principles of 18th-century Whigs. In the words of the Boston Town meeting: "The raising or keeping a standing army within the kingdom in time of peace, unless it be with the consent of Parliament, is *against the law* . . . ."[207] The prohibition of standing armies was hence added to the principle of self-taxation and the right of jury trial as a legally binding constitutional restraint on Parliament's power in Whig constitutional doctrine.

As events moved from crisis to crisis, culminating in the Intolerable Acts of 1774, the American constitutional consensus position developed in the direction suggested by Whately and Hicks. From condemnation of taxation, standing armies, writs of assistance, denial of jury trial, and the other violations of particular traditional rights, it evolved into a challenge to all parliamentary authority. The Boston Port Act was not a tax, nor did it violate any other traditional right. It simply completely closed the Port of Boston to all trade, and the colonists perceived this as an intolerable act of tyranny. In 1774 no less than today, once Americans felt something to be intolerable, they soon found an argument that it was unconstitutional. The argument was simply a natural extension of the underlying principle behind all the colonial arguments—the principle that lawful government must be founded upon the consent of the governed.

The new consensus position appeared in the usual rash of pamphlets in 1774, the three best known of which were written by John Adams, James Wilson and Thomas Jefferson.[208] The constitu-

206. Hicks, *The Nature and Extent of Parliamentary Power Considered*, in TRACTS OF THE AMERICAN REVOLUTION 164, 175 (M. Jensen ed. 1967).

207. *See* B. Bailyn, *supra* note 20, at 113.

208. Adams, *Novanglus*, in 4 THE WORKS OF JOHN ADAMS 11–177 (C. Adams ed. 1851);

tional views articulated in the three pamphlets were in essence the same; all three reflected the legalist appeal to unwritten fundamental law that had characterized the earlier polemics of Otis, Dulany, Dickinson, and Samuel Adams. Wilson's argument can be taken as representative.

Wilson began by noting that Tories often defended Parliament's supremacy on the basis of the Blackstonian dogma that in every state there must be a single supreme sovereign.[209] That important principle, he argued, was no logical necessity, but rather a practical device for settling conflicts peacefully, and thus advancing the "ultimate end of all government," which was "the happiness of the society."[210] Governmental legitimacy was founded upon the consent of the governed, and the people consented to government in order to advance their happiness.[211] But, argued Wilson, the legal supremacy of Parliament was more conducive to the happiness of Englishmen than Americans, who were not, and as a practical matter could not be, represented in the House of Commons:[212] Americans could not fairly be asked to submit to parliamentary rule, trusting to the English respect for the "dictates of natural justice."[213] After all, "a very little share of experience will sufficiently convince us, that a regard to justice is by no means the ruling principle in human nature."[214]

Not only was the theory of parliamentary sovereignty over America contrary to "the essential maxims of jurisprudence" and "the genius of the British constitution," but, in Wilson's view, it was "not less repugnant to the voice of her laws."[215] Wilson's complex legal argument rested primarily on the authority of Lord Coke's observation in *Calvin's Case*[216] that English statutes did not apply in Ireland, because the Irish were not represented in Parliament.[217]

Jefferson, *A Summary View of the Rights of British America*, in TRACTS OF THE AMERICAN REVOLUTION, *supra* note 206, at 256–276; Wilson, *Considerations on the Nature and Extent of the Legislative Authority of the British Parliament*, in 2 THE WORKS OF JAMES WILSON 721–746 (R. McCloskey ed. 1967).

209. 2 THE WORKS OF JAMES WILSON, *supra* note 208, at 723.

210. *Id.* (citing Burlamaqui). Note the similar view taken by James Iredell in his 1774 *Address to the People of Great Britain*, in 1 LIFE AND CORRESPONDENCE OF JAMES IREDELL 217–19 (G. McRee ed. 1949).

211. 2 THE WORKS OF JAMES WILSON, *supra* note 208, at 723.

212. *Id.* at 724-34.

213. *Id.* at 734.

214. *Id.*

215. *Id.* at 735.

216. 77 Eng. Rep. 377 (K.B. 1609).

217. 2 THE WORKS OF JAMES WILSON, *supra* note 208, at 738-740. The details of the

Wilson, like Adams and Jefferson, concluded that as a matter of British constitutional law, Americans were subjects of the King of England and bore personal allegiance to him, but were entirely free of the legislative authority of the British Parliament.

The theory had two important legal implications. First, the Intolerable Acts, along with all other parliamentary legislation, were of no binding effect in America. For Wilson, those laws were "unconstitutional and void";[218] for Jefferson they were "nugatory";[219] for Adams they were "null and void."[220] Second, the theory disowned total independence, establishing a British empire structured along the lines of a federal system. Americans would retain control over internal legislation and taxation, but Parliament would have the authority to enact trade regulations of concern to the whole empire. This authority would not rest on any original sovereign authority in Parliament, but rather on the free grant by the legislatively independent American states. The colonies would be bound to England as distinct states under one monarch, connected by a "treaty of commerce" under the terms of which Americans would agree to accept the restrictions of the Navigation Act system in return for its commercial advantages.[221]

That the views of Adams, Jefferson and Wilson reflected a genuine consensus of American views in 1774 is confirmed by the actions of the broadly representative First Continental Congress, which met in Philadelphia in the fall of that year. The Congress—which in characteristic 18th-century fashion debated its theoretical position at length in the midst of the crisis—finally declared that the Americans "by the immutable laws of nature, the principles of the English constitution, and the several charters or compacts" had the rights to "life, liberty and property," which "no one had a right to dispose of without their consent.[222] Most important, reflecting the

---

argument based on the legal status of the colonies and dominions are exhaustively canvassed in C. McIlwain, *supra* note 122, at 18–137 and reexamined, in the light of subsequent criticism, in Black, *The Constitution of Empire: The Case for the Colonists*, 124 U. Pa. L. Rev. 1157 (1976).

218. 2 The Works of James Wilson, *supra* note 208, at 752.

219. Tracts of the American Revolution, *supra* note 206, at 268.

220. 4 The Works of John Adams, *supra* note 208, at 89.

221. *See, e.g., id.* at 114.

222. 1 Journals of the Continental Congress 67 (W. Ford ed. 1904). An interesting debate took place in the Continental Congress over whether to include the "law of nature" along with the constitution and the colonial charters as the basis of the rights claimed. The debate was as much tactical as philosophical; appeal to the "law of nature" foreshadowed ultimate claims of independence in the minds of the more conservative delegates. Thus,

views of Wilson, Adams, and Jefferson, the Congress claimed for Americans "a free and exclusive power of legislation in their several provincial legislatures, . . . in all cases of taxation *and internal policy*, subject only to the negative of their sovereign.[223] Finally, the assembled colonial leaders reasserted, as always, the legal character of their grievances: the rights claimed for Americans could not be "*legally* taken from them, altered, or abridged by any power whatever, without their consent. . . ."[224]

In the same fall of 1774, English voters elected a House of Commons whose makeup ensured that the American proposals would be rejected. One of the few members who supported conciliation was Edmund Burke, who in a memorable but futile speech favoring acceptance of the American proposals gave what remains the best description and explanation of the peculiarly legalistic temper of the American Whig movement. Burke observed that in no country was the law so generally studied as in America; almost every American who could read knew some law, and Blackstone's Commentaries had sold nearly as many copies in the colonies as in England.[225] Where the interests of lawyers were not tied to the prevailing order, Burke said, legal education was a "formidable adversary to government."[226] He continued in oft-quoted words:

> This study renders men acute, inquisitive, dexterous, prompt in attack, ready in defence, full of resources. In other countries, the people, more simple, and of a less mercurial cast, judge of an ill principle in government only by an actual grievance; here they anticipate the evil, and judge of the pressure of the grievance by the badness of the principle. They augur misgovernment at a distance, and snuff the approach of tyranny in every tainted breeze.[227]

The American Whig literature of the pre-independence period confirms Burke's observation. That literature varied greatly in the measures of resistance to English policy it urged—from the caution of Otis and Dulany to the radicalism of the Sons of Liberty and the false Virginia Resolves—and in the specific objects of its protest—

Rutledge argued that "[t]he first emigrants could not be considered as in a state of nature; they had no right to elect a new king." 1 LETTERS OF MEMBERS OF THE CONTINENTAL CONGRESS 22 (E. Burnett ed. 1921). On the other side, John Jay said, "It is necessary to recur to the law of nature . . . . The constitution of Great Britain will not apply to some of the charter rights. A mother country surcharged with inhabitants, they have a right to emigrate. . . . [E]migrants have a right to erect what government they please." *Id.* at 20.

223. *Id.* at 68 (emphasis added).

224. *Id.* at 71 (emphasis added).

225. SELECTED WRITING AND SPEECHES OF EDMUND BURKE 161 (P. Stanlis ed. 1963).

226. *Id.*

227. *Id.* Compare these words with Dickinson's. *See* text accompanying note 195 *supra*.

taxes, non-jury trials, standing armies and the closing of the Port of Boston. But throughout the period, and over the whole range of spokesmen and issues, the American position was characteristically stated in legal terms. The condemned British policies were not merely attacked as unjust or untraditional or even "unconstitutional" in the extra-legal sense of that term.[228] They were said to be *illegal*—and the law to which the colonists appealed was the unwritten fundamental law of reasonable custom and customary reason that made up the British constitution.

G. *The Decision for Independence*

After the British rejection of all proposals for conciliation, the conflict erupted into war. At this point—for a few short months during the first half of 1776—the forensic controversy moved outside the arena of law and constitutional principles. The remaining dispute among American Whigs was whether the conflict should be regarded as a war for national independence, or as civil war whose aim was British recognition of the loose imperial ties the Americans had claimed in 1774. After that dispute was resolved in favor of independence, it became the task of the American spokesmen to justify that decision to the world.

The case for independence could not be made in legal terms. While still within the British constitution Americans could and did argue that legally they were entirely free from *parliamentary* authority. But for Americans to decide for independence meant to forswear allegiance to the King, and thereby to remove themselves from the circle of those to whom that constitution applied. The justification of the decision for independence therefore had to be based entirely upon extra-legal considerations of utility and political philosophy. That case was made in the two best known of all the writings of the revolutionary period, Thomas Paine's *Common Sense*, which played so large a part in persuading Americans to choose independence, and the Declaration of Independence, which was meant as the official justification of the decision once it was made. Paine's pamphlet claimed a natural right of self-government, and argued in practical terms that independence was preferable to dominion status.[229] Jefferson's Declaration stated the justification for independence in terms of Lockean natural rights, and the ultimate power

228. *See* note 102 *supra*.

229. Paine, *Common Sense, reprinted in* THE ESSENTIAL THOMAS PAINE 24–26, 36–47 (S. Hook ed. 1969).

and moral right of the people to "alter or abolish" governments that were "destructive" of these rights.

The Declaration recited at length the actions of the Crown which had led the Americans to break with England—many of which actions Americans had denounced over the previous dozen years as unconstitutional and illegal—but it placed no emphasis on legal argument.[230] This was not only because independence could not be seen as a legal remedy for unconstitutional laws and policies, but also because the Declaration was not primarily addressed to either Englishmen or Americans. Its audience was indicated in its own words; it was "submitted to a candid world." The appeal to the great world outside the British empire had to be stated in terms of standards to which all would give assent. In the western world of 1776, these standards were the self-evident truths and inalienable rights of rationalist Enlightenment philosophy—the standards on which Jefferson relied in the familiar opening lines of the Declaration.

IV. Conclusion: After Independence

The Declaration of Independence and Paine's *Common Sense*, if read in isolation from other Whig literature, give a distorted view of the political and constitutional ideas of revolutionary Americans. These documents are characteristic of the political literature of the few months between January 1776 and Independence Day, a period during which the American cause was necessarily articulated in extra-legal terms. Jefferson and Paine thus justified the break with England by reference to natural rights that were regarded as purely ethical limitations on government, and were thought of as accessible to all by direct intuition.[231] This view of natural law suggests the principles of majoritarian democracy, and hence provides little basis for claims of superior access to fundamental law on the part of specially trained elite judges. Egalitarian natural law ideas of this kind have been associated with the Jeffersonian, Jacksonian and

230. Daniel Boorstin has said that the Declaration of Independence was "a bill of indictment against the king, written in the language of British constitutionalism." D. Boorstin, The Genius of American Politics 84 (1953). It is true that many of the grievances set out in the main body of the Declaration criticize actions which colonists had attacked as illegal—abridgment of jury trial, taxation without representation and the like. But the Declaration did not characterize these actions as illegal, or suggest that an important ground of objection to them was their inconsistency with the British constitution.

231. This strand of thought traces back to Locke's theory of natural rights, *see* note 73 *supra* and accompanying text, but flows more directly out of the thought of the radical natural law thinkers of mid-18th-century England, such as Burgh, Price and Priestley. *See generally* S. Lynd, Intellectual Origins of American Radicalism 17–63 (1968).

populist movements, with their suspicion of unwritten law, judicial independence and judicial review of all kinds throughout American history.[232]

But this was by no means the dominant view of natural or fundamental law among revolutionary Americans. As I have shown in this article, the fundamental law ideas that largely animated American Whig thought during the pre-1776 independence struggle differed substantially from this extra-legal and egalitarian conception. Through the 1760's and early 1770's, Whigs ranging from the conservative John Dickinson to the radical Samual Adams primarily articulated a "revolutionary legalist" view flowing out of the English fundamental law tradition. Under that view, fundamental law prevented legislative infringements of *legal* rights—primarily common law property rights, and rights to traditional institutional arrangements and legal procedures. These rights were the products of social evolution, modified by precedent and ratified by the special "artificial reason" of the law. Thus, although these rights were commonly regarded as dictates of natural law, it was a natural law more accessible to the legally learned than to the commonsense intuition of the laity.

It remains to examine in detail the place of these two different conceptions of higher law during the 15 years following independence, the years in which Americans established the constitutional basis of their new republic. As might be expected, the legalist and elitist conception of fundamental law would more often be identified with the conservative forces in American society—those who favored a strong central government, a strong executive and judiciary, limitations on the electoral franchise, hard money, and creditors' rights. By contrast, the purely ethical and egalitarian conception was more often associated with those who favored state autonomy, a broad franchise, legislative supremacy, and paper money. In the great contest over the ratification of the United States Constitution, it was primarily the former group who became Federalists, favoring ratification, while the latter set of views was more often associated with antifederalism and opposition to ratification.[233]

---

232. *See* R. COVER, JUSTICE ACCUSED 131–48 (1975); R. ELLIS, THE JEFFERSONIAN CRISIS: COURTS AND POLITICS IN THE YOUNG REPUBLIC 113–22 (1971); P. MILLER, THE LIFE OF THE MIND IN AMERICA 99–268 (1965). These ideas also influenced the Garrisonian wing of the antislavery movement. R. COVER, *supra*, at 149–58; A. KRADITOR, MEANS AND ENDS IN AMERICAN ABOLITIONISM 185–217 (1970).

233. The exact nature and extent of the identification of the Federalists with political

This is not to say simply that ratification and the triumph of federalism entailed acceptance of the legalist or conservative view of unwritten fundamental law, the view which best supports noninterpretive judicial review. The new practice of establishing a written constitution, drawn up by a special representative convention and ratified by the people influenced the place of unwritten law in constitutional theory. The effect of this new practice—accepted as much by conservatives and Federalists as by democrats and Antifederalists—on the idea that judicially ascertainable fundamental law could itself have constitutional status remains to be carefully analyzed. In the ratification struggle, moreover, the Federalists adopted and indeed exploited the theory and rhetoric of popular sovereignty, and it remains to be shown that an acceptance of noninterpretive judicial review was consistent with this development.[234]

The ultimate place of unwritten fundamental law in the constitutional scheme established by the framers thus requires further examination. It has been my purpose in this article to lay the foundation for that examination by determining the framework of constitutional thought within which Americans operated as they became self-governing. There can be little doubt that a prominent part of that framework was the traditional idea of a legally binding and unwritten constitution that had played so central a role in the dispute that led to independence. Those ideas formed the status quo in constitutional theory in 1776.

---

conservatism and the Anti-federalists with radicalism or democracy has been one of the most contested issues among the historians of the period. *Compare* Kenyon, *Men of Little Faith: The Anti-Federalists on the Nature of Representative Government*, in THE REINTERPRETATION OF THE AMERICAN REVOLUTION, *supra* note 21 at 526-66 (Anti-federalists characterized by fear of government, timidity, extreme desires for checks and balances), *with* G. WOOD, THE CREATION OF THE AMERICAN REPUBLIC, 1776-1787, at 483-89 (1969) (Federalists elitist and aristocratic).

234. The adoption by the Federalists of the theory of popular sovereignty is the central theme of the recent and masterful survey of the political thought of the 1776–1787 period, G. WOOD, *supra* note 242.

Popular Sovereignty, the Origins of Judicial Review, and the Revival of Unwritten Law

Leslie Friedman Goldstein
University of Delaware

This essay draws together research from a variety of sources to argue that American constitutional theory in the 1776-1803 period underwent a profound transformation. Central to that transformation were changes concerning the meaning and importance of the concept of government by consent of the governed. As the significance of popular sovereignty within our constitutional theory increased, the place of unwritten law in judicial review commensurately shrank. Moreover, this judicial move away from reliance on unwritten law appears to have contributed to a rapid increase in the popularity of the institution of judicial review. These very dramatic changes point to the need for public law scholars to reconsider currently influential arguments about the unwritten law origins of judicial review.

Although the modern Supreme Court has not dared to say it aloud, a good deal of the current scholarship on the Court (e.g., Grey, 1974 and 1978; Miller, 1982; Perry, 1982; Bobbitt, 1982) maintains that unwritten law is a perfectly legitimate basis on which the Court may declare statutes void. The contribution of the natural law tradition to the original development of the judicial review element of American constitutional history is an old story (e.g., McLaughlin, 1912; Corwin, 1928-9, 1957 and 1963, Wright, 1931; Haines, 1932; Rossiter, 1953; Bailyn, 1967, pp. 189-9).[1] What has been

*I wish to acknowledge the research assistance of Laurie J. Shannon and the support of the University of Delaware Undergraduate Research Program.

[1] The recent criticism of this tradition by Walter Berns (1983) on the grounds that none of these scholars understood the true meaning of "the doctrine of modern natural rights and natural law from which . . . we derive . . . our constitutionalism"—however powerful Berns' elucidation of Locke, Hobbes, Vattel and Pufendorf may be—is somewhat beside the point. The question is not the true import of Locke's theories, but rather what those theories meant to our revolutionary framers. When a man as well-read and as serious in his scholarship as John Adams could assert that Locke, Cicero and Aristotle all taught the same thing about natural law—not to mention dozens of lesser figures who exhibit the same confusion—it does not really matter that Berns is correct in realizing that Locke intended to reject rather than endorse the tradition of Cicero and Aquinas.

Rossiter (1953, p. 353), for instance, quotes Adams: "Natural law and right are . . . revolution principles. They are the principles of Aristotle and Plato, of Livy and Cicero, and Sidney, Harrington, and Locke: the principles of nature and eternal reason; the principles on which the whole government over us now stands."

revived is the view that even after the United States adopted a written Constitution ratified by popularly elected conventions, many of its framers and ratifiers continued to believe that judges should enforce unwritten rights—rights neither mentioned nor implied in that document—against laws enacted by popularly elected legislatures.

Unwritten law theories of judicial review experienced a heyday during the first few decades of the twentieth century (McLaughlin, 1912; Corwin, 1914; Haines, 1932), but fell into disfavor with the decline of economic substantive due process. After the Supreme Court accepted the New Deal, public law orthodoxy in the U.S. returned to the outlook that took its bearings, first, from the well-known defenses of judicial review in Hamilton's Federalist #78 and John Marshall's opinion in *Marbury v. Madison*, both of which ground the judges' power to strike down statute law firmly in the higher power of the sovereign people who adopted the supreme legal rules of the Constitutional text, and, second, from the well-known discussion at the Constitutional Convention, exhibiting a consensus that foresaw judicial review as a safeguard of the written Constitution that was about to be ratified by the people (Farrand, 1913, I, pp. 97, 109; II, pp. 28, 73, 76, 78, 93, 248, 299, 376, 428; III, p. 220. Also, Haines, 1932, pp. 126-135; Corwin, 1963, pp. 10-13; but cf. Levy, 1967). According to this position, after tentative experiments with an unwritten natural law or common law approach to judicial review (e.g., *Fletcher v. Peck* in 1810), the Supreme Court abandoned its reliance on unwritten rights in favor of reliance on the constitutional text, since the latter had a firmer grounding in American constitutional theory (see, e.g., Gunther, 1980, p. 506).

In the 1970s, apparently stimulated by the *Griswold-Eisenstadt-Roe* series of right-to-privacy decisions, as the earlier generation had been inspired by the economic substantive due process decisions,[2] a group of prominent judicial scholars once again took up the cause of unwritten law judicial review. Both Thomas Grey (1974, 1978) and Walter Murphy (1978) argued that it was the conscious intent of the framers and the widespread understanding of the ratifying generation that written constitutions could not completely codify the higher law, and they claim textual support for this view in the Ninth Amendment. Their arguments, along with a variety

[2] Neither in *Griswold v. Connecticut*, *Eisenstadt v. Baird*, nor *Roe v. Wade* did any justice ever say in so many words, "It is our job to discover the unwritten natural rights of Americans and enforce them as fundamental law." Instead (with the exceptions of Justices Douglas and Clark, who struggled valiantly and unpersuasively in *Griswold* to demonstrate that the right of married couples to use contraceptive devices was implied in the words of the First, Third, Fourth, Fifth, Ninth, and Fourteenth Amendments), the justices adopted or returned to the theory that the due process clauses (Fifth and Fourteenth Amendments) require them to identify the most important liberties for Americans and to guard these against undue legislative invasion. Although they do not spell it out, this "identifying" process amounts to an invocation of unwritten law.

of other factors including the policy preferences of scholars, appear to have been influential; the 1980s have spawned many new defenses of unwritten law judicial review. (For a review and critique of this literature, see Goldstein, 1985.) Thomas Grey's argument (1978) covered the period up to and including the Revolution of 1776; Walter Murphy's argument (1978) sweeps more broadly, covering Supreme Court history from 1789 to the present. This article focuses more narrowly on the critical period between 1776 and 1789 and assesses the impact that the new American political institutions had upon the idea, popular in the 1760s and 1770s, that judges could and should strike down statutes that conflicted with the unwritten fundamental law of reason and custom.

In 1787 the American people institutionalized popular sovereignty at the national level with a set of practices not in effect in 1776: they established a written constitution, drawn up by a specially elected set of representatives, and ratified by the people via another set of specially elected delegates. These practices emerged gradually and unevenly among the thirteen states after the Revolution, and their emergence was accompanied by an evolution in American constitutional theory. This article analyzes both the transition in American constitutional theory that took place between 1776 and the writing of the Constitution in 1787, and the effect upon judicial review of the new practices concerning constitution writing and ratification in the period from 1787 until 1803, the date of the landmark *Marbury v. Madison* decision. My thesis is that American constitutional theory underwent a rapid and profound evolution during that quarter century. In particular, the significance attached to the concept of "government by consent of the governed" rose dramatically, even as that concept itself took on a transformed meaning. This process was accompanied by a notable decline of the outlook that it was appropriate for judges to strike down statutes on the basis of unwritten law, and by a dramatic increase in the acceptance of judicial review.[3]

The evidence for this thesis appears in a variety of disparate sources which have never before been all drawn together. These strands of evidence include the work of historians such as Bernard Bailyn (1967) and Gordon Wood (1969a, 1969b) on early American political ideology; the work on early American state constitutions by Donald Lutz (1980), Willi Paul Adams (1980) and others; and opinions by early state supreme courts and the eighteenth century federal courts, analyzed relatively often by traditional public law scholars, most recently in a prize-winning essay by Sylvia Snowiss (1981).

[3] My thesis thus drastically curtails the import of the (1978) work of Thomas Grey as a useful guide for current Supreme Court practice. To curtail similarly the import of Walter Murphy's (1978) essay would be beyond the scope of this piece; it would require an extended analysis of all the nineteenth-century cases that he cites and of the public and scholarly reaction to them. As this essay, however, should suggest, that analysis is one worth doing.

Once woven together, these strands create a convincing pattern of argument that challenges the assumption that extratextual judicial review was understood to be the norm by 1791, much less that it was the prevailing norm by 1803. My argument points to profound changes during 1776-1803 on the American answer to four questions: (1) the meaning of "government by consent of the governed"; (2) the relationship between that concept and the practice of writing and ratifying constitutions; (3) the relationship between that concept and the age-old debate over legislative versus judicial supremacy; and (4) the relationship between that concept and the debate (reintensified by Grey's and Murphy's scholarship) over textual versus extratextual judicial review.

These changes produce the conclusion that the correlation by the early 1800s between the increased popularity of judicial review and the increased reliance on government-by-consent-of-the-governed to justify that review was not mere coincidence. Rather, the new combination is best understood as a reflection of the new constitutional theory and practice prevalent in America by that time.

I. 1776-1786: The First Decade of Free Republicanism

No one seriously doubts that some conception of a higher law of natural justice influenced the colonists during the heated decade of the 1760s and in the years leading immediately to the revolution. John Adams's remark about the politically catalyzing influence of James Otis's protestation against the Writs of Assistance to the effect that "an Act against the Constitution is void: an Act against natural Equity is void . . ." is well known. Adams's comment was that all who heard Otis left the meeting "ready to take arms . . . then and there the child Independence was born" (Adams, II, p. 521; X, pp. 247-8). After the break from England, however, as popular sovereignty took on an increasingly dominant role both in the legislative process and in the constitution-making process, the public understanding of the restraining role to be played by a higher law of nature or of ancient custom seems to have shifted accordingly.

A. Government by Consent of the Governed re: Legislation

Although "government by consent of the governed" has been a political shibboleth in America at least since the seventeenth century (Lutz, 1980, pp. 24-31), its meaning has undergone some twists and turns over the past 300 years. Since the early colonies were settled by groups organized as stockholder companies, their company/colonial charters generally granted voting rights to the adult males[4] who belonged. These voters selected local

[4] The exclusion of females from the body politic was rarely discussed. For a few exceptions during the founding era see John Adams (1856, IX, pp. 375-8, commenting in 1776); James Wilson (1967, I, pp. 85-9, commenting in 1790-1); and Thomas Jefferson (1854, VII, pp. 36, commenting in 1816).

governing bodies who were generally left alone by the British authorities (Lutz, pp. 24-26 and 100-101; Goebel, 1971, pp. 3-4, 85; W.P. Adams, 1980, pp. 230-233).

What began as virtually universal manhood suffrage accompanying virtual home rule in the early 1600s became radically transformed by the early 1700s, as more and more people immigrated who belonged neither to the local company nor the local church. By the early eighteenth century property and religious requirements for suffrage were fairly stringent, resulting in an essentially oligarchical system, yet Americans still spoke and wrote of living under "government by consent of the governed." During this period the assumption of a homogeneous community which shared a single "common good" prevailed. This view supported the notion, controversial during the break with England but later reasserted for domestic circumstances, that the non-voters could be virtually represented as the voters were actually represented (Lutz, 1980, pp. 100-5; Bailyn, 1967, pp. 161-175; Wood, 1969a, pp. 167-185).

By the 1770s popular consent in the sense of suffrage rights for adult males had yet again transformed itself; religious exclusion had become quite lax and the ready availability of property had caused the electorate, at least of the northern colonies, to include substantial majorities of the adult male population. Despite mild property qualifications, voter turnout rates for adult males in the North in the 1770s compare favorably with those in the contemporary U.S. (Lutz, 1980, pp. 24-6, 100-5. Cf. Haskins, 1981, p. 41; Williamson, 1960; J.R. Pole, 1966; and Hyneman, 1977, pp. 15-16).

The dispute with England over virtual representation did not really destroy the concept in America, although it put the idea under enough of a shadow that suffrage restrictions were somewhat loosened in the early postrevolution constitutions. Vermont instituted universal manhood suffrage and New Hampshire, Delaware, Georgia, and North Carolina lifted restrictions to the point that one scholar describes them as having "virtually guaranteed" universal manhood suffrage (in the cases of the latter three, for non-slaves). Moreover Pennsylvania changed its rules to the point that 90% of adult males qualified. Kentucky entered the union with universal adult white male suffrage in the 1790s (Lutz, 1980, pp. 105-8). Also significantly, after the revolution the size of state legislative bodies was greatly expanded, sometimes doubled or tripled. The logic here was to put the people in closer touch with their representative, and the expansion apparently had the effect, fostered also by changes in popular attitudes brought about by the revolution, of bringing a much larger portion of the socially "common" element into state legislatures (Douglass, 1955; Main, 1966; Lutz, 1980, pp. 106-110; Wood, 1969a, pp. 167-8).

By the late 1770s then, the colonial maxim of "government by consent of the governed" was already referring to a rather dramatically new reality, produced by America's peculiar history and revolutionary experience. In the British theory the House of Commons was thought to "re-present" the people and to act in their behalf, as distinguished from by their instructions. The people being re-presented were thought of as having a homogeneous interest and as sending the most virtuous and honorable of their number off to Commons to speak for them. The manner of selection (who participated, what size election districts, etc.) was not particularly important, except that all who participated in the selection needed to have an independent will and a stake in the community (read: property). The sense in which "the people" were thought to give consent to public policy was that they shared in the lawmaking process—Commons had to consent in the name of the people, as did Lords in the name of the nobility or property and the monarch in the name of the whole nation.

The American colonies, of course, had no house of aristocrats, and until the crises of the 1760s the king had left them pretty much to be ruled by their own assemblies. These assemblies did generally have an upper house, appointed by the crown, and also had to work with a governor appointed by the crown, but these colonial upper houses were not really second legislative chambers in the full sense. Although they had some legislative responsibilities, they functioned largely as advisers to the governor (Lutz, 1980, p. 102). Thus, the legislative house elected by the people here had a much more dominant role over policy than in England (Adams, 1980, p. 231). Moreover, property requirements for voters that were essentially the same in the colonies as in England produced an electorate that was a much greater proportion of the population because land was so much more readily available here (Lutz, 1980, pp. 87-8).

The revolution intensified these already large differences from the British pattern by bringing about the deliberate expansions of the electorate and of the size of the legislatures. Also, the legislatures themselves were radically democratized by making even the upper chamber elective, and by generally allowing the same people to vote for its members who voted for the lower house members (Adams, 1980, pp. 293-307).[5]

One additional change greatly enhanced the role of popular consent in the legislative process. Accustomed to thinking of the crown as peculiarly the ruler and the judges as his lackeys (for judges had been less politically independent in the colonies than in England), the early postrevolution state

[5] Gestures were made in the direction of having an upper house that would represent "Property" in accordance with traditional Anglo-American Whig theories of balanced government (i.e., balanced between the principles of human numbers and property), by imposing much stiffer property requirements on candidates for the upper house than on candidates for the lower house. These gestures proved futile, because the groups of voters were the same, and the resulting state senates proved indistinguishable in behavior from the state assemblies (Lutz, 1980, pp. 88-89, 108-9, 207-8; Wood, 1969a, pp. 206-214; Main, 1967).

constitutions radically weakened both the executive and judicial branches, and tended to place them under the thumb of the legislatures (Wood, 1969a, pp. 135-150, 160-173; Lutz, 1980, p. 44). With an independent executive veto out of the picture, legislation really could be viewed as the will of the people (at least if one considers "people" in the sense of the majority of males).

B. Consent of the Governed to the Constitution of Government

The Pilgrim Code of 1636 stated, "We . . . freeborn subjects of the state of England . . . do ordain constitute and enact that no act imposition law or ordinance be . . . imposed upon us . . . but such as shall be imposed by consent of the body of associates or their representatives legally assembled" (Ward, 1973, p. 17). This is an assertion of a right of popular consent to legislation, or to government policy, not of a right in the people to determine the structure of government and the limits of its power. The notion of the latter evolved more slowly in America. It was stimulated by a variety of historical circumstances, by the social contract theories of Hobbes, Pufendorf, Vattel, and Locke, and by the tradition of corporate charters—originally granted by the crown, but later written by the colonists, often for their own consumption (Lutz, 1980, pp. 27-9, presents a list of these charters.) But is was also impeded by the higher law tradition of natural and common law exemplified by Sir Edward Coke and by the eighteenth century theory that viewed the legislature as embodying the people.

The sixteenth and early seventeenth century colonial charters gradually evolved from authorizations for commercial (and religious) enterprises into frames for local government (Bailyn, 1967, pp. 189-193; Goebel, 1971, pp. 3-4; McLaughlin, 1912, pp. 249-265). Also, the distance from England and the absence of a professional American bar in the seventeenth century made it useful to compile in writing the basic legal rights and privileges of Englishmen, which were in turn understood to be derived from the principles of human nature and/or from the Judaeo-Christian moral code (Bailyn, 1967, pp. 193-8 and 187-9). Thus, the seventeenth century had familiarized Americans with the practice of having their elected representatives draw up charters of the people's liberties; these were understood to be declarations of the common understanding, rather than grants of rights as such.

The Lockean principles embodied in the Declaration of Independence put forth as self-evident truth the idea that individuals by nature are equally free and freely choose to empower government to secure their natural rights. Moreover, they retain an indefeasible right to "alter or abolish" their "form" of government if they decide that it has become destructive of their rights. With this pronouncement, it became the acknowledged birthright of all Americans to live under a form of government to which they had given consent. A paraphrase of this conception of popular sovereignty can be found in eight of the fourteen (counting Vermont) state constitutions adopted between 1776 and 1780 (Hyneman, 1977, pp. 15-16; Peters, 1977, p. 174; Adams, 1980, pp. 63-5, 138).

It may thus come as a surprise to the untutored reader that the first six constitutions adopted by the American states were adopted not by any extraordinary act of the people but rather by the state legislatures (Lutz, 1980, p. 45; Peters, 1977, pp. 171-2). Even after Delaware (1776), North Carolina (1776), and New York (1777) innovated by having constitutions drawn up by conventions specially elected for the purpose, four additional states continued the pattern of having the legislative body write the constitution. Not until 1780 did the technique of specially elected constitutional drafting conventions become *de riguer* in every state (Lutz, 1980, p. 83). And not until the Massachusetts Constitution of 1780 was the additional step of ratification directly by the people tacked on to the process. This new technique was employed for only five of the ten constitutions adopted between 1780 and 1800 (Massachusetts, Pennsylvania, two New Hampshire constitutions, and the U.S. Constitution with the indirect mechanism of elected ratifying conventions) (Lutz, 1980, pp. 45, 65-9, 71-5, 81-4. Cf. Peters, 1977, p. 172).[6] During the late 1770s and early 1780s state legislatures amended constitutions, claimed power authoritatively to interpret them, and in a substantial number of cases flagrantly violated them (Lutz, 1980, pp. 62-5, 121; Wood, 1969a, pp. 274-5, 279; Snowiss, 1981, pp. 13-4; Goebel, p. 101, 142; Corwin, 1925, pp. 511-520).

Apart from the legislature's power over the writing of the constitution, the very meaning of a constitution as a restraint on government was quite different in the late 1770s from what it became in the nineteenth century. While scholars (compare Grey, 1978, with Bailyn, 1967, ch. 5; see also Storing, 1981, p. 37) can debate the question whether more Americans sided with Coke or with Blackstone as to the issue of Parliament's supremacy against the courts as final interpreter of the British "constitution,"[7] the way that American state constitutions were worded before 1787 makes it difficult to read them as placing any effective restraints upon legislatures. The constitutions of those years contained

[6] Charles Warren suggests that "The States" in 1776 introduced the idea that only extra-legislative bodies have proper authority to write or amend constitutions (1925, pp. 16-17). In fact, the popular acceptance of this idea, as measured by its institutionalization into constitutions, took much longer than he indicates. Stourzh, by contrast, acknowledges the gradualism of the transition (1776-1788) but provides none of the evidence in support of his correct insight (1984, p. 166).

[7] Henry St. John Viscount Bolingbroke defined the constitution in 1735 as "that assemblage of laws, institutions and customs, derived from certain fixed principles of reason, directed to certain fixed objects of public good, that compose the general system, according to which the community hath agreed to be governed" (Letter X, p. 108).

Declarations of Rights that were often worded in the form of moral admonitions; some of their clauses called upon government to adhere firmly "to justice, moderation, temperance, frugality, and virtue" (e.g. Virginia, 1776). Where the 1787 U.S. Constitution has the imperative commands "shall" or "shall not," these earlier state documents would have "ought" or "recommend" (as in "freedom of the press ought not to be restrained"—1776 Pennsylvania). Probably most telling, almost all the early state constitutions suggested circumstances where the legislature would be permitted to violate what were being declared to be "rights": "But no part of a man's property shall be taken from him . . . without his own consent, *or that of the legislative body of the people*" (New Hampshire, 1784, Art. XII, emphasis added). (Lutz, 1980, pp. 61-68, 49, 35; Wood 1969a, pp. 271-3; Peters, 1977, pp. 176-7; cf. Stourzh, 1984, pp. 168-9.) Finally, it is at least suggestive that while executives' oaths of office in these early constitutions included the duty to uphold the document, the oaths of legislators and judges did not (Goebel, 1971, p. 108).

This legislative power over constitutions stemmed from the prevailing assumption in 1776 that the legislature re-presented the people. That "ruler" whose arbitrary power the revolutionaries wanted to hem in had been eliminated from the picture. Thus, it was to take time for the idea to dawn on Americans that they might have use for constitutions which could check themselves qua rulers. It seemed in 1776 that constitutions could be used instead for expressing the public consensus on how government would be arranged and what it should be doing.

The old idea of a higher law that limited government had not disappeared; in fact, writing down that law was one way that Americans believed they were improving upon the British system. Although some—like James Otis in 1765 (Bailyn, 1967, p. 189; Wood, 1969a, p. 277), and Ellsworth and James Wilson opposing the *ex post facto* laws clauses at the Constitutional Convention (Farrand, 1913, II, p. 376)—argued that it would be a mistake to try to codify the basic privileges available to all Anglo-Americans as a matter of "right reason," most were persuaded that explicit confirmation of those rights in a visible, concrete document would be beneficial (Bailyn, 1967, pp. 189-190, 192; Wood, 1969a, pp. 266-8; Snowiss, 1981, p. 16; Jacobsohn, 1984; and the frequently cited opinion of Judge Tucker in *Kamper v. Hawkins*, 1793). But the prevailing idea in 1776 was not that we had these rights *because* the written constitutions embodied them; rather the idea was that we had them because right reason, as applied to human nature and as evolved through the Anglo-American tradition, told us they were true. The state constitutions' declarations of rights were just that: they were announcements of rights that would exist with or without the announcement; they were not viewed as witholdings of powers from the government, because powers over those rights were not viewed as transferable or alienable.[8] As one of the more striking examples of this outlook one can cite arguments from the 1786 Rhode Island Supreme Court case of *Trevett v. Weeden*. Trial by jury had been denied to certain defendants, and the state constitution, adapted from the colonial charter virtually unchanged by the legislature (Goebel, 1971, p. 139 at n. 147), had no explicit guarantee of trial by jury but did guarantee "all liberties and immunities of free and natural subjects . . . [of] England" (Thorpe, 1909, VI, p. 3220). The attorney James Varnum used this clause to argue that the right was "a fundamental a constitutional right," and one the courts must enforce, but, in the fashion of the times, he buttressed his argument with allusions to natural rights.[9] He traced the right to jury trial back to the Magna Carta and to custom even older than that and argued that it was an institution for providing practical security to people's natural right to equal liberty. His argument explicitly assumes that the rule that judges must enforce natural rights is even more obvious than the rule that they must enforce constitutional ones (p. 29).[10] The court tried to duck a direct clash with the legislature and resolved the case by denying their own jurisdiction, but the case nonetheless aroused much controversy.

[8] Grey, 1978, is the latest treatment, but much evidence of this is in the older work cited in the first paragraph of this essay. See also Wood, 1969a, pp. 456-7; and Storing, 1981, p. 37.

[9] His argument was published in a pamphlet which was widely publicized and was being sold in Philadelphia during the Constitutional Convention (McLaughlin, 1912, pp. 44-5; Crosskey, 1953, II, pp. 962-965).

[10] Varnum's pamphlet provides further evidence of the confusion about natural law philosophy in the minds of the eighteenth-century statesmen that underlies the disagreement between Walter Berns and Thomas Grey (see note 1). In order to establish judicial duty to declare the statute void, Varnum first invoked Locke's *Second Treatise* for the principle that government may not violate the inalienable natural right of the people to life, liberty, and the security of property (pp. 20-22). He then paraphrased and quoted at some length E. de Vattel's *The Law of Nations or Principles of the Law of Nature* (1758), to make the point that the people through a social compact establish the fundamental law, or constitution, which then operates as a limit upon the legislators, who are only the deputies of the people and who derive their commission through the constitution. Thus their power is limited thereby (pp. 23-25). Varnum was applying this argument to a constitution adopted by the legislature! Probably aware that the argument's applicability to Rhode Island was, to state it mildly, questionable, Varnum tried to buttress his case with the argument that, obviously, judges could not or should not enforce statutes that violate natural law or divine law. He gave as a hypothetical instance of the former an order that a man vacate his home for six months, and, as an instance of the latter, an order that a man kill his own child. He then tried to tie these assertions to Vattel's theory by an argument that says, essentially, higher authority is higher authority; whether it is God or the people qua-sovereign, judges must obey it: "But the judges, and all others, are bound by the laws of nature in preference to any human laws, because they were ordained by God himself anterior to any civil or political institutions. They are bound, in like manner, by the principles of the constitution in preference to any acts of the General Assembly, because they were ordained by the people [!] anterior to and created the powers of the General Assembly" (p. 29).

C. Changes in the 1780s

That the mid-1780s were a period of genuine political crisis in the United States is by now well documented. Abuses of legislative power were legion: paper money schemes, tender laws, suspension of debt collection, legislative interferences with trial by jury, bills of attainder, grants of exemption from the standing laws, etc. (Corwin, 1925, pp. 511-520; Wood, 1969a, pp. 403-425; Lutz, 1980, pp. 116-122. See also James Madison's essay of 1787 in 1901 ed., II, p. 361 ff.) One scholar documents repeated instances of legislative interference with ongoing trials in at least three states and cites Jefferson for authority that this also went on in a fourth (Goebel, 1971, pp. 98-9). In the course of this crisis, the dominant American political ideology underwent a profound shift.

The first and crucial change was that the people developed a sense of themselves as separate from the legislative body. This gradually led to a number of important shifts after 1780. First, drafters of state constitutions, realizing that the legislature did have the power of "rulers" and that such power could usefully be checked, moved toward strengthening the executive and judicial branches (Lutz, 1980, p. 45; Wood, 1969a, pp. 161, 447-463). Second, beginning with the Massachusetts Constitution of 1780, states moved, albeit haltingly, toward combining the writing of constitutions by specially elected bodies with the ratification of them by the people (Lutz, 1980, pp. 62-5, 71-5, 81-3; Stourzh, 1984, p. 166).[11] Once the constitution really did emerge out of popular consent, the institutional groundwork was laid for a popular-sovereignty-based theory of higher law and of judicial review. Just such a theory emerged in the mid-1780s. In addition, popular sovereignty was working its way into the authoritative structuring of constitutions and into legislative activities; the American tradition of petitioning legislators evolved into a custom of delivering insistent and binding "instructions." The power to give such instructions was enshrined in constitutions, and legislators took these instructions quite seriously (Lutz, 1980, pp. 115-118; Wood, 1969a, pp. 363-389; Adams, 1980, pp. 246-9). Thus in a paradoxical development, the 1780s was a period of an increase in the direct power of the people to legislate through instructions and an increase in the power of the people to check legislation through their role as authors of binding constitutions.

The first full-blown American theory of popular control over government through a written constitution appears to have been developed in the pamphlet "Conciliatory Hints" by Thomas Tudor Tucker in 1784 (Wood, 1969a, pp. 280-2). In calling for a constitutional convention in South

[11] See Wood, 1969a, chapter 8 for a brillant discussion of how the American extra-legislative and sub-legislative tradition of political activities by the people "out-of-doors" became transubstantiated in the 1780s into supra-legislative authority.

Carolina to replace the legislatively adopted charter with one that would have more legitimacy, Tudor reasoned, "In a true commonwealth . . . all authority is derived from the people at large, held only during their pleasure. . . . No man has any privilege above his fellow-citizens, except . . . what they have thought proper to vest in him . . . ." Thus, a constitution should be based "on the firm and proper foundation of the *express consent of the people, unalterable by the legislature*, or any other authority but that by which it is to be framed . . . [and] it should be declared to be paramount to all acts of the legislature . . ." (Wood, 1969a, p. 281, emphasis added). Within a year, Govenor Morris similarly expressed the sentiment that if the Constitution can be changed by the legislature, it is no constitution (Haines, 1932, p. 95). Once this outlook became widespread, the legislature could be viewed as neither the "rulers" nor the "people" but as the deputies of the people. This idea had been implicit in Locke and in the Declaration and explicit in the writings of Samuel Pufendorf and E. de Vattel, with which educated, politically active Americans were familiar (Berns, 1983, pp. 66-74; Wood 1969a, p. 284; McLaughlin, 1912, pp. 68-74). However, not until the 1780s did the idea begin to find institutional expression in America via constitutional conventions and extralegislative ratifications.

The earliest experiments with judicial review also occurred in the 1780s in state supreme court cases, and, as with the theory of consent to the constitution, a role for popular sovereignty emerged only gradually.[12] It was not unusual for arguments and court opinions for these cases to rely on unwritten "constitutional" rights, as well as on written texts. For instance, in 1784 attorney Alexander Hamilton argued in *Rutgers v. Waddington* that the New York law at issue was void on the ground that it conflicted with the Articles of Confederation, the Treaty of Peace and the unwritten law of nations (Goebel, 1964, pp. 282-315, 393-419).

During this period and continuing into the decade of the nineties, judicial review was extremely controversial. Opposition to it ranged from denial of its legitimacy by opposing counsel (in *Rutgers v. Waddington* and *Commonwealth of Va. v. Caton*, 1782, Haines, 1932, pp. 98-104; Corwin, 1911, pp. 110-120), to questioning of it by judges on the bench (in *Commonwealth v. Caton*, Haines, 1932, pp. 95-98; Crosskey, 1953, pp. 952-961; Goebel, 1971, pp. 126-8; and in *Rutgers v. Waddington*, Haines, 1932, pp. 98-104; Crosskey, 1953, pp. 962-965). There were also more extreme reactions of popular mass protest meetings against it (*Rutgers v. Waddington*, Haines, 1932, pp. 98-104; Crosskey, 1953, pp. 962-965), and popular petitions to state legislatures against it (*Holmes v. Walton*, N.J.,

[12] These court decisions were generally not published. They are reviewed in Haines, 1932, ch. 4-7; Snowiss, 1981, pp. 10-16; Corwin, 1911, pp. 110-120; Goebel, 1971, pp. 124-141, McLaughlin, 1912, pp. 41-50; Crosskey, 1953, II, pp. 944-975; and Warren, 1925, pp. 43-48. The most thorough are Haines, Goebel, and Crosskey.

1780, Haines, 1932, pp. 92-5; Crosskey, 1953, pp. 948-952). Legislatures, too, opposed judicial review by votes of censure upon its exercise, or perceived exercise (*Rutgers v. Waddington*, Haines, pp. 98-104; Crosskey, pp. 962-5; *Trevett v. Weeden*, R.I., 1786, Haines, pp. 105-112; Goebel, 1971, pp. 137-141), and through attempts to outlaw it, (*Bayard v. Singleton*, N.Car., 1786-7, Haines, pp. 112-120; Crosskey, pp. 971-5; and *Holmes v. Walton*, Haines pp. 92-5). In some instances legislatures insisted that judges accused of engaging in judicial review present themselves at the legislature to account for their (mis)behavior (*Bayard v. Singleton*, Haines, pp. 112-120; Crosskey, pp. 971-975; and *Trevett v. Weeden*, Haines, pp. 105-112; Goegel, pp. 137-141), and there were even serious efforts to impeach and remove from office such judges (*Trevett v. Weeden*, Haines, pp. 105-112; Goebel, pp. 137-141 and *The New Hampshire Ten-Pound Act Case*, 1786-7, Crosskey, pp. 968-971).

In sum, the first decade of independence was a period of extreme commitment to popular sovereignty. Judges and attorneys, however, sometimes argued for a judicial power to reject popularly supported statutes that conflicted with an unwritten higher law. And judicial review during this period—a period in which it was *not* understood to be limited to the enforcement of a popularly adopted written text—was highly controversial.

II. 1787-1803: The Merger of Majority Will and Wisdom

Popular sovereignty was very much in the air in 1787, but whether it could be saved from itself was an open question. Leading statesmen were in despair over the lack of republican virtue that our republics had produced; what had been thought a contradiction in terms in 1776, "democratic despotism," seemed to be on our doorstep (Wood, 1969a, p. 404, paraphrasing John Adams).

The ingenious Federalist solution to the problem, to make a very long story short, was to turn the people against themselves. The people *qua* nation would be used to limit the people *qua* states. Within the nation majority rule would prevail, but the majority would be sliced three ways, once for the House, once for the Senate, and once for the President. Similarly, for ascertaining the voice of "the people" to amend the Constitution, extraordinary majorities would be sliced three ways: 2/3 in the House, 2/3 in Senate, and 3/4 of the state legislatures.

Any of these three embodiments of "the people" would be given the power to block action by the parallel other versions of "the people." Thus, by making the sense of the community very deliberate indeed, the Federalists hoped to make it more likely that majority will would approximate civic wisdom, thereby bringing about at the level of public policy (if not in the individual soul) at least an analogue for republican virtue. True to the essence of this solution, the Federalist scheme for adoption of the Constitution utilized popular approval through ratifying conventions. This enhanced the potential acceptability of popular-sovereignty-based theories of judicial review to be applied at the national level.

As was the case with the argument that only a written constitution could properly allow for popular control over legislatures, the germ of the idea that judicial review should be viewed as an instrument of popular sovereignty seems to have first been published in America in Thomas Tudor Tucker's (1784) pamphlet, "Conciliatory Hints" (Tucker, 1983).[13] In that pamphlet Tucker rehearsed the familiar Lockean arguments on reasons for entry into the social compact, on the delegating of power from the people to the government, and on the idea that if the legislature "should exceed the powers vested in them, their act is no longer the act of their constituents" (Tucker, 1983, pp. 612-4, 622-3). But Tucker added certain suggestions that pointed toward an American improvement upon the Lockean theory that had justified our revolution. He criticized the British "constitution" as lacking a peaceful remedy for oppression: Parliament's "privileges are undefinable, because it is impossible to say, how far they may be extended without rousing the people to a tumultuous opposition or civil war; for with them there is no other remedy against tyranny and oppression" (p. 612). Americans now had the heaven-sent opportunity for an express statement from the people as to the limits of legislative power. Moreover, we would be well-advised to contrive "the terms of the compact or constitution . . . to provide a remedy . . . without outrage, noise or tumult" for all cases where the rulers resort to a "traitorous abuse of trust" (p. 614). Although Tucker does not detail that remedy for avoiding appeal to the sword, he does in the same pamphlet suggest that a problem which had recently occurred in a sister state—inadvertent transgression of the constitution by the legislature—could have been avoided had only that constitution "expressly declare[d] that no act of the legislature contravening it should be of force" in the courts of law (p. 627). Tucker thus suggests that judicial review might serve as the peaceful alternative to revolution and also as the institutional guardian of the people's sovereignty.

In 1786 in preparation for a state supreme court case, *Bayard V. Singleton*, the attorney James Iredell elaborated a more complete theory along those lines in a North Carolina newspaper; moreover, he outlined the same arguments in a letter in August 1787 to Richard Spaight, a delegate then attending the Constitutional Convention. Sylvia Snowiss (1981) has recently made a convincing case that Iredell's arguments provided the

[13] Although Wood (1969a, pp. 280-282) originally drew my attention to this Tucker essay, he does not note its formative contribution to an American theory of judicial review.

inspirations both for Hamilton's explanation of judicial review in Federalist #78 and for James Wilson's explanation of it in his lectures in law, delivered in 1790-91 but published in 1793 (1981, p. 16. See related speculations in Wood, 1969a, pp. 460-1; Goebel, 1971, p. 130; Haines, 1932, pp. 116-120; McLaughlin, 1912, pp. 74-5, n. 1; and Stourzh, 1984, pp. 169-172). Both Hamilton and Wilson were enormously influential in shaping the American understanding of judicial review and its relation to popular sovereignty. Iredell's newspaper argument was as follows:

The power of the Assembly is limited and defined by the Constitution. It is a creature of the Constitution . . . . The *people* have chosen to be governed under such and such principles. They have not chosen to be governed, not promised to submit upon any other; and the Assembly have no . . . right to obedience on other terms . . . .

The (judicial) duty . . . I conceive, in all cases is to decide according to the *laws of the State*. It will not be denied, I suppose, that the constitution is a *law* of *the State*, as well as an act of Assembly, with this difference only, that it is the *fundamental* law, and unalterable by the legislature, which derives all its power from it. One act of Assembly may repeal another act of Assembly. For this reason, the latter act is to be obeyed, and not the former. An act of Assembly cannot repeal the constitution, or any part of it. For that reason, an act of Assembly, inconsistent with the constitution, is *void*, and cannot be obeyed, without disobeying the superior law to which we were previously and irrevocably bound. The judges, therefore, must take care at their peril, that every act of Assembly they presume to enforce is warranted by the constitution, since if it is not, they act without lawful authority. This is not a usurped or a discretionary power, but one inevitably resulting from the constitution of their office, they being judges for the benefit *of the whole people, not mere servants of the Assembly*. (Emphasis in original. McRee, ed., 1949, II, pp. 145-149.)

This argument echoes that of Varnum of 1786, but it significantly omits the Locke-based natural rights argument and the divine law argument, standing instead squarely on the Vattel-based constitutional theory of popular consent as source of limits on legislative power. It fleshes out Thomas Tudor Tucker's skeletal suggestion that the people's written constitutional limits on legislatures can be enforced by courts of law.

Although Iredell indicated his awareness of, and seemed at this time to endorse, the natural-justice-based version of judicial review as well (a version he was later explicitly to disavow[14]), he made a point of noting the singular advantage of a judicial review power grounded squarely in a written constitution:

Without an expressed constitution the powers of the legislature would undoubtedly have been absolute (as the Parliament of Great Britain is said to be) and any act passed, *not inconsistent with natural justice (for that curb is avowed* by the judges even in England) would have been

[14] In *Calder v. Bull* (1798, p. 398) he wrote: "If a government . . . were established by a Constitution which imposed no limits on the legislative power, the consequence would *inevitably* be, that *whatever* the legislative power chose to enact, would be lawfully enacted, and the judicial power could *never* interpose to pronounce it void. It is true that some speculative jurists have held, that a legislative act against natural justice must, in itself, be void, but I cannot think that, under such a government, any court of Justice would possess a power to declare it so."

binding on the people. The experience of the evils . . . attending an absolute power in a legislative body suggested the propriety of a *real* original contract between the people and their future government . . . .

It really appears to me, the exercise of the [judicial] power is unavoidable, the Constitution *not being a mere imaginary thing, about which ten thousand different opinions may be formed, but a written document* to which all may have recourse . . . . (All emphasis added. McRee, 1949, II, pp. 148, 173-4.)

It was this kind of judicial review that the principle of popular sovereignty now supported.

Iredell's description of judicial review required that judges "take notice of" any direct clash between a statute and a constitution and consider the constitution as a law of superior obligation, because it comes from "the whole people" (Letter to Spaight, 1787, in McRee, 1949, p. 173).

Hamilton's famous version of the argument, from Federalist 78, was:

Every act of a delegated authority, contrary to the tenor of the commission under which it is excercised, is void. No legislative act, therefore, contrary to the Constitution, can be valid. To deny this would be to affirm that the deputy is greater than his principal; that the servant is above his master; that the representatives of the people are superior to the people themselves . . . . If there should happen to be an irreconcilable variance between [a statute and the Constitution], that which has the superior obligation and validity ought, of course, to be preferred . . . .

Wilson's was:

From the constitution, the legislative department, as well as every other part of government derives its power: by the constitution, the legislative, as every other department, must be directed; of the constitution, no alteration by the legislature can be made or authorized . . . . The constitution is the supreme law of the land: to that supreme law every other power must be inferior and subordinate.

Now, let us suppose, that the legislature should pass an act manifestly repugnant to some part of the constitution; and that the operation and validity of both should come regularly in question before a court, forming a part of the judicial department. In that department, the "judicial power of the United States is vested" by the "people," who "ordained and established" the constitution . . . . Two contradictory rules . . . cannot possibly be administered . . . . The supreme power of the United States has given one rule: a subordinate power . . ., a contradictory rule: the former is the law of the land: as a necessary consequence, the latter is void . . . . In this manner . . . it is the duty of a court of justice, under the constitution of the United States, to decide. (1967, I, pp. 329-331.)

Subsequent to the development and propagation of these popular-sovereignty-based rationales for judicial review, a rather dramatic transformation of its legitimacy can be observed. Judicial review lost its controversial status during the 1790s and gained acceptance not only among the judiciary but also in state and federal legislatures, and, presumably, in the popular mind. Legislative attacks on the principle of judicial review died out.[15] In contrast to mass protests and impeachment

[15] State supreme court cases exercising judicial review on the basis of state constitutions after 1789 are canvassed in Haines, 1932, ch. 7 and McLaughlin, 1912, pp. 19-30.

attempts, one reads of instances where legislatures amended statutes in order to comply with judicial objections (for example, *Kamper v. Hawkins*, 1793, Haines, 1932, pp. 152-7). During the early years of the U.S. Congress, repeated allusions were made to the propriety of judicial examination of the question of the constitutionality of federal statutes (Warren, 1925, ch. 4; cf. Crosskey, 1953, pp. 1028-1046). In 1799, when several state legislatures announced replies to the Virginia and Kentucky Resolutions' interposition doctrine, they pointedly spoke of the U.S. Supreme Court as the final interpreter of the U.S. Constitution (McLaughlin, 1912, pp. 16-17; Haines, 1932, pp. 189-191).

By 1802, high courts in eight of the states had endorsed judicial review (Corwin, 1963), and federal courts had followed suit, endorsing the concept of judicial review in a number of instances prior to 1803 (Warren, 1923, ch. 1; McLaughlin, 1912, pp. 10-16; Haines, 1932, ch. 8; Goebel, 1971, pp. 778-784).[16] In the judicial decisions where judicial review was discussed at any length, the prominence of the Iredell-Hamilton-Wilson popular consent theory is unmistakable.[17] In the fifteen state supreme court cases between 1789 and 1802 where judicial review was arguably at issue (see Haines, 1932, ch. 7; McLaughlin, 1912, pp. 19-30), nine contained judicial defenses of the power. Of those, seven either quoted or paraphrased the Iredell-Hamilton-Wilson rationale. The two that presented an alternative argument, quoting Coke and relying on the Magna Carta and "common right and reason," were both South Carolina cases, *Ham v. M'Claws*, 1789; *Bowman v. Middleton*, 1792. It is instructive that in two subsequent South Carolina cases, *Lindsay v. Commissioners*, 1796, and *White v. Kendrick*, 1805, the Coke approach is dropped and replaced by the will-of-the-people-as-higher-law argument.

During the 1790s judicial review not only gained a mighty ally in the Iredell-Hamilton-Wilson argument concerning popular consent to the rules of the constitution, it also gained renewed strength from tougher wording in the state constitutions. Copying the example of the U.S. Constitution, the six post-1790 eighteenth-century constitutions adopted "shall" in bills of rights in place of the formerly preferred "ought." In sum, the 1790s in America witnessed a change in the very concept of written constitutions. Now they were written in a language meant to be binding, and they were viewed as binding at least in part because they expressed "the consent of the governed." To a nation which took its bearings from the Declaration of Independence, this was no small addition to the argument.

[16] The Supreme Court cases were: *Cooper v. Telfair*, 1800; *Calder v. Bull*, 1798; *Hollingsworth v. Virginia*, 1798; *Hylton v. U.S.*, 1796; *Van Horne's Lessee v. Dorrance*, 1795. The lower federal court cases were: *The First Hayburn Case*, 1792; *Ogden v. Witherspoon*, 1802; *Minge v. Gilmour*, 1798; and *U.S. v. Callender*, 1800.

[17] This point is also made by Snowiss (1981, pp. 18-19), but she presents none of the evidence.

III. 1803 AND THE FUTURE

According to Snowiss (1981), when John Marshall established judicial review over congressional statutes in *Marbury v. Madison*, although he restricted judicial power to the enforcement of written rules, he transformed the court's power from one limited to Iredell's concept of "a clear and urgent case" of clashing provisions (see Iredell, concurring, in *Calder v. Bull*, 1798, p. 399) to a power to expound the various doubtful meanings of the Constitution. In his hands it became a judicial power to choose one interpretation against other reasonable, conflicting ones that the legislature may have chosen. Paradoxically, Snowiss (1981, pp. 2, 4-5) sees this as clearly an expansion of judicial power over the earlier version of judicial review, which, although based upon unwritten law concepts, was limited to a narrow range of fundamental natural/common law rights (see also Jacobsohn, 1984, pp. 25-7; Berns, 1983). By contrast, the versions of unwritten higher law of contemporary scholars like Thomas Grey and Walter Murphy would take judicial power altitudes beyond Marshall's plateau of judicial exposition of the written constitutional text. Grey would have us learn from the Supreme Court the content of our "basic national ideals of individual liberty and fair treatment" (1974, p. 706), and Murphy would allow the Court to strike down any law that conflicted wtih the justices' notion of the "dignity of the individual" (1978, pp. 155-9).

The higher-written-law background of judicial review, which Grey traces up until 1776, did not disappear in 1787 after the Constitution was drafted. It appears as influential in judges' decisions well into the nineteenth century. The opinion of Justice Chase for *Calder v. Bull* (1798) and the opinion of Chief Justice Marshall in *Fletcher v. Peck* (1810) exhibit the transitional trait of acknowledging natural law/common law support for their position and also grounding it in exposition of the constitutional text. Justice Chase explains that the *ex post facto* laws clauses of the constitution do not apply to the statute at hand, and he explains why, but he also says that "the genius, nature, and the spirit of our state governments, amount to a prohibition of [fundamentally unjust] laws: and the great principles of law and reason forbid them" (p. 388). These unwritten principles would make such acts of our legislatures void even "if they had not been expressly restrained" (p. 388). But the clear implication is that our constitution does expressly forbid violations of fundamental justice. Marshall, too, covered his bets both ways, declaring in *Fletcher* that "either by general principles which are common to our free institutions, or by the particular provisions of the Constitution of the United States," the law in question was void (p. 139).

As American society became less homogeneous, presumably less consensual, and scholars became more positivistic in their outlook during the nineteenth century, these unwritten-law justifications gradually disappeared, although they later resurfaced in the form of extremely controversial "noninterpretive" readings of the constitutional text, most notoriously in the doctrine of substantive due process (but cf. Murphy, 1978). Perhaps that disappearance is related to the fact that Americans were starting to view natural justice as that which Iredell had described as "a mere imaginary thing, about which ten thousand different opinions may be formed" (McRee, 1949, II, pp. 173-4). But the *political* success of a judicial review anchored firmly in the theory of popular consent to the constitutional text was very likely also a factor in the judges' shift.

This essay has been essentially an account of the relative weakness of judicial review in the first decade of the Confederation, when it was based primarily on unwritten natural rights, and an account of its rapid flourishing starting in the mid-1780s once it was grounded in a constitutional theory that stressed popular consent to government as articulated in a written, boundary-setting document. There is currently a boom in scholarly commentary that views judicial review as a more or less unbounded charter to judges to fill in for Americans the content of our unwritten "national ideals" (to name but a few examples, Miller, 1982; Perry, 1982; Bobbitt, 1982; Carter, 1985). Perhaps this account of the early days of judicial review will prove a cautionary tale for such scholars.

Case References

Bayard v. Singleton, 1 Martin 42 (N. Car., 1786-7).
Bowman v. Middleton, 1 Bay 252 (1792).
Calder v. Bull, 3 Dallas 386 (1798).
Commonwealth v. Caton, (VA., 1782).
Cooper v. Telfair, 4 Dallas 14 (1800).
Eisenstadt v. Baird, 405 U.S. 438 (1972).
Fletcher v. Peck, 10 U.S. 87 (1810).
Griswold v. Connecticut, 381 U.S. 479 (1965).
Ham v. M'Claws, 1 Bay 93 (S. Car., 1789).
The First Hayburn Case, 2 Dallas 406 (1792).
Hollingsworth v. Virginia, 3 Dallas 387 (1798).
Holmes v. Walton (N.J., 1780).
Hylton v. U.S., 3 Dallas 171 (1796).
Kamper v. Hawkins, 1 Va. Cases 20 (1793).
Lindsay v. Commissioners, 2 Bay 61 (1796).
Marbury v. Madison, 11 Cranch 138 (1803).
Minge v. Gilmour, Fed. Cases No. 9, 631 (1798).
The N.H. "Ten-Pound" Act Case, (N.H., 1786-7).
Ogden v. Saunders, 12 Wheaton 213 (1827).
Ogden v. Witherspoon, Fed. Cases No. 10, 461 and 3 N.C. 404 (1802).
Roe v. Wade, 410 U.S. 113 (1973).
Rutgers v. Waddington (N.Y., 1784).
Trevett v. Weeden (R.I., 1876).
U.S. v. Callender, Fed. Cases No. 14, "09 (1800).
Van Horne's Lessee v. Dorrance, 2 Dallas 304 (1795).

References

Adams, John. 1856. *The Works of John Adams*. C. F. Adams, ed. Boston: Little, Brown.

Adams, Willi Paul. 1980. *The First American Constitutions*. Rita and Robert Kimler, trans. Chapel Hill: University of North Carolina Press.

Bailyn, Bernard. 1967. *Ideological Origins of the American Revolution*. Cambridge: Harvard University Press.

Berns, Walter. 1983. Judicial Review and the Rights and the Laws of Nature. In Philip Kurland et al., eds., *1982 The Supreme Court Review*. Chicago: University of Chicago Press.

Bobbitt, Philip. 1982. *Constitutional Fate*. New York: Oxford University Press.

Bolingbroke, Henry St. John Viscount. 1735. *A Dissertation Upon Parties*. 3rd ed. London: H. Haines.

Carter, Lief H. 1985. *Contemporary Constitutional Lawmaking*. New York: Pergamon.

Corwin, Edward S. 1911. The Establishment of Judicial Review. *Michigan Law Review*, 9: 102-125.

———. 1914. A Basic Doctrine of American Law. *Michigan Law Review*, 12: 247-276.

——— . 1925. The Progress of Constitutional Theory Between the Declaration of Independence and the Meeting of the Philadelphia Convention. *American Historical Review*, 30: 511-536.

———. 1928-9. The Higher Law Background of American Constitutional Law. *Harvard Law Review*, 42: 149-185, 365-409.

———. 1957. *Court Over Constitution*. Gloucester, MA: Peter Smith. (Reprint of 1938 ed.)

———. 1963. *The Doctrine of Judicial Review*. Gloucester, MA: Peter Smith. (Reprint of 1914 ed.)

Crosskey, William W. 1953. *Politics and the Constitution in the History of the United States*. Chicago: University of Chicago Press.

Douglass, Elisha. 1935. *Rebels and Democrats*. Chapel Hill: University of North Carolina Press.

Ely, John. 1980. *Democracy and Distrust*. Cambridge: Harvard University Press.

Farrand, Max. 1913. *Records of the Federal Convention*. New Haven: Yale University Press.

Goebel, Julius, ed. 1964. *The Law Practice of Alexander Hamilton*. New York: Columbia University Press.

———. 1971. *Volume I of the Oliver Wendell Holmes Devise History of the Supreme Court of the U.S.: Antecedents and Beginnings to 1801*. New York: MacMillan.

Goldstein, Leslie F. 1985. Judicial Review and Modern Judicial Scholarship. Paper presented at annual meeting of Midwest Political Science Association, Chicago.

Grey, Thomas. 1974. Do We Have an Unwritten Constitution? *Stanford Law Review*, 27: 703-718.

——— . 1978. Origins of the Unwritten Constitution: Fundamental Law in American Revolutionary Thought. *Stanford Law Review*, 30: 843-893.

Gunther, Gerald. 1980. *Cases and Materials in Constitutional Law*. 10th ed. Mineola, NY: Foundation.

Haines, Charles H. 1932. *The American Doctrine of Judicial Supremacy*. Berkeley: University of California Press.

Haskins, George Lee. 1981. *Part One of Volume II of Holmes Devise History of the Supreme Court of the U.S.* New York: Macmillan.

Hyneman, Charles S. 1977. Republican Government in America: The Idea and Its Realization. In George and Scarlett Graham, eds., *Founding Principles of American Government: Two Hundred Years of Democracy on Trial*. Bloomington: Indiana University Press.

Jacobsohn, Gary. 1984. E.T.: The Extra-Textual in Constitutional Interpretation. *Constitutional Commentary*, I: 21-42.

Jefferson, Thomas. 1854. *The Writings of Thomas Jefferson*. H.A. Washington, ed. Washington, DC: Taylor and Maury.
Levy, Leonard. 1967. Judicial Review, History, and Democracy: An Introduction. In Leonard Levy, ed., *Judicial Review and the Supreme Court*. New York: Harper and Row.
Lutz, Donald. 1980. *Popular Consent and Popular Control*. Baton Rouge: Louisiana State University Press.
McLaughlin, Andrew. 1912. *The Court, the Constitution, and Parties*. Chicago: University of Chicago Press.
McRee, Griffith, ed. 1949. *Life and Correspondence of James Iredell*. New York: Peter Smith. (Reprint of 1858 ed.)
Madison, James. 1901. *The Writings of James Madison*. Gaillard Hunt, ed. New York: G.P. Putnam's Sons.
Main, Jackson T. 1966. Government by the People: The American Revolution and the Democratization of the Legislature. *William and Mary Quarterly*, 3rd Series, 23: 391-407.
______. 1967. *The Upper House in Revolutionary America*. Madison: University of Wisconsin Press.
Miller, Arthur S. 1982. *Toward Increased Judicial Activism*. Chicago: Greenwood.
Murphy, Walter. 1978. The Act of Constitutional Interpretation. In M. Judd Harmon, ed., *Essays on The Constitution of the United States*. Port Washington, NY: Kennikat.
Perry, Michael S. 1982. *The Constitution, the Courts, and Human Rights*. New Haven: Yale University Press.
Peters, Ronald M. 1977. The Written Constitution. In George and Scarlett Graham, eds., *Founding Principles of American Government*. Bloomington: Indiana University Press.
Pole, J.R. 1966. *Political Representation*. New York: St. Martin's.
Rossiter, Clinton. 1953. *Seedtime of the Republic*. New York: Harcourt Brace.
Snowiss, Sylvia. 1981. From Fundamental Law to Supreme Law of the Land: A Reinterpretation of the Origin of Judicial Review in the U.S. Paper presented at annual meeting of American Political Science Association, New York.
Storing, Herert. 1981. The Constitution and the Bill of Rights. In Ralph Rossum and Gary McDowell, eds., *The American Founding*. Port Washington, NY: Kennikat.
Stourzh, Gerald. 1984. The American Revolution, Modern Constitutionalism, and the Protection of Human Rights. In Kenneth Thompson and Robert Myers, eds., *Truth and Tragedy: A Tribute to Hans Morgenthau*. New Brunswick: Transaction Books.
Thorpe, F.N. 1909. *The Federal and State Constitutions, Colonial Charters, and Other Organic Laws of the States, Territories, and Colonies*. Washington, DC: Government Printing Office.
Tucker, Thomas Tudor. 1983. Conciliatory Hints Attempting . . . to Remove Party Prejudice. In Charles S. Hyneman and Donald S. Lutz, eds., *American Political Writing During the Founding Era 1760-1805*. Indianapolis: Liberty Press. (Reprint of 1784 ed.)
Varnum, James. 1787. *The Case Trevett against Weeden*. Providence: John Carter.
Ward, Harry M. 1973. *Stastism in Plymouth Colony*. Port Washington, NY: Kennikat.
Warren, Charles. 1923. *The Supreme Court in U.S. History*. Boston: Little Brown.
______. 1925. *Congress, the Constitution and the Supreme Court*. Boston: Little, Brown.
Williamson, Chilton. 1960. *American Suffrage from Property to Democracy*. Princeton: Princeton University Press.
Wilson, James. 1967. *The Works of James Wilson*. Robert McCloskey, ed. Cambridge: Harvard University Press.
Wood, Gordon. 1969a. *The Creation of the American Republic 1776-1787*. Chapel Hill: University of North Carolina Press.
______. 1969b. *Representation in the American Revolution*. Charlottesville: University of Virginia Press.
Wright, Benjamin F. 1931. *American Interpretations of Natural Law*. Cambridge: Harvard University Press.

"A TUB TO THE WHALE": THE FOUNDING FATHERS AND ADOPTION OF THE FEDERAL BILL OF RIGHTS

Kenneth R. Bowling

Seamen have a custom, when they meet a whale, to fling him out an empty tub by way of amusement, to divert him from laying violent hands upon the ship. Jonathan Swift, *Tale of a Tub* (1704)

Like a barrel thrown to the whale, the people were to be amused with fancied amendments, until the harpoon of power, should secure its prey and render resistance ineffectual. [Samuel Bryan], "Centinel No. 19," (Philadelphia) *Independent Gazetteer*, October 7, 1788

The constitutional role of the federal Bill of Rights has been monumental. This fact would surprise most members of the First Federal Congress, the body which reluctantly proposed to the states the constitutional amendments later called the Bill of Rights.[1] The Federalist

Mr. Bowling is a member of the First Federal Congress Project at George Washington University, Washington, D.C. This article is based upon a chapter in his "Politics in the First Congress, 1789-1791" (Ph.D. diss., University of Wisconsin 1968). Additional research was conducted under a grant from the National Endowment for the Humanities.

[1] Although much has been written about the Bill of Rights, very little of it relates to the legislative history of its adoption. This is particularly true about the political aspects, most of which are contained in previously unstudied manuscripts. Robert A. Rutland, *The Birth of the Bill of Rights, 1776-1791* (Chapel Hill 1955), which focuses on the background of the amendments, aptly summarizes its passage through the First Federal Congress. Irving Brant, *The Bill of Rights: Its Origin and Meaning* (Indianapolis 1965), contains primarily a brief analysis of some of the rhetoric of the debate. His *James Madison: Father of the Constitution, 1787-1800* (Indianapolis 1950) includes a short legislative history, effectively making the point that Madison was the force behind adoption of a federal Bill of Rights. Leonard W. Levy's thesis is clearly stated in Leonard W. Levy, Kenneth L. Karst, and Dennis J. Mahoney, eds., *Encyclopedia of the American Constitution* (4 vols., New York 1986), I, 113-116. Levy concludes in his essay on the Bill of Rights that it arose from political necessity

JOURNAL OF THE EARLY REPUBLIC, 8 (Fall 1988).

majority considered amendments an unnecessary political expedient of little constitutional importance, and the time spent on their adoption as wasted. Antifederal members saw them as an impediment to the changes in the structure and power of the new federal government that they sought. Many law clerks and scholars have searched in vain through the congressional debate over the first ten amendments for comment on their constitutional or philosophical implications. Instead of inspiring rhetoric and thoughtful analysis about the rights of man, they find only political fights: the most important, between James Madison of Virginia and his fellow Federalists in the House of Representatives; the most bitter, between the Federalists and the Antifederalists in the House; and, finally, the least divisive, between the House and the Senate.

Leonard Levy aptly states that Madison is even more entitled to be known as the father of the Bill of Rights than of the Constitution. Without Madison's commitment there would have been no federal Bill of Rights in 1791, but even he did not envision a separate bill of rights. Although he had long been convinced of the necessity of bills of rights to protect civil liberties, practical political concerns were his primary motivation. He believed rights-related amendments would satisfy enough Antifederalists to protect the new Constitution from both the structural amendments and the second Federal Convention which Antifederal leaders demanded, and to secure ratification by Rhode Island and particularly North Carolina. In addition he had to consider his political survival in Virginia. Forced upon him more by the political climate of late 1788 than by the arguments of his friend Thomas Jefferson, Madison's proposals, as both Federalists and Antifederalists quickly declared, tossed a tub to the whale.

---

and that Madison is even more entitled to be known as the father of the Bill of Rights than of the Constitution. Julius Goebel, Jr., *History of the Supreme Court of the United States*, vol. 1, *Antecedents and Beginnings to 1801* (New York 1971), ch. 10, is the most detailed narrative on the adoption of the amendments. One of the author's theses is that while certain proposed amendments protected civil liberty, others (the alterations or structural ones) were merely "political" (414). This statement ignores the fact that the movement for amendments was in itself political and that many Federalists considered the rights-related ones in particular nothing more than a political tactic cynically employed by self-serving Antifederal leaders to whip up opposition to the Constitution among the populace. It is also important to remember that some amendments which do not appear to us to be rights-related were so considered in the eighteenth century. Charles Warren's "New Light on the History of the Federal Judiciary Act of 1789," *Harvard Law Review*, 37 (Nov. 1923), 49-132, fails to establish as intimate a connection between the Judiciary Act and the first ten amendments as it asserts.

Noah Webster, although not a member of Congress, expressed the point of view of many of its Federalist members in an anonymous attack on Madison, published while the Virginian was leading the floor fight for amendments. "It seems to be agreed on all hands," he wrote, "that paper declarations of rights are trifling things and no real security to liberty. In general they are a subject of ridicule." The people regret that "Congress should spend their time in throwing out an empty tub to catch people, either factious or uninformed, who might be taken more honorably by reason and equitable laws. They regret particularly that Mr. Madison's talents should be employed to bring forward amendments, which, at best can have little effect upon the merits of the constitution, and may sow the seeds of discord from New-Hampshire to Georgia."[2]

Madison and other leaders in the fight to strengthen the federal government during the 1780s made a critical—almost fatal—error at the Federal Convention by not attaching a bill of rights to the proposed Constitution when Antifederalists George Mason of Virginia and Elbridge Gerry of Massachusetts had called for one. Even in the face of Mason's advice that "it would give great quiet to the people," all the states in attendance voted against adding a bill of rights. Antifederalist Richard Henry Lee of Virginia unsuccessfully attempted to attach several hastily drafted amendments to the Constitution in September 1787 before the Confederation Congress submitted it to the states for ratification. His recommendations, however, were not confined to guarantees of personal liberty; he wanted to change the structure and curtail the power of the new federal government as well.[3] Thus an ambiguity in the meaning of the word "amendment" arose at the start of the ratification debate and remained throughout. Support for amendments could indicate either a desire that personal liberties be protected, or that fundamental changes in the balance of

---

[2] William T. Hutchinson *et al.*, eds., *The Papers of James Madison* (15 + vols., Chicago and Charlottesville 1962-), XII, 334-345. I identified Webster as the author based on the fact that "A Free Mechanic" (New York *Journal*, Aug. 20, 1789) in replying to the piece signed "Pacificus" referred to its author as a noted grammarian; in addition, "Pacificus'" thoughts on bills of rights are identical to those Webster wrote anonymously in 1787 and 1788 and then copyrighted in 1790 under his own name. See also Julian P. Boyd *et al.*, eds., *The Papers of Thomas Jefferson* (23 + vols., Princeton 1950-), XVIII, 131-135.

[3] Max Farrand, ed., *The Records of the Federal Convention of 1787* (4 vols., New Haven 1937), II, 587-588; Merrill Jensen, ed., *The Documentary History of the Ratification of the Constitution*, vol. I, *Constitutional Documents and Records, 1776-1787* (Madison, Wisc. 1976), 322-353.

power between the state and federal governments and in the structure of the federal government be made, or both. As time passed some participants in the debate over the Constitution sought to clarify the confusion by replacing "amendment" with "bill or declaration of rights" for the former sense and "alteration" for the latter. Each of the last four states to ratify proposed their amendments in two lists to reflect this distinction. In this article I use "amendment" to refer to both types and "alteration" and "bill of rights" or "rights-related amendments" to distinguish between them.

Having failed to attach amendments in the Confederation Congress, Antifederalists demanded them from the ratifying conventions. Party leaders stressed the absence of a bill of rights similar to those which existed in most states. Many Federalists considered the eloquent demands of Antifederal leaders for a bill of rights during the ratification campaign as merely a ruse to cover their opposition to a Constitution which restricted state sovereignty and thereby threatened their political bases. Such a motive cannot be attributed to George Mason, the author of the 1776 Virginia Declaration of Rights. To suggest it for Patrick Henry, the chief opponent of Madison and Jefferson in their ten-year struggle for religious liberty in Virginia, is another matter.

In reply to Antifederal demands for a bill of rights, Federalists asserted that since all powers not delegated to the federal government remained with the states there was no need for a federal bill of rights because Congress had no power to interfere with personal liberties. Further, some argued, a federal bill of rights might endanger liberties not only because it protected only certain specified rights, but also because it implied that the central government had the power to decide which rights to guarantee. Pennsylvanian James Wilson's widely reprinted speech of October 1787 is generally seen as the first statement of this critical Federalist argument, but it had been used earlier by both Roger Sherman of Connecticut in the Federal Convention, and Madison in the Confederation Congress. It was a shrewd argument, but hardly convincing to men who knew history and who found in the "necessary and proper" and "supremacy" clauses of the Constitution a multitude of scenarios for tyranny. In the Federal Convention and in his Objections, Mason countered that since the laws of the United States were paramount to state bills of rights, the state protections provided little security. The two sides repeated their positions ad infinitum during the months that the Constitution was before the states.

Delaware, New Jersey, Georgia, and Connecticut ratified without the issue of amendments creating much stir. In Pennsylvania Antifederalists unsuccessfully urged the ratification convention to propose fifteen primarily rights-related amendments in conjunction with its adoption. Although published by the minority, the proposals had no legal standing. But in February the Massachusetts Convention became the first to adopt amendments, proposing nine "amendments and alterations" which were basically the latter and did not even include protections for the freedoms of press, speech, assembly, or religion. The idea of conditional ratification, requiring that the amendments be adopted by the necessary number of states prior to Massachusetts' ratification becoming effective, was rejected in favor of amendments merely recommendatory. Like Pennsylvania, Maryland's Convention rejected the efforts of its Antifederalists to adopt amendments and the minority then published them. Although many of the twenty-eight proposals were alterations, they included far more rights-related amendments than either those of Massachusetts or the Pennsylvania minority. The South Carolina Convention recommended four alterations. Its decision to omit rights-related amendments may have arisen from the warning of one member that bills of rights generally began with a statement that all men are born free and equal, a condition not the case in South Carolina. When, at the end of June 1788, New Hampshire became the critical ninth state to ratify, its convention adopted the nine Massachusetts amendments almost verbatim, added three protecting personal liberty, and defeated an attempt to make its ratification conditional on their subsequent adoption.

Four states remained out of the new Union. Each had large Antifederal constituencies, perhaps majorities, and their conventions proposed fundamental alterations. Virginia Federalists had to accept such recommendations as the price of securing ratification without the demand for prior amendments. Virginia proposed twenty alterations and a separate bill of rights consisting of twenty items. Modeled on George Mason's 1776 Virginia Declaration of Rights, the proposed federal bill of rights which Virginia recommended was the first complete and integrated bill. The New York Convention in July called for twenty-two alterations and a bill of rights of twenty-three provisions. In addition, New York Federalists, in order to avert a conditional ratification or an outright rejection, bowed to Antifederal demands for a circular letter to the states calling for a second federal convention to adopt amendments. The movement for a second convention, an Antifederal goal from the beginning, now became decidedly more threatening. The North Carolina Convention adopted all of Virginia's amendments, added six of its own, insisted that these amendments be added to the Constitution prior to its ratification, provided for delegates to a second state convention, and adjourned in August. Rhode Island Antifederalists defeated the Constitution in a freeholders' election and prevented the calling of a convention several times prior to 1789.[4]

What was the nature of the alterations which the Federalists so feared and which threatened to overturn the constitutional revolution of 1787? The majorities and minorities of eight of the twelve state ratifying conventions that met prior to the First Federal Congress put forth 210 amendments.[5] While many duplicated each other, some varied significantly in detail, enough so that one Federalist newspaper predicted that if the absurd and contrary proposals ever came to the floor of Congress, they would "immediately like Swift's books, give battle to each other, and soon destroy themselves." About 100 separate proposals can be distinguished. Alterations formed a clear majority of both the 210 and the 100. A precise division is impossible because certain amendments protected political or personal rights while altering the powers of the central government; for example, the prohibition of standing armies in peacetime. The alterations expressed a decentralist, republican political philosophy rooted in English tradition and American experience. First and foremost, they sought to alter the balance of power in the new system in order to make the states more equal with the federal government. One New York amendment succinctly expressed this: all federal officials should be bound by oath not to violate the rights and constitutions of the states. Secondly, the alterations aimed at a pure separation of powers between the judicial, executive, and legislative branches, with the

---

[4] The work of John P. Kaminski, Gaspare J. Saladino, and Richard Leffler, eds., *The Documentary History of the Ratification of the Constitution*, vols. XIII-XVII, *Commentaries on the Constitution* (Madison, Wisc. 1981-), has brought together all of the important source material from the unofficial debate over whether the proposed Constitution needed to be amended; they are in the process of publishing all of the official debate as well. See "M.C." (XIII, 502-503) for an early advocate of a bill of rights who argued that it would drive a wedge between the Antifederal leaders and their followers.

[5] (Philadelphia) *Federal Gazette*, Mar. 10, 1789. The most convenient compilation of these amendments is Edward Dumbauld, *The Bill of Rights* (Norman, Okla. 1957), 173-205. Cecelia M. Kenyon, ed., "Introduction," *The Antifederalists* (Indianapolis 1966), provides an excellent analysis of the immediate and long range political and theoretical implications of the proposed amendments.

latter being dominant. Finally, southern Antifederalists sought to further institutionalize sectionalism in the new system.

The Federal Convention did not make the difficult decisions necessary to flesh out Article III creating the federal judiciary. Instead it left that responsibility to the First Congress. Antifederalists consequently proposed amendments designed to limit the options of Congress and enervate the federal judiciary. Its original jurisdiction would be limited to cases involving the United States as a party, two or more states, foreign nations, and admiralty and maritime law. Admiralty courts were to be the only inferior federal courts of original jurisdiction; state courts would hear others issues, with only certain ones appealable to the federal judiciary. Finally, if a decision of the Supreme Court dissatisfied a litigant, the president, under congressional regulations, could appoint a commission to review the decision.

Antifederalists found the president and the executive branch created by Article II far too powerful. Their proposals sought to limit both its monarchical trappings and the possibility of the president assuming dictatorial powers either on his own or in collusion with the Senate to which he had a connection in violation of the doctrine of separation of powers. The president would serve no more than two terms, have an accountable council to advise him, and have his powers of pardon and command of the army in the field curtailed. New York proposed that he be convicted of impeachment by a simple majority of those present.

Despite their commitment to legislative supremacy, the Antifederalists did not ignore the powers delegated under Article I to a distant and small (relative to its constituency) Congress. Specifically to be denied Congress was the establishment of monopolies, regulation of state militias, ratification of treaties contradictory to state constitutions, granting of titles of nobility, and adoption of direct taxes or excises (except on ardent spirits) unless other sources of revenue proved insufficient and the states failed to meet special requisitions. Congress's control over elections and the federal city would be abridged. Several states proposed a two-thirds or three-fourths majority—usually but not always indicating sectional motives—to maintain a standing army in times of peace, to pass commercial laws, and to ratify commercial treaties or treaties contracting American territorial claims. Six states wanted congressional districts limited to 30,000 constituents until such time as the size of the House reached 200 after which this limitation could be raised. Finally, and most important of all the amendments, six states proposed that all powers not expressly or clearly delegated to Congress be reserved to the states. This had been the language of the Articles of Confederation and if attached to the Constitution would have eliminated the doctrine of implied powers.

Ratification by eleven states had legitimized the Federal Convention, but Federalists had little time for celebration since they saw ahead an Antifederal leviathan poised to attack the ship of state. Refusal to accept a Bill of Rights at the Federal Convention had cost Federalists dearly: in Massachusetts, acceptance of the idea of subsequent amendment; in Virginia, recommendations for fundamental alterations; in New York, a circular letter to the states calling for a federal convention; and in North Carolina, prior amendments. In addition, four states, including Virginia, had instructed their delegations to the First Congress to devote every effort to obtaining amendments. August and September 1788 provided new threats. A group of New Yorkers attempted to unite Antifederalists up and down the coast. Congress deadlocked over where the First Congress should meet. And Pennsylvania Antifederalists had called the first statewide political party convention in American history for the purpose of adopting amendments and selecting a slate of candidates to support them in the first House of Representatives. Federalists began to fear that Antifederalists might take control of the First Congress. George Washington lamented to Madison that "to be shipwrecked in sight of the Port would be the severest of all possible aggravations to our misery."[6]

No national issues arose during the first congressional election in the winter of 1788-1789 aside from that of amendments. Having failed to obtain changes before ratification, and being uncertain whether a second convention would be called, Antifederal leaders sought to ensure them by means of electing a Congress that would, in the opinion of Madison, commit suicide. All the Antifederalist candidates promised support for amendments, both alterations and rights-related. In some cases, Federalist candidates pledged themselves to amendments, although usually remaining vague about which ones they might support. Despite Federalist fears, Antifederalists did not fare well in the election. Americans, by virtue of a general willingness to try the new system, an expectation of amendments, and partisan election laws in some states, swept Federalists into the First Congress from all states except Massachusetts, New York, Virginia, and South Carolina. (North Carolina and Rhode Island did not hold

[6] Sept. 23, 1788, *Papers of Madison*, XI, 262.

their elections until after the first session of the First Congress.) Those four states sent ten Antifederalists to a 59-man House and Virginia sent two Antifederalists to a 22-man Senate.[7]

The major contest—and the one with the most national coverage—occurred in the Virginia Piedmont during January and February 1789. There, James Madison ran against James Monroe, a moderate Antifederalist. The congressional district had been carefully constructed by Patrick Henry to keep the nationally known and respected Federalist out of the House of Representatives. Monroe advocated amendments to a sympathetic constituency which had been led to believe that Madison was "dogmatically attached to the Constitution in every clause, syllable and letter." Such an opinion about Madison had a firm foundation, but it failed to acknowledge a shift that had gradually taken place in his thinking since he had condemned the subsequent amendments of Massachusetts as a blemish and convincingly argued to a Virginia political ally against a federal bill of rights. In the Virginia Convention, Madison had repeated the stock Federalist argument that a bill of rights was unnecessary if not dangerous, but in the end gave tacit support to the convention's amendments even though many were highly objectionable. The New York call for a second convention had frightened Madison much more, but even as late as early August 1788 he still desired a trial period of a few years to demonstrate what amendments the Constitution needed.[8]

North Carolina's refusal to ratify without amendments and the Antifederalist resurgence as the autumn of 1788 approached converted Madison. It had taken him a year to accept the reality of the drastic mistake that had been made at the Federal Convention. At the end of September he informed Jefferson, then American Minister to France, that "safeguards to liberty ag[ain]st which no objections can be raised" should be introduced in Congress. "My own opinion has always been in favor of a bill of rights" he asserted a month later in a comprehensive letter to Jefferson, whose letters during the

---

[7] On the first congressional election see Kenneth R. Bowling, "Federalists and Antifederalists After Ratification: The First Congressional Election" (M.A. thesis, University of Wisconsin 1964), and Gordon DenBoer, Lucy Trumbull Brown, Robert A. Becker, and Merrill Jensen, eds., *The Documentary History of the First Federal Elections, 1788-1790* (3 + vols., Madison, Wisc. 1976-).

[8] To Washington, Feb. 15, 1788, Jan. 14, 1789, to Edmund Randolph, Apr. 10, 1788, to Hamilton, June 27, 1788, from George Lee Turberville, Apr. 16, 1788, to Washington, Aug. 24, 1788, to Jefferson, Aug. 10, 1788, *Papers of Madison*, X, 510, XI, 18-19, 23, 181, 226, 240-41, 418.

preceding year had helped to ease the pain of the turnabout by providing a sophisticated rationale. "At the same time," he continued, "I have never thought the omission a material defect, nor been anxious to supply it even by subsequent amendment, for any other reason than that it is anxiously desired by others. I have favored it because I supposed it might be of use, and if properly executed could not be of disservice."[9] Early in November, as Virginia had prepared to elect its first Senators, candidate Madison, an obvious choice for the Senate, wrote from the Confederation Congress at New York to a friend in the legislature at Richmond announcing that he did not consider the Constitution faultless. Madison managed to discourse at length in this letter without mentioning one specific amendment that he supported. "The universal cry is for amendments, & the Federals are obliged to join in it; but whether to amuse, or conceal other views seems dubious," mused Henry, who led the opposition to Madison's reluctant and unsuccessful senatorial candidacy. Henry contended that anyone who wished for amendments wasted a vote on Madison, and told the legislature his election would produce "rivulets of blood throughout the land."[10]

Finding himself the underdog in the congressional campaign against Monroe, Madison rode painfully home from Philadelphia, where he had sought treatment for hemorrhoids. Joining Monroe in a series of debates, Madison stressed his long struggle for separation of church and state in Virginia. Also, he declared in letters to influential constituents, publicly read around the district and printed in newspapers throughout the United States, that with the Constitution safely ratified, amendments could be considered. Specifically, he favored congressional approval—rather than a second convention—of amendments to safeguard all the "essential rights," to provide for the periodic increase of the House of Representatives, and to protect the people against nuisance appeals by the wealthy to a distant United States Supreme Court. "In a number of other particulars," Madison believed, "alterations are eligible either on their own account, or on

[9] To Jefferson, Sept. 21, Oct. 17, *ibid.*, XI, 257-58, 297. Adrienne Koch discusses the important differences between Madison and Jefferson on the Constitution and Bill of Rights in *Jefferson and Madison: The Great Collaboration* (New York 1964), ch. 3.

[10] To George Lee Turberbville, Nov. 2, 1788, *Papers of Madison*, XI, 330-332; Henry to Richard Henry Lee, Nov. 15, 1788, in William Wirt Henry, *Patrick Henry: Life, Correspondence and Speeches* (3 vols., New York 1891), II, 429; Henry Lee to Madison, Nov. 19, 1788, *Papers of Madison*, XI, 356-357.

account of those who wish for them." While clearly refuting the allegation that he opposed any amendments, that statement left vague how many and which alterations he would support. Madison defeated Monroe, 1,308 to 972. The fact that he had given his word during the campaign underlies all the reasons he later gave for supporting amendments.[11]

Virginia Antifederalists continued to question the sincerity of Madison's conversion. George Mason emphasized that Madison would never have been elected without making some promises and had now become "the ostensible Patron of Amendments. Perhaps some Milk & Water Propositions may be made . . . by Way of th[r]owing out a Tub to the Whale; but of important & substantial Amendments, I have not the least Hope." Senator Richard Henry Lee wrote his old ally Henry that Madison's "ideas, and those of our convention, on this subject, are not similiar."[12]

An Antifederal newspaper called on members of the First Congress to adopt amendments as their first order of business. "The interest of this new empire requires a union of sentiment, and Congress can do much that way, if the subject of amendments has that proper attention paid to it, which from its importance it naturally claims." But the Federalist press, having contributed to an election landslide, ridiculed the idea of amendments, especially alterations. "The worship of the ox, the crocodile, and the cat, in ancient time, and the belief in astrology and witchcraft by more modern nations, did not prostrate the human understanding more than the numerous asburdities" proposed as amendments, proclaimed one. An anonymous twenty-eight-part essay analyzing the state proposals concluded that "if we must have amendments, I pray for merely amusing amendments, a little frothy garnish."[13] When Congress achieved a quorum in April, Madison naively expected no great difficulty

---

[11] *Documentary History of the First Federal Elections*, II, 317-349, (quotation at 339); Brant, *Madison: Father of the Constitution*, 240-242.

[12] George Mason to John Mason, July 31, 1789, in Robert A. Rutland, ed., *The Papers of George Mason, 1725-1792* (3 vols., Chapel Hill 1970), III, 1164, and Richard Henry Lee to Patrick Henry, May 28, 1789, *Henry Correspondence*, III, 387-388.

[13] (Philadelphia) *Freeman's Journal*, Mar. 4, 1789; (Boston) *Massachusetts Centinel*, Mar. 11, 1789; [Nicholas Collin], "Foreign Spectator," *Federal Gazette*, Oct. 21, 1788-Feb. 16, 1789. The latter series of essays was republished at New York in the midst of the House debate over amendments; see New York *Daily Gazette*, June 3-July 7, 1789.

in getting the Federalist Congress to adopt amendments. Those which "I am known to have espoused, will as far as I can gather, be attainable from the federalists . . . ." These selected proposals would "extinguish opposition to the system, or at least break the force of it, by detaching the deluded opponents from their designing leaders."[14]

On May 4, a month after the session opened and in order to draw attention from Virginia's application for a second convention which was submitted the next day, Madison gave notice that he would offer amendments in three weeks. He later agreed to two postponements to allow the revenue debate to proceed. Finally, on June 8, informing his colleagues that he felt bound by honor and duty, Madison moved that the House sit as a Committee of the Whole to receive and debate his proposals. But his colleagues let him know quickly that they did not consider the matter as urgent as he. They were not expressing opposition to the protection of civil liberties. On the contrary, almost all—even Madison's most vocal critics—held advanced libertarian ideas for their times. They had other reasons for opposing the debate: amendments meant alterations as well as protections for civil liberty; Congress had more important business; and the debate might produce the first public display of the sectional division within the young republic. Most Federalists, basking in their election sweep, believed amendments unnecessary either as a political stratagem or because personal rights needed protection at the federal level. Forgetting their fears of six months earlier, Federalists called for postponement to allow a trial period for the new system. As Roger Sherman, the House's most vocal opponent of amendments expressed it, if the people had really wanted amendments they would have secured them prior

---

[14] To Edmund Randolph, Apr. 12, 1789, to Jefferson, Mar. 29, 1789, *Papers of Madison*, XII, 76, 38. See also to Edmund Pendleton, Apr. 8, 1789, *ibid.*, XII, 51. For lack of interest in devoting Congress's time to amendments, see the comments of the following Federalists, all but the first of whom were members of it: Samuel A. Otis to Nathan Dane, Mar. 28, 1789, Personal Papers Miscellany (Library of Congress [LC], Washington, D.C.); Farewell Celebration for Jonathan Elmer, Mar. 26, 1789 (Glassboro State College Library, Glassboro, N.J.); Abraham Baldwin to Joel Barlow, Mar. 1, 1789, Miscellaneous Manuscript Collection (Yale University [Yale], New Haven, Conn.); Richard Bland Lee to Powell, Mar. 28, 1789, Leven Powell Papers, LC; Paine Wingate to Pickering, Mar. 25, 1789, Timothy Pickering Papers (Massachusetts Historical Society [MHS], Boston, Mass.); Ralph Izard to Jefferson, Apr. 3, 1789, *Papers of Jefferson*, XV, 22; and Thomas Hartley to Stephen Chambers, Mar. 30, 1789, Stauffer Collection (Historical Society of Pennsylvania [HSP], Philadelphia, Penn.)

to ratification. Antifederalists also wanted postponement because they suspected Madison's proposals would fall far short of the alterations they sought. Madison's only support came from two Virginia Federalists who understood Henry's influence.[15]

In response to this reluctance, Madison delivered a long speech defending his motives and arguing for the expediency of amendments. Every motive of prudence argued for them, he pleaded; large numbers of Antifederalists would thereafter support the Constitution and North Carolina and Rhode Island would rejoin the Union. He claimed his proposals aimed at not only curbing abuses by government against the people but also, most importantly, at protecting minorities against majorities. Publicly abandoning the stock Federalist argument that in a government of delegated powers no civil liberties could be infringed, Madison noted as an example that since Congress had all the power necessary and proper to collect revenue it might issue general search warrants as a means. He argued that no serious objection could be raised about the items he promised to recommend, for they were chosen carefully to secure a two-thirds vote in Congress and ratification by three fourths of the states. Madison refused to support alterations. To be sure, he contended, some respectable individuals had sought such amendments but the mass of the people had been concerned only about encroachments on their liberties. In conclusion, he offered and discussed in detail each of his proposals.[16]

Relying heavily on the Virginia Convention's bill of rights, and therefore on George Mason's 1776 Virginia Declaration of Rights, Madison incorporated into his June 8 proposals most of the rights-related amendments recommended by the states. He did omit free and frequent elections unencumbered by poll taxes, a declaration of civilian control of the military, freedom from the suspension of laws or their unauthorized execution, and freedom to hunt and fish in

---

[15] *Papers of Madison*, XII, 125. The legislative history of amendments, and all the relevant documents, can be found in Charlene Bangs Bickford and Helen E. Veit, eds., *Documentary History of the First Federal Congress*, vol. IV, *Legislative Histories* (Baltimore 1986), 1-48. All references in this article to the legislative process are from that source. References and quotations from the debates can be found in Joseph Gales and W.W. Seaton, comps., *The Debates and Proceedings in the Congress of the United States. . .* [*Annals*] (42 vols., Washington 1834-1856); in this case at I, 424-431. During the debate, ten members participated with frequency. They were Madison, Sedgwick, Vining, Smith of South Carolina, Ames and Sherman from the side which eventually supported amendments, and Gerry, Tucker, Livermore and Burke from the other side.

[16] *Papers of Madison*, XII, 193-209.

seasonable times. Madison included two rights-related proposals not recommended by any state: no person could be forced to give up private property without just compensation and no state could infringe the equal rights of conscience, freedom of the press, or trial by jury in criminal cases. Of the proposed alterations Madison included only a handful, some of which were rights-related as well: one regulating the apportionment of the House in order to set a limit on its size and to facilitate constituent access, one confirming separation of powers, one regulating the compensation of congressmen to prevent salary grabs, one setting a minimum monetary value on cases which could be appealed to the Supreme Court to prevent vexatious appeals against the poor, and one declaring that all powers not delegated were reserved to the states. The latter proposal significantly lacked the word "expressly" between "not" and "delegated." In sending off copies of his amendments to acquaintances in Virginia and North Carolina, Madison insisted that he designed them to touch "the structure & stamina of the Govt." as little as possible. Yet, they were "important in the eyes of many" and "objectionable in those of none."[17]

Despite Madison's long and comprehensive speech, neither Federalists nor Antifederalists seemed inclined to proceed with the business. Madison had "done his duty," Federalist William L. Smith of South Carolina had smugly told the House earlier, "and if he did not succeed, he was not to blame." Antifederalists again urged a postponement until the new government had been organized and the House could take up all the amendments of the states rather than merely those "few propositions brought forward by an individual gentleman." The respect that many members felt for Madison—who acted as a sort of prime minister during the first session of Congress—rather than the Antifederal threat to bring forward alterations resulted in the House referring Madison's proposals to the Committee of the Whole.[18]

Federalist Representative George Clymer of Philadelphia had reflected in a letter just before the speech on whether Madison meant "merely a tub to the whale, a declaration about the press, liberty of conscience &c. or will suffer himself to be so far frightened with the antifederalism of his own state as to attempt to lop off essentials . . . ." A postscript added after the speech summed up the view

---

[17] To Edmund Randolph, June 15, 1789, to Samuel Johnston, June 21, 1789, *ibid.*, XII, 219, 250.

[18] *Annals*, I, 429-449.

of almost everyone: Madison "has proved a tub" on amendments. Later Clymer described Madison as "a sensible physician" who "has given his malades imaginaires bread pills, powder of paste and neutral mixtures."[19]

Other Federalist representatives characterized the proposals as innocent, nugatory, premature, or unnecessary.[20] Fisher Ames, the most carping critic of bills of rights in general, believed they "may do some good towards quieting men, who attend to sounds only, and may get the mover some popularity, which he wishes." Theodore Sedgwick thought their introduction unwise and of no value politically. On and off the floor of Congress, both of these Massachusetts Federalists questioned Madison's motives, complained about his timidity and lack of nerve when confronted by popular clamors, and declared bills of rights to be of no constitutional importance. At the same time, both men, despite harassing Madison on the floor, let friends know early in the debate that they intended in the end to support a modification of what Sedgwick termed Madison's water gruel amendments.[21]

Madison's proposals had become public throughout the country after they were published in the New York *Daily Advertiser* on June 12. A Boston Antifederalist reported that Federalists there openly expressed disappointment with "the great Man from Virginia. They think he appears too serious in his motion for amendments." Antifederalists at Boston on the other hand complained that Madison had laid "aside the amendments proposed by the several states in order to prevent any thing being done on the subject." The *Gazette of the United States*, a Federalist organ, later criticized the proposals more than once. Nevertheless, a letter to a newspaper predicted that "they will give general satisfaction, and quiet the minds of many well disposed citizens."[22]

---

[19] To Peters, June [8], 1789, Richard Peters Papers, HSP; to Coxe, June 28, 1789, Tench Coxe Papers, HSP.

[20] George Gale to [William Tilghman], June 17, 1789, Tilghman Papers, HSP; Thomas FitzSimons to [Benjamin Rush], June 15, 1789, excerpt, *Parke-Bernet Sale Catalog 468* (New York 1943), 34; Benjamin Contee to Gov. John Eagar Howard, June 12, 1789, Executive Papers (Maryland Hall of Records, Annapolis, Md.).

[21] Ames to Thomas Dwight, June 11, 1789, to George R. Minot, July 2, 23, 1789, Seth Ames, ed., *Works of Fisher Ames* (2 vols., Boston, 1854), I, 53 (quotation), 58, 65; Sedgwick to Pamela Sedgwick, Aug. 20, 1789, Ames to Sedgwick, Oct. 6, 1789, Sedgwick Papers, MHS; Sedgwick to Lincoln, July 19, 1789, Benjamin Lincoln Papers, MHS; Sedgwick to Lincoln, Aug. 14, 1789, Fogg Autograph Collection (Maine Historical Society, Portland, Me.).

[22] Peter Muhlenberg to Benjamin Rush, June 25, 1789, Sol Feinstone

Madison received a great deal of reaction. "I like it as far as it goes; but I should have been for going further," wrote his gently critical mentor, Jefferson. Others suggested Madison include the power for Congress to declare where canals should be cut, a two-thirds majority for commercial laws, and a three-fourths majority for treaties surrendering American territorial claims.[23] "If Chips must be put into the Porridge," wrote Richard Peters, Speaker of the Pennsylvania Assembly, "I would let the bad Cooks put them into the Pot, nor should any throw out Tubs but those who were afraid of the Whale." Madison understood all too well about tubs and whales, but he questioned Peters about the porridge. Madison soon received a fable entitled "The Wise Cooks and Foolish Guests." Eleven cooks carefully prepared an excellent soup. Dissatisfied, some of the guests proposed changes in the recipe to the extent that the soup became unrecognizable. "Had you lived in the Days of these Cooks," Peters pointedly teased, "your Easiness of Temper . . . would have prompted you to indulge the Anti Soupites in some of their Whims of an innocent Nature especially if they had been some of your Neighbours."

Madison, delighting in his correspondence with the witty Peters and seeking to change his disapproving mind, argued the necessity of amendments. "As an honest man" he felt bound by the fact that the Constitution was adopted in Virginia and other states with the tacit understanding of subsequent amendment. Further, he insisted that if the Virginia candidates in the congressional election had not taken a conciliatory stand on the issue, the delegation would have been almost wholly disaffected; that if the Federalist side of the House had not acted, the Antifederal side would have; that if adopted his amendments would destroy the opposition everywhere, enable the administration to venture into measures not otherwise safe, and prevent Antifederal leaders from blowing "the trumpet for a second Convention." Finally, obtaining North Carolina's ratification required some amendments. Peters remained unconvinced, believing Madison's apprehensions too highly wrought and his amendments merely a banner

---

Collection (American Philosophical Society, Philadelphia, Penn.); James Sullivan to Gerry, June 28, 1789 (James S. Copley Library, LaJolla, Calif.); (New York) *Gazette of the United States*, Aug. 15, 19, 1789; John Fenno to [Joseph Ward], July 5, 1789, Ward Papers (Chicago Historical Society); New York *Daily Gazette*, Aug. 7, 1789.

[23] From Tench Coxe, June 18, 1789, from John Dawson, June 28, 1789, from Jefferson, Aug. 28, 1789, *Papers of Madison*, XII, 240, 264, 363-364.

for the Antifederal leaders to raise because the alterations they sought were excluded.[24]

Madison's incoming letters also brought the news he hoped to hear. The "honest" Antifederalists as well as the Federalists at Philadelphia were pleased, reported Tench Coxe, Madison's mouthpiece in the Philadelphia press. The designing and less honest opponents had been stripped of their arguments, Coxe insisted.[25] Virginia Antifederalists and Federalists approved.[26] Although details of Madison's proposals were unknown in North Carolina, news from there particularly encouraged him. That state's Antifederal leadership wanted amendments which confined Congress to *expressly* delegated powers, but Federalist Samuel Johnston, soon to be elected to the first United States Senate, thought "a little Flourish & Dressing without injuring the substantial part or adding much to its intrinsic value, such as a pompous Declaration of Rights" might be enough to obtain a Federalist victory at the state's upcoming second ratification convention.[27]

Six weeks later—July 21—Madison "begged" the House to take up his proposals. It spent the day debating whether to free the Committee of the Whole from its assignment and to appoint a select committee instead. Federalists could see no good purpose in discussing the subject below crowded public galleries so they established a select committee composed of a member from each state, despite the Antifederal call for a public debate.

The committee, whose members were unsympathetic to amendments, reported back to the House a week later. It discussed the missing state proposals, but, as chairman John Vining observed, it "conceived some of them superfluous or dangerous, and found many of them so contradictory that it was impossible to make any thing of them."[28] It retained Madison's plan of incorporating the amendments into the body of the Constitution itself, rather than appending them at the end as committee member Roger Sherman urged. The

---

[24] From Richard Peters, July 5, 20, Aug. 24, 1789, to Peters, Aug. 19, 1789, *ibid.*, XII, 283, 301-303, 353-356, 346-347.

[25] From Tench Coxe, June 18, 1789, *ibid.*, XII, 239-240. See Coxe's writings signed "A Pennsylvanian" in the *Federal Gazette*, June 18, 30, 1789.

[26] From Edward Stevens, June 25, 1789, from Edmund Randolph, June 30, 1789, from Archibald Stuart, July 31, 1789, *Papers of Madison*, XII, 261, 273, 319.

[27] From William R. Davie, June 10, 1789, from Hugh Williamson, July 2, 1789, from Benjamin Hawkins, [July] 3, 1789, from Samuel Johnston, July 8, 1789, *ibid.*, XII, 210-211, 274-275, 284-285.

[28] *Annals*, I, 672, 741.

report also tightened Madison's prose, rearranged his proposals, and narrowed considerably the absolute guarantees of religious freedom and the equal rights of conscience. Most prominently, it gutted Madison's majestic natural law preamble by omitting the right of the people "to reform or change their government, whenever it be found adverse or inadequate to the purposes of its institution"; the statement "that all power is originally vested in, and consequently derived from the people"; and the list of benefits that people derive from government: enjoyment of life and liberty, acquiring and using property, pursuing and obtaining happiness and safety.

The report reflected the Federalist viewpoint of 1789, that support of government stability rather than the right of revolution proved uppermost. The principles of 1776, enunciated by Mason in the Virginia Declaration of Rights and Jefferson in the Declaration of Independence, need not be added to the Constitution. Madison, firmly attached to his own ideas if not his own words, showed displeasure with the revision although he admitted some things had perhaps been changed for the better. Sherman, reported to have opposed civilian control of the military in the committee, thought the proposals probably "harmless and satisfactory to those who are fond of Bills of rights." William Loughton Smith found them inoffensive and perhaps of some strategic benefit.[29]

On August 13 two Virginians moved to go into Committee of the Whole on the select committee's report of two weeks earlier. Once again, spokesmen from both parties urged postponement. Even select committee chairman Vining expressed ambivalence, but being "impressed by the anxiety which the honorable gentleman from Virginia had discovered for having the subject" debated, Vining would support its consideration instead of the land office bill which "in point of importance, every candid mind would acknowledge . . . preference." Elbridge Gerry considered the proposals so inadequate that they, and the many others which would be offered on the floor, would require a lengthy debate. Madison insisted that adoption of amendments before the session ended was vital, and that any proposals in addition to his would waste the House's time. Once again the members yielded to

---

[29] Madison to Jefferson, Aug. 2, 1788, *Papers of Jefferson*, XV, 324-325; Sherman's Amendments, July 1789, Madison Papers, LC; Sherman to Henry Gibbs, Aug. 4, 1789, Gibbs Family Papers, Yale; Richard Henry Lee to Samuel Adams, Aug. 8, 1789, James C. Ballagh, ed., *The Letters of Richard Henry Lee* (2 vols., New York 1911-14), II, 496; William Loughton Smith to Edward Rutledge, Aug. 9-15, 1789, *South Carolina Historical Magazine*, 69 (Jan. 1968), 14.

Madison and postponement failed. The first motion set off a long debate as Sherman attempted without success to place any amendments at the end, rather than within the body, of the Constitution.[30]

From August 13 to 18 the Committee of the Whole considered each proposal individually. The high point of the debate took place on August 15, a sweltering Saturday. The debate was between Federalists and Antifederalists except for Sedgwick's complaint that to guarantee the right of assembly descended into minutia and his suggestion that the Constitution might just as well protect a man's freedom to go to bed when he chose. Led by Gerry, the other Antifederal spokesmen were Aedanus Burke, Thomas Tudor Tucker, and Thomas Sumter of South Carolina. Gerry and Sumter accused the select committee of being so attached to its own work that it would not tolerate any change. Burke declared that the proposals before the Committee of the Whole would never satisfy the people—that Madison's amendments were "frothy and full of wind, formed only to please the palate; or they are like a tub thrown out to a whale, to secure the freight of the ship and its peaceable voyage." Madison responded to the attack. Had not the people been told that they should oppose the Constitution until they secured these very rights? Had not the amendments he proposed been the ones most strenuously advocated by Antifederal leaders? Who, he implied, was deceiving whom? Burke did not argue that point, but instead held up copies of the amendments of several state conventions to show their difference from those on the floor, concluding that all the important amendments had been omitted. Federalist William Smith summarized the day's debate as more ill-humored and rude than any other that had occurred in Congress. Likely, it was during this day's debate that members of both sides challenged opponents to duels.[31]

When the Committee of the Whole reconvened after its Sunday adjournment, Burke proposed that it add to the select committee report a popular item from the Virginia ratifying convention's proposed bill of rights: civilian control of the military and a prohibition against standing armies in time of peace except from necessity. The motion failed. Tucker took offense at Madison's proposal to prevent the states from infringing on certain specified rights of American citizens

---

[30] *Annals*, I, 704-717.

[31] *Ibid.*, 729-749; William Smith to Williams, Aug. 17, 1789, Otho Holland Williams Papers (Maryland Historical Society, Baltimore, Md.); William L. Smith to Edward Rutledge, Aug. 9-15, 1789, *South Carolina Historical Magazine*, 69 (Jan. 1968), 24; Elbridge to Samuel R. Gerry, June 30, 1790, S.R. Gerry Papers, MHS.

and moved without success that it be struck. Gerry moved that all of the amendments of the states not contained in substance in the select committee report be referred to the Committee of the Whole, and that it adopt a report incorporating them with the work of the select committee. Tucker threatened a second convention in support of the motion; nevertheless, it lost 34 to 16. After a heated debate, with frequent calls to order, the Committee of the Whole rose and submitted the select committee's report to the House, having made only minor changes in it. The House began its consideration immediately. Tucker moved to refer seventeen of the alterations recommended by the states to a new Committee of the Whole, but the House easily defeated the motion.[32]

Apparently none of the select committee's amendments had received the two-thirds majority in the Committee of the Whole necessary to gain approval by the full House. Somewhere Madison would have to locate the votes. President Washington, who had urged Congress in his inaugural address to adopt amendments promoting the rights of freemen without altering the system, had given Madison a letter of support. Washington thought some of the proposals unimportant, but "not foreseeing any evil consequences that can result from their adoption, they have my wishes for a favorable reception in both houses."[33] Lukewarm though it was, the note probably influenced House Federalists to unite behind Madison's amendments. In addition, their postponement or defeat at that stage of the process might provide Antifederalists with new ammunition by which to conduct a campaign for a second convention.

Madison paid a price for the Federalist votes he secured in order to assure the necessary two-thirds majority. Federalists voted out the little that remained of Madison's preamble and agreed to Sherman's motion that the amendments be placed at the end of the Constitution. Madison considered the latter change "an unavoidable sacrifice to *a few* who knew their concurrence to be necessary, to the despatch if not the success of the business . . . ." He feared that the placement would lead to ambiguities about how far the original Constitution had been superseded by the amendments. Actually the change set a precedent for isolating amendments, broadened their role in constitutional law, and made it possible to point to a body of amendments known as the federal Bill of Rights.[34]

---

[32] *Annals*, I, 749-764.
[33] To Madison, [c. May 31, 1789], *Papers of Maidson*, XII, 191.
[34] Madison to Alexander White, Aug. 24, 1789, *Papers of Madison*, XII, 352-353;

On August 20 and 21 the House made only minor changes while moving rapidly through the proposals. When what became the Tenth Amendment limiting the central government to only those powers delegated came up for approval, Gerry moved to add the word "expressly" between "powers" and "delegated," thus bringing reservation of powers into conformity with the Articles of Confederation and the amendments proposed by six states and eliminating the doctrine of implied powers. William Smith and another southern Federalist voted with the Antifederal minority because they believed adding the word would go a long way to prevent Congress from interfering with slavery.

Burke proposed without success that Congress be stripped of its power to interfere with state regulation of congressional elections unless a state proved unable, neglected, or refused to hold elections. In the long debate which ensued, Madison expressed opposition not so much to the popular proposal as to the timing of its introduction. Gerry saw no reason for omitting it except to establish an arbitrary government "to which the present system is pointed in no very indirect manner." Burke decried the assertion, often heard in the House, "that this revolution, or adoption of the new Constitution, was agreeable to the public mind, and [that] those who had opposed it at first are now satisifed with it." On the contrary, he claimed, Americans had parted with their liberties out of patriotism, relying on future amendment by Congress to restore them. Having failed to secure the recommendation of such a popular amendment, Antifederalists had little hope left. Irritated, Madison noted privately at the end of the day that the Antifederalists were trying to "defeat by delaying a plan short of their wishes, but likely to satisfy a great part of their companions in opposition." The last eight days, he complained, had been "extremely difficult and fatiguing" and "exceedingly wearisome."

By August 22 both the heat and the ill humor had subsided. Tucker moved the adoption of one more amendment: Congress shall not impose direct taxes except when duties, imports, and excises proved insufficient and then only after a state had refused to pay a congressional requisition. Many Federalists, Madison included, saw the elimination of Congress's power to lay direct taxes as the chief Antifederal goal. Samuel Livermore of New Hampshire, besides William Floyd of New York the only Federalist voting consistently with

---

Annals, I, 767. For an analysis of Sherman's role see Christopher Collier, *Roger Sherman's Connecticut: Yankee Politics and the American Revolution* (Middletown, Conn. 1971).

the Antifederalists, declared it to be the most important amendment to come before the House. "Unless something more effectual was done to improve the Constitution, he knew his constituents would be dissatisfied. As to the amendments already agreed to, they would not value them more than a pinch of snuff; they went to secure rights never in danger." Gerry and Sumter warned that the states would be annihilated if the power of direct taxation remained with Congress, but the motion failed. With the defeat of four more proposals on voice votes, House Antifederalists gave up the fight for alterations.[35] The two Antifederalists who had spoken against Madison's proposals most frequently expressed their dissatisfaction privately. Gerry confirmed Madison's analysis that a real difference existed between Antifederal spokesmen and their followers: the House proposals had no "other purposes than to reconcile those who had no adequate idea of the essential defects of the Constitution." Tucker fumed that they were "calculated merely to amuse, or rather to deceive."[36]

On August 24 the House transmitted seventeen amendments to the Senate. Madison found them little changed from the report of the select committee.[37] The two Philadelphia representatives advised their fellow townsman, Senator Robert Morris, that the Senate "adopt the whole of them by lump as containing neither good or harm, being perfectly innocent." Morris, who held Madison responsible for all the time which the House had wasted on amendments, disagreed. "Poor Madison took one wrong step in Virginia by publishing a letter respecting *amendments*, and you . . . know what a cursed thing it is to write *a Book*," he joshed Richard Peters, concluding at the end of the Senate debate that "they are what Centinel calls them, a 'tub for the whale.'" Senator Pierce Butler of South Carolina agreed that Madison had offered only "*milk-and-water*" propositions; "I suppose . . .

---

[35] *Annals*, I, 795-808; William L. Smith to Edward Rutledge, Aug. 9-15, 1789, *South Carolina Historical Magazine*, 69 (Jan. 1968), 20-21; Madison to Edmund Randolph, Madison to Edmund Pendleton, Aug. 21, 1789, *Papers of Madison*, XII, 348-349; William Smith to Williams, Aug. 22, 1789, Otho Holland Williams Papers. On the importance of the direct taxation issue see Madison to Tench Coxe, July 30, 1788, Edmund Randolph to Madison, Aug. 18, 1789, Madison to Washington, Dec. 5, 1789, *Papers of Madison*, XI, 210, XII, 345, 459; and David Stuart to Washington, Sept. 12, 1789, Washington Papers, LC.

[36] Gerry to John Wendell, Sept. 14, 1789, Fogg Autograph Collection; Tucker to St. George Tucker, Oct. 2, 1789, Charles Roberts Autograph Letters Collection (Haverford College, Haverford, Penn.).

[37] To Alexander White, Aug. 24, 1789, *Papers of Madison*, XII, 352-353.

to keep his promise with his constituents."[38] The Senate met in secret, and the unofficial recorder of the debates, Federalist William Maclay of Pennsylvania, was bedridden for all but the first day's debate. He noted in his diary then that Senators Morris, Ralph Izard of South Carolina, and John Langdon of New Hampshire treated the amendments contemptuously and unsuccessfully urged a postponement until the next session. Senator Richard Henry Lee of Virginia reported a debate over whether liberty of speech and freedom of the press should be struck from the amendments on the grounds that they only tended to encourage licentiousness. He was also probably the source for the asertion that a simple, but not the necessary two-thirds, majority of the Senate opposed the right of the militia to bear arms.[39]

The two Antifederalist senators, Virginia's Lee and William Grayson, faced overwhelming odds. Earlier in the session, when Grayson had proposed laying the Virginia Convention amendments before the Senate, Lee persuaded him to wait until the House acted, and both men closely observed proceedings there. Grayson complained that Madison's proposals "effect personal liberty alone, leaving the great points of the Judiciary, direct taxation, and etc., to stand as they are." The strategy of such a tactic, the Senator reasoned, was merely to break the spirit of the Antifederal party by dividing it. Lee believed that the Federalists, having gained their new government, wished "to neglect the condition upon which probably their success was founded." Lee and Grayson failed to preserve and strengthen the House proposals, and to add one-by-one the Virginia amendments omitted by Madison.[40]

When it completed work on the amendments on September 14, the Senate had made twenty-six changes. Aside from tightening language, the Senate rearranged and compressed the seventeen articles

---

[38] To Peters, Aug. 24, Sept. 13, 1789, Peters Papers, HSP; to Hopkinson, Aug. 15, 1789, Francis Hopkinson Papers, HSP; to James Wilson, Aug. 23, 1789, Willing, Morris and Swanwick Papers (Pennsylvania Historical and Museum Commission, Harrisburg, Penn.); Butler to James Iredell, Aug. 11, 1789, Griffith J. McRee, *Life and Correspondence of James Iredell* (2 vols., New York 1857-1858), II, 265.

[39] Kenneth R. Bowling and Helen E. Veit, eds., *Documentary History of the First Federal Congress*, vol. IX, *The Diary of William Maclay and Other Notes on Senate Debates* (Baltimore 1988), 133; Thomas B. Randolph to St. George Tucker, Sept. 12, 1789, Brock Collection (Henry E. Huntington Library, San Marino, Calif.); John Randolph to St. George Tucker, Sept. 11, 1789, Tucker Papers, LC.

[40] Grayson to Patrick Henry, June 12, 1789, *Henry Correspondence*, III, 391; Richard Henry Lee to Charles Lee, Aug. 28, 1789, to Samuel Adams, Apr. 25, 1789, *R. H. Lee Letters*, II, 499, 484.

into twelve and made significant changes in content. Struck from the House amendments were ones forbidding the states from infringing certain rights of Americans, asserting separation of powers as a principle of the United States government, guaranteeing freedom of conscience, exempting from military service those with religious objections, and the vicinage requirements in criminal trials, the monetary minimum for appeals to the Supreme Court, and the provision for trials of crimes committed in a place in possession of an enemy. The Senate added a minimum of twenty dollars at issue to ensure a jury trial in common law suits, weakened the guarantees of the religious liberty clause, and, significantly, added "or to the people" at the end of the reservation of powers amendment. The Senate also inserted a preamble describing the amendments as a response to the state ratification conventions and as a means of extending public confidence in the government. Senator Lee understandably found the statement ironic. He believed the Senate had "mutilated and enfeebled" the House proposals, and assured Patrick Henry that he and Grayson had made every effort to secure the adoption of the Virginia amendments. "We might as well have attempted to move Mount Atlas upon our shoulders"; in fact, echoing the warning of the "Federal Farmer" two years earlier, he lamented, that not insisting on prior amendment of the Constitution had been little better than committing suicide. "The lower house sent up amendments which held out a safeguard to personal liberty in [a] great many instances, but this disgusted the senate," Grayson reported to Henry; "they are so mutilated and gutted that in fact they are good for nothing, and I believe, as many others do, that they will do more harm than benefit."[41]

Also angered by the Senate changes, Madison claimed they struck at his most salutary proposals. Reports circulated that he had declared the amendments stripped of their sedative virtue and that none wsa better than those agreed to by the Senate. Predictably, Sherman and several other congressmen who had reluctantly supported Madison welcomed the amending hand of the Senate. And, when President Washington forwarded the twelve amendments to the states in early October, most of the Senate changes remained.[42]

---

[41] Richard Henry Lee to Patrick Henry, Sept. 14, 1789, William Grayson to Henry, Sept. 29, 1789, *Henry Correspondence*, III, 339, 406; Richard Henry Lee to [Francis Lightfoot Lee?], Sept. 13, 1789, *R. H. Lee Letters*, II, 500.

[42] Madison to Edmund Pendleton, Sept. 14, 23, 1789, *Papers of Madison*, XII, 402, 418-419; Sherman to Gov. Samuel Huntington, Sept. 17, 1789, Lane Memorial

Little is recorded about the ratification process within the states. The Antifederal leviathan had submerged and no new, unified opposition had replaced it. Other issues such as the assumption of the states' revolutionary war debts by the central government and the location of the federal capital had captured public attention. Although nine states ratified the amendments within ten months, it took more than two years before the necessary tenth state acted. Several states rejected either the first or second of the proposed amendments—on apportionment of the House and on compensation to members of Congress—and so, to Madison's further chagrin, the twelve became ten.[43]

In the four states where Antifederalism had never been a major force, New Jersey and Delaware ratified the amendments just as quickly as they had the Constitution itself, while Connecticut and Georgia waited until the 1939 sesquicentennial of the Bill of Rights. Although important but not always effective Antifederal parties had existed in Maryland, South Carolina, and New Hampshire, all three states ratified the amendments between December 1789 and January 1790.

Pennsylvania had influential Antifederalists, but it ratified the amendments in March 1790 despite Samuel Bryan's revival of "Centinel." Bryan repeated familiar arguments about the kinds of changes that the Constitution really required and described the twelve amendments as an opiate prescribed to subjugate the people. In his view, Madison had rendered Machiavelli piddling by comparison. In Massachusetts the Antifederal leadership unsuccessfully proposed an additional twelve alterations in the legislature, and a last minute disagreement between the two houses prevented adoption of the amendments. Finally convinced that it had never ratified the Bill of Rights, Massachusetts did so in 1939.[44]

Collection, Yale; Abraham Baldwin to Joel Barlow, Sept. 13, 1789, Miscellaneous Manuscripts Collection, Yale; Fisher Ames to Caleb Strong, 15 Sept. 1789, Thompson Autograph Collection (Hartford Seminary Foundation, Hartford, Conn.); Paine Wingate to John Langdon, Sept. 17, 1789, Dreer Collection, HSP.

[43] Douglas Adair, ed., "James Madison's Autobiography," *William and Mary Quarterly*, 2 (Apr. 1945), 204. Delaware and Pennsylvania did not adopt the first amendment (on apportionment) and New York, New Jersey, and New Hampshire did not adopt the second (on congressional compensation).

[44] "Centinel Revived," (Philadelphia) *Independent Gazetteer*, Aug. 27, 29, Sept. 9, 1789; *Report of the Committee of Both Houses Appointed to Consider Further Amendments to the Constitution of the United States* (Boston 1790), Shipton Imprints No. 22655; Henry

Most of the complaints about the amendments came from the four states with the strongest Antifederal parties. New York Antifederal leaders found them trivial, equivocal, and unimportant since the people and the states lacked the power to enforce them. New York, however, agreed to them in February 1790.[45] In North Carolina the amendments helped bring the state back into the Union as Madison and others had hoped. Nevertheless, the November 1789 convention, which ratified the Constitution a month prior to the legislature's adoption of the amendments, had demanded that its congressmen seek eight additional amendments. These provided further guarantees of personal liberty, but primarily altered the structure and powers of the federal government in order to further protect state interests. North Carolina's representatives attempted without success to bring the proposals before the House in March and May 1790. In November 1790 the North Carolina Senate killed a resolution for a second Federal Convention.[46]

Rhode Island informed the federal government in September 1789 that the amendments "already afforded some relief and satisfaction to the minds of the people of this state," but it did not ratify the Constitution until May 1790. With its ratification, Rhode Island sent a list of twenty-one alterations and eighteen rights-related amendments which the state assumed to be unimpaired by the Federal Constitution. Among the novel alterations it proposed were an end to the importation of slaves as soon as possible and a provision that no amendment to the Constitution could take place after 1793 unless eleven of the original thirteen states agreed to it. Rhode Island adopted all but one of Congress's Amendments two weeks after it ratified the Constitution itself.[47]

Jackson to Knox, Mar. 7, 1790, Henry Knox Papers, MHS; Christopher Gore to Thomas Jefferson, Aug. 18, 1791, *Papers of Jefferson*, XXII, 16n; Leverett Saltonstall to Cordell Hull, Mar. 3, 1789, General Constitutional Records, RG 11 (National Archives [NA], Washington, D.C.).

[45] Staughton Lynd, "Abraham Yates's 'History of the Movement for the United States Constitution,'" *Class Conflict, Slavery, and the United States Constitution* (Indianapolis 1967), 222; DeWitt Clinton to Charles Clinton, Feb. 8, 1790, Miscellaneous Manuscripts (New-York Historical Society, New York, N.Y.).

[46] New York *Packet*, Oct. 8, 15, 1789; *State of North Carolina. In Convention, November 23, 1789*, Shipton Imprints No. 22039; John Steele to Joseph Winston, May 22, July 20, 1790, in H. M. Wagstaff, ed., *The Papers of John Steele* (2 vols., Raleigh, N.C. 1924), I, 61-62, 70-71; Thomas Blount to John Gray Blount, Nov. 27, 1790, Alice B. Keith, ed., *The John Gray Blount Papers* (2 vols., Raleigh, N.C. 1959), II, 147.

[47] John Collins to Washington, [Sept. 19, 1789], Miscellaneous Records,

Virginia's response to the amendments was crucial both to Madison politically and to the continuance of an Antifederal movement. Opponents of the Constitution, particularly in the heavily Antifederal counties south of the James River, not only became reconciled to the document as a result of the amendments, but also praised Madison as having been their patron. The state's Antifederal leaders remained dissatisfied nevertheless.[48] Henry claimed the Amendments injured rather than served the cause of liberty, and he promised to continue the fight. He insisted they acted only to lull suspicion and cast an impediment in the way of those who wished to "retrench the exorbitancy of power granted away . . . from the people" to the central government.[49] More moderate than Henry, George Mason, who must have recognized much from his Virginia Declaration of Rights in Madison's proposals, gained satisfaction from them as they had stood before the Senate revised them. With a few more alterations he could support the new system. Jefferson, by his own words in 1787 "not a friend to a very energetic government," had not been forced to take sides in the ratification debate because of his absence in France. Although he had claimed to be more of a Federalist than an Antifederalist, his unyielding support for a bill of rights, and his widely circulated suggestion that once nine states had ratified the Constitution the others should withhold their consent until such a bill was added, proved him a moderate Federalist at most. Jefferson agreed with Mason that amendments additional to those sent to the states should be pressed in order to fix the government on a more republican basis.[50]

Department of State Records, RG 59, NA. The Rhode Island amendments can be found in William Staples, *Rhode Island in the Continental Congress* (Providence 1870), 674-680.

[48] Edmund Pendleton to Madison, Sept. 2, 1789, Edward Carrington to Madison, Sept. 9, 1789, Madison to Washington, Nov. 20, 1789, *Papers of Madison*, XII, 368-369, 393, 453.

[49] Patrick Henry to Richard Henry Lee, Aug. 28, 1789, Jan. 29, 1790, Richard Henry Lee to Patrick Henry, Sept. 27, 1789, June 10, 1790, *Henry Correspondence*, III, 397-398, 402-404, 414, 421-422; Henry to Monroe, Jan. 24, 1791, James Monroe Papers, LC.

[50] Washington to James Craik, Sept. 8, 1789, Washington Papers, LC; Henry Lee to Madison, [c. Dec. 20, 1787], Madison to Jefferson, Oct. 24, 1787, *Papers of Madison,* X, 215-216, 339; Mason to Samuel Griffin, Sept. 8, 1789, Mason to Jefferson, Mar. 16, 1790, *Mason Papers*, III, 1172, 1189; Jefferson to Madison, Dec. 20, 1787, Jefferson to Francis Hopkinson, Mar. 13, 1789, Jefferson to Mason, June 13, 1790, *Papers of Madison*, XII, 442, XIV, 649-651, XVI, 493.

The amendments first came before the Virginia legislature during the closing weeks of 1789. Henry urged postponement; nevertheless, reacting out of anger or the recognition of defeat, he avoided the debate by going home. The resolution for postponement lost overwhelmingly, although an attempt to ask Congress to adopt the remainder of the Virginia Convention amendments failed by only one vote. The two houses disagreed over which of the twelve amendments to reject, and it did not ratify until December 1791. Appropriately, this made Virginia the tenth state to ratify and therefore gave legal effect to the first ten amendments, by then widely referred to as the Bill of Rights.[51]

Senators Grayson and Lee jointly had sent two official letters to the state in September 1789 insisting that they had done all they could to have "radical" amendments adopted. Fearing a loss of civil liberty and a tendency toward national rather than federal government, they expressed "real grief that we now send forward propositions inadequate to the purpose of real and substantial amendments, and so far short of the wishes of" Virginia. Their letters seriously misread the public reaction to Madison's amendments, and the legislature refused to order them printed. Leaked to the press at the end of 1789, the letters appeared in newspapers throughout the United States, where, in light of Madison's effectiveness, they served as the funeral oration for the Antifederalist party. "Some few indeed had gone such lengths in their declarations of hostility that they feel it awkward perhaps to come over," Secretary of State Jefferson informed the Marquis de Lafayette, "but the amendments proposed by Congress, have brought over almost all their followers."[52]

As Madison had predicted the amendments did detach the Antifederalists from their leaders and thereby prevented immediate structural revision of the Constitution.[53] The opposition party which

---

[51] Madison to Washington, Nov. 20, 1789, Henry Lee to Madison, Nov. 25, 1788, Hardin Burnley to Madison, Nov. 28, 1789, Edward Carrington to Madison, Dec. 20, 1789, *Papers of Madison*, XII, 453-456, 463-464; Henry Lee to Hamilton, Nov. 16, 1789, in Harold C. Syrett and Jacob E. Cooke, eds., *The Papers of Alexander Hamilton* (26 vols., New York, 1961-1979), V, 517.

[52] Richard Henry Lee and William Grayson to Governor of Virginia, Sept. 28, 1789, *idem* to Speaker of House of Delegates, Sept. 28, 1789, *Federal Gazette*, Dec. 28, 1789; John Fenno to Ward, Jan. 31, 1790, Ward Papers; David Stuart to Washington, Dec. 3, 1789, Washington Papers, LC; Ames to George R. Minot, Jan. 13, 1790, *Ames' Works*, I, 72; Jefferson to Lafayette, Apr. 2, 1790, *Papers of Jefferson*, XVI, 293.

[53] Several amendments designed to alter the federal judiciary were postponed until the Second Congress by the House on March 3, 1791.

replaced the Antifederalists was led by Madison and Jefferson and not Henry, who preferred to become a Federalist rather than associate with his old political enemies. The new party accepted the Constitution and challenged its interpretation rather than its essence. In one of the first pamphlets to attack the new party, Federalist William Smith argued that it was Madison "who advised that no other amendments to the Constitution should be offered to the people but a few milk and water propositions . . . ." Alexander Hamilton, after a decade of violent party politics, reflected that Madison's amendments met "scarcely any of the important objections which were urged, leaving the structure of the government, and the mass and distribution of its powers where they were, [and] are too insignificant to be with any sensible man a reason for being reconciled to the system if he thought it originally bad."[54]

The constitutional role as well as the consecrated status of the federal Bill of Rights today is due less to the foresight of the Founding Fathers than to the vigilance of a concerned citizenry, and especially to what Jefferson had called to Madison's attention in 1789 as an argument of "great weight" in favor of a bill of rights, "the legal check which it puts into the hands of the judiciary."[55]

---

[54] [William L. Smith], *The Politics and Views of a Certain Party, Displayed* (n.p. 1792), Shipton Imprints No. 24801, 22-23; "An Address to the Electors of the State of New-York," [Mar. 21, 1801], *Papers of Hamilton*, XXV, 356.

[55] Jefferson to Madison, Mar. 15, 1789, *Papers of Jefferson*, XIV, 659.

The Second Amendment and the Historiography of the Bill of Rights

*by David T. Hardy**

The second amendment to the Constitution of the United States recognizes that "[a] well regulated militia being necessary to the security of a free state, the right of the people to keep and bear arms shall not be infringed."[1] That there is controversy surrounding the interpretation of the second amendment, or any provision of the Bill of Rights, is hardly surprising. While the disputes relating to the first, fourth and remaining amendments focus upon their detailed application, the conflict over the second amendment concerns the question of its very subject matter. One school of thought contends that the second amendment protects a collective right, a narrow guarantee of a state right to maintain organized reserve military units.[2] This interpretation emphasizes the phrase "A well regulated militia being necessary to a free state," and maintains that the subsequent recognition of the people's right to bear arms is a mere restatement of this collective (i.e., state) right. The other school of thought contends that the amendment recognizes an individual right to possess and use arms.[3] This interpretation empha-

* Staff Attorney, Office of the Solicitor, United States Department of the Interior, Washington, D.C. The views expressed are solely those of the author and do not reflect those of his department.

[1] The second amendment's capitalization and punctuation is not uniformly reported; another version has four commas, after "militia," "state," and "arms." Since documents were at that time copied by hand, variations in punctuation and capitalization are common, and the copy retained by the first Congress, the copies transmitted by it to the state legislatures, and the ratifications returned by them show wide variations in such details. Letter from Marlene McGuirl, Chief, British-American Law Division, Library of Congress (Oct. 29, 1976).

[2] See, e.g., Beschle, Reconsidering the Second Amendment: Constitutional Protection For Right of Security, 9 Hamline L. Rev. 69 (1986); Cress, An Armed Community: The Origins and Meaning of the Right to Bear Arms, 71 J. Am. Hist. 22 (1984); Levin, The Right to Bear Arms: The Development of the American Experience, 48 Chi. Kent L. Rev. 148 (1971); Note, The Right to Bear Arms, 19 S.C.L. Rev. 402 (1967).

[3] This approach fell into disfavor in the early twentieth century, but its resurgence in recent years

sizes the phrase "the right of the people to keep and bear arms shall not be infringed," and maintains that the preceding description of the militia (i.e., all individuals capable of armsbearing) is a mere explanation of one objective of this guarantee.[4]

The works of neither school entertain the possibility that an "either/or" test may be a gross oversimplification of what are in fact two different sets of constitutional priorities. Yet the fact that prior to 1788 the Framers who proposed protections for individuals' arms did not propose to protect the militia, and those desirous of protecting the militia did not propose safeguards of individual arms, suggests the quixotic nature of previous attempts to demonstrate that the Framers, as a whole, had a single intent. Is it reasonable to assume that John Adams, obsessed with the risk of mob rule, and Thomas Jefferson, who so lightly praised the virtues of frequent revolutions, were of a single mind when it came to popular armaments? When Virginia constitutionalized the principle that a well-regulated militia was necessary to the proper defense of a free state, and Pennsylvania instead guaranteed that the people had a right to bear arms for defense of themselves and the state, was there in fact

---

has altered constitutional interpretation. While advocates of collective rights approaches have for a decade failed to produce much in the way of original thought or research, the last five years have seen an explosion of original research supporting the individual rights approach. See, e.g., Caplan, The Right of the Individual to Bear Arms: A Recent Judicial Trend, 1982 Det. C.L. Rev. 789; Dowlut, The Right to Arms: Does the Constitution or the Predilection of Judges Reign?, 36 Okla. L. Rev. 65 (1983); Dowlut & Knoop, State Constitutions and the Right to Keep and Bear Arms, 7 Okla. City U.L. Rev. 177 (1982); S. Halbrook, That Every Man Be Armed: The Evolution of a Constitutional Right (1984); Subcomm. on the Constitution of the Sen. Judiciary Comm., The Right to Keep and Bear Arms, 97th Con., 2d Sess. (Comm. Print 1982); Halbrook, The Right to Bear Arms in the First State Bills of Rights: Pennsylvania, North Carolina, Vermont, and Massachusetts, 10 Vt. L. Rev. 255 (1985) [hereinafter The Right to Bear Arms]; Halbrook, To Keep and Bear Their Private Arms: The Adoption of the Second Amendment 1787-1791, 10 N. Ky. L. Rev. 13 (1982); Hardy, Armed Citizens, Citizen Armies: Toward a Jurisprudence of the Second Amendment, 9 Harv. J.L. & Pub. Pol'y 559 (1986) [hereinafter Armed Citizens]; D. Hardy, Origins and Development of the Second Amendment (1986); Kates, Handgun Prohibition and the Original Meaning of the Second Amendment, 82 Mich. L. Rev. 204 (1983); Malcolm, The Right of the People to Keep and Bear Arms: The Common Law Tradition, 10 Hastings Const. L.Q. 285 (1983); Shalhope, The Ideological Origins of the Second Amendment, 69 J. Am. Hist. 599 (1982). The author is also informed that Joyce Malcolm, a historian specializing in early modern British history, is in the final drafting of a treatise on the common law right to arms, which alone is likely to double the available original research on the history of that right.

[4] The author has suggested a third school of thought, advocating a "hybrid" right, in which the right is individual but its source is collective. In this view, individuals are seen as having a right to possess arms suitable for organized military reserve duty. See Hardy, Armed Citizens supra note 3, at 615-622.

an identical understanding which motivated each statement? Both existing formulations of the second amendment require us to assume precisely that. As a consequence, no existing analysis of that amendment has attempted a critical examination of the proposals for the second amendment against the varied backgrounds and philosophies of their authors, and none has taken account of recent research demonstrating that the different state conventions were dominated by radically differing political philosophies.

It is the purpose of this article to suggest that in fact ***neither*** the collective nor individual school of thought is correct insofar as it claims to ***entirely*** explain the second amendment, and ***both*** are correct, insofar as they purport to offer partial explanations. The second amendment was not intended to recognize only a single principle; rather, like the first, fourth, fifth, and sixth amendments, it was intended as a composite of constitutional provisions. Its militia component and its right to bear arms recognition have in fact different origins and theoretical underpinnings. One is a legacy of the Renaissance, brought to fruition by the "Classical Republicans;" the other is the creation of seventeenth century English experience, brought to fruition in the Enlightenment. At the time of the framing of our Constitution, the militia statement found its primary constituency among the gentry, particularly that of Virginia. The individual right to bear arms provision was primarily advanced by the Radical movement, particularly in Pennsylvania and Massachusetts. Only after the Constitution had received its crucial ninth ratification were the two precepts joined into a single sentence, thereby creating a constitutional "package" which addressed the demands of both schools of thought. Thus neither the militia nor the right to bear arms provision can be taken in isolation as a sufficient explanation of the second amendment, a fact made obvious by the first Congress' retention of both clauses during its extensive paring of Madison's proposals.[8] The second amendment therefore has histori-

[8] Madison's original proposal took no fewer than 46 words to describe the rights involved: "The right of the people to keep and bear arms shall not be infringed; a well-armed, and well-regulated militia being the best security of a free country: but no person religiously scrupulous of bearing arms, shall be compelled to render military service in person." 12 The Papers of James Madison 201 (R. Rutland & C. Hobson eds. 1979). The version finally voted out by the Congress uses only 24 words. Madison's original version also illustrates his approach of grouping several rights into a single amendment, since it incorporated not only a militia and a right to arms component, but would have added a

cal interest which extends beyond militia and arms issues. It is, metaphorically speaking, a fault line in the bedrock of the Constitution; the one place where a rough joinder of related ideas enables us today to discern a turning point between two entirely different American approaches to statecraft.

To be sure, militia systems and individual armament have always been related concerns with a practical interaction. An armed citizenry was the basis of the militia the Framers sought, and the functioning of such a militia was the most obvious *political* purpose of citizen armament. Such an interaction is hardly unique; the first amendment guarantees freedom of expression and the right to petition the legislature. At the same time, neither of the interrelated rights can fully express the purposes of the Framers. Indeed, the overlap between the militia concept and the right to arms concept has not prevented a certain rivalry between the two, a rivalry especially pronounced during the formative years of our own nation. Supporters of one view may not have disputed the principle of the other, but they certainly disputed whether it deserved high political-constitutional priority.

One group, influenced by the Classical Republicans, saw the establishment of a stable republic that could survive in a hostile environment as the highest priority. For this group, to emphasize citizens' rights *against* such a republic was to place the cart before the horse. The other group, influenced by Enlightenment thought, saw the establishment of the rights of man, around which a free republic or democracy might be construed, as the main priority. A statement, rather than a command, regarding the value of the militia "to a free state" appealed to the first group; a command that the right "of the people" to bear arms shall not be infringed appealed to the second.

In order to fully understand *both* purposes of the second amendment it will be necessary to examine first the origins of the militia concept, second, the origins of an individual right to bear arms, and third, the eventual merger of the two concepts which led to the present second amendment.

---

constitutional right to conscientious objection.

I. The Militia as Essential to a Free Republic

A. A Digression: Modern Historiography, the Classical Republicans and the Radicals

Only a few decades ago, the ideology of the American Revolution could have been neatly summarized as a commentary on John Locke's *First Treatise on Civil Government.* While acknowledging that more state-centered Republicans emerged during the seventeenth century (largely as a result of the English Civil War and the Protectorate of Oliver Cromwell which followed), this view assumes that their ideas had been discredited in the late seventeenth century and were disregarded in the eighteenth.[6] Thus before Locke there was nothing, so far as the theoretics of the Framers were concerned.

Recent research has forced a reevaluation of this view, suggesting both that Locke's role was overstated[7] and that eighteenth century American thought was heavily influenced by pre-Lockean republican views.[8] These "Classical Republicans" (largely identified with the Whig Party) contributed greatly to late eighteenth century American political thought. Although largely forgotten today, the names of eminent Republicans such as Sidney, Harrington and Fletcher were commonplace to the Framers and their contemporaries.[9] Indeed, modern students of this movement maintain that the

---

[6] Shalhope cites, as typical, a 1940 conclusion that "Americans in 1776 had little if any knowledge of past republics and that consideration of these was clearly irrelevant to the discussion of the origins of republican institutions in America." Shalhope, Toward a Republican Synthesis: The Emergence of an Understanding of Republicanism in American Historiography, 29 Wm. & Mary Q. (3d Ser.) 49, 50 (1972).

[7] See generally J. Pocock, The Machiavellian Moment: Florentine Political Thought and the Atlantic Republican Tradition (1970).

[8] The works most crucial to this recognition were: Pamphlets of the American Revolution (B. Bailyn ed. 1965); H. Colbourn, The Lamp of Experience: Whig History and the Intellectual Origins of the American Revolution (1965); C. Robbins, The Eighteenth Century Commonwealthman: Studies in the Transmission, Development and Circumstance of English Liberal Thought from the Restoration of Charles II until the War with the Thirteen Colonies (1959); and G. Wood, The Creation of the American Republic 1776-1787 (1969). The best historiographical works include Banning, Republican Ideology and the Triumph of the Constitution, 1789 to 1793, 31 Wm. & Mary Q. (3d Ser.) 167 (1974); Pocock, Machiavelli, Harrington and English Political Ideologies in the Eighteenth Century, 22 Wm. & Mary Q. (3d Ser.) 549 (1965); Shalhope, Republicanism and Early American Historiography 39 Wm. & Mary Q. (3d Ser.) 334 (1982); and Shalhope, supra note 6.

[9] See B. Bailyn, The Ideological Origins of the American Revolution 85 (1967); H. Colbourn, supra note 8, at 60, 78, 127.

Framers were immersed in Classical Republican thought:

> No man's thought is altogether free. Men are born into an intellectual universe where some ideas are native and others are difficult to conceive. Sometimes this intellectual universe is so well structured and has so strong a hold that it can virtually determine not only the ways in which a society will express its hopes and discontents but also the central problems with which it will be concerned. In 1789 Americans lived in such a world. The heritage of classical republicanism and English opposition thought, shaped and hardened in the furnace of a great Revolution, left few men free.[10]

Yet the rediscoverers of Classical Republican thought did not have the last word in the effort to discern the political thought of the Framers. The seventeenth century had its Populists and Democrats (the Diggers and the Levelers) and one of the effects of the Classical Republican emphasis has been the study of their counterparts (albeit not direct descendants), the Radical thinkers of revolutionary America.[11] However unappealing such radicalism may have been to the gentry, its values and thought explain the stance of Sam Adams, Thomas Paine, and the urban patriots of Boston and Philadelphia to a far greater degree than the Classical Republicans' emphasis on agrarian, freeholding society. Morever, since one of the Radical legacies was an emphasis on individual rights, as distinguished from the Classical Republicans' emphasis on a well-ordered society, their thought is of special relevance to our Bill of Rights, not to mention the Jeffersonian/Jacksonian democracy of the early republic.

To be sure, when we speak of Republicans and Democrats, Conservatives and Radicals, we do so in a quite subjective manner. Few, if any, statesmen of 1787-1791 would have admitted to being anything but a "Republican." Indeed, those whom we would view as "Radicals" today were among the most ardent supporters of "Republicanism." Few would have cared to be called "Radical." These terms of art thus have little relation to how the labelled individuals described themselves at the time. Moreover, to categorize so

---

[10] Banning, supra note 8, at 178-79.

[11] Probably the best treatment of American Radical thought is The American Revolution: Explorations in the History of American Radicalism (A. Young ed. 1976). See also Shalhope, supra note 8, at 338-39.

varied a band of thinkers is to understate the diversity of their thought and impose upon that group a particular perspective. The views of Jefferson, the agrarian Radical, differed subtly from those of Sam Adams, the urban Radical; neither man would have cared for too close an association with the views of Sam's aristocratic cousin, John Adams. Richard Henry Lee and Elbridge Gerry, both ardent Republicans, are to our eyes hardly compatriots of Carter Braxton, the reluctant revolutionary and Monarchist. Yet all these otherwise disparate individuals put their names to the Declaration of Independence, and all (whether Monarchist or Democrat, Conservative or Radical) would have been similarly Radical to a Tory of the time. Recognizing these limitations, it is still plausible to distinguish between "Conservative Revolutionaries" such as George Mason, and their Radical brethren such as Sam Adams, and between those who gave priority to establishing a stable republic and those who gave priority to defining and guaranteeing rights against even such a government.

B. The Free State and a Well Regulated Militia

The existence of an English militia, comprised not of specialized units but of essentially the entire male population, far antedates even the Norman Conquest.[12] By 1181, every English freeman was required annually to prove ownership of arms proportionate to his landholdings.[13] In 1253, even serfs were required to prove annually that they owned a spear and dagger.[14] Subsequent enactments ordered all healthy Englishmen to own longbows, to train their sons in archery from age seven, and to abstain from a variety of outdoor sports that diverted commoners from the archery ranges.[15] By the fifteenth century, Englishmen already regarded universal armament for national defense as a critical element in their development of "government under law."[16] This perception of citizen armament as

---

[12] A duty of all freeman to serve in the fyrd, or militia, is traceable at least to the seventh century, and may well antedate even the Saxon invasions. See J. Bagley & P. Rowley, A Documentary History of England 1066-1540, at 152 (1965).

[13] J. Bagley & P. Rowley, supra note 12, at 154-56.

[14] Id. at 155-156.

[15] See generally Hardy, Armed Citizens, supra note 3, at 564-66.

[16] Many may think these concepts are recent creations. In fact, Sir John Fortescue, who fought in

a peculiarly English virtue was thereafter reinforced by the rise of royal absolutism on the Continent,[17] with consequent limitation on firearm possession in France and the Empire. Long after her continental counterparts had banned or severely restricted firearms ownership,[18] Elizabeth still struggled to stop her subjects from drawing pistols in church, or firing them in the churchyard.[19]

While the results of citizen armament may thus have been annoying to sundry clerics, they did much to restrain excessive royal power. An English king had to remember that his "'gentleman pensioners' and his yeoman of the guard were but a handful, and bills or bows were in every farm and cottage."[20] Conversely, a popular monarch could count upon a massive reserve army, maintained at little or no cost to the state: in the 1580s, Elizabeth could main-

---

the War of the Roses, distinguished in the 1470s between France's "jus regale" and England's "jus regale et polliticum." "Jus Regale" can be rendered "royal law" or "law of the king"; "polliticum" can be rendered as "of the State," "national," or even "of the republic" (Latin translation of Plato's Republic rendered the title as "Politia"). Fortescue argued that the French peasants were starved and impoverished so that they were "crokyd" and "feble," and unable to defend the realm: "nor thai have wepen, nor money to bie them wepen withall." Thus the French king, unable to use his unreliable nobility or his weak and unarmed peasants, was forced to rely on mercenaries: "Lo, this is the frute of his Jus regale. Yf the reaume of Englonde, wich is an Ile, and therfor mey not lyghtly geyte soucore of other landes, were rulid vnder such a lawe and vnder such a prince, it wolde be a pray to all oper nacions pat wolde conqwer, robbe or deuouir it." Fortunately, Englishmen were healthy, wealthy and armed to the teeth, "wherfore thai ben myghty, and able to resiste the adversaries of this realme, and to beete oper reaumes that do, or woldee do them wronge. Lo, this is the fruty of Jus polliticum et regale, under wich we live." J. Fortescue, The Governance of England, Otherwise Called The Difference Between an Absolute and a Limited Monarchy 114-15 (C. Plummer rev. ed. 1885).

[17] See generally M. Beloff, The Age of Absolutism 1660-1815 (1962).

[18] For example, the Holy Roman Emperor banned wheelock firearms throughout the Empire in 1518, while unauthorized manufacture of firearms or gunpowder in France soon became a capital offense. Blair, Further Notes on the Origin of the Wheelock, *in* Arms and Armor Annual 29, 35-36 (1973); L. Kennett & A. Anderson, The Gun in America 12, 15 (1975); N. Perrin, Giving Up the Gun 58 (1975).

[19] Proclamation Enforcing Peace in Churches and Churchyards (Oct. 30, 1561), 2 Tudor Royal Proclamations 177-78 (P. Hughes & J. Larkin eds. 1969).

> For avoiding of divers outrageous and unseemly behaviors. . . and for the better and speedy reducing of the same churches to the godly uses for Thee which the same were builded, . . . Her Majesty's pleasure is that if any person shall make any fray or quarrel, or draw, or put out his hand to any weapon for that purpose, or shoot any handgun or dag within the cathedral church of St. Paul . . . or within any other church or churchyard, [he] . . . shall suffer imprisonment by the space of two months without bail or mainprize. . . .

Id. Henry VIII had briefly experimented with prohibiting firearms shooting by all but the wealthy, but soon abandoned the attempt in the face both of massive noncompliance and of new military needs. See Hardy, Armed Citizens, supra note 3, at 566-69.

[20] C. Oman, A History of the Art of War in the Sixteenth Century 288 (1937).

tain 120,000 men on duty throughout the summer.[21] Such a force was almost entirely for defensive use because, since the twelfth century, English kings had relied upon mercenaries for foreign military service.[22] Mercenaries were not tied to a home district; they were better trained and, while on the offensive, could be compensated by plunder. But after the loss of British holdings in France during the mid-fifteenth century, England stood mainly on the defensive, and mercenary forces dwindled to a handful of bodyguards and coastal garrisons.

This decline paralleled an expansion and perfection of the militia system under the late Tudors.[23] The system all but collapsed under the reign of the pacifistic James I, who acquiesced in the repeal of the militia statutes. The civil war which came during the reign of his son, Charles I, saw both sides dependent upon standing armies (sometimes equipped by disarming local militias). The end result of the war was a military dictatorship.[24] The dictatorship ended in turn with the restoration of Charles II, who restored only a limited royalist militia backed by standing forces. This turmoil predictably inspired various theoreticians to suggest various ideal political systems. Unlike many thinkers from that period in history, the Classical Republicans, who drew inspiration largely from the Greek and Roman republics, left an enduring legacy.

To the early Classical Republicans, the militia concept was more than simple tradition. The belief that such a militia was "necessary to a free State" soon became central to their political thought. They drew inspiration from Nicolo Machiavelli, who had both explained and attempted to implement a national militia centuries before. Writing to an Italy which had seen its city-states and their mercenary armies crushed in detail by French and Spanish professionals, Machiavelli advocated an Italian nation, led by a popular prince and based on a national militia. Such a prince, he explained, would found his state upon: "good laws and good arms. And as there cannot be good laws where there are not good arms, and where there

---

[21] L. Boynton, The Elizabethan Militia 8-9 (1967).

[22] B. Lyon, A Constitutional and Legal History of Medieval Britain 271-73 (2d ed. 1980). See L. Boynton, supra note 21.

[23] See L. Boynton, supra note 21.

[24] See generally Hardy, Armed Citizens, supra note 3, at 572-575.

are good arms there must be good laws, I will not now discuss the laws, but will speak of the arms."[25] Mercenaries were to be categorically condemned; they were "disunited, ambitious, without discipline, faithless, bold amongst friends, cowardly amongst enemies, they have no fear of God, and keep no faith with men."[26] These faults were inherent in all mercenaries; their lack of patriotism left no motivation beyond wages, which were not enough to motivate men to die.[27] More fundamentally, any mercenary army powerful enough to defend a state must be more than powerful enough to subjugate it.[28] According to Machiavelli, only a nation defended by a militia can escape this dilemma: "Rome and Sparta were for many centuries well armed and free. The Swiss are well armed and enjoy great freedom."[29]

The great Florentine expanded these themes in his *Art of War*. A prince who relies upon mercenaries must either remain embroiled in wars, or risk overthrow when mercenaries become unemployed with the advent of peace.

> A prince, therefore, who would reign in security, ought to select only such men for his infantry as will cheerfully serve him in war when it is necessary, and be as glad to return home when it is over. This will always be the case with those who have other occupations and employments by which to live.[30]

Such a militia stabilizes the state, whatever its form:

> it is certain that no subjects or citizens, when legally armed and kept in due order by their masters, ever did the least mischief to any state . . . Rome remained free for four hundred years and Sparta eight hundred, although their citizens were armed all that time; but many other states that have been disarmed have lost their liberties in less than forty years.[31]

---

[25] N. Machiavelli, The Prince and the Discourses 44 (Mod. Library ed. 1950) (1513).

[26] See id. at 44-45.

[27] See id. at 45.

[28] "Mercenary captains are either very capable men or not; if they are, you cannot rely upon them, for they will always aspire to their own greatness, either by oppressing you, their master, or by oppressing others against your intentions; but if the captain is not an able man, he will generally ruin you." Id.

[29] Id. at 46.

[30] N. Machiavelli, The Art of War 21 (rev. ed. 1965) (1521).

[31] Id. at 30.

Knowledge of Machiavelli's writings spread rapidly. An English translation of his *Art of War* went through no fewer than three printings by 1588,[32] yet long before the translations his writings were common currency among the English statesmen.[33] Machiavelli's greatest impact upon English thought came, however, through the writings of James Harrington. Harrington applied Machiavelli's *realpolitik* to seventeenth century England, substituting a republic of freeholders for rule by a popular prince. The outcome was a stable republic populated, ruled and defended by a militia of its freeholders.[34] Ownership of land gives independence; unlike a feudal landholder, the modern freeholder owns in fee simple, is not obliged as a condition of tenure to fight for a superior, and thus can defend his own rights and interests.

> [T]he power whose distributics in society [Harrington] was trying to chart was essentially the possession of land that gave a man independence, this independence being in the last analysis measured by his ability to bear arms and use them in his own quarrels. Harrington's democracy was a republic of freeholders owning their own lands and weapons. . . .[35]

Indeed, Harrington's rejection of monarchy is intertwined with his belief that land, political power and military force must be in the same hands:

> Harrington's entire theory of monarchy can be reduced to two propositions: first, that the King's agents and servants must be supported either upon the land as a feudal aristocracy, or about his person, as praetorians or janissaries; second, that whichever of these methods is adopted, relations between the military class and the King will be so prone to tensions that monarchy can never be a stable form of government.[36]

---

[32] Id. at xxx.

[33] See generally F. Rabb, The English Face of Machiavelli 48-51 (1964). Rabb cites, for example, quotations and paraphrases in English diplomatic dispatches dating from as early as 1537.

[34] Harrington's major works were Oceana published in 1656 and The Prerogative of Popular Government published in 1658. The best current collection is The Political Works of James Harrington 210, 389 (J.G.A. Pocock ed. 1977). Harrington has proven to be a bit of a political visionary. He predicted the independence of British and Spanish colonies, the French Revolution, and advocated universal free education, voting by secret ballot, and tax exemptions for dependents. C. Hill, The Century of Revolution 1603-1714, 310 (1962).

[35] Pocock, supra note 34 at 553-554.

[36] Id. at 559.

This, Harrington argued, could be contrasted to his stable republic where property, political power, and arms were all in the same hands. Such a republic faced few internal threats, since those with arms also had the greatest economic and political interest in maintaining the state. Nor were external threats to be feared:

> inasmuch as, the commonwealth being equal, [an invader] must needs to find them united, but in regard that such citizens, being all soldiers or trained up unto their arms, which they use not for the defense of slavery but of liberty (a condition not in this world to be bettered), they have more especially upon this occasion the highest soul of courage and (if their territory be of any extent) the vastest body of a well disciplined militia that is possible in nature. Wherefore an example of such an one overcome by the arms of a monarch, is not to be found in the world . . . [F]or the reasons why a government of citizens . . . is the hardest to be held, there needs no more than that men accustomed unto their arms and their liberties will never endure the yoke.[37]

Harrington wrote during the Protectorate, when efforts to maintain a standing army were indeed destabilizing the nation. After 1660, the army played a different role, that of maintaining royal power. Harrington's postulate that an army could not be adequately financed and subordinated was compromised. Harrington's followers, particularly Henry Neville, modified his critique. Whereas Harrington had assumed a standing army could not stabilize a government, good or bad, Neville and other post-1675 Harringtonians saw it as all too capable of stabilizing an autocratic one.[38] Conversely, by arming the people at large democracies could obtain an incomparable advantage: "democracy is much more powerful than aristocracy, because the latter cannot arm the people for fear they could seize upon the government."[39] Harrington's followers also recast his utopia in a conservative light, by arguing that traditional English practices had in fact been republican. "The arming and training of all the freeholders of England, as it is our undoubted

---

[37] Id. at 442-443.

[38] Neville's great work, Plato Redivus, Or a Dialogue Concerning Government, may be conveniently found in Two English Republican Tracts (C. Robbins ed. 1969). See generally C. Hill, supra note 34, at 223.

[39] C. Hill, Some Intellectual Origins of the English Revolution 27 (1980) (citing Neville, supra note 38).

ancient Constitution, and consequently our Right," argued Robert Molesworth, "so it is the Opinion of most Whigs, that it ought to be out in Practice."[40] Thus the Classical Republicans ultimately cast the militia not only as part of the republican utopia but also an underpinning of the existing English constitution.

C. The Standing Army Controversy

Yet as Harrington's successors refined the argument for the militia vis-a-vis the standing army, they were being overtaken by events. In 1688 James II relied upon his army, which was financed out of his own personal funds rather than Parliamentary appropriations, and staffed by handpicked officers. Too late, James discovered his mistake. England was "invaded" by William of Orange, supported by some 12,000 troops. Although James mustered more than twice that number, dissension (particularly among the officers) prevented James from offering battle, and he fled into exile.[41]

This "Glorious Revolution" and William and Mary's acceptance of the throne offered by Parliament did nothing to reduce the support for the standing army. For England to accept William also meant being drawn into the ongoing struggle between Holland and France and facing the risk of James' return with a French army. The need for the projection of force on the continent had returned and, as always, the militia was totally unsuited to this task.

English policy makers had to face several other realities, none of which favored reliance on the militia. An invasion, if it came, would be spearheaded by well-trained French troops, at a time when such training was of increasing importance. Technical improvements over the course of the seventeenth century had immensely complicated the role of the average infantryman. At the beginning of the century, the customary infantry weapons of musket or pike (an eighteen-foot spear held by men formed in a dense mass) had required a moderate amount of training; an army of that time

---

[40] Molesworth, Forward to F. Hotman, Franco Gallia at xxvi (R. Molesworth trans., London 1711).

[41] See generally G. Trevelyan, The English Revolution 1688-1689, at 63 (1939). Crucial to the army's failure was an officers' conspiracy led by none other than John Churchill, James' commander-in-chief, who defected to William during the confrontation.

maneuvered slowly in "tercios" or "battles" of about 3,000 men. During the first third of the seventeenth century, armies were constructed around a "battalion" of about 500 men trained to execute a multitude of orders: "officers became not merely leaders, but trainers of men; diligent practice in peace-time, and in winter, became essential; and drill, for the first time in modern history became the precondition for the military success. . . ."[42] Conversely, the financial revolution of the 1690's, which saw the creation of a national bank and acceptance of a national debt, made it possible to fund a large enough standing force.[43] Increasing tactical and economic sophistication were paralleled by the realization of political means to guarantee legislative control of the army. Parliament could keep a tight rein on the standing army by limiting appropriations and enacting "Mutiny Acts" of intentionally short duration.[44]

The increased viability of a true standing army suddenly forced the post-1688 Whigs to face the prospect of becoming members of the establishment they had formerly opposed.[45] Some, like Molesworth, hedged:

> A Whig is against the raising or keeping up a Standing Army in Time of Peace; but with this Distinction, that if at any time an Army (tho even in Time of Peace) should be necessary to the Support of the very Maxim, a Whig is not for being too hasty to destroy that which is to be the Defender of his Liberty.[46]

---

[42] M. Roberts, The Military Revolution 1560-1660, Inaugural Lecture delivered before the Queen's University of Belfast 9-11 (copy in possession of author). The earlier use of the pike had led to no improvements in organization. Fifteenth century pikemen were generally launched *en masse* at the enemy.

[43] See generally Pocock, supra note 7, at 64-65.

[44] The Mutiny Acts authorized the imposition of martial law on persons enlisted in the military. Absent their sanctions, a deserting soldier could be punished by a civil suit for breach of contract, or at most, prosecution as a runaway apprentice; one who struck an officer might face misdemeanor assault charges in the civilian courts. C. Barnett, Britain's Army 1503-1970, at 124 (1970). The post-1688 Mutiny Acts were generally of one year's duration, ensuring that without annual parliamentary reauthorization army discipline would be almost unattainable.

[45] To be sure, the events of 1688 cannot be represented as an unqualified Whig victory. William's policies favored neither party, and those of his successor Ann strongly favored Tories. Only with the accession of George I in 1714 did the Whigs attain a dominant hand. See generally B. Williams, The Whig Supremacy 1714-1760 (2nd ed. 1962). At the same time, for Whigs after 1688 the destruction of the government would likely mean replacement of a generally unsympathetic Tory establishment with an oppressive and vengeful Jacobite one, and the loss of their gains made during the Glorious Revolution.

[46] Molesworth, supra note 40, at xxv.

Others continued to defend the renaissance ideal of the citizen-freeholder-soldier, and argued that treating military skills as a specialization would lead inevitably to tyranny and corruption. While their views, as will be shown, gained great currency in America, in England they became simply the "Opposition."[47]

In the years after 1688, a standing army thus became more acceptable to Englishmen, if not to their American counterparts. Macaulay sums up the experience:

> What had been at first tolerated as an exception began to be considered as the rule. Not a session passed without a mutiny bill, regarded merely as an occasion on which hopeful young orators fresh from Christchurch were to deliver maiden speeches, setting forth how the guards of Pisistratus seized the citadel of Athens, and how the Praetorian cohorts sold the Roman empire to Didius. At length these declamations became too ridiculous to be repeated. The most old fashioned, the most eccentric, politician could hardly, in the reign of George the Third, contend that there ought to be no regular soldiers. . . .[48]

The acceptance of a standing army was paralleled by the atrophy of the militia system in England. Indeed, the rural disorders of the 1760s inspired fear in the gentry of the militia-trained portion of the populace. Lord Barrington, for instance, feared that "a few soldiers, commanded by a weak, ignorant subaltern, might be defeated by a very large mob, full of men lately used to arms in the army and militia."[49] The general militia in England was steadily supplanted by a select militia which achieved efficiency by a sacrifice of almost every traditional attribute. The 1761 Militia Act, for instance, authorized mustering of only a few hundred men from each county. Those chosen were, if wealthy, able to hire another to serve as a substitute; those actually serving were issued government arms, stored by the officers under lock and key. The Lieutenant of the county (or his deputies) was authorized "to employ such Person

---

[47] Even under William, who relied heavily upon Whig ministers, "[t]he honeymoon did not last. . . . [A] flood of publications reminded Englishmen of the ancient system they were supposedly reviving, including a Saxon-style militia. Yet William believed that military common sense dictated a standing army." H. Colbourn, supra note 8, at 48. Under the Tory administrations which followed, these views became truly the "opposition theory [which] provided a model for an American version." Banning, supra note 8 at 183.

[48] 3 T. Macaulay, The History of England from the Accession of James the Second 47 (1856).

[49] T. Hayter, The Army and the Crowd in Mid-Georgian England 117 (1978).

or Persons as he or they shall think fit, to seize and remove the arms, clothes and accoutrements belonging to the militia, whenever [they] shall adjudge it necessary to the peace of the kingdom. . . ."[50] It thus is no surprise that a few years later the Whig mayor of London would inform Parliament that the militia "could no longer be deemed a constitutional defence, under the immediate controul and direction of the people; for by that bill they were rendered a standing army to all intents and purposes whatever. . . ."[51]

II. The People's Right to Keep and Bear Arms

As noted above, Classical Republicanism strongly influenced American revolutionary ideology. Nevertheless, while the views of Harrington and Neville may go far toward explaining the outlook of John Adams and George Mason, but they are less illuminating in explaining the views of Sam Adams, Thomas Paine, Thomas Jefferson, and their fellows.

> Alongside the Machievellian conception of citizenship, order and liberty, there grew up another paradigm . . . . Classical theory asserted the predominance of politics over all other aspects of social life. In exactly the way Pocock has described the creation of all matrices of language, [eighteenth century] writers decomposed old meanings about civil order and recomposed the elements of time, citizenship, and the distribution of authority. Outside the [classical] polity, they constructed a model of economic life that borrowed its order from nature — the newly conceptualized nature of predictable regularity. As the economy absorbed more and more of the attention of men and women it supplied a new identity for them. By the end of the eighteenth century the individual with wide-ranging needs and abstract rights appeared to challenge the citizen with concrete obligations and prescribed privileges.
>
> In the 1790's, when the Jeffersonian Republicans and Federalists confronted each other, the battle lines had been drawn around opposing conceptions of civil society.[52]

---

[50] "An Act to explain, amend, and reduce into one act of Parliament the Several Laws, now in being, Relating to the Raising and Training the Militia Within that part of Great Britain called England," 20 Geo. 3, ch. 20, § 105 (1761).

[51] The North British Intelligencer 20 (Edinburgh 1776) (reporting speech by Lord Mayor of London, attacking the Scottish Militia Bill) (Lib. of Congress Rare Books Collection).

[52] Appleby, Republicanism in Old and New Contexts, 43 Wm. & Mary Q. (3d Ser.) 20, 31-32 (1986).

Although Anglo-Saxon society had long placed particular emphasis on the individual, especially toward property,[53] the concept of individual political rights was of relatively late birth. To print a work on politics or religion required a royal permit as late as 1695.[54] Most colonies retained the permit requirement into the 1730's;[55] even after these measures lapsed, it was illegal to print a work reflecting on an action of Parliament or the person of a member without prior authorization.[56] The 1661 Act Against Tumultuous Petitioning prohibited petitioning the King or Parliament for changes in the established law, absent a permit from a justice of the peace.[57] The 1673 Test Act, which generally barred non-Anglicans from civil or military office, remained on the books until 1829;[58] searches based on general warrants, issued by the executive, were

---

[53] See generally A. Macfarlane, The Origins of English Individualism (1978); C. Morris, The Discovery of the Individual 1050-1200 (1972).

[54] C. Hill, supra note 34, at 248-49. When the Licensing Act briefly lapsed in 1679, the royal courts asserted a common law basis for the prohibition against most political publications, the Chief Justice stating that it extended to "all Persons that do Write or Print or Sell any Pamphlet that is either Scandalous to Public or Private Persons." G. Sensenbaugh, That Grand Whig Milton 56 (1952). Judge Allybone's jury instructions in the Seven Bishop's Case are instructive. "In the first place, . . . no man can take upon him to write against the actual exercise of the government, unless he have leave from the government. If he does, he makes a libel, be what he says true or false; if we once come to impeach the Government by way of argument, it is argument that makes government or no government. . . . . My next position is, that no private man can take upon him to write concerning the government at all, for what has any private man to do with the government. It is the business of the Government to manage matters relating to the government; it is the business of subjects to manage only their private affairs. . . . when I intrude myself into matters which do not concern my particular interest, I am a libeller." 2 Lord Campbell, Lives of the Lord Chief Justices 362 (7th ed. 1878).

[55] From 1686 to 1732, the standard royal command authorizing colonial governors to assume their post ordered them to ban not only printing, but also possession of a printing press, without a license. "You are to provide by all necessary orders that no person keep any press for printing, nor that any book, pamphlet or other matters whatsoever be printed without your especial leave and license first obtained." C. Rossiter, Seedtime of the Republic 29 (1953).

[56] In 1762, the author of a legal treatise was threatened with prosecution for including in his work passages criticizing rulings of the House of Lords, without having obtained the Lords' consent; a century later, a biographer obtained statutory authorization to publish a history of judges, some of whom had sat in Parliament. 5 Lord Campbell, Lives of the Lord Chancellors and Keepers of the Great Seal of England 26 (7th ed. 1878).

[57] J.R. Jones, Country and Court 143 (1978). Even authorized petitioners ran a risk; the "Seven Bishops" were prosecuted for seditious libel based upon a petition handed directly to the king. In 1701, the "Kentish Petitioners," who presented a mild petition requesting passage of a spending bill, were imprisoned on the spot for contempt of Parliament. E.N. Williams, The Eighteenth Century Constitution 410-11 (1960).

[58] G. Trevelyan, The English Revolution 1688-1689, at 27-28 (1939). While the Toleration Acts relieved certain non-Anglican protestant religions from the risk of criminal prosecution for non-adherence, those acts did not permit their communicants to hold office.

universally accepted until the 1760s.[59] Most of our Bill of Rights are, in short, of quite recent vintage. It should therefore come as no surprise that the concept of a right to keep and bear arms has a later point of origin than that of the militia. Conversely, a specifically individual right to arms, separate and apart from the militia system, was one of the earliest of the *individual* civil rights to gain acceptance.

In fact, the origins of the concept of an individual right to arms lies not in the eighteenth century Enlightenment, but in the turmoil of the seventeenth century. As Joyce Malcolm has demonstrated,[60] Englishmen of all classes and loyalties were shocked when, hard pressed for arms at the outset of the English Civil War, both Royal and Parliamentary forces disarmed suspected opponents and even supporters.[61] The end of the fighting brought no end to the risk. In 1659, the Protectorate for the first time gave formal statutory authorization to disarm Englishmen *en masse*: officials were authorized to search for and seize all arms possessed by veterans of the Royal armies or by "any other person whom the Commissioners shall judge dangerous to the peace of the Commonwealth."[62] Nor were supporters of the Commonwealth safe for long. The following year, the Commonwealth fell and Charles II was restored to the throne. One of his first acts was to order the Lords Lieutenant of the militia to disarm all likely opponents. The *Calendar of State Papers* summary of his order ends: "officers to be numerous, disaffected persons watched and not allowed to assemble, and their arms seized."[63]

The order was executed so zealously as to antagonize even Charles' supporters. The failure of his attempts to secure a compre-

---

[59] 6 Lord Campbell, Lives of the Lords Chancellor and Keepers of the Great Seal of England 305-09 (7th ed. 1878).

[60] Malcolm, supra note 3. Dr. Malcolm's work has also appeared in a paper, J. Malcolm, "Disarmed: The Loss of the Right to Bear Arms in Restoration England" (Mary Ingraham Bunting Institute of Radcliffe College 1980), and is now being prepared in treatise form.

[61] J. Malcolm, supra note 3, at 294-96. See also Hardy, Armed Citizens, supra note 3, at 572.

[62] Ordinances and Acts of the Commonwealth and Protectorate 1317-1319 (London 1911).

[63] 8 Calendar of State Papers (Domestic) 150, Charles II, No. 188 (July 1660). Using the militia for such tasks was not unusual; in addition to being a military force, it was used for domestic law enforcement. However, the same order makes it clear that the Lords Lieutenants were to "stack" the militia, relying not upon a general muster of the populace but upon volunteers "who offer assistance," who were to be "formed in troops apart and trained."

hensive militia bill in 1661 is primarily attributable to resentments aroused among members of the royalist Restoration Parliament.[64] Only after strenuous effort was Charles able in 1662 to secure passage of a suitable Militia Act. The 1662 Act broadly authorized actions which Charles had previously undertaken by prerogative. Rather than draw its membership from the entire body of the people, the militia was to be a limited, organized group of Royalists;[65] most critically for the purposes of this article, the Lieutenants and their deputies were to "search for And seize all Arms in the custody or possession of any person or persons whom the said Lieutenants or any two or more of their deputies shall judge dangerous to the peace of the Kingdom. . . ."[66] In support of these provisions, gunsmiths and carriers were ordered by proclamation to file weekly reports on firearms sold and transported.[67] Furthermore, in 1671, the Hunting Act was amended to restrict arms possession by all but the landed gentry. The Hunting Acts had long barred all but the relatively wealthy from ownership of hunting implements, such as traps, nets and hunting dogs. The 1671 Act added all firearms to the list of contraband, and extended the ban to all persons not owning lands with an annual rental value exceeding 100 pounds sterling.[68] Anyone possessing property with greater value was authorized to search residences for weapons on his own initiative.[69] Both Charles and his successor, James II, vigorously implemented these firearms proscriptions.[70] In December 1686, James issued duplicate orders to six Lords Lieutenant of the militia, stating that he was

---

[64] J.R. Western, The English Militia in the Eighteenth Century 12-14 (1965).

[65] Statutes at Large, 14 Car. 2, ch. 3, § 2 (1662). Apart from numerical limitations, members were required to swear that "it is not lawful upon any pretence whatsoever to take arms against the King." Id. at § 19.

[66] Id. at § 14. The search was to be between dawn and sunset, unless the warrant issued by the Lieutenant or his deputies indicated otherwise. Force could be used in the event of resistance.

[67] Malcolm, supra note 3, at 285, 299-300.

[68] Statutes at Large, 22 & 23 Car.2, ch. 25, §§ 2-3 (1670). This was fifty times the property requirement for voting, and marked a 250% increase over the previous hunting requirement. Hardy, Armed Citizens, supra note 3, at 576. Well into the next century, barely 3% of Englishmen could boast lands of this value. C. Hill, Some Intellectual Consequences of the English Revolution 9 (1980).

[69] The 1671 Acts in fact marked a major act of self-assertion by the gentry. Not only the poor were disarmed, but the wealthy tradesmen and others who failed to invest in land. The gentry, not the King, now controlled game and hunting and enforced the law. See P. B. Munsche, Gentlemen and Poachers: The English Game Laws 1671-1831, at 12-18 (1981).

[70] See generally Hardy, Armed Citizens, supra note 3, at 578-79.

informed "that a great many persons not qualified by law under pretense of shooting matches keep muskets or other guns in their houses" and that they should instruct their deputies "to cause strict search to be made for such muskets or guns and to seize and safely keep them till further order."[71] The searches were intended to keep the Anti-Royalists under control and on the defensive.[72] The reconstituted Royalist militia was used for enforcement, and sometimes engaged in mass searches.[73]

As noted above, neither such disarmaments nor James' personally-financed standing army were sufficient to sustain him in power. James lost his throne but retained his head, for the 1688 Glorious Revolution[74] was accomplished without a single fatality. Parliament, meeting on its own initiative as a "convention," formulated a "Declaration of Rights" which William and Mary, its nominees, were required to accept prior to taking the throne.[75] The Declaration was intended to reflect the very core of traditional English rights which must be observed in the future; it embodied only the most indisputable and critical rights.[76] A century later, an American Congress would use much of the Declaration as a basis for an American bill of rights.[77]

---

[71] 2 Calendar of State Papers (Domestic) 314, James II, No. 1212 (Dec. 6, 1686).

[72] See J.R. Western, supra note 64 at 31.

[73] One contemporary Londoner reports, "The militia for the citty [sic] of London went from house to house to search for arms, and 'tis said at some places quantities were seized." 1 N. Lutterell, A Brief Historical Relation of State Affairs from September 1678 to April 1714, at 263 (Oxford 1857).

[74] If "revolution" seems a strange term to apply to the actions of a predominantly conservative, thoroughly "establishment" Englishman, it must be remembered that the term was invented to describe this particular event and (being taken from the mechanical arts) was meant to describe a return to the constitutional point of origin. James, the term implied, had reversed constitutional norms: the "revolutionaries" sought to restore them through further action. See J.R. Western, supra note 64, at 1.

[75] Following their acceptance, they summoned a proper Parliament which, being thus empowered to enact legislation, enacted the Declaration of Rights as a bill of rights. 1 W.& M., ch. 1, § 2 (1688). See generally G. Trevelyan, supra note 58, at 149-151.

[76] The concentration upon fundamentals, and matters of consensus, had a practical basis. Until the Declaration could be drafted, the throne could not be offered to William and Mary. James might at any point return, either through negotiation or through invasion. William began to hint that, absent a prompt offer, he was prepared to return to the Continent. Accordingly, a statement of the most vital rights had to be quickly prepared and had to be limited to such as all factions would agree upon. G. Trevelyan, supra note 58, at 149-151.

[77] Guarantees of rights to petition, prohibitions on excessive bail or fines and protections against cruel and unusual punishments are obvious examples of safeguards embodied in the Bill of Rights. Other guarantees of the Declaration were written into our Constitution itself. Bans on levying of taxes without legislative consent, guarantees that "parliaments ought to be held frequently," and that free-

The Parliamentary debates over the Declaration mark the first acceptance of an indisputably individual right to keep and bear arms. The debates in the House of Commons[78] show that arms confiscations under the Militia Act were a widespread grievance. Sir Richard Temple, for example, criticized the militia bill as containing the power to disarm all England.[79] Mr. Boscawen's crucial speech focused upon the oppressive acts of Parliament as well as those of the King.[80] Sergeant Maynard[81] complained that "an Act of Parliament was made to disarm all Englishmen, whom the lieutenant should suspect, by day or by night, by force or otherwise."[82] Others seconded his complaints of oppressive enactments before Maynard returned to the floor:

> Some particulars well propounded — Some gross grievances for which we are beholden to a Parliament, who care not what was done, so their pensions were paid. — Militia Act — an abominable thing to disarm the nation, to set up a standing army — Corporation Act carried into execution with a high hand.[83]

---

dom of debate in Parliament "ought not to be impeached or questioned in any court or place out of parliament" all reflect concepts written into our 1787 Constitution.

[78] These debates were fortuitously preserved in a pencilled outline of speeches. See 2 P. Yorke, Lord of Hardwicke, Miscellaneous State Papers from 1501 to 1726, at 399 (London 1778). The notes were made by Lord Somers, who headed the committee charged with drafting the Lords' version of the Declaration. They survived a 1752 fire at Lincoln Inn which destroyed most of the remainder of Somers' papers.

[79] Id. at 416.

[80] Bowscawen also added a personal element to Temple's complaints of disarmament: "Acts of the Long Parliament — Corporation Act — That the same with the resolution — The most loyal or deserving, turned out. — Militia — Imprisoning without reason; disarming — Himself disarmed." Id. The reference to the Long Parliament is ambiguous; that would normally identify the Parliament which sat from 1640-1649, during the Civil War, and was dissolved by Cromwell. By adding in the various "rump" Parliaments under the Protectorate, it can be extended to 1660. Might Boscawen have been refering to Charles II's first Parliament, the "Cavalier" or "Pensioner" Parliament? Since it met intermittently from 1661 to 1679, it certainly was a long Parliament, if not the "Long Parliament," and it enacted the Corporation Act (which turned non-royalists out of all city governments) as well as the Militia Act, both of which Boscawen names as grievances.

[81] Maynard would later successfully argue that Parliament ought to proceed both to fill the throne and secure their rights. Id. at 417. Sergeant was then, incidentally, a very high legal rank; in court, a Sergeant-at-law was entitled to speak first, before even the Attorney or Solicitor General, and was entitled to be addressed as "brother" by the bench; while all others uncovered their heads in the Royal presence, the Sergeant retained his coif, lest it be thought that the law must humble itself before a monarch. C. Bowen, The Lion and the Throne 278 (1957).

[82] 2 P. Yorke, supra note 78, at 407.

[83] Id. at 414, 415, 417. Some of the listed complaints were, "fundamentals too may be destroyed, by corrupting Parliaments;" "In the year 1660, there were many hard laws made, grievous to the people . . . Militia Act . . . Corporation Act was arbitrary." Id.

The House of Commons voted out a Declaration, in the form of a list of grievances and parallel rights. The list of grievances included a statement that "The Acts concerning the militia are grievous to the subjects." Although this would clearly focus upon the rights of the individual, or "subject," Commons clouded the issue in the rights recognitions of its draft: "[T]he Subjects which are Protestants, should provide and keep arms for the common defense; and that the arms which have been seized and taken from them be restored."[84] The House of Lords found this combination of individual right and remedy with a collective purpose unacceptable. The grievance section of Commons' draft was altered into a general indictment of James' policies. He had endeavored "to subvert and extirpate" the "laws and liberties of this kingdom" by, inter alia, "causing several good subjects, being protestants, to be disarmed, at the same time when papists were both armed and employed contrary to law."[85] The second passage was even more profoundly altered. The "common defense" proviso was replaced with a recognition that individuals might possess arms "for their defense." The Lords declared: "For the vindicating and asserting their ancient rights and liberties. . . . [t]hat the subjects, which are protestants, may have arms for their defense suitable to their conditions and as allowed by law."[86] Lest there be confusion over the "as allowed by law" proviso, Parliament promptly amended the Hunting Acts to delete firearms from the list of contraband.[87] The House of Commons paralleled this with an amendment to the Militia Act which

[84] Journal of the House of Commons from December 26, 1688 to October 26, 1693, at 21-22 (London 1742) (Lib. of Congress Rare Books Collection).

[85] The proviso regarding armament of Catholics was inserted, the Lords explained in conference, because "[t]his is a further aggravation fit to be added to the clause." Id. at 25.

[86] 1 W. & M., ch. 2 (1689).

[87] 4 W. & M., ch. 2 (1692). See generally Hardy, Armed Citizens, supra note 3 at 581. As Dr. Malcolm notes, "The provision in the Declaration of Rights that Protestant subjects had a right to have arms suitable to their conditions and as allowed by law was interpreted to mean that all Protestants, whatever their condition, were permitted to have arms." Malcolm, supra note 3 at 16. The extension of rights such as these to all Protestants was a legacy of the Protestant dissenters' contribution to the Glorious Revolution. Previously, non-Anglican Protestants had been viewed as a public danger; the Presbyterians and Independents had, after all, been the mainstay of Cromwell's Protectorate and were often lumped in with Catholics as persons who believed monarchs might be overthrown for religious reasons. One seventeenth century sermon indeed charged that Jesuits and Calvinists were "sworn brothers in Iniquity, to plot and conspire the death and ruine of Princes." G. Sensenbaugh, supra note 54, at 75. It would be interesting to have the reactions of Jean Calvin and Ignatius Loyola to that accusation.

repealed all power to seize firearms; unfortunately, the bill was lost in the House of Lords when William dissolved Parliament.[88] Nevertheless, its provisions were soon incorporated into colonial militia statutes.[89]

The Lords' changes, which prevailed in conference, thus emphasized the individual character of the right to arms. The final form of the Declaration does not so much as mention the militia. Standing armies are mentioned, but the objection is only that they were maintained "without consent of Parliment;" a purely royal army is contrary to law, one created by Parliment is quite consistent with the Constitution.

The Declaration in turn formed the core of the following century's conception of individual rights. In his famed *Commentaries*, Blackstone discussed the absolute rights of life, liberty and property, and the auxiliary rights which protect them. After discussing such auxiliary rights as those to petition and to legal process he concluded, in words which would have been read and re-read by Jefferson, Madison and almost any colonist with a claim to constitutional insight:

> The fifth and last auxiliary right of the subject, that I shall at present mention, is that of having arms for their defense, suitable to their condition and degree and as allowed by law. Which is also declared by the same Statute 1 W&M s. 2 c.2 and is indeed a public allowance under due restrictions, of the natural right of resistance and self preservation, when the sanctions of society and the laws are found insufficient to restrain the violence of oppression.[90]

In brief, it is apparent that the common law recognized an individual right to keep and bear arms, and that this was separate and apart from the related concept (whether or not it be considered a "collective" or an "individual right") that a militia was an especially appropriate way of defending a free republic. The "collective/

---

[88] Malcolm, supra note 3, at 309 & n.139.

[89] Maryland's colonial militia code of 1692 paralleled the 1662 Militia Act, but added a proviso that "no pressmaster or any persons whatsoever shall presume at any time to seize, press or carry away from the inhabitant resident in this province any arms or ammunition of any kind whatsoever. . .any law, statute or usage to the contrary notwithstanding." 13 Archives of Maryland: Proceedings and Acts of the General Assembly of Maryland, April 1684 - June 1692, at 557 (W. Browne ed. 1894).

[90] 1 W. Blackstone, Commentaries *144.

individual" distinction was not unknown at this point, but Englishmen approached it by stressing that their system endorsed *both* concepts. As the Recorder of London noted, when called upon to determine the legality of privately-established military reserve units:

> The right of his majesty's Protestant subjects, to have arms for their own defense, and to use them for lawful purposes, is most clear and undeniable. It seems, indeed, to be considered, by the ancient laws of this kingdom, not only as a right, but as a duty . . . And that this right, which every Protestant most unquestionably possesses individually, may, and in many cases must, be exercised collectively, is likewise a point which I conceive to be most clearly established by the authority of judicial decisions and ancient acts of Parliment, as well as by reason and common sense.[91]

III. The Militia and the Rights to Arms in Pre-Revolutionary America

A. Decline of the Militia System

While the militia as an institution declined in Britain during the eighteenth century,[92] it retained vitality in the colonies. Unlike the mother country, the colonies lacked both the need to project military force beyond their borders, and an economy which could support a significant standing force. The colonists quickly adapted the militia system to Indian conflicts, instituting rapid response units and long-range patrols.[93] They also assimilated the views of the English Whigs and Classical Republicans,[94] with their stress upon the militia's role in a free republic.[95] To Harrington, an army was too unstable to support any government; to Neville, it was so stable as to support a tyrannical one; to many colonists, it was capable of corrupting a republican government into a tyranny. Had not James Burgh, their favorite Whig,[96] laid their troubles with the mother

[91] W. Blizard, Desultory Reflections on Police 59-60 (London 1785) (copy in possession of author). See also Malcolm, supra note 3, at 313; Hardy, Armed Citizens, supra note 3, at 587.

[92] See generally supra notes 41-48 and accompanying text.

[93] See generally J. Gavin, The Minute Men 1-46 (1967).

[94] See C. Rossiter, The Political Thought of the American Revolution 55 (1963). See generally B. Bailyn, supra note 9; H. Colbourn, supra note 8.

[95] See generally supra notes 36-39 and accompanying text.

[96] Burgh's most popular work, Political-Disquisitions, infra note 97, was quickly reprinted in the

country at the feet of the English standing army?[97] The Revolution's origins reinforced these views. The most critical preparation for the conflict came in 1774, when revolutionaries took over virtually every colony's militia organization. The British attempts to raid militia arsenals at Concord and Williamsburg ensured the alliance of Massachusetts and Virginia and converted local grievances into a continental war.[98]

The conclusion of the American Revolution left Americans in a position similar to that of post-1689 English Whigs: the former opponents were now in control. Many now found a limited standing army acceptable. Hamilton later observed that exclusive dependence on the militia: "had like to have cost us our independence. . . . The steady operations of war against a regular and disciplined army can only be successfully conducted by a force of the same kind."[99] These views prevailed in the early republic: a small professional army was kept afoot, and it was expanded as needed to meet sundry emergencies.[100] As in post-1689 England, the standing army was denounced,

---

colonies by Benjamin Franklin. Major printed works at that time were sold by pre-publication subscription; the signatories to Burgh's subscription list read like those to the Declaration of Independence: George Washington, Thomas Jefferson, John Adams, John Hancock and John Dickinson. L. Cress, Citizens in Arms: The Army and the Militia in American Society to the War of 1812, at 35 (1982).

[97] "Had we at this time no standing army, we should not think of forcing money out of the pockets of three millions of our subjects. We should not think of punishing with military execution, unconvicted and un-heard, our brave American children, our surest friends and best customers. . . . We should not—but there is no end to observations on the difference between the measures likely to be pursued by a minister backed by a standing army, and those of a Court awed by the fear of an armed people." 2 J. Burgh, Political-Disquisitions: An Enquiry into Public Errors, Defects and Abuses 475-476 (reprint 1971) (London 1774).

[98] In 1774, the British government banned export of arms and ammunition to the colonies, and instructed General Gage to disarm rebellious areas. After several attempts to raid militia arsenals in the Boston area, some successful and some unsuccessful, an intended raid on the Concord arsenal brought about the outbreak of war at Lexington and Concord. At almost the same time, British authorities in Virginia secretly emptied the powder magazine at Williamsburg, but were discovered as they made off. The Virginians responded by mustering militia units, confronting British officials, and seizing 200 muskets from the governor's mansion. The unusually bad timing of the two raids thus brought Massachusetts and Virginia (which otherwise had little in common) into an alliance in revolution, thus uniting the leadership of New England and the South. See generally Hardy, Armed Citizens, supra note 3, at 591-593.

[99] The Federalist No. 25, at 166 (A. Hamilton) (C. Rossiter ed. 1961).

[100] Initially, one regiment was maintained; a second was added in 1791. During the 1798 quasi-war with France, this was expanded to four regiments. W. Millis, Arms and Men 46, 50-53 (1956). A decade later, Jefferson's administration began with 4,000-5,000 men on duty and eventually doubled this authorized strength. R. Weigley, Towards an American Army: Military Thought from Washington to Marshall 27-28 (1962). The 1820 report by Secretary of War Calhoun, a dedicated

derided, and retained.

The parallel Whig view, which stressed the desirability of a true militia, had a longer lease on life. Pre-1789 American political thought had stressed the need to enroll all citizens, or at least all free holders, for militia duty, and had rejected any idea of a "select militia" in which only a portion of the population was enrolled.[101] Provisions authorizing Congress to provide for the arming and organizing of the national militia were seen as allowing it to require that all citizens possess arms of uniform caliber and conform to a standard of drill.[102] In practice, while various administrations prepared detailed plans along these lines, Congress refused to enact them.[103] Washington's first annual address acknowledged: "[a] free people ought not only to be armed, but disciplined; to which end a uniform and well-digested plan is requisite."[104] His second address courteously hinted that the "establishment of a militia" was among the "subjects which I presume you will resume of course, and which

---

Jeffersonian, called for reducing the importance of the militia, which were incapable "of meeting in the open field the regular troops of Europe" and instead creating an expansible army. Id. at 31-33.

[101] A few examples: Richard Henry Lee charged that a select militia would "answer all the purposes of an army" and that therefore the "Constitution ought to secure a genuine and guard against a select militia." Letters from the Federal Farmer to the Republican 21-22, 124 (W. Bennet ed. 1978). In the Pennsylvania federal ratifying convention, John Smilie expressed concern that "Congress may give us a select militia which will in fact, be a standing army." 2 The Documentary History of the Ratificaction of the Constitution 509 (M. Jensen ed. 1976). When Baron von Steuben, the Prussian expatriate who became Washington's Inspector General, proposed a select militia, one Connecticut newspaper was able to complain that the congressional power over the militia "looks too much like Baron Steuben's militia, by which a standing army was meant and intended," 3 Id. at 378. A Pennsylvania newspaper complained that the Federalists sought: "1. The liberty of the press abolished. 2. A standing army. 3. A Prussian militia." J. McMaster & F. Stone, Pennsylvania and the Federal Constitution 1787-1788, at 141 (1888).

[102] At the Constitutional Convention, a delegate explained that "by *organizing*, the Committee meant proportioning the officers and men—by *arming*, specifying the kind, size, and calibre of arms—and by *disciplining*, prescribing the manual exercise, evolutions, ..." 5 J. Elliot, Debates in the Several State Conventions on the Adoption of the Federal Constitution 344 (1966) (2d ed. 1836). In the Pennsylvania convention, James Wilson explained: "If a soldier drops his musket, and his companion, unfurnished with one, takes it up, it is of no service, because his cartridges do not fit it. By means of this system, a uniformity of arms and discipline will prevail throughout the United States." 2 id. at 521.

[103] Major plans included Steuben's of 1784; Knox's of 1786; and Washington's of 1790. The last, submitted to Congress in January 1790, was drafted, redrafted, debated and, after a year and a half of work, enacted in emasculated form as the Militia Act of 1792. J. Palmer, Washington, Lincoln, Wilson: Three War Statesmen 87-89, 104-05, 107-123 (1930). See also L. Cress, supra note 96, at 78-93, 116-129.

[104] 1 Messages and Papers of the Presidents 57 (1897) [hereinafter Messages].

are abundantly urged by their own importance."[105] One year later, Washington again listed militia legislation as "a matter of primary importance whether viewed in reference to the national security to the satisfaction of the community or to the preservation of order."[106] In 1792, Congress voted out the first (and, until 1903, the last) national Militia Act.[107] While this Act required all white males of military age to possess a rifle or musket (or, if enrolled in cavalry or artillery units, pistols and a sword), it did nothing to guarantee uniformity of calibers, fixed no standard of national drill, and failed even to provide a penalty for noncompliance. The subsequent presidential calls for detailed organization of a national citizen army [108] went unheeded. The original ideal of the militia thus ultimately went the way of the standing army controversy: "The ideological assumptions of revolutionary republicanism would no longer play an important role in the debate over the republic's military requirements."[109]

B. The Dominance of the Right to Arms

Conversely, even as the republican militia concept weakened throughout the eighteenth century, the concept of an individual right to arms became more firmly entrenched in American thought. To a great extent, this was a part of a larger intellectual movement. The primary legacy of the 1689 settlement in England had been the supremacy of Parliament. Bodin's maxim that in every government

---

[105] Id. at 75.

[106] Id. at 99.

[107] Act of May 8, 1792, 1 Stat. 271.

[108] 1 Messages, supra note 104, at 132 (Washington, 1793: suggests examination of the Militia Act is "an inquiry which cannot be too solemnly pursued"); id. at 176 (Washington, 1795); id. at 317 (Jefferson, 1801: Congress should "at every session continue to amend the defects which from time to time shew themselves in the laws for regulating the militia"); id. at 333 (Jefferson, 1802: considering the importance of the militia, "you will doubtless think this institution worthy of a review, and give it those improvements of which you find it susceptible"); id. at 360 (Jefferson, 1804: "Should any improvement occur in the militia system, that will be always seasonable"). After all these efforts, Congress still failed to attempt any significant improvements. By 1805, even Jefferson was reduced to asking for a select militia, which had been anathema even to conservatives a few years before: "I can not, then, but earnestly recommend to your early consideration the expediency of so modifying our militia system as, be a separation of the more active part from that which is less so, we may draw from it when necessary an efficient corps fit for real and active service, and to be called to it in regular rotation." Id. at 373.

[109] L. Cress, supra note 96, at 176.

there must be a single, ultimate repository of sovereignty was accepted,[110] and that repository was fixed as Parliament. While Parliament must heed the "Constitution", the Constitution was (with apologies to a later Chief Justice) what Parliament said it was.[111] The colonists, whose initial conflict was with Parliament and not the King,[112] necessarily had to take issue. One counter was to amplify the concept of rights which existed somehow beyond the scope of *any* governmental interference.

The most historical approach involved deriving such right from common law. This involved accepting Coke's position that the common law was immemorial and suprahuman, the product not of any one legislator or legislative act, but of the collective intelligence and experience of Englishmen over a millenium or more.[113] Few dicta have had as great an impact on legal history as the equivocal passage Coke slid into *Dr. Bonham's Case*:

---

[110] B. Bailyn, supra note 9, at 200-05.

[111] As a modern British writer put it:

> It follows from all this that there is nothing rigid or static about the English Constitution. Not being set out or declared in any sacrosanct document nor hedged in by some special procedure of amendment, it can be changed or modified in any or every particular by the ordinary process of legislation. It can be reformed in any part by an ordinary Act of Parliament assented to in the ordinary way.

S. B. Chrimes, English Constitutional History 9 (2d ed. 1953). Madison's attack on the Alien and Sedition Acts still stands as an impeccable sketch of the difference between the English and American understandings:

> In the British Government the danger of encroachment on the rights of the people is understood to be confined to the executive magistrate. The representatives of the people in the Legislature are not only exempt themselves from distrust, but are considered as sufficient guardians of the rights of their constituents against the danger from the Executive. Hence it is a principle, that the Parliament is unlimited in its power; or, in their own language, is omnipotent. Hence too, all the ramparts for protecting the rights of the people — such as the Magna Carta, their Bill of Rights, [etc.] — are not reared against the Parliament, but against the royal prerogative . . .. In the United States, the case is altogether different. The People, not the Government, possess the absolute sovereignty. The Legislature, no less than the Executive, is under limitations of power.

R. Buel, Securing the Revolution: Ideology in American Politics 1789-1815, at 249 (1972).

[112] See generally, H. Colbourn, supra note 8, at 166-67. As Franklin wrote in 1770, "The sovereignty of the Crown I understand the sovereignty of Britain I do not understand. . . . We have the same King, but not the same legislature." Namier, King George III: A Study of Personality, *in* Causes and Consequences of the American Revolution 193, 197 (E. Wright ed. 1966). The notion that the colonists' fight was with Parliament and its ministers and not with George III was hard dying. Even after the fighting at Concord, Washington would write of "the Ministerial Troops (for we do not, nor cannot yet prevail upon ourselves to call them the King's troops)." 3 Writings of George Washington 291 (J. Fitzpatrick ed. 1931).

[113] J.G.A. Pocock, The Ancient Constitution and the Feudal Law 36-55 (1967). See generally C. Bowen, The Lion and the Throne (1957).

> And it appears in our books, that in many cases, the common law will controul Acts of Parliament, and sometimes adjudge them to be utterly void: for when an act of Parliament is against common right an reason, or repugnant, or impossible to be performed, the common law controul it, and such Act to be void. . . .[114]

Coke's language led to his removal as Chief Justice,[115] and his holding was overruled by proclamation,[116] but his words became sacred writ to the Americans.[117]

Derivation of a common law right to arms took little effort. Even the earliest common law jurists had recognized a right to self-defense and to the possession of arms for that purpose.[118] The recognition of an individual right to arms in the 1689 Declaration made the matter all but indisputable. The colonists took to heart Blackstone's derivation of an individual right to arms from both these sources. When, during the Stamp Act crisis, objection was raised to a call for all citizens to procure arms, newspaper articles published throughout the colonies[119] proclaimed:

> It is a natural right which the people have reserved to themselves, confirmed by the Bill of Rights, to keep arms for their own defence; and as Mr. Blackstone observes, it is to be made use of when the sanctions of society and law are found insufficient to restrain the violence of oppression.[120]

In similar vein, members of the Continental Congress exhorted the Committees of Safety that "[i]t is the Right of every English subject to be prepared with Weapons for his Defense."[121]

But the common law was not the only source of rights theory,

---

[114] Dr. Bonham's Case, 77 Eng. Rep. 646, 652 (1610).

[115] C. Bowen, supra note 113, at 381-83.

[116] J. Baker, An Introduction to English Legal History 92-93 (1979).

[117] In the Stamp Act crisis alone, the passage was cited by James Otis, John Adams, and Patrick Henry. C. Bowen, supra note 113, at 315-16.

[118] Blackstone, for instance, noted: "Both the life and limbs of a man are of such high value, in the estimation of the law of England, that it pardons even homicide committed se defendo (in self defense) or in order to preserve them." 1 W. Blackstone, Commentaries *310. See generally Caplan, The Right of the Individual to Bear Arms: A Recent Judicial Trend, 4 Det. C.L. Rev. 789, 804-06 (1982).

[119] The article was one of the "Journal of the Times," which was written anonymously in Boston, published there and in New York and Philadelphia, and thereafter reprinted widely throughout the colonies. B. Bailyn, supra note 9, at 115 n.21.

[120] O. Dickerson, Boston Under Military Rule 79 (1936).

[121] Halbrook, supra note 3, at 280 (citing North Carolina Gazette (Newburn), July 7, 1775 at 2, col. 3).

particularly when, after 1776, the conflict became one with the entire British system and not merely Parliament.[122] Some Americans reconciled their views with tradition by claiming that American views were a purified common law which lacked later British corruptions.[123] Others went behind the common law, claiming it only declared some natural rights.[124] The major American thinkers were even bolder. Washington wrote with pride that "the foundation of our empire was not laid in the gloomy age of ignorance and superstition," and Madison calmly explained that our Constitution declined to incorporate the common law because many of its principles were anti-republican.[125] One source of the new rights theory lay in the various "compact" theories of government, which sought the origins of the state in implicit agreements rather than in divine commands. The civilian jurist Hotman had initially argued for such a view in his 1572 work *Franco Gallia*[126] which became available in English through Molesworth's 1711 translation.[127] To Hotman, the compact theory represented liberation from autocracy founded upon "divine right" or supposed tradition: his research sought to trace government among what became the French people to democratic tribal arrangements, which in turn were suppressed by usurping monarchs.[128]

A more abstract (and less democractic) view was taken by Thomas Hobbes in his 1651 *Leviathan*.[129] To him, government was founded upon a compact of mutual protection. The fundamental rule of nature was "to seek peace and follow it" and, conversely,

---

[122] H. Colbourn, supra note 8, at 190.

[123] Id. at 126, 190.

[124] C. Rossiter, supra note 94, at 352.

[125] Id. at 377; 1 B. Schwartz, infra note 142, at 448.

[126] J.G.A. Pocock, supra note 113, at 20.

[127] F. Hotman, Franco Gallia (R. Molesworth trans., London 1711).

[128] The compact theorists were not burdened with the data generated by modern archaeology, which suggest that the choice of tribal leaders occured among Cro-Magnons, some tens of millenia ago. See Pfeiffer, Cro-Magnon Hunters Were Really Us, Working Out Strategies for Survivial, 17 Smithsonian 74, 82 (1986).

[129] Hobbes' appeal to power and consent as the basis of dominion upset the royalists, while his assertion that popular consent once given could never be modified or revoked (absent failure of the sovereign to perform the sole duty of protection) alienated their opposition. Hobbes was concerned, after the Restoration, that Royalists might have him burned for heresy; as it was, they settled for burning his books at Oxford. C. Hill, supra note 34, at 249. During our own colonial period, he was "denounced as frequently by loyalists as by patriots." B. Bailyn, supra note 9, at 28-29.

"the second, the sum of the right of nature" was "by all means we can, to defend ourselves."[130] This right was so fundamental that it could not be included in the compact: "A Covenant not to defend my selfe from force, by force, is alwayes vod. For (as I have shewd before) no man can transfere, or lay down his Right to save himselfe from Death. . . ."[131] While Hobbes is often seen as laying the foundations for absolute monarchy,[132] he in fact admits one circumstance under which the monarch may justly be replaced by his subjects:

> The Obligation of Subjects to the Sovereign is understood to last as long, and no longer, than the power lasteth, by which he is able to protect them. For the right men have by Nature to protect themselves, when none else can protect them, can by no Covenant be relinquished.[133]

A different rationalist basis for colonial derivations of rights encompassed supernatural origins, whether seen as God or nature. The Anglican church, hamstrung by its acceptance of non-resistance,[134] was unable to make much contribution here, but the slack was more than taken up by the Congregationalist, Baptist and Presbyterian divines who played so major a role in promoting the pa-

---

[130] T. Hobbes, Leviathan ch. 14 at 107 (reprint 1950) (1651).

[131] Id. at 116.

[132] This view is not completely fair: Hobbes in fact admits that his sovereign can be a democratic government: "The legislator in all Common-wealths, is only the Soveraign, be he one Man, as in a Monarchy, or one Assembly of men, as in a Democracy, or Aristocracy." Id., ch. 26 at 226. Hobbes also seems to accept that a government might be one of limited powers, although he clearly regards this as a mistake: "Amongst the Infirmities therefore of a Common-wealth . . . this is one, That a man to obtain a Kingdome is sometimes content with lesse power, than to the Peace, and defence of the Common-wealth is necessarily required. From whence it commeth to passe that when the exercise of the Power layd by, is for the publique safety to be resumed, it hath the resemblance of an unjust act. . . ." Id., ch. 29 at 276.

[133] Id., ch. 21 at 117.

[134] The doctrine of nonresistance (which was derived from the Pauline epistles and early Christian martyrology) maintained that Christians were required to submit to a ruler, no matter how unjust; indeed, the reliance upon the submission of early Christians to martyrdom indicated that submission was required even to a pagan ruler bent upon extirpating Christianity. See generally G. Senssbaugh, That Grand Whig Milton (1952). The seriousness with which this was taken can be seen in the aftermath of the Seven Bishops' Case, in which James II prosecuted seven Anglican bishops for seditious libel. After James was overthrown in the Glorious Revolution, a majority of the seven were forced to resign by the new government because they were "nonjurors," unable in conscience to take an oath recognizing William and Mary as sovereigns. Whatever his actions toward them, their nation or their church, James was still their monarch, to whom submission was due. C. Hill, supra note 34, at 238.

triot cause.[185] Joel Barlow, a chaplain in Washington's army, thus derived a right to arms:

> Only admit the original, unalterable truth, ***that all men are equal in their rights***, and the foundation of every thing is laid; to build the superstructure requires no effort but that of natural deduction. The first necessary deduction will be, that the people will form an equal representative government. . . . Another deduction follows, That the people will be universally armed: they will assume those weapons for security, which the art of war has invented for destruction.[186]

Many colonists also consulted European natural law theorists in hopes of defining the rights of men.[187] These thinkers commonly stressed an individual right or duty to self defense as the very core of individuality. Pufendorf, deriving natural law from man's instincts toward society, concluded that (at least for a person with dependents) a failure to use necessary deadly force to defend himself is a violation of natural law and a sin:

> Nor indeed should it be thought that the law of nature, instituted as it was for the safety of man, favors such a peace as would cause his immediate destruction, and bring about anything but a social life. . . . Now there are some who would carry this command so far that it could not be abrogated even by civil law, maintaining that the man who allows himself to be killed when he could have defended himself, can be condemned on the same score as if he had killed himself. . . . To us it seems necessary to consider first of all, whether it is of any great concern to others that the person who is attacked survive, or whether, as a matter of fact, he apparently lives only to himself. We hold that in the former case the man is ***obligated*** to secure his own protection by every means possible, but, in the latter case we maintain that it is only ***permissible***. . . .[188]

---

[185] See generally Morgan, The American Revolution Considered as an Intellectual Movement, *in* Causes and Consequences of the American Revolution 172, 182-86 (E. Wright ed. 1966).

[186] J. Barlow, Advice to the Privileged Orders in the Several States of Europe, Resulting from the Necessity and Propriety of a General Revolution in the Principle of Government 46 (reprint 1956) (London 1792).

[187] See generally B. Bailyn, supra note 9, at 27. See also C. Rossiter, supra note 94. "In pamphlet after pamphlet, American writers cited . . . Beccaria on the reform of the criminal law, Grotius, Pufendorf, Burlamqui and Vattel on the laws of nature and of nations, and on the principles of civil government. The pervasiveness of such citations at times astonishing." Id. at 359.

[188] Pufendorf, De Jure Naturae et Gentium: Libri Octo (C. & W. Oldfather trans.) *in* The Classics of International Law 265-266 (J. Scott ed. 1934).

Burlamaqui went farther, maintaining the natural law of self-preservation might be deduced from reason as well as social instincts. "Let us suppose man in solitude; he would still have several duties to discharge, such as to love and honour God, to preserve himself, to cultivate his faculties. . . ."[139]

Thus, the intellectual bases for an individual right to bear arms expanded at the same time that the practical bases for the militia system declined. Both principles, however, are immortalized in the second amendment to the Constitution. We might suspect that this is the remnant of a period in which the decline of the republican militia ideal overlapped the origin of the Enlightenment and Jeffersonian/Jacksonian democracy. To test this hypothesis will require a detailed examination of both the militia and the right to arms concepts during the formation of the American republic.

IV. The American Right to Arms

A. The Prototypes: Virginia, Pennsylvania and Massachusetts

In the summer of 1776, the Continental Congress recommended that the former colonies "adopt such governments as shall, in the opinion of the representatives of the people, best conduce to the happiness and safety of their consitituents, and Americans in general."[140] While not every state responded with a bill of rights (or, for that matter, a new constitution), a significant number did so as to enable us to trace the process whereby certain rights became codified in declarations of rights. Since drafters of each declaration were conversant with the work of their predecessors and duplicated or differed as they saw fit, it also becomes possible to compare how different factions phrased particular rights.

The ancestry of the second amendment can be found in the declarations of rights adopted by Virginia, Pennsylvania and Massachusetts. The different approaches taken by each state give insight into

---

[139] J.J. Burlamaqui, The Principles of Natural and Politic Law (Nugent trans. 5th ed. Cambridge 1807). The jurist goes on to note that "To kill a man, for instance, is a bad action in a robber, but is lawful or good . . . in a citizen or soldier, who defends his life or country. . . ." Id. at 121.

[140] 4 Journals of the Continental Congress 342 (W. Ford ed. 1906).

the differences of opinion over which component, militia or right to arms, was most deserving of recognition.

1. Virginia and the Well-Regulated Militia

Virginia's Constitution and Bill of Rights were the first adopted after the Declaration of Independence. While records of the actual deliberations are limited, it is known that Thomas Jefferson drafted a document worthy of the Enlightenment. Jefferson's draft would have extended the franchise to any taxpayer, divided state lands among the landless citizens, ended importation of slaves, and banned the establishment of religion. His proposal did not mention the militia or its role in a republic, but did include a clearly individual right to arms: "No freeman shall ever be debarred the use of arms."[141]

Virginia's legislature chose instead a constitution and bill of rights drafted by committee, and taken predominantly from the proposals of the more conservative George Mason.[142] The prevailing version omitted any mention of individual arms and substituted a recognition that: "A well-regulated militia, composed of the body of the people, trained to arms, is the proper, natural, and safe defence of a free State."[143]

It is unlikely that the choice was dictated in this case by a conflict

---

[141] 1 Papers of Thomas Jefferson 344 (J. Boyd ed. 1950). Jefferson's draft indicates he toyed with adding the words "within his own lands" at the end of this guarantee. See id. at 353. Like many Virginia landowners, Jefferson had probably had troubles with trespass and poaching. Washington, for example, had to post notices, publish handbills, and write letters to his neighbors in vain efforts to stop such poaching. See 37 Writings of George Washington 194 (J. Fitzpatrick ed. 1940). Jefferson's proposals also would have divided State lands among persons owning no lands, or less than fifty acres apiece, would have provided that they would be held in fee simple (a reflection of his opposition to fee tail, which was still permitted in Virginia), and would have barred transfer of State lands "until purchased of the Indian native proprietors". 1 Papers of Thomas Jefferson, supra, at 362.

[142] Traditionally, the Bill of Rights is ascribed to Mason. This attribution is based in large part on Edmund Randolph's recollection that Mason's proposals "swallowed up all the rest." 1 B. Schwartz, The Bill of Rights: A Documentary History 247 (1971). Recent evidence suggests, however, that the relevant portion was added by the committee, albeit taken almost verbatim from Mason's Fairfax Resolves. See H. Miller, George Mason: Gentleman Revolutionary 148 (1975). On the other hand, there also is evidence that the Fairfax Resolves were more of a committee effort than has previously been supposed. See Sweig, A New-Found Washington Letter of 1774 and the Fairfax Resolves, 40 Wm. & Mary Q. (3d. Ser.) 283 (1983). It is clear in any event that the body of the Virginia Constitution was in fact a committee effort, based on submission of a number of plans. See 1 Papers of Thomas Jefferson, supra note 141, at 337.

[143] 7 F. Thorpe, The Federal and State Constitutions 3814 (1909).

of values. Jefferson, who had served on the committee to organize the Virginia militia,[144] was an unlikely opponent of the militia concept. Mason, who was a firearms collector and George Washington's hunting partner,[145] was an improbable supporter of individual disarmament. The difference is more one of emphasis. The Constitution as adopted looks predominantly to maintenance of the status quo. This was predictable since the members of the committee charged with the initial drafting were predominantly large landowners.[146] Mason's original draft contained a substantial property requirement for legislators — only citizens owning 1,000 pounds worth of real estate could run for the lower house, while only those with twice that freehold could run for the upper.[147]

In more general terms, the primary concern of the 1776 constitution is (as it was with Harrington and his followers) the establishment of a stable republic. Indeed, the original draft did not recognize a "right" to freedom of religion, but rather a "toleration of the exercise of religion,"[148] along the lines of the British Toleration Act, which for practical grounds exempted certain faiths from the ban on non-establishment churches.[149] Only the intervention of the novice legislator James Madison[150] enabled an American president to later boast: "It is now no more that toleration is spoken of, as if it was by the indulgence of one class of people, that another enjoyed the exercise of their inherent natural rights."[151] The Virginia Declaration

---

[144] D. Malone, Jefferson the Virginian 195 (1948).

[145] K. Rowland, Life of George Mason 104 (1892); 83 The Diaries of George Washington 71 (D. Jackson ed. 1978) ("[November] 27. [1771.] Set off before sunrise with John Custis for Colo. Masons and went a driving [deer] in his Neck after breakfast—2 deer killed. [November] 28. Went a driving again with Colo. Mason—killed nothing.").

[146] J. Main, The Sovereign States 1775-1783, at 156 (1973).

[147] Id. at 157; 1 Papers of Thomas Jefferson, supra note 141, at 366.

[148] Hunt, James Madison and Religious Liberty, Proceedings of the 17th Annual Meeting of the American Historical Society 165, 166-67 (1901). Madison later recollected that Mason had "inadvertently adopted" the word "toleration." 1 Papers of Thomas Jefferson, supra note 141, at 250. This is consistent with the hypothesis that Mason differed from Jefferson and the Radicals not so much in values as in perspective. To Mason, the object was to establish a stable republic, which would naturally respect individual rights, while to Jefferson the object was to reserve the rights and let the republic form within those reservations.

[149] Toleration Act, 1 W. & M. 18 (1689). The Act begins: "Forasmuch as some ease to scrupulous consciences in the exercise of religion may be an effectual means to unite their Majesties' protestant subjects in interest and affection . . . ."

[150] See generally Hunt, supra note 148.

[151] 31 Writings of George Washington 93 (J. Fitzpatrick ed. 1939).

thus looks backward to the classical republic and concern for the state; Jefferson's unsuccessful draft, in contrast, looked forward to the form of democracy which would take his name. The gap between the Harringtonian republic and Jeffersonian democracy was clearly demonstrated in Jefferson's explanation of his draft:

> I was extending the right of suffrage (or in other words the rights of a citizen) to all who had a permanent intention of living in the country. Take what circumstance you please as evidence of this, either the having resided a certain time, or having a family, or having property, any or all of them. Whoever intends to live in a country must wish that country well, and has a natural right of assisting in the preservation of it.[152]

The contrast between Mason's and Jefferson's proposals highlights a correlation which will be found in later efforts by other states. Those constitutions which maintained the Classical Republican link between land ownership and electoral participation also stressed its ideal of militia institutions. Those constitutions which accepted the Radical foundation of near-universal manhood suffrage largely ignored the militia ideal but stressed individual rights to arms.

2. Pennsylvania and the Individual Right to Arms

Pennsylvania adopted a bill of rights only a few months after Virginia, yet its political situation was nearly opposite that present in Mason's state. While Virginia's establishment became the leadership of its revolutionary movement, the Pennsylvania establishment lagged behind and was overthrown by the Quaker State's revolutionary movement. The pre-1776 legislature was dominated by the wealthier families; unlike Virginia's ruling gentry, their wealth was primarily based on shipping and commerce. The threat to trade posed by the split with Britain understandably made such men wary of independence.[153] The revolutionary movement, in contrast, had its primary strongholds in the more sparsely populated, agrarian West, as well as a secondary base among the apprentices and "mechanics" (in modern terms, the labor movement) of Philadel-

[152] 1 Papers of Thomas Jefferson, supra note 141, at 504.

[153] See generally Doerflinger, Philadelphia Merchants and the Logic of Moderation 1760-1775, 40 Wm. & Mary Q. (3d Ser.) 197 (1983).

phia.[154] As one writer of the last century, himself sympathetic to the aristocracy, phrased it:

> At the beginning of the contest with Great Britain the control of affairs in Pennsylvania was still in the hands of the aristocratic element of the province, which centered in Philadelphia and the richer and more thickly settled counties adjacent thereto, and whose power politically was supported by the requirement of a 50 pound property qualification for the franchise . . . [T]he assembly lent but a lukewarm support to the patriot cause, and many measures earnestly desired by the patriot leaders failed in that body because of the innate caution and conservatism of its members.
>
> There was, however, another element well suited by temper and circumstances to play the part desired by the radical leaders, if only power in proportion to its numbers could be given it. This was the democracy, the party of the country, as the other was the party of the city. Its strength lay chiefly in the back counties, where the independent life of the settler and farmer, and the practical uniformity of material conditions, naturally stimulated the democratic instinct.[155]

The Radical forces launched a successful assault on the opposition. Following the Continental Congress' call for new state constitutions, the Committees of Safety arranged extralegal elections for representatives to a constitutional convention. Each county would elect an equal number of delegates (thus weighting the convention against the more populous eastern counties) and the property requirement was waived for the militia,[156] who comprised much of those counties' revolutionary element.[157] In the meantime, Radical members of

---

[154] See generally J. Selsam, The Pennsylvania Constitution of 1776: A Study in Revolutionary Democracy (1936); Gough, Notes on the Pennsylvania Revolutionaries of 1776, 96 Pa. Mag. 89 (1972).

[155] Harding, Party Struggles Over the First Pennsylvania Constitution, Annual Report of the American Historical Association 371-72 (1895).

[156] Id. at 374.

[157] One historian noted in a recent work:

> Aristocratic Whigs described the militia privates as "in general damn'd riff raff — dirty, mutinous and disaffected." The militia described themselves as "composed of tradesmen and others, who earn their living by their industry . . ." [A] check of one militia company roster against the published tax lists for Philadelphia reveals that of sixty-seven names, almost half (twenty-nine) appeared on no tax list between 1769 and 1781 . . . . For such men, participation in the militia was the first step in the transition from crowd activity to organized politics. Like the New Model Army of the English Civil War, the militia was a "school of political democracy."

E. Foner, Tom Paine and Revolutionary America 63-64 (1976).

the assembly absented themselves; their departure deprived that body of a quorum and paralyzed any possible counterattack. The aristocratic elements were neatly trapped; to run for the constitutional convention would be to endorse its legitimacy without gaining any reasonable chance of winning its control. Many instead sat out the election, leading to a convention as dominated by the Radicals as Virginia's had been by the gentry.

The convention's product has been described as the "most democratic form of government ever tried by an American State."[158] The fifty pound franchise requirement was replaced with one that enfranchised any taxpayer over the age of twenty-one.[159] It was probably Benjamin Rush, one of the losing aristocrats, who complained of the power placed in the hands of the citizenry: "They call it a democracy — a mobocracy in my opinion would be more proper. All our laws breathe the spirit of town meetings and porter shops."[160]

Pennsylvania became the second state to adopt a bill of rights; a comparison with Virginia's product is all the more instructive since the Pennsylvania convention obtained copies of the Virginia Bill of Rights and were able to use it as a model.[161] Indeed, John Adams later noted that their "bill of rights is almost verbatim from that of Virginia."[162] "Almost" is, however, a word that bears emphasis. Individual rights are given greater scope in the Pennsylvania declaration than in that of Virginia.[163]

Pennsylvania clearly departed from the Virginia approach when it deleted the Virginia reference to well regulated militias and added a new recognition: "That the people have a right to bear arms for the defense of themselves and the State. . . ."[164] The "themselves

---

[158] Harding, supra note 155, at 376.

[159] Pa. Const. § 6 (1776), reprinted *in* 5 F. Thorpe, supra note 143, at 3084.

[160] Harding, supra note 155, at 386. Harding himself complains that the supporters of the 1776 document were men of obscure birth, of little education or property, and of the narrowest views, "the party of the democracy — suspicious, bigoted, easily swayed by demogogues . . . ." Id. at 383-84.

[161] 1 B. Schwartz, supra note 142, at 262.

[162] J. Adams, Diary and Autobiography 391 (L. H. Butterfield ed. 1964).

[163] Most noticeably, Pennsylvania added rights to freedom of speech (Virginia recognized, probably through oversight, only that of the press) and assembly. See 1 B. Schwartz, supra note 142, at 262-263.

[164] Pa. Declaration of Rights, § 12 (1776), reprinted *in* 5 F. Thorpe, supra note 143, at 3083. The constitution itself did provide for the militia — but with businesslike statements that all "freeman"

and the State" proviso seems superfluous, but it reinforces the distinction between the Radicals' recognition of an individual right (against, it should be noted, even the government they now dominated) and the Virginia gentry's simple praise of a militia system as necessary to their "republic." The Radicals of the Pennsylvania convention thus repudiated Mason's Harringtonian model (which linked land ownership, political rights, and militia duty) in favor of the Jeffersonian formula of universal suffrage and an individual right to arms.

The future federal second amendment was thus the direct descendant, not of any one model, but of two distinct products of two different political outlooks. The militia component is ultimately derived from the work of the Virginia convention, which made no effort to define a right to arms. The second amendment's right to arms component is a direct descendant of the work of the Pennsylvania Radicals, who sought an unquestionably individual right and considered a militia statement superfluous.

3. North Carolina, Massachusetts and the Unsuccessful Compromise

A third approach deserves mention, not because it was a progenitor of the second amendment, but because it was available as a model in 1791 and was specifically rejected by the first Congress. This approach was taken, only a few months after the Pennsylvania convention, by North Carolina. That state's convention was split between Republican and Democratic elements, and its product reflected the need for compromise.[165] Under the constitution they voted out, all taxpayers could vote for the lower house, while those with fifty acres or more of land could vote for the upper as well. On the other hand, the actual candidates were subject to stricter requirements; the governor must own 1,000 pounds worth of land, members of the upper and lower houses 300 and 100 acres, respec-

shall be "trained and armed" under legislative direction. Pa. Const. § 5 (1776), reprinted in 5 F. Thorpe, supra note 143, at 3084. There is no statement of the militia's necessity or role in a republic, but simply a practical provision for its organization.

[165] J. Main, supra note 146, at 166-69. Main points out that some counties sent delegates with a mandate to "oppose everything that leans to aristocracy" while other delegates noted that their main concern was "how to establish a check on the representatives of the people."

tively.[166] The franchise was thus quite broad, while the privilege of seeking office was considerably narrowed. The convention took a similarly eclectic approach to a bill of rights.

North Carolina took its Declaration of Rights primarily from Virginia. However, it replaced Mason's paean to the militia with a variant of the Pennsylvania approach: "[T]he people have a right to bear arms, for the defense of the state. . . ."[167] The omission of the militia statement on the one hand, and the recognition of an individual right — but only for defense of the State — seems an uneasy balance between the Virginia and the Pennsylvania models. Massachusetts' 1780 Constitution expanded upon this third approach. Its chief author was John Adams, probably the colonies' most devout Harringtonian[168] whose fears that excessive democracy would lead to anarchy[169] gave force to Jefferson's accusations that Adams was a closet Monarchist.[170]

The Massachusetts Constitution and Bill of Rights drew heavily upon those of Virginia. Members of the lower house were required to have freehold estates of 100 pounds, and those of the upper house were required to own 300 pounds.[171] The Bill of Rights largely focused upon the nature of the government, occasionally going so far as to codify its powers rather than restrain them.[172]

Adams chose an unusual mode of coping with the question of arms and militia provisions. He took the language of the Pennsylvania convention, expanded it somewhat by recognizing for the first time a right to "keep" as well as to "bear" arms, but then qualified

---

[166] N.C. Const. §§ 5, 6, 15 (1776, amended 1835), reprinted *in* 5 F. Thorpe, supra note 143, at 2790-2791.

[167] N. C. Declaration of Rights § 17 (1776), reprinted *in* 5 F. Thorpe, supra note 143, at 2788.

[168] See Z. Haraszti, John Adams and The Prophets of Progress 34-35 (1952).

[169] Id. at 35-37.

[170] Id. at 37-40. It is difficult to find a sharper contrast than that between Jefferson's defense of near-universal sufferage—"my observations do not enable me to say I think integrity the characteristic of wealth. In general I believe the decisions of the people, in a body, will be more honest and more disinterested than those of wealthy men . . . ." 1 Papers of Thomas Jefferson, supra note 141, at 504, and Adams' argument that "the men in general, who are wholly destitute of property, are also too little acquanted with public affairs to form a right judgment . . . ." Z. Haraszti, supra note 168, at 36.

[171] Mass. Const. art. V, § 2 and art. III, § 3 (1780, amended 1840)), reprinted *in* 3 F. Thorpe, supra note 143, at 1897-98.

[172] For example, provisions were included which authorized support of "public Protestant teachers of piety, religion and morality"; they also noted that "Each individual of the society . . . is obliged, consequently, to contribute his share to the expense of this protection . . . ." Mass. Const. arts. III, X (1780, amended 1911), reprinted *in* 3 F. Thorpe, supra note 143, at 1890-91.

the entire provision by recognizing the resulting right only with regard to the common defense.[173] Given Adams' outstandingly Harrington viewpoint, the qualifier is hardly a surprise, although how it can be reconciled with his original proposal to recognize a right to "keep" arms is unclear. Possibly, to Adams, the proviso was meant simply as an explanation along the lines of the statements of social duty mentioned above, and not as an operative qualifier. Perhaps Adams simply felt a need to reconcile his creation with his philosophy and thus added a clause tying a radically-conceived right into a Harringtonian set of political values. The most likely explanation lies, however, in Adams' legal background and in his general suspicion of the people and of mobs. To "keep" arms was, after all, a more precise rendition of the 1689 English Declaration than the "to bear" language used in the other state conventions. The 1670 English Hunting Act, prohibiting arms to the poor, had used the phrase "have or keep," and the phrase "keep arms" recurs in post-1692 English case law interpreting the Act as modified after the Declaration of Rights.[174] To this extent, Adams' work was what we would expect from one of the premier attorneys of the colonies. The qualifier "for the common defense" may share similar roots. If Adams was going to recognize, in precise legal terms, a right to own or carry firearms as a citizen pleased, he was going to reserve the power to suppress armed riots. Some seven years later, in his *Defense of the Constitution*, Adams would write:

> To suppose arms in the hands of citizens, to be used at individual discretion, except in private self-defense, or by partial orders of towns, countries or districts of a state, is to demolish every constitution, and lay the laws prostrate, so that liberty can be enjoyed by no man; it is a dissolution of the government. The fundamental law of the militia is, that it be created, directed and commanded by the laws, and ever for the support of the laws.[175]

Adams was thus mindful of the uses of arms (i.e., legitimate self-

---

[173] "The people have a right to keep and to bear arms for the common defence." Mass. Const. pt. I, art. XVII, reprinted *in* 3 F. Thorpe, supra note 143, at 1892.

[174] See J. Smith, Constitutional Right to Bear Arms 16-26 (1959) (unpublished manuscript).

[175] 6 Works of John Adams, Second President of the U.S. 197 (C. Adams ed. 1851). Adams, however, was not a defender of the select militia concept. See Halbrook, The Right to Bear Arms, supra note 3, at 314 (citing Adams in 1823: "The American states have owed their existence to the militia for more than two hundred years. A select militia will soon become a standing army . . . .").

defense and militia duty) and concerned about misuse for mob action or anarchy. With far greater precision than is typical in constitutional processes, he sought both to ensure the breadth of the right he desired and to fix its boundaries.

The popular reaction to his proposal illustrates forcefully that many ordinary citizens did not share his fears of the people, and on the contrary feared the exercise of government power that might be allowed under his "common defense" proviso. A meeting of the citizens of Williamsburg objected to the language, noting that "we deem it an essential privilege to keep Arms in our Houses for Our Own Defense" and that the qualifier might be read to allow government to "Confine all the fire Arms to some publick Magazine."[176] In Northampton, an objection was raised that the right to keep and bear arms "is not expressed with that ample and manly openess and latitude which the importance of the right merits" and should be changed to "The People have a right to keep and bear arms, as well, for their Own as the Common defence . . . ."[177]

In sum, by 1780 there were three major state models for dealing with the question of popular armaments: the Virginia or Harrington/Gentry model, stressing a well-regulated militia; the Pennsylvania or Jeffersonian/Radical model, stressing an individual right to bear arms; and the Massachusetts development of the North Carolina model, stressing a right both to keep and to bear arms, but only for the common defense. It is worth noting that at the state level, only the Pennsylvania model withstood the test of time. After 1780, both the Virginia and the Massachusetts models fell into complete disuse,[178] while the Pennsylvania model thrived in the age of Jeffer-

---

[176] The Popular Sources of Political Authority: Documents on the Massachusetts Convention of 1780, at 624 (O. & M. Handlin eds. 1966).

[177] Clune, Joseph Hawley's Criticism of the Constitution of Massachusetts, 3 Smith C. Stud. Hist. 15 (1917).

[178] Virginia's approach prevailed only in Maryland, whose 1776 constitution recognizes that "a well-regulated militia is the proper and natural defence of a free government." Maryland Declaration of Rights § 25 (1776), reprinted *in* 3 F. Thorpe, supra note 143, at 1688. Maryland's 1776 Constitution also imposed varying property requirements for voting and candidacy, ranging from 50 acres of land to vote for the lower house, to 1000 acres for a state senator or any representative to the Continental Congress. Id. at 1691, 1695, 1696. "The property requirements contained in the Maryland constitution excluded almost 90 per cent of Maryland's male taxpaying population from holding provincial office. Because of these restrictions, only ten percent could qualify for the lower house and seven percent for the upper. The elite's dominance of the constitution accurately reflected the class structure of the society." Hoffman, The "Disaffected" in the Revolutionary South, reprinted *in* The

sonian democracy.[179]

B. Militia and Individual Armament in the American Bill of Rights

In 1787, the Continental Congress summoned a convention to propose amendments to the Articles of Confederation. The decision by the delegates to the Constitutional Convention to instead draft a replacement compact offered Americans a rare and unique opportunity to dictate, consciously and in some detail, the terms by which they would be governed. With the exception of the Article I section 9 limitations on ex post facto laws, bills of attainder and peacetime suspensions of habeus corpus, the convention's proposal did little to recognize individual rights. Conversely, it did expressly grant Congress the power to raise and support armies, with no restriction save a two-year limit on any appropriations for that purpose, and also gave the power to provide for the organizing, arming and disciplining of the militia.[180] The contrast between the breadth of these powers and the traditional views of standing armies and militia organization predictably led to conflicts in the ratifying conventions which were called in each state. It is out of these conflicts that our Bill of Rights arose.

1. Ratification Conventions Demand a Federal Bill of Rights

The omission of a bill of rights was a weak point of the proposed Constitution, and soon became the focus of opposition. The early conflicts critical to the gestation of the Bill of Rights came in Pennsylvania, Massachusetts and New Hampshire. These were soon followed by a series of similar demands from Virginia, New York, and North Carolina. Each of these proposals therefore merits consideration.

American Revolution: Explorations in the History of American Radicalism 280 (A. Young ed. 1976). Today, the Massachusetts "common defense" model is followed in only 4 states of the 39 that have "right to arms" constitutional provisions: Maine, Massachusetts, Arkansas, and Tennessee. Dowlut & Knoop, supra note 3, at 177, 203.

[179] It was adopted, for example, in Kentucky in 1792, in Indiana in 1816, in Connecticut in 1818, and in Missouri in 1820. Hardy, Armed Citizens, supra note 3, at 597 n.188.

[180] U.S. Const. art. I, sec. 8.

a. The Pennsylvania Minority

The Pennsylvania convention was the first to consider major criticism of the absence of a federal bill of rights. The criticism did not prevail, and the state ratified the Constitution without reservation. This action seems inconsistent with the same state's 1776 enumeration of rights and stress upon protections of the individual.[181] The explanation is simple: by 1787, the Philadelphia commercial "empire" had struck back; the ratifying convention was heavily dominated by the eastern counties and their commercial aristocracy which, some three years later, would replace the 1776 Constitution.[182] In the 1790 state convention, the defending minority would include several of the men who in 1787 pressed unsuccessfully for a federal bill of rights — Robert Whitehill, John Smilie and William Findley.[183]

In any event, the leaders of the aristocracy who dominated the 1787 convention had little reason to sympathize with an individual right to arms. Benjamin Rush's complaint that the 1776 Pennsylvania Constitution institutionalized "mobocracy" has already been mentioned. James Wilson, leader of the pro-ratification forces, had recently been on the receiving end of the "Fort Wilson Incident," in which a firefight broke out between his supporters, barricaded in his house, and a body of Radical militiamen marching past in protest over the lack of price controls.[184] His opponents, as noted previously, were largely supporters of the 1776 Radical-Democratic Constitution.[185]

Available records of the Pennsylvania convention[186] indicate that

---

[181] See supra notes 154-163 and accompanying text.

[182] See generally Harding, supra note 155.

[183] See id. at 383; 1 & 2 J. McMaster & F. Stone, supra note 101, at 419, 421, 482.

[184] See generally Alexander, The Fort William Incident of 1779: A Case Study of the Revolutionary Crowd, 31 Wm. & Mary Q. (3d Ser.) 589 (1974). The militia/citizen group was marching in support of price controls, which they argued were necessitated by merchant specualtion. In anticipation of the march, Wilson's home (nicknamed due to the sturdiness of its construction, "Fort Wilson") was occupied by thirty or so of his supporters. During the march, a firefight broke out between the occupants of the house and the militia; one occupant and several militiamen were killed. Although this may seem a comparatively tame affair by our standards, it was seen at the time as quite stunning; contemporaries wrote of "a convulsion among the people" and "[m]any flying the city for fear of [v]engeance." Id. at 589.

[185] See J. McMaster & F. Stone, supra note 101.

[186] The following discussions are based heavily upon J. McMaster and F. Stone, supra note 101.

the lack of a federal bill of rights was an important issue, and perhaps the most important issue from the outset.[187] The dispute came to a head when Whitehill, seconded by Smilie, moved for a federal bill of rights.[188] The motion failed, 46-23, and the Federalist majority refused even to permit it or the vote to be entered in the convention's journal.[189] Whitehill and Smilie, joined by Findley and other delegates, published a pamphlet setting out their amendments and rationale; the pamphlet was in turn reprinted in Pennsylvania newspapers.[190]

The minority's argument was hardly Harringtonian. The limited number of representatives under the new Constitution would, they argued, present the danger that "men of the most elevated rank will be chosen. The other orders in society, such as farmers, traders and mechanics . . . shall be totally unrepresented."[191] This was not a criticism that would have moved John Adams, or likely George Mason, but Whitehill was a small farmer and a Jeffersonian[192] and Findley had declined appointment to the federal Constitutional Convention out of poverty.[193]

While they considered a standing army objectionable,[194] the Pennsylvania minority had scarcely a good word for the militia. Indeed, to them the danger was not that the Congress would fail to adequately discipline the militia and thereby allow the republican tradition to lapse, but that Congress might endanger individual liberties by too forcefully using its powers. Militia discipline to them posed a danger to the individual:

For most ratifying conventions, the standard reference is The Debates in the Several State Conventions on the Adoption of the Federal Constitution (reprint 1966) (J. Elliot 2d ed. 1836). This work reports but little of the Pennsylvania convention, since Elliot relied upon reports published by a reporter apparently bribed by the Federalists to publish only the speeches of the two leaders of their group. J. McMaster & F. Stone, supra note 101, at v, 14-15. The relevant portions of the Pennsylvania proceedings are also reproduced at 1 B. Schwartz, supra note 142, at 627-62.

[187] See, e.g., J. McMaster & F. Stone, supra note 101, at 116, 190, 314, 419, 421, 482.

[188] Id. at 420, 425. The exact nature of Whitehill's motion is unclear. He is stated to have moved the articles "which might either be taken collectively, as a bill of rights, or separately, as amendments to the general form of government proposed." Id. at 421. Presumably, he sought ratification of an amended version of the proposed Constitution, which might well have raised problems in itself.

[189] Id. at vi.

[190] Id. at 454.

[191] Id. at 472.

[192] Id. at 756.

[193] William Findley of Westmoreland, Pa., 5 Pennsylvania Magazine 444 (1881).

[194] J. McMaster & F. Stone, supra note 101, at 480.

> [T]he personal liberty of every man, probably from sixteen to sixty years of age, may be destroyed by the power Congress have in organizing and governing of the militia. As militia they may be subjected to fines of any amount, levied in a military manner; they may be subjected to corporal punishments of the most disgraceful and humiliating nature; and to death itself, by the sentence of a court-martial.[195]

We are here a long way from the worries of the later, more conservative Virginia convention; to them, the predominant danger was that Congress would neglect the militia, or use it to supplant state governments.[196] To the Pennsylvanians, these were secondary concerns; the primary danger was to the individual as such. It is not surprising that, while the Pennsylvania proposals mirror almost every provision of the later federal bill of rights,[197] any recognition of the necessity of a militia, or other analog to the militia component of the second amendment, is pointedly omitted. The militia is mentioned only in the eleventh proposal, which would simply provide that its organization, armament and training would remain a state responsibility, and that no militiamen may be forced to serve outside their state of residence.[198]

The Pennsylvania minority did not similarly neglect the right to arms. Indeed, consistent with their emphasis on individual rights, their seventh proposal sought recognition:

> That the people have a right to bear arms for the defense of themselves and their own State, or of the United States, or for the purpose of killing game; and no law shall be passed for disarming the people or any of them, unless for crimes committed, or real danger of public injury from individuals.[199]

---

[195] Id.

[196] See infra notes 222, 225.

[197] The later fifth and eighth amendments are taken almost verbatim from the Pennsylvania wording; the Pennsylvania proposals also called for recognition of freedom of conscience, speech, press, and the establishment of protection against warrants unsupported by evidence or not particularly describing the property to be seized. J. McMaster & F. Stone, supra note 101, at 461-63.

[198] Id. at 462-63.

[199] Id. at 462. Their proposals also, remarkably, added a guarantee that "the inhabitants of the several States shall have liberty to fowl and hunt in seasonable time on the lands they hold, and on all other lands in the United States not inclosed, and in like manner to fish in all navigible waters . . . ." Id. This provision was adapted from a similar guarantee in the 1776 State constitution, which was defended at the time as barring British-style Hunting Acts which could be used to disarm the populace. See Hardy, Armed Citizens, supra note 3, at 596-97, 603 n.218.

The Pennsylvania proposals did not prevail in that state's convention, but the publicity accorded them ensured that they were considered by members of later conventions.[200] When, two years later, James Madison sat down to draft the federal bill of rights, he considered Pennsylvania's minority proposals along with those of other states.[201]

b. Samuel Adams and the Massachusetts Minority

The Massachusetts convention saw the next proposal for a bill of rights. In that state, however, Federalist leaders faced an extremely close fight. Anxious for every vote, they accepted a limited proposal for a bill of rights, which was successfully introduced by John Hancock.[202] The rights recognized by Hancock's draft were primarily economic (limiting direct taxes and federally-created monopolies) or aimed at protecting states' rights. The only individual rights guaranteed were those to indictment by grand jury and jury trial in civil cases.[203]

Samuel Adams, the famed Radical leader, unsuccessfully proposed the addition of a paragraph containing a multitude of individual rights:

> [T]hat the said Constitution be never construed to authorize Congress to infringe the just liberty of the press, or the rights of conscience; or to prevent the people of the United States, who are peaceable citizens, from keeping their own arms; or to raise standing armies, except when necessary for the defense of the United States, or of some one or more of them; or to prevent the people from petitioning, in a peaceable and orderly manner, the federal legislature for a redress of grievances; or to subject the people to unreasonable searches and seizures of their persons, papers or possessions.[204]

Adams' motion was unsuccessful,[205] but it is noteworthy that this

---

[200] See E. Dumbauld, The Bill of Rights and What It Means Today 11 (1957).

[201] See I. Brant, James Madison: Father of the Constitution 264 (1950). Madison's amendments were drawn almost entirely from forty Virginia propositions. Id. at 265.

[202] 2 B. Schwartz, supra note 142, at 674.

[203] Debates and Proceedings in the Convention of the Commonwealth of Massachusetts Held in the Year 1788, at 79-81 (Boston 1856).

[204] Id. at 86-87.

[205] The Journal of the convention shows Adams' motion as losing on a voice vote. Id. at 87. The

Radical, whose constituency was the urban "mechanics" and small tradesmen,[206] did not consider the militia worthy of mention, while a clearly individual right to arms merited a detailed guarantee. Even his limitation on standing armies was no more than a statement of the obvious — that they should not be maintained where not necessary to defense. Although Sam Adams had a model in his state constitution, written by his aristocratic cousin John, he preferred an unlimited individual right to bear arms to John's citation of arms bearing "for the common defense."[207]

c. New Hampshire: the Bill of Rights Carries a Majority

The Pennsylvania minority's position and that of Sam Adams were ultimately absorbed into the New Hampshire proposals, attached to that state's crucial ratification.[208] We know that the vote in New Hampshire was expected to be close — so close that the Federalists had to obtain a temporary adjournment to muster the votes needed to avoid defeat.[209] Unfortunately, we know almost nothing of that state's deliberations.[210] It is apparent that New Hampshire borrowed "almost verbatim" most of its proposals from those advanced by Hancock in Massachusetts.[211] However, the New Hampshire delegates added three proposals of their own, perhaps taken from Samuel Adams' proposed supplement. The first would have barred standing armies, or their quartering in private homes during peacetime, except with consent of three-fourths of the Con-

---

record of the debates indicates he withdrew his motion. Id. at 266. The former version is not only more authoritative, but more logical; the motion came at the very end of the convention, when Adams had nothing to lose by pushing the matter to a vote. Moreover, the report of the debates bore a caveat: "The printers who took the minutes of the preceding Debates, are conscious that there are some inaccuracies, and many omissions made in them. It could not be otherwise, as they were inexperienced in the business, and had not a very eligible situation to hear in the Convention." Id. at "Note to the First Edition of the Debates" (unpaginated).

[206] Daniel Webster later recollected that Adams' statement that his position on the Constitution was changed by the resolution of a large meeting of Boston's "mechanics," Adams' primary constituency. P. Lewis, The Grand Incendiary 359-60 (1973).

[207] See supra note 173 and accompanying text.

[208] New Hampshire gave the Constitution its ninth ratification and thus made it binding upon the states already signatories. See The Federal Convention and the Formation of the Union of the American States 375 (W. Solberg ed. 1958).

[209] 1 B. Schwartz, supra note 142, at 758.

[210] A fragment of one speech is all that survives of the record of its debates. Id.

[211] Id.

gress. New Hampshire's second addition prohibited federal laws affecting religion or infringing rights of conscience. The third provided that: "Congress shall never disarm any Citizen except such as are or have been in Actual Rebellion."[212] Like the concepts advanced by Sam Adams and by the Pennsylvania minority, the New Hampshire proposals made no mention of a well-regulated militia.

Thus, at the time of the ninth ratification, three major proposals for a bill of rights had surfaced.[213] All sought a clearly individual right to bear arms, and none lauded the necessity of a militia. The Radical-Republican division visible in the state bills of rights is apparent here as well; the two demands whose origins can be traced were advanced by the Radical leadership in each state.

d. Virginia, New York, North Carolina: the Merger of Republicans and Radicals

New Hampshire's ratification did not end the battle, although by giving the Constitution its ninth ratification, it bound the states which had already signed the Constitution. Among the several states which had not ratified were the major commercial states of Virginia and New York. Few states boasted the intellect arrayed in Virginia, and in few was ratification as much in doubt.

The Federalists' task was complicated by Virginia's unusual, perhaps unique, political alignment on the federal constitutional issues. Leaders in the call for a bill of rights, and in opposition to the unamended Constitution, came from varied backgrounds. Conservative George Mason and Democrat Thomas Jefferson joined forces to promote a bill of rights,[214] despite their earlier differences as to what such a bill ought to contain.[215] They were joined by the firebrand Patrick Henry and the more staid Richard Henry Lee, both of whom defy simple classification.[216]

---

[212] Id. at 761.

[213] There was also an unsuccessful committee report, and a minority report, from Maryland: neither, however, proposed either a militia or a right to arms clause. Id. at 729-35.

[214] Jefferson, then an ambassador to France, had suggested that it would be best if the Constitution were ratified by the requisite nine States, and the remainder then held out for a bill of rights. See D. Malone, Jefferson and the Rights of Man 168-169, 171 (1951).

[215] See generally supra notes 141-147, 152 and accompanying text.

[216] A modern historian classifies Henry as "firmly attached to the world of the gentry." Isaac, Preachers and Patriots: Popular Culture and the Revolution in Virginia, reprinted *in* The American

Mason's position is perhaps the most simply stated. To him, the priority was protection of the militia, and the restriction of a standing army. Yet preserving the militia required a delicate balance: a government bent upon destroying it might do so either by too lax a regime, by "neglect[ing] to provide for arming and disciplining the Militia," or by too strict a one, "subjecting them to unnecessary severity of discipline in time of peace, confining them under martial law, and disgusting them so much as to make them cry out, 'give us an army.' "[217] Patrick Henry shared similar fears. The "militia is our ultimate safety,"[218] he wrote, yet it might be undermined if either the national government made no provision for the militia or if its provisions added too much to the citizens' burdens. To Henry, the militia ideal involved a good deal of personal freedom to obtain arms. Excessive requirements (e.g., requirement of a special firearm for federal duty) might hinder rather than aid the goal. "The great object is that every man be armed," he argued, asking on the other hand, "but can the people afford to pay for double sets of arms?"[219] To Lee, the danger was more one-sided. Congress might well create a select militia, "distinct bodies of military men, not having permanent interests and attachments in the community."[220] Having done this, it would naturally neglect the militia proper, so that "the yeomanry of the country [who] possess the lands, the weight of property, possess arms, and are too strong a body of men to be openly offended . . . may in twenty or thirty years be by means imperceptible to them, totally deprived of that boasted weight and

---

Revolution 128, 153 (A. Young ed. 1976). Jefferson, who knew him, would have differed. "Whenever the courts were closed for the winter session, he would make up a party of poor hunters of his neighborhood, would go off with them in the piny woods of Fluvanna, and pass weeks in hunting deer . . . wearing the same shirt the whole time, and covering all the dirt of his dress with a hunting shirt." M. Tyler, Patrick Henry 29-30 (reprint 1980) (1898). Richard Henry Lee's background would mark him as a member of the innermost circles of planter aristocracy. Yet this can hardly explain his objection to the proposed constitution that "the lower and middle classes of people would have no great share [in taxation decisions]", nor his contemplated move to New England: "The hasty, unpersevering, aristocratic genius of the south suits not my disposition, and is inconsistent with my ideas of what must constitute social happiness." See Letters from the Federal Farmer, supra note 101, at 20; E. Morgan, The Challenge of the American Revolution 119 (1976).

[217] D. Robertson, Debates and Other Proceedings of the Convention of Virginia 270-271 (2d ed. Richmond 1805).

[218] Id. at 274.

[219] Id. at 275.

[220] Letters from the Federal Farmer to the Republican, supra note 101, at 124.

strength."[221]

Yet an analysis of only the militia question does an injustice to all three advocates. Even those who would normally be considered conservative or Harringtonian placed new emphasis on individual rights. This may have been a result of their alliance with the Radicals (Jefferson was no longer a young delegate justifying a radical constitution, but a former governor charged with the most delicate diplomatic affairs) or due to the emphasis on individual rights in past conventions, or simply because the political climate of 1788 was different from that of twelve years before. To Mason, loss of the militia system was no longer the ultimate risk, but merely an evil means to a worse end:

> Forty years ago, when the resolution of enslaving America was formed in Great Britian, the British parliament was advised by an artful man, who was governor of Pennsylvania, to disarm the people—that was the best and most effectual way to enslave them—but that they should not do it openly; but to weaken them and let them sink gradually, by totally disusing and neglecting the militia.[222]

Henry shared these feelings. On the one hand, "the militia, sir, is our ultimate safety," on the other, "[t]he great object is that every man be armed . . . every one who is able may have a gun."[223] Richard Henry Lee concluded his republican paean to the militia with a passage no Jeffersonian Democrat could have bettered. "[T]o preserve liberty, it is essential that the whole body of the people always possess arms, and be taught alike, espcially when young, how to use them."[224] Perhaps to Lee "the young and ardent part of the community, possessed of but little or no property" could not be relied upon as the militia[225], but they certainly should have been armed.

Virginia's ratification was secured, albeit by a close vote of 88-80, and only at the price of simultaneous proposals for a bill of rights.[226] The proposals were drafted by a committee that included

---

[221] Id. at 21.
[222] D. Robertson, supra note 217, at 270.
[223] Id. at 274-275.
[224] Letters from the Federal Farmer to the Republican, supra note 101, at 124.
[225] Id. at 22.
[226] See C. Bowen, Miracle at Philadelphia 304 (1986).

Antifederalists Lee and Mason, as well as Federalists James Madison, John Marshall, and John Wythe.[227] Madison had always tended to emphasize individual rights in general and individual armament in particular. At the outset of the Revolution, he had noted his skill with the rifle;[228] in Federalist No. 46 he would praise the "advantage of being armed, which the Americans possess over the people of almost every other nation" and note that European governments "are afraid to trust their people with arms;[229] nearly half a century later, the former President, legislator and "Father of the Constitution" would attack aristocracy on the ground it could never be safe "without a standing army, an enslaved press and a disarmed populace."[230]

The committee took an unusual approach to the militia arms concept. Previous proposals had emphasized either the importance of the militia or recognized an individual right to arms. The Virginia committee chose to do both, and spliced together wide ranging provisions from earlier proposals. From Virginia's Bill of Rights came the militia component; while Mason's presence on the committee made this expected, it is noteworthy because this was the first time a federal ratifying convention had so stressed the need for a militia. The right to arms may have been drawn almost verbatim from the Massachusetts Declaration of Rights, employing its broad reference to rights to keep as well as to bear arms, while deleting its qualifier "for the common defense," or it may have been assembled from the Pennsylvania minority's recognition of a people's right to bear arms, joined to Sam Adams' proposal of a federal right of "keeping their own arms."[231] Whatever the origin, it is apparent that Virginia meant to extend broad protections both to militia needs and individual rights when it called for recognition "that the people have the right to keep and bear arms; that a well regulated militia, composed of the body of the people trained to arms, is the proper, natural and safe defence of a free state . . . ."[232]

---

[227] 2 B. Schwartz, supra note 142, at 765.

[228] Madison wrote that he could hit a small target from 100 yards, but that he was far from the best marksman. James Madison: A Biography in His Own Words 38 (M. Peterson ed. 1974).

[229] The Federalist No. 46, at 310-311 (J. Madison) (Modern Library ed. 1947).

[230] R. Ketcham, James Madison: A Biography 640 (1970).

[231] See supra note 204 and accompanying text.

[232] 1 B. Schwartz, supra note 142, at 842.

The Virginia approach of combining a militia recognition with a statement of individual rights could have been expected to have a broader appeal than either provision taken alone. It is thus hardly surprising that it supplanted the previous models, and was employed almost verbatim in the ratifying conventions in New York and North Carolina.[233]

V. Drafting of the Federal Bill of Rights

When James Madison found himself cast in the unlikely role of father of the national bill of rights,[234] he was not forced to write upon a clean slate. His first step was to obtain a pamphlet which conveniently listed all state proposals, from the Pennsylvania minority onward.[235] The problem became one of editing; out of hundreds of proposals, many redundant and some questionable, a hard core of usable proposals had to be selected. The barriers to be surmounted required discarding all controversial proposals. As he informed Jefferson, "every thing of a controvertible nature that might endanger the concurrence of two-thirds of each House and three quarters of the States was studiously avoided."[236] After excluding the controversial propositions, Madison still had to single out the most desirable proposal, and then (where several different proposals had been made to a single end) select the specific terms of the guarantee. Finally, he had to decide how to assemble and group the rights into a number of amendments. The last task was to a certain extent governed by Madison's plan (which had been retained in committee) to

[233] See id. at 912, 968. Yet of the two, only New York ratified. North Carolina is best described as declining to ratify, since that state's convention simply refused, pending a bill of rights, either to ratify or to repudiate the proposed Constitution. Id. at 966.

[234] Madison had argued against a bill of rights in his contributions to the Federalist Papers. See The Federalist, supra note 229, at 238. At the Virginia convention, he argued that "A bill of rights would be a poor protection for liberty." 1 B. Schwartz, supra note 142, at 764. Even after introducing his bill of rights, he informed Jefferson "My own opinion has always been in favor of a bill of rights. . . . At the same time I have never thought the omission of a material defect, nor been anxious to supply it even by subsequent amendment, for any other reason than that it is anxiously desired by others." 11 Papers of James Madison 297 (R. Rutland & C. Hobson eds. 1977). Yet this and later tendencies to downplay the bill of rights as an improvement on the Constitution may have been an attempt to avoid accusations of inconsistency. No one could complain if Madison, who had expressed his personal beliefs that a bill of rights was unnecessary, was later to advocate one simply because his constitutents demanded it.

[235] 12 Papers of James Madison, supra note 234, at 58.

[236] Id. at 272.

interweave the amendments into the text of the constitution, in the manner of a modern "pocket part."[237]

Madison's decision to include a right to arms in his federal bill of rights is hardly surprising. Such a right had been demanded in virtually every call for a bill of rights; indeed, it had received twice the number of demands accorded freedom of speech.[238] Language praising the militia had received much less support, essentially having been appended to the right to arms clause in Virginia and the two following conventions.[239] But an adaptation of the Virginia/New York/North Carolina wording combining the two held unusual promise. One of Madison's major objectives was to "bring in" North Carolina.[240] He hoped to convince it to ratify the Constitution by offering an acceptable bill of rights. North Carolina could hardly object to a nearly verbatim acceptance of its demand.

A combination of a militia statement with individual right recognition fitted Madison's objectives perfectly. The militia statement, standing alone, would likely be unacceptable to groups typified by the Pennsylvania minority, Sam Adams and his supporters, the New Hampshire majority, and possibly Jefferson himself, all of whom had advocated an individual right to arms clause and none of whose efforts had so much as mentioned the militia. An individual right to arms clause standing alone might well have irritated militia supporters such as George Mason and possibly Richard Henry Lee, both powerful Virginians with whom Madison still had to deal and who would vote on his proposal, Mason in the Virginia legislature and Lee in the federal Senate.[241]

It is doubtful that a militia statement had too much appeal for Madison himself, although he certainly backed the militia concept and its necessity to the republic.[242] Madison was somewhat skepti-

---

[237] See 1 Annals of Congress 450-53 (J. Gales ed. 1789).

[238] See 1 B Schwartz, supra note 142, at 1167.

[239] See supra notes 231-32.

[240] 12 Papers of James Madison, supra note 234, at 193 (outline prepared by Madison of a speech on the Bill of Rights).

[241] Madison was also walking a fine line between the Federalist and Antifederalist camps. He strove to propose amendments which would appease the Antifederalists, thus heading off some of their likely proposals which might impair Federalist aims. The tactic was suggested to him by Henry Lee, Richard Henry Lee's brother.

[242] "When Madison became President he did everything in his power to carry a sound militia policy through Congress. In every message he urged establishment of a well regulated militia; as it

cal of bills of rights in general — "parchment barriers," he called them, violated at will by majorities "in every state."[243] How much more skeptical must he have been of an unenforceable declaration that a militia when "well" regulated is "necessary" to a free state? Interestingly, while employing imperative phrasing (i.e., "Congress shall make no law") in the remainder of the Bill of Rights, Madison did not try his handiwork on the militia statement. Instead, he let stand George Mason's original, declaratory form.[244]

Further, when Madison outlined the improvements at which the Bill of Rights were aimed, he cited freedom of press and conscience, the right to arms, and other liberties; he gave not a word to the militia.[245] Whatever its value in Madison's eyes, Mason's proclamation that the militia "is the proper, natural and safe defense of a free state" would stay in, albeit with modification and abbreviation.[246]

Madison's choice for the right to keep and bear arms component was less complex. Madison knew from experience that the Virginia/New York/North Carolina model had proven acceptable to all factions in Virginia; indeed, the committee that drafted it had included himself and Richard Henry Lee, one of the Constitution's most prominent opponents. It also had been endorsed by New York and always-vital North Carolina. Moreover, the concise wording of the statement "the people have a right to keep and bear arms," required little editing. A Madisonian touch adding a command that it "shall not be infringed," was all that was needed.

The breadth of this language would likely please the Pennsylvania, Massachusetts, and New Hampshire delegates who had sought

---

had been accurately defined by Washington, Hamilton and Jefferson." J. Palmer, supra note 103, at 129.

[243] 11 Papers of James Madison, supra note 234, at 297.

[244] Indeed, deciding upon the structure of the federal militia had been one of the most divisive questions of the young republic. It would have been hard for Madison to have made the militia statement specific and enforcable and at the same time avoid controversy. See generally supra notes 93-101.

[245] 12 Papers of James Madison, supra note 234, at 193-94. The outline was used for Madison's June 8 speech in the House; in outlining the reasons why the English Declaration of Rights cannot be relied upon as an adequate statement of individual rights, it notes "arms to Protts," an apparent reference to the Declaration's statement that "the subjects which are protestant" may have arms.

[246] The difficulties in wording the militia statement as a command also highlight its unique status: it is the only portion of the bill of rights which essentially calls for government action, rather than prohibiting it.

an individual right to arms. With any fortune at all, these delegates would view Madison's language as incorporating their ideas.[247] The wording of the militia clause was, after all, a combination of the broadest terms employed in the state bills of rights. From Pennsylvania had come the recognition of a popular right to bear arms;[248] from Massachusetts had come the right to keep them; yet the controversial Massachusetts limitation to keeping and bearing "for the common defense"[249] was conspicuously omitted.[250] Merging the militia declaration with an individual arms clause would thus have been expected to please George Mason and Samuel Adams alike, nicely reconciling Harringtonians and Jeffersonians, Conservatives and Radicals.

The related issues were dealt with more quickly. Subjection of the militia to martial law was restricted in what became the fifth amendment by guaranteeing jury trial to militiamen not in actual service during time of war or public danger.[251] Conscientious objection would be taken care of in an addendum to the militia statement, although that addendum was removed by the Senate.[252] Thus

---

[247] This in fact happened. For example, a Massachusetts newpaper described Madison's draft as incorporating Adams' proposals, including that for a right to arms. The Massachusetts articles were reprinted in the Philadelphia Independent Gazeteer, Aug. 20, 1789, at 2, col. 2. See generally Hardy, Origins and Development of the Second Amendment, supra note 3, at 250; Halbrook, Right to Bear Arms, supra note 3, at 309-10. A Pennsylvania newspaper explained that in Madison's draft "the people are confirmed by the next article in the right to keep and bear their private arms." The Federal Gazette & Philadelphia Evening Post, June 18, 1789, at 2, col. 1. The article was written by Tenche Coxe, a friend of Madison. Coxe mailed a copy to Madison on the day of publication; Madison took time from the debates to reply with appreciation and note that it had already appeared "in the Gazettes here." Hardy, Armed Citizens, supra note 3, at 610.

[248] See supra note 164.

[249] See supra note 173.

[250] The absence was not inadvertant; the Senate rejected, by voice vote, a proposal to add "for the common defense" to the right to arms clause. Journal of the First Session of the Senate of the United States of America 77 (Washington 1820) ("On motion to amend article the fifth, by inserting these words, 'for the common defense,' next to the words 'bear arms': It passed in the negative.").

[251] Madison's original proposals would have included the following: "The trial of all crimes (except in cases of impeachments, and cases arising in the land or naval forces, or the militia when on actual service, in time of war or public danger) shall be by an impartial jury of freeholders of the vicinage, with the requisite unanimity . . . and in all crimes punishable with loss of life or member, presentment or indictmentby a grand jury shall be an essential preliminary. . . ." 1 Journal of Congress 452 (J. Gales ed. 1789). This proposal was ultimately divided into the fifth and sixth amendments, the first of which applies his armed forces and active militia exception to the requirement of indictment by grand jury.

[252] Journal of the First Session of the Senate of the United States of America 71 (Washington 1820).

four arms and military related concerns raised by the ratifying conventions could be resolved entirely.

Significantly, the one military concern not addressed by Madison was the call for limitations on a standing army. As discussed above, Americans by 1789 had crossed the line the English Whigs had passed a century before: a standing army might be a nuisance, but now it was an American nuisance. Statesmen would still condemn it, but also continue to authorize it. Moreover, unlike the right to arms and need for a militia, the details of limiting the army were eminently "controvertible." Federalists in the conventions had strongly opposed any limitations[253] and no consensus had developed among the supporters of such limitations.[254] Madison wisely avoided inserting such limitations in his draft; when others proposed them in the Senate their motions were uniformly defeated.[255] The one objective the future second amendment would *not* seek was a barrier to a standing army.

Having structured his proposals, Madison faced one last choice. While the Constitution provided for the amendment process, it said nothing regarding the form of amendments. Madison planned to offer nine amendments, each containing several paragraphs. Each amendment would be designated for insertion at a different, specific point in the text of the Constitution. The first amendment would add a prefix to the Constitution, recognizing that all power is derived from the people. The second and third (which were ultimately

---

[253] See, e.g., 1 B. Schwartz, supra note 142, at 455-56; J. McMaster & F. Stone, supra note 101, at 409 (James Wilson, in the Pennsylvania convention: "It may be frequently necessary to keep up standing armies in time of peace. The present Congress have . . . [gone] farther and raise[d] an army without communicating to the public the purpose . . . . When the commotions existed in Massachusetts, they gave orders for enlisting an additional body of two thousand men . . . . [O]ught Congress to be deprived of power to prepare for the defense and safety of our country?").

[254] Virginia's Bill of Rights, for instance, merely provided that standing armies in time of peace "should be avoided." Maryland's provided that standing armies (presumably in war as in peace) ought not to be kept up "without the consent of the legislature." Massachusetts provided that standing armies in time of peace ought not to be kept upwithout the consent of the legislature. See 3 F. Thorpe, supra note 143, at 3814, 1688, 1892. The Pennsylvania minority desired to ban all standing armies in peacetime, while Sam Adams desired to bar them only when not "necessary." See J. McMaster & F. Stone, supra note 101, at 462.

[255] A proposal to add to what became the second amendment a recognition that such armies are "dangerous to liberty," should be avoided as far as possible, and would be authorized in peace only upon a two-thirds vote of each house of Congress was lost six to nine. Four days later, an amendment stating more concisely that a two-thirds majority was necessary was lost on a voice vote. Journal of First Session of the Senate of the United States 71, 75 (Washington 1820).

rejected by the states) would expand membership of the House and fix their compensation, and would be added to Article I in sections 2 and 6. The third amendment would have grouped together ten paragraphs and inserted them in Article I, section 9, immediately following the Constitution's existing guarantees of individual rights (viz., restrictions on suspension of habeas corpus, bills of attainder and ex post facto laws).[256] Interestingly, Madison intended the future second amendment, also containing individual rights, as a general limitation of legislative power, rather than as a modification to Congress' militia powers under Article I, section 8. While insertion of militia language might have pleased George Mason, there is little doubt that the individual right component predominated in Madison's mind.

Madison's handiwork underwent substantial editings in both House and Senate. The effect was to pare the guarantees to a minimum. Madison's expansive guarantee of freedom of expression, "the people shall not be deprived or abridged of their right to speak, to write, or to publish their sentiments; and the freedom of the press, as one of the great bulwarks of liberty, shall be inviolable,"[257] became simply "Congress shall make no law . . . abridging the freedom of speech, or of the press."[258] Madison's militia and arms provisions fared better. His proposal that "the right of the people to keep and bear arms shall not be infringed; a well armed and well regulated militia being the best security of a free country. . ."[259] became "[a] well regulated militia, composed of the body of the people, being the best security of a free state, the right of the people to keep and bear arms, shall not be infringed," as ultimately passed by the House.[260] Although the first casualties of the House's editorial

[256] 1 Journal of Congress 451-53 (J. Gales ed. 1789). The remaining amendments were dealt with as follows: a provision forbidding state interference with rights of conscience or press, or to jury trial, would be inserted in article I, § 10, following the existing restrictions on state powers; a right to civil jury trial and limitation on federal appeal would be inserted in article III, § 2, following the existing definition of federal judicial power; a detailed guarantee of criminal jury trial and grand jury indictment would be substituted for the existing jury guarantees in that same section; and a new article VII would be added, expressly codifying the seperation of powers.

[257] Id. at 451.

[258] U.S. Const. amend. I.

[259] Journal of Congress, supra note 256, at 451.

[260] Journal of the First Session of the Senate of the United States 63, 64 (Washington 1820) (citing bill as passed by the House).

process were Madison's preambles and explanations,[261] the militia statement and the right to arms guarantee were both retained. The first House apparently did not feel that either portion of the ultimate second amendment was redundant. The Senate did not either, for it emphasized the differing natures of each provision. On the one hand, it refused to add "for the common defense" to the right to arms guarantee,[262] which would have suggested that the guarantee's purpose was linked solely to the militia; on the other, it replaced the House's statement that the militia was "the best security" of a free state with a stronger statement that it was "necessary" to that security.[263]

VI. Conclusion

The second amendment to the Constitution had two objectives. The first purpose was to recognize in general terms the importance of a militia to a free state. This recognition derives from the very core of Classical Republican thought; its "constituency" among the Framers was found primarily among conservatives, particularly Virginia's landed gentry. Indeed, prior to Virginia's proposal, no federal ratifying convention had called for such recognition. The second purpose was to guarantee an individual right to own and carry arms. This right stemmed both from the English Declaration of Rights and from Enlightenment sources. Its primary supporters came from the Radical-Democratic movement, whether based among the small farmers of western Pennsylvania or the urban mechanics of Massachusetts. Only by incorporating both provisions

---

[261] Lost, for example, were Madison's proposed preamble to the Constitution, stating that "Government is instituted and ought to be exercised for the good of the people; which consists in the enjoyment of life and liberty . . ."; his explanation that freedom of the press is "one of the great bulwarks of liberty"; and the explanation that the express guarantees ought not be read to rule out other rights retained by the people, since they were inserted "either as actual limitations of such powers, or as inserted merely for greater caution." 1 Annals of Congress 451 (J. Gales ed. 1789). The House was apparently more interested in stating concisely the limitations upon federal power than in explaining why the limitations were created.

[262] Journal of the First Session of the Senate of the United States 77 (Washington 1820) ("On motion to amend article the fifth, by inserting these words: 'for the common defense' next to the words 'to bear arms'; it passed in the negative.").

[263] Id. at 77. In the House, Elbridge Gerry had unsuccessfully argued that the "best security" language was inadequate since it admitted that other measures, e.g., a standing army, would be acceptable as secondary securities. 1 Annals of Congress 751 (J. Gales ed. 1789).

could the first Congress reconcile the priorities of Sam Adams with those of George Mason, and lessen the "disquietude" both of the Pennsylvania and Massachusetts minorities and those of the Virginia and New York majorities. The dual purpose of the second amendment was recognized by all early constitutional commentators;[264] the assumption that the second amendment had but a single objective is in fact an innovation born of historical ignorance.

The distinction between the second amendment's purposes enables us to avoid the pitfalls of the collective rights view, which would hold that the entire amendment was meant solely to protect a "collective right" to have a militia.[265] The militia component of the second amendment was not meant as a "right", collective or individual, except in the sense that structural provisions (e.g., requirements that money bills originate in the House, or military appropriations not exceed two years) are considered collective "rights." Indeed, the militia component was meant to invoke the exertion of governmental power over the citizen, to inspire it to require citizens to assume the burdens of militia duty. In this respect it differs radically from any other provision of the Bill of Rights. To read what was a recognition of an individual right, the right to arms, as subsumed within the militia recognition is thus not only permitting the tail to wag the dog, but to annihilate what was intended as a right.[266] As the one

---

[264] For example, St. George Tucker, a Revolutionary War veteran who went on to an extraordinary legal and scholarly career, began his discussion of the second amendment with the note that "The right of self defense is the first law of nature," went on to discuss the dangers of standing armies, and closed with a note that the British government had disarmed its citizens under the Hunting Acts. See Blackstone's Commentaries, with Notes of Reference to the Constitution and Laws 300 (St. George Tucker ed. 1803). William Rawle, a noted legal scholar who sat in a State convention which ratified the Bill of Rights, drew a still clearer distinction between the two clauses:

> In the Second Article, it is declared that a well regulated militia is necessary to the security of a free state: a proposition from which few will dissent. Although in actual war, the services of regular troops are confessedly more valuable, yet . . . the militia form the palladium of the country . . . . The corollary from the first position is, that the right of the people to keep and bear arms shall not be infringed. The prohibition is general. No clause in the Constitution could by any rule of construction be conceived to give Congress a right to disarm the people.

W. Rawle, A View of the Constitution 125 (2d ed. 1829). Similar understandings were later voiced by Storey and Cooley. See 3 J. Story, Commmentaries on the Constitution of the United States 746-47 (1833); T. Cooley, General Principles of Constitutional Law 298-99 (3d ed. 1898). See generally Hardy, Armed Citizens, supra note 3, at 611-15.

[265] See supra note 2.

[266] Acceptance of the collective rights view, moreover, edges us into morass after morass. First, who may raise the issue? The only political "collective rights" with which the author is familiar are those

provision of the Bill of Rights which encourages rather than restricts governmental action, the militia component's terms were necessarily vague and its phrasing a reminder rather than a command.[267]

The right to arms portion of the second amendment, in contrast, was meant to be a prohibition, as fully binding as those in the remainder of the Bill of Rights. Madison intended that the second amendment be read as incorporating the individual rights proposals put forward by the Pennsylvania minority and by Sam Adams and the New Hampshire convention. Judging from contemporary discussion in Massachusetts and Pennsylvania, he succeeded.[268] If either clause can be accorded primacy, it is the right to arms clause; only in Virginia, at the eleventh hour of the ratification process, was a militia clause appended to a federal bill of rights proposal.

Reading the entirety of the second amendment as militia-related, based upon some contemporary references to the need for constitu-

---

of various Indian tribes, which as sovereigns negotiated treaties with the national government. It has been held that individual members of the tribes have standing to raise these tribal rights as a defense to a criminal action. See, e.g., United States v. Dion, 106 U.S. 2216, 2220 n.6 (1986); United States v. Winans, 198 U.S. 371, 381 (1905). Second, what does the second amendment bar? Does it repeal by implication the federal power to call forth the militia? Might an individual or a state object to any nationalization of military reserve units? Does it restrict the federal power to maintain an army, or require, as a prerequisite to such maintenance, a finding that militia would not better serve the need? If it does none of these things, then why did so many Americans, and the first Congress, spend so much time advocating it?

[267] The militia recognition, examined carefully, thus stands out from the remainder of the Bill of Rights; it is the only such "recognition," the only provision lacking Madison's strongly prohibitory language, the only provision calling for federal action, the only provision phrased in such ambiguous tones. The author frankly suspects that Madison inserted it primarily to appease George Mason and perhaps Richard Henry Lee. Mason's belief in the efficacy of such recognition has been discussed above, as has his tendency to phrase provisions in terms of what "ought" to be done by a free government, rather than what "shall" not be done. Madison was quite familiar with Mason's outlook, having sat with him on the committee which drafted Virginia's proposals for the federal Bill of Rights. Mason was then a man with considerable power among the dominant gentry in Virginia; Madison was more than a bit suspect among that group for his federalist beliefs — in fact, he had been denied a seat in the first Senate by vote of the legislature. Patrick Henry, with characteristic excess, informed the legislature that placing Madison in the Senate would "terminate in producing rivulets of blood through out the land." R. Ketchum, James Madison: An Autobiography 275 (1970). Fortunately, his election to the House produced not even a minor insurrection. To entirely omit a clause so close to Mason's heart as this one would hardly have been very wise. Conversely, if the objective was to please Mason, and the issue not one important to Madison himself, there would be no reason to spend time working out details or firming up language with commands. Mason could hardly complain about a slight paraphrase of his own work, and its very vagueness would avoid conflict which might pull down the guarantees of individual rights for which Madison was so deeply concerned.

[268] See supra note 247.

tional recognition of the militia concept, confuses the purpose of one provision with the text of another. The second amendment, in short, cannot be explained simply as a last avowal of the classical ideal, as "the last act of the Renaissance."[269] Rather, it is a bridge between the decline of that ideal and the rise of the liberal democracy. Part of the second amendment looks backward to the worlds of Polybius and Machiavelli; but part looks forward, to the worlds of Jefferson and Jackson. Only a recognition of the dual nature of the second amendment will enable us to give meaning to the aspirations of Thomas Jefferson and Samuel Adams as well as those of George Mason.[270]

---

[269] During a seminar sponsored by the American Academy of Political and Social Sciences in 1986, Professor Lawrence Cress maintained that the second amendment was purely militia-related and was "the last act of the Renaissance." The author replied that this was true only of its militia component, sponsored by the convservative framers, and not at all of its right to arms component, which was endorsed by radicals. The second amendment was not the last act of the Renaissance, but a bridge between the Renaissance concept of a republic and the Jeffersonian/Jacksonian concept of democracy. Out of that exchange grew the present article.

[270] We may be forgiven the suspicion that many advocates of the "collective rights" approach in fact desire the militia statement to subsume the right to arms recognition only because they recognize the militia statement is unenforceable and, ultimately, all but meaningless. It is doubtful that most collective right proponents would react favorably to case law finding an enforceable duty to require all citizens to purchase and stockpile M-14's, M-16's or any other standard military firearm, to force each to participate in basic training, and to organize every adult into a reserve military unit. The supposed endorsement of the militia component thus becomes simply an expedient way of negating every provision of the second amendment, and nullifying both the objectives of the conservatives and those of the radicals.

The Contract Clause and the Evolution of American Federalism, 1789-1815

Steven R. Boyd

ARTICLE I, Section 10, of the United States Constitution declares that no state "shall enter into any Treaty, Alliance, or Confederation; grant Letters of Marque and Reprisal; coin Money; emit Bills of Credit; make any Thing but gold and silver Coin a Tender in Payment of Debts; pass any Bill of Attainder, ex post facto Law, or Law impairing the Obligation of Contracts, or grant any Title of Nobility."

One portion of that section, the prohibition on states passing laws that impair the obligation of contracts, has proven particularly important in American constitutional history and in the development of American federalism.[1] Few men at the time of the adoption of the Constitution foresaw this crucial role for the contract clause. It attracted little comment during the ratification debate, while those who did consider it usually linked it with the companion prohibition on bills of credit or the ban on "any Thing but gold and silver" being made "a Tender in Payment of Debts."[2] They made this connection because during the Confederation debtors in some states used depreciated paper money to pay their obligations. This action, sanctioned by various states that declared their

Mr. Boyd is an associate professor of history at the University of Texas at San Antonio. He wishes to thank Robert Becker, James Broussard, John P. Kaminski, and Sandra Van Burkleo for assistance in preparing this article.

[1] The standard work on the contract clause is Benjamin Fletcher Wright, *The Contract Clause of the Constitution* (Cambridge, Mass., 1938). Forrest McDonald's *Novus Ordo Seclorum: The Intellectual Origins of the Constitution* (Lawrence, Kan., 1985), esp. 270-275, focuses on the Constitutional Convention and the question of the authorship of the clause. On the development of the clause during the early national period see, in addition to Wright, Peter Magrath, *Yazoo: Law and Politics in the New Republic: The Case of Fletcher v. Peck* (Providence, R.I., 1966). On federalism see Martin Diamond, "What the Framers Meant by Federalism," in Robert A. Goldwin, ed., *A Nation of States: Essays on the American Federal System* (Chicago, 1963).

[2] See, for example, "A Citizen of Philadelphia" [Pelatiah Webster], "Remarks on the Address of Sixteen Members," in Merrill Jensen, John P. Kaminski, and Gaspare J. Saladino, eds., *The Documentary History of the Ratification of the Constitution* (Madison, Wis., 1976-), XIII, 302, hereafter cited as *History of Ratification.*

paper issues to be legal tender, was part of a broad pattern of state interference in private contracts.[3] The proponents of constitutional change argued that such policies were unjust, iniquitous, and unacceptable.

In fact, opposition to debtor-oriented state policies was a major factor in the call for the Federal Convention. In the fall of 1787 James Madison advised Thomas Jefferson that the "mutability of the laws of the States," especially laws involving paper emissions and affecting contracts, "contributed more to that uneasiness which produced the Convention, and prepared the public mind for a general reform" than any other single source.[4] James Wilson later declared on the floor of the Pennsylvania state convention, "If only the following lines [including the contract clause] were inserted in this Constitution, I think it would be worth our adoption."[5]

Historians generally have agreed with Madison that the states' economic policies played an important role in the decision to call the convention. Charles A. Beard, for example, declared that "of the forces which created the Constitution, those property interests seeking protection against omnipotent legislatures were the most active."[6] Beard concluded, citing Madison as well as Alexander Hamilton and John Marshall, that the contract clause was "designed to bring under the ban substantially all legislation which affected personalty adversely."[7] Merrill Jensen and Forrest McDonald shared Beard's view. Both stressed the importance the framers attached to the prevention of such state legislation and the role of the contract clause in accomplishing that end.[8] Indeed, with the exception of Benjamin Fletcher Wright, who demonstrated that Chief Justice Marshall's expansion of the clause to include public contracts ran counter to the expectations of some of the framers, most historians have assumed that the federal courts' interpretation of the contract clause realized the framers' intentions.[9] The brief discussion of the clause during the ratification debate, because it did not explicitly contradict this idea, seems to reinforce the prevailing interpretation.

[3] Allan Nevins, *The American States during and after the Revolution, 1775-1789* (New York, 1924).

[4] Madison to Jefferson, Oct. 24, Nov. 1, 1787, in *History of Ratification*, XIII, 447.

[5] *Ibid.*, II, 500. The lines, which included the contract clause, were "No state shall hereafter *emit bills of credit;* make any thing but gold and silver coin, a *tender* in payment of debts; pass any bills of attainder; ex post facto law; or *law impairing the obligation of contracts*" (*ibid.*).

[6] Beard, *An Economic Interpretation of the Constitution of the United States* (New York, 1913), 178.

[7] *Ibid.*, 182.

[8] Jensen, *The Making of the American Constitution* (New York, 1964), 97; McDonald, *E Pluribus Unum: The Formation of the American Republic, 1776-1790* (Boston, 1965), 186-187.

[9] Wright, *Contract Clause*, chap. 1.

If, however, one examines the early history of the contract clause from the Constitutional Convention through the ratification debates and into the initial legislative, executive, and judicial interpretations, a far more complex picture emerges. Federalists and Antifederalists held a wide range of opinions about the meaning of the clause. Furthermore, during the first quarter century under the Constitution no one idea of the meaning of the clause held sway. Instead, state legislatures pursued a variety of contradictory policies. These policies in turn illustrate that there was no single, monolithic intent of the framers. The men who wrote the Constitution, like the men who adopted and implemented it, held a vast range of ideas (including, some of them, no opinion at all) of what the various parts of the Constitution meant.

The initial attempts to bring meaning to the language of the document took place, for issues related to the contract clause, in the states and only secondarily in the federal courts. Furthermore, within the states all three branches of government grappled with notions of the meaning of the clause prevalent in each state. In acting upon these conflicting conceptions, state policymakers also sought to establish their conception of proper federal-state relations. The ultimate configuration of the system of federalism, which Madison insisted was neither wholly national nor wholly federal, lay in the balance as state policymakers debated the meaning of the contract clause.

The clause meant different things to different men in 1787-1788 and throughout the early national period. To Federalist William Gardner, a Portsmouth, New Hampshire, merchant, it meant that the election of "anticommercial" and "dogmatical" Antifederalists to the state legislatures was of little consequence. The "wings of the legislature" had been "pretty well clipped," he advised Nicholas Gilman, a New Hampshire Federalist, former member of the Constitutional Convention, and later a member of the First Congress. Once the "much wished for federal government" was set in "motion," it would render the state legislatures impotent, their "unfit" members incapable of inflicting damage.[10]

Six weeks later, William R. Davie, who had served as one of North Carolina's delegates to the Federal Convention, offered a far different notion of the meaning of the clause. At the North Carolina convention, during a discussion of the paper money provision of Article I, Section 10, he insisted that the clause would not affect that state's existing paper money or public securities. The clause applied, he assured the delegates, "merely to contracts between individuals." It was this limited meaning, Davie added, that made the clause the "best in the Constitution."[11]

Although Gardner and Davie agreed on the merit of the contract clause, their understandings of it varied enormously. Gardner praised the Con-

[10] Gardner to Gilman, June 14, 1788, Gardner Papers, New-York Historical Society, New York City.

[11] Max Farrand, ed., *The Records of the Federal Convention of 1787*, 4 vols., rev. ed. (New Haven, Conn., 1937), III, 350.

stitution because it materially restricted the power of the state legislatures. Davie, on the other hand, insisted that the clause applied only to private contracts, leaving the state legislatures free to act in a broad range of areas.

This ambiguity was in part a result of the way in which the contract clause became a part of the Constitution. When delegates to the Federal Convention assembled in May 1787, none of the resolutions they considered resembled Article I, Section 10. The Virginia Plan, which formed the basis for discussion for the first two months of the convention, proposed to empower the national legislature "to negative all laws passed by the several States contravening, in the opinion of the national legislature, the articles of union; or any treaties subsisting under authority of the Union."[12] Although that broad grant of authority was originally agreed to without debate or dissent, the delegates eliminated it on July 17.[13] Every subsequent attempt to add it to the Constitution failed. Instead of a general restraint on state action imposed at the discretion of the national legislature, the Constitution they drafted imposed more precise limits enforceable only in response to specific state action.

The restriction on the states that denied to them the power to impair the obligation of contracts was first proposed late in the deliberations, on August 28, when Rufus King of Massachusetts "moved to add, in the words used in the Ordinance of Cong[res]s establishing new States, a prohibition on the States to interfere in private contracts."[14] King's reference was to the Northwest Ordinance, which declared that "no law ought ever to be made or have force in the said territory that shall, in any manner whatever, interfere with or affect private contracts, or engagements bona fide, and without fraud previously performed."[15]

Two delegates spoke against King's motion. Gouverneur Morris of Pennsylvania thought it "would be going too far," for there were "a thousand laws relating to bringing actions—limitations of actions & which affect contracts." George Mason of Virginia raised a similar objection, while Madison, although in favor of the motion, still preferred a "negative on the State laws [which] could alone secure the effect." In response to these objections, Wilson asserted that only "*retrospective*" interferences would be prohibited. Madison countered that retrospective interferences were already precluded by the "prohibition of ex post facto laws, which will oblige the Judges to declare such interferences null & void." The delegates then approved by a vote of seven states to three an amendment offered by John Rutledge of South Carolina that transformed King's resolution into a denial of the right of the states to pass bills of attainder or retrospective laws.[16] That prohibition was materially expanded by the

[12] *Ibid.*, I, 225.

[13] *Ibid.*, II, 21-22.

[14] *Ibid.*, 439.

[15] *The People Shall Judge: Readings in the Formation of American Policy* (Chicago, 1949), I, 252-253.

[16] Farrand, ed., *Records*, II, 439-440.

committee on style to prohibit the states from "altering or impairing the obligation of contracts." On September 14 the delegates deleted the word "altering" and the contract clause became part of the Constitution.[17]

Although the debates in Philadelphia shed little light on the framers' understanding of the clause, the arguments of Federalists and Antifederalists during the contest over ratification, comments by other observers, and calls for legislative action after individual state ratifications and before the inauguration of the new government all indicate a diversity of opinions about the meaning and prospective impact of the clause.

One version of what the clause meant linked it to the other monetary provisions in Article I, Section 10. William Maclaine of North Carolina, for example, tied it to the prohibition of further emissions of state paper money.[18] So did Pelatiah Webster, a Philadelphia merchant and pamphleteer, who argued that the Constitution "obliged" people to "fulfil their contracts, and not avoid them by tenders of any thing less than the value stipulated."[19] A group of citizens from Northampton County, Pennsylvania, also understood the Constitution in these terms.[20] On the other hand, Roger Sherman and Oliver Ellsworth, two of Connecticut's delegates to the convention, declared in a letter to the governor that Article I, Section 10, denied to the states the power to impair "the obligation of contracts by *ex post facto* laws."[21]

Others assumed that the prohibition applied only to state interferences in private contracts. Gov. Edmund Randolph of Virginia, a member of the Federal Convention and the Virginia state convention, insisted that the clause applied only to "private contracts."[22] So did William R. Davie, who declared in the North Carolina convention that the clause only limited state authority to interfere in "contracts between individuals."[23]

Precisely what kinds of interference in private contracts would be precluded was a matter of some discussion. In *Federalist* No. 44 Madison insisted that the "sober people" of America were "weary" of state legislative interferences in "cases affecting personal rights."[24] One specific kind of interference Madison condemned was installment legislation. Of a 1786 Virginia court bill that allowed debtors to pay their obligations in three annual installments, he remarked that "such an interposition of the law in private contracts is not to be vindicated on any legislative principle

[17] *Ibid.*, 597, 619.

[18] Jonathan Elliot, ed., *The Debates in the Several State Conventions on the Adoption of the Federal Constitution* . . . , 5 vols., 2d ed. (Philadelphia, 1861), IV, 477.

[19] "A Citizen of Philadelphia," "Remarks on the Address of Sixteen Members," in *History of Ratification*, XIII, 302.

[20] *Ibid.*, II, 648.

[21] Sherman and Ellsworth to Gov. Samuel Huntington, Sept. 26, 1787, *ibid.*, XIII, 471.

[22] Elliot, ed., *Debates*, IV, 477.

[23] Farrand, ed., *Records*, III, 350.

[24] Jacob E. Cooke, ed., *The Federalist* (Middletown, Conn., 1961), 301-302.

within my knowledge."[25] Installment laws like the Virginia bill, stay laws (postponing the time for the payment of debts beyond their contractual limits), and commodity payment laws (allowing payment in specified commodities at a proportion of their appraised value) were all, Madison recalled late in life, laws impairing the obligation of contracts as he understood the ban.[26]

Others seemingly agreed. Wilson, for example, in discussing types of state legislation that were proscribed, insisted to the Pennsylvania state convention that the Constitution prohibited not only installment laws but "other acts of a similar effect."[27] Charles Cotesworth Pinckney, a South Carolina framer, remarked in an "Extract of a letter from an eminent Member of the late Convention at Philadelphia," published in the Charleston *Columbian Herald,* that the Constitution was an honest one and that the limitations on the states found in Article I, Section 10, meant "that in future we shall be free from the apprehensions of paper money, pine barren acts [commodity payment laws], and installment laws."[28] Antoine de la Forest, the French vice consul in New York City, reported to the comte de Montmorin in September 1787 that "the creation of Paper money, the laws that stay the operation of obligations and Contracts, those that authorize the payment of debts in property or depreciated paper, can no longer take place."[29]

Some public figures, while agreeing that the Constitution prohibited these types of legislation in the future, insisted that the state legislatures nonetheless could and should act to protect the interest of debtors while they still had power to do so. In Georgia, for example, "Tullius" wrote in an essay published in the *Gazette of the State of Georgia* in June 1788 that "the period is now fast approaching when, from the limited authority left in each individual state by the new Constitution, we shall be deprived of the power and opportunity, which now present themselves, of doing an act which will at once be an important piece of justice to many of our best citizens and, at the same time, bring the most extensive advantages to the state at large." The act to which "Tullius" alluded was one "lately talked of in conversation," namely, a law for the payment of debts in installments. "Tullius" called on the Georgia executive council to summon the legislature into session so that it could enact such a law before the ratification of the Constitution by nine states would deny forever any state legislature the right to so interfere in debtor-creditor relations.[30]

There is no indication that the executive council considered this proposal, but Edward Telfair, governor of Georgia in 1786-1787 and

[25] James Madison to James Madison, Sr., Dec. 12, 1786, in Robert A. Rutland *et al.,* eds., *The Papers of James Madison,* IX (Chicago, 1975), 205.

[26] "Preface to Debates in the Convention of 1787," Farrand, ed., *Records,* III, 548.

[27] *History of Ratification,* II, 519.

[28] *Ibid.,* XIII, 274n.

[29] La Forest to comte de Montmorin, Sept. 28, 1787, *ibid.,* 259.

[30] *Ibid.,* III, 300-301.

1789-1793, did respond unofficially. Writing as "A Planter," Telfair argued that once the Constitution was adopted, any state legislation contrary to it—including the proposed installment measure—would not "continue in force." In lieu of an ineffective installment law, Telfair proposed an allotment system, or commodity payment plan, by which debtors could transfer a portion of their property at its real value to creditors before the commencement of the new government. This measure, too, required prompt action, for it also would be prohibited by Article I, Section 10.[31] Despite such urgings, the executive council did not call the legislature into special session. By January 1789, when the legislature did meet, the opportunity to act had passed.

Proponents of debtor relief were more successful in South Carolina, where in November 1788 the legislature enacted an installment law that made all debts contracted before January 1, 1787, recoverable in five annual installments beginning in March 1789. A similar measure, passed the year before, made the first installment due in March 1788. The 1788 legislation provided that any payments made under the 1787 law would be credited under the new act. As in Georgia, some Federalists argued that the new law was unconstitutional since the Constitution prohibited such legislation. Proponents of the measure, Federalist and Antifederalist alike, argued the contrary, insisting that the Constitution would not bind the states until the new government was set in motion, and that state laws passed before that date would not be affected by the constitutional ban.[32]

The simple language of the Constitution, along with statements made by its proponents during the convention and ratification debates, indicates a widespread belief that certain forms of debtor-relief legislation that had been permissible during the Confederation era would be precluded following establishment of the new federal government in 1789. Some Federalists and Antifederalists understood the clause to encompass far more than that. A New Hampshire Federalist, for example, argued in the Portsmouth *New-Hampshire Spy* (November 3, 1787) that the Constitution "expressly prohibits those destructive laws in the several states which alter or impair the obligation of contracts; so that in future anyone may be certain of an exact fulfillment of any contract that may be entered into or the penalty that may be stipulated in case of failure." This writer was not precise, but the inference from his statement is that the states' power to pass bankruptcy and insolvency legislation, as well as stay, installment, and commodity payment laws, would be eliminated by the Constitution.

Although no other Federalist made such a broad assertion of the

[31] *Ibid.*, 304-307.

[32] "An Act to Regulate the Payment and Recovery of Debts . . . ," in Thomas Cooper and David J. McCord, eds., *The Statutes at Large of South Carolina*, 10 vols. (Columbia, S.C., 1836-1841), V, 88-92. The debates are printed in the *City Gazette, or the Daily Advertiser* (Charleston), Oct. 24, 27, 28, 1788. For a discussion of South Carolina's debtor policies see Jerome J. Nadelhaft, *The Disorders of War: The Revolution in South Carolina* (Orono, Maine, 1981), 192-200.

inclusive force of Article I, Section 10, several Antifederalists did. Luther Martin, a Maryland delegate to the Constitutional Convention, in a speech to the Maryland legislature later published as an Antifederalist pamphlet, suggested that the Constitution threatened that state's existing insolvency legislation.[33] A Pennsylvania Antifederalist, "Deliberator," warned that under the Constitution "no state can give relief to insolvent debtors, however distressing their situation may be; since Congress will have the exclusive right of establishing uniform laws on the subject of bankruptcies throughout the United States; and the particular states are expressly prohibited from passing any law impairing the obligation of contracts."[34] Richard Henry Lee ultimately concluded that the power of Congress to pass uniform codes of bankruptcy posed a threat to the states' bankruptcy power and therefore opposed it.[35] And Antifederalists in the New York state convention sent a circular letter to the state legislatures that included an amendment stipulating that "the Power of Congress to pass uniform Laws concerning Bankruptcy shall only extend to Merchants and other Traders; and that the States respectively may pass Laws for the relief of other Insolvent Debtors."[36]

Did the clause apply to public contracts or only to private ones? Did it extend to all debtor-relief legislation or only to particular kinds? Did it affect legislation enacted before the Constitution was ratified or only laws passed afterward? The language of the Constitution led men to different conclusions. And while William Symmes, an Antifederalist delegate to the Massachusetts convention, acknowledged that he did not "at present understand what effect it [the contract clause] will have," his modesty was atypical.[37] In large measure unaware of this diversity of views, most men believed that they understood the clause. They also assumed that their understanding coincided with that of the majority of the framers and anticipated that it would be the basis of public policy in the immediate future.

[33] Martin, "The Genuine Information Delivered to the Legislature of the State of Maryland . . . ," in Herbert J. Storing, ed., *The Complete Anti-Federalist*, 7 vols. (Chicago, 1981), II, 19-82.

[34] *Freeman's Journal* (Philadelphia), Feb. 20, 1788, *ibid.*, III, 180.

[35] *Ibid.*, II, 343-344.

[36] Linda Grant De Pauw, *The Eleventh Pillar: New York State and the Federal Constitution* (Ithaca, N.Y., 1966), appendix B, 300.

[37] Symmes to Peter Osgood, Jr., Nov. 15, 1787, in *History of Ratification*, XIV, 113. It should also be noted that there was some agreement on what the clause did not do. It did not diminish the equity power of state jurists, who could abrogate private contracts if they were "unjust." The literature on the rapid shift in private law from this just-price notion to a modern one that stresses the sanctity of a contract unless fraud is proven occurred independently of the constitutional mandate of Article I, Section 10, which only restricted the lawmaking authority of the legislature. On the development of modern contract law see Morton J. Horwitz, *The Transformation of American Law, 1780-1860* (Cambridge, Mass., 1977), chap. 6. On the preservation of state equity power see Hamilton, *Federalist* No. 80.

TABLE I
STATE LAWS IMPAIRING THE OBLIGATION OF CONTRACTS,
BY YEAR IN FORCE, 1789-1815

Year	*Vt.*	*R.I.*	*Conn.*	*N.Y.*	*N.J.*	*Pa.*	*Md.*	*Va.*	*N.C.*	*S.C.*	*Ga.*
1789	SB	SB	B	B		B	B	S	B	IB	
1790	SB	SB	B	B		B	B	S	B	IB	
1791	SB	SB	B	B	B	B	B	S	B	IB	
1792	SB	SB	B	B	B	B	B	S	B	IB	
1793	SB	B	B	B	B	B	B	S	B	IB	
1794	SB	B	B	B	B		B	S		B	
1795	SB	B	B	B	B		B	S		B	
1796	SB	B	B	B			B	S		B	
1797	SB	B	B	B			B	S		B	
1798	SB	B	B	B			B	S		B	
1799	SB	B	B	B			B	S		B	
1800	SB	B	B	B		S	B	S		B	
1801	SB	B	B	B		S	B	S		B	
1802	SB	B	B	B		S	B	S		B	
1803	SB	B	B	B		S	B	S		B	
1804	SB	B	B	B		S	B	S		B	
1805	SB	B	B	B		S	B	S		B	
1806	SB	B	B	B		S	B	S		B	
1807	SB	B	B	B		S	B	S		B	
1808	SB	B	B	B		S	B	S	S	B	S
1809	SB	B	B	B		S	B	S	S	B	S
1810	SB	B	B	B			B	S		B	
1811	SB	B	B	B			B	S		B	
1812	SB	B	B	B		B	B	S	S	B	S
1813	SB	B	B	B		B	B	S	S	B	S
1814	SB	B	B	B		SB	B	S	S	B	S
1815	SB	B	B	B		SB	B	S			

S = Stay, I = Installment, B = Bankruptcy. The statutes are cited in the notes attached to discussion of them in the text or in Coleman, *Debtors and Creditors*, and Feller, "Moratory Legislation," *Harvard Law Rev.*, XLVI (1933), 1061-1085.

The implications of these different understandings of the scope of the contract clause are important. If, at its broadest, all state interferences in contracts public and private were precluded (including interferences created by existing legislation), the role of the states in the new constitutional order would be substantially diminished. Furthermore, if the states could not act, then the federal power to pass bankruptcy statutes was exclusive, and the role of the federal government in the operation of the economy would be quite broad. If, on the other hand, the clause restricted only particular types of state legislative interference in private contracts henceforth, then the power of the states in regulating the economic life of the nation remained significant.

The resolution of these ambiguities, and thus of the shape of federal-state relations, came only gradually as state legislatures and state and federal courts moved to establish their notions of constitutional policy in the new republic. The legislatures necessarily took the lead in defining areas of permissible state action. Between 1788 and 1815 they implemented their standard of constitutional right and political authority by continuing existing legislation respecting contracts and by supplementing it with additional stay and bankruptcy measures.

Historians have long been aware of some aspects of state interference in contracts following ratification of the Constitution. Peter J. Coleman, for example, analyzed all state bankruptcy legislation from the founding of the colonies to the close of the nineteenth century in *Debtors and Creditors in America: Insolvency, Imprisonment for Debt, and Bankruptcy, 1607-1900.*[38] Other historians have also noted specific statutes as did Louis Hartz in *Economic Policy and Democratic Thought: Pennsylvania, 1776-1860.*[39] Legal scholars, too, have identified state laws interfering with contracts following ratification.[40] Table I, which incorporates all of this research as well as my own in the published state statutes, illustrates the extent to which stay, installment, and bankruptcy legislation remained a part of state public policy during the early national period.

In some states such policies represented a continuation of debtor-relief measures adopted in the 1780s. In 1787, for example, the South Carolina legislature approved an installment law. It did so over the objections of Federalist David Ramsay, who maintained that the measure was "unconstitutional" because the "power of all legislative bodies was limited by the eternal laws of justice and reason."[41] The act allowed repayment of existing debts over a three-year period. Eighteen months later, the legislature revised the law to allow debtors to pay over five years and to permit any payments made under the 1787 act to be credited under the new law. Proponents of the revised installment act, including Charles Pinckney and Pierce Butler, both of whom had been delegates to the Federal Convention, were not persuaded by the argument of Jacob Read, another convention delegate, that the new Constitution, having been ratified by nine states, was already binding. The bill, as finally approved, allowed payment of debts, some of which were already thirty years old, over five years beginning in March 1789, a date that fortuitously coincided with the commencement of the new federal government.[42]

After 1800, Pennsylvania, as part of a "radical program of judicial reform,"[43] allowed petty debtors to stay executions of debts under one hundred dollars for three to nine months. Although the act was vetoed by

[38] Coleman, *Debtors and Creditors* (Madison, Wis., 1974).

[39] Hartz, *Economic Policy and Democratic Thought* (Cambridge, Mass., 1948).

[40] A. H. Feller, "Moratory Legislation: A Comparative Study," *Harvard Law Review*, XLVI (1933), 1061-1085.

[41] Report of House Debates, *Massachusetts Gazette* (Boston), Mar. 27, 1787.

[42] Cooper and McCord, eds., *Statutes*, V, 88-92; *City Gaz.* (Charleston), Oct. 24, 27, 28, 1788.

[43] Richard E. Ellis, *The Jeffersonian Crisis: Courts and Politics in the Young Republic* (New York, 1971), 161.

Gov. Thomas McKean and then repassed over his veto, and though it was the subject of considerable public debate, no one objected to its stay provision. Furthermore, this policy was broadened in 1804 and 1806 to protect any debtor for a period of three to twelve months if the debtor was a freeholder or could provide adequate security for the amount of the debt, interest, and court costs.[44] Finally, in 1814, the state authorized a seven-year stay of execution if a majority of a debtor's creditors agreed.[45]

The North Carolina legislature enacted measures in 1809 and again in 1812 that mandated a three-month stay of execution, provided the debtor secured the endorsement of two freeholders as securities.[46] The Georgia legislature required similar security in measures of 1808 and 1809, as well as a one-third payment in order to obtain a stay.[47] The Virginia legislature did the same in 1808 and 1814 when it provided for "stay bonds, to be taken on judgements, decrees, deeds of trust and conditioned for the payment of the debt at the expiration or repeal of the act."[48] This legislation supplemented a policy that allowed debtors to defer the collection of debts for three to twelve months by use of a replevy bond. Under that system, which operated in Virginia from 1748 to 1817, a debtor who obtained the signature of a solvent individual as guarantor of the debt could secure a stay of execution.[49]

Not all states adopted general relief measures. For example, Vermont and Rhode Island after 1789 received petitions from debtors seeking relief. In Vermont most of those petitioners were granted a stay of execution of up to ten years, while a smaller number secured a bankruptcy act.[50] The Rhode Island legislature granted bankruptcy relief to a larger share of petitioners than did Vermont, but in some cases allowed a stay of execution for periods of a few months to several years. In 1792, creditors challenged the latter procedure in federal circuit court. Alexander Champion and Thomas Dickason argued that such a stay impaired the obligation of the contract of debt owed to them by Silas Casey. Justices John Jay and Henry Marchant agreed. In one of the earliest exercises of judicial review

[44] "An Act for the Recovery of Debts and Demands not exceeding one Hundred Dollars . . . ," *Laws of the Commonwealth of Pennsylvania* (Philadelphia, 1804, 1806), VI, 383-400, VIII, 558-569. See the discussion of the act in Ellis, *Jeffersonian Crisis*, 160-164, 167-168.

[45] John Purdon, comp., *The Digest of the Laws of Pennsylvania, 1700-1830* (Philadelphia, 1831), 388-389.

[46] *Laws of North Carolina* (Raleigh, N.C., 1809, 1812), chaps. 1, 8.

[47] "An Act to Alleviate the Condition of Debtors . . . ," *Acts of the General Assembly of the State of Georgia* (Milledgeville, Ga., 1809), 16-18; "An Act to Alleviate the Condition of Debtors . . . ," *ibid.* (1810), 29-31.

[48] "An Act Concerning the Sale of Property Under Executions . . . ," *Acts Passed at a General Assembly* . . . (Richmond, Va., 1808), 14-15; "An Act Concerning Executions," *ibid.* (1815), 68-75.

[49] "An act to reduce into one act the several acts concerning executions, and for the relief of insolvent debtors," *The Revised Code of the Laws of Virginia* . . . (Richmond, Va., 1819), 524-547.

[50] Coleman, *Debtors and Creditors*, 69-71.

of a state law, they held that Rhode Island's act granting a stay of execution to Casey violated the contract clause and was therefore void. The principal record of the case, a notice in the *Providence Gazette*, reported that the legislature, then in session, agreed to cease granting such stays in the future. The legislature continued to grant bankruptcy relief to roughly half the debtors who petitioned for it and a stay of execution to all petitioners pending legislative action on their request.[51]

The contract clause places restrictions upon the states only. The Constitution in Article I, Section 8, gives Congress authority to establish a uniform system of bankruptcy legislation. Congress did not, however, exercise that authority until 1800, and the statute it then passed was repealed in 1803.[52] In the absence of federal legislation, states continued to act in this area as they had during the Confederation.

South Carolina, for example, continued measures first adopted in 1759, by which an insolvent could obtain a discharge if his creditors accepted a share of his property in settlement for his debt. He then received a one-year stay of suits from any creditors unwilling to accept a partial settlement. This statute, with minor revisions, remained the basis for South Carolina's bankruptcy policy throughout the nineteenth century.[53]

Pennsylvania, too, built on its colonial experience by amending several times in the 1780s a statute first passed in 1750. The statute expired, however, in 1793, and not until 1812 did the state reenter the field. Then it approved a short-lived law that extended bankruptcy relief to residents of the city and county of Philadelphia and made the system voluntary. The law proved so unpopular that it was repealed within a year. In 1814 a federal district court declared it an unconstitutional impairment of the obligation of contracts.[54]

North Carolina's experience paralleled Pennsylvania's. The legislature expanded colonial practice in 1777 and 1778 by allowing debtors to obtain discharge from their obligations by taking an oath of poverty. These laws expired in 1793.[55]

New York in 1788 and New Jersey in 1791 also adopted general bankruptcy legislation, although New Jersey's law lapsed in 1795. New York's statute allowed a debtor to be discharged of all obligations with the consent of three-fourths of his creditors by value. The law, amended several times, survived until 1813, when it was replaced by one that allowed a discharge with the consent of two-thirds of the creditors by

[51] June 23, 1792; Coleman, *Debtors and Creditors*, 95.

[52] Charles Warren, *Bankruptcy in United States History* (Cambridge, 1935), 10-22.

[53] Cooper and McCord, eds., *Statutes*, IV, 86-94. The discussion of state bankruptcy legislation that follows is based in large measure on Coleman, *Debtors and Creditors*. For his discussion of South Carolina legislation see chap. 13.

[54] "An act for the relief of insolvent debtors, in city and county of Philadelphia, passed March 13, 1812" (Philadelphia, 1812); *Golden* v. *Prince*, 10 Federal Cases 542-547 [1814].

[55] Coleman, *Debtors and Creditors*, chap. 16.

value. This statute was nullified in 1819 by the United States Supreme Court decision in *Sturgis* v. *Crowninshield* as an unconstitutional impairment of the obligation of contracts.[56]

Other states preferred different policies. Maryland, after a one-year experiment with a general bankruptcy statute in 1787, abandoned it in favor of granting bankruptcy by special petition. Between 1789 and 1805, 1,456 debtors had their obligations discharged before the state again adopted a general bankruptcy statute. That 1805 statute continued in operation to 1854.[57]

Rhode Island and Connecticut also preferred a policy of discharging debtors only by special petition. Unlike Maryland, however, where the burden of hearing large numbers of petitions compelled the legislature to transfer this function to the courts, the legislatures of these two states continued to hear such requests to 1828 and 1818 respectively. In those years the legislatures repealed all forms of bankruptcy legislation.[58]

In summary, then, the "thou shalt nots" of the Constitution did not prevent the states from continuing established policies regarding bankruptcy and debtor relief. The question is: how could men embrace a document that potentially at least prohibited such policies and still pursue them?

A partial explanation is that the Constitution was not perceived to be controlling until the inauguration of the new government. Therefore, so the proponents of debtor relief in the states argued, legislation approved during the Confederation era avoided the constitutional prohibition. This was the view of the majority in the 1788 South Carolina legislature. Chief Justice John Louis Taylor of the North Carolina Supreme Court held it too.[59] In Georgia "Tullius" and former governor Telfair agreed that the state legislature could act on matters affecting contracts only until the commencement of the new government, although Telfair also believed that any such legislation had to be executed before that date in order to escape the constitutional prohibition.[60] John Brown Cutting of Massachusetts, a commercial agent in Charleston, agreed with Telfair in this: he advised John Rutledge in the spring of 1789 that he doubted that the South Carolina installment act of 1788 could continue in operation once the new government was set in motion.[61]

[56] For New Jersey see *ibid.*, 136. The New York statutes are summarized in William P. Van Ness and John Woodworth, eds., *Laws of the State of New York . . .*, 2 vols. (Albany, N.Y., 1813), I, 460n. *Sturgis* v. *Crowninshield* is printed in 4 Wheaton 122-208 (1819).

[57] Coleman, *Debtors and Creditors*, chap. 12.

[58] See the tables *ibid.*, 81, 96.

[59] *City Gaz.* (Charleston), Oct. 24, 27, 1788. See also the discussion of this in the Jan. 1788 session of the legislature in *Debates which Arose in the House of Representatives . . .* (Charleston, S.C., 1831), 14-15, 17. *Jones* v. *Crittenden*, 4 North Carolina Reports 60 (1814).

[60] *History of Ratification*, III, 300, 304-307.

[61] Cutting to Rutledge, Feb. 21, 1789, in Merrill Jensen and Robert A. Becker,

Opinions varied on this point. Opponents of debtor-relief legislation in South Carolina argued that such statutory relief was precluded by the state's act of ratification. Francis Corbin, attorney general of Virginia, held that the Constitution was the supreme law of the land as early as August 1788, when the required number of states had ratified it.[62] Not until 1821 did the United States Supreme Court resolve the question: in *Owings* v. *Speed* it held that statutes adopted before the inauguration of the new government were constitutional, even if such laws continued to be enforced after March 1789. What determined constitutionality, the Court held, was the date of enactment.[63]

Most legislatures enacted debtor-relief legislation only after the federal government was inaugurated. They did so over the vociferous objections of men who insisted that stay laws, installment laws, commodity payment laws, and the like violated the constitutional ban of Article I, Section 10. In 1809, for example, a number of North Carolina legislators led by William Gaston, a prominent Federalist and later state judge, opposed their state's "bill for the relief of debtors." That measure proposed a one-year stay if the debtor paid one-half the principal, the entire interest due, and court costs, and provided security for the remainder of the obligation. Gaston argued that the Constitution of the United States was "so very clear and explicit, that it must stand obvious to all, an insuperable bar to the passage of the bill."[64]

The judges of the North Carolina Supreme Court also proved critical of debtor-relief legislation. In *Jones* v. *Crittenden*, decided in January 1814, Chief Justice Taylor held for the court that the state's 1812 act "to suspend executions for a limited time" impaired the obligation of contracts and was therefore unconstitutional.[65] The court declared that the framers intended to prohibit stay laws, that the policy inherent in such legislation was unwise, and that the prohibition was absolute.

In Virginia "Asconius" voiced the same view when that state's legislature considered a stay law in 1814. He insisted that such measures were "unconstitutional, iniquitous, and impolitic" as well as "a violation of the principles of natural justice."[66] In Georgia the editor of the *Augusta Herald* repeatedly attacked that state's 1808 debtor-relief measure, and the state's 1814 act was similarly condemned in other newspapers as immoral, unnecessary, and unconstitutional.[67]

---

eds., *The Documentary History of the First Federal Elections, 1788-1790* (Madison, Wis., 1976-), I, 214.

[62] Aug. 5, 1788, Executive Papers, Virginia State Library, Richmond.

[63] 6 Wheaton 420-424 (1821).

[64] "State Legislative Debate in the House of Commons of North Carolina, on the Bill for the Relief of Debtors," *Star* (Raleigh), Dec. 22, 1808.

[65] 4 North Carolina Reports 55-68 (1814).

[66] *Virginia Gazette* (Winchester), Mar. 11, 1809.

[67] May 26, June 2, 1808. See also "Lucius," *Columbian Museum & Savannah*

In light of these arguments, on what grounds could state laws affecting contracts be found *not* to violate the federal Constitution? First, it should be noted that not all opponents of such laws held that the states could not pass them. Instead, they argued that some particular measure was impractical or unwise. For example, the editor of the *Augusta Herald,* who assailed the Georgia act of 1808, observed that the measure, if approved, would stop nearly all civil business of the courts for approximately seven months, "which is certainly extending *relief* beyond what the circumstances of the case required."[68] A year and a half later, commenting upon a new bill then pending, the same editor argued that "the less legislative bodies take upon themselves to interfere with the private contracts of individuals, the better."[69] Federalist Shaler Hillyer, an Augusta merchant, likewise condemned the Georgia legislature for approving the 1808 statute, which he found "oppressive and immoral" but not unconstitutional.[70] Clearly, the implication is that on some occasions legislative interferences could be justified as constitutional.

One such occasion, in the minds of some state legislators, resulted from renewal of warfare in Europe after 1800. Legislators in the North Carolina House of Commons argued that Jefferson's embargo necessitated an "indulgence" for their "suffering constituents." Furthermore, when confronted with the contention that a proposed stay law was unconstitutional, spokesmen for the majority maintained it was not. W. R. King insisted that a suspension act passed the previous session, and by implication the one proposed, "was constitutional," for were it not, the judges "would have refused to carry it into effect."[71] The bill, which provided for a ninety-day suspension, was approved by a ten-vote margin.

In 1814 a Caroline County, Virginia, farmer offered the same justification for debtor-relief legislation—that it was constitutional because it was necessary. He called upon the Virginia legislature to close that state's courts because of disruptions brought by the War of 1812. To allow the courts to stay open at a time when "specie is so scarce," he warned, would mean that the "few holders of it in each county" would "have the upper hand over debtors, quite unfairly."[72]

This view was widely held. Thus, while several state and federal courts struck down state laws as unconstitutional impairments of the obligation of contract, other judges viewed these matters differently. For example, in April 1808, Paul Grimball, a Georgia planter, petitioned the superior court for an injunction to halt a forced sale to satisfy a judgment against

Advertiser, Aug. 2, 1808; "Wilkes," *Monitor* (Washington, Ga.), Oct. 13, 1813; and the "Grand Jury of Richmond County," *Columbian Museum,* May 26, 1814.

[68] May 26, 1808.

[69] Nov. 23, 1809.

[70] Hillyer to Oliver Whyte, June 19, 1808, Hillyer Papers, University of Georgia, Athens.

[71] "Debate in the House of Commons," *Star* (Raleigh), Dec. 22, 1808.

[72] *Virginia Patriot* (Richmond), Oct. 22, 1814.

him. The basis for Grimball's petition was the unfairness of the proceeding, which "would prove ruinous to the complaintant, inasmuch as nearly double the property would be sacrificed now, at a forced sale, which it would have required only four months ago, to pay these judgements." Grimball's attorney argued that the court should intervene on the ground of "public utility," since it would be profoundly unfair for Grimball to be compelled to sacrifice a substantial share of his property at forced sale at a time when prices were artificially depressed because of the federal embargo.[73] Opposing counsel did not deny the legitimacy of Grimball's complaint but contended that an injunction should not be issued because "no levy and sale was yet ordered." They also argued that if Judge Thomas Charlton did grant Grimball relief, Grimball should then be required to give security "before the relief prayed for could be obtained."[74]

After a careful review of the court's equity power, Judge Charlton declared "that cases of this description involve hardship and oppression; that they are against equity and conscience; that they are promotive of injury to the public; that they enable monied men to accumulate usurious wealth; and that they tend to convert a *just* and *salutary* measure of the government [the embargo], into an engine of political disaffection, through the medium of distressed and persecuted debtors."[75] He then issued an injunction to stay the forced sale while requiring Grimball to deposit with the sheriff "sufficient property, the valuation of which to be ascertained by the price at market three months preceding the embargo act," as security for the debt in question.[76] Charlton acted in his capacity as a superior court judge with equity powers. His analysis nonetheless sheds light on the motives of legislators who argued the state could act in extraordinary situations to ensure justice for hard-pressed debtors.

During the spring of 1808 the Georgia legislature did precisely that when they approved "An act to alleviate the condition of debtors and afford them temporary relief." The act provided a stay of any judgment from the date of passage of the bill, May 23, 1808, to December 25, 1808, provided the defendant entered "good and sufficient freehold security . . . for the ultimate payment of the debt, cost and interest, and upon paying one third part of the judgement and one third part of the costs."[77]

In November of the same year the constitutionality of that measure was challenged on the ground that it impaired the obligation of a contract. In a comprehensive evaluation of the contract clause Charlton forcefully articulated the constitutional understanding of the proponents of debtor-relief legislation. In his ruling he acknowledged that Article I, Section 10, denied the states the authority to pass laws that impaired the obligation of

[73] *Ex Parte Paul Grimball,* Cases in the Superior Courts in the State of Georgia 153 (1808).

[74] *Ibid.*

[75] *Ibid.,* 158.

[76] *Ibid.*

[77] *Acts of the General Assembly of Georgia* (1809), 16-18.

contracts. But, he asked, "What is meant by the term 'impairing the obligation of contracts?' " His answer: "any measure . . . that gives them a diminished value, takes from them any of the essential properties of contracts, or which divests them of that priority of lien, obligation or recovery . . . must impair the obligation of the contract." The Georgia act was constitutional, he insisted, because it did none of those things. Charlton acknowledged that the law extended the period "at which contracts were heretofore enforced" and suspended the means of recovery. But the obligation "remained entire, and a bond or covenant is as valuable, and on the score of the obligation, is as operative now, as before the passing of the act."[78]

In effect, Charlton distinguished between the obligation of the contract, which was protected, and the means of enforcing it (remedies available to the creditor for failure to fulfill the obligation), which could be altered. This distinction between the obligation of a contract and its remedies had existed at the time of the adoption of the Constitution, may have been tacitly recognized in the revision of the contract clause on the floor of the Federal Convention, and underlay much of the state action described above.

In the spring of 1787, for example, members of the Maryland Senate, a conservative and soon to become an overwhelmingly Federalist body, argued against a state emission of paper money proposed by the state House of Delegates. The senators warned that such a measure was unwise in that it "violated the first principles of justice and legislation, by infringing the contracts of individuals."[79] Supporters of the Senate in the ensuing public debate went farther in their attack, explaining that the House of Delegates bill "changes the nature of past contracts, and suggests a mode [of relief] ruinous to creditors, repugnant to justice and good faith, disreputable to government, and fatal to our commercial interests." These were harsh words, indeed, albeit standard ones among the critics of such debtor-relief measures. What is remarkable, however, is not the language of the Senate's supporters but their proposed alternative. They called for a "law obliging debtor and creditor to enter into a reasonable composition, proposed by either party, placing the one on a certainty of receiving his due at stipulated periods, and securing the other against suits before the expiration of the term."[80] Some Marylanders opposed as a breach of the obligation of contracts a state issue of paper money that they believed would depreciate and would then be used to pay legitimate debts at full face value. But the same men believed that it was not a breach of contract to use state authority to compel debtors and creditors to agree to a

[78] *P. Grimball* v. *F. Ross*, Cases in the Superior Courts 180-181 (1808).

[79] "The Reply of the Senate," in Melvin Yazawa, ed., *Representative Government and the Revolution: The Maryland Constitutional Crisis of 1787* (Baltimore, 1975), 50.

[80] "A Proposal from Anne Arundel County," *Maryland Gazette* (Annapolis), Feb. 8, 1787, *ibid.*, 54.

moratorium during which a debtor could not be arrested or his property attached, as long as there was a guarantee that the creditor eventually would be compensated.

Joseph Jones, a Virginia Federalist, reported a similar view in that state: that alterations in the remedy intended to protect the debtor and guarantee payment at a later date were not impairments of contract. In December 1787, he informed Madison, then at the Confederation Congress meeting in New York, that the Virginia House of Delegates had adopted a court bill that set a minimum on the value at which goods could be sold at auction in execution of a judgment. If goods did not sell at three-fourths of their value, the execution could be postponed for twelve months, provided the debtor posted bond or otherwise provided adequate security. Such a minimum appraisal law, Jones commented, was held to be no "direct interference with private contracts."[81]

This distinction between the obligation of a contract and the remedies available to a creditor if the debtor failed to fulfill the obligation may have underlain the revisions in the contract clause made on the floor of the Federal Convention. The report of the committee on style denied the states the power of "altering or impairing the obligation of contracts." The elimination of the words "altering or" may have signified a tacit recognition by the delegates that some changes not diminishing the obligation could be legitimate.[82]

Not all agreed. In the legislative debate over the 1808 debtor-relief bill in North Carolina, opponents argued vociferously against the idea that "by passing this bill we should not impair the contract itself, but deprive one of the parties of the opportunity of enforcing it." Such "a quibble," William Gaston insisted, "would satisfy no man's understanding" and was a mere "miserable subterfuge."[83] The observer for the Raleigh *Star* who covered the debate reported principally the comments of the bill's opponents, but the implication is clear. The proponents of the bill assumed that what Gaston saw as a "miserable subterfuge" was in fact a legitimate distinction.

That distinction gained formal recognition in 1819 when Chief Justice Marshall stated his opinion in *Sturgis* v. *Crowninshield* that "the distinction between the obligation of a contract and the remedy given by the legislature to enforce that obligation has been taken at the bar, and exists in the nature of things. Without impairing the obligation of the contract the remedy may certainly be modified."[84] Marshall nonetheless declared unconstitutional the law in question, a New York state bankruptcy act. He did so, first, because it affected contracts entered into before the passage of the law, and, second, because he personally opposed all bankruptcy

[81] Dec. 18, 1787, in Rutland *et al.*, eds., *Madison Papers*, X, 329-330.

[82] The "mystery" of the contract clause is discussed in McDonald, *Novus Ordo Seclorum*, 270-275, although he does not suggest the hypothesis advanced here.

[83] *Star* (Raleigh), Dec. 22, 1808.

[84] 4 Wheaton 122-208 (1819).

legislation. Other members of the Court did not share Marshall's view, and in *Ogden* v. *Saunders*, in 1827, he was overruled as to bankruptcy laws affecting contracts entered into after passage of a state bankruptcy act.[85]

The majority in that case argued that if a state passes a bankruptcy act, that law becomes an implicit part of the contract, affecting the remedies available to the creditor if the debtor fails to perform the obligation. The distinction between the obligation and remedies justified, in Marshall's opinion in *Sturgis* v. *Crowninshield*, the abolition of imprisonment for debt. Building on that opinion, Justice Bushrod Washington held for the majority in *Ogden* v. *Saunders* that a discharge could include not only the body of a debtor but his future earnings as well. Such a discharge, he held, did not impair the obligation of a contract.[86]

The Court's conclusion in *Ogden* v. *Saunders* had been reached by some judges earlier. For example, Justice Brockholst Livingston, a New York Federalist, upheld state bankruptcy legislation in *Adams* v. *Storey*, a case decided in 1817. He maintained that at the time of the writing of the Constitution the states had a right to pass insolvency and bankruptcy laws, and that neither Article I, Section 10, nor Article I, Section 8, restricted that right. Article I, Livingston held, was intended to prevent certain types of state policies arising from the calamities of war—legal tender paper money, installment laws, and commodity payment laws. In contrast, insolvency and bankruptcy laws arose as an "encouragement to trade," were universal among the states, and served a legitimate function that distinguished them from the types of action prohibited by Article I, Section 10.[87] For Livingston, in contrast to the United States Supreme Court, those means that "encouraged trade" were constitutional.

Livingston did not sanction or proscribe stay laws in his decision in *Adams* v. *Storey*. Neither did the Supreme Court in 1819 or 1827. But state legislatures and judges had previously, and would in future, justify such laws on the same grounds that had been used to justify state bankruptcy legislation.[88] Such legislation did not impair the obligation of contract for it merely altered the remedy, which was compatible with the intentions of the framers. Furthermore, such legislation was necessary and just. It protected individuals from the deleterious effects of governmental policies, even as it encouraged the legitimate efforts of farmers and merchants.

So, what can we say about the effects of the prohibitions of Article I, Section 10, on state economic policy during the early national period? Clearly, the broad potential envisioned by some Federalists and Antifederalists was not realized. Neither Congress nor the federal courts

[85] 12 Wheaton 213-369 (1827).

[86] *Ibid.*

[87] 1 Federal Cases 141-152 [1817].

[88] In addition to the material cited above see Murray N. Rothbard, *The Panic of 1819: Reactions and Policies* (New York, 1962), chap. 2.

moved to prohibit state bankruptcy legislation, except in a limited fashion, and then only after 1815. The potential for the absolute sanctity of contracts, free from state interference through any form of debtor-relief legislation, which Antifederalists had predicted, and some Federalists may have preferred, was not achieved.

Even so, the states did resort to fewer interferences in contracts, and in more limited ways, after 1789 than they had during the Confederation period. No state adopted a commodity payment law after 1789, and the only installment law operating during the early national period was passed before the establishment of the new government. Furthermore, some legislatures rejected calls for stay and other forms of debtor-relief legislation, in part because of Article I, Section 10. Still, the impact of the ban was smaller than the language of the Constitution would seem to suggest, for stay and bankruptcy legislation continued to be adopted following ratification of the Constitution.

More broadly, the early history of the contract clause confirms Madison's argument in *The Federalist* that the Constitution was neither "wholly national nor wholly federal." Because of the ambiguity of Article I, Section 10, Federalists and Antifederalists came to widely differing conclusions about the prospective impact of the contract clause. Some interpreted the clause to mean that most or all state debtor relief legislation would be proscribed. Others, Federalist and Antifederalist alike, anticipated a far narrower effect. This host of conflicting interpretations, the previous experience of the colonies and states with such policies, and the reactive nature of the federal judiciary, which could respond to state initiatives only when deciding cases alleging a state violation of the Constitution, created a vacuum that states filled by continuing and initiating new stay, installment, and bankruptcy programs.

These state initiatives profoundly affected the ultimate shape of federalism. Thus, while the federal courts after 1815 moved to deny the constitutionality of stay and installment laws, they accepted such debtor-relief legislation if it had been adopted before the inauguration of the new government. The experience of the states during the first quarter century under the new government also signaled to future state legislatures that stay and other forms of debtor-relief laws could be adopted as short-term responses to immediate economic crises with little likelihood of federal review. Finally, the federal courts affirmed the constitutionality of state bankruptcy legislation that affected only future contracts. The Constitution, as a result of state legislative initiatives that built on the ambiguity of the document and of the diversity of the framers' intentions, proved incapable of establishing exclusive federal control over state economic policy after 1789.

THE RECOVERY OF BRITISH DEBTS IN THE FEDERAL CIRCUIT COURT OF VIRGINIA, 1790 to 1797

by CHARLES F. HOBSON*

"I observe that the British Merchants, have begun to prosecute the Recovery of their old debts before the people are in a situation to pay," wrote Virginia merchant (and debtor) Thomas Pleasants, Jr., in July 1790, alluding to the lawsuits recently begun in the United States Circuit Court, District of Virginia. The fourth article of the treaty of peace between the United States and Great Britain, concluded 3 September 1783, stipulated that creditors on either side were to "meet with no lawful impediment to the recovery of the full value in sterling money, of all *bona fide* debts heretofore contracted." Until the federal circuit court opened in the spring of 1790, this article had been a dead letter as far as British creditors of Virginia citizens were concerned. Now, it appeared, Virginians would finally have to face up to the prospect of judgments at law to enforce the payment of their debts contracted before the war of independence.[1]

The British debt litigation in Virginia during the 1790s reveals the inability of courts to resolve a conflict that was never simply a matter of law. The recovery of the prewar debts was at once a series of private disputes and an inseparable part of the larger public controversy between the United States and Great Britain over the enforcement of the treaty. The inclusion of the fourth article in itself showed that both nations regarded the payment of debts as at least partly a public responsibility. At the same time, however, the commissioners who negotiated the treaty were unwilling themselves to make a serious attempt to settle the problem. Instead they placed the entire burden of enforcing the fourth article on the courts and the full liability for payment on the individual debtors. This disposition of the debts question as if it were strictly an issue of law proved unrealistic. The parties to British debt suits acted not only as private litigants; in effect they became public symbols, representatives of the sovereignty and dignity of the nations to which they belonged. The American debtor thus grounded his defense on

*Mr. Hobson is editor of the Papers of John Marshall. He wishes to thank George H. Hoemann for his helpful comments on a draft of this article. An earlier version of the article was presented to the colloquium of the Institute of Early American History and Culture.

[1] Pleasants to James Madison, 10 July 1790 (William T. Hutchinson et al., eds., *The Papers of James Madison* [Chicago and Charlottesville, 1962-], XIII, 273); Hunter Miller, ed., *Treaties and Other International Acts of the United States of America, 1776-1863* (8 vols.; Washington, D.C., 1931-48), II, 154.

the fact that the plaintiff was a subject of Great Britain and thereby answerable for the bad faith and misconduct of his king toward the United States.

In Virginia, where indebtedness to British merchants was most highly concentrated, the political passions and antagonisms generated by the Revolution were too intense and pervasive to allow the courts and especially the juries to act as impartial arbiters in cases of British debt. This was true not only of the state courts, but also to a large extent of the federal circuit court as well. British plaintiffs who turned to this court beginning in 1790 were much less successful than has generally been understood.[2] As soon as suits were brought, lawyers for the Virginia debtors raised elaborate special defenses that were essentially political rather than legal in nature. These special defenses effectively prevented any judgment on a British debt case until 1793. Even after the circuit court in 1793 and the Supreme Court in 1796 overruled the debtors' special pleas, British creditors continued to encounter obstacles to the recovery of their debts.[3]

The most important measure dealing with British debts adopted by the Virginia General Assembly during the war was the 1777 act for "Sequestering British Property." Undei this law citizens could pay all or part of their debts owed to British subjects into the state loan office. Upon making his payment the debtor received a certificate, which he then delivered to the

[2] Earlier studies of the British debt controversy in post-Revolutionary Virginia tend to break off at the point where litigation begins, apparently on the assumption that these legal proceedings were merely the denouement of a conflict that had already ended largely in the British creditors' favor. According to the standard view, the adoption of the Constitution and the creation of a federal court system secured the interests of the creditors, who thereafter enjoyed "amazing success" in the courts. The most authoritative treatment of the subject concludes that by 1796 "the question of repayment was resolved. No legal impediments stood in the way of the British creditor, and he or his executors did very well in the vast majority of suits against Virginia debtors" (see Isaac Samuel Harrell, *Loyalism in Virginia: Chapters in the Economic History of the Revolution* [Durham, 1926], pp. 173-77 [quotation on p. 177]; Emory G. Evans, "Private Indebtedness and the Revolution in Virginia, 1776 to 1796," *William and Mary Quarterly*, 3d ser., XXVIII [1971], 373).

[3] Two principal sources were used for this study. One is the records of the United States Circuit Court, Virginia District, Ended Cases, which are deposited in the Virginia State Library, Richmond. They consist of order books, record books, rule books, and original case papers, along with an index to the ended cases. The other is the papers submitted by British merchants to the claims commissions under the Jay Treaty of 1794 and the Convention of 1802. They include memorials, affidavits, correspondence, and transcripts of court cases and are in Treasury Group, Class 79 (hereafter cited as T. 79), Public Record Office (hereafter cited as P.R.O.). The claims papers form part of the Virginia Colonial Records Project microfilm, which I have used at the Research Library, Colonial Williamsburg Foundation, Williamsburg.

These sources, particularly the court records, are still largely unexploited. In researching the article cited above and an earlier one ("Planter Indebtedness and the Coming of the Revolution in Virginia," *WMQ*, 3d ser., XIX [1962], 511-33), Emory Evans culled both sources extensively for correspondence between merchants and planters. Isaac Harrell did not have access to the claims commission papers, if indeed their existence was known at the time he wrote his monograph. He did sample some of the court records, which had just been discovered (*Loyalism in Virginia*, pp. 162-63, 185).

Governor and Council and obtained a receipt that would "discharge him from so much of the debt." [4] In passing this act the legislature evidently had in mind a money-raising scheme, not unlike a public loan, to bolster the state's depleted finances. Because paper money was a legal tender, the legislators also hoped to maintain the value of this currency by allowing debtors to pay it into the loan office. In this regard the act was a notable failure. Remarkably few citizens chose to pay off their British debts in this manner, and the expected financial boon did not materialize. Unless moved by patriotism, debtors had little incentive to pay since British creditors could not recover from them during the war. The great depreciation of the paper money, however, soon made it possible for Virginians to pay off their debts at a fraction of their real value. Not surprisingly most of the payments occurred during the last two months of the act, when the depreciation was sixty to one.[5]

Even at the height of the depreciation, the number of debtors taking advantage of the sequestration law was strikingly small. Of those who did, some undoubtedly saw an easy opportunity to escape their indebtedness. Others simply tried to protect themselves by depositing in the loan office the depreciated paper which they as creditors were required by law to accept from their own debtors. Thomas Jefferson, for example, made two payments in discharge of John Wayles's debts totaling £2,666 (about £90 specie)—an amount, he later explained, that was identical to what he had received in depreciated currency for lands sold in 1776 "before a shilling of paper money was emitted." Another Virginian informed his British creditor that he did not wish "a farthing advantage" by his loan office payment, but only to make good the currency he had been obliged to receive for real value.[6]

Lawyers for Virginia debtors later contended that loan office payments constituted a valid discharge of British debts despite the fourth article of the peace treaty. Another act under which Virginians claimed exemption from British debts was that of May 1782 "to repeal so much of a former act as suspends the issuing of executions upon certain judgments." One section of this act declared "that no debt or demand whatsoever, originally due to

---

[4] William Waller Hening, ed., *The Statutes at Large . . . of Virginia . . .* (13 vols.; Richmond, Philadelphia, and New York, 1809-23), IX, 379-80.

[5] For the best discussion of the sequestration law, see Evans, "Private Indebtedness," *WMQ*, 3d ser., XXVIII (1971), 354-57. The scale of depreciation was established by a 1781 act (Hening, *Statutes*, X, 472-73).

[6] List of Paper Money Paid in at Loan Office on Account of Farell and Jones (Claim of John Tyndale Ware, T. 79/30); Jefferson to William Jones, 5 Jan. 1787 (Julian P. Boyd et al., eds., *The Papers of Thomas Jefferson* [Princeton, 1950-], XI, 16); Robert Hart to George Anderson, July 1784 (Claim of Anderson and Daiziell, T. 79/32).

a subject of Great-Britain, shall be recoverable in any court in this commonwealth, although the same may be transferred to a citizen of this state, or to any other person capable of maintaining such action, unless the assignment" was made before 1 May 1777.[7] Among lawyers, opinions differed as to the meaning of this law. Some regarded it as merely a temporary war measure to prevent recovery of debts assigned to citizens, one that the legislature had at least implicitly repealed by subsequent acts. Others insisted that the law continued in full force as a general prohibition against the recovery of all British debts.[8] The latter view, needless to say, predominated in Virginia during the decade following the peace. Virginians and British creditors alike assumed that until the assembly expressly repealed this law, no court in the commonwealth would hear a suit for the recovery of a British debt.

The state courts remained closed to British creditors after the treaty of 1783—if not officially by wartime legislative enactments, then virtually by the refusal of the judges to hear any case for the payment of prewar debts. Having so recently witnessed the widespread destruction and loss of lands and personal property at the hands of an invading British army, Virginians could not easily be reconciled to opening the courts of justice to their former enemies. No action angered them more than the carrying off of their slaves and the subsequent refusal in the spring of 1783 of British Commanding General Carleton to return them. Although the Virginia assembly at first seemed predisposed to give effect to the treaty, the failure to return the slaves, along with the continuing British occupation of the Northwest posts, both contrary to the stipulations of the seventh article of the treaty, turned the majority of citizens against payment of British debts. Beginning in 1784 the legislature defeated successive attempts to remove legal impediments to recovery, in each instance making it clear that no steps would be taken on the debts until Great Britain made satisfaction for the slaves.[9] Even if Great Britain had returned the slaves (or made compensation for them) and evacuated the posts, Virginians never contemplated a literal compliance with the stipulations of the fourth article. Immediate and full payment of £2,000,000 sterling, the amount owed by Virginians, was an economic

[7] Hening, *Statutes*, XI, 75-76.

[8] William Nelson, Jr., to Jefferson, 4 Feb. 1791 (Boyd et al., *Papers of Jefferson*, XIX, 244-45).

[9] Evans, "Private Indebtedness," *WMQ*, 3d ser., XXVIII (1971), 358-67. See also Thomas Underwood to Madison, 4 Jan. 1790; Walter Jones to Madison, 5 Feb. 1790; Thomas Pleasants, Jr., to Madison, 10 July 1790 (Hutchinson et al., *Papers of Madison*, XII, 468; XIII, 28, 273-74). For later action by the Virginia legislature on this subject, see the resolutions adopted in 1791 and 1793 (*Journal of the House of Delegates of the Commonwealth of Virginia* ... [Richmond, 1791], Oct. 1791, pp. 21, 42, 58; ibid. [Richmond, 1793], Oct. 1793, pp. 101, 124-25, 128).

impossibility in the war-ravaged commonwealth.[10] The best the legislature was prepared to offer was payment by installments over seven years with interest deducted for eight years of the war. This proposal was not adopted, however, though its terms formed the basis of numerous private agreements between creditors and debtors after the war.

From the beginning of the controversy the courts of the commonwealth showed no inclination to resist the legislative will on the subject of British debts. According to Edmund Pendleton, president of the court of appeals and highest judicial officer of the state, it was the province of the legislature "to determine how the treaty is to be performed." [11] When the courts, closed since 1774, reopened in 1777, suits brought before the war for the recovery of British debts were placed on the so-called "British docket." There they languished until well into the 1790s.[12] While the old cases remained suspended and the legislature refused to repeal its wartime acts preventing recovery, British creditors saw little point in instituting new suits. One agent for a British merchant firm stated that it would have been irresponsible to put his clients "to the expense of prosecuting suits, which at the very moment of instituting them, I knew would not be tried." Only in the rare instances in which the defendant agreed not to plead "British debt," did British creditors bother to bring suit.[13] The attitude of Virginia judges was summed up by Judge John Tyler, who at the Fredericksburg District Court in 1790 declared "that he would preside at the Trial of no Cause, where a British Subject was plaintiff, and the Plea was such." Tyler refused even to hear cases between two Virginians that indirectly involved debts owed to British subjects. The state courts of Virginia remained effectively closed to British plaintiffs seeking recovery of prewar debts until after the Jay Treaty of 1794. The prevailing opinion of the Virginia judiciary was that notwithstanding the treaty of 1783 and the Constitution of 1787, the state legislature would have to repeal its wartime laws before British subjects could sue for recovery.[14]

The first occasion in which a Virginia judge acting in his official capacity expressed an opinion in favor of British creditors was the case of *Page* v.

---

[10] Evans, "Planter Indebtedness," *WMQ*, 3d ser., XIX (1962), 511.

[11] Pendleton to Madison, 31 Mar. 1783 (Hutchinson et al., *Papers of Madison*, VI, 422-23).

[12] Hening, *Statutes*, IX, 368, 380; John Warden to William Hay, 22 June 1799 (Claim of John Hay and Co., T. 79/27).

[13] Deposition of Benjamin Waller, Jr., 12 Sept. 1810, p. 2 (Claim of Robert Cary and Co., T. 79/3); William Hay to William Moore Smith, 3 Feb. 1799 (Claim of John Hay and Co., T. 79/27).

[14] John Warden to William Hay, 22 June 1799 (Claim of John Hay and Co., T. 79/27); William Nelson, Jr., to Jefferson, 22 Nov. 1790 (Boyd et al., *Papers of Jefferson*, XVIII, 57).

Pendleton, decided on 3 May 1793 in the High Court of Chancery. Chancellor George Wythe forthrightly declared that payments made by the plaintiff's testator into the state loan office under the sequestration law of 1777 did not discharge the testator's debts to British creditors. This suit, however, could not properly be called one for the recovery of a British debt. Both parties were Virginians, and the purpose of the decree was to instruct the plaintiff as executor not to distinguish between British and other creditors in distributing the assets of the estate. Wythe's opinion established no precedent, for when word of it circulated soon after at the sitting of the federal circuit court, the chancellor was rebuked for "having officiously given Opinions on Points, which he was not bound in that Case, to decide." [15] At that very term the federal court upheld loan office payments as a lawful discharge of British debts.[16]

The establishment of a federal court system in 1789 opened a new and brighter prospect of recovery to British merchants. Jurisdiction of civil suits between foreigners and American citizens for claims exceeding $500 was vested in circuit courts, which were held in districts corresponding to each of the states. The bench consisted of any two justices of the federal Supreme Court and the judge of the federal district court, any two of whom constituted a quorum. The Supreme Court justices associated with the district court judge changed from term to term, as they rode circuit on a rotating basis—an arrangement that was not well designed for the efficient dispatch of business. The court in Virginia—officially called the Court of the United States, Middle Circuit, District of Virginia—convened on 22 May and 22 November of each year, at first alternately in Charlottesville and Williamsburg, then permanently at Richmond. It held its first session in May 1790 at Charlottesville.[17]

To British plaintiffs the restriction of federal jurisdiction to claims above $500, or £150 Virginia currency, was a serious drawback, particularly to the Scottish merchants. The largest class of debts in Virginia was contracted at stores throughout the Piedmont region operated by factors for Scottish

---

[15] George Wythe, *Decisions of Cases in Virginia by the High Court of Chancery*... (Richmond, 1852), pp. 211-18; William Hay to William Moore Smith, 3 Feb. 1799; John Warden to William Hay, 22 June 1799 (Claim of John Hay and Co., T. 79/27).

[16] This was the case of *Ware, Administrator of Jones, v. Hylton*, discussed below.

[17] *The Public Statutes at Large of the United States of America*... (17 vols.; Boston, 1848-73), I, 75; Julius Goebel, Jr., *Antecedents and Beginnings to 1801*, in *The Oliver Wendell Holmes Devise History of the Supreme Court of the United States*, ed. Paul A. Freund, I (New York, 1971), 472, 554-59; U.S. Circuit Court, Va., Order Book (hereafter cited as O.B.) I, 1. After meeting once in Charlottesville and Williamsburg, the court settled permanently at Richmond beginning at the May 1791 term (*U.S. Statutes at Large*, I, 217).

firms. Most of these debts fell below the federal jurisdictional amount.[18] Nevertheless, the accumulated interest and rate of exchange on many smaller debts brought them up to the required sum. A bond to secure payment of £75 also qualified because the suit was brought for the penal sum of £150.[19]

The great majority of cases filed in the federal circuit court of Virginia during its early years were for the recovery of prewar British debts. More than a hundred were brought at the first term and within a year the docket exceeded two hundred. This was not a large number of cases, however, and many more eligible creditors apparently preferred to wait for a ruling on the special defenses put in by the Virginia debtors.[20] The most conspicuous plaintiffs in the early cases were William Jones, surviving partner of the Bristol firm of Farell and Jones, and James and Robert Donald and Company of Glasgow. Before the war Farell and Jones traded extensively with the larger Tidewater planters and merchants on terms typical of the commission or consignment system: In return for shipments of tobacco or other produce, the Bristol firm sold the produce, shipped goods and paid the insurance on return cargoes, and paid bills of exchange drawn on them. J. and R. Donald and Company conducted business by direct purchase of tobacco and sale of goods and supplies within the colony through resident factors, who managed a network of stores throughout the Piedmont and central Southside regions of the colony.[21]

Whether they traded on consignment with English merchants or by direct purchase with Scottish factors, Virginia planters incurred indebtedness through liberal extensions of credit. Accounts were settled annually, with the planter's indebtedness either carried to a new ledger or (if the balance had become too large) liquidated by means of a bond. In giving

---

[18] Evans, "Private Indebtedness," *WMQ*, 3d ser., XXVIII (1971), 349-50; William Hay, Remarks on the Answer of the Attorney General of the United States to the Memorial of William Cunningham & Company . . . , 15 May 1798, p. 24 (Claim of John Hay and Co., T. 79/27).

[19] Richard Hanson to William Jones, 10 July 1790, 17 Aug. 1791 (Claim of J. T. Ware, T. 79/30).

[20] U.S. Circuit Court, Va., Rule Book (hereafter cited as R.B.) I, 1-51. James Monroe to Jefferson, 1 May 1792 (*American State Papers: Documents, Legislative and Executive, of the Congress of the United States . . . ,Class I: Foreign Relations,* I [Washington, D.C., 1833], 234).

[21] During the first three terms, Farell and Jones brought thirty cases; J. and R. Donald and Co. brought forty-eight (U.S. Circuit Court, Va., R.B. I, 1-51). On Farell and Jones, see W. E. Minchinton, *The Trade of Bristol in the Eighteenth Century* (Bristol, 1957), pp. 170-71; Memorial of John Tyndale Ware, 16 Oct. 1798 (Claim of J. T. Ware, T. 79/30). On J. and R. Donald and Co., see Memorial of Robert Donald, Sr., Andrew Donald, and Alexander Donald, Sr., surviving partners of J. and R. Donald and Co., 18 May 1799 (Claim of J. and R. Donald and Co., T. 79/15). For a succinct discussion of the consignment and the Scottish factor methods of trading in colonial Virginia, see Richard B. Sheridan, "The British Credit Crisis of 1772 and the American Colonies," *Journal of Economic History*, XX (1960), 168-69, and sources cited there.

his personal bond the planter solemnly bound himself to pay a certain sum of money by a certain day. Suits brought on defaulted bonds constituted the largest class of British debt cases in the federal court. Bond debts enjoyed the highest priority and dignity in law and could be proved simply by producing the original written instrument in court. Another large category of cases arose on unsettled or open accounts. Proving these debts involved considerable trouble and expense—"they are what I most dread," wrote the agent of Farell and Jones.[22] A third type of British debt case, occurring much less frequently than the other two, consisted of those brought on bills of exchange protested for nonacceptance or nonpayment. These debts were more or less self-evident as long as the plaintiff produced the bill and notarized protest.

For each of these three kinds of cases there was an appropriate form of action at common law, in which the plaintiff filed his "declaration" and the defendant his "pleas." The purpose of these pleadings, which could go through several stages of alternating statements, responses, and denials, was to arrive at some specific issue or issues of fact for a jury to decide or of law for the judges to decide. The distinctive feature of the British debt cases, what defined them as such, was that in addition to the regular common law pleas, the Virginia debtors entered a set of special pleas grounded on the plaintiff's being a subject of Great Britain. Couched in the peculiar forms and language of the law, these special pleas in effect restated the Virginians' long-held opinions concerning the meaning and effect of the treaty of 1783. As presented in court the British debt pleas raised matters of "law" that would have to be decided before any issues of fact could be referred to a jury. If these special pleas were upheld, no jury trial would be needed; if not, the case would then proceed like any other debt case. Although in many of these cases, particularly those brought on bonds or bills, the debtor had no real defense other than the British debt pleas, his attorney always put in a general denial of indebtedness. Thus if he lost on the special pleas, the debtor would be assured of a trial by his Virginia peers, who in turn could be expected to bestow every advantage within their power upon the defendant.

When British plaintiffs sued out their writs in the spring of 1790, the lawyer most sought after by the debtors was John Marshall, the future chief justice, whose reputation as a practitioner placed him at the top of the Virginia bar. For whatever reasons—personal preference, political con-

[22] Richard Hanson to William Jones, 22 Oct. 1791 (Claim of J. T. Ware, T. 79/30).

Virginia Historical Society

John Marshall (1755-1835)

siderations, or simply because the debtors approached him first—Marshall decided to employ his professional talents in defending these suits. The entry of cases brought at the first term of the federal court shows his name for the defendant almost to the exclusion of any other.[23] Among those represented by Marshall were members of the political and social elite of Virginia: the Randolphs, Harrisons, Byrds, Carter Braxton, and Thomas Jefferson (as an executor of John Wayles). His clients were planters, great and small, and merchants such as the Richmond firms of Daniel L. Hylton and Pleasants and Company; the Manchester house of Trents, Crump and Bates; Roger Atkinson of Petersburg; and Williamsburg apothecary John M. Galt.[24]

As closely identified as he was with defending Virginians indebted to British merchants, Marshall unquestionably had major responsibility for drafting the special British debt pleas. So numerous were his cases and so lengthy were the texts of these pleadings that he soon found it necessary to have them printed. The case for the defendants originally consisted of two British debt pleas, later expanded to four. The first and (as the event showed) most important of these declared that the debtor's payment into the state loan office under the sequestration law of 1777 legally discharged him from the debt.[25] This plea of course was entered only where debtors had actually made loan office payments. Of the cases defended by Marshall approximately twenty included this defense. The other three special pleas were routinely filed in all cases. The second special plea interposed two other wartime acts of the General Assembly: that of 1779 "concerning escheats and forfeitures," which vested in the commonwealth all real and personal property belonging to British subjects; and that of 1782 prohibiting the recovery of British debts unless assigned to a citizen before 1 May 1777. Both acts were declared to be "unrepealed and still in force." The third plea alleged British infractions of the seventh article of the treaty, namely, the carrying off of the slaves and the continuing occupation of the Northwest posts, and other hostile acts such as supplying arms to Indian tribes at war with the United States. The purpose of this lengthy recital, which restated in legal phraseology the familiar refrain of the Virginia legislature, was to

---

[23] U.S. Circuit Court, Va., R.B. I, 1-14. For the plaintiff the names of Jerman Baker and Andrew Ronald predominate.

[24] The editors of the Papers of John Marshall are preparing a volume on Marshall's law practice, which will include a selection of his British debt cases.

[25] *Jones* v. *Walker*, U.S. Circuit Court, Va., Ended Cases (Restored), 1797. The pleas are in the hand of John Marshall, attorney for Thomas Walker. The printed forms survive in great numbers among the suit papers of the federal circuit court.

show that the treaty of peace was void and that a state of war still existed. The last and briefest of the British debt pleas simply asserted that the right of the plaintiff was "totally annulled" by the dissolution of the "then subsisting government" on 4 July 1776.

Once the debtor put in these special British debt defenses, all the cases followed a set ritual, suggesting a preconcerted agreement by counsel for both parties. The plaintiff joined issue on the defendant's general denial of indebtedness, which question was referred to the decision of a jury. The special pleas all terminated in "demurrers"; the plaintiff denied that these pleas, even if the facts alleged in them were true, were sufficient in law to bar him from recovering his debt. To the second, third, and fourth British debt pleas the plaintiff demurred immediately. The pleadings on the first, alleging loan office payments as a discharge of the debt, passed through several stages before reaching this point. Instead of demurring to the loan office plea, the plaintiff replied by setting up the fourth article of the treaty and the "supreme law" clause of the Constitution. The defendant thereupon "rejoined" by reciting British infractions of the peace treaty and asserting that the sum claimed by the plaintiff was not a bona fide debt due within the meaning of the treaty. The plaintiff then brought the pleadings to a close by demurring to this rejoinder. In this cumbersome way the parties insured that certain questions would come squarely before the judges as "legal" issues to decide.[26]

Did Marshall and other attorneys for the Virginia debtors seriously believe they could win on one or more of these special British debt pleas? Or did they employ them simply to drag out the proceedings as long as they could? If delay was the principal motive, then these pleas effectively served the purpose. Before a case could be placed on the court docket for trial, pleadings had to be filed at monthly meetings of the "rules" in the clerk's office. The additional special pleas made it more likely that a British debt case would linger at the rules beyond the time normally required for a debt case. Once all the issues of law and fact were joined and the case was transferred to the court docket, plaintiffs encountered another source of delay: the reluctance of the judges to rule on the merits of the pleas. No arguments were heard until November 1791, eighteen months after the first suits were

[26] For the subsequent pleadings on the loan office plea, see the report of *Ware* v. *Hylton*, decided at the Feb. 1796 term of the Supreme Court (Alexander J. Dallas, *Reports of Cases Ruled and Adjudged in the Several Courts of the United States, and of Pennsylvania*... [4 vols.; Philadelphia, 1790-1807], III, 202-7). Although the treaty question was presented in the pleadings on the loan office plea, it was necessary to have a separate plea on this point for the cases in which the loan office plea did not apply.

brought. Another eighteen months (three terms of court) elapsed before the court pronounced judgment. This prolonged silence of the judges bespoke the uncomfortable dilemma imposed upon them by the British debt pleas. Embedded in the formal, legalistic language were questions of great public moment that required the court to move beyond its accustomed role of applying and interpreting the common law. Were the laws of Virginia to yield to the treaty as the "supreme law of the land"? If the treaty automatically repealed conflicting state laws, did its operation extend beyond repeal to nullify actions (e.g., loan office payments) taken under them? Was the treaty of 1783 void and of no effect? Was it the province of the judiciary to declare treaties broken? Forced to venture into controversial areas of public policy, to decide issues that went to the definition of the newly created federal system, the judges procrastinated as long as they decently could.

The first hearing of arguments on the British debt pleas began on 24 November 1791 and continued for more than a week in the courtroom of the Capitol in Richmond. The federal circuit court at this term included two Virginians: District Court Judge Cyrus Griffin and Associate Justice John Blair. The third member of the bench was Associate Justice Thomas Johnson of Maryland. The case selected for the purpose was *Jones* v. *Walker*, one of the suits brought by the surviving partner of Farell and Jones. The defendant, Dr. Thomas Walker, a noted physician, soldier, explorer, and land speculator, had made a loan office payment of £2,150 (equivalent to £107 specie) on 25 May 1779 in discharge of his debt to the Bristol firm. The original attorneys in the case, Jerman Baker and John Marshall, were joined at the hearing by six of their colleagues, so that each side was represented by four of the ablest counsel of the Virginia bar: Baker, Andrew Ronald, John Wickham, and Burwell Starke for the plaintiff; Marshall, Patrick Henry, Alexander Campbell, and James Innes for the defendant.[27] A stenographic report of *Jones* v. *Walker* taken by David Robertson, the reporter of the Virginia ratifying convention debates of 1788, is unfortunately no longer extant. The only surviving record is the speech of Patrick Henry, as published in 1817 by William Wirt, who had access to Robertson's manuscript.[28]

Exploiting his knack for translating dry questions of law into personal terms, Henry predictably used the occasion to arraign the conduct of Great Britain during the war and since the peace—his purpose being to show that

[27] *Jones* v. *Walker*, U.S. Circuit Court, Va., Ended Cases (Restored), 1797; William Wirt, *Sketches of the Life and Character of Patrick Henry* (3d ed.; Philadelphia, 1818), pp. 318-19.
[28] Wirt, *Patrick Henry*, pp. 312-13.

the plaintiff's right of recovery was forfeited by the hostile acts of his monarch. " 'Those animosities, which the injustice of the British nation hath produced,' " he remarked at the outset of his impassioned address, " 'are necessarily brought forth. The conduct of that nation, which bore so hard upon us in the late contest, becomes once more the subject of investigation.' "[29] The defensive pleas had been artfully composed to make the case part and parcel of the continuing dispute between Great Britain and the United States over the enforcement of the peace treaty. Henry made the most of the situation, leaving no doubt among his audience as to who the real parties were before the bar of the court. For three days he held forth in the crowded courtroom, amplifying the points raised in the pleas: that debts were liable to confiscation in war; that Virginia was an independent nation competent to exercise the power to confiscate British debts and had in fact done so; that the debts were not revived by the treaty, which had been annulled and was of no effect; and that if it did remain in force, its operation did not extend to debts discharged by loan office payments.[30] Aside from affording public entertainment, the brilliant forensic efforts of Henry and his fellow attorneys were wasted. Judge Blair left the bench before the arguments commenced on account of his son's death and did not return until the end of the term. He was also reportedly unwilling to sit in the case because of a personal stake in the loan office payments. In Blair's absence Griffin and Johnson declined to give their opinions.[31]

Jones v. *Walker* was continued to the May 1792 term, when Griffin was joined by just one Supreme Court justice, James Wilson of Pennsylvania. Much to the disappointment of British plaintiffs, Wilson refused to decide on the points argued at the last term or to hear any suits for British debts, though more than a hundred were set for trial. The court adjourned after meeting only a week. Again at the November 1792 term only two judges attended, Griffin and William Cushing of Massachusetts. Illness prevented Chief Justice John Jay from accompanying Cushing—a "political sickness," muttered one frustrated creditor. The result was another suspension of the British business for want of a full court, though two made a quorum.[32] Finally, at the May 1793 term a full court was present: Griffin, Jay, and

[29] Ibid., p. 321.

[30] Ibid., pp. 321-69.

[31] U.S. Circuit Court, Va., O.B. I, 55, 81; William Madison to James Madison, 3 Dec. 1791 (Hutchinson et al., *Papers of Madison*, XIV, 136); Richard Hanson to William Jones, 29 Jan. 1792 (Claim of J. T. Ware, T. 79/30); James Monroe to Jefferson, 1 May 1792 (*Amer. State Papers: For. Rel.*, I, 234).

[32] U.S. Circuit Court, Va., O.B. I, 92, 121, 122; Richard Hanson to William Jones, 1 June, 14 Dec. 1792 (Claim of J. T. Ware, T. 79/30).

James Iredell of North Carolina. The plaintiff William Jones had since died, however, which meant that his numerous suits had to be revived by special writs in the name of his administrator, John Tyndale Ware. This could not be done before the session began, but to prevent still another postponement the court, with the defendant's consent, ordered one of the cases to be revived in Ware's name: the suit against Richmond merchant Daniel L. Hylton, which accordingly became the new test case.[33]

A second hearing on the British debt pleas took place between 24 May and 7 June 1793. On the latter date the court struck down three of the pleas, but on the loan office plea Iredell and Griffin overruled Jay, whose sympathy for the creditors was public knowledge, and declared that payments under Virginia's sequestration law were a lawful discharge of the debt.[34] Although no report of the attorneys' arguments was taken, the opinions of Iredell and Jay survive in published form.[35] That of Judge Iredell was included in the report of the appeal of *Ware* v. *Hylton* as heard by the Supreme Court in 1796. Jay's opinion, though published more than a century ago, has escaped scholarly attention because it appeared under another title in a volume of reports of cases in the federal circuit court of New York.[36]

Of the four special British debt pleas, the judges had the least difficulty dismissing the last, which alleged that the debt was annulled by the dis-

---

[33] U.S. Circuit Court, Va., O.B. I, 141.

[34] James Iredell to Mrs. Iredell, 20 May 1793 (Griffith J. McRee, *Life and Correspondence of James Iredell*, II [New York, 1858], 394-95; *Virginia Gazette and Richmond Manchester Advertiser*, 10 June 1793). In 1786 Jay as secretary for foreign affairs had written a report urging repeal of state laws in conflict with the treaty (Worthington Chauncey Ford et al., eds., *Journals of the Continental Congress, 1774-1789*, XXXI [Washington, D.C., 1934], 781-874).

[35] David Robertson did not report the second hearing because "he was informed by the counsel, that it would be nothing more than a repetition of the first; and he adds, that he was afterwards told it was much inferior" (Wirt, *Patrick Henry*, p. 313). Iredell kept notes of the trial, written in a minute scrawl that is nearly impossible to read. A surviving manuscript notebook, with a rough transcription by J. A. C. Grant, is now at the Law Library of the Library of Congress. It begins with Henry's recapitulation on 29 May, followed by the arguments of Marshall (29-30 May), Campbell (30 May), Innes (31 May), and Wickham (31 May-1 June). I am indebted to John Semonche of the University of North Carolina and to James R. Perry of the Documentary History of the Supreme Court of the United States, 1789-1801, for identifying and locating this source.

[36] Iredell did not participate in the decision of the appeal but did read his circuit court opinion, which Dallas included in his report (Dallas, *Reports*, III, 256 n.). Jay's opinion was published under the title of *Jones* v. *Walker*, the original test case (Elijah Paine, Jr., *Reports, Circuit Court, United States, Second Circuit*. . . [2 vols.; New York, 1827-56], II, 688). The editor of the second volume noted that the case was from the federal circuit court of Virginia, but no date was given. The statement of facts preceding the opinion describes the Walker case, but the opinion itself was clearly the one Jay delivered in *Ware* v. *Hylton* in June 1793. A likely explanation is that Jay wrote his opinion beforehand on the assumption that Walker would still be the test case. No manuscript has been located, and the circumstances of its publication in Paine are unknown. Subsequent citations of this opinion are to the text as reprinted in *Federal Cases [1789-1880]* (30 vols.; St. Paul, 1894-97), XIII, No. 7, 507, 1059-69. No opinion, if one ever existed, by Judge Griffin has been found.

solution of the former government. This was, in fact, given up during the course of argument, inconsistent as it was with the acts recited in the other pleas that explicitly recognized the continued existence of British debts. Also quickly abandoned was that part of the second plea grounded on the 1779 act "concerning escheats and forfeitures from British subjects," vesting in the state the real and personal property of British subjects. Though the plea alleged that British debts were personal property, by its very words the act was not "to extend to debts due to British subjects, and payable into the loan office." As Jay charitably remarked, this act "must have been inadvertently pleaded." [37]

This left the other two acts of Virginia pleaded in bar to the plaintiff's action: the 1777 sequestration law and the 1782 act prohibiting recovery of British debts unless assigned to a citizen before 1 May 1777. First, however, the court had to confront the allegations of British infractions of the peace treaty made in the third plea and also in the subsequent pleadings on the loan office plea. If this plea was good, there was no need to consider the others. Because the formalities of pleading required him to demur, the plaintiff in a technical sense admitted the truth of the allegations. The real question was whether these facts had any legal consequences. Did they show that a state of war still existed and that the plaintiff as an alien enemy was barred from American courts, or that the treaty was void and the plaintiff could claim no benefit under it? Neither Jay nor Iredell seriously regarded the notion that the two countries were at war, but each gave close and careful attention to the matter of the treaty's voidability. Both judges adroitly rejected the expansive view of judicial power that necessarily resulted from admitting the sufficiency of this plea. Granting that questions concerning the validity of treaties properly fell within the cognizance of the judiciary, Jay reasoned that this power extended only to "judicial" concerns such as whether they had been made and ratified according to prescribed forms. Courts, said Iredell, were "entirely incompetent" to decide the policy questions "of extreme magnitude" involved in pronouncing a treaty void. Even admitting that the treaty had become "voidable" by the infractions, the court had to consider it valid and obligatory until either Congress or the president and Senate declared it void by some positive act.[38]

With the treaty held to be in full force, the only remaining props supporting the debtors' cause were the Virginia laws. Jay easily disposed of

[37] Hening, *Statutes*, X, 70; Dallas, *Reports*, III, 257-58; *Federal Cases*, XIII, No. 7, 507, 1061, 1064.

[38] *Federal Cases*, XIII, No. 7, 507, 1061-63; Dallas, *Reports*, III, 258-62 (quotations on p. 260).

the 1782 act on the ground that the legislature intended it to operate only during the war and for the purpose of preventing alien enemies from recovering their debts by fraudulent assignments. He insisted that the plaintiff had a good right to bring his action after the war even without the fourth article. Iredell allowed the act its fullest operation as a general prohibition against recovery of all British debts, but held that it was repealed by the treaty of peace. He conceded, however, that the repeal became effective only with the adoption of the Constitution. Until then the act remained in force as a bar to recovery by British creditors.[39]

The case for the debtors thus came down to the first plea, that payments into the loan office discharged the debtor. Much the greater portion of the judges' opinions centered on this plea, no doubt reflecting a proportionate share of attention in the arguments at the bar. In allowing the sufficiency of this plea, Iredell accepted the defense argument that Virginia had full authority to enact the sequestration law by virtue of a general right of confiscation belonging to all nations at war. Confiscation, he admitted, was contrary to the "customary" law of nations adopted by civilized countries but was de facto binding if enacted by sovereign authority. The sequestration law, he believed, did not amount to an outright confiscation or complete extinguishing of the debt. Its effect rather was to substitute the state in place of the British creditor. It exonerated the debtor, though it did not take away the right of the creditor to apply to the commonwealth for payment. As for the treaty, the North Carolina jurist contended that it could not retrospectively destroy the private rights of Virginians acquired while the sequestration law was in force unless the text contained express words to that effect. In short, the debts contemplated by the fourth article did not include those discharged by loan office payments.[40]

Jay opposed Iredell at every point. While giving the fullest operation to the treaty to annul loan office payments and insisting that the words of the fourth article unambiguously comprehended debts discharged in this manner, the chief justice went even further to suggest that independently of the treaty the sequestration law did not constitute a bar to recovery. The preamble, he noted, explicitly disavowed any intention to confiscate debts as contrary to "the law and usages of nations." A close scrutiny of the enacting clauses satisfied him that British debts, as distinguished from other property mentioned in the act, were not even to be sequestered. The pay-

---

[39] *Federal Cases*, XIII, No. 7, 507, 1064; Dallas, *Reports*, III, 258, 276-78.

[40] Dallas, *Reports*, III, 262-80.

ments into the loan office, for example, were to be voluntary. Jay concluded that the Virginia assembly regarded itself as bound by the customary law of nations and intended only to prevent payment to British creditors during the war.[41]

In the end the difference between Iredell and Jay was this: The former would have the creditor seek redress by petitioning the state, the latter by suing the original debtor. To the parties, however, the practical consequences of this difference were of great importance. In 1788 the assembly had enacted legislation reducing the commonwealth's liability for sums paid into the loan office to the actual specie amount. Who was to suffer the loss resulting from the depreciation of paper money? Interestingly, the 1788 act did not identify the party to whom the state was liable, explaining that "it belongs not to the legislature to decide particular questions, of which the judiciary have cognizance, and it is therefore unfit for them to determine whether the payments so made into the loan office . . . be good or void between the creditor and debtor."[42]

The decision of *Ware* v. *Hylton* on 7 June 1793 cleared away all but one of the special British debt defenses. Jay's dissent on the loan office plea persuaded the plaintiff's agent to appeal that part of the decision to the Supreme Court. He was unable to bring an immediate appeal, however, because a formal judgment in the case could not be rendered at this term of the federal circuit court. After ruling on the special pleas, the court referred to a jury the issue of payment of that portion of Hylton's debt that had not been paid into the loan office. Jay charged the jurors to bring in a verdict for the principal and full interest. The jury found for the creditor on the principal, but despite their instructions could not agree on whether to disallow interest for the eight years of the war. The upshot was that judgment—and thus an appeal—in the Hylton case was postponed for another year. The Supreme Court did not finally hear the appeal until February 1796, when the four sitting justices—Samuel Chase, William Paterson, James Wilson, and William Cushing—unanimously reversed the circuit court's decision and threw out the last of the special pleas.[43]

---

[41] Hening, *Statutes*, IX, 378; *Federal Cases*, XIII, No. 7, 507, 1064-69.

[42] Hening, *Statutes*, XII, 529-30. Jay cited this act as proof that the Virginia legislature considered debts paid into the loan office as still subsisting after the war: "Here, then, the legislature of Virginia recognizes the plaintiff in the capacity of creditor, and the defendant in that of debtor, although, with great delicacy, they forbear touching the question in difference between them" (*Federal Cases*, XIII, No. 7, 507, 1068). In 1784 a bill was introduced into the legislature making the debtors who made loan office payments liable for deficiency between paper money and specie (Madison to Jefferson, 9 Jan. 1785 [Hutchinson et al., *Papers of Madison*, VIII, 231]).

[43] Richard Hanson to John Tyndale Ware, 9 June 1793 (Claim of J. T. Ware, T. 79/30);

Possessing at best only dubious legal merit, the British debt pleas nonetheless brilliantly succeeded in delaying the day of reckoning for the Virginia debtors. The strategic purpose Marshall and other lawyers for the debtors had in mind seems clear enough. They meant to keep the cases tied up in court as long as possible in the hope that diplomacy might resolve the British debt problem—preferably by an agreement that would shift the burden of liability from the individual debtors to the public at large. At the very least the long postponement of a decision by the court would give the debtors breathing space to recover some measure of prosperity and regain the means of paying their debts.

With all but one of the special defenses declared invalid by the federal circuit court in June 1793, British creditors at the ensuing November term regularly began to obtain judgments on liquidated debts such as bonds and protested bills of exchange.[44] Although these cases, stripped of their special pleas, were now supposedly on the same footing as any other debt cases, juries soon gave notice that British debts would continue to receive distinctive treatment. A hung jury in *Ware* v. *Hylton* left unresolved the question of deducting interest during the war years. At the November 1793 term presiding judge William Paterson, like Jay before him, instructed the jury to allow full interest on British debts. This time the jurors unanimously deducted eight years' interest, following the example of the Virginia legislature's proposed installment plan of 1784. Judge Paterson at first refused to accept this verdict. He sent the jurors back repeatedly, but they were "all interested" and refused to yield. In all subsequent verdicts in British debt cases, juries routinely subtracted war interest.[45]

No issue in the politics and law of British debts was more bitterly disputed than the suspension of war interest. However divided in opinion they may have been concerning their obligation to pay the principal, Virginians were nearly unanimous in believing that they were morally and legally absolved from paying this interest. In deducting it Virginia juries could point to a practice that was common in private settlements after the war. In

---

Phineas Bond to Lord Grenville, 25 June 1793 ("Letters of Phineas Bond," *Annual Report of the American Historical Association for the Year 1897* [Washington, D.C., 1898], p. 534); *Ware* v. *Hylton* (Dallas, *Reports*, III, 199-285).

[44] Cases involving loan office payments were suspended until after the Supreme Court decided *Ware* v. *Hylton* in 1796.

[45] John Hamilton to Lord Grenville, 11 Dec. 1793 (Foreign Office [hereafter cited as F.O.], Class 5/ Vol. 2, P.R.O.); A Brief State of the Case of the British Merchants Trading to North America Previous to the Year 1776, 18 Mar. 1794 (F.O. 95/512). The 1784 plan disallowed interest for the period of hostilities, 19 Apr. 1775 to 3 Mar. 1783 (Madison to James Monroe, 4 Dec. 1784 [Hutchinson et al., *Papers of Madison*, VIII, 175]).

many instances British creditors did relinquish accumulated war interest—as, for example, the agent of Farell and Jones did in settling with the executors of John Wayles. This usually happened, however, only when the creditor had a good prospect of receiving the principal. Those who were forced to pursue their debtors into court for payment of the principal refused this indulgence, regarding war interest as a just penalty for being kept out of their debts for so long.[46]

The most elaborate exposition of the Virginia point of view was penned by Secretary of State Thomas Jefferson in his diplomatic correspondence with British minister George Hammond in 1792, which was published about the time the federal court in Virginia began to give judgments in British debt cases.[47] The secretary of state, a trained lawyer, put forward an array of legal and equitable arguments to justify the denial of full interest to British creditors. His main contention was that "interest is not part of the debt, neither comprehended in the thing, nor in the term," a maxim that he insisted held true in every country, even a commercially advanced one like England. Citing numerous precedents from English law, Jefferson observed that the allowance of interest in that country was not based on express law, "but rests on the *discretion of judges and juries*, as the arbiters of damages." They awarded or withheld interest according to the particular circumstances of each case. The "universal devastation" that occurred in many of the states during the war and consequent destruction of profits from lands were circumstances that weighed heavily in American minds in favor of suspending interest, the secretary explained.[48]

In essence Jefferson's views amounted to "no slaves, no interest." Virginia juries no doubt acted on this simple equation in reaching their verdicts in British debt cases. The practice of deducting war interest eventually received judicial sanction in the highest court of the commonwealth. In 1797 the court of appeals, echoing Jefferson, held that juries had broad equitable powers to determine what was due of principal and interest on bond debts. The judges readily concurred with the jury's abatement of war interest even though there had been no payment of principal. Presiding judge Edmund

---

[46] "Memorandum of Agreement between Richard Hanson and Executors of John Wayles," 7 Feb. 1790 (Boyd et al., *Papers of Jefferson*, XV, 675); Phineas Bond to Lord Grenville, 12 Oct. 1792 ("Letters of Phineas Bond," *A.H.A. Annual Report*, pp. 518-19).

[47] Jefferson to Hammond, 29 May 1792 (*Amer. State Papers: For. Rel.*, I, 201-37), originally published as an appendix to *A Message of the President of the United States to Congress Relative to France and Great-Britain, Delivered December 5, 1793*... (Philadelphia, 1793).

[48] *Amer. State Papers: For. Rel.*, I, 213-14. Jefferson went on to show that the deduction of war interest was the general practice in American courts, though not a universal one.

Pendleton delivered a tartly worded opinion that read more like an inflammatory political tract than a solemn judicial pronouncement. Independent of the treaty, he said, British creditors "were not entitled in justice to recover one shilling of their *principal* debts from the debtors." These he conceded were recoverable by the treaty, but interest formed no part of the debt. Reminded by counsel for the creditor of Chief Justice Jay's charge to the jury in the Hylton case, Pendleton was unmoved: "I have no doubt but he gave that opinion with the like sincerity, as I have delivered mine to the contrary, and mankind if they think it worth while, will judge between us."[49]

In the federal court, justices like Jay and Paterson might instruct juries that plaintiffs were in law entitled to full interest, but they were virtually powerless to overrule general verdicts. All they could do was order a new trial, which answered no good purpose since the result would probably be the same. In *Ware* v. *Hylton* the plaintiff's counsel proposed a special verdict, which would have referred the question of interest to the court, but the jurors refused.[50] Since at common law, errors in a general verdict could only be corrected by a new trial, the disallowance of war interest that formed part of this verdict could not be appealed to a higher court. This weighty question was thus never presented for adjudication to the Supreme Court. The appeal in *Ware* v. *Hylton* determined only the question of law arising from the loan office plea.[51]

Unable to recover war interest on judgments for debts due by bond or protested bills of exchange, British merchants could not without great difficulty even secure judgments on unliquidated debts arising upon open accounts. Suits for the recovery of these debts could be defeated by the statute of limitations and the strict enforcement of the rules for proving "book debts." These obstacles worked particular hardship on the Scottish firms in the retail trade before the war. Since the limitation of actions applied equally to American and British merchants and the same evidence was required of both to establish book debts, these were not overt legal impediments to recovery. Their effect, complained the British, was nevertheless discriminatory

---

49 *McCall* v. *Turner* (Daniel Call, *Reports of Cases Argued and Decided in the Court of Appeals of Virginia* [6 vols.; Richmond, 1801-33], I, 133-47 [quotations on pp. 143, 146]).

50 Richard Hanson to John Tyndale Ware, 9 June 1793 (Claim of J. T. Ware, T. 79/30).

51 Lawyers presumably could have contrived some means of bringing the question up to the high court, but no case embracing this issue was decided. See the remarks of Justice Bushrod Washington in the case of *Conn* v. *Penn*, decided in 1818 in the federal circuit court of Pennsylvania (Richard Peters, Jr., *Reports of Cases Argued and Determined in the Circuit Court of the United States, for the Third Circuit* . . . [Philadelphia, 1819], pp. 523-24).

and discouraged them from bringing suits. One attorney advised his British clients not to sue unless they could produce evidence of a renewed assumption of the debt since the peace.[52]

In Virginia the limitation for actions brought on open account was five years. A saving clause protected foreigners "beyond the sea, or out of the country" from the operation of the statute, but foreign merchants with resident factors—e.g., the Scottish firms—were not exempted.[53] Although the assembly subtracted five years from the limitation computation owing to the closing of the courts during the war, this suspension was of little benefit to British plaintiffs bringing suit in the 1790s. In cases where the plaintiff had not obtained a new promise to pay or had not sued his debtor immediately after the war, the statute of limitations was successfully pleaded in both state and federal courts. To no avail were the counter pleadings by plaintiffs that they were ordered out of Virginia during the war, that they were effectively excluded from the courts after the peace, and that they were creditors within the meaning of the treaty.[54]

Not all Virginians rushed to take full advantage of the statute of limitations. The bitter experience of the war had not completely vitiated their sense of honor or concern for reputation. In some instances, at least, they pleaded limitation or threatened to do so not to escape payment altogether but to obtain favorable terms from their creditors.[55] The British objections to pleading the act of limitations were ultimately sustained, but not until after the Convention of 1802 reaffirmed the fourth article of the 1783 treaty. The Supreme Court in 1806 ruled that the statute of limitations could not bar recovery of British debts contracted less than five years before the Revolution.[56]

If his case was not barred by the general statute of limitations, the open account creditor still had to prove his debt. Here he unhappily discovered that proof of his books by his own oath would not be admitted as evidence. Such ex parte proof had been routinely accepted in the courts before the

---

[52] Affidavit of James Webb, 24 Jan. 1804 (Claim of McCall and Shedden, T. 79/7).

[53] Hening, *Statutes*, III, 381-84; VI, 481; Samuel Shepherd, *The Statutes at Large of Virginia ... in Three Volumes*, I (Richmond, 1835), 29.

[54] John Bassett Moore, ed., *International Adjudications, Ancient and Modern: History and Documents ...* (8 vols.; New York, 1929-36), III, 64-66. For a case in the federal court in which Marshall successfully pleaded the statute of limitations, see *Asselby* v. *Pleasants*, U.S. Circuit Court, Va., Ended Cases (Restored), 1793.

[55] Roger Atkinson, Jr., to Robert Fearon, 3 Feb. 1794 (Claim of Richard Hanson, T. 79/17). In the Asselby case cited in the preceding note, the defendants confessed judgment after working out a compromise with their creditor.

[56] *Hopkirk* v. *Bell* (William Cranch, *Reports of Cases Argued and Adjudged in the Supreme Court of the United States [1801-1815]* [9 vols.; Washington, D.C., 1804-17], III, 454; IV, 194).

Revolution and indeed was sanctioned by law. The Virginia statute "prescribing the method of proving book debts," enacted in 1748, permitted a merchant to submit his store books, proved by his oath, as good evidence if he brought his action within two years of delivering the articles charged.[57] This statutory departure from common law rules of evidence greatly facilitated the retail trade by promoting easy credit. The merchant, confident of proving his debts, liberally extended credit from year to year, demanding a bond (regarded as a "mark of distrust") only in "perilous cases." The courts, in turn, equitably interpreted the law, customarily ignoring the two-year limitation for bringing suit as long as the merchant proved his books before a magistrate within that time. Indeed, this was the usual means of proving such debts, and the courts even disallowed costs for witnesses because the plaintiff could prove his accounts by his own oath.[58]

British merchants bringing suit after the war continued to have the benefit of the 1748 law, though the assembly in 1779 had eliminated the merchant's oath as admissible proof for debts contracted after 1 May 1780.[59] The old law was of little use to them, however, for the courts, both state and federal, now strictly enforced the two-year limitation on this kind of evidence. In effect plaintiffs had to fall back on common law rules of evidence, either by proving the delivery of the articles or by proving the handwriting of the factors, clerks, storekeepers, or agents—many of whom were now dead or had departed to distant places—who kept the books before the war. Without these proofs or a positive acknowledgment of the debt, suits brought on open account would not succeed in the courts.[60]

For British creditors the actual results of litigation in the federal circuit court of Virginia between 1790 and 1797 fell far short of their expectations of justice. The favorable rulings of 1793 and 1796 in the case of *Ware* v. *Hylton* failed to remove all the impediments to recovery. To be sure, by 1797 British plaintiffs were routinely winning judgments, though always with a deduction of interest for the war. A tally of the British debt cases decided during these years would show that the vast majority of judgments,

---

[57] Hening, *Statutes*, VI, 53-55.

[58] *The Reply of William Cunningham & Co. to the Answer of the United States*... (Philadelphia, 1798), pp. 25-26; William Hay, Considerations on the various Subjects of Enquiry..., 19 Feb. 1798, pp. 6-9 (Claim of John Hay and Co., T. 79/27).

[59] Hening, *Statutes*, X, 133.

[60] See the report of a federal case, *Bowman* v. *Patteson*, 1797 (Claim of Speirs, Bowman and Co., T. 79/11). For a state case, *McCall and Shedden* v. *Moore's Administrator*, King and Queen District Court, 1797, see St. George Tucker to William Davies, 9 Dec. 1798 (Claim of John Hay and Co., T. 79/27). See also Opinion of David Robertson, 4 Apr. 1806 (Claim of Buchanan, Hastie and Co., T. 79/25).

including open account suits, were in favor of the plaintiff. It is misleading, however, to measure the success of British creditors by the number of judgments won. They did not go to trial unless they had a good prospect of winning. The debtors, even if they expected to lose, wanted a jury trial in order to have the war interest deducted. Thus, a high winning percentage for British plaintiffs was to be expected. What this fails to show, of course, is how many creditors, particularly those by open account, were discouraged from bringing suits in the first place.

Those who gained judgments, moreover, were by no means assured of collecting their money. Owing to insolvencies, emigration, deaths, and alienation of property since the peace, executions—some for enormous sums—often yielded little or nothing to British creditors by the time they began to obtain judgments in 1793. A common complaint was that the estates of their debtors had already been absorbed in satisfying judgments previously obtained by Virginia or other American creditors, who of course had enjoyed access to the courts since the war.[61] The federal court was powerless to compensate British creditors for losses they had already sustained from the long delay in adjudicating their claims. Even an impartial hearing of their cases during the 1790s could not have done full justice to them at that late date.

Virginians were no more pleased with the proceedings in the federal court than were British litigants. As Anglo-American relations rapidly deteriorated toward crisis following outbreak of the European war in 1793 and declaration of American neutrality, anti-British hostility in the commonwealth intensified to a pitch of war fever. In December 1793, simultaneously

[61] On the difficulties in collecting British debt judgments, see Remarks on the Claim of Gibson Donaldson & Hamilton (Claim of Gibson Donaldson and Hamilton, T. 79/11); Deposition of Benjamin Waller, Jr., 12 Sept. 1810 (Claim of Robert Cary and Co., T. 79/3); Memorial of William Robertson Lidderdale (Claim of W. R. Lidderdale, T. 79/32). Among the largest class of claims brought before the British debt commissions were those in which the debtors had become insolvent, died, or removed to unknown parts since 1783. Accompanying the claims were long lists of names of debtors, with notations that the estate was "insolvent" or had been "squandered," that the debtor or his representative had moved away (often to Kentucky), and that executions on judgments had been returned "no effects." See Statement of Debts in Suit (Claim of J. and R. Donald and Co., T. 79/15). Richard Randolph and Thomas Mann Randolph, two of the richest planters in Virginia before the Revolution, died after the war deeply in debt to British merchants, having distributed most of their property to members of their families or to Virginia creditors. By 1797, when their British creditors finally obtained judgments in the federal court (two against Richard Randolph for $54,000 and four against Thomas M. Randolph amounting to almost $80,000), the executors were able to plead successfully that they had "fully administered" the assets of the estates. This meant that no execution could be levied except on such assets as might happen to come in at a later time. See *Ware, Administrator of Jones, v. R. Randolph's Executors* (two cases); *Ware, Administrator of Jones, v. T. M. Randolph's Executors*; and *Lidderdale's Executor v. T. M. Randolph's Executors* (three cases), U.S. Circuit Court, Va., Record Book, V, 360-74; VI, 126-62; VIII, 37-52; Moore, *International Adjudications*, III, 226-28.

with the first judgments in favor of British creditors in the federal court, the General Assembly called for a suspension of the fourth article of the peace treaty until Britain fulfilled its treaty obligations. The grand jury of the federal court soon echoed the legislature's sentiments by presenting "as a national grievance" the recovery of British debts until the British government complied with the treaty and made reparation for violations of American neutrality.[62] It was clear by the mid-1790s, if not earlier, that a resolution of the debts controversy could only come about as part of a general diplomatic settlement of all the outstanding points in dispute between the two countries.

With the signing of a new treaty in 1794, negotiated for the United States by John Jay, British debts were referred to an arbitration commission. The Jay Treaty also provided for the withdrawal of the British from the Northwest, removing one obstacle to the payment of the debts, though it was silent as to compensation for the slaves. The debts commission was to hear claims for losses allegedly arising from the operation of lawful impediments to recovery by British creditors since 1783 and for which full compensation could not be obtained "in the ordinary course of justice." Consisting of three British and two American members (the fifth seat fell by lot to a British subject), the commission was to determine cases according to "equity and justice." When the mixed commission began its work at Philadelphia in the spring of 1797, British claimants immediately shifted their attention from the courts to this quasi-judicial body. Arbitration, however, was not the answer. After two years the commission was dissolved by the withdrawal of the American members, who had consistently dissented from a series of rulings favorable to the claimants, including one that restored war interest.[63]

The proceedings at Philadelphia were only a temporary setback to the general rapprochement between the United States and Great Britain that began in the mid-1790s and lasted through Jefferson's first administration. In 1802 the two governments agreed to the expedient of a lump sum payment to the merchants. By the Convention of 1802 the United States paid Britain £600,000, which was distributed through a domestic commission that heard claims between 1803 and 1811. Though this sum was considerably less than that claimed by the merchants, the convention also reaffirmed

[62] *Journal of Va. House of Delegates*, Oct. 1793, pp. 101, 124-25, 128; Presentment of Grand Jury, May 1794, U.S. Circuit Court, Va., Ended Cases, 1794; O.B. I, 358.

[63] Miller, *Treaties and Other International Acts*, III, 249-51. The story of this commission is fully documented in Moore, *International Adjudications*, III.

the fourth article of the peace treaty, which in its future operation was "to be binding and obligatory."[64] The American courts were to remain open to British creditors for the recovery of their old debts, and the reaffirmation of the fourth article promised to place them on a more secure footing than they had been during the preceding two decades. In keeping with the spirit of this new understanding, the Supreme Court soon disallowed the statute of limitations as a defense against recovery.[65] This ultimate resolution of the British debts issue by means of a public diplomatic settlement and continued private litigation reflected the dual political and legal dimensions of the controversy that had been present since the beginning.

[64] Bradford Perkins, *The First Rapprochement: England and the United States, 1795-1805* (Philadelphia, 1955), pp. 138-41; Moore, *International Adjudications*, III, 359-433. The domestic commission eventually approved claims amounting to £1,400,000; hence the dividend on a successful claim was less than 50 percent. The British never made compensation for the slaves, though this might have been taken into account in arriving at the sum agreed to as compensation for the debts.

[65] *Hopkirk* v. *Bell*, decided in 1806 (Cranch, *Reports*, III, 454; IV, 164).

The First Federal Question Case

Wythe Holt

What is a 'federal question'? Section two of article three of the Constitution grants jurisdiction to federal courts over, among other items, 'all cases in law and equity, arising under this Constitution, the laws of the United States, and treaties made . . . under their authority'.[1] This has become generally known as the grant of 'federal question' jurisdiction. The present statute giving such jurisdiction to federal courts dates only from 1875;[2] not only has it been restrictively construed,[3] but existing federal schemes of benefits, rights, and regulations provide us with a familiar, pat, confining notion of the nature of federal questions. What sorts of matters might have

Wythe Holt is Professor of Law at the University of Alabama. This essay was delivered in earlier forms at Emory University School of Law and the University of Chicago Law School. Funding for research was thankfully provided by grants from Dean Charles W. Gamble and the University of Alabama School of Law. Pleasant, efficient, and necessary support was given by Mary Ann Hawkins, Charles Reeves, and others on the staff of the Federal Archives and Records Center in East Point, Georgia; by Robert Plowman and others on the staff of the Federal Archives and Records Center in Philadelphia; by the staff at the Federal Archives and Records Center in Waltham, Massachusetts; and by the staffs at the Library of Congress, the Massachusetts Historical Society, and the libraries of Emory University, the University of North Carolina, the University of Georgia, the University of Virginia, and the College of William and Mary, for all of which the author is most grateful. The author also wishes to thank Professors Kathryn Preyer, Wilfred Ritz, Larry Yackle, and John Langbein for their helpful suggestions and their support.

1. U.S. Const. Art. III, §2.
2. Judiciary Act of Mar. 3, 1875, ch. 137, §§1, 2, 18 Stat. 470.
3. See, e.g., Al Katz, 'The Jurisprudence of Remedies: Constitutional Legality and the Law of Torts in *Bell v. Hood*', 117 *University of Pennsylvania Law Review* 1 (1968); Paul J. Mishkin, 'The Federal "Question" in the District Courts', 53 *Columbia Law Review* 157 (1953); James H. Chadbourn and A. Leo Levin, 'Original Jurisdiction of Federal Questions', 90 *University of Pennsylvania Law Review* 639 (1942); Note, 'The Outer Limits of "Arising Under"', 54 *New York University Law Review* 978 (1979). See also infra note 43 and accompanying text.

been expected to constitute federal questions in 1787, when the Constitution was written, and when such schemes were not contemplated much less established?

It is my thesis that great potential was hidden in those vague but suggestive words by the Framers, a potential that could be exploited by those who wished to have a strong centralized government. Further, it is my contention that the Federalist Party, in making the first grant of 'federal question' jurisdiction (in the Judiciary Act of 1801[4]), exploited those words to the fullest. Only one case was ever brought under that Act in which its limits and meaning might have been tested,[5] since the Jeffersonians quickly repealed it when they came into power; but that case helps to demonstrate the vast possibilities inherent in the Constitutional concept of 'federal questions'.

I

The problem is cast in the best light only when we forget modern connotations and transport ourselves back into the language of the past. We must also look outside the 'law' to its social and political context, to the federalism debates of the 1780s, 1790s, and 1800s. Founders and other citizens tended to polarize over the question of the power and authority of the new federal government relative to those of the governments of the sovereign states which adopted the Constitution.[6] Many (including most of those who wrote the Constitution) found serious flaws in the loose Confederacy which won the Revolution, and thought the solution to be a strong, powerful, active central government. Many others were fearful of the dangers which a powerful central force posed; they were aggressively happy with the notion that the various states would provide what strength of government proved to be necessary.

Engulfed in the debate over federalism, the first Congress did not make any explicit reference to 'arising under' jurisdiction in the Judiciary Act of 1789.[7] When Congress in the 1790s legislated, pursuant to its Constitution-

4. Judiciary Act of Feb. 13, 1801, ch. 4, 2 Stat. 89.

5. *Hobby v. Day*, discussed in parts II and III, infra note 29.

6. See generally, e.g., Peter S. Onuf, *The Origins of the Federal Republic: Jurisdictional Controversies in the United States 1775-1787*, (Philadelphia, 1983) 149-209. I am indebted to Sandra vanBurkleo and Tony Freyer for bringing this volume to my attention.

7. Today, usage demands that important statutes allocating federal jurisdiction be called 'Judiciary Acts'. Congress did not utilize this term in the early period, nor was apparently it a term of common parlance then. The first act dealing with the federal courts was called 'An Act to establish the Judicial Courts of the United States', Sept. 24, 1789, ch. 20, 1 Stat. 73, while the Federalist statute which revised the scheme in large part was called 'An Act to provide for the more convenient organization of the Courts of the United States', Feb. 13, 1801, ch. 4, 2 Stat. 89. These have come respectively to be known, however, as the Judiciary Act of 1789 and the Judiciary Act of 1801, and so they

ally-granted powers, to make laws concerning patents and copyrights,[8] and to 'establish . . . uniform laws on the subject of bankruptcies',[9] each act carried with it a special grant of federal jurisdiction,[10] lessening the possibility that an aggrieved party might claim that a contract dispute over a patent or a tort dispute during a bankruptcy was one 'arising under' federal laws and thus arguably within the competency of the federal courts.[11] At times federal plaintiffs during the 1790s were careless or imprecise (under modern standards) in their allegations concerning jurisdiction, and at times they used fictions (such as a fictitious allegation of the amount in controversy) to obtain federal jurisdiction,[12] but I have been unable to discover a single attempt by a bold litigant or attorney to claim federal jurisdiction in a civil case on what they might have called, or what we would now call, 'federal question' grounds before 1801.[13]

---

will be called (and cited to) henceforth in this essay. This usage is also followed with other similar Acts.

The Judiciary Act of 1789 made no reference to cases 'arising under' federal law, not even in its grant of appellate jurisdiction from state courts to the Supreme Court. See Judiciary Act of 1789, §25.

8. U.S. Const. Art. I, §8, cl. 7.

9. U.S. Const. Art. I, §8, cl. 3.

10. See An Act to promote the progress of the useful Arts; and to repeal the act heretofore made for that purpose, Feb. 21, 1793, ch. 11, §§5, 6, 1 Stat. 322; An Act to establish an uniform System of Bankruptcies throughout the United States, Apr. 4, 1800, ch. 19, §58, 2 Stat. 35 [hereinafter cited as Bankruptcy Act of 1800]. See also Judiciary Act of 1801, §12 (backstop grant of bankruptcy jurisdiction).

11. Wilfred Ritz has argued that the absence of an express 'arising under' grant of jurisdiction in the Judiciary Act of 1789 did not necessarily mean that there was no federal question jurisdiction in the federal courts. The constitutional provision might have been deemed mandatory or self-executing. See Wilfred J. Ritz, 'Rewriting the History of the Judiciary Act of 1789: Exposing Myths, Challenging Premises, and Using New Evidence', 67-75 (unpublished manuscript, 1983 version, in possession of its author); Robert N. Clinton, 'A Mandatory View of Federal Court Jurisdiction: A Guided Quest for the Original Understanding of Article III', 132 *University of Pennsylvania Law Review* 741 (1984). I am most grateful to Professor Ritz for his invitation to read his work in manuscript.

12. Wilfred Ritz has made a careful and convincing study of these cases and problems, insofar as evidence of sloppiness or fictitious allegations to obtain jurisdiction is given in early Supreme Court decisions. See Wilfred J. Ritz, 'The Expansion of Federal Court Jurisdiction in 1789-1798 By the Use of Jurisdictional Fictions', esp. pp. 17-21 (unpublished manuscript, 1983 version, in its author's possession). See also Julius Goebel, Jr., *History of the Supreme Court of the United States: vol. I, Antecedents and Beginnings to 1801*, (New York, 1971) 586-89, 683-85.

13. In a very important sense, I have already violated my own canon of construction, in the manner in which I have catered to modern thinking in the paragraph in the text preceding this superscript. The rhetoric of this paragraph *presumes* that federal jurisdictional grants are to be closely and strictly construed, so that plaintiff's allegations concerning jurisdiction must be precise. That is the sense of things ingrained into us by our modern legal

By 1800 many members of the Federalist Party, which then controlled the Presidency and both Houses of Congress, were apprehensive that Thomas Jefferson, and what they took to be his dangerous Jacobin Democrats, would carry the national elections set for November of that year. They viewed the states-rights and anti-commercial[14] principles of the Jeffersonians with an extremely jaundiced eye, typically predicting the downfall of American civilization, the destruction of the Constitution, and the end of economic progress should the Jeffersonians prevail.[15] Following the lead of Alexander Hamilton, these Federalists attempted to establish for the good of themselves and for the good of the country—matters which they viewed as synonymous—a safe haven of power in the federal judiciary, 'now almost the only security left to us—and it [the judiciary] is at all times the most important branch of the federal government', as the Federalist chair of the House judiciary committee wrote.[16] Another Federalist Congressman wrote, '[I]f this hostile spirit in the States should increase, the federal judicial system must increase with it.'[17]

---

education and experience, but it is anachronistic to transport this assumption back into the 1790s, using it to characterize plaintiffs' jurisdictional allegations as 'loose' or 'fictitious'.

Those in favor of strong central government would have concomitantly desired a broad and generous federal court jurisdiction, and not only would they have tended to file at least somewhat broadly or 'loosely' phrased pleadings as a matter of course but they would have also had an expectation of generous construction by sympathetic judges. Those of the states' rights persuasion would have desired a restricted federal court jurisdiction and would have argued for a strict, narrow approach to allegations concerning jurisdiction. Since this was a matter of serious dispute, it is misleading to use language which in effect takes one side of that dispute as being correct or timelessly 'normal'. I have occasionally used such language nevertheless since the lulling effect of its familiarity heightens the dramatic tension of an otherwise pedestrian legal history essay when finally contrasted with the strange, outlandish nature of the Federalist views of jurisdiction in 1800-02.

14. Here I am guilty of shorthand of a different sort. Many budding urban entrepreneurs, shopkeepers, and other more modern capitalists were adherents of Jefferson and of laissez-faire, but the banking, land-speculating, aristocratic 'old' wealth which provided much of the support for the Federalist vision of a government-nurtured and controlled economy did not cotton much to the newcomers' version of 'commerce', and thus concluded that the Jeffersonians were 'anti-commercial'. See generally Joyce Appleby, *Capitalism and a New Social Order: The Republican Vision of the 1790s*, (New York and London, 1984), 88-94, *passim*; Gary B. Nash, *The Urban Crucible: Social Change, Political Consciousness, and the Origins of the American Revolution* (Cambridge and London, 1979).

15. A flavor of the extreme fears and apprehensions entertained by the Federalist Party in the period 1800-02 can be gained by reading the debates in Congress over repeal of the Judiciary Act of 1801. See *Debates and Proceedings in the Congress of the United States* Vols., (Washington, 1851) xi, 23-184, 362-65, 475-81, 510-985 [hereinafter cited as *Annals of 7th Congress*, without cross-reference to this footnote].

16. Samuel Sewall to Theodore Sedgwick, Dec. 29, 1800, in Sedgwick I Collection, Massachusetts Historical Society.

17. Leven Powell to Burr Powell, Mar. 26, 1800, Leven Powell Papers, Tucker-Coleman Collection, The College of William and Mary.

The resulting Judiciary Act of 1801[18] is remembered chiefly by Jefferson's sobriquet of the 'midnight judges act', since it provided for the doubling of the federal judiciary, and since during the last days of his Presidency John Adams assiduously appointed only the most solid of Federalists to the new positions.[19] But judges without power are useless: the heart of the 1801 Act lay in its enormous accretions to federal jurisdiction, and chief among these were clauses which granted federal circuit courts jurisdiction over 'all cases in law or equity, arising under the constitution and laws of the United States' and 'also of all actions, or suits, matters or things cognizable by the judicial authority of the United States'.[20] For the first time, federal courts had been explicitly granted 'federal question' jurisdiction. It remained to be seen how such new power might be used.

II

The struggle between the Jeffersonians and the Federalists was an acrimonious one, in which partisans on each side regularly reviled each other scurrilously. Moreover, both sides used the law of libel to persecute the most effective propagandists on the other side.[21] It is thus fitting that the first case in which the new type of federal jurisdiction might have been applied was a civil libel suit brought in December 1801 by William J. Hobby, the Federalist postmaster of Augusta, Georgia, against Ambrose Day and James Hely, the Jeffersonian editors of the *Louisville* Georgia *Gazette and Republican Trumpet*. Hobby sought the then gigantic sum of $10,000 in damages. His pleading alleged that the *Trumpet* had accused the 'avowed Tory' Hobby of mismanaging the mail in a viciously partisan way, by detaining letters to Jeffersonians, by opening their packages, and by misdirecting, destroying, or holding 'until they become useless' the Jeffersonian newspapers which provided to their partisans most of the political intelligence of the times. Hobby also alleged that he had been called 'an ungrateful wretch' who wrongfully continued to 'feed at the public trough', since he did not resign his post when Jefferson took office.[22]

18. Ch. 4, 2 Stat. 89.

19. See generally Kathryn Turner, 'The Midnight Judges', 109 *University of Pennsylvania Law Review* 494 (1961).

20. Judiciary Act of 1801, §11.

21. See generally Stephen B. Presser & Jamil S. Zainaldin, *Law and American History: Cases and Materials* (St. Paul, 1980) 208-34; James Morton Smith, *Freedom's Fetters: The Alien and Sedition Laws and American Civil Liberties*, (Ithaca, 1956), esp. pp. 202-220, 385-90; Leonard Williams Levy, *Jefferson and Civil Liberties: The Darker Side* (Cambridge, 1963) 42-69; Dumas Malone, *Jefferson the President: First Term, 1801-1805* (Boston, 1970) 225-35. I am indebted to Kathryn Preyer and Steven Hochman for this point.

22. Those records of the case which survive are to be found in the Federal Archives and Records Center in East Point, Georgia. The minute books of the Fifth Circuit, accessible also on microfilm, record the procedural outlines and dates of court action in each case; the minutes contain, for example, the nature of the jurisdictional claim made by the

Postmasters were in a strategic position, since they personally handled all of the mails. In the tense and agitated atmosphere surrounding the campaign of 1800 and its bitter aftermath, people on each side habitually suspected the other of tampering with the mails. 'I dare not through the channel of the post hazard a word to you on the subject of the election', Jefferson wrote by personal messenger to his primary confidante, James Madison, in February 1801. '[I]ndeed the interception & publication of my letters exposes the republican cause as well as myself personally to so much obloquy that I have come to a resolution never to write another sentence of politics in a letter.'[23] In one of history's notably magnanimous and potentially healing political decisions, Jefferson, once elected, did not immediately sweep from office all Federalists, but indeed retained most of them at the lower levels of government, something which many of his supporters did not fully understand. However Jefferson did gradually dismiss many Federalists who continued to use their offices in a partisan manner, and soon after Hobby filed his suit Jefferson had Postmaster General Gideon Granger fire him. Granger explained lamely to Hobby that, since Federalist postmasters who were also newspaper printers might misuse the franking privilege or might suppress the dissemination of news to rival printers, they could not be continued in office and all would be replaced.[24] Hobby replied, in an angry public letter, that he neither was nor had been the printer or editor of any newspaper, nor had he ever abused his office.[25]

Hobby's protestations seem disingenuous. He was apparently one of the staunchest of Federalist partisans and propagandists in Georgia, and he was closely connected with, if not the actual printer and editor of, the *Augusta Herald*, a Federalist organ. The Jeffersonian *Georgia Republican* later printed an affidavit of its printer's devil, formerly apprenticed to the *Herald*, who swore that newspapers directed to Day and Hely had been 'several times' delivered to William J. Bunce, editor and printer of record of the *Herald* (and at the time master of the deposing apprentice); that Hobby often wrote for and edited the *Herald*; that Bunce was the 'tool' of Hobby; and

---

defendants' plea to jurisdiction, namely that all of the parties were Georgia citizens. The details of the pleading, and the history of the marshal's several attempts to execute the judgment, are to be found in the file of the case. The quotations in the text are taken from Hobby's pleading.

23. Thomas Jefferson to James Madison, Feb. 1, 1801, James Madison Papers, Library of Congress. See also Uriah Tracy to Theodore Sedgwick, Jan. 29, 1802, John Rutledge to Sedgwick, Feb. 17, 1803, both in Sedgwick I Collection, Massachusetts Historical Society (both worrying about Republican tampering with Federalist mail in the post offices).

24. Gideon Granger to W.J. Hobby, Jan. 16, 1802, *Augusta Herald*, Feb. 3, 1802, reprinted in *Washington Federalist*, Feb. 19, 1802. Hobby printed Granger's letter and his own reply (see the next footnote) in the *Augusta Herald*, and they were then picked up and printed by the Federalist press elsewhere.

25. W.J. Hobby to Gideon Granger, Feb. 1, 1802, *Augusta Herald*, Feb. 3, 1802, reprinted in *Washington Federalist*, Feb. 19, 1802.

that Hobby, 'in general, exhibited as much anxiety as if the paper had been published on his own account'.[26] The *Herald*'s records demonstrate that in July 1804, about a year after the jury verdict in his libel case, Hobby became coprinter and coeditor of the *Herald* with Bunce, a position he retained for thirteen years.[27] The Congressman from Georgia, a Jeffersonian, noted in 1802 on the floor of Congress that 'the editorial part of the paper, called the *Augusta Herald*, was supposed to come from the pen of Mr. Hobby; . . . that the press was generally considered to be under his control; and that the paper teemed with invective against the principal officers of the present Administration'.[28]

Hobby's libel action was called up on December 18, 1801, as the last case heard on the last day of the December term of the Fifth Circuit, sitting at Augusta. Hobby had alleged that the two defendants were 'aliens and subjects of the King of Great Britain', thus attempting to found the case upon alienage jurisdiction, a noncontroversial head of jurisdiction granted in the 1789 Act. Day and Hely vigorously denied this allegation, however. Their pleas to jurisdiction indignantly averred that each was 'also a citizen of the same State of Georgia' as was the plaintiff. Noting pointedly that the 1801 Act 'was at the time of instituting said action of force and unrepealed', Day and Hely argued that federal jurisdiction could not exist under any other part of the 1801 Act. '[B]y the Constitution of the United States the Judicial Authority thereof is not vested with power or cognizance' over a libel action 'between citizens of the same State', they concluded, refusing to accept any argument that such a suit might be brought under the 'federal question' grant.[29]

It was the fourth time that jurisdiction had been questioned during that session, a number apparently so high that on the previous day the court had issued from the bench a special rule concerning pleading to jurisdiction.[30] No such rule had been felt necessary before that time, perhaps an indication of a newfound awareness of the potential involved in an assertion of federal jurisdiction.[31]

26. [Savannah] *Georgia Republican & State Intelligencer* May 2, 1803. See also *Augusta Herald*, June 1, 1803.

27. Clarence S. Brigham, *History and Bibliography of American Newspapers 1690-1820*, 2 vols. (Worcester, 1947) i, 115.

28. *Annals of 7th Congress* 796-97 (remarks of John Milledge of Georgia). See also ibid. at 753 (remarks of John Rutledge of South Carolina).

29. Plaintiff's pleading and defendants' pleas to jurisdiction, Case File, Hobby v. Day, Fifth Circuit, Federal Archives and Records Center, East Point, Georgia.

30. See Minute Book, Fifth Circuit, Dec. 17, 1801, Federal Archives and Records Center, East Point, Georgia. Two of the other pleas to jurisdiction were upheld, but they did not deal with an attempted assertion of federal question jurisdiction. I have been unable to locate the papers in the fourth case. The actual text of the rule is also not extant; all we have is the notation made in the minute book.

31. Cf. Wilfred Ritz, 'Jurisdictional Fictions', supra note 12, 56-72.

The judges who issued the new rule and who heard argument on the defendants' pleas to jurisdiction were both Jeffersonian appointees, Dominic Augustin Hall of South Carolina and Henry Potter of North Carolina. Adams had selected Federalists for the Fifth Circuit, but each had declined the honor of appointment too late for Adams to nominate other Federalists.[32] In order to ensure the continuity of justice, Jefferson had been forced to make appointments to that circuit despite his antipathy toward the Judiciary Act of 1801 under which their authority existed, an antipathy which would make repeal of the Act the first order of business of his administration when Congress met again in December 1801.[33] All of the other Adamsite Federalist appointees to the new circuit positions created by the Act had accepted. Thus, the first question of the meaning and constitutionality of the expansive jurisdictional provisions of the 1801 Act was brought before the only federal circuit bench in the country whose judges were Jeffersonians, supposedly by 'party discipline' if not by conviction opposed to the extension of jurisdiction and federal power portended by its provisions. After having heard argument on the pleas to jurisdiction, these Jeffersonian appointees upheld federal jurisdiction over Hobby's libel action.

As was usual in those times, argument on preliminary motions exhausted the preparation of the lawyers involved and trial of the cause was postponed until the succeeding term of court. The Jeffersonian majority in the new Congress meanwhile in February repealed the Judiciary Act of 1801, effective July 1, 1802,[34] which made almost meaningless the spring term of the circuit courts whose judges would disappear from office soon thereafter. Only Chief Judge Hall showed up to hold the lame-duck term of the Fifth Circuit in April in Savannah, and a single circuit judge had no authority to try cases under the 1801 Act, so *Hobby v. Day* had to be postponed once again. After another delay for unknown reasons in December, 1802, the cause finally came on for trial before a panel consisting of Federalist Supreme Court Justice Alfred Moore and Jeffersonian District Court Judge

32. For the full story of Adams' 'midnight' appointments to the federal bench in February 1801, see my forthcoming article concerning the Judiciary Act of 1801. There were supposed to be three judges in the Fifth Circuit, but Jefferson never appointed a Circuit Judge for Georgia. See, e.g., *Augusta Herald*, Jan. 19, 1802. He advised his own Fifth Circuit appointees that he considered their tenure to be temporary, as he began to work for repeal of the Judiciary Act of 1801 (which created their offices) from the moment he became President. See, e.g., Thomas Jefferson to Nathaniel Macon, May 14, 1801, Nathaniel Macon Papers, University of Virginia. (Jefferson used the advice of his party lieutenants in the Southern states concerning these key appointments, and Congressman (soon Speaker) Nathaniel Macon was his chief henchman in North Carolina; thus the letter went to Macon instead of Potter.)

33. See supra note 32 and infra note 70 and accompanying text.

34. An act to repeal certain acts respecting the organization of the Courts of the United States; and for other purposes, Mar. 8, 1802, ch. 8, 2 Stat. 132; see my forthcoming article which will deal with the Jeffersonians' repeal of the Judiciary Act of 1801 and passage of their own Judiciary Act of 1802.

William Stephens, in May 1803.[35] Hobby was awarded a breathtaking $2000 judgment when the defendants put on no witnesses; the deposing apprentice apparently would not testify in open court.[36] Writs of execution against Day and Hely were returned unsatisfied ('no goods to be found') by the marshal (presumably a Jeffersonian partisan) for the next several years.[37] The marshal's return of May 1806 notes an agreement signed by

35. It is somewhat surprising, if jurisdiction was sustained on 'federal question' grounds, that the suit was not dismissed in 1803 for want of jurisdiction, since the 'federal question' grant had by then been repealed, but perhaps ambiguous language in the repealer was held to sustain the suit. The repealing legislation clumsily provided that all suits which had been brought under the 1801 Act 'shall be . . . continued over' to courts established by the repealer, restoring federal jurisdiction as it had been under the 1789 Act. An Act to repeal certain acts respecting the organization of the Courts of the United States; and for other purposes, Mar. 8, 1802, ch. 8, §4, 2 Stat. 132. This could have been construed to prevent abatement, although it could also have been construed either to apply only to actions under the 1801 Act which would have been proper under the 1789 Act or to permit the new courts to apply rules of abatement as they saw fit.

In one of the few other cases in which the question of abatement due to repeal might have been raised, Justice Samuel Chase riding circuit in Delaware in 1804 dismissed a suit brought under the 1801 Act when it appeared that the amount in controversy required for federal jurisdiction in such suits by the 1789 Act, but not required in such suits by the 1801 Act, was lacking. See Penn's Lessees v. Pennington, minute book, Third Circuit, Federal Archives and Records Center, Philadelphia, Pennsylvania (case files do not survive); Richard S. Rodney, 'The End of the Penn's Claim to the Delaware: Some Forgotten Lawsuits', *Pennsylvania Magazine of History and Biography*, lxi (1937) 182 (discussion of Chase's bench opinion, which survives in notes taken at trial by one of the lawyers). The heirs of William Penn claimed title to all of Delaware, but the legal means of asserting this staggering claim was a series of ejectment suits founded on diversity of citizenship, in each of which the title to a single plot of land was at issue. Pennington was one of those ejectment suits. The 1789 Act required a $500 minimum amount in controversy for diversity suits, but the 1801 Act expressly waived any minimum amount in controversy for suits involving title to land, and apparently none of the Delaware plots was individually worth $500. Compare Judiciary Act of 1789, §11, with Judiciary Act of 1801, §11.

At least three other nondiversity cases were retained in federal court after the 1802 repeal, two of them despite counsel's argument that jurisdiction had been destroyed by repeal, but all three were bankruptcy cases and the Bankruptcy Act of 1800 (not repealed until 1803) contained its own grant of jurisdiction, see Bankruptcy Act of 1800, §58; supra note 6 and accompanying text, so that the repeal of the backstop grant of bankruptcy jurisdiction contained in section 12 of the 1801 Act did not withdraw federal jurisdiction over such actions. See Rogers v. Sullivan; Sullivan v. Lowell, case files & minute book, First Circuit, Federal Archives and Records Center, Waltham, Massachusetts (pleas to jurisdiction argued in October 1802 term); Barnes v. Billington, case file & minute book, Third Circuit, Federal Archives and Records Center, Philadelphia (case brought in October 1801, tried in October 1803; no plea to jurisdiction noted).

36. See *Augusta Herald*, May 18, 1803. The apprentice apparently would have been a shaky witness. See ibid., May 18, June 1, 1803.

37. Despite their refusal to pay the judgment, Day and Hely apparently ran into financial difficulty, as they suspended publication of the *Trumpet* after the jury verdict from June until November 1803. Clarence S. Brigham, *American Newspapers*, supra note 27, 117-18.

Hobby's lawyer that 'you need not levy for more than the costs, until further orders'.[38] Apparently Hobby gave up trying to collect his pound of flesh, having won at least a significant moral victory.

III

Neither the case records nor available contemporary newspapers[39] give us a clue about what seems to us to be the most important issue raised in *Hobby v. Day*: if the defendants were correct in believing themselves to have been Georgia citizens and not British subjects (and they should have known),[40] upon what theory was federal jurisdiction upheld? Why might *Hobby v. Day* have been seen by the court to have involved a *federal* question? The suit was a simple common-law libel action in form, fully cognizable in the Georgia state courts. It was not founded upon any substantive federal statute, and contained no disputed ingredient of or controversy over federal law.

Two theories of federal jurisdiction advance themselves. Both would be difficult to sustain today, although the first is certainly less odd to the modern mind than is the second. One theory is that a federal employee or officer should be given access to a federal court, at least when the employee wishes to sue over a question of the conduct of the office. Congress has to

38. Case file, Hobby v. Day, Fifth Circuit, Federal Archives and Records Center, East Point, Georgia.

39. No minutes of the court's opinion on the jurisdictional question survive in the case files. The pleas to jurisdiction merely bear the notation 'overruled'. No number of the *Trumpet* survives for the period December 1801 through November 1803. No newspaper of which we do have surviving numbers recorded or reported on the jurisdictional arguments made in December 1801, not even the *Herald*.

40. It is possible that the defendants might have erroneously believed themselves to be Georgia citizens. Citizenship was not clearly defined at that time; Georgia was still a raw frontier state, recently populated, with many of its residents transients or born elsewhere. Persons who considered themselves citizens of a state might not have been adjudged so by a court.

The famous Jeffersonian newspaper editor William Duane was sued in the fall of 1801 for libel by a Federalist editor. Duane defended on grounds that neither diversity jurisdiction nor alienage jurisdiction existed, since he was, he thought, a citizen of Pennsylvania just like the plaintiff. Duane had been born in what became Vermont, and had spent much of his youth in Pennsylvania, but had been taken by his mother back to Ireland (her home) when he was about 13 years old, in 1774. He did not return to the United States until 1795, when he settled in Philadelphia. The three Federalist circuit judges of the Third Circuit had no difficulty in holding him to be a subject of the British King, finding neither the locale of his birth (which was of course British at the time) nor his later resumption of Pennsylvania residence to be sufficient to negate the facts that he did not reside on United States soil when independence was declared (even though his removal was involuntary), and that he did not aver a declaration of loyalty to the United States when he reached 21. Hollingsworth v. Duane, J.B. Wallace 51 (C.C.D. Pa. 1801). Still protesting, Duane soon took out naturalization papers. James Morton Smith, *Freedom's Fetters*, supra note 21, 278, n.4.

date not granted blanket permission for any federal agent who so desires to become a federal court plaintiff, although there are specific statutes which give some officials entry,[41] and there are provisions for removal by federal officials when sued in state courts.[42] Access to federal court under the *present* general federal question statute (passed in 1875) on the ground that the suit concerns the official conduct of a federal officer has generally been denied,[43] since the present statutory language has usually been restrictively construed to require that the plaintiff's pleading present a substantial and controverted issue of federal *law* before the case will be seen to contain a 'federal question'.[44] While there are cases to the contrary,[45] deriving primarily from Chief Justice John Marshall's expansive 1824 construction of the Constitutional 'arising under' language in *Osborn v. Bank of the United States*[46] to allow federal jurisdiction if there were somewhere in the back-

41. See 28 U.S.C. §§1339 ('any civil action arising under any Act of Congress relating to the postal service'); 1340 ('any civil action arising under any Act of Congress providing for internal revenue, or revenue from imports and tonnage'); 1345 ('all civil actions, suits or proceedings commenced by the United States, or by any agency or officer thereof expressly authorized to sue by Act of Congress'); 1352 ('any action on a bond executed under any law of the United States'); 1355 ('any action or proceeding for the recovery or enforcement of any fine, penalty, or forfeiture, pecuniary or otherwise, incurred under any Act of Congress'); 1357 ('any civil action . . . to recover damages for any injury to his person or property on account of any act done by him, under any Act of Congress, for the protection or collection of any of the revenues, or to enforce the right of citizens of the United States to vote in any State') (1983).

42. See 28 U.S.C. §1442 (1983) (limited to United States officers who are officers of courts, for acts under color of office; to officers of either House of Congress, for the discharge of official duties; and to officers who apprehend or punish criminals and who collect revenue, for acts under color of office or on account of authority vested in them).

43. See, e.g., *Martin v. Wyzanski*, 262 F. Supp. 925 (D. Mass. 1967) (no federal question jurisdiction over libel suit brought against a federal judge, where there was no controverted issue of federal law). See also, e.g., *Johnston v. Earle*, 245 F.2d 793, 795 (9th Cir. 1957) ('the mere fact that a suit is against a federal officer does not support original jurisdiction . . . on the ground that it is a case arising under the laws of the United States'); *Viles v. Symes*, 129 F.2d 828 (10th Cir. 1942). These cases all involve attempts to assert federal jurisdiction over federal officials as *defendant*, but the principle should apply equally well to cases like that brought by Hobby, and the very absence of instances of attempted suit by federal officials indicates a great deal about their acceptability.

44. 'Two things are necessary to the existence of a federal question: first, an actual dispute between the parties as to the meaning of some law of the United States; second, materiality of the construction of such law to a determination of the cause.' *California Oil Co. v. Miller*, 96 Fed. 12 (C.C.D. Cal. 1899). Leading cases are: *Gully v. First Nat'l Bank*, 299 U.S. 109 (1936); *Tennessee v. Union & Planters Bank*, 152 U.S. 454 (1894); *Gold-Washing & Water Co. v. Keyes*, 96 U.S. 199 (1878). See also *Cohens v. Virginia*, 19 U.S. (6 Wheat.) 264 (1821).

45. See, e.g., *Blevins v. Hines*, 264 Fed. 1005 (W.D. Va. 1920).

46. 22 U.S. (9 Wheat.) 738 (1824). As Part III of this essay will demonstrate, Marshall's expansiveness in *Osborn* by no means interpreted the Constitution as broadly as might have been done. Marshall, one of the drafters of the Judiciary Act of 1801, presumably was aware of the broader arguments before he wrote *Osborn*, but they are not alluded to in his opinion.

ground of the case an issue of federal law which might have been controverted (such as whether Postmaster Hobby had been correctly appointed to office), it is safe to conclude that neither Congress nor the federal courts today imagine that a libel suit brought by a federal minion concerning conduct in office would or should constitute a federal question 'arising under' the laws of the United States. If Judges Hall and Potter accepted jurisdiction in *Hobby v. Day* under this theory, the holding is significant.

It is not impossible, however, that an even broader theory of jurisdiction was upheld by these two judges. The broader theory was the Federalist notion of the expansive possibilities inherent in the 'arising under' language of Article III, section 2 which they had copied into the Judiciary Act of 1801. Unfettered by our modern pinched understanding of what a 'federal question' is, and desiring to expand the power of the federal courts, a number of Federalists in 1800 had come to believe that the common law itself was, in the language of the Constitution, a 'law[] of the United States' since it was an inherent part of the heritage of each of the colonies, and thus of the nation made from the colonies. Since each component state adhered to the common law, then so did the new nation as a whole (the argument went).[47]

47. One reasonably concise presentation of what has been and will be herein called the Federalist position, since no Jeffersonian is on record as accepting it, is given in the speech of Representative Roger Griswold of Connecticut during the momentous debate of repeal of the Judiciary Act of 1801. See *Annals of 7th Congress* 767-71 ff. Some Federalists had made similar arguments with respect to the common law of crimes during the 1798 debates on adoption of the Sedition Act. See Julius Goebel, Jr., *Antecedents and Beginnings*, supra note 12, 634.

Not all Federalists accepted this argument, however. Robert Goodloe Harper, who was to be one of the Federalist drafters of the 1801 Act, rejected the notion of a federal common law jurisdiction during the just-mentioned 1798 debates. See Kathryn Preyer, 'Joseph Story, The Supreme Court and the Question of Federal Common Law Jurisdiction over Crimes', 9 and n.22 (unpublished essay, 1983 version, in its author's possession). Justice Samuel Chase expostulated against the existence of such a jurisdiction in his famous opinion in *United States v. Worrall*, 28 Fed. Cas. 774, 778-79 (No. 16766) (C.C.D. Pa. 1798), but it is significant that in the same case 'after a short consultation', ibid. at 780, Chase permitted the defendant charged with a common-law offense to be pronounced guilty and sentenced to prison. The speculation of Francis Wharton that Chase hastily sought the views of his Federalist Supreme Court brethren, who in 1798 would have also been in Philadelphia, and who were probably among those 'surprised' at his apostasy, Francis Wharton, *State Trials of the United States During the Administrations of Washington and Adams* (Philadelphia, 1849) 199n., is I think a sound interpretation of events. It is clear that Chief Justices John Jay and Oliver Ellsworth (principal draftsperson of the 1789 Act) and Justices James Iredell and William Paterson all understood a federal common-law criminal jurisdiction to exist, and it is probable that Justices James Wilson and Bushrod Washington, that is to say six of the 12 Justices (all Federalists) who sat upon the Supreme Court up to 1801, accepted this position. Only the chameleon Chase is on record as opposed to it, among all Federalist judges during this period. I think that, while many Federalists and those who would become Federalists might have taken an equivocal or even a states' rights position on the issue of a federal common-law jurisdiction during the early and mid-1790s, between 1798 and 1801 the dangers of a Jacobin takeover pushed many toward the position shared by Ellsworth.

Internal and external evidence cements the conclusion that the *possibility* of judicial adoption of this broad meaning was written into the first grant of 'arising under' jurisdiction in the 1801 Act. The federal courts had notoriously exercised common law jurisdiction in *criminal* cases prior to 1801. The Judiciary Act of 1789 had granted to federal courts jurisdiction over 'all crimes and offenses that shall be cognizable under the authority of the United States'.[48] Federalist judges had in effect construed that language broadly,[49] as referring to and including the common law of crimes, and holding in at least two instances that federal courts could entertain crimes indictable at common law.[50] The Judiciary Act of 1801, as its first-

---

Congressman James A. Bayard of Delaware, and others in the party which accepted something of the notion of a federal common law competency.

48. Judiciary Act of 1789, §§9 (district court jurisdiction), 11 (circuit court jurisdiction).

49. Actually, given the Federalists' tendency to construe the Constitution generously with regard to the powers of the federal government, see supra note 13, most arguments for a federal common-law jurisdiction made by Federalist judges and district attorneys seemed to sound in theories of the inherent or natural powers of the United States, rather than to make statutory arguments in response to the Jeffersonian position, repeated in case after case, that:

> In relation to crimes and punishments, the objects of the delegated power of the United States are enumerated and fixed. . . . Every power is [a] matter of definite and positive grant; and the very powers that are granted cannot take effect until they are exercised through the medium of a law. Congress undoubtedly had a power to make a law, which should render it criminal to offer a bribe to the commissioner of the revenue; but not having made the law[,] the crime is not recognized by the federal code, constitutional or legislative. . . .

United States v. Worrall, 28 Fed. Cas. 774, 777-78 (C.C.D. Pa. 1798) (No. 16766) (argument of Alexander J. Dallas for the defense). After Chase's peroration agreeing with Dallas in that case, the Federalist District Judge Richard Peters sitting with him on the trial made the appropriate argument that Congress had enacted such a statute: 'Whenever an offence aims at the subversion of any Federal institution, or at the corruption of its public officers, it is an offence against the well-being of the United States; from its very nature, it is cognizable under their authority; and, consequently, it is within the jurisdiction of this court, by virtue of the 11th section of the judicial act [of 1789].' Ibid. at 779-80.

50. See *United States v. Henfield*, 11 Fed. Cas. 1099, 1100-01 (C.C.D. Pa. 1793) (No. 6360) (reporting a grand jury charge of Jay, C.J., delivered before the Federal Crimes Act of 1790 had been passed, when the only federal criminal authority in existence must have been a common-law jurisdiction); *United States v. Henfield*, Ibid. at 1106-08 (grand jury charge of Wilson, J., claiming to state the views of Iredell, J.); *United States v. Ravara*, 27 Fed. Cas. 714 (C.C.D. Pa. 1794) (No. 16122) (Jay, C.J.); *Williams' Case*, 29 Fed. Cas. 1330 (C.C.D. Conn. 1799) (No. 17708) (Ellsworth, C.J.); *United States v. Worrall*, 28 Fed. Cas. 774 (C.C.D. Pa. 1798) (No. 16766), discussed supra notes 47 & 49, and cases collected or mentioned in Kathryn Preyer, 'Joseph Story', supra note 47, 48 and nn.3-14, 17, 31. Only in *Williams* and *Worrall* was federal common-law jurisdiction over crimes declared to be full in extent. See generally Stephen B. Presser, 'A Tale of Two Judges: Richard Peters, Samuel Chase, and the Broken Promise of Federalist Jurisprudence', 73 *Northwestern University Law Review* 26, 46-72 (1978).

mentioned head of jurisdiction, repeated verbatim this recently construed language concerning federal criminal jurisdiction from the 1789 Act[51] and followed it immediately, as the second head, with the new grant of 'arising under' jurisdiction. Finally, the 1801 Act used almost precisely the same words as had the 1789 grant of criminal jurisdiction in its backstop, catch-all, intention-revealing extension of federal jurisdiction to '*all* actions, or suits, matters or things *cognizable* by the judicial *authority of the United States*'.[52]

Given the heightened political tensions of the time and especially the beleaguered and desperate situation which the Federalists perceived themselves to have been forced into, and given the fact that the drafters of the 1801 Act were shrewd, experienced, and intelligent Federalist lawyers (particularly James A. Bayard of Delaware), the phrasing and location of these jurisdictional grants cannot have been coincidental or haphazard. The Act was designed (as it stated in blunt language) so that it could be construed to extend federal jurisdiction to the limits constitutionally permissible. Congressman Joseph Hopper Nicholson of Maryland, one of the most astute Jeffersonians in the House, noted that he had 'often heard [Bayard] maintain upon this floor an opinion that the common law of England was the common law of the United States in their national capacity, and that therefore the Federal courts have a general common law jurisdiction'.[53] The Act was written so that it could be so construed by the friendly Federalists then almost universally populating the federal bench.[54]

Such a construction would have enormous consequences. The relations between the states and the federal government, and the relations among the branches of the federal government, would have been quite different from those we know today had this potential federalization of common-law jurisdiction been accepted by federal judges and then carried to its most far-reaching conclusions. *All ordinary common-law suits between citizens could have been brought in the federal courts, rather than in the state courts.*

Although the complete atrophy of state courts was an ultimate possibility, this was not the real concern or goal of the Federalists. They wanted, at

51. See supra note 49.

52. Judiciary Act of 1801, §11 (emphasis added).

53. *Annals of 7th Congress* 806.

54. See generally William Winslow Crosskey, *Politics and the Constitution in the History of the United States*, 3 vols. (Chicago, 1953, 1980) ii, 543-674. Crosskey, however, ignores the 1801 Act. The argument in favor of this reading of the Judiciary Act of 1801 is extended and amplified in my detailed discussion of that Act, in my forthcoming article on that subject. It ought to be noted here, however, that the section of the 1801 Act which granted the power to take writs of error from the new circuit courts to the Supreme Court described them as being taken from 'all final judgments in civil actions *at common law*, in any of the circuit courts hereby established'. Judiciary Act of 1801, §34 (emphasis added).

bottom, for suits arising from interstate commercial dealings to be able to be taken before judges of their own kind, less likely to be tied to localistic, nonbusiness, or more democratic interests.[55] Alexander Hamilton, defending the Judiciary Act of 1801 in a series of newspaper essays, asserted that federal courts were designed for instances 'where there would exist some distrust of the State Courts, . . . especially . . . [for] the merchants in our Commercial States'. The 'existence alone' of the federal courts, he continued, 'has a powerful and salutary effect. The liberty to use them, even where it is not often exercised, inspires confidence in the intercourse of business. They are viewed as beneficent guardians whose protection may be claimed when necessary.'[56]

Of course, tort actions against obstreperous and irreverent Jeffersonians, such as the libel suit in *Hobby v. Day*, might also need to be brought in locales friendlier than state courts. The arch-Federalist Theodore Sedgwick, thinking no doubt of criminal as well as civil common-law jurisdiction, had wanted an expanded federal jurisdiction 'so as to render the justice of the nation acceptable to the people, to aid [the] national economy, to overawe the licentious, [and] to punish the guilty'.[57] Federal courts with their greater powers would be benign watchdogs over the Federalist version of the Constitution and helpmates to interstate business, keeping unruly Democrats in check, promoting Federalist interests, construing their jurisdiction only as broadly as the times demanded, awaiting the presumably inevitable reaccession to national power they expected to occur in four years. Federalist judges would be avuncular potential dictators, with their potential mostly kept in reserve.

A federal common-law jurisdiction was anathema to the states-rights' Jeffersonians, who found the Federalists power-hungry, aristocratic, smug, and dangerous, not benign. The Jeffersonians understood the breadth of potential jurisdiction inherent in the 1801 Act. 'Is not the jurisdiction of the Federal court extremely limited from the true and genuine construction of the Constitution'? Congressman Philip Thompson of Virginia demanded to know. 'Have we not State courts diffused in abundance over every commonwealth composing this Union? Are they not competent to the decision of all cases of controversy between citizen and citizen'?[58] But worse than this, to the Jeffersonians, were two other aspects of the Federalist argument: first, the legislative nature of common-law adjudication, and second, the Federalist doctrine of judicial supremacy. Common-law judges use essentially un-

55. See supra note 14.

56. [Alexander Hamilton], 'The Examination', Pts. V & VI, in *The* [Hartford] *Connecticut Courant*, Jan. 18, 1802.

57. Theodore Sedgwick to Rufus King, Nov. 15, 1799, in Charles R. King, ed. *The Life and Correspondence of Rufus King*, 6 vols. (New York, 1894-1900) i, 147.

58. *Annals of 7th Congress* 552. See also the aware writings of Jefferson and Madison, cited in Kathryn Preyer, 'Joseph Story', supra note 47, nn.24 & 25.

fettered discretion to create the substantive rules of law which they apply. 'The common law extends to all persons and all things', Thompson continued. 'The judges have a right of adopting this law, or such parts as they may deem applicable; they can annul your laws. . . . [I]f these powers should ever be conceded, they would without doubt possess an unlimited, an uncontrollable power of legislation.'[59] 'Is it not legislation to all intents and purposes', queried Nicholson, 'when your judges are authorized to introduce at pleasure the laws of a foreign country [the common law, which the Jeffersonians always identified as emanating from their recent enemy, Great Britain], to arm themselves with power'?[60]

Moreover, the Federalists claimed that the courts were the proper part of the federal government to establish the meaning of the Constitution, finally and without recourse to any elected officials, federal or state. If the Constitution included the common law as one of the 'laws of the United States' which federal cases might 'arise under', then the federal courts would be able to regard all common-law decisions as *constitutional* ones and would be able to override both state and federal legislatures to have the final say over any issue of law in the United States.[61] Thompson summed up the argument against such a construction:

> Give the Judiciary this check upon the Legislature, allow them the power to declare your laws null and void; allow the common law, a system extending to all persons and to all things, to be attached to the Constitution, as I understand it is contended; and in vain have the people placed you upon this floor to legislate; your laws will be nullified, your proceedings will be checked.[62]

John Randolph of Roanoke, the brilliant and acerbic Jeffersonian Congressional leader, put the problem in characteristically concise, acute, yet provocative language. The Federalist judiciary,

> are said to be harmless, unaspiring men. Their humble pretensions extend only to a complete exemption from Legislative control; to the exercise of an inquisitorial authority over the Cabinet of the Executive [referring to the mandamus asked for in *Marbury v. Madison*[63]], and the veto of the Roman Tribunate upon all your laws, together with the establishing any body of laws which they may choose to declare a part of the Constitution.[64]

59. *Annals of 7th Congress* 554.

60. Ibid. at 806.

61. '[A]nother [difficulty] . . . immediately presents itself. If the Constitution adopted the common law, or the common law attached itself to the Constitution, it immediately became a law of the United States, and is paramount to the laws and constitutions of the individual States.' Ibid. at 810 (remarks of Nicholson).

62. Ibid. at 552-53.

63. 5 U.S. (1 Cranch) 137 (1803).

64. *Annals of 7th Congress* 662.

To acknowledge that any case at common law was one 'arising under . . . the laws of the United States' was, to the Jeffersonians, a nullification of the election of 1800.

The Federalists, in response, essentially demurred rather than answered. They denied that Federalist judges were or would be unfair. They claimed that the Judiciary Act of 1801 was enacted pursuant to and within the terms and intent of the 1787 Constitution. And they quite frankly acknowledged that they had strengthened the federal judiciary out of fear that Jefferson's election would unleash a torrent of excess and abuse in the name of democracy. 'We believed Mr. Jefferson radically and on principle hostile to the national Constitution', Congressman John Rutledge admitted.[65] Bayard was even blunter:

> The independence of the judiciary was the felicity of our Constitution. It was this principle which was to curb the fury of party upon sudden changes. . . . Raised above the storm, it was the Judiciary which was to control the fiery zeal, and to quell the fierce passions of a victorious faction. We are standing on the brink of that revolutionary torrent, which deluged in blood one of the fairest countries of Europe [France]. . . . Prostrate your judges at the feet of party, and you break down the mounds which defend you from this torrent.[66]

The Federalists went further, for they believed that Jefferson and his party were engaged in destroying the Constitution and the promise of America before their very eyes. 'The fears which I then felt [at the election] have not been dispelled, but multiplied by what I have since seen', cried Bayard. 'I observe the institutions of the Government falling around me, and where the work of destruction is to end God alone knows.'[67]

The Federalists implicitly acknowledged the general truth of the Jeffersonian assertions concerning the great accretion to federal jurisdiction contained in the 1801 Act by not denying those assertions, and by reiterating their own assertion that the federal courts alone stood between the destructive Jeffersonians and the Constitution. Cutting to the heart of the Constitutionally-founded contradiction we disguise under the term 'separation of powers', Bayard exemplified this position when he challenged his opponents with judicial review itself:

> You have a right to abolish, by a law, the offices of the judges of the circuit court; they have a right to declare the law void. It unavoidably follows, in the exercise of these rights, either that you destroy their rights, or that they destroy yours. . . . If you pass the bill upon your table [to repeal the 1801 Act] the judges have a Constitutional right to declare it void. I hope they will have the courage to exercise that right.[68]

65. Ibid. at 750.

66. Ibid. at 650.

67. Ibid. at 628.

68. Ibid. at 648.

The Federalists did not really dispute the Jeffersonian claims concerning the degree of the increase in federal jurisdiction granted by the 1801 Act. They *were* certain that the Jeffersonians portended an evil excess of democracy, that the judges who exercised power under their expanded jurisdiction would do so wisely and well, and that the expansion was necessary in order to preserve their version of the Constitution. The Jeffersonian Speaker of the House, Nathaniel Macon of North Carolina, arrowed in directly on these fundamental differences between the two parties simply by saying that 'the people there [in his state] behave decently without having Federal judges or standing armies to protect them against themselves'.[69]

The expansion of federal judicial authority contained in the 1801 Act was, however, only a matter of *potential* until litigants, attorneys, and judges invoked and then explicated it. The suggestive but vague language of the Act had to be interpreted broadly before the fears of the Jeffersonians or the hopes of the Federalists would be realized. Due in large part to the tensions and uncertainties surrounding the passage of the Act, particularly the fact of Jefferson's determination to have it repealed as soon as possible (a determination widely understood and soon realized),[70] the only vehicle which ever presented itself to the federal judiciary for the accomplishment of that interpretation was *Hobby v. Day*. The two Jeffersonian judges who sat in that case accepted jurisdiction, as we have seen.

How could it be possible that Jeffersonians would agree with the Federalist position that federal jurisdiction existed on the ground that the 1801 Act authorized federal courts to try common-law actions because the common law was a 'law of the United States'? At least two plausible explanations exist. First, Hall and Potter may have concluded that such was the intent of the Federalist Congress which passed the law and, adhering to Jefferson's views on the powers of federal judges, they were bound to bow to the will of the legislature without being able to exercise any power of judicial review to overturn it. Jeffersonians in 1800-02 rejected the Federalists' notion of judicial review, arguing that the proper avenue of appeal for an unconstitutional law was to take the question to the people in an election. Hall and Potter may thus have presumed themselves unable to avoid application of the 1801 Act. Or, secondly, they may have wished to create a cause celebre which would result in public outcry and, eventually, would have contributed support for the abolition of their own offices.[71]

69. Ibid. at 709. See generally Joyce Appleby, *Capitalism*, supra note 14.

70. See, e.g., the contemporaneous commentary of a well-known Jeffersonian jurisprude: 'As soon as the question [passage of the Judiciary Act of 1801] had been . . . carried in the house of representatives, a member gave notice, which was laid upon the table, that at the next session he should move for a repeal of the act. . . . The question whether a succeeding congress could repeal the law, and by so doing remove the newly appointed judges from office, soon became a popular topic of discussion, in many parts of the United States'. St. George Tucker, ed. *Blackstone's Commentaries*, 5 vols., (Philadelphia, 1803), iv, Appendix I, 24-25.

71. A third possibility, brought to my attention by Kathryn Preyer, is that these two Jeffersonians might not have agreed with Jefferson's position on the jurisdictional expansion of

If Judges Hall and Potter did hold that the common law was a 'law of the United States', and thus that the Constitution extended federal jurisdiction to all cases, then the first federal question case was perhaps the most significant case in all our early jurisprudence. *Hobby v. Day* would also be a demonstration of the overly narrow rigidity of the interpretivist approach to the meaning of the Constitution, since the interpretivists' strict-constructionist belief in the necessary existence of a single, clearly-defined meaning for each Constitutional phrase founders when the open-ended language of Article III is focused upon. Gouverneur Morris, who probably was the principal draftsperson of the final version of Article III, and who was a leader among the diehard Federalist proponents and defenders of the expansionist Judiciary Act of 1801 as Senator from New York,[72] asserted as

---

the federal courts. Party 'lines' were looser then than now and political communication was more haphazard, it is true, and of course many of Jefferson's adherents did not agree with all or even much that he believed or said.

However, the crucially important nature of the question involved, the mode of selection of the only two Jeffersonian circuit court appointees, and the favors subsequently bestowed upon them by the Jeffersonians make it unlikely that they would have acted to disagree with their party leader on this issue. First, Jefferson viewed the 1801 Act, plus the Federalists' nearly complete retention of control of the federal judiciary, as the primary targets of his campaign to rid the nation of its aristocratic pretenders and to 'restore' his version of the 1787 Constitution. It would have been exceedingly strange for two of his appointees to fail to adhere to this position, at the inception of his term in office, in offices themselves so close to the substance of the issue. The topic of repeal of the 1801 Act was widely mooted publicly, especially in the South. See, e.g., Henry de Saussere to John Rutledge, Feb. 17, 1802, John Rutledge Papers, Southern Historical Collection, University of North Carolina; supra note 70.

Second, Jefferson made it clear to his lieutenants in North and South Carolina (and Georgia) that he wanted to appoint to the Fifth Circuit only persons who were regular Jeffersonians. See, e.g., Thomas Jefferson to Nathaniel Macon, May 14, 1801, Nathaniel Macon Papers, University of Virginia. Third, both Potter and Hall were generously rewarded by Jefferson and his party for their service, which might not have happened had either bucked the President in this, the first crucial issue of his administration, one which to Jefferson symbolized the fundamental differences between the two parties, and one which vitally concerned the jobs of Potter and Hall. Potter was given the federal district judgeship in North Carolina when it chanced to fall vacant in the spring of 1802 (he remained in that position until his death 55 years later, a staunch Jeffersonian to the end). See generally Wilson Grandy Briggs, *Henry Potter 1766-1857*, (Chapel Hill, 1953) 3-7. Hall was given a Louisiana Territorial Judgeship in 1803 by Jefferson when Louisiana was purchased and organized; later President Madison made him the first District Judge there when Louisiana was admitted to the Union and a federal court was created for it. I think it fair to conclude that Potter and Hall were loyal Jeffersonians.

Two other possibilities have been urged upon me by Wilfred Ritz. The jurisdictional plea may have been overruled simply because it was technically deficient, or because the judges were willing to accept federal jurisdiction based on some legal fiction not apparent in the meager record we have. While I think both unlikely, both are certainly possible explanations since we know so little about the case.

72. In the Senate, where the final vote to repeal the 1801 Act was only by a 16-15 margin thanks to the defection of South Carolina's Jeffersonian Senator John Ewing Colhoun to the other side, see *Annals of 7th Congress* 183, Morris was viewed as one of the principal defenders of the 1801 Act, speaking to the issue on five separate occasions. See Ibid. at 36-41, 76-92, 157, 159, 180-82.

much years later when he implied that 'redundant and equivocal terms' characterized 'a part of what relates to the judiciary' in the Constitution.[73] The Framers had to equivocate, since most of the public never would have accepted a Constitution explicitly giving such broad powers to a federal judiciary, but Morris himself was certain that the vague words he had put into Article III encompassed the vague words broadly empowering the federal courts in the 1801 Act.[74] This study of the first federal question case

73. Morris to Timothy Pickering, Dec. 22, 1814, in Max Farrand, ed., *The Records of the Federal Convention of 1787*, 4 vols., revised edition (New Haven and London, 1937) iii. 420. Morris should be quoted more fully:

> [The Constitution, he modestly admitted,] was written by the fingers, which write this letter. Having rejected redundant and equivocal terms, I believed it to be as clear as our language would permit; excepting, nevertheless, a part of which relates to the judiciary. On that subject, conflicting opinions had been maintained with so much professional astuteness, that it became necessary to select phrases, which expressing my own notions would not alarm others, nor shock their self-love. . . .

Morris can be taken as saying that he wrote his own centralizing views of federal jurisdiction into the Constitution, using equivocation (or, perhaps we should say, open-ended phraseology) in order to keep 'others' from seeing the expansionist possibilities inherent therein.

74. The arguments of the wily, immensely astute Morris in defense of the 1801 Act bear close scrutiny. First, Morris argued that the Constitution had been written by centralizers, who despaired that solutions for national problems would ever emanate from a group of equal but fractious states, during a short time when the proponents of states' rights were asleep, a time not likely to be duplicated:

> There are some honorable gentlemen now present [he said to the Senate in January 1802] who sat in the Convention which formed this Constitution. I appeal to their recollection, if they have not seen the time when the fate of America was suspended by a hair? my life for it, if another convention be assembled, they will part without doing anything. Never, in the flow of time, was a moment so propitious, as that in which the Convention assembled. The States had been convinced, by melancholy experience [Shays' Rebellion?], how inadequate they were to the management of our national concerns. The passions of the people were lulled to sleep; State pride slumbered; the Constitution was promulgated; and then it awoke, and opposition was formed; but it was in vain. The people of America bound the States down by this great compact.

Annals of 7th Congress 40. The Constitution thus rejected a states' rights position and subordinated the states to the federal government, even to the extent of having deprived them of their sovereign immunity, since Morris next lamented the passage of the Eleventh Amendment: 'One great provision of the Constitution—a provision that exhibited the sublime spectacle of a great State bowing before the tribunal of justice—is gone!' Ibid. at 40-41. The impetus for an expansionist federal government, particularly for an expansionist federal judiciary, was (Morris thought) the potential in a republic for an excess of popular domocracy, which might control the states and might even gain control of the new national legislature. He aimed directly at the states-rights Jeffersonians and their leader:

has, throughout, reminded us that law is politics, not something magically cut off from its living context.[75]

> Look into the records of time [Morris continued], see what has been the ruin of every Republic. The vile love of popularity. Why are we here? To save the people from their most dangerous enemy; to save them from themselves. What caused the ruin of the Republics of Greece and Rome? Demagogues, who, by flattery, gained the aid of the populace to establish despotism.

Ibid. at 41. To save the people from themselves, Morris continued in a later speech, if the checks on popular will provided by two legislative branches and a Presidency populated by 'men selected from their fellow-citizens for their talents, for their virtue; [by] men advanced in age, and of matured judgment' were to 'prove insufficient, and alas! such is the condition of human nature, that I fear they will not always be sufficient, the Constitution has given us one more', an 'independent' judiciary which can declare the acts of those two branches unconstitutional. Ibid. at 83-84. But what sort of trial jurisdiction had been vested in that judiciary?

> [W]e find [Morris said] that the judicial power shall extend to a great variety of cases. . . . [T]he Constitution did not merely contemplate, but did, by express words, reserve to the national tribunals a right to decide, and did secure to the citizens of America a right to demand their decision, in many cases evidently cognizable in the State courts. And what are those cases? They are those in respect to which it is by the Constitution presumed that the State courts would not always make a cool and calm investigation, a fair and just decision.

Ibid. at 78. In *every* head of jurisdiction in Article III, therefore, the centralizing Constitution granted to federal judges the power to hear cases in which state justice might be suspect, and granted to American citizens a right to demand access in order to avoid the suspected state prejudice. Morris' words about the language he himself drafted, see supra note 73, imply a very broad grant of federal jurisdiction indeed, a protective jurisdiction to be sure, a backstop and curative jurisdiction rather than a mandatorily all-encompassing one, but a potentially omnivorous federal jurisdiction *capable* of hearing, if necessary, 'a great variety of cases'. Morris was, I believe, defending an Act which permitted federal jurisdiction over *Hobby v. Day*, that is, the 1801 Act described in these pages.

75. Cf. Mark V. Tushnet, 'Following the Rules Laid Down: A Critique of Interpretivism and Neutral Principles', 96 *Harvard Law Review* 781 (1983).

SUPREME COURT APPOINTMENTS, 1789-1801: CRITERIA, PRESIDENTIAL STYLE, AND THE PRESS OF EVENTS

James R. Perry

What factors influence appointments to the Supreme Court? Too often, studies emphasize a straightforward process of measuring candidates against a set of criteria, including professional qualifications, character, public service, party affiliation, and state of residence. Less often studied is the impact of a president's style of decision-making. Does he decide alone or with the advice of others? If he consults with others, who are they and what influence do they have on his final choice? Studies also frequently neglect the specific context—political, legal, and temporal—within which the decision is made. The press of events is a far more important factor than is suggested by a review of the literature on appointments.

The present study examines Supreme Court appointments made during the presidencies of George Washington and John Adams. Although both presidents were Federalists, the criteria they applied to candidate differed and so did their styles of decision-making. Most important, this study explores the appointment process within a fully delineated early national context, including the influence of state and national politics, the constraints of judicial legislation, and, in general, the press of events. The result illuminates much about the leadership of Washington and Adams, the relationship between state and federal politics, the struggle between Federalists and Republicans, and the forces shaping membership on the Court.

The Supreme Court—indeed the entire federal judiciary—was a novel creation. The Articles of Confederation had provided for no

---

Mr. Perry, formerly co-editor of *The Documentary History of the Supreme Court of the United States, 1789-1800*, is a free-lance writer and editor in Washington, D.C.

JOURNAL OF THE EARLY REPUBLIC, 6 (Winter 1986).

federal judiciary. In 1780 Congress created a three-member Court of Appeals in Cases of Capture, which had an appellate jurisdiction limited to resolving disputes among state admiralty courts. At the Constitutional Convention, delegates had far less to say about the judicial than about the executive and legislative branches. As finally approved, Article 3 of the Constitution established a Supreme Court, defined its original and appellate jurisdiction, and provided a bit vaguely for "such inferior Courts as the Congress may from time to time ordain and establish." During the ensuing struggle over ratification, Antifederalists voiced alarm over the potential threat of the federal judiciary to state courts. And in the first session of Congress, concern that the federal judiciary would swallow the state judiciaries permeated debate over legislation establishing inferior federal courts.[1]

As George Washington considered candidates for appointment to the Supreme Court, he was aware of these fears about the federal judiciary. His hopes for the new system of government and his belief in the importance of the federal judiciary to the government's success were shadowed by the opposition of the Antifederalists. The president knew that he had to tread carefully.

On September 24, 1789, Washington submitted to the Senate his nominations for the six seats on the Supreme Court. For chief justice, he nominated John Jay of New York; for associate justices, John Rutledge of South Carolina, James Wilson of Pennsylvania, William Cushing of Massachusetts, Robert H. Harrison of Maryland, and John Blair of Virginia. On September 26 the Senate confirmed all of the nominees.[2] How had the president chosen these six men? Scholars writing about Washington's appointments generally agree on the criteria most important to him in making nominations to the Court. First, he considered the candidate's fitness, including his character, health, training, experience, and public recognition or fame. Second, given the jealous localism of the states, he sought a balanced geographic distribution on the high bench. Third, he gave due consideration to a candidate's sacrifice attendant upon the war for independence. And, finally, he chose candidates who supported the new government established under the Constitution; this gradually evolved into partisanship as the labels of Federalist and Antifederalist gave way to

---

[1] Henry J. Bourguignon, *The First Federal Court: The Federal Appellate Prize Court of the American Revolution, 1775-1787* (Philadelphia 1977), 40; Julius Goebel, Jr., *History of the Supreme Court of the United States*, vol. 1, *Antecedents and Beginnings to 1801* (New York 1971), 171, 205-206, 280-291, and chs. 7, 8, 9, and 11.

[2] *Journal of the Executive Proceedings of the Senate of the United States of America* (32 vols., Washington, D.C. 1828-1909), I, 29-30.

Federalist and Republican.[3] Washington's first nominees to the Supreme Court exemplified these criteria.[4] But other individuals also fit this profile. The question remains: how did the president select these six?

Washington's style of decision-making shaped his choice of nominees. He encouraged all interested candidates to make their desires known, but he responded noncommittally to all applications. He did not want to nominate men who would then decline to serve, because this would damage severely the infant government's image. He inquired freely of senators and congressmen as to qualified individuals in their states. About specific applicants, he consulted with trusted advisers, particularly James Madison and Robert Morris. But despite all the consultations, Washington kept secret the names of his nominees until the list was given to the Senate.[5] As Washington wrote some years later in reference to his Supreme Court nominations: "although

---

[3] Lucy M. Salmon, *History of the Appointing Power of the President* (New York 1886), 25; Gaillard Hunt, "Office-Seeking during Washington's Administration," *American Historical Review*, 1 (Jan. 1896), 275-278; Carl Russell Fish, *The Civil Service and the Patronage* (New York 1905), 6-10; Frank L. Esterquest, "State Adjustments to the Federal Constitution, 1789-1800" (Ph.D. diss., University of Chicago 1940), 267; James Hart, *The American Presidency in Action: 1789* (New York 1948), 112-122, 131-133; Leonard D. White, *The Federalists: A Study in Administrative History* (New York 1948), 258-261, 271, 272, 276; Daniel S. McHargue, "Appointments to the Supreme Court of the United States: The Factors that Have Affected Appointments, 1789-1932" (Ph.D. diss., University of California, Los Angeles 1949), 5; John C. Miller, *The Federalist Era, 1789-1801* (1960; rep. New York 1963), 31; Henry J. Abraham, *Justices and Presidents: A Political History of Appointments to the Supreme Court* (2nd ed., New York 1985), 71-72; William J. Daniels, "The Geographic Factor in Appointments to the United States Supreme Court: 1789-1976," *Western Political Quarterly*, 31 (June 1978), 226-237; Carl E. Prince, *The Federalists and the Origins of the U.S. Civil Service* (New York 1977), 2-10.

[4] Biographical information readily available in the *Dictionary of American Biography* or the *Biographical Directory of the American Congress, 1774-1961*, is not noted here.

[5] For Washington's noncommital responses and caution, see Edmund Randolph to James Madison, July 19, 1789, James Madison Papers (Library of Congress [LC], Washington, D.C.); Richard Morris to George Washington, July 23, 1789, George Washington Papers, LC; John Lowell to Elbridge Gerry, July 20, 1789, Gerry II Collection (Massachusetts Historical Society [MHS], Boston); for Washington's inquiries and consultations, see Fisher Ames to John Lowell, July 28, 1789, Sol Feinstone Collection (David Library of the American Revolution, Washington Crossing, Penn.); Edmund Randolph to James Madison, July 19, 1789, Madison Papers; Elbridge Gerry's Recommendations for Offices in Massachusetts [before July 20, 1789?], Washington Papers [for dating, see Maeva Marcus and James R. Perry, eds., *The Documentary History of the Supreme Court of the United States, 1789-1800* (1 vol. to date, New York 1985), I, 636-637]; Ralph Izard to Edward Rutledge, Sept. 26, 1789, *American Historical Review*, 14 (July 1909), 777; George Washington to James Madison,

I do— at all times— make the best enquiries my opportunities afford, to come at the fittest characters for offices, where *my own* knowledge does not give a *decided* preference . . . no one knows my ultimate determination until the moment arrives when the nomination is to be laid before the Senate.— My resolution, not to create an expectation, which thereafter might embarass my own conduct (by such a commitment to any one as might subject me to the charge of deception) is co-eval with my inauguration; and in no instance have I departed from it." Thus, less than a week before Washington submitted his first nominations to the Senate, even Vice President John Adams could write "how the President will decide, on the judiciary Appointments I know not."[6]

Yet, while Adams did not know who the president would nominate, he may have provided general principles that guided the final selection. In a letter dated September 21 (three days before the president sent his nominations to the Senate), Adams wrote that "It would have an happy effect if all the judges of the national supréme Court, could be taken from the chief Justices of the several states. The superiority of the national government would in this way be decidedly acknowledged. All the judges of the states would look up to the national bench as their ultimate object.— As there is great danger of collisions between the national and state judiciaries, if the state judges are men possesed of larger portions of the people's confidence than the national judges, the latter will become unpopular." Washington echoed the vice president's view in the official cover letter sent to the justices with their commissions: "Considering the Judicial System as the chief Pillar upon which our national Government must rest, I have thought it my duty to nominate, for the high Offices in that department, such men as I conceived would give dignity and lustre to our National Character." Later Washington wrote that "in the Person of a Judge, the World will look for a character and reputation founded on service

---

Aug. 9, 1789, Madison Papers; George Washington to James Madison [Aug. 20-Sept. 11, 1789] (Rosenbach Foundation, Philadelphia, Penn.) [see Marcus and Perry, eds., *Documentary History of the Supreme Court*, I, 651-652 for dating]; Paine Wingate to Timothy Pickering, Sept. 14, 1789, Timothy Pickering Papers, MHS; Robert Morris to Mary Morris, Sept. 25, 1789, Robert Morris File (Henry E. Huntington Library, San Marino, Calif.); George Washington to James Madison [before Sept. 24, 1789], Madison Papers [see Marcus and Perry, eds., *Documentary History of the Supreme Court*, I, 665-666 for dating]; and, for Washington's secrecy, see Fisher Ames to Caleb Strong, Sept. 15, 1789, Thompson's Collection of Autograph Letters (Hartford Seminary Foundation, Hartford, Conn.).

[6] Washington to Edmund Pendleton, Mar. 17, 1794, Washburn Papers, MHS; Adams to William Tudor, Sept. 18, 1789, Tudor Papers, MHS.

and experience" and that "In such important appointments as the Judiciary, much confidence is necessary."[7]

And so it is not surprising that Washington favored the appointment of state chief justices or other high judicial officers—present or former. Jay, Rutledge, and Cushing each was or had been his respective state's chief judicial officer. Harrison was chief judge of the Maryland General Court. Blair, although not chief judge of the Virginia Court of Appeals, sat on that bench as well as being chief justice of the General Court and former chancellor of the High Court of Chancery. (He was nominated by the president in lieu of the presiding judge of the Court of Appeals, Edmund Pendleton, whose poor health prevented him from accepting appointment to the Supreme Court.) James Wilson had never held state judicial office, but his indisputable brilliance as a legal scholar and unparalleled exertions in support of the Constitution were powerful incentives to nominate him; in addition, Wilson benefited from the position of his friend, Robert Morris, close to the president. Washington's decision to appoint Jay to head the Supreme Court may have been influenced by Jay's skills not only in the legal field but also in political and diplomatic arenas, skills that would be sorely needed in dealing with fractious state judiciaries.[8]

Thus, Washington's nominations resulted from a careful consideration of appropriate criteria, as well as from a highly consultative process. But other factors also affected his nominations. One of the most important was the pressure of public interest and scrutiny. Washington quickly discovered that there would be no shortage of candidates, both self-proclaimed and popularly acclaimed. During the spring and summer of 1789 candidates and their friends sought the support of the president and those thought to have influence with him.

The efforts on behalf of candidates reveal political pressures specific to the early 1790s. The support for James Wilson illustrates both the techniques used to forward a candidate's claim and the political pressures underlying those efforts. In early 1789 Wilson was the man most frequently mentioned for chief justice. Possessed of a brilliant legal mind, he was unpopular in Pennsylvania because of his opposition to the radically democratic government established in that state

---

[7] Adams to Stephen Higginson, letterbook copy in Adams Papers, MHS; Washington to John Rutledge, Sept. 30, 1789, and Washington to Otho H. Williams, Nov. 22, 1789, letterbook copies in Washington Papers.

[8] George Washington to James Madison [before Sept. 24, 1789], Madison Papers; George Washington to Edmund Pendleton, Sept. 28, 1789, letterbook copy in Washington Papers; Charles Warren, *The Supreme Court in United States History* (3 vols., Boston 1923), I, 36.

in 1776. Antifederalists in Pennsylvania disliked Wilson because of his outspoken support of the federal cause, both in the Constitutional Convention and at the Pennsylvania state ratifying convention. His lack of a broad constituency precluded his election either as a senator or congressman.

Wilson's friends therefore sought his appointment as chief justice. Benjamin Rush of Philadelphia, who had joined Wilson in fighting for ratification in Pennsylvania, took a leading role; Pennsylvania's Senator Robert Morris, a close ally of Wilson, also lent his support.[9] On March 9, 1789, Philadelphia's *Federal Gazette* extolled Wilson's public sacrifices and his virtues: "A new system of federal jurisprudence must be formed; a new region in the administration of justice must be explored, in which genius alone can supply the defect of precedent; and who so equal to those great and original undertakings as that favorite son of Pennsylvania, James Wilson, esq." Who, indeed? The New-York *Journal* responded on April 16 that there were many men more deserving than Wilson of the chief justiceship and listed seven.

Wilson and his friends increased their efforts. Wilson wrote to the president that he desired appointment as chief justice. Washington's answer, as to all such applications, was noncommittal. On the same day that Washington wrote to Wilson, he sent an equally noncommittal answer to Thomas McKean, chief justice of the Pennsylvania Supreme Court, who also had written soliciting a position in the judiciary. Unlike Wilson's pretensions, McKean's were not supported by a number of advocates. Moreover, McKean had been the subject of an impeachment effort the previous year, and he had earned the enmity of Pennsylvania Antifederalists for the virulence of his attacks on them.[10]

The day after Wilson sent his application to the president, Benjamin Rush wrote to the vice president explaining Wilson's situation in Pennsylvania, reminding him of Wilson's contributions to the federal

---

[9] Rush to Tench Coxe, Jan. 31, Feb. 26, 1789, Tench Coxe Papers (Historical Society of Pennsylvania [HSP], Philadelphia); Frederick Muhlenberg to Rush, Mar. 21, 1789, Gratz Collection, HSP; Janet Montgomery to Robert R. Livingston [before July 4, 1789], Robert R. Livingston Papers (New-York Historical Society, New York); Morris to Francis Hopkinson, Aug. 15, 1789, Hopkinson Papers, HSP.

[10] Wilson to Washington, Apr. 21, 1789, Washington Papers; Washington to Wilson, May 9, 1789, copy in Miscellaneous Letters, RG 59 (National Archives [NA], Washington, D.C.); McKean to Washington, Apr. 27, 1789, Washington Papers; Washington to McKean, May 9, 1789, Hampton Carson Collection, HSP; G.S. Rowe, *Thomas McKean: The Shaping of an American Republicanism* (Boulder, Colo. 1978), 246-249, 255-256.

cause, and trying to allay any concerns he might have about "the deranged state" of Wilson's finances. Noting Adams' influence as president of the Senate, Rush added none too subtly that Adams "had not a more zealous friend . . . in the late election of vice president in this state, than Mr Wilson." In response, Adams denied any influence in the Senate and added curtly that "I am not obliged to vote for a Man because he voted for me." Furthermore, Adams wrote that "Services, Hazards, Abilities and Popularity, all properly weighed, the Ballance, is in favour of Mr Jay.— one of the Judges, I wish Mr Wilson to be: and the difference is not great between the first and the other Judges."[11] Adams thereby foretold the outcome of the competition for chief justice.

Wilson's appointment was an exception to Washington's rule of nominating experienced jurists from the high courts of the states. The rule is illustrated by the outcome of the intense competition for appointment that took place in Massachusetts beginning in June 1789. Most prominent Federalists there supported the appointment of John Lowell, a highly qualified jurist who had sat already on the Court of Appeals in Cases of Capture. Francis Dana, associate justice of the Massachusetts Supreme Judicial Court, wrote to the vice president on June 26 in support of Lowell's appointment; Dana also withdrew his own name from consideration, because it was clear by then that Supreme Court justices would have to ride extensive circuits and Dana's health was poor. In response, Adams wrote that William Cushing, chief justice of the Massachusetts Supreme Judicial Court, also had been mentioned as a potential appointee, and he continued that "For my own part I only wish that the best and ablest men may be brought into the public service, such as have the clearest and fairest reputations, are known to the people and have acquired weight and consequence in their estimation."[12]

Lowell's partisans kept up their pressure. Massachusetts Congressman Elbridge Gerry noted Lowell's credentials and popular support on a list of Massachusetts applicants for federal office that he gave to the president. On July 18 Benjamin Lincoln, formerly lieutenant governor of Massachusetts, wrote to Secretary of War Henry Knox and the president in support of Lowell. In drafting his response,

---

[11] Rush to Adams, Apr. 22, 1789, Adams Papers; Adams to Rush, May 17, 1789, photostat in Benjamin Rush Papers, LC.

[12] Dana to Adams, Adams Papers; Adams to Dana, July 10, 1789, letterbook copy, *ibid.*

Knox wrote and then crossed out that he knew "the opinion of the Senators here to be highly favorable to Mr Lowell." Presumably Knox meant the Massachusetts senators; Congressman Fisher Ames of Massachusetts believed that the entire Massachusetts delegation in Congress supported Lowell. In reference to Cushing's candidacy, Ames wrote "by what influence the nomination will be supported I am not able to discover." Boston lawyer Christopher Gore wrote to Rufus King, senator from New York and a former Massachusetts resident, that to pass over Lowell, who had sat on the Court of Appeals in Cases of Capture, for a position of "similar rank" would be seen as disgraceful to Lowell; besides, Cushing was too old for the post.[13]

But Lowell's professional credentials, previous service on the Court of Appeals in Cases of Capture, and relative youth do not explain fully why his Federalist supporters favored his appointment over that of William Cushing. State politics must be taken into account. Cushing's appointment would remove him as chief justice of the Massachusetts Supreme Judicial Court. The opponents of Governor John Hancock feared that Hancock would alter the Federalist makeup of that bench by filling Cushing's vacancy with a jurist so obnoxious as to induce the resignation of several justices, thereby creating an opportunity to appoint additional politically sympathetic justices. This argument was presented to John Adams by Francis Dana, former governor James Bowdoin, Stephen Higginson (a bitter opponent of Governor Hancock), and by John Lowell himself.[14]

In early August the effort to get Lowell appointed lost momentum. In a letter to Elbridge Gerry dated August 8, Lowell suggested that the opposition of Lieutenant Governor Samuel Adams and an unnamed "Gentleman" might have been blocking the appointment.

---

[13] Elbridge Gerry's Recommendations for Offices in Massachusetts [before July 20, 1789], Washington Papers; Lincoln to Knox, Henry Knox Papers, MHS; Lincoln to Washington, Washington Papers; Knox to Lincoln, July 26, 1789, draft in Knox Papers; Ames to John Lowell, July 28, 1789, Feinstone Collection; Gore to King, Aug. 6, 1789, Rufus King Papers (New-York Historical Society). Cushing was 57 (Gore wrote 56) and Lowell was 46. The question of Cushing's ability to ride circuit was raised also by John Lowell in a letter to John Adams, Aug. 7, 1789, Adams Papers.

[14] Dana to Adams, July 31, 1789, Bowdoin to Adams, Aug. 10, 1789, Higginson to Adams, Aug. 10, 1789, Lowell to Adams, Aug. 7, 1789, Adams Papers. There is little doubt that these letters were part of an organized offensive; two days before Bowdoin wrote his letter from Boston, Lowell mentioned to Elbridge Gerry in a letter written from Roxbury that "I rather think Mr Bowdoin has written to the V. Presidt on the Subject." Aug. 8, 1789, Gerry II Collection.

Thereafter Lowell's supporters focused on securing for him appointment as federal district judge for Massachusetts.[15]

In sum, President Washington's first nominations to the Supreme Court were made after careful consideration of appropriate criteria and after extensive consultation with those who knew the candidates. But the process of selection did not occur in a vacuum. Instead, as exemplified by the efforts of Wilson's and Lowell's friends, state and federal politics intervened. Favorable public response to the appointments justified Washington's care in selection.[16]

In making these first appointments to the Supreme Court, Washington enjoyed a luxury he would not always have thereafter. That luxury was time—leisurely time to consult with state leaders and close advisers, time to determine whether a candidate would accept. For the rest of his first term and all of his second, Washington chose most of his nominees under pressure, either to assure a sufficient number of justices on the Supreme Court itself or to make certain that the justices' circuit-riding was not disrupted. This latter requirement was particularly constraining. The Judiciary Act of 1789 generally defined each state as a federal district and grouped the districts into three circuits. It further specified that two justices join each district judge twice each year to form a circuit court for that district. Although this was revised in 1793 so that only one justice was required to sit with each district judge, keeping the circuits manned still pressured Washington's decision-making.[17] Furthermore, unforeseen events upset some of his most careful calculations.

Washington was fortunate in the circumstances attending the first vacancy on the Supreme Court. The vacancy resulted when, after prolonged negotiations, Robert H. Harrison decided that he was not well enough to serve as associate justice. He informed the president of his decision on January 21, 1790, less than two weeks before the opening of the Court's first term.[18] In the meantime, North Carolina finally

---

[15] Lowell to Gerry, Gerry II Collection; Fisher Ames to George Richards Minot, Aug. 12, 1789, in *Works of Fisher Ames*, ed. Seth Ames (2 vols., Boston 1854), I, 66-68; Christopher Gore to Rufus King, Aug. 22, 1789, King Papers; Fisher Ames to Caleb Strong, Sept. 15, 1789, Thompson's Collection of Autograph Letters. Lowell was appointed federal judge for the district of Massachusetts on Sept. 26, 1789. *Senate Executive Journal*, I, 30.

[16] Ralph Izard to Edward Rutledge, Sept. 26, 1789, *American Historical Review*, 14 (July 1909), 777; Boston *Massachusetts Centinel*, Oct. 3, 1789; Edward Rutledge to George Washington, Oct. 31, 1789, Gratz Collection; David Humphreys to George Washington, Oct. 28, 1789, Washington Papers.

[17] *Statutes at Large of the United States*, I, 73-75, 333-334.

[18] Harrison to Washington, Oct. 27, 1789, RG 360, NA; Harrison to Washington,

had ratified the Constitution in a second state convention held in November 1789. Washington thought it expedient to appoint a prominent North Carolinian to the national government in order to strengthen the bond between the two. There was no question who that individual should be. James Iredell, a wartime attorney general and Superior Court judge of North Carolina, had taken a leading role in the ratification struggle in that state. With William R. Davie, he had published the debates of the first North Carolina ratifying convention. This had brought Iredell to the attention of Congress in the summer of 1789, and at that time there were hints of a judicial appointment for him outside of North Carolina. Iredell had not discouraged the inquiries. Hugh Williamson, a North Carolinian who had sat in the Constitutional Convention and worked with Iredell for ratification in North Carolina, had informed Washington of Iredell's qualifications and suggested that the president contact South Carolina's Senator Pierce Butler should he want further information.[19]

Therefore, when Washington learned of Harrison's declination, he could act quickly. His nomination of a replacement is particularly revealing because of the full documentation concerning how he came to select Iredell. On February 4, 1790, two days after the Supreme Court opened, Washington invited to dinner the justices then in New York, Vice President John Adams, Attorney General Edmund Randolph, Secretary of War Henry Knox, and Secretary of the Treasury Alexander Hamilton, as well as the judge, marshal, attorney, and clerk of the federal district court for New York. Significantly, the only senators present were Benjamin Hawkins and Samuel Johnston of North

Oct. 27, 1789, Letters of Resignation and Declination from Federal Office, RG 59, NA; James McHenry to Washington, Nov. 14, 1789, Washington Papers; Washington to Harrison, Nov. 25, 1789, Harrison to Washington, Jan. 21, 1790, Library of Congress Special Collection, RG 233, NA; Alexander Hamilton to Harrison, Nov. 27, 1789, transcript in John C. Hamilton Transcripts (Columbia University, New York); Washington to James McHenry, Nov. 30, 1789, George Washington Papers (Henry E. Huntington Library); James McHenry to Washington, Dec. 10, 1789, Washington Papers, LC.

[19] *Proceedings and debates of the Convention of North-Carolina, convened at Hillsborough, on Monday the 21st day of July, 1788, for the purpose of deliberating and determining on the Constitution recommended by the general Convention at Philadelphia, the 17th day of September, 1787. To which is prefixed the said Constitution* (Edenton 1789); Williamson to Iredell, Aug. 12, 1789, Charles E. Johnson Collection (North Carolina State Department of Archives and History, Raleigh); Iredell to Williamson, Aug. 29, 1789, draft in Johnson Collection; Williamson to Washington, Sept. 19, 1789, Washington Papers, LC.

Carolina.[20] Immediately upon arriving home from the dinner, Senator Johnston, who was James Iredell's brother-in-law, wrote that "The President enquired particularly after you and spoke of you in a manner that gave me great pleasure." Two days later President Washington, in an unusually revealing passage written in his diary, noted that in filling the vacancy "I determined after contemplating every character which presented itself to my view to name Mr Iredall of No Carolina; because, in addition to the reputation he sustains for abilities, legal knowledge and respectability of character he is of a State of some importance in the Union that has given *No* character to a federal Office.__ In ascertaining the character of this Gentleman I had recourse to every means of information in my power and found them all concurring in his favor."[21]

Three days after this entry was made, the Senate received the president's nomination of Iredell. The Senate considered the nomination on February 10. Senator Johnston wrote to Iredell that "it was necessary, as you was not generally known to the Members, that some Member should inform them of your qualifications to execute that Office." Senator Pierce Butler spoke in Iredell's favor. But "a Member from New Hampshire . . . wished to hear the Sentiments of the Gentlemen from the State where you resided, upon this Mr Hawkins confirmed what Majr Butler had said and added something of his own." The Senate then voted unanimously to confirm the nomination.[22]

Washington acted quickly in nominating Iredell, in contrast with his leisurely investigation of candidates and their qualifications the year before. The swiftness of his choice was made possible by three factors. First, he believed it important to choose a respected North Carolinian for appointment to a high federal position, and this narrowed his choice. Second, there were individuals in New York to provide information on Iredell's qualifications. Third, the president knew that Iredell would accept the appointment.

A year later, when Washington had to fill another vacancy on the Court, he acted much more slowly than he had in choosing Iredell. On March 5, 1791, John Rutledge forwarded his resignation to the

---

[20] Donald Jackson and Dorothy Twohig, eds., *The Diaries of George Washington* (6 vols., Charlottesville 1976-1979), VI, 28.

[21] Johnston to Iredell, Feb. 4, 1790, James Iredell Sr. and Jr. Papers (Duke University, Durham, N. C.); George Washington Diary, Feb. 6, 1790, Washington Papers, LC.

[22] Johnston to Iredell, Feb. 11, 1790, Johnson Collection; *Senate Executive Journal*, I, 38, 40.

president. He was resigning in order to accept appointment as chief justice of South Carolina's Court of Common Pleas.[23] Assuming that the president would nominate a justice either from South Carolina or Georgia, candidates from those states proclaimed themselves or were named by others.[24]

The president postponed any action, because he would be touring through the southern states in the spring and could investigate candidates himself. While in Columbia, South Carolina, he made up his mind. In an unusual letter dated May 24, 1791, and sent to Charles Cotesworth Pinckney and Edward Rutledge, Washington offered to appoint one of them to the bench. The president had seen both just three weeks before. Pinckney and Rutledge were brothers-in-law, and the president relied on their "friendship for each other" in this "singular" offer.[25] Both had trained in the Middle Temple before the revolution, both had long public careers, and both declined Washington's offer. In a joint letter to the president on June 12, they explained that "We think we can be of more real Advantage to the General Government & to our own State Government by remaining in the Legislature."[26]

The president probably received this letter at Mount Vernon in late June;[27] only one month remained before the Supreme Court would convene in Philadelphia on August 1. Concern to fill the vacancy before then may have prompted Washington to turn his attention to Thomas Johnson in Maryland. Johnson had replaced Robert H. Harrison as chief judge of the Maryland General Court after Harrison died in April

---

[23] Miscellaneous Letters, RG 59, NA.

[24] Jacob Read to Washington, Feb. 10, 1791, Miscellaneous Letters, *ibid.*; James Gunn to Washington, Mar. 7, 1791, and Charles Pinckney to Washington, Mar. 8, 1791, Washington Papers, LC. In particular, Nathaniel Pendleton, briefly chief justice of the Georgia Superior Court and then United States judge for the district of Georgia, began an extensive campaign to secure appointment. Pendleton to James Iredell, Mar. 5, 1791, Iredell Papers; Pendleton to [Henry Knox], Mar. 5, 1791, J.S.H. Fogg Collection (Maine Historical Society, Portland) [see Marcus and Perry, eds., *Documentary History of the Supreme Court*, I, 720-722, for identification of recipient]; Pendleton to George Washington, Mar. 5, and Apr. 10, 1791, Washington Papers, LC; Edmund Pendleton to Thomas Jefferson, July 13, 1791, Thomas Jefferson Papers, LC; Edmund Pendleton to James Madison, July 13, 1791, Washington Papers, LC.

[25] George Washington Papers (Charleston Library Society, Charleston, S. C.); Jackson and Twohig, eds., *Diaries of George Washington*, VI, 126.

[26] Washington Papers, LC.

[27] He was there from June 12 to June 27. Jackson and Twohig, eds., *Diaries of George Washington*, VI, 163-164.

1790. The president had known Johnson from the early days of the revolution, thus making unnecessary an investigation of his qualifications. Furthermore, Washington saw Johnson for several days at the end of June when the president met with the commissioners of the federal city. (Johnson had been a commissioner since January 1791.) Johnson also traveled through Maryland with Washington as the president made his way to Philadelphia.[28] The president arrived in Philadelphia on July 6 and wrote to Johnson eight days later offering to appoint him to the Court and requesting an answer as soon as possible.[29] Johnson responded in two letters—one of July 27 and one of July 30/August 1—that he was concerned about having to ride the southern circuit given his age (58) and "weak Frame." Urgent business called him to Georgetown, and he wrote that "I feel real Unesiness that my Embarrassment should occasion delay in your filling up this Office as the Time is now so short."[30] It was already too late for Washington to find someone in time to sit with the Court in August. He consulted with the justices, who agreed to relieve Johnson from having to ride the ensuing southern circuit. Furthermore, there was a general opinion that Congress would soon relieve the justices from the burden of riding circuit. Washington explained the results of his inquiries to Johnson in a letter of August 7 and forwarded a temporary commission, which Johnson accepted. He thereby became the first recess appointee to the Court. On November 7 the Senate confirmed Johnson's nomination, and he received a permanent commission.[31]

But despite the expectation that Congress would free the justices from riding circuit, no such change was made; and as Johnson had

---

[28] Lyman H. Butterfield, ed., *Diary and Autobiography of John Adams* (4 vols., Cambridge, Mass. 1961), II, 150; Jackson and Twohig, eds., *Diaries of George Washington*, VI, 164-166; Herbert Alan Johnson, "Thomas Johnson," in *The Justices of the United States Supreme Court, 1789-1978*, ed. Leon Friedman and Fred L. Israel (1978; rep. 5 vols., New York 1980), I, 149, 157; Edward S. Delaplaine, *The Life of Thomas Johnson* (New York 1927), 150, 472.

[29] Jackson and Twohig, eds., *Diaries of George Washington*, VI, 169n; George Washington to Thomas Johnson, July 14, 1791, Dreer Collection, HSP.

[30] Miscellaneous Letters, RG 59, NA.

[31] The consultation took place at a dinner, which probably occurred on August 3 or 4. John Jay to Sally Jay, Aug. 3, 1791, Washburn Papers; Temporary Commission, Aug. 5, 1791, Thomas Johnson Letters (C. Burr Artz Public Library, Frederick, Md.); Washington to Johnson, Aug. 7, 1791, letterbook copy in Washington Papers, LC; Johnson to Washington, Aug. 13, 1791, Miscellaneous Letters, RG 59, NA; *Senate Executive Journal*, I, 86, 88; Commission, Nov. 7, 1791, photostat in Gift Collection (Maryland Hall of Records, Annapolis).

anticipated, his health did not allow him to continue as a justice. He resigned on January 16, 1793. Washington's response reflected his frustration at the turnover of personnel on the Supreme Court: "besides the difficulty of finding characters to fill the dignified & important station of Judge, in whom are combined the necessary professional, local & other requisites, the resignation of persons holding that high Office conveys to the public mind a want of stability in that Department, where it is perhaps more essential than in any other."[32]

Having received Johnson's resignation so late in January, Washington had no time to recruit another candidate before the Court's next scheduled meeting on the first Monday of February. On February 18 the president sought the advice of Attorney General Edmund Randolph, who favored the appointment of William Paterson, governor of New Jersey. Formerly attorney general of that state and a member of the Constitutional Convention, Paterson had served as one of New Jersey's first senators and had played an important role in the drafting of the Judiciary Act. Secretary of State Jefferson concurred in Randolph's opinion of Paterson. Washington offered a place on the Court to Paterson, the latter accepted, and the Senate confirmed the nomination.[33]

The Court's membership remained stable for two years. But in 1795 Washington was faced with two vacancies on the bench, and his efforts to fill them were complicated by national politics, constraints imposed by the Judiciary Act of 1789, and uncommonly bad timing. His problems began in April 1794, when Chief Justice Jay was appointed envoy extraordinary to negotiate a resolution of disputes between the United States and Great Britain. When Jay returned to New York in late May 1795, he found that in his absence New York Federalists had entered him in the election for governor of that state.

---

[32] Washington to Johnson, Feb. 1, 1793, letterbook copy in Washington Papers, LC. See also Johnson to James Wilson, Mar. 1, 1792, Hampton L. Carson Collection (Free Library of Philadelphia, Penn.); Johnson to James Iredell, Mar. 31, 1792, Johnson Collection; and Johnson to Washington, Jan. 16, 1793, Miscellaneous Letters, RG 59, NA. Congress did nothing to relieve the justices of riding circuit until after Johnson resigned from the Court. On March 2, 1793, an act was passed requiring only one justice—rather than two—to attend each circuit. *Statutes at Large*, I, 333-334.

[33] Randolph to Washington, Feb. 18, 1793, and George Washington Journal, Feb. 19, 1793, Washington Papers, LC; Washington to Paterson, Feb. 20, 1793, George Washington Papers (Princeton University, Princeton, N. J.); Paterson to Washington, Feb. 25, 1793, Miscellaneous Letters, RG 59, NA; *Senate Executive Journal*, I, 38. The president's executive journal records, for January 26, 1793, that Johnson's resignation had been received "a few days ago." Washington Papers, LC.

On June 5 he was declared the victor, but not until June 29 did he write to the president resigning as chief justice.[34]

Coincidentally, the same day Washington received Jay's resignation, a letter arrived from former Associate Justice John Rutledge stating that, if nominated to replace Jay, he would accept. Rutledge had written on June 12 in Charleston, where early results indicated Jay had been elected governor, and Rutledge assumed that the chief justice would resign to accept the new post. The president quickly decided on the recess appointment of Rutledge. On July 1, 1795, Washington wrote from Philadelphia that "without hesitating a moment, after knowing you would accept . . . I directed the Secretary of State to make you an official offer of this honorable appointment." Pointedly he noted "my desire & the advantages that would attend your being in this city the first monday in August (at which time the next session of the supreme Court will commence)." Secretary of State Edmund Randolph in his official letter also urged Rutledge to hasten to the capital, where Rutledge would receive his commission, dated July 1. Having arranged a replacement for Jay and completed other business, the president set off for Mount Vernon on July 15.[35]

If Washington thought that replacing a chief justice was so simple, others did not. There was a question whether the chief justice's successor should come from the ranks of the associate justices, and, more specifically, whether the senior associate justice, William Cushing, should be promoted. Some opposed setting such a precedent. As Tench Coxe had written three years before: "The man of the first abilities, that can be found should be induced into the Station . . . dull seniority and length of service should be considered as nothing." Attorney General William Bradford, Jr., speculating on who would replace Jay, wrote on June 4, 1795, that "the principle of Rotation would be the least exceptionable . . . but as cases may often occur in which the succession of the eldest puisne judge would be wholly improper, it will be impossible to establish such a system. The public voice seems already to have excluded Mr C[ushing] who stands next to Mr Jay— & it is even supposed by some that neither h[e?] nor his friends for him would desire it." Cushing's ill health probably was the main obstacle. He had missed many days of the February 1795 term because

---

[34] *Senate Executive Journal*, I, 151-152; Frank Monaghan, *John Jay* (New York 1935), 405; Jay to Washington, Washington Papers, LC.

[35] Rutledge to Washington, Washington Papers, LC; Washington to Rutledge, letterbook copy, *ibid.*; Randolph to Rutledge, July 1, 1795, letterbook copy in Domestic Letters, RG 59, NA; Jackson and Twohig, eds., *Diaries of George Washington*, VI, 204.

of a cancer on his lip, and he frequently missed Court terms entirely. Some, moreover, had a harsh opinion of Cushing; New Hampshire Congressman Jeremiah Smith thought him "superannuated & contemptible." Other individuals mentioned to replace Jay included former Secretary of the Treasury Alexander Hamilton and Secretary of State Randolph.[36]

As late as mid-July the choice of Rutledge as chief justice was known by few,[37] but it is likely that Rutledge had received the letters from President Washington and Secretary of State Randolph when, on July 16, he delivered a vehement speech in Charleston opposing the treaty negotiated by Jay in England. The details of the Jay Treaty had remained secret during its consideration by the Senate in June, but the Philadelphia *Aurora* had published an abstract of the treaty on June 29, and the full text appeared in the Philadelphia *Gazette* two days later. The pro-French party was incensed by what it read. By July 11, the treaty's terms were known at Charleston, and they were published the next day in Charleston's *City Gazette Extraordinary*. It is probable, therefore, that Rutledge had heard of his recess appointment (which was concurrent with the revelation of the treaty) before he spoke to an assembly of Charlestonians on July 16.[38] As reported

[36] Coxe to Richard Henry Lee, [Apr. 11, 1792?], Lee Family Papers (University of Virginia, Charlottesville) [see Marcus and Perry, eds., *Documentary History of the Supreme Court*, I, 735-736, for dating]; Bradford to Samuel Bayard, Gratz Collection; Jeremiah Smith to William Plumer, Feb. 7, Feb. 24, 1795 [quotation], Plumer Papers (New Hampshire State Library, Concord); John Adams to Abigail Adams, Feb. 9, 1795, Adams Papers; William Bradford, Jr., to Alexander Hamilton, July 2, 1795, Alexander Hamilton Papers, LC. With no evidence, Charles Warren, *Supreme Court in United States History*, I, 124-125, contends that Bradford was writing to offer the chief justiceship to Hamilton on behalf of the president. Yet Bradford makes clear that he was writing on his own initiative. Warren's contention has been repeated and given great meaning by subsequent historians: Charles Kerr, "If Spencer Roane Had Been Appointed Chief Justice Instead of John Marshall," *American Bar Association Journal*, 20 (Mar. 1934), 167, 168; McHargue, "Appointments to the Supreme Court of the United States," 24.

[37] William Bradford, Jr., to Samuel Bayard, July 16, 1795, Gratz Collection.

[38] Harold C. Syrett, ed., *The Papers of Alexander Hamilton* (26 vols., New York 1961-1979), XVIII, 389-390n; George C. Rogers, Jr., *Evolution of a Federalist: William Loughton Smith of Charleston (1758-1812)* (Columbia, S.C. 1962), 276. Charles Warren is the main proponent (with slim evidence) that Rutledge did not know of his recess appointment. *Supreme Court in United States History*, I, 129. Arrayed against Warren are Henry Flanders, *The Lives and Times of the Chief Justices of the Supreme Court of the United States* (2 vols., New York 1875), I, 632-633; Richard Barry, *Mr. Rutledge of South Carolina* (New York 1942), 355; Rogers, *Evolution of a Federalist*, 276; and Leon Friedman, "John Rutledge," in *The Justices of the United States Supreme Court, 1789-1978*,

in Charleston's *South-Carolina State-Gazette* on July 17, 1795, Rutledge attacked the Jay Treaty in most intemperate language. He voiced distrust of England and in contrast praised the bravery of the French.

Three days before news of Rutledge's speech reached Philadelphia, Secretary of State Randolph reported to the president about Rutledge that "it is very seriously whispered, that within these two months he is believed in Charleston to be deranged in his mind." This report came from a letter that Henry William DeSaussure, a prominent and respected Charleston lawyer, had received "from a practising lawyer, of some eminence there."[39] It should be noted that rumors of Rutledge being "deranged" were current *before* Rutledge's speech appeared in any newspapers outside of Charleston. Concern about his mental stability was *fueled by*, rather than *caused by*, reports of his speech.

On July 28 two Philadelphia newspapers—*Dunlap's American Daily Advertiser* and the Philadelphia *Gazette*—became the first to publish reports of Rutledge's speech.[40] That very day, Secretary of the Treasury Oliver Wolcott, Jr., wrote to Alexander Hamilton that "to my astonishment, I am recently told that Mr Rutledge has had a tender of the office of Chief Justice__ By the favour of heaven the Com[missio]n is not issued, and now I presume it will not be."[41] The inference is clear that the Anglophile treasury secretary had opposed the Rutledge appointment before the arrival of reports from Charleston, but that the latter rendered the appointment impossible. On July 29 Randolph wrote to the president that "The conduct of the intended Chief Justice is so extraordinary, that Mr Wolcott and Colo Pickering conceive it to be a proof of the imputation of insanity."[42] (Timothy Pickering was secretary of war.)

---

ed. Friedman and Israel, I, 45. A caveat, however, must be entered here: Barry's biography of Rutledge is marred by innumerable factual errors and hagiographical bias (*e.g.*, he never mentions Rutledge's mental instability and suicide attempts), and Friedman relies heavily on Barry. The best account of the Rutledge imbroglio is Rogers, *Evolution of a Federalist*, 281-284. Even if Rutledge had not known of his recess appointment, he did know it was a possibility; after all, he had written to the president asking for it. Therefore, whether or not he knew of the president's action, Rutledge exhibited poor judgment in commenting publicly on a treaty that could become involved in litigation before the Supreme Court.

[39] Randolph to Washington, July 25, 1795, Washington Papers, LC.

[40] For a fuller listing of newspapers reprinting the Rutledge speech, see Marcus and Perry, eds., *Documentary History of the Supreme Court*, I, 767-768.

[41] Hamilton Papers. Oliver Wolcott, Jr., wrote a similar passage to his father, Oliver Wolcott, Sr., on August 10, 1795. Oliver Wolcott, Jr. Papers (Connecticut Historical Society, Hartford).

[42] Washington Papers, LC.

In the period before Rutledge arrived in Philadelphia, many hoped that the reports of his incompetence would convince the president to change his mind and not deliver the temporary commission. Attorney General William Bradford, Jr., wrote to Alexander Hamilton that "The crazy speech of Mr Rutledge joined to certain information that he is daily sinking into debility of mind & body, will probably prevent him to receiving the appointment I mentioned to you." Secretary of War Pickering advised the president to withhold the commission. Secretary of State Randolph wrote to the president that "No answer has been received from Mr Rutledge; but the reports of his attachment to his bottle, his puerility, and extravagances, together with a variety of indecorums and imprudencies multiply daily."[43]

On August 10 Rutledge arrived in Philadelphia; a day later the president returned from Mount Vernon. But Washington could not focus his attention on Rutledge's recess appointment. Immediately the president was faced with a crisis in his cabinet. With the Jay Treaty still unsigned, Secretary of State Randolph was accused of being involved with French envoy Jean Antoine Joseph Fauchet in a bribery plot.[44] In the highly charged political atmosphere resulting from public debate over the Jay Treaty, Randolph's purported indiscretion was a potentially explosive spark. Randolph, seriously compromised by the scandal, became a political and administrative liability. Undoubtedly the pro-French party would see Randolph's departure from the cabinet as a sign of pro-British leanings in the administration. They would be doubly angry if Rutledge were denied the promised commission, an action that would be seen as resulting from his opposition to the treaty. But if he received his commission, the anger of the Francophiles might be softened. The relationship of the Randolph and Rutledge crises, previously unnoticed by historians, is clear.

On the day after the president's arrival in Philadelphia, Randolph gave Rutledge his commission, and Rutledge took his seat on the bench. Oliver Wolcott, Jr., commented that "the Prest was pledged in such a degree, that the Comn could not be denied." He continued that "the Senate will have to determine, when a permanent appointment is made, whether Mr R. shall be the man."[45] And so attention shifted to how the Senate would vote when it met in December.

---

[43] Bradford to Hamilton, Aug. 4, 1795, Hamilton Papers; Pickering to Washington, July 31, 1795, and Randolph to Washington, Aug. 5, 1795, Washington Papers, LC.

[44] Philadelphia *Gazette*, Aug. 12, 1795; Jackson and Twohig, eds., *Diaries of George Washington*, VI, 209; Syrett, ed., *Papers of Alexander Hamilton*, XVIII, 527-528n.

[45] Randolph to Rutledge, Aug. 12, 1795, letterbook copy in Domestic Letters,

During the ensuing months Rutledge was the topic of many newspaper articles. Some viewed his speech against the Jay Treaty as intemperate; some thought it an honest expression of personal belief. His republicanism and support of France, his mental condition, and his personal finances were the subjects of attack and counterattack.[46] In addition there were rumors that Rutledge had changed his mind and decided to support the Jay Treaty. These rumors were denounced by the opponents of the treaty,[47] but were given credence by others. From Charleston, South Carolina, Congressman William L. Smith wrote to Oliver Wolcott, Jr., that he believed that Rutledge repented delivering his speech. Former New Jersey Congressman Elias Boudinot wrote that "Nothing can excuse this instance of democratic fury, but the reported state of Mind, of this once worthy Man— I am told, but cannot answer for the truth of it, that he is now much ashamed of his Conduct."[48]

One question rises above the charges and countercharges, the rumors and denials: what reliable evidence did senators have when they voted on the Rutledge nomination? On November 17 former Senator Ralph Izard wrote from Charleston to South Carolina's Senator Jacob Read: "No man could be more afflicted than I was at the part Mr Rutledge took in opposition to the Treaty. I am sure he is now very sorry for it himself. After the death of his Wife, his mind was frequently so much deranged, as to be in a great measure deprived of his senses; & I am persuaded he was in that situation when the Treaty was under consideration[.] I have frequently been in company with him since his return, & find him totally altered." Izard asked Read "to communicate my opinion on this business" to his "Friends": Senators George Cabot and Caleb Strong of Massachusetts, Senator Oliver Ellsworth of Connecticut, and Senator Frederick Frelinghuysen of New Jersey. The senators probably derived little solace from the

---

RG 59, NA; James Iredell to Hannah Iredell, Aug. 13, 1795, Johnson Collection; Oliver Wolcott, Jr., to Oliver Wolcott, Sr., Aug. 17, 1795, Wolcott Papers.

[46] Most of the debate originated in Boston and Philadelphia newspapers: New York *Argus*, Aug. 5, 1795; Boston *Federal Orrery*, Aug. 6, 1795; Boston *Independent Chronicle*, Aug. 13, 17, 27, Sept. 3, 1795; Philadelphia *Aurora*, Aug. 21, Sept. 8, Oct. 20, 1795; Boston *Columbian Centinel*, Aug. 26, Sept. 2, 5, 1795; Boston *Gazette*, Sept. 7, 1795; Richmond *Virginia Gazette, and General Advertiser*, Sept. 30, 1795; Rutland *Herald*, Oct. 5, 1795; Philadelphia *Gazette of the United States*, Nov. 12, 1795.

[47] Philadelphia *Aurora*, Aug. 21, Sept. 8, 1795.

[48] Smith to Wolcott, in *Memoirs of the Administrations of Washington and John Adams, Edited from the Papers of Oliver Wolcott, Secretary of the Treasury*, ed. George Gibbs (2 vols., New York 1846), I, 230-231; Boudinot to Samuel Bayard, Oct. 17, 1795, Bradford Papers (Princeton University).

news that Rutledge was still suffering mentally from the loss of his wife, who had died over three years before. Read responded to Izard's letter on December 10, noting that "I believe with you that a weakness of the moment not to be accounted for was the Cause of that unwise Speech & Violent Conduct which has Indeed done great mischief." Read had spoken with South Carolina Congressman William L. Smith and Senator Cabot, but the latter gave him no hope for cooperation.[49]

On December 10 the Senate received President Washington's nomination of Rutledge as chief justice and immediately postponed consideration until December 15. On that date the nomination was rejected by a vote of 14 to 10. The senators from South Carolina, North Carolina, and Virginia stood by Rutledge; he also picked up a vote each from Kentucky, New York, Vermont, and New Hampshire. Georgia Senator George Walton later claimed that if he and his fellow Georgian James Gunn had arrived in time for the vote, they would have cast their votes against Rutledge (probably because they had recent evidence of Rutledge's mental instability); the same was claimed of Rhode Island's William Bradford and Delaware's John Vining.[50] The vote then would have been 18 to 10, excluding only the Maryland senators whose leanings are unknown.

Jacob Read provides the most detailed account of what happened in the Senate. He wrote that the senators thought "it woud be very unwise in Gouvernment to put that man in the first Seat of Justice in the Union who had headed a Town meeting & urged & excited the Citizens to do what woud in a very little time if pursued totally destroy all gouvernment & defeat our respresentative System intirely." Read continued that "very full reports of his pecuniary embarrassments were also circulated but these formed a very inferiour objection." Read was the only senator to speak in favor of Rutledge; no one spoke in opposition. This reticence may have resulted from the fact that just six days before (on December 9) the Senate had opened its doors to the public for the first time in its six-year history.[51]

Although Read did not mention the reports of mental instability, they undoubtedly influenced the senators' thinking. Such reports had

---

[49] Izard to Read, Emmet Collection (New York Public Library, New York); Mabel L. Webber, comp., "Dr. John Rutledge and His Descendants," *South Carolina Historical and Genealogical Magazine*, 31 (Jan. 1930), 15; Read to Izard, Ralph Izard Papers (University of South Carolina, Columbia).

[50] *Senate Executive Journal*, I, 194, 195-196; John Adams to Abigail Adams, Dec. 21, 1795, Adams Papers; Jacob Read to Ralph Izard, Dec. 19, 1795, Izard Papers.

[51] Read to Ralph Izard, Dec. 19, 1795, Izard Papers; *Journal of the Senate of the United States of America* (Philadelphia 1795 [1796]), 16-17.

been current even before it was known that Rutledge had delivered his speech. They had been mentioned prominently since. On December 14 Alexander Hamilton in New York City had written a letter to one of that state's senators, Rufus King, in response to King's request for advice. While the letter did not reach King before the Senate vote, it expresses in a reasoned fashion the concerns of many: "If there was nothing in the case but his imprudent sally upon a certain occasion I should think the reasons for letting him pass would outweigh those for opposing his passage__ But if it be really true__ that he is sottish or that his mind is otherwise deranged, or that he exposed himself by improper conduct in pecuniary transactions, the byass of my judgment would be to negative."[52] Contrary to the opinion of most historians, the Senate's rejection of Rutledge was influenced by concern about his fitness for office more than by political considerations.[53]

While Rutledge's opponents exulted and his proponents complained,[54] news arriving from the South suggested that the Senate had

---

[52] King Papers. This letter is postmarked "N-York DEC. 15," the day the Senate rejected the Rutledge nomination.

[53] Historians who have attributed the Senate's action to partisan motives include John Belton O'Neall, *Biographical Sketches of the Bench and Bar of South Carolina* (1859; rep., 2 vols., Spartanburg, S.C. 1975), I, 27; George Van Santvoord, *Sketches of the Lives, Times and Judicial Services of the Chief Justices of the Supreme Court of the United States* (2d ed., Albany, N.Y. 1882), 209-210; Warren, *Supreme Court in United States History*, I, 127-139; Barry, *Mr. Rutledge of South Carolina*, 357; McHargue, "Appointments to the Supreme Court of the United States," 27-28; George S. McCowan, Jr., "Chief Justice John Rutledge and the Jay Treaty," *South Carolina Historical Magazine*, 62 (Jan. 1961), 23; Goebel, *Antecedents and Beginnings to 1801*, 748; Abraham, *Justices and Presidents*, 41, 73; Kent R. Middleton, "The Partisan Press and the Rejection of a Chief Justice," *Journalism Quarterly*, 53 (Spring 1976), 107, 109-110; Walter B. Edgar and N. Louise Bailey, eds., *Biographical Directory of the South Carolina House of Representatives* (4 vols., Columbia, S.C. 1974-1984), II, 580; and Robert L. Meriwether's sketch of Rutledge in *Dictionary of American Biography*, XVI, 258-260. As usual, Barry's account has serious factual errors as does McGowan's; Friedman, "John Rutledge," I, 48, is also unreliable. The most balanced assessment is that of Flanders, *Lives and Times of the Chief Justices*, I, 641. Rogers, *Evolution of a Federalist*, 281-284, also plays down partisan motives. Ralph Izard foresaw that Republicans would ascribe Rutledge's rejection to party purposes: "By the accounts from the Northward I find that the enemies of the Government are making every possible exertion to do mischief. They are in hopes that the Senate will not confirm the appointment of Mr Rutledge as Chief Justice; & if so, will immediately raise a clamor, & endeavor to ascribe the rejection to party"; Izard to Jacob Read, Nov. 17, 1795, Emmet Collection. This is exactly what happened, and historians have adopted the Republican explanation.

[54] John Adams to Abigail Adams, Dec. 16, 17, 1795, Adams Papers; Jeremiah Smith to William Plumer, Dec. 16, 1795, Plumer Papers; Robert R. Livington to Edward Livingston, Dec. 20, 1795, Robert R. Livingston Papers.

made the right decision—Rutledge *was* mentally unstable. Georgia's Senator Walton, arriving in Philadelphia after the Senate's vote, reported "a Disarrangement of Intellect certainly exists and has been more decissive lately than formerly." Rutledge had not been able to hold the circuit courts in Georgia and North Carolina.[55] And he had even attempted suicide. Walton added that "Mr R's Conduct, as Chief Justice of the state of S. Carolina has been lately so unsatisfactory that several Grand Juries have presented him for what they thought Misconduct or at least Negligence of his Duty. The Embarrassment of his private affairs has lately pressed harder upon him than ever and produced or at least accellerated and increased the Disorder of his Mind."[56] On December 26 Rutledge again tried to take his life.[57] Two days later Rutledge—unaware of the Senate rejection—wrote to Washington to resign for reasons of "ill Health."[58]

Washington's effort to replace Chief Justice Jay had turned into an embarrassing public fiasco—an unfortunate combination of Rutledge's weakness, a heated political climate resulting from conflict over the Jay Treaty, and the Randolph scandal. And to make matters worse, with the Court scheduled to meet on the first Monday in February, the president had to find a chief justice *and* an associate justice. On October 25 John Blair had resigned. He had been in poor health for several months and quit in October in order to give the president time to appoint a successor.[59]

---

[55] John Adams to Abigail Adams, Dec. 21, 1795, Adams Papers. John Rutledge, in a letter to George Washington on December 28, 1795, explained that he had not been able to hold the Circuit Court for the district of Georgia because of the death of the clerk, the lack of records, and the absence of the district judge, who was empowered to appoint a new clerk. Miscellaneous Letters, RG 59, NA.

[56] John Adams to Abigail Adams, Dec. 21, 1795, Adams Papers. Others also noted news of Rutledge's deterioration: William Vans Murray to James McHenry, Dec. 24, 1795, James McHenry Papers, LC; New York *American Minerva*, Dec. 24, 1795.

[57] William Read to Jacob Read, Dec. 29, 1795, Jacob Read Papers (University of South Carolina). William Read thought the attempted suicide had occurred on Dec. 27, but the correct date can be determined by a letter from Benjamin Moodie to Jacob Read, Dec. 29, 1795, Jacob Read Miscellaneous Papers (New York Public Library), and an article in the Baltimore *Federal Gazette*, Jan. 8, 1796.

[58] Dec. 28, 1795, Miscellaneous Letters, RG 59, NA.

[59] Blair to Washington, Oct. 25, 1795, *ibid.* For Blair's worsening health, see John Blair to William Cushing, June 12, 1795, Robert Treat Paine Papers, MHS; William Bradford, Jr., to Samuel Bayard, July 16, 1795, Gratz Collection; Blair to James Iredell, Sept. 14, Oct. 10, 1795, *Life and Correspondence of James Iredell*, ed. Griffith J. McRee (2 vols., New York 1857; rep. in 1 vol., New York 1949), II, 454-455.

But Washington had not acted. Apparently anticipating that the Senate might not confirm Rutledge, the president hoped to enlist Patrick Henry as chief justice. Henry had been a leading opponent of the Constitution in Virginia; but during the 1790s he came to support the Washington administration and the Federalists. As early as 1794 Virginia's Governor Henry Lee had corresponded with Washington and explained Patrick Henry's position. The president was willing to consider Henry for some appointment, but he made it clear that he needed assurances that Henry would accept any appointment that might be proffered.[60] At the end of September 1795, when Rutledge's troubles were escalating, Lee wrote to Henry to find out whether he would be willing to have Lee contact the president about nominating Henry as chief justice. Patrick Henry did not answer. In mid-December 1795 Lee contacted Henry again to solicit a commitment, and he wrote to the president that he would forward Henry's decision soon. Lee repeated his efforts in late December.[61]

President Washington refused to make the offer until Henry indicated that he would accept. Already there was a perception—as noted by Virginia's Senator Henry Tazewell—of "the embarrassments experienced by the Executive in filling the high offices of ye Government."[62] Washington did not want to exacerbate this perception with a highly publicized refusal by Patrick Henry.

By mid-January time and the president's patience both were running out. Washington wrote to Henry Lee on January 11 that the lack of news about Patrick Henry's inclinations was "embarrassing in the extreme." He was delaying nominations for chief justice, associate justice, and secretary of war until he received word from Henry. As Washington had noted in late December, "I am waiting [expecting] information to make a general arangement_ or rather distribution of these offices before I decide upon either separately." Furthermore, the Supreme Court was to convene in just a few weeks and "for particular reasons the bench ought to be full."[63] The Court's docket was

---

[60] Lee to Washington, Aug. 17, 1794, Washington Papers, LC; Washington to Lee, Aug. 26, 1794, Lee Family Papers (Virginia Historical Society, Richmond).

[61] Lee to Henry, Sept. 30, Dec. 17, 1795, in *Patrick Henry: Life, Correspondence and Speeches*, ed. William Wirt Henry (3 vols., New York 1891), II, 561-562; Lee to Washington, Dec. 9, 1795, Washington Papers, LC; Lee to Henry, Dec. 26, 1795, Mss. Acc. 594 (Boston Public Library, Mass.); Lee to Washington, Dec. 26, 1795, Washington Papers, LC.

[62] Tazewell to James Monroe, Dec. 26, 1795, James Monroe Papers (New York Public Library).

[63] Washington to Lee, Lee Family Papers; Washington to Edward Carrington,

crowded and the cases to be heard included *Ware* v. *Hylton* (the British debt question) and *Hylton* v. *United States* (the carriage tax case).[64] In the draft of his January 11 letter to Lee, Washington wrote and then crossed out "I am really at a loss to know what measures *now* to adopt; could I have supposed that it would have taken 'till this time to have ascertained the opinion of a certain character I should have relinquished the idea altogether."[65]

In the meantime the Philadelphia *Aurora* published (and republished from other newspapers) article after article attacking the Federalist partisanship it claimed was responsible for the Rutledge rejection.[66] These are the articles that the president would have seen during the weeks he was waiting to hear from Patrick Henry. They may in fact have strengthened his resolve to wait, for surely Republicans would be mollified if Henry—with solid credentials as an early Antifederalist—were nominated chief justice. But finally the president could wait no longer.

On January 26, 1796, he submitted to the Senate the nominations of Associate Justice William Cushing for chief justice, Samuel Chase of Maryland for associate, and James McHenry for secretary of war. The Senate confirmed the nominations the next day.[67] Washington may have elevated Cushing because there was little time to find a new candidate before the Court was to sit. The Supreme Court had lacked a fully commissioned and sitting chief justice since February 1794, when Jay had last attended, and the president may have been concerned that a chief justice be presiding during the February 1796 term when the politically explosive British debt case would be argued.

Expediency also may have dictated Chase's appointment. With Patrick Henry out of the running, Washington may have viewed Chase as someone who would mollify the same constituency. An early revolutionary, Chase (like Henry in Virginia) had opposed the Constitution in Maryland; but after ratification Chase became an ardent Federalist. In September 1789 he had applied to Washington for appointment as associate justice, but his opposition to the Constitution was too recent and he had not yet held high judicial position. The latter obstacle was removed in 1791, when Chase was appointed chief judge of the

---

Dec. 23, 1795, letterbook copy in Washington Papers, LC.

[64] Jeremiah Smith to William Plumer, Feb. 17, 1796, Plumer Papers.

[65] Washington Papers, LC.

[66] Philadelphia *Aurora*, January 2, 7, 9, 15, 1796. Federalist newspapers in Philadelphia were strangely quiet, not even reprinting those articles that appeared elsewhere: Boston *Columbian Centinel*, Dec. 26, 1795, Jan. 23, 1796.

[67] *Senate Executive Journal*, I, 198.

Maryland General Court.[68] On June 14, 1795, James McHenry wrote to the president to report Chase's conversion to Federalism and to seek Chase's appointment to the Court; but there was no vacancy at that time. In the fall Washington considered appointing Chase attorney general but was concerned by the heated partisan opposition to Chase in Maryland and by the lingering taint of a speculation scandal involving Chase during the revolution. In the meantime Maryland Congressman Williams Vans Murray also made known his support of Chase. Whatever Washington's misgivings about Chase's reputation the preceding year, he overcame them by January 20, 1796, when he wrote to McHenry asking him to find out whether Chase would accept appointment as associate justice. Washington emphasized the importance of Chase setting off immediately in order to attend Court in Philadelphia. McHenry received this letter the next day and on January 24 reported to the president that Chase had accepted the offer and would be in Philadelphia in time for the Court's sitting.[69] On January 28, 1796, Washington wrote to McHenry that the Senate had consented to Chase's nomination and that Chase must hurry to Philadelphia, because "without him, there is no certainty of a sufficient number of Judges to constitute [the Supreme Court]."[70]

The president had killed two birds with one stone. He had appointed someone with early Antifederalist credentials to mute the accusation of partisanship following the Rutledge rejection,[71] and he had secured the services of someone who could reach Philadelphia for the Court's February term.[72] Although it has not previously been noted

---

[68] James Haw *et al.*, *Stormy Patriot: The Life of Samuel Chase* (Baltimore 1980), 145-155, 164, 166-168; Chase to Washington, Sept. 3, 1789, Gratz Collection.

[69] McHenry to Washington, Washington Papers; Washington to Alexander Hamilton, Oct. 29, 1795, Hamilton Papers; Haw *et al.*, *Stormy Patriot*, 105-109; Murray to McHenry, Dec. 24, 1795, McHenry Papers; Murray to Washington, Jan. 24, 1796, Washington Papers, LC; Washington to McHenry, Jan. 20, 1796, McHenry Papers; McHenry to Washington, Jan. 21, 24, 1796, Washington Papers, LC. Henry Abraham, *Justices and Presidents*, 76, states that Washington considered appointing Chase chief justice after the rejection of Rutledge. There is no evidence to substantiate this.

[70] McHenry Papers.

[71] Reaction to Chase's appointment partially defeated this goal. On February 2, 1796, the Philadelphia *Aurora* noted Chase's early Antifederalism but then explained that he had been vocally supportive of the Jay Treaty, and "this will wash an antifederalist whiter than snow." In a letter to James Monroe on February 26, 1796, James Madison also mentioned that Chase was a member of the "treaty party." Madison Papers.

[72] In this he was successful. Court convened on February 3 and Chase joined it the next day. Minutes, Feb. 3, 4, 1796, General Records, RG 267, NA.

by historians, political context and temporal constraints strongly shaped Chase's appointment.[73] There is no other way to explain why Washington would appoint as associate justice someone whom he had refused to nominate as attorney general. Despite Chase's confirmation by the Senate, however, the announcement of the appointment met with virtually unanimous disfavor. Rumors of a drinking problem and continuing reports of Chase's questionable moral character were widespread.[74]

But the president's problems were not over. Even if William Cushing accepted promotion to the chief justiceship, Washington would have to appoint an associate justice to fill the resulting vacancy. And on February 2 Cushing declined to accept his promotion on account of age and poor health.[75] Washington next turned his attention to Connecticut's Senator Oliver Ellsworth. In contrast to Chase, Ellsworth boasted an enviable set of credentials. A former member of Connecticut's Supreme Court of Appeals and Superior Court, Ellsworth had had an important role in the shaping of the Constitution in Philadelphia and in its ratification in his home state. Elected a senator to the first

---

[73] Most accounts have failed to note these influences. See Edward S. Corwin's sketch of Chase in *Dictionary of American Biography*, IV, 34-37; Warren, *Supreme Court in United States History*, I, 142-144; Robert R. Bair and Robin D. Coblentz, "The Trials of Mr. Justice Samuel Chase," *Maryland Law Review*, 27 (Winter 1967), 370-371; Irving Dilliard, "Samuel Chase," in *The Justices of the United States Supreme Court*, ed. Friedman and Israel, I, 189; Haw *et al.*, *Stormy Patriot* , 175-176; and Jane Shaffer Elsmere, *Justice Samuel Chase* (Muncie, Ind. 1980), 54-57. Daniel S. McHargue's account of the Chase nomination is the only other one that suggests that the need for another justice on the bench quickly may have been a factor in the choice of Chase. See "Appointments to the Supreme Court of the United States," 30-33.

[74] Jeremiah Smith to William Plumer, Jan. 29, 1796, Plumer Papers; John Adams to Abigail Adams, Feb. 6, 1796, Adams Papers; Oliver Wolcott, Sr., to Oliver Wolcott, Jr., Feb. 15, 1796, Wolcott Papers; William Plumer to Jeremiah Smith, Feb. 19, 1796, letterbook copy in William Plumer Papers, LC; Abigail Adams to John Adams, Feb. 21, 1796, Adams Papers. Samuel Johnston wrote that "I have no personal acquaintance with Mr Chase, but am not impressed with a very favorable opinion of his moral Character whatever his professional Abilities may be"; Johnston to James Iredell, Feb. 27, 1796, Johnson Collection. It is worth noting that Charles Warren misattributed Johnston's unflattering comments and stated that they were the words of Associate Justice Iredell, thereby suggesting that Chase joined a Court none too happy to have him. Warren's mistake has been cited repeatedly since. Warren, *Supreme Court in United States History*, I, 143-144; Dilliard, "Samuel Chase," I, 189; Haw *et al.*, *Stormy Patriot*, 176; George Lee Haskins and Herbert A. Johnson, *History of the Supreme Court of the United States*, vol. 2, *Foundations of Power: John Marshall, 1801-15* (New York 1981), 93.

[75] Cushing to Washington, photostat of draft (Scituate Historical Society, Massachusetts); John Adams to Abigail Adams, Feb. 2, 1796, Adams Papers.

Congress, he was the principal author of the Judiciary Act of 1789. On March 3, 1796, President Washington nominated Ellsworth for the chief justiceship. The next day, the Senate voted 21 to 1 for confirmation.[76] Public reaction was overwhelmingly favorable.[77] Oliver Ellsworth was President Washington's last nominee to the Supreme Court.

During Washington's presidency, several factors influenced his choice of appointees. In selecting his nominees, Washington looked for highly qualified jurists with established reputations, men who had made sacrifices for the revolutionary cause and supported the Constitution. He also maintained a geographic balance on the Court. Washington's decision-making style was distinctive. He encouraged applicants to make known their aspirations. He consulted with those knowledgeable about prospective nominees and discussed candidates with his own advisers. Before nominating anyone, he usually sought assurances that the nominee would accept in order that the federal judiciary not be embarrassed by refusals to serve. Finally, Washington kept his decision secret until the nomination was presented to the Senate or the recess appointment was tendered to the candidate.

But repeatedly after his first nominations in September 1789, President Washington's careful style of selecting nominees had been pressured by time or disrupted by events. In particular, the requirement that there be a sufficient number of justices to attend the Court or to travel on circuits disrupted his careful calculations. The appointments of Thomas Johnson, John Rutledge (as chief justice), Samuel Chase, and William Cushing (as chief justice) all reveal signs of haste. Also, partisanship on the national level increasingly affected nominations. While the nominations of James Wilson and William Cushing had been influenced by state politics, the appointments of John Rutledge (as chief justice) and Samuel Chase as well as the courting of Patrick Henry were affected by conflict between Federalists and Republicans. The same factors would impinge upon and shape the appointments of the next president, John Adams.

---

[76] *Senate Executive Journal*, I, 203-204.

[77] John Adams to Abigail Adams, Mar. 5, 1796, Adams Papers; Jeremiah Smith to William Plumer, Mar. 5, 1796, Plumer Papers (New Hampshire State Library); see also Jonathan Trumbull to John Trumbull, Mar. 4, 1796, Hubbard Collection (Connecticut State Library, Hartford); Oliver Wolcott, Sr., to Jonathan Trumbull, Mar. 14, 1796, copy in Oliver Wolcott, Sr. Papers (Connecticut Historical Society); Peleg Coffin, Jr., to Dwight Foster, Mar. 28, 1796, Ch. F 3.13 (Boston Public Library); William Plumer to Jeremiah Smith, Mar. 31, 1796, letterbook copy in Plumer Papers, LC.

For two years Adams did not have to concern himself with filling a Court vacancy. But he knew early in his administration that one of the justices might have to leave the bench. James Wilson, caught in a complex web of debt and speculative investments, was a fugitive from justice beginning in the summer of 1797. On August 25, 1798, Associate Justice Iredell wrote from his home in Edenton, North Carolina, to let Secretary of State Timothy Pickering know that Wilson had died in a nearby tavern four days before. Iredell stressed the importance of appointing a replacement quickly. A great deal of important business was due to come before the southern circuit that fall, and Iredell could not preside in North Carolina because he was involved in suits to be argued there. Pickering received this news in Trenton, New Jersey, on September 5 and forwarded it the next day to the president, who was at his home in Quincy, Massachusetts.[78]

Adams' reaction to news of a vacancy on the Court was in stark contrast to President Washington's style. Adams did not consult with advisers, communicate with individuals knowledgeable about proposed candidates, or contact the candidates themselves. Instead President Adams, immediately upon receiving Pickering's letter, wrote back that the position should be offered first to John Marshall, and then, if Marshall refused, to Bushrod Washington. Adams explained that "Marshall is first in Age, Rank and public services, probably not Second in Talents." On September 20, Pickering received the president's instructions and complied at once.[79] But he doubted whether Marshall would accept. He had talked with Marshall in late June and did not think that he would forfeit the substantial income from a thriving law practice for the salary of a justice.[80]

Pickering, assuming that Marshall would decline, tried to expedite the offer to Bushrod Washington. In a private letter to Marshall on September 20, the secretary of state asked him to find out whether Washington would accept the offer. That same day, Pickering wrote

---

[78] Charles Page Smith, *James Wilson: Founding Father, 1742-1798* (Chapel Hill 1956), 383-385; Iredell to Pickering, draft in James Iredell Sr. and Jr. Papers; Pickering to Adams, Adams Papers.

[79] Adams to Pickering, Sept. 13, 1798, Adams Family Collection, LC; Adams to Pickering, Sept. 14, 1798, Miscellaneous Letters, RG 59, NA; Pickering to Marshall, Sept. 20, 1798, letterbook copy in Domestic Letters, RG 59, NA.

[80] Pickering to Marshall, Sept. 20, 1798, Gray-Glines Collection (Connecticut State Library); Timothy Pickering to John Adams, Sept. 20, 1798, Adams Papers. Marshall had been in Philadelphia from June 19 to June 25. Herbert Johnson, Charles T. Cullen *et al.*, eds., *The Papers of John Marshall* (4 vols. to date, Chapel Hill 1974-1984), III, xxix, 467.

to Adams that "Virginia should fill the vacant seat; and if General Marshall should decline, Mr Washington has decidedly a superior claim to any other gentleman there of the profession." The day before, Pickering had forwarded to the president a letter received from Attorney General Charles Lee, in which the latter endorsed the appointment of Bushrod Washington. When Adams received Pickering's letter with Lee's letter enclosed, he wrote to the secretary of state explaining his preference for Marshall. His explanation reveals much about his criteria for choosing a justice. He wrote that, as one of three special envoys to France, "the Conduct of Marshall alone has been entirely Satisfactory, and ought to be marked by the most decided approbation of the Public, He has raised the American People, in their own Esteem. And if the Influences of Truth and Justice, Reason and Argument is not lost in Europe he has raised the Consideration of the United States in that quarter of the world. He is older at the Bar than Mr Washington, and you and I know by Experience that Seniority at the Bar, is nearly as much regarded, as it is in the Army. If Mr Marshall should decline I should next think of Mr Washington."[81]

As Pickering had anticipated, Marshall declined the associate justiceship. But he reported that Bushrod Washington would accept and added his own approval of the choice. Pickering forwarded this news to the president on October 5, 1798, one month—and a flurry of letters—after receiving Associate Justice Iredell's news of James Wilson's death. The next day, Bushrod Washington's commission was on its way south. The latter received the news on October 15, accepted the offer, and quickly traveled south to attend the southern circuit. Bushrod Washington's recess appointment was confirmed by the Senate on December 19, 1798.[82]

Adams' first Supreme Court appointment reveals much about his criteria for and style of choosing candidates. Like George Washington, Adams sought a highly qualified and respected lawyer (Bushrod Washington, however, had never been a judge). Moreover, he chose one in sympathy with his brand of Federalism. Finally, Adams maintained a geographic balance on the Court by filling Wilson's seat with

---

[81] Pickering to Marshall, Gray-Glines Collection; Pickering to Adams, Sept. 20, 1798, Lee to Pickering, Sept. 13, 1798, Adams Papers; Adams to Pickering, Sept. 26, 1798, Miscellaneous Letters, RG 59, NA.

[82] Marshall to Pickering, Sept. 28, 1798, Pickering to Adams, Adams Papers; Pickering to Washington, presscopy in Pickering Papers; Washington to Pickering, Oct. 16, 1798, General Records of the Department of State, RG 59, NA; *Senate Executive Journal*, I, 297.

someone else from the middle circuit and from a state not currently represented on the Court. But most notable about Adams' first appointment to the Court was his style of decision-making. In contrast to George Washington, Adams did not wait for applicants to make known their desire for appointment. He made his decision without contacting either John Marshall or Bushrod Washington. And he did not discuss the nominations with knowledgeable friends of the candidates or with his own advisers.

What accounts for the vivid contrast between Washington's and Adams' styles? Washington had been a superb politician who tried to proceed cautiously in selecting and determining the support for his nominees. Furthermore, he was not familiar with the world of jurists and courts. Adams, on the other hand, was familiar with courts and the practice of law and was therefore in a better position to weigh the merits of different candidates. Also, Adams thought a president should make appointments independently. As early as 1789, in a series of letters to Roger Sherman, he had stated his belief that the Constitution was flawed in mixing the executive and legislative branches in the appointment process. Among other reasons, Adams asserted that the executive's responsibility for choosing poor candidates was thereby lessened, that the Senate's involvement would excite ambition and the possibility of corruption among the senators, and that it would encourage regional and party rivalry.[83] Believing this, he was not inclined to consult with members of Congress on candidates for the Supreme Court.[84] He was particularly unlikely to do so given the state of party politics during his administration. From the day he took the oath of office, Adams was faced with an increasingly polarized Federalist party. The tension was epitomized at the highest level of the executive branch in the split between Adams and the High Federalists in his own cabinet. Adams' independence, honesty, and

---

[83] Charles Francis Adams, ed., *The Works of John Adams, Second President of the United States* (10 vols., Boston 1850-1856), VI, 432-436. Lucy M. Salmon, *History of the Appointing Power of the President*, 13n, 27, was the first to note Adams' independence in making appointments. See also Prince, *The Federalists and the Origins of the U.S. Civil Service*, 10-11.

[84] Some historians have stated that, in making nominations to federal office, President Adams did consult with local leaders and members of Congress. These historians generally fail to distinguish between lesser positions and more important ones; Adams made his Supreme Court nominations quite independently. Fish, *The Civil Service and the Patronage*, 24; White, *The Federalists*, 83, 85; Joseph P. Harris, *The Advice and Consent of the Senate: A Study of the Confirmation of Appointments by the United States Senate* (Berkeley 1953), 44.

forthrightness left him ill-equipped to moderate the political in-fighting. More and more during his administration, Adams became an isolated figure.[85]

In making his second appointment to the Supreme Court, Adams was more subject to lobbying because he was in Philadelphia and accessible to interested parties and their supporters. On October 20, 1799, barely a year after Bushrod Washington's appointment, James Iredell died at his home in North Carolina. Iredell had been in ill health since the summer and had missed the August term of the Court.[86] While several candidates were mentioned,[87] Alfred Moore of North Carolina had an active sponsor. John Steele, formerly a congressman from North Carolina, was comptroller of the treasury and living in Philadelphia. In several letters to John Haywood, a justice on the North Carolina Superior Court, Steele described his plans and then his efforts on Moore's behalf. On November 13 Steele wrote that he had decided to mention Moore's name to the president. On November 21 he reported that "I had a good opp[ortunit]y of conversing on the subject at Head quarters, and stated exactly what kind of man he [Moore] was when I left the State. If he is the same man still he is without doubt to be appointed." Finally, on November 30 Steele promised that "The moment that a successor to Iredell is fixed upon, I will let you hear from me. Moore I still think and hope will be the man."[88] Steele's efforts bore fruit.

On December 4 President Adams nominated Moore. After postponing consideration of the nomination several times, the Senate finally confirmed on December 10.[89] The senators may have hesitated because Moore was not very well known outside of North Carolina. Formerly that state's attorney general, Moore had been elected to the North Carolina Superior Court just one year before his elevation to the Supreme Court. The president may have been influenced by Moore's support of ratification in North Carolina or by the tradition of maintaining a geographic balance on the Court. Whatever Adams' motivation, he acted decisively and quickly, as he had in the nomination

---

[85] Manning J. Dauer, *The Adams Federalists* (1953; rep. Baltimore 1968), 122-124, 212-259, 265; Miller, *The Federalist Era*, 244-245; Peter Shaw, *The Character of John Adams* (Chapel Hill 1976), 237-240, 247-248.

[86] Raleigh *North-Carolina Minerva*, Oct. 29, 1799; Samuel Johnston to Hannah Iredell, July 27, 1799, Johnson Collection; Philadelphia *Gazette*, Aug. 5, 1799.

[87] John Steele to John Haywood, Nov. 13, 1799, Ernest Haywood Collection (University of North Carolina, Chapel Hill); Philadelphia *Aurora*, Dec. 3, 1799.

[88] Haywood Collection.

[89] *Senate Executive Journal*, I, 325, 327.

of Bushrod Washington the year before. In this instance, however, he may have relied more on the recommendations of those who knew the candidate.

Adams' tendency to submit nominations quickly was evidenced again the next year. The vacancy resulted when Chief Justice Ellsworth resigned. One of three envoys extraordinary appointed to negotiate differences with France, Ellsworth's health was weakened by his exertions. On October 16, 1800, he sent his resignation from Le Havre, France. The president received it on December 15, by which time it was clear that Adams would not be serving a second term. With breathtaking speed, Adams nominated John Jay on December 18, and the Senate confirmed the nomination on December 19.[90]

Jay's reappointment surprised most and pleased few. It was widely known that Jay wanted to retire from public life. Just the month before, he had announced to the New York legislature his decision not to run for a third term as governor because of his age and declining health.[91] North Carolina Congressman Richard Dobbs Spaight asked sarcastically, "is there no man in the U.S. fit for this appointment but Jno Jay, that we must re-appoint a man who has before held it & given it up?" Secretary of the Treasury Oliver Wolcott, Jr., wrote to former Secretary of State Timothy Pickering that "The nomination is here considered as having been made in one of those 'sportive' humours for which our Chief is distinguished." Wolcott thought it unlikely that Jay would accept. On January 8, 1801, the Philadelphia *Aurora* acidly commented that "*John Jay* after having thro' decay of age become incompetent to discharge the duties of Governor, has been appointed to the *sinecure* of *Chief Justice* of the United States." At first Thomas Jefferson reacted calmly: "we were afraid of something worse." But soon he viewed Jay's reappointment as part of a Federalist plot to thwart the results of the recent election and prevent the Republicans from taking control of the government.[92]

Why had Adams chosen Jay? Notifying Jay of his appointment, Adams wrote that the chief justiceship was "independent of the inconstancy of the people, as it is of the will of a President. In the future

---

[90] *Ibid.*, I, 317, 326, 327, 360; Ellsworth to Adams, Adams Papers.

[91] Monaghan, *John Jay*, 424; Robert Troup to Rufus King, Dec. 31, 1800, Timothy Pickering to Rufus King, Jan. 5, 1801, King Papers.

[92] Spaight to John G. Blount, Dec. 22, 1800, John Gray Blount Papers (North Carolina State Department of Archives and History); Wolcott to Pickering, Dec. 28, 1800, Pickering Papers; Jefferson to James Madison, Dec. 19, 26, 1800, Madison Papers.

administration of our Country, the firmest security we can have, against the effects of visionary schemes or fluctuating theories, will be in a solid judiciary & nothing will cheer the hopes of the best men so much, as your acceptance of this appointment." Perhaps Adams thought this appeal to patriotism would convince Jay. He also may have hoped that a long-desired revision of the Judiciary Act under consideration in Congress would relieve the justices of riding circuit, thereby making the job less physically demanding and more acceptable to Jay. Above all, the nomination reflected Adams' respect for Jay.[93]

But Jay dashed Adams' hopes. In a letter of January 2, 1801, Jay thanked the president for the nomination, which "so strongly manifests your Esteem." But he continued that the failure of Congress to alter the Judiciary Act of 1789 in such a way as to relieve the justices of circuit-riding was unacceptable: "I left the Bench perfectly convinced that under a System so defective, it would not obtain the Energy weight and Dignity which are essential to its affording due support to the national Governmt; nor acquire the public Confidence and Respect, which, as the last Resort of the Justice of the nation, it should possess. Hence I am induced to doubt both the Propriety and Expediency of my returning to the Bench under the present System, especially as it would give some Countenance to the neglect and Indifference with which the opinions & Remonstrances of the Judges on this important Subject have been treated."[94] Despite his desire to return to private life, Jay seriously considered the offer, but the requirement of riding circuit was determinative: "I find that, independent of other Considerations, the State of my Health removes every Doubt— it being clearly and decidedly incompetent to the fatigues incident to the office."[95]

While Adams waited for Jay's decision, he made contingency plans. On December 23, 1800, Adams wrote to his son Thomas in Philadelphia that, should Jay refuse, "I shall follow the Line of Judges most probably and then there will be a vacancy." He requested his son to inquire whether Jared Ingersoll would accept appointment as associate justice. Ingersoll, formerly Pennsylvania's attorney general

---

[93] Adams to Jay, Dec. 19, 1800, letterbook copy in Adams Papers.

[94] Jay to Adams, Adams Papers. For the efforts of the justices to end circuit-riding, see Goebel, *Antecedents and Beginnings to 1801*, 554-569.

[95] Jay to Adams, Adams Papers. This raises the question of whether Jay might have accepted the appointment had Congress already passed the Judiciary Act of 1801, which did abolish circuit-riding. The act passed on February 13, 1801. *Statutes at Large*, II, 89-100.

and then United States attorney for the district of Pennsylvania, was a highly respected lawyer with extensive experience arguing before the Supreme Court. Two days after the president wrote, his wife Abigail confirmed the plan in a letter to Thomas Adams: "The president has appointed mr Jay chief Justice if he refuses as I fear he will, mr Cushing will be offered it, but if he declines, then mr patterson will be appointed— I know it to be the intention of the president to appoint mr Ingersoll a Judge if a vacancy offers."[96]

Although Cushing might be offered first refusal of the chief justiceship, it could be assumed that he would refuse again, as he had in 1796. At least, most people hoped he would. In addition to those opposed to Cushing's elevation in 1796, Secretary of State John Marshall did not think Cushing a good choice for chief justice. There was even some feeling that Cushing should resign, thereby allowing President Adams—rather than the next president—to nominate his replacement.[97] In any event, Cushing's refusal would present an opportunity to elevate William Paterson. Many had favored this in 1796; at that time, however, it would have required skipping over James Wilson, who had desired the chief justiceship for himself.[98] Now that Wilson was dead, Paterson was the next senior associate justice, and his appointment as chief justice would be very popular.[99]

Thomas Adams, following his father's instructions, asked Jared Ingersoll whether he would accept appointment as an associate justice. Ingersoll wanted time to think about it. His major concern was having to ride circuit. As Thomas Adams informed his mother, "his greatest difficulty arises from the uncertainty whether any change will

---

[96] John Adams to Thomas B. Adams, and Abigail Adams to Thomas B. Adams, Adams Papers.

[97] Marshall to Charles C. Pinckney, Dec. 18, 1800, Charles C. Pinckney Papers, LC; Thomas B. Adams to Abigail Adams, Dec. 20, 1800, Adams Papers; Samuel Sewall to Theodore Sedgwick, Dec. 29, 1800, Theodore Sedgwick Papers, MHS.

[98] Jeremiah Smith to William Plumer, Feb. 24, 1795, Feb. 17, 1796, Plumer Papers (New Hampshire State Library); Uriah Tracy to Oliver Wolcott, Sr., Feb. 10, 1796, Wolcott, Jr. Papers; Samuel Johnston to James Iredell, Feb. 27, 1796, and James Iredell to Hannah Iredell, Mar. 3-4, 1796, Johnson Collection; John Adams to Abigail Adams, Mar. 5, 1796, Adams Papers.

[99] Theodore Sedgwick to Caleb Strong, Dec. 17, 1800, Caleb Strong Papers, MHS; James Gunn to Alexander Hamilton, Dec. 18, 1800, Hamilton Papers; Thomas B. Adams to Abigail Adams, Dec. 20, 1800, Adams Papers; Samuel Sewall to Theodore Sedgwick, Dec. 29, 1800, Sedgwick Papers; Timothy Pickering to Rufus King, Jan. 5, 1801, King Papers; Jonas Platt to James Kent, Jan. 16, 1801, James Kent Papers, LC; John Marshall to Joseph Story, 1827 (William L. Clements Library, Ann Arbor, Mich.).

take place in the Judiciary system, during this Session." Adams added pointedly that "Mr Ingersoll will be at Washington in February at the Supreme Court." On January 9, 1800, the young Adams was still waiting for Ingersoll to make up his mind.[100]

President Adams' plans were thwarted by events. It is not known when he received Jay's declination, written on January 2 in Albany, but Washington and Georgetown newspapers began to report the news on January 13 and 14.[101] Yet Adams did not follow his plan to offer the chief justiceship first to Cushing and then to Paterson. The reason he did not is tied to the progress of the judiciary bill in Congress. On January 19, 1801, the president received a note from Secretary of the Navy Benjamin Stoddert that the House of Representatives would have a final reading of the judiciary bill the next day: "As the bill proposes a reduction of the Judges to five__ and as there are already five Judges in commission, it is suggested that there might be more difficulty in appointing a chief Justice without taking him from the present Judges, after the passage of this bill even by one Branch of the Legislature, than before."[102] Adams had to act quickly if he was to leave behind a Supreme Court consisting of six justices, thereby preventing his successor from appointing one until two left the bench.

Given subsequent events as described by John Marshall, it can be presumed that Adams knew the contents of Stoddert's note before deciding on nominating Marshall himself. In 1827 Marshall recounted events as follows:

> On the resignation of Chief Justice Ellsworth I recommended Judge Patteson as his successor. The President objected to him, and assigned as his ground of objection that the feelings of Judge Cushing would be wounded by passing him and selecting a junior member of the bench. I never heard him assign any other objection to Judge Patteson, though it was afterwards suspected by many that he was believed to be connected with the party which opposed the second attempt at negotiation with France. The President himself mentioned Mr Jay, and he was

---

[100] Thomas B. Adams to John Adams, Dec. 28, 1800, Thomas B. Adams to Abigail Adams, Dec. 30, 1800, Thomas B. Adams to John Adams, Jan. 9, 1801, Adams Papers.

[101] Georgetown *Washington Federalist*, Jan. 13, 1801; Georgetown *Museum* and Washington *National Intelligencer*, Jan. 14, 1801.

[102] Adams Papers. The centrality of progress on the judiciary bill to the eventual appointment of John Marshall has been discussed in Kathryn Turner, "The Appointment of Chief Justice Marshall," *William and Mary Quarterly*, 17 (Apr. 1960), 149-150, 153-154.

nominated to the Senate. When I waited on the President with Mr Jays letter declining the appointment he said thoughtfully "Who shall I nominate now?" I replied that I could not tell, as I supposed that his objection to Judge Patteson remained. He said in a decided tone "I shall not nominate him." After a moments hesitation he said "I believe I must nominate you." I had never before heard my self named for the office and had not even thought of it. I was pleased as well as surprized, and bowed in silence. Next day I was nominated.[103]

This account—over twenty-five years after the events transpired—requires clarification. First, the president had every intention of offering the chief justiceship to William Paterson, but only *after* it had been offered first to the senior associate justice (and Adams' old friend), William Cushing. Now, with the House of Representatives about to vote on a bill to limit the number of justices to five, there was no time to carry out his plan to elevate Paterson and fill Paterson's place with Ingersoll. The major problem was that Ingersoll had not yet agreed to accept appointment as associate justice. He was waiting to see what changes Congress would make in the judiciary. Adams was trying to fill the bench before those alterations were approved by even one house. Marshall's suggestion that Paterson had never been in contention is not borne out by surviving documentation. It is more likely that John Adams had confided his plan to his immediate family but not to the secretary of state.

Second, Marshall mentions rumors of Paterson's supposed involvement with "the party which opposed the second attempt at negotiation with France" in 1799 and leaves the impression that Adams might have been adversely influenced by this. Included in the "party" referred to were Alexander Hamilton and members of Adams' own cabinet.[104] In fact, the same accusation was made on the very day that Adams nominated Jay, when Georgia's Senator James Gunn wrote to Hamilton that "Mr Jay having once declined the office of Cheif Judge it is no compliment to re-appoint him to that office, nor was it decent to wound the feelings of Judge Patterson." Gunn explained Adams' overlooking Paterson by the latter's friendship with Hamilton.[105] But Gunn

---

[103] John Marshall to Joseph Story, 1827 (William L. Clements Library).

[104] Syrett, ed., *Papers of Alexander Hamilton*, XXIII, 545-547n.

[105] Dec. 18, 1800, Hamilton Papers. Michael Kraus asserts without evidence that Adams passed by Paterson because of the latter's relationship to Hamilton. See his "William Paterson" in *The Justices of the United States Supreme Court*, ed. Friedman and Israel, I, 172. Henry J. Abraham, *Justices and Presidents*, 81, repeats this error, among several others marring his treatment of the Marshall appointment. Equally unsubstantiated is John E. O'Connor's speculation that Adams may have preferred

was wrong in 1800, and Marshall was equally incorrect in 1827. If Adams suspected Paterson of disloyalty, then it did not affect the president's plan during late December and early January to offer the chief justiceship to him should Jay and Cushing decline.

Finally, Marshall, by writing that "I waited on the President with Mr Jays letter declining the appointment," suggests that the president was just learning of Jay's action on January 19. In fact, Adams had known about it for at least five days. Is this a case of faulty memory on Marshall's part? Or did Marshall mean simply that he was carrying Jay's letter, not that it was the first time the president heard of Jay's declination? Or, more tantalizing, did Marshall remember incorrectly—was he actually carrying Stoddert's letter notifying the president of the House's impending vote on the judiciary bill? We will never know.

What we do know is that Paterson's supporters were shocked and angered by Adams' nomination of Marshall on January 20. New Jersey Senator Jonathan Dayton, although respectful of Marshall's "talents & standing," knew that the appointment of Paterson "would have been the most acceptable to our country." Others concurred.[106] Dayton and other Federalists complained about what they thought were crazy nominations.[107] He therefore led a movement in the Senate to have Paterson appointed chief justice and Marshall an associate justice. But without the agreement of President Adams all such efforts were doomed to failure.[108] As Dayton phrased it in a letter to Paterson, the president without elaborating "declared that he would never nominate you."[109] Whether Adams was so bald in his explanation is unknown. Given Congress's progress on the judiciary bill, however, which limited the Court to five members, the president was in no position to revoke the nomination of Marshall and then submit two nominations (one

---

Marshall over Paterson because the former was ten years younger than the latter and seemingly healthier. *William Paterson: Lawyer and Statesman, 1745-1806* (New Brunswick, N.J. 1979), 261.

[106] *Senate Executive Journal*, I, 371; Dayton to Paterson, Jan. 20 [quotation], 28, 1801, William Paterson Papers (Rutgers University, New Brunswick, N.J.); James McHenry to Oliver Wolcott, Jr., Jan. 22, 1801, Wolcott, Jr. Papers; James A. Bayard to Andrew Bayard, Jan. 26, 1801, Bayard Family Papers, LC; James Hillhouse to Simeon Baldwin, Jan. 31, 1801, Baldwin Family Papers (Yale University, New Haven, Conn.); Henry Van Schaack to Theodore Sedgwick, Feb. 17, 1801, Sedgwick Papers.

[107] Jonathan Dayton to William Paterson, Jan. 20, 28, 1801, Paterson Papers; James McHenry to Oliver Wolcott, Jr., Jan. 22, 1801, Wolcott, Jr. Papers.

[108] Jonathan Dayton to William Paterson, Jan. 20, 28, 1801, Paterson Papers; James A. Bayard to Andrew Bayard, Jan. 26, 1801, Bayard Family Papers.

[109] Dayton to Paterson, Jan. 28, 1801, Paterson Papers.

for chief justice and one for associate justice). Adams also may have been abrupt because he opposed interference by the legislative branch with appointments to office.

In any event, on January 27, 1801, the Senate unanimously confirmed the nomination of John Marshall to be chief justice.[110] Paterson tried to mollify the anger of his adherents. In a letter to Dayton, Paterson wrote that "With respect to the office of chief-justice, I have always considered myself as being out of the question. I long ago made up my mind on the subject, and have invariably and repeatedly declared, that if appointed to that office I would not accept." Whether Paterson meant this seriously or wrote it simply to placate his supporters is unknown. If Paterson had so declared himself, the Adams family had not heard him. The plan to elevate Paterson to the chief justiceship obviously required his willingness to accept. In Paterson's letter to Dayton, he continued that "Mr Marshall is a man of genius, of strong reasoning powers, and a sound, correct lawyer. His talents have at once the lustre and solidity of gold. I have no doubt, that he will discharge the duties of the office with ability and honor." Paterson also wrote to Marshall to congratulate him.[111] In the end, people focused on Marshall's unquestionable qualifications, which had been evident as early as February 1796, when Marshall had first argued a case before the Supreme Court.[112] Charles Cotesworth Pinckney summed up Marshall's strengths: "Elevated talents, sound federal principles, & unshaken firmness."[113]

Interestingly, William Paterson was the only person who commented that, for the first time, one state had two justices on the Court: Bushrod Washington and John Marshall both were from Virginia. Paterson, in the letter to Dayton quoted above, wrote that "the nomination was unexpected, because the late president [Washington] laid it down for a rule, which I presumed the present had adopted, not to select two judges from the same state."[114] But President Adams did

---

[110] *Senate Executive Journal*, I, 374. The unanimous vote was noted in Jonathan Dayton to William Paterson, Jan. 28, 1801, Paterson Papers, and in the Boston *Columbian Centinel*, Feb. 14, 1801.

[111] Paterson to Dayton, Jan. 25, 1801, Gratz Collection; Marshall to Paterson, Feb. 2, 1801, Paterson Papers.

[112] Jeremiah Smith to William Plumer, Feb. 17, 1796, Plumer Papers (New Hampshire State Library); Richard Stockton to John Adams, Feb. 2, 1801, Adams Papers; David Stone to Samuel Johnston, Feb. 28, 1801, Hayes Collection (University of North Carolina).

[113] Pinckney to Theodore Sedgwick, Feb. 12, 1801, Sedgwick Papers.

[114] Paterson to Dayton, Jan. 25, 1801, Gratz Collection. Incredibly, Paterson

not feel bound to maintain a geographical distribution of appointments to the Court. As Thomas Adams had written the month before, speculating whether Oliver Ellsworth of Connecticut would be replaced by someone from that state: "If the old rule of locality is to have its weight, Connecticutt may perhaps be looked to for a character, but I think the President will obey the dictates of his own opinion in this instance, without regard to the narrow principle which has heretofore prevailed with respect to such appointments, & which I know was never approved by him."[115]

In making nominations to the Supreme Court, John Adams differed from George Washington in more ways than simply on the relative importance each gave to maintaining a geographic balance on the Court. Consistently, Adams made his decisions quickly and without consultation with advisers, a contrast to Washington's more cautious and consultative approach. To some extent, this difference resulted from the increasing intraparty strains among the Federalists during the Adams administration. It also may be attributed to Adams' greater experience in, and familiarity with, the legal field. This allowed him to proceed without the degree of consultation required by Washington. In addition, Adams opposed interference in a president's decisions

---

wrote that he had expected Timothy Pickering would be appointed chief justice. Given Pickering's ties to Hamilton, opposition to the president, and recent ouster as secretary of state, this expectation seems seriously out of touch with political reality. But one bit of evidence suggests that Paterson may not have been entirely wrong. On July 8, 1811, Benjamin Waterhouse wrote a letter to John Adams, in which he mentioned a conversation with Samuel Dexter, who "related to me your efforts to give this resentful man [Pickering] a comfortable living in the station of a Judge, but that it was concluded by others that the Colonel was not quite adequate to the station of a judge." Worthington Chauncey Ford, ed., *Statesman and Friend: Correspondence of John Adams with Benjamin Waterhouse, 1784-1822* (Boston 1927), 59. It is not clear when Adams considered Pickering for a judicial post, but Peter Shaw, *The Character of John Adams*, 266, assumes that it occurred after Pickering's dismissal in May 1800.

[115] Thomas B. Adams to Abigail Adams, Dec. 20, 1800, Adams Papers. Turner, "Appointment of Chief Justice Marshall," 156n., discounts Thomas Adams' statement by noting the following passage written by President Adams in 1798, when he was trying to fill the seat left vacant by the death of Pennsylvania's James Wilson: "As Virginia has no judge at present, she is as much entitled as Pennsylvania to attention." Turner fails to note that President Adams—one and a half years into his administration and hoping for another—was constrained politically in a way that he was not as a lame duck president with only months to serve. He had nothing to lose in early 1801 by acting on his belief that geographic balance was not of paramount importance. The only other historian to mention that the appointment of Marshall violated the principle of geographic distribution is Daniel S. McHargue, "Appointments to the Supreme Court of the United States," 502.

regarding appointment to office. But Adams' quick decision-making had its pitfalls: witness John Jay's refusal to accept the chief justiceship in 1800.[116] Furthermore, because Adams proceeded without consulting others and preparing the ground for his nominations, his nominees frequently ran into difficulty. This happened when the Senate delayed confirmation of Alfred Moore pending further information about this relative unknown, and it happened again when Marshall's nomination surprised a Senate expecting Paterson's promotion to the chief justiceship.

While Presidents Washington and Adams differed significantly in their style of deciding on nominations to the Court, they both used similar criteria in reaching their decisions. Although Adams gave less weight to geographic distribution, both he and Washington sought fit characters with records of service and a political outlook that would support the development of the nascent federal government. But most significantly—and generally neglected by historians—both Washington and Adams made their decisions under the twin pressures of time and events. Especially after the first appointments in September 1789, neither of them enjoyed the luxury of a leisurely consideration of all potential candidates. Circuits had to be attended to, the Court itself had to have a quorum, and unpredicatable events upset plans. It is this last set of conditioning factors—the press of time and events—that has too often been ignored by those writing about appointments to the Court. They provide a perspective that reveals much about appointments during the Federalist period and would prove equally fruitful for the era that followed.

---

[116] Two of President Washington's thirteen nominees who were confirmed by the Senate declined to serve: Harrision as associate justice and Cushing as chief justice. In neither instance did Washington have the advance indication of a likely declination that Adams had with Jay in late 1800.